Teaching through
Radio and Television

Teaching through

Radio and Television

◇◇◇

REVISED EDITION BY

William B. Levenson, Ph.D.

> Deputy Superintendent, Cleveland Public Schools; Former
> Director, Station WBOE, Cleveland; Past President, Associa-
> tion for Education by Radio-Television

Edward Stasheff, M.A.

> Associate Professor of Speech, University of Michigan; For-
> merly Assistant Program Manager TV Station WPIX, New
> York

GREENWOOD PRESS, PUBLISHERS
NEW YORK

Dedicated to the memory of

EDWIN FROST HELMAN
1901–1950
Director, Station WBOE
Cleveland Public Schools
1947–1950

. . . his many friends in radio education are
better men and women for having known him.

Preface

THE RECEPTION ACCORDED the earlier edition of this book has made clear the growing interest on the part of American education in the aims, function, and use of school broadcasting.

The twofold purpose of the publication remains: the improvement of school broadcasting and the encouragement of more effective use of educational programs.

The modern teacher has something to look forward to. She has, at present, many tools, but two of them lie shining and comparatively unused upon the workbench. Radio and Television have existed for some time but never have they been utilized to the fullest in education.

Television, still in its experimental stage, educationally offers possibilities as a tool to fire the imagination of our teachers and educators. They have only to understand their tool, imagine its possibilities and go to work. For television has the hearing appeal of radio and sight besides.

It is to make known these possibilities, to stimulate the imagination, to create a thorough knowledge of the working implements—radio and TV—that this book has been written.

How can educators utilize a tool with which they are not completely familiar? How can they utilize a tool unless they are conscious of its dangers and limitations?

In the past five years the remarkable rise of television has made its impact not alone on the stock market, movies, and sports, but also on many thousands of families and to an already discernible extent in more and more classrooms. In planning this revision the need was recognized for a discussion of the school implications of the current status of TV and its probable growth.

This edition incorporates authoritative television data in each chapter as seen by a practical telecaster who has had commercial as well as educational experience.

For the end papers we are indebted to Eva E. Mizerek and the publishers of *Scholastic Teacher*, in the pages of which they first appeared.

The numerous other changes and additions in this volume are the result of helpful suggestions by many leaders in educational broadcasting who have been using the text in their classes. To them and particularly to the staffs of Stations WBOE and WNYE, the authors wish to express their heartfelt thanks.

WILLIAM B. LEVENSON
EDWARD STASHEFF

Cleveland, Ohio
New York City
March, 1952

Preface to the First Edition

◇◇

THE PURPOSE OF this volume is twofold: the improvement of school broadcasting and the encouragement of more effective use of educational radio programs.

The material herein presented is an outgrowth of the writer's experience in the classroom use of radio and in directing the operations of Station WBOE, which is owned and operated by the Cleveland Board of Education. The organization of the subject matter has been evolved through application in teacher training courses which are presented on the undergraduate and graduate school levels.

It is obvious that a well-rounded treatment of this field cannot be presented entirely by print. Several aspects of the subject can be learned successfully only by firsthand experience. The production of programs, for instance, requires some knowledge of studio equipment and this in turn necessitates actual demonstration and laboratory practice. Even effective classroom utilization practices require that the teacher know how to tune a receiver properly and use a playback machine correctly. Discussion, demonstration, and direct experience are essential.

The writer wishes to express his gratitude for the opportunity he has had to serve under an alert progressive school administration. The inspiration of Superintendent Charles H. Lake and Assistant Superintendent H. M. Buckley has been stimulating. It is understood that the opinions expressed here do not represent those of any institution, but only those of the writer. Whatever shortcomings are noted should be attributed to him alone.

To his colleagues at WBOE the writer wishes to acknowledge his heartfelt thanks. It has been a privilege to share their enthusiasm and the joy of accomplishment.

Appreciation is hereby expressed also to I. H. Conley for his help in reading the manuscript.

W. B. L.

Cleveland, Ohio
June, 1945

Contents

List of Illustrations

◇◇

Teaching through
Radio and Television

1

The Contributions of Broadcasting to Teaching

◇◇◇

What is the influence of broadcasting?

How can radio and television help in teaching?

What special assistance can television provide?

What are the chief limitations in using broadcasts?

◇◇◇◇◇◇◇◇THE SECOND HALF of the twentieth century witnesses the Industrial Revolution proceeding at an accelerated tempo. More than ever it becomes apparent that every basic scientific advance contributes directly to fundamental social change.

The illustrations are familiar: the development of movable type was closely related to the spread of literacy; the application of steam power was a major factor in the rise of urban industrial communities; the use of the internal-combustion engine increased the mobility of modern life.

The process is repeated. In the field of communications, for example, the influence of electronic applications will be equally widespread. The long-range effects must remain in the realm of speculation; however, in one generation we have seen a remarkable transformation in the agencies of mass communication.

Most teachers are aware of the vital nature of communication. For the conveyance of intelligence is the first essential of cooperation, and without it, social life as we know it could not exist. The exchange of meanings is the essence of teaching. If it were not for communication, every generation would have to start anew to understand, control, and conquer nature.

Especially for us, as teachers in a democratic society, this process is essential. Our efforts will determine in large measure the success or failure of one of mankind's greatest experiments—the attempt to draw everyone into the process of government.

If the products of the American schools are to justify the underlying faith of our way of life—that most of the people will be right most of the time—then we need to be sure that the social changes that will invariably take place in the wake of these scientific marvels are conditioned to a maximum degree by our active interest and participation.

The good teacher cannot afford to be a mere spectator of the social scene. If it is true, as some have said, that cultural influences are shifting from church and school to press, films, radio and television, then the significance of such change has real meaning for the truly professional educator.

So it is that education as a part of life becomes each day more complicated. All the products of the new technologies—aviation, atomic power—sooner or later affect the curriculum. Some of the developments are introduced in terms of content, some such as films and broadcasting have already influenced methods.

Imaginative teachers have always sought to utilize the resources of the community to serve the needs of the pupils. The first instructor to bring a printed page into a classroom five hundred years ago was probably regarded as radical by his colleagues. True, it is almost natural to be suspicious of the unfamiliar but it is likewise true that today's innovation becomes familiar tomorrow.

From the hornbook to the modern textbook and from the slate to the motion picture, these tools for learning have ever been changing. Though not all change is progress, and though education has had more than its share of proposed cure-alls, it is undeniably true that some lasting contributions have been made.

Just as industry has learned that it must use modern tools for efficient production, so education has learned that the teacher must be provided with the latest devices to prepare the children to live happily in a complex society. The school day is a fairly long one. The years of learning required for effective participation in the modern society are already many, and as more education and specialized training are demanded, those responsible for the education of youth will need to employ the best tools available. Radio and television are among these. Neither one is a panacea, but there is ample evidence that, when used judiciously, each can be a dynamic force in teaching.

Broadcasting Is an Influence of Vital Importance

In the days of radio's infancy a famous university president was asked whether his institution would care to present a series of educational programs. He bluntly refused, adding, "Radio is just another gadget. It will be forgotten in a few years."

Those few years have passed and the "gadget" is still with us. Today it is a rare American home that does not have one or more radio sets. More people spend more time tuned in to radio than on anything but work and sleep. More than 2,700 stations are in operation in the United States. In one year realistic businessmen spend over $400 million for the use of time to sell products. Broadcasting (the term as used in this volume includes radio and television), press, and motion pictures are the mass communications media of the twentieth century.

But statistics alone do not demonstrate the enormous influence of radio upon the thinking and conduct of people. No other medium reaches so many people simultaneously or has so direct and intimate an appeal.

Numerous surveys, such as the one conducted by *Fortune*, have shown that nearly two-fifths of the nation has found it can get most of its news without turning to newspapers.

When the voice quality and radio style of a presidential candidate are significant factors in the success of a political campaign, when the radio is used by nations as a prime weapon in psychological warfare, when thousands of Americans from coast to coast discuss a news commentary of last night or repeat Bob Hope's latest story, then the influence of radio—whether it be for good or otherwise—must be recognized as a powerful force.

Too often when commercial radio broadcasting is mentioned to school people, they shrug their shoulders and with seeming indifference exclaim, "I seldom listen; it's all silly, anyhow." Yet the fact is that the great majority of the American public does listen regularly, and radio definitely affects its mental patterns.

As for television, still in its infancy (though a lusty, sprawling infant) at mid-century, its rapid growth and habit-forming impact should not be discounted. Even though the beginning of 1952 found only fifty areas served by 108 television stations, with 5 million sets installed in all, there was already evidence of television's hold on the public. A Hofstra College survey of suburban New Yorkers revealed a tremendous drop in radio listening in most television families, with smaller drops in movie going and reading. A mail survey of 500 Chicago television homes reported by *Billboard* disclosed that 94 per cent of the children aged ten and older viewed television for more than 3 hours per day. This time was being taken from other activities, obviously, and educators and sociologists were both pointing with pride and viewing with alarm. The influence of television on homework, for example, will come in for closer examination in Chapter 12, "The Commercial Program for Children."

It is an established fact, and probably a disturbing one, that the typical American school child spends hours every day of the year listening to the radio or watching the television set, or possibly doing both. Add to that the weekly movie, the comic books, and the daily newspaper, and the teacher can readily understand why the comparatively few hours spent in the classroom are but a limited phase of the child's educational experience. The knowing teacher also faces the disturbing fact that of all these influences the two most popular and possibly the strongest are, as Edgar Dale suggests, the comic books and television. Why? Says Dr. Dale, "Comic strips are 'read' because they are personal, concrete, and real. They are not impersonal, abstract, and unreal. Television too is personal, concrete, real."

Assuming, then, that the capable teacher recognizes that she is dealing with a 24-hour, and not a 5-hour, child, several questions arise: What can the schools do to make these outside experiences helpful? How can the child's natural interest in broadcasting be used to further his educational growth? And, more definitely, what contributions can radio and television make to teaching? It is with the last question that this chapter will deal primarily.

Radio and Television Can Become New Tools of Education

The measure of broadcasting's specific contributions to education can be gauged only by its relation to the general objectives of education. The latter have been discussed so extensively that any analysis here would be repetitious; however, the aid that these media can provide in achieving such goals is not so well known. These contributions, though they overlap, may be grouped as follows:

Broadcasts Are Timely. It has been said that "What aviation is to transportation, radio is to education in its fullest meaning." The need for timeliness is obvious in the study of current events, for example. Radio presents and interprets the event while it is still current and before it becomes history, whereas textbooks and even magazines cannot do that. As pupils listen to selected news broadcasts and discussions of crucial issues, they become increasingly aware of the complex problems they will meet as citizens.

Many organizations, both commercial and educational, have presented effective news programs to young listeners. *People in the News* presented through the Empire State FM School of the Air, *It's Your World* offered by Indiana University, and *Youth Looks at the News* presented by Station KDKA of Pittsburgh are examples of successful efforts.

This is a time when the United Nations is struggling to remain on its feet, when organizations such as UNESCO need the understanding of all, young and old. Thus it is heartening to note that agencies such as Station WDTR of the Detroit Public Schools are presenting such series as *The United Nations and UNESCO*. At the same time across the border in Canada the Maritime School Broadcasts present its programs *From Their World to Ours*. Both are using radio for this common goal. Other noteworthy examples could easily be added. The N.A.E.B. Tape Network is also serving this purpose.

Timeliness is essential, too, in other areas of study. Vocational guidance, for instance, can have but limited value if it is not closely related to the changing needs of the community and the current demands of industry. It is often difficult for teachers who are somewhat removed from industrial activity to keep informed of these continuous changes, and here the radio has been used to good effect. Several educational radio stations, such as KUOM of the University of Minnesota and WOI of Iowa State College, have broadcast interviews with personnel managers and employment counselors as well as with men on the job. Current local needs and present local opportunities have been emphasized, and responses from high schools have indicated that a definite need is being served. The radio provides the last page of the newest textbook.

In educational guidance also, it is necessary that the data used be current. The series, *College Advisement*, presented to high school pupils by Station WBGO of the Newark Public Schools, *So You're Thinking about College* broadcast by WTDS, the Toledo School Station, and *Mapping Your Future* on New York's WNYE illustrate this contribution.

During the war years the timeliness of radio was particularly demonstrated. The United States Office of Education cooperated with one of the networks to present a series of programs which contributed a great deal to the rapid formation of the High School Victory Corps throughout the country and to an understanding of its need and purposes.

The application of educational radio to meet an emergency need was illustrated in several communities where programs were presented to help provide preinduction training. Local authorities discussed principles of flight, newer concepts of global geography, and aspects of military life that would be helpful to the potential draftee. WBOE, the Cleveland School Station, broadcast practice lessons in code, using Signal Corps transcriptions. WBEZ, operated by the Chicago Public Schools, presented a timely radio series entitled *New Worlds for Old*, which interpreted the geography of the air age.

Television too can leap into the breach. The modern television station needs only 4 to 6 hours to shoot, process, edit, and broadcast film, with narration and background music added "live" as the silent film unrolls.

In September, 1949, the City of New York found itself facing a growing incidence of infantile paralysis. All media, from placards on telephone poles to newsreels, were mobilized to alert the public to the menace and yet to avoid panic. A series of programs on Station WPIX stressed the few simple rules of cleanliness, but reassured anxious parents by showing recently made films of the latest polio therapy, and reminded them that immediate treatment might well prevent lasting effects. In early December of the same year, during an acute water shortage, WPIX cameramen made a special documentary film, showing aerial views and close-ups of the depleted reservoirs, and brief object lessons of tightened taps, simpler dishwashing and other aids to water conservation.

In fostering a spirit of national unity, in launching various community drives, in alerting citizens to a great variety of emergencies from polio and rabies to water shortages and impending floods, the timeliness of radio and the immediacy of television have enabled them to make significant contributions to the schools of America.

Broadcasting Conquers Space. In a shrinking world, where air travel is changing former concepts of geography and no region is more than sixty hours from Main Street, corresponding developments in communication are needed more than ever before. Radio's ability to transmit the spoken word with the speed of light is of vital significance in modern life. The lonely fur trapper of the Far North can hear Toscanini's music at the same time that the spectators in the rear of the NBC Music Hall can. With radio, the most isolated classroom can hear the world. Geography is translated into terms meaningful to the child. The life and customs, the people and their forms of expression the world over assume concrete shape. The unfamiliar, which is so often misunderstood and more often distrusted, can be brought closer home and effectively interpreted by an intelligent use of radio. To be sure, events have shown that the contrary also is true; however, the tool itself is neutral. Its use determines its value. In a postwar world which has discovered that international understanding is the salvation of mankind, broadcasting must come to play an even greater part.

In cooperation with the BBC the pupils of several American school systems have participated in two-way transatlantic discussions with European youth. Station WLS contributed to international understanding at the child's level through a series of *Visiting Day Programs* which were transcribed overseas and presented to classrooms in the American Midwest.

Various commentators speak daily from abroad but as yet, international broadcasting for regular home and classroom listening is still in its early development. The trend is evident. With improved facilities and more delayed broadcasts using transcriptions, such programs will become more common.

Even on a more limited national scale, radio's seven-league boots still have a long way to go. Regional misunderstandings persist. Provincialism is still apparent. In helping to remove these barriers, the wide-awake teacher will use radio to travel with her class. And where television is available, she will watch local stations and their schedules for programs dealing with other lands and other customs, particularly in holiday seasons when stations often show foreign observances of world-wide holidays. She will take advantage of "on the spot" pickups of the opening of Congress or the State Legislature, of Mardi Gras in New Orleans, and of the Mummers' Parade in Philadelphia.

In communities where religious and racial tensions provide problems, the teacher may find it possible to recommend such programs as WPIX's *Television Chapel,* or the CBS series, *Lamp unto My Feet* in which a different faith presents its tenets and ceremonials each Sunday. A visit to churches of different denominations is not always feasible; visiting by television is hampered only by availability of receivers, the problem which haunts and will haunt educational television for some time to come.

In short, radio and television provide the classroom with windows on the world, with magic carpets that transport pupils to other lands, to other sections of their own land, and to new and different climates of opinion and culture.

Broadcasting Can Give Pupils a Sense of Participation. The qualified teacher knows that direct, more than indirect, experiences are productive of learning. The carefully selected pupil activity, the well-planned field trip, the practical problem which grows out of a felt need—all these are participatory in nature and effective educationally. But life is too short and society too complex for the average child to obtain immediate knowledge of many things.

It is inevitable that symbols be used for some experiences, and yet the danger is that as experiences become increasingly vicarious, teaching tends to become a verbal outpouring, and learning, a feat of memory. The joy of self-discovery and the pleasures of personal association are lacking.

Radio can help to overcome this tendency by opening the doors of the classroom to the world outside. When the child hears an "actuality" program, such as a presidential inauguration or the opening session of Congress, he has a feeling of participation in the event and history becomes a living, vibrant experience. The pupils who heard Norman Corwin's memorable program on the Bill of Rights shared consciously the trials of the founding fathers, as well as their nation's pride in a monumental achievement.

Listeners to the remarkable CBS series, *You Are There*, turned the clock back as through the power of a stirred and guided imagination they participated in the milestones of history. Likewise the children in England who listened to BBC's, *How Things Began* became part of a great adventure. For them the story of man was more than a mass of dates to be memorized.

Any moviegoer knows that sound coupled with sight can create a world of illusion. Add to that the actuality of television and it becomes obvious that, even more than radio, this newest medium can give pupils a sense of participation. True, the promise of TV is still greater than its practice and there are as yet few programs that might be cited; nevertheless the potentials are there.

It will be noted, therefore, that because of the still emerging pattern of TV's growth the emphasis in the subsequent discussion of value will remain on radio.

Those who saw as well as heard the dedication of the United Nations, for example, or the President's Inauguration are aware of television's power to create a sense of being present as history is made. "Experiment in the Desert," a documentary drama presented by CBS re-creating the explosion of the first atom bomb in Los Alamos, illustrated vividly television's potential contribution as an educational influence.

Broadcasting Can Be an Emotional Force in the Creation of Desirable Attitudes. Radio is thought of frequently as a teaching aid which can accelerate the accumulation of facts. There is much evidence to support that claim. However, facts alone are not the aim of education. The decisive factor is what the learner *does* with the facts. To illustrate simply, the jaywalker knows that the red traffic light means "stop"; but if knowledge of the fact does not affect his attitude concerning safety and, in turn, his habits, then the fact is incidental.

Not only in safety, health, etc., but in the whole process of democratic living, attitudes, not facts, are paramount. In the vital matter of promoting harmonious interracial relations, Rachel Davis DuBois in *Get Together, Americans* points out: "When working in the area of racial and cultural conflicts one should remember that people do not change their attitudes about other groups of people by merely acquiring facts. People do not act according to what they know but according to how they *feel* about what they know."

The conveyance of information is a comparatively simple phase of teaching. Far more difficult is the development of desirable attitudes. Even in the days before Herr Goebbels, psychologists knew that attitudes do not result from reasoning alone. Emotional drives have a powerful influence. Here is where radio can be of great help to the teacher, for radio has learned to use drama and music, two potent forces for creating an emotional impact.

There have been many radio presentations which accomplished this. The following are good examples:

The CBS program, *Between the Dark and the Daylight*, made excellent use of on-the-scene recordings to present the plight of children in war-torn countries.

The crucial matter of race relations was treated in vital, compelling fashion by Station WMAQ of Chicago with its series, *Destination Freedom*. A courageous, hard-hitting dramatic series dealing with the same topic was presented by Station WMCA of New York with its well-known, *New World A-Coming*.

The public's indifference to an increasingly important problem—the conservation of natural resources—was challenged by Station WLW of Cincinnati with its stirring series, *Generation on Trial*.

Station KHJ of Los Angeles delivered a powerful message on behalf of safety with its program, *And Sudden Death*. Perhaps too shocking for immature listeners, it was nevertheless a fearful and necessary reminder for their elders.

Television has demonstrated its value here also. For example, some time ago on a Lincoln's birthday observance, CBS produced "The Face of Lincoln" using his own writings and illustrated largely by photographic studies of his memorable face. The narrator was not shown until the end. He was Gordon Heath, the fine Negro actor. The final picture made its own point.

Broadcasting Can Add Authority.   Few teachers, however conscientious they may be, can hope to be experts in every phase of the subject matter they teach. The mass of available information is multiplying constantly. The search for the best sources and the lack of time make it difficult for the already burdened classroom teacher to exploit all the possibilities. Here, too, the services of radio and television can be enlisted.

The occasional appearance of an authority whose material is planned to relate to the interests, needs, and capacities of pupils, can be of active assistance to the teacher. As the leaders of contemporary life—political, scientific, industrial, and educational—deliver their messages, they become members of the teaching staff. And thus, as Darrow puts it, one can "substitute first-hand enthusiasm and mastery for second-hand interest and half-digested information."

There have been many radio programs of this type, some for classroom use and others primarily for home listening. Station WNYC offered *City Rent Laws* to help clarify a social problem which affected many families. Skillful use was made of authoritative information which held the listener's interest. The same station presented *U. N. Proceedings*, which featured members of the United Nations in informative yet dramatic presentations of their activities, in remote pick-ups from Lake Success. In the field of health, Station WFBR of Baltimore broadcast *Keeping Well*—reliable content presented in a framework of enjoyable drama. The WHA series, *Afield with Ranger Mac*, has been heard by a generation of Wisconsin school children. The elementary grades of Kansas City, Missouri, have responded enthusiastically to the KMBC-KFRM series, *The Art Lesson*.

A successful series, which has been presented by Station WOSU for several years, has been the *Science Club of the Air* in which classroom experiments are motivated and guided by the broadcaster. For advanced students *Invitation to Learning* presented by CBS is certainly noteworthy.

The classroom visit of an authority made possible through radio has been used effectively in various subject fields. For example, music in Nashville, Tennessee; conservation in Portland, Oregon; and Spanish in Evansville, Indiana. Yet radio's help in contributing authenticity does not depend upon the microphone appearance of a specialist. Several dramatic programs have been of real significance to the school, because they combined the fruits of a research staff with the talents of a dramatic cast. Several of the *Cavalcade of America* programs presented by DuPont over NBC have been noteworthy in this regard.

Television's role in this area is now being explored but already there are several noteworthy examples. The DuMont series, *Johns Hopkins Science Review*, originating in Baltimore from the laboratories of Johns Hopkins University, and Dr. Roy K. Marshall's series on NBC-TV are indicative of programs to come. The outstanding ABC film series *Crusade in Europe* can also be included in this classification.

Broadcasting Can Integrate the Learner's Experiences. As noted earlier, the correlation of the child's activities in school with those he undergoes after school has become increasingly difficult. Another aspect of integration which the teacher faces is the coordination of the knowledge obtained in various classrooms. The meanings acquired in the mathematics class relate to those of the physics laboratory. Music and art are based on fundamental principles common to both. Geography, history, and economics are likewise interrelated and the same can be said of practically all subjects. The synthesis of newly acquired meanings is an essential step in the learning process and yet it is here that much classroom teaching falls down. The pressure of time, a narrow course of study, the teacher's specialization, preparation for college examinations, the departmental system—many reasons are given, but the fact remains that the "wholeness" of knowledge, a recognized aim, is seldom achieved.

In this regard, too, radio is no panacea but it can help a great deal. The Standard School Broadcast series, which has been heard on the West Coast since 1928, has on many occasions emphasized the relationship between music and art. The series *Look What We Found* offered to elementary classes by Station KUOM of the University of Minnesota was a productive experiment in relating various fields of knowledge at the child's level of understanding. The University of Wisconsin series, *Let's Draw* has, for several years, demonstrated how a skillful teacher can use one art form to motivate creation in another field. *Science is Fun* heard by the Philadelphia schools through Station WFIL presented dramatized biographies and the stories behind great inventions. The former WBEZ series *Let the Artist Speak* pointed out the effects of life in Latin America upon resultant art forms. Many other programs of this nature have shown how radio can contribute to an amalgamation of what the child may consider unrelated knowledge.

Broadcasting Can Challenge Dogmatic Teaching. Passive learning and dogmatic teaching are much too common in many classrooms. Only the rare child will question the wisdom of the teacher's point of view, evaluate the presence of bias in a textbook, and analyze the prevailing beliefs in his community. The upsetting of preconceived notions often irritates but it likewise stimulates. When the child hears a radio program in which a belief which he has hitherto accepted is questioned by apparent authorities who provide supporting evidence to the contrary, he learns the real meaning of suspended judgment. When he views a forum program in which even the experts disagree, he comes to understand that truth is not easily arrived at.

The American radio program structure abounds with examples of programs that challenge points of view. *America's Town Meeting,* the *People's Platform,* and the *University of Chicago Round Table* are some of the better known network programs of this type. More recently, *Town Meeting* and the *People's Platform* have been seen as well as heard, in "simulcasts," the term used to describe programs broadcast on radio and television simultaneously.

Several local stations have also broadcast discussions of this nature. One of the most successful has been *Labor Arbitration* presented by Station WMCA, New York City. *City Club Forum* offered by Station WGAR of Cleveland is another good example.

For younger listeners the rapid rise of the *Junior Town Meeting League* is an interesting development. Programs dealing with crucial issues, national and international, are discussed by pupil speakers who support differing points of view. After the formal talks they respond to questions from the pupil audience. Broadcasts of this type have been presented in Boston, Cincinnati, Newark, Cleveland, Philadelphia, Akron, and Toledo. These school-presented programs have been fine demonstrations of radio's capacity to encourage a more scientific attitude toward social problems.

Television has given programs of this type a tremendous impetus, with the earnest features of the school participants adding immeasurably to the impact of their ideas. Not only Junior Town Meetings, but earlier school forums such as *There Ought to Be a Law* and *It's High Time* in New York City; *A View to Education* in Chicago; *The Young Idea* in Detroit have drawn general, as well as school, audiences to the television screen.

Broadcasting Can Be Used to Develop Discrimination. The development of good taste and the ability to make intelligent choices are closely related to the previous discussion. These aspects of the child's growth are vital, yet unfortunately as educational objectives they have been slighted in many schools.

Edgar Dale's observation of several years ago deserves repetition today:

People can be roughly divided into two classes—the sponge-minded and the critically minded. The sponge-minded absorb with equal gullibility what they see at the movies, what they read in the newspapers, what they hear over the radio. They are the passive viewers, readers, listeners. Fair game for advertisers, they it is who put down $350,000,000 for patent medicines each year. Even in their student days, they accepted without a flicker of mistrust what the textbook said or what they heard from the lecture platform. Porous as a sponge, for a brief time their minds absorb but do not assimilate.

The critically minded are active, not passive, in their reception of the printed and spoken word or the motion picture. They constantly ask: "Is it true? Where's your evidence?" and "What do you mean by 'true'?" They search out hidden assumptions, unwarranted inferences, false analogies. They are the good-natured sceptics and sometimes, unfortunately, the soured cynics. They give the ill-informed and inaccurate teacher many an evil moment. They are our only hope for progress.[1]

It has been demonstrated by Fawcett, Biddle, and others that with continued selective exposure and follow-up analysis it is possible to shift students from the passive group to the active.

Skillful teachers in many parts of the country have used radio to help attain such goals. By first determining the present tastes of their pupils, then by evaluating with them the program elements that make for quality, and finally by suggesting superior programs for home listening, teachers have helped many students to become selective in their listening and critical of what they hear and see.

In several high schools commercial announcements are recorded and then analyzed by the children. Thus, consumer education is undertaken in realistic fashion. Some schools use recordings of selected commercial programs to call attention to examples of good acting, superior speech, expert production, etc.

There was a time when good music and drama could be had only in the big cities. Today the children of the Arkansas farmer, like their more sophisticated contemporaries of Manhattan, have an opportunity to hear the best. The growing attendance at concerts, the support of orchestras, and the success of road tours are attributable in large measure to radio's achievement in elevating standards of taste.

Programs such as the *Firestone Hour*, the *Metropolitan Opera*, *New York Philharmonic*, the *Family Hour*, and others of like quality have contributed much to the cultural life of America. By encouraging

---

[1] Edgar Dale, "Discrimination," *The News Letter*, November, 1936, p. 1.

listening to such programs, the classroom teacher can enrich the child's growth immeasurably.

In the field of serious music, TV also makes its contribution. Not only can the cameras accentuate the instrumental structure of a symphony by focusing on the section which is featured at any given point in the composition, but the effect of seeing Toscanini superimposed over the NBC Symphony as he conducts gives the viewer in living room or classroom a musician's-eye view of the noted conductor. Students of music have much to gain by seeing and hearing the great conductors and orchestras of our time.

Some optimists suggest that television may do as much to popularize ballet as radio has done for fine music. Not only have our leading ballet companies and premier dancers come before the cameras and thus been made available to communities seldom exposed to ballet before, but several variety programs now include serious ballet. Within a period of one month, one of the authors encountered three little girls who were teaching themselves ballet by watching television. Their reach far exceeded their grasp, of course, but the impulse was there. The Ford program *Through the Crystal Ball*, which featured a ballet series, was short-lived, but it may be that it came before its time.

Broadcasting Can Help in Continuous Curriculum Revision. No curriculum worthy of the name can remain static while an ever-changing society makes new demands upon its members. Constant and continuous curriculum revision is an accepted ideal in modern education. Its attainment is another matter. The lure of inertia is great and change is not always welcomed.

Committees which have labored conscientiously in revising courses of study find all too often that months after the materials have been prepared and issued, the classroom practices in some schools remain unchanged. Somewhere along the line the distribution and acceptance of the product breakdown, and even bales of mimeographed material will not solve the problem. The results of concerted effort by a few upon the improvement of procedures by the many are often apt to be disappointing. Obviously, this difficulty is basically a question of the teacher's attitude toward change. However, there is ample evidence that for specific localities several well-spaced radio programs can be effective in distributing the findings of such committees. It has been found that with the use of the radio and adequate teacher guides, curricular revision is more than a "scissors and paste" technique. As the teacher and her class utilize the program which introduces a new topic or changes the emphasis of old material, the revision means something to her. In evaluating the programs, she and her colleagues contribute democratically to this reorganization.

When some schools decided to place additional emphasis on the study of Latin America, radio was used to good advantage in several communities, among them Grand Rapids and Forth Worth. The implications of harnessed atomic power have been discussed in numerous programs presented to science classes. The place of creative poetry in the curriculum was highlighted in a San Diego school series. Literature was very well handled by the Newark School Station, WBGO. A notable service to rural schools is being rendered by Station WSUI of the State University of Iowa. Kansas State Teachers College is active similarly in cooperation with a network of commercial stations in that state. Music's place in the curriculum was the topic of a series broadcast by the Alabama State College for Women. Toledo's school station WTDS presented the story of transportation to the intermediate grades. In Newark the Director of Elementary Education used WBGO to present the *New Arithmetic Curriculum* to some 1,500 teachers.

The safety course of study in Cleveland was introduced by a series of demonstration radio lessons. These are but a few examples of radio's function in this regard. Furthermore, it is true generally that every educational radio program contributes to curriculum revision by adding information or by new emphasis.

Broadcasting Can "Up-Grade" Teaching Skills. Industry's recent and successful use of teaching aids to improve skills while on the job has been followed with great interest by administrators. In a few communities radio has been used in the schools with a similar purpose in mind, namely, the improvement of teaching methods. If this use of radio seems to be emphasized in this volume, it is because the writers feel strongly that (a) radio's function as an aid to the supervisor has not been explored thoroughly and (b) as more school-owned radio stations are established and greater attention is given to doing the specialized school job, some modifications of this demonstration approach will become more common.

Those who have felt that radio can demonstrate good teaching, as well as contribute the other values described earlier, hold this point of view: radio is primarily an agency of distribution. It can enable many to hear the best. For the children it means that inspiration derived from the talented teacher can be shared by many. Given an expert teacher and the time to prepare an excellent lesson, plus the opportunity to reach many classes rather than one, is it not likely that the results of such teaching will be highly productive?

As this process of teaching with the help of radio takes place, the teacher in the classroom has a unique opportunity to observe the methods of an expert being applied in her own room. Though supervision is, in many instances, a matter of personality adjustment, nevertheless, there are basic suggestions in instructional procedures that can be broadcast to teachers. As a timesaver the radio thus can be of real service, for, as supervisors in any large school system will testify, "just getting around" consumes much valuable time.

One common form of supervision is to sit at the rear of the room and tell the teacher later what is thought of her efforts. Perhaps it is more important to have the expert actually demonstrate just what is wanted. Granted that the radio visit does not represent a typical classroom situation, still there are common problems of supervision that can be approached in this manner. The appalling waste of time on nonessentials in the average classroom is known. A well-organized lesson moving along from step to step and reaching worth-while goals in less time cannot help influencing the teaching staff.

The radio can also provide in-service teacher training in other ways. Every well-selected educational program affects the teacher indirectly and so contributes to her growth and teaching proficiency. But in a more direct manner radio has been used, for example, by the National Education Association to broadcast educational conferences. Several communities have invited specialists in pedagogy to address teachers by radio after school hours. In Michigan, Dr. Joseph Maddy has for years used radio to demonstrate methods of teaching in the field of

music. WBOE in Cleveland, WABE in Atlanta, and WIP in Philadelphia present programs which demonstrate teaching techniques.

Several school television programs have re-created classroom situations in a double-barreled attempt to present subject matter attrac-
tively and to show the community what is going on in the schools.
While a class conducted before the cameras is scarcely typical, nevertheless the techniques of a really expert teacher can be shared with
other colleagues in this way. Columbia University's Teachers College
has installed television receivers in special viewing rooms, chiefly to
keep interested students abreast of video developments. Such a setup,
however, could be used for observation of superior teaching.

On the whole, the services of radio and television as teacher training
media on a large scale have yet to be enlisted, although their contributions have already proved effective.

*Broadcasting Can Interpret the Schools to the Commu-
nity.* Another service which broadcasts, audio or video, can render
the schools derives from their unique ability to interpret school activities to the public. Advertisers know that radio sells merchandise and
certainly it can and does publicize institutional services as well. In
the past, educators generally have been reluctant to engage in public
relations activities. But that point of view is changing. The need for
acquainting the citizen with the school product he is receiving for his
tax dollar is greater than ever before. The day has passed when teachers
can complacently assume that tax levies will be renewed automatically.
The burden of federal taxation will remain a heavy one regardless of
changes in administration. Public sentiment toward the little red
schoolhouse is rapidly vanishing, and John Q. Public wants to be
shown what the modern schools are accomplishing and why additional
support is necessary. The schools have an obligation to provide the
answers. In this process the radio has shown its worth.

Public relations broadcasting by schools does not imply high-
pressure salesmanship. An effective program serving this end can be
in good taste and yet good listening. Every school program affects
public relations but a school presentation designed specifically for
adult consumption can more likely produce these desired ends.

Numerous school systems and universities have shown how radio can be used in this manner. Several good examples are *News and Views of Schools Today* over San Diego's Station WFMB; *The Suburban School Round-up* broadcast by WIBG in Philadelphia; in Portland, Oregon, KEX's *Your Schools and You* and KOIN's, *Spotlight on Youth.* WBOE in Cleveland presented *We, the Pupils,* and *Ask the Teacher.*

In television, the Chicago school station WBEZ was doing a similar job over Television Station WBKB as long ago as 1945–1946. The initial and experimental series, *A View to Education,* provided a cross section of educational activities on all levels and in many subject areas. New York City's Television Unit cooperated with Station WPIX in a bimonthly series, *This Is Your City,* several programs of which were devoted to the city schools. In other cities, such a project, interpreting the workings of the city's government to the taxpayer, might well be a function of the schools. In the college field, faculty and students of the University of Miami prepared a 20-minute documentary film dealing with student life and recreational activities, as well as teaching methods, new courses, and specially designed tropical architecture.

Because of the growing importance of this type of activity, Chapter 11 will be devoted exclusively to public relations broadcasting.

Other Values—CLOSER OBSERVATION OF INDIVIDUAL CHILDREN. In addition to the contributions noted above, there are several related services which broadcasting can render. It provides the teacher with a chance for closer observation of individual children, their listening habits, their ability to comprehend, and their special interests. As the children react to a stimulus provided by someone other than herself, the teacher has a rare opportunity to analyze such pupil reactions.

SOUND IS HELPFUL IN TEACHING. There is another aspect of radio to consider. For many centuries teaching was done largely by means of a teacher's voice. With the invention of the printing press greater emphasis was placed upon using the eyes, and wide reading was the gateway to scholarship. Today, sound has once more come into its own through the great influence of radio. Psychologists have noted that not all children learn equally well from the printed word; to some sound is very helpful.[2] To these children, as well as to those with poor sight whose reading habits must be guarded, a school without a radio receiver is indeed an educational tragedy.

SERVICE TO HANDICAPPED CHILDREN. Finally, in this discussion of values, mention should be made of radio's services to the handicapped children who must remain at home. In every community there are shut-in children who because of illness or injury cannot attend school. For them, a radio series that is both interesting and informative is of immense value educationally and perhaps therapeutically as well. The Indianapolis series *School Ship of the Air*, which was planned primarily for such children, was a delightful travelogue and heartily welcomed by the young listeners at home. More recently, New York City's school station WNYE offered a *High School of the Air for Home Instruction*, in which courses in all four years of English, world history and American history, and general science were specifically designed for homebound pupils, with mimeographed materials including assignments, listening aids, and suggestions mailed to students every two weeks.

The increased efficiency of such instruction by television is self-apparent; the difficulty, once again, is the availability of a television receiver in the bedroom of the homebound student. . . . Yet a survey of five hundred homebound high school students in New York City revealed that 82 per cent had television sets in their homes. Accordingly, the thrice-a-week Board of Education series over WPIX, *The Living Blackboard*, was planned not for classroom viewing but primarily for children in homes and hospitals who were not able to attend school in the normal fashion. Within two months after the inception of the programs in the fall of 1951, communities in New Jersey and Connecticut were using the telecasts for their homebound pupils.

Television Can Teach Skills. Television's great advantage has been emphasized by Dr. Franklin Dunham, Chief of Radio, United States Office of Education. "Television has a greater potentiality for education," said Dr. Dunham, "than it has for entertain-

---

[2] M. D. Vernon, Chapter V, "The Influence of Attitudinal Factors upon Perception," in *Visual Perception*, Cambridge University Press, 1937.

Anne Anastasi, Chapter X, "Variations within the Individual," in *Differential Psychology*, The Macmillan Company, 1937.

ment. In its very essence it can do what we have long hoped we could accomplish with radio—it can teach skills." This factor has been utilized in adult education, on an irregular basis, and in several commercial programs. Surgical operations, frequently in color, have been scanned by a camera immediately over the operating table. They have been seen by groups of doctors in viewing rooms far more clearly and in greater detail than the same operation could be seen in the front row of the operating room. On one occasion, such an operation was beamed on a special circuit to a large audience of physicians in Atlantic City's Convention Hall. Two years later, a similar closed circuit was seen by doctors from coast to coast, through the use of coaxial telecast cable and microwave relay.

Commercial programs dealing with cooking have proved popular, as have those devoted to interior decorating, dress making and knitting. The carving of the family turkey is a hardy Thanksgiving perennial on many stations in many cities. And Jon Gnagy's *You Are an Artist* was one of the first how-to-do-it programs to win general acceptance, as well as one of the first to combine instruction in the principles of art and art appreciation with actual practice in pencil sketching.

True, such efforts to teach skills have not been organized; they have been sporadic and occasional, or have been aimed at improving the domestic skills of the housewife. However, they have already served to demonstrate television's power to teach skills to many over an area as wide as the coaxial cable can reach. Summed up then, broadcasting can help in the following ways:

1. Broadcasting is timely.
2. Broadcasting conquers space.
3. Broadcasting can give pupils a sense of participation.
4. Broadcasting can be an emotional force in the creation of desirable attitudes.
5. Broadcasting can add authority.
6. Broadcasting can integrate the learners' experiences.
7. Broadcasting can challenge dogmatic teaching.
8. Broadcasting can be used to develop discrimination.
9. Broadcasting can help in continuous curriculum revision.
10. Broadcasting can "up-grade" teaching skills.
11. Broadcasting can interpret the schools to the community.
12. Broadcasting offers closer observation of individual children.
13. Sound is helpful in teaching.

14. Broadcasting offers a service to handicapped children.
15. Television can teach skills.

There Are Limitations in Teaching by Broadcast

Neither Radio Nor Television Can Replace Teachers. In spite of its many possible values, the use of radio in teaching does not imply that "nonsense spoken into the microphone will emerge as wisdom from a loudspeaker." As in all phases of human endeavor, the results of teaching with radio are dependent upon preliminary planning and preparation. Values are inherent in no instrument, and the radio is no exception. The same is true of television.

The value of the program is dependent to a large degree upon the use the classroom teacher makes of it. It is evident that broadcasting will never supplant the teacher; the most it can do is to supplement and reinforce her efforts. Even with color television, facsimile, and other developments, the classroom procedures of the future will in all probability still consist largely of the teacher's personal approach.

Dean Uhl's observations are to the point when he states:

Certainly the fear about the displacement of books and even of teachers by radio programs is groundless. At this point one may refer briefly to the history of fear in connection with other educational innovations. During Matthew Arnold's life, for example, apparently his own sweetness and light were changed at times to fear when he contemplated the displacement of literary classics by science as advocated then by Spencer and Huxley. Greater fear had accompanied the displacement of certain Latin materials by more vitally humanistic materials in the fifteenth century. Even greater fear was aroused in the various countries by the possibility that any vernacular might become a vehicle of high literary experience or of accepted instruction of pupils beyond the rudiments. The English language was such a stimulus of fear for three centuries. The deepest fear about an educational innovation seems to have been aroused by the invention of printing and the possibility that students might have access to printed materials. That fear has prompted the opposition to innovations is one of the accepted facts of the history of education. Skillful and intelligent use of the radio in a classroom has already indicated the broadened rather than the restricted place that superior teachers can occupy when that modern innovation is properly used.[3]

---

[3] Willis L. Uhl, "Psychological Factors in Education by Radio," *The Phi Delta Kappan*, March, 1939, p. 338.

Further Limitations. The chief limitations of the radio teaching program were recognized from the outset. The following handicaps which were noted by Charters in 1930 are not yet entirely overcome:

1. Synchronization of time. A standardization of schedules must be worked out so that an appreciable number of schools can receive the same program at the same time.
2. Timeliness. The material offered by radio must relate, at least, to its proper place in the yearly curriculum.
3. Utilization. It is not sufficient for the children to hear a lesson; some use must be made of it.
4. Program form. The lecture method has certain limitations which may be minimized by adapting it to this new medium.[4]

It is true that with the increased use of transcriptions, "repeat" programs, the growth of local educational stations, improved teacher guides, and more radio experience in general, some of the above handicaps have been reduced, but certain it is that much more remains to be done.

Aside from purely practical considerations, there are other handicaps concerning radio instruction which have been noted.

From the psychological point of view Cantril and Allport, after noting the advantages of radio, list the following disadvantages:

It [radio] cannot count upon the habits of disciplined and attentive listening that the classroom calls forth since it is usually regarded as a medium of entertainment rather than instruction.

All visual aids in education are absent, save only the aid of visual imagery.

Spontaneous questions are impossible.

Humor is less appreciated.

Circular phenomena are absent, and the invention of new ideas from class discussion becomes impossible.

There is less opportunity for the students to analyze and dissect the presentation.

Suggestibility is enhanced though perhaps no more so than in a congregate face-to-face assembly.

Lectures are impersonal with a consequent loss in friendliness and human interest.

---

[4] W. W. Charters, "Radio in Elementary and Secondary Schools," *Education on the Air*, Ohio State University, 1930, pp. 129–130.

Students do not, as inquiry shows, favor radio education as an exclusive substitute for classwork.[5]

Again, in recognition of these disadvantages, experimenters in radio education have developed techniques which, although they do not eliminate certain objections, have minimized many of them. For example, the use of visual materials with the radio broadcast, the "cooperative" radio lesson, skillful production, and improved script writing have aided greatly in this direction.

Lack of good reception has been a frequent complaint in more than one classroom, and many a fine radio program has not been productive because of this fault. Without at least satisfactory reception, teaching with radio merely substitutes expectation for realization, and nothing is more disheartening to both pupils and teachers.

Other limitations should be noted. The need for recognizing individual differences is apparent when dealing with an instrument for mass communication. However, satisfactory adjustments can be made through provision for varied types of follow-up work as suggested in the radio program guides. Unless specific adaptations are made in classroom procedures, not only a radio program but even a fine textbook may be said by some to disregard individual differences. The radio visit seldom comes more than once or twice a week and the rest of the time the classroom teacher is free to make whatever adjustments are needed. Indeed, if she feels that the radio material is not suited to the needs and capacities of her pupils, then she should be perfectly free not to receive it. Compulsion would certainly be a poor approach to use in the introduction of a new tool. The initial feeling of antagonism would interfere with achievement.

Mere passive listening is liable to be a weakness with certain types of radio material. Hearing and listening are not synonymous. Even with radio, the telling method is not real teaching. Worth-while pupil activity, particularly in the lower grades, is believed by some to stimulate learning. This activity may take a variety of forms—writing, computing, observing visual materials, answering questions, etc. An alert classroom teacher, who is aware of the possible weaknesses in a radio lesson, can do much to overcome them.

---

[5] Hadley Cantril and G. W. Allport, *Psychology of Radio*, Harper & Brothers, 1935, p. 253.

The best way to teach, it has been said, is in a number of ways. That, briefly, is radio's contribution to the teacher. It adds a new and vivid approach. Perhaps the best test is to ask whether the average teacher accomplishes as much in the same amount of time. Not whether she *can* accomplish as much, but whether she actually *does*. There is quite a gap between the potential and the actual, in teaching also.

And so in the final analysis the contributions and limitations of teaching with radio are both dependent upon a preliminary evaluation of the possible contribution that can be made by this medium. Undoubtedly it can serve in education. Conclusive evidence to that effect is shown as every day passes.

Basic and worth-while developments in the field of learning have not come about by any sudden revelation; rather they have emerged from years of trial and error. The initial period of indifference or opposition which later mellowed to curiosity and finally led to general acceptance suggests that the use of radio in the schools is repeating with striking similarity the story of the introduction of other methods and fields of study—laboratory instruction, physical education, manual arts, journalism, etc.

There is no denying that a healthy skepticism is essential for genuine and enduring advance. Yet within one generation radio broadcasting has come to have a recognized place in the American home and school.

And surely an even healthier skepticism is justified in regard to television. The lack of suitable programs during daytime hours, caused in part by the sheer expense of television production and in part by the lack of classroom receivers, gives many of us pause. But as Edgar Dale wrote in 1949,

. . . prophecy about television for even the next ten years is hazardous, and bad guesses about radio some twenty years ago make many persons cautious about new prophecies. We may claim too little rather than too much. . . . Our society has been producing excellent ideas much faster than we can distribute them. We have developed and used lots of ideas to improve technical competence, but have lagged far behind in improving social competence. Through television we can break the log jam, decrease the distance between technical and social competence.

As this edition goes to press, the combination of coaxial cable and microwave relays has spanned the continent, and more than three-quarters of the population of America has access to television. Programs are exchanged with stations in Canada by kinescope recording, and live programs come across our northern and southern borders in both directions. Of the 257 noncommercial stations authorized by the FCC, fewer than 10 per cent are on the air at this time, but the influence of those few is already far-reaching. Nearly a hundred schools and colleges are "feeding" TV programs to local commercial stations, many of them rehearsing the programs in well-equipped studios on their own campuses. The low-cost vidicon camera has given the less wealthy colleges and universities new hope, since they can now set up closed circuit studios for something like $25,000, instead of a quarter of a million, as before. Under the aegis of the Fund for the Advancement of Education numerous colleges are experimenting with closed circuit television as one possible answer to the rapidly approaching teacher and classroom shortage caused by the oncoming tidal wave of students. All in all, educational television is already beginning to make its contributions felt, and undoubtedly will, like educational radio, be a fully going concern by 1960.

2

The Development of Broadcasting in Schools

◇◇

Why has government regulation been necessary?

What is the FCC? Its scope? Some of the problems faced?

What is the history of early experimentation with educational radio?

What signs are there of the beginnings of educational television?

What is an educational program?

What are the obstacles to overcome?

◇◇◇◇◇◇◇◇COMPARED WITH THE HISTORIES of other forms of communication, that of radio is relatively brief. In 1873 the Scottish mathematician, James Clerk Maxwell, in his work *Electricity and Magnetism,* outlined theoretically and predicted the action of electromagnetic waves.

Fourteen years later Dr. Heinrich Rudolph Hertz demonstrated the existence of such waves and showed that they could be sent through space with the speed of light. Though he accomplished little of a practical nature, he pointed the way.

Sir Oliver Lodge, Nikola Tesla, Sir William Preece, and other continued the experiments. In 1895, Guglielmo Marconi sent and received wireless signals at his home in Bologna, Italy. By the turn of the century, messages were being transmitted from shore to ships, and on December 7, 1902, Marconi sent the first west-east transatlantic wireless messages from Glace Bay to England.

Several demonstrations given by Marconi before the officials of the United States Naval Board aroused great interest in this country. Outstanding among the American investigators were Profesor Reginald Fessenden and Dr. Lee De Forest. The latter hastened progress by inventing the audion, a three-element vacuum tube, having filament, plate, and grid. With the discoveries by E. H. Armstrong and the perfection of the vacuum tube by Dr. I. Langmuir, successful communication was established between the United States and Europe. The coming of the First World War and governmental control of radio communication facilities to meet the emergency gave impetus to the industry. When amateur operators formed societies and "listened in," radio broadcasting was founded. Whether the pioneer broadcasting station was KDKA in Pittsburgh or WWJ in Detroit has not been determined, but widespread public interest in broadcasting was not aroused until 1920, when returns were broadcast on the election of President Harding. Big business was quick to see the possibilities of radio, and in 1921 the Westinghouse Manufacturing Company established what is now Station WJZ at New York City. A year later the American Telephone and Telegraph Company opened Station WEAF, also in New York (now WNBC). At first the broadcasting groups expected to gain their revenue from the sale of receiving sets.

30

The thought of advertising did not come until later. During 1922 there was a mushroom growth of radio stations and nearly six hundred were organized.

In 1926 radio avertising was organized on a national basis when the National Broadcasting Company was formed by three leading public utilities. Station WEAF became the key station of the "Red" network and, later, WJZ was made the nucleus of the "Blue" network. The following year the Columbia Broadcasting System was organized around WABC (now WCBS). Soon other national and regional networks were in operation, such as Mutual, Yankee, and Don Lee.

Government Regulation Appears

Even in the early stages of broadcasting it was recognized that some type of governmental control over radio was essential. The Radio Act of 1912 had provided that every transmitter should be licensed, and a limit was placed on the frequency range of a station's operation. However, with the coming of the World War, private broadcasting was prohibited, and radio was placed under complete control of the government.

The period from 1920 to 1926 has been designated as one of "chaos in the airwaves." It was readily apparent that, as experimental transmitters began to fill the air, the Radio Act of 1912 was inadequate for satisfactory regulation of this new medium.

During the period from 1922 to 1925, Secretary of Commerce Herbert Hoover called a series of four annual conferences composed of representatives in the various fields of radio. These conferences laid the groundwork for future radio legislation, and four basic principles were evolved: (a) the control and regulation of radio should rest in the hands of the American people; (b) freedom of speech must be protected; (c) radio must be regulated so that the ideals and interests of the people are protected; (d) broadcasting in this country must be financed, largely if not entirely, by private enterprise.

Duties assigned to the Secretary of Commerce were as follows: (a) to classify stations, (b) to fix call letters, (c) to allocate power, (d) to set the time of operation, (e) to assign wave lengths, (f) to determine character of emission and the duration of licenses.

With this basic legislation established, it was hoped that the so-called chaotic conditions in radio would be reduced, but when the courts ruled that the Department of Commerce had no such powers and that anyone could broadcast any time anywhere, bedlam ensued. With stations selecting their own frequency as well as the hours of broadcasting, it was soon apparent that radio needed a traffic cop.

The Radio Act of 1927, which created the Federal Radio Commission of five members, assigned specific duties of the type noted above. Although it had no direct power of censorship, the commission could control the character of broadcasting, and at its own discrimination determine whether or not licenses were to be renewed. From concepts developed in previous public-utility legislation, it was agreed that radio regulation must be aimed for the "public interest, convenience, or necessity." This federal legislation assured broadcasters of a definite legal status and, as a result, the creation of the present American radio structure was begun.

In 1934 the Federal Communications Commission replaced the Federal Radio Commission, and under its jurisdiction were included telephone and telegraph activities as well as broadcasting.

Duties and Problems of the FCC

Organization.   As the government agency which regulates the operations of two potentially powerful educational influences—radio and television—it is highly desirable that teachers be familiar with its activities.

This administrative body is directed by seven commissioners each serving seven-year terms. Appointments are made by the president with the approval of the Senate, and both major political parties are represented.

Scope.   A major task of the Federal Communications Commission (FCC) is to allocate bands of frequencies to the various radio services. It would be wasteful and chaotic to attempt to operate a broadcast station on one frequency, a police station on the frequency immediately adjoining, an aircraft station on the frequency next to that, and a ship station next to that. There must be bands of frequencies for each of the thirty-nine radio services with which the commission deals, and within these bands assignments can be made to individual stations.

Thus, there must be bands for radio broadcasting, there must be bands for aircraft radio, for police radio, for fire department radio, for ships at sea, for railroad radio, and for television. There must be bands for radar and other navigation aids. There must be portions of the radio spectrum in which industrial, scientific, and medical equipment such as diathermy machines and radio heating devices, can operate without causing interference to important communication services. There must be bands for international broadcasting and bands for amateurs. Dividing the radio spectrum into bands of frequencies for the various radio services is also an international problem.

And once there is international agreement as to what the bands for the various services shall be, there must be a division of the assignments within the bands. For example, the bands set aside for radiotelephone and radiotelegraph in the world master plan must be shared by the stations of the United States with the stations of all the countries of the world. The ship bands must be shared, so must the aviation bands and the international broadcasting bands.

However, the assignment of frequencies is only a part of the FCC's activity. In the final analysis, broadcasting's service to the public must be measured largely in terms of programs and so, directly or indirectly, this agency is concerned with what the listener and viewer receive.

By the terms of the Communications Act, American radio and television stations have broad freedom. They are held not to be common carriers; that is, they may take or refuse specific programs as they please. The Commission is prohibited from censorship of programs. Contrary to what many educators believe, stations are not required to present any specified percentage of so-called public-service programs. However, the stations are required to operate in the public interest. This arrangement involves the use of discretion by both the licensees and the commission, and, of course, here is where disagreements arise.

Problems—INTERPRETATION OF FCC FUNCTIONS. Their function, say the government representatives, is to make the American broadcasting system a more nearly perfect instrument of democracy. The central problem, they point out, is how to obtain a wider diversification of expression over the air waves that will be more truly representative of *all* the segments of society.

Some industry representatives reply that this is another instance of increasing bureaucratic regimentation, that regulation can too readily become control and that the foundation of free American broadcasting is threatened. Statements such as the following are quite common, "Radio gives the people what they want. If their tastes are low, then radio is necessarily low-brow."

Wayne Coy, Chairman of the FCC, defines the function of that body in this manner: "In drawing that boundary line between the claims of the usually articulate and ably-represented private interests and the rights of the often inarticulate, unrepresented general public, the administrative agencies find their greatest opportunity for service."

Several moves have been made by the commission to clarify the meaning of public interest, convenience, or necessity and to determine the boundary line mentioned above.

One step taken more than a decade ago, and upheld by the Supreme Court, was the requirement that the National Broadcasting Company divest itself of one of its networks. The commission argued that this was too much concentration of control. It also banned practices which, it claimed, handicapped chain-affiliated stations in the development of programs to serve local community needs.

During the thirties, the general question of joint control of newspapers and broadcast stations was drawing the attention of Congress. It was also arising from time to time in connection with particular decisions of the commission. The commission held an extensive hearing on this problem in 1941. During this inquiry it was brought out that of 800 standard broadcast stations, 200 were owned to the extent of 50 per cent or more by newspaper interests, and 48 others were in a greater or lesser degree associated with newspapers. It was also discovered that, in more than 90 communities, the only radio station was licensed to, or associated with, the only newspaper.

The commission decided not to adopt any general rule with respect to newspaper ownership of radio stations. It stated that it did not desire to discourage legally qualified persons from applying for licenses, but that it did desire to encourage the maximum number of qualified persons to enter the field of mass communications and to permit them the use of modern inventions and improvements in the art, to ensure good public service. It announced that its policy would be to dispose of future newspaper applications on a case-by-case basis, taking care not to grant licenses that would result in placing control in the hands of the few to the exclusion of the many.

As a general policy, the commission, when it is confronted by two applications from a community, prefers the nonnewspaper application, other things being substantially equal.

Another barrier in the free flow of information, according to the FCC, has been the concentration of ownership of broadcasting stations. Commission rules now provide that no one person or company may own more than one station in its broadcasting radius. The rules also provide that no person may own more than a total of six FM stations or five television stations throughout the country as a whole.

In 1946 the FCC issued a report entitled, "Public Service Responsibility of Broadcast Licensees" which rocked the radio industry. This so-called "Blue Book" provided a wealth of detail on the increasing tendency of some broadcasters to backslide on their public-service responsibility by failing to live up to the promises they made to the commission when seeking their original licenses.

The commission announced that, thereafter, before renewing any station license, it would expect a showing of stricter compliance with a licensee's representations as to the public service he would render to the community. The commission emphasized that, under the law, it is the licensee himself who must discharge the responsibility of rendering a service to the community in which he operates. He cannot relieve himself of that responsibility by delegating the task of program making to the networks or others. He cannot discharge that responsibility if he ignores the availability of talent in his community and fails to give it a radio outlet. He cannot adequately live up to that responsibility if he operates his station solely for private gain in a manner marked by advertising excesses. And he cannot affirmatively fulfill that responsibility if he fails to make his station available for the airing of issues of importance to the community and the rendition of other sustaining service directed to the vital interests of the community. The commission, therefore, served notice that in issuing and in renewing the licenses of broadcast stations it would look to see whether that responsibility had been fulfilled.

Other FCC rulings have dealt with give-away programs, station editorializing, and censorship. As developments in television continue it is apparent that further governmental action will take place.

REGULATORY PROBLEMS. Today, over twenty years after the FCC was established, there remains an obvious current of unrest and often bitter opposition to several practices and trends in American broadcasting. Criticisms have been voiced by men in public office and various social agencies as well as by broadcasters themselves. Generally speaking, one group states that radio is tending toward monopoly control by a few and that such control of public opinion in a democracy is a potential danger. They advocate more stringent government regulation. Another group insists that such complaints are made largely to secure more and more government control of radio and that such control would be fatal to the basic American right of free speech.

The comments expressed by former Commissioner C. J. Durr at the 1947 Institute for Education by Radio are indicative of one point of view: "Some feel the test of a 'democratic' radio depends largely upon the size of its audience. Others argue, the test is how well radio serves the ends of a democratic society—an enlightened people capable of making intelligent choices."

As to the public acceptance of current radio offerings Wayne Coy, referred to earlier, stated,

All this talk of 85,000,000 sets and 2,700 stations is very heady and heartening but it's apt to be so misleading. After all, we are supposed to be getting radio service to people, not measuring our success by sets purchased or stations put on the air. I don't know what the up-to-date figures are but a network vice-president a while back stated that at night 75 percent of the sets are turned off and in the daytime 86 percent are turned off. As a member of the FCC which is supported not just by constant listeners but by all the taxpayers, I don't feel I can be complacent about a situation even approximating that.

A recent example of the FCC's policy-making function was its action in regard to color television. It was announced by the FCC on October 13, 1950, that CBS might proceed with commercial broadcasting, using the color television system devised by this particular broadcasting system through years of research. The ruling was disapproved by many on the grounds that color television was not yet perfected, and that to allow CBS to proceed with a method which might soon be obsolete would be fair neither to the public nor to other broadcasting systems. The courts upheld the FCC, and CBS began commercial broadcasts in color in midyear of 1951.* Before that year was out, however, material shortages compelled the government to request a stoppage of further color development and CBS voluntarily abandoned color broadcasting. Half a year was too short a space in which to tell whether the public wanted color enough to warrant the switchover from black-and-white set manufacture, and whether the FCC was justified in its decision. The one fact that stands out now is that, barring further military emergencies, television will develop faster than many had anticipated, and that interest in the development of this new means of communication stems from every small homeowner as well as the government. Even if nothing comes of color television in the near future, the FCC ruling has stimulated interest which may in itself be educational—the interest of a free people who intend to keep their right of free speech through new developments of all its tools—the press, radio, and video.

It is not the purpose here to pass judgment upon the justifications for such criticism or to debate the relative merits of the present plan as compared with a quasi-governmental scheme as recommended by some. The point is that the pattern of American broadcasting is still evolving. Many questions remain, such as: What shall be the relationship between government and the broadcasting industry? What are the criteria for judging whether or not a station is actually serving the public interest, convenience, and necessity? To what extent shall newspaper and motion-picture interests control radio, television, and facsimile? At what point do network radio and television submerge local interests? How free shall commentators be? To what extent shall the government operate international short-wave stations? In terms of public interest, what is the desired relationship between advertising agency and station operator? Are self-imposed "codes" enough in assuring public interest? Should any part of the program schedule

---

* Since this time, the picture has changed. The RCA compatible color system, permitting reception of color programs in black-and-white on standard receivers is now approved and used by all networks.

be reserved for nonsponsored public service programs? These and other questions await satisfactory solution. Educators will follow with great interest and no little concern the maturation of the Fifth Estate.

Early Considerations of Radio as an Educational Medium

From the very beginning of broadcasting, professional educators thought of radio as a cultural medium. Much of the leadership in this direction came, as it still does, from the United States Office of Education. Only four years after the first commercial broadcast, Dr. John J. Tigert, then Commissioner of Education, evidenced keen and early interest in the possibilities of radio in education. He wrote:

The school, the library, and the newspaper are usually ranked as the three great educational agencies. The radio promises to take its place as the fourth, and it appears to be fast fulfilling that promise. . . .

Even the details of his [the child's] instrument stimulate scientific inquiry, and every adjustment is an experiment in physics. The child who saves his pennies, buys materials from the ten-cent store, and constructs an instrument that will enable him to hear conversations a mile away has learned lessons in thrift, in handiwork, and in science that the best teachers in the land might well contemplate with envy. And what he receives through that instrument afterwards contributes to his appreciation of music, his acquaintance with literature, and his knowledge of world affairs in a way which effectively supplements the instruction which he receives in school, though it may be lacking in organization and sequence.[1]

Various state departments of education also recognized the possibilities of this medium and soon courses were broadcast which were more or less systematically organized. The pioneering efforts of Ben Darrow in organizing the *Ohio School of the Air* are well known.[2] The activities of the Massachusetts State Department of Education, Division of University Extension, are likewise noteworthy.

Growth of Radio in Schools. The public schools were not slow in experimentation and soon here and there throughout the land evidences of real accomplishment were apparent. To list definitely in chronological order these developments is a difficult and perhaps im-

---

[1] Armstrong Perry, *Radio in Education*, The Payne Fund, 1929, pp. 41–42.

[2] Ben Darrow, *Radio, The Assistant Teacher*, R. G. Adams and Co., 1936, and *Radio Trailblazing*, College Book Co., 1940.

possible task, since some of the experiments were not widely publicized. The following list is quoted from a Federal Writers' Project publication.

1. Haaren High School, New York City, claims the honor of being the first public school to broadcast regularly scheduled instruction classes by radio. It started with the broadcast of accounting lessons in 1923 and gained such momentum by the following year that its radio activities were made the subject of a 254 page report by the New York City Board of Education.

2. Buffalo, N.Y., 1922: Vocational School pupils built a complete radio station which was utilized to broadcast programs by pupils from the city's schools.

3. Atlantic City, N.J., 1923: School news and musical programs were broadcast by municipal broadcasting station located in a high school.

4. Los Angeles, Calif., 1923: Mrs. Grace C. Stanley, Commissioner of Elementary Schools, broadcast talks on history and geography of that state. These talks were scheduled to start the school day and records indicated that they were responsible for a material reduction in the percentage of tardiness in schools equipped for radio.

5. Oakland, Calif., 1924: Dr. Virgil E. Dickson started series of lessons on physical training, penmanship, arithmetic, history, literature, English, geography, etc., consisting of twenty-minute lessons preceded by four minutes of music. Fifty-six lessons were presented in 1924–1925 and the lessons were continued for several years.

6. Cook County, Ill., 1924: *Little Red School House* was started by Station WLS as a weekly program for schools of the county. Talks were given on corn, dairying, birds, automobiles, achievements of boys and girls, etc. Papers were prepared and read by pupils and music was furnished by them. Parent-teacher groups equipped the schools with radio receivers.

7. Kansas State Agricultural College, Station KSAC, October 5, 1925: *College of the Air* with courses in psychology, English, sociology, community organization, literature, economics, journalism, and vocational education was started. Lectures were supplemented by home study and examinations taken under supervision of county superintendents for credits amounting to one year of college attendance.

8. Cleveland, Ohio, 1925: First radio courses in music appreciation were organized by Miss Alice Keith of the Cleveland Public

Schools. Cleveland Symphony Orchestra played for upper grades and high school with other music provided for primary and intermediate grades. Miss Keith introduced the first radio music textbook written by herself for use in the course, and records showed a 100 per cent increase in attendance at children's concerts of the Cleveland Symphony Orchestra as a result.

9. Atlanta, Ga., 1926: A *Public School of the Air* was presented with 30-minute daily programs prepared by an executive committee consisting of the city superintendent, supervisors, principals, and teachers. Additional programs were presented in the evenings for parent-teacher associations and parents and children in the homes. Radio receivers were supplied by a local dealer.

10. Arkansas, 1926: A. B. Hill, State Superintendent of Schools, utilized a commercial station to reach 112 Smith-Hughes centers in that state—more than he was able to visit by automobile in three months.

11. Upton, Mass., 1927: Principal Stewart B. Atkinson, of the Upton High School, submitted a report indicating that 53 of the 253 Massachusetts high schools were equipped with radio receivers and that twenty-nine of the sets had been made in the schools.

12. Hartford, Conn., 1926: The Connecticut State Board of Education initiated a music appreciation series with lessons broadcast by a commercial station. The lessons were received by groups of 600 to 800 pupils and it was estimated that the average audience numbered at least 25,000.[3]

Various organizations soon were formed to promote the cultural use of radio.

In 1930 the National Advisory Council on Radio in Education was organized to stimulate an interest in radio education.

Another organization, the National Committee on Education by Radio, which was supported by the Payne Fund, was somewhat more aggressive in its methods. Since it felt that certain commercial groups were at times unfriendly to the development of educational broadcasting, it demanded that a share of the broadcasting frequencies be set aside for educational purposes.

From various sources comments were heard of a "cultural reawakening" and a "spiritual rebirth" due to radio's influence. Leading civic and educational bodies adopted resolutions. Meetings and institutes

<hr />

[3] *Radio in Education*, Department of Public Instruction, Harrisburg, Pa., 1939, pp. 5–6.

were common, and the future of radio as a cultural agency seemed bright.[4]

Characteristic of the hopeful outlook were expressions such as the following:

Glenn Frank, former president of the University of Wisconsin:

I have an exalted conception of what radio can mean to the American future. I think the invention of the radio equals in significance the invention of the printing press. Specifically, the radio promises to render two important services to the American future: (1) it promises to unify us as a people, and (2) it promises to debunk our leadership.[5]

The National Committee on Education by Radio:

Colleges and universities with radio broadcasting stations have in their possession one of the most powerful and effective tools for popular education which exists at the present time. Ohio is the first state to maintain from public funds a state school of the air. Our children's children will honor Ohio for her pioneering vision.[6]

Historian James T. Shotwell, Columbia University:

Challenging situations will continue to arise with every new orientation of society, but I am confident that through the use of radio there will be brought to their solution a more direct, a more rational, a more intelligent technique than has ever been used in the realm of politics in the past.[7]

"Radio is in its infancy, and infancy is a poor time to decide what character the adult is going to have," said Raymond Swing to the Sixth Annual Institute for Education by Radio. A new social mechanism could hardly be expected to reach maximum efficiency in a single decade.

Today, more than three decades after modern broadcasting began, the same comments might well be repeated. The once infant radio, now grown to adolescence, is often awkward, occasionally precocious, but still growing rapidly. And the pattern of its growth, the educator must admit, has not been fashioned greatly by formalized educational

---

[4] Wm. B. Levenson, *The Training of Radio Personnel: An Analytical Approach,* Western Reserve University, 1937, p. 34.

[5] *Education by Radio,* II, No. 19 (June 9, 1932), 72.

[6] *Ibid.,* II, No. 16 (April 28, 1932), 63.

[7] James T. Shotwell, "Radio in Historical Perspective," in *Radio and Education,* University of Chicago Press, 1931, p. 23.

influences but rather by commercial advertisers. Yet none will doubt that, though a major objective of the radio "show" is to distribute merchandise, still it may, and often does, have definite cultural values.

Educational Television Is Growing Slowly

Television's "potential" for education was even more loudly proclaimed by educators, manufacturers and broadcasters than that of radio or film. With sound and sight, plus motion, actuality and immediacy placed at the service of the teacher, it seemed to provide the answer to many a school broadcaster's prayer. Yet, fifteen years after television was working in the laboratories, ten years after it was made commercially available to homes in the New York City, Chicago, and Los Angeles areas, video's most ardent apologists were constrained to admit that television in the classrooms was still more potential than actual, even by the mid-point of the twentieth century.

One naturally asks: Why is not television used more? Perhaps George Seldes suggests the answer: "The arts live by daily bread."

Educational radio programs are provided by university and community owned stations, paid for out of public funds, or they are supplied by commercial stations who pay for these usually sustaining programs out of the profits made on sponsored shows. Few if any television stations will have excess profits before 1955; at the present writing (1951) any station that is "in the black" for any month proudly proclaims it in the trade press.

And anyone who has watched a television program go on the air from a studio, realizes that the cost of producing a video program is far greater than that of presenting one by radio. More (and highly expensive) equipment and a larger technical force are necessary, since, in addition to operating engineers, the TV staff must include cameramen, dolly pushers, microphone-boom operators, stage hands, prop men, electricians, and projectionists to handle film and slides. There is the cost of scenery, lighting equipment, "props," film, slides, and special art work. In a dramatic presentation, the cast must memorize lines and exact positions before the cameras, and that means longer rehearsals. Make-up is now used almost universally; costumes might well be needed in a historical program.

Thus, with commercial television programs barely paying their way, it can readily be seen that educational video might well result in considerable financial loss. The remarkable thing is that so many broadcasters have been willing to incur this loss; it is natural that they have sought to ensure as large an audience as possible for their public service ventures. And here we come to the crux of the problem: stations are unwilling to schedule programs during school hours when there are few or no television receivers in the schools, while school authorities are understandably reluctant to invest in expensive receiving equipment when there are few or no programs available.

This familiar cycle has been broken in several instances on an experimental basis by school systems which have borrowed receivers from far-sighted manufacturers or distributors for a period of several months, during which local stations have planned, in cooperation with school experts, one or more series aimed at these temporarily equipped classrooms. Chicago schools in 1945–1946, Philadelphia and Baltimore schools in 1949, took part in such experiments.

When one recalls that American television, like that of other nations, was brought to a standstill during the war years and did not make truly nation-wide progress, either in receiver installations or in transmitter availability, until 1947, the hopeful student may well be encouraged by the recent signs of interest in educational video's brief history.

One of the earliest uses of television as an education medium occurred at the State University of Iowa. Many of the topics which were presented by the experimental television transmitter at the University have since been repeated countless times by unconscious imitators, showing how fundamentally sound was this early approach.

The subjects described in a 1934 report by E. B. Kurtz included:

Oral hygiene—Dentistry Department—illustrating correct method of brushing teeth

Identifying trees—Botany Department—leaves used for identification

Equilibrium—Physics Department—diagrams and models used

Reading, architectural—Engineering drawings—symbols used and detail drawings shown

Trail marking—Girl Scout lecture—diagrams of trail markings shown

Shorthand—Commerce Department—shorthand symbols and differences

Charcoal sketching—Art Department—portrait drawn during discussion

The University of Iowa Publications—statistical charts, pen and ink drawings of buildings, and pictures of president and deans shown

Spring birds—museum, mounted specimens shown

French pronunciation—Romance Languages Department—speaker illustrated lip and tongue movements

The constellations—Astronomy Department—diagrams of constellations shown

Iowa wild-life series—museum—mounted animals shown

Graded art lesson series—Art Department—elementary art taught and illustrated [8]

The war, which inhibited the growth and expansion of television, also provided two unusual instances of the value of television in mass education. When the need to train large numbers of air-raid wardens arose in New York City, RCA installed receivers in numerous police stations. Classes of air-raid wardens met there for training in enemy-aircraft recognition, methods of dealing with incendiary bombs, and first aid. NBC and CBS also broadcast for the general public, few of whom had receivers, instructions for dealing with incendiary bombs and also an extended series on first aid.

Shortly after the war's end, Station WBKB and the Chicago Public Schools cooperated in two series, *Young Chicago* and *A View to Education*. Receivers of two different screen sizes were borrowed from a local manufacturer, and "television classrooms" were set up to evaluate the broadcasts. (Incidentally, more recent investigations point to the 16-inch screen as the minimum for classroom use.)

At about the same time, CBS Television cooperated with the New York Board of Education's radio station WNYE in the presentation of *There Ought to Be a Law*, a high-school discussion program. This series ran on the average of twice a month for nearly two years. It was presented in the early evening and aimed at the general viewing audience.

In the following fall (1946) NBC and the Board of Education experimented with two elaborate science programs, one dealing with

[8] E. B. Kurtz, "Teaching by Television," *Education on the Air*, Ohio State University, 1934, pp. 258–262.

atomic energy, the other with theories of flight. One hundred selected junior high-school students were pretested on the subject matter covered by each broadcast. They viewed the programs at NBC on large-screen receivers and discussed the broadcasts. Then they were re-examined. In addition, control groups of matched ability in general science were given the same tests. The experiment was not continued for a sufficient time to provide definite results, but all indications pointed to great effectiveness and rapid learning.

In 1948, Creighton University, Omaha, Nebraska, in cooperation with Station WOW-TV, broadcast a series of programs on microscopic life, applying a modification of the microphotographic projector to television.

Perhaps the most extensive experiment in the use of television for educational purposes yet attempted was undertaken by the Special Training Devices Section of the United States Navy for the greater part of 1949. With special observers from the Army and Air Forces in attendance, special courses in technical subjects such as Naval Ordinance and Gunnery were taught by outstanding naval instructors in a television studio operated by the Navy's Special Devices Center at Sands Point, Port Washington, Long Island. These were transmitted by microwave to classroom receivers in the Merchant Marine Academy at King's Point, Long Island, a few miles away. In addition to some 130 programs done on this closed circuit, a series of eighteen hour-long programs was presented for use in training reservists through NBC to WNBT, New York; WPTZ, Philadelphia; and WNBW, Washington, D.C.

At the Merchant Marine Academy, the junior class was divided at random into five sections of about twenty students each. Two sections were taught by television and three face to face, in the usual way. In as many classes as possible, the same instructor taught the remote classes and the face-to-face groups, to eliminate the factor of instructor differential.

Individual subjects covered in the TV lessons included radar, sonar, battery alignment, and CIC. Fordham University cooperated by setting up pre- and postinstruction tests to compare teaching by (a) television, (b) television instructors face to face in the classroom, (c) normal classroom instruction, (d) kinescope recordings. Students and instructors rated the broadcasts as well, and specimen rating sheets are shown in Chapter 8, "Measuring the Results."

The results of the evaluation, as reported by Professor Robert T. Rock, Jr., of Fordham University, are most revealing. For the officers tested, television teaching was more effective than teaching by local instructors in 50 per cent of the comparisons made. In another 38 per cent of the comparisons, it was just as effective. For the enlisted men, television was more effective in 53 per cent of the cases and just as effective in another 20 per cent. In all, 80 per cent of comparisons showed television as good or better than local instructors. TV recordings or kinescopes were judged as good or better than local instructors in 75 per cent of the comparisons, and kinescopes were reported as satisfactory as live programs in 84 per cent of the comparisons. It should be pointed out that only two comparisons could be made: *gain in knowledge* and *amount of knowledge,* in adults of common interest. General education admittedly is concerned with many more factors.

One unusual feature, not available to most such projects, was a talk-back microphone in each classroom whereby students might ask questions of the television instructor. The voice of the student came into the studio, was heard by all viewers, and the question could then be answered by the teacher. Of course, only on such a closed circuit could such facilities be provided. With a large number of classrooms such a procedure seems unlikely with present technical facilities.

Recognizing that television could not replace the teacher, but could only supplement her work, the schools of Philadelphia and Baltimore took steps in 1949 to move educational programs from the evening hours into the school day. Programs orginating from WBAL-TV were received on thirty-six sets loaned by a local set distributor. In Philadelphia, some sixty sets were made available by manufacturers, besides another dozen in Camden schools, and an over-all program of five broadcasts a week arranged with three Philadelphia stations. The following year saw eight programs a week, about which more details are given in Chapters 4 and 7.

This may be the pattern of the future—television sets borrowed for the schools, so that programs will be made available. Then, sets purchased as more programs are provided, and so on until in-school telecasts are accepted by public, schools, and stations. Thus is the early history of radio being repeated. For there, too, PTA gifts, for example, first brought radio into many a classroom.

Educational Programs Fall into Two Divisions

The meaning of the term "educational program" has been discussed extensively by school men. In fact, the search for a definition has been the subject of many conferences. In a very general sense *all* broadcasts may be called educational. The eminent radio speaker, professor, and former legislator, T. V. Smith, indicates that a program is educational "when intelligent people talk about something important." Whether all educational programs need be of the "talk" type is, of course, open to question. The definition presented by W. W. Charters has been accepted generally. He defines an educational program as "One whose purpose it is to raise standards of taste, to increase the range of valuable information, or to stimulate audiences to undertake worth while activities."

Using the term "educational" in a general sense, two major divisions of such cultural programs may be recognized:

1. Broadcasting part of a formal curriculum into the schoolroom. Examples of this type are the programs prepared by various city school systems such as Chicago, Rochester, Cleveland, and Detroit. Less formal in nature, yet of definite classroom value, are the regular school programs sponsored by radio networks, such as the Standard School Broadcast of the NBC Pacific coast chain. The school offerings of the various college-owned radio stations are generally included in this first division.
2. The other major division of educational programs includes a wide variety of more informal presentations. The former chairman of the board of the Radio Corporation of America, General James G. Harbord, speaking at the University of Chattanooga, listed these: "Outstanding news events, eye-witness accounts 'on scene,' speeches, music and dramatizations." Although in a narrow sense the educational value of *some* dramatizations, *some* music, and *some* speeches. might be questioned, yet the classification seems reasonable.

In the field of television, the term "educational" is even more frequently and more loosely applied, since there are as yet far more "informally educative," than specifically instructional, programs on the air. However, there can be no dispute about the educational value of the fine dramas and literary adaptations to be seen on such programs as *Kraft Theatre, Studio One, Philco Playhouse,* or *Ford Theatre.* Nor will any educator question the value of Edward R. Murrow's unusual presentation of events on the CBS television series, *See It Now.*

Similarly, the art instructions of Jon Gnagy (*You Are an Artist*) and the scientific demonstrations of Dr. Roy K. Marshall (*The Nature of Things*) and Ivan Sanderson (*Treasures of Earth*) are educational programs by any standard. Film classics and good travelogues will pass muster, as must remote pickups from Washington or the headquarters of the United Nations. On the whole, then, television would seem to fall into the same classifications as those given above for radio.

University Radio Stations. At one time there were more than one hundred licensed educational stations in the United States. By May, 1927, the number of such stations, as shown by the records of the former Federal Radio Commission, had decreased to ninety-four. According to the National Committee on Education by Radio, twenty-three educational stations were forced to suspend operations between January 1 and August 1, 1930. By the following fall the number of college stations was reduced to forty-nine. In 1950 there were again over 100 educational radio stations. It is significant that, as the number of college-owned radio stations has decreased, there has been at the same time a slow but steady increase in the number of short-wave radio stations owned and operated by local boards of education. A brief history of this development will be noted later.

The majority of college stations have endured similar experiences. Some have fallen by the wayside while others, through years of experience, have developed satisfactory and often excellent program services. President Tyson suggests that the story of these institutions can be divided into separate and distinct stages of development.[9]

In the beginning the college station was either an "experimental plaything" or a laboratory for engineering courses. Later, when the

---

[9] Levering Tyson, *Education Tunes In*, American Association for Adult Education, 1930, p. 40.

apparatus was developed, programs were needed and the administrators then saw that some use could be made of the station. A director was appointed, usually one with limited experience. The novelty of the new instrument had great appeal. The faculty members were anxious to take part. Enthusiasm ran high, and lectures and program plans were readily forthcoming. However, this enthusiasm was of short duration. Faculty members began to wonder whether the results were really worth their efforts. Program plans became scarce and the administrators began to doubt the educational values claimed for broadcasting. A critical stage in the life of the station was reached.

New difficulties appeared in the form of commercial stations which were being established. Very often interference was so great that the college station could not be heard and the number of listeners began to drop off. The Federal Radio Commission, in attempting to eliminate station interference, required that the institutionally owned station had to present a continuous supply of programs on the air in order to retain its license. "Faced with the necessity of filling this air time somehow," says Tyson, "the amateur director took the only course that was open to him. He resorted to entertainment."

At this stage the administrators of the school began to wonder whether the radio station was really worth its cost. The depression, in several cases, forced the issue. The stations were closed. Some schools, however, retained their radio stations as public relations agencies and others effected a reorganization of policy, added cultural programs, and provided additional aid to remunerate lecturers and other station talent. Some of these stations secured a new wave length and installed modern equipment. They served the cultural needs of their community, promoted their institutions, and trained students. For many college stations, however, this metamorphosis was too trying and, as has been noted, their total number dwindled.

Use in School Systems. The development of educational broadcasting by city school systems differs in some respects from that of colleges and universities. The use of radio, at least as a public relations medium, is generally accepted by the larger systems. In a survey of 100 large cities in 1938 it was found that 87 per cent were making some use of radio to interpret the schools to the public. Continuous programs throughout the year were presented by 56 per cent of the schools.[10]

Aside from this public relations aspect, the movement for a continuous plan of programs designed for in-school consumption has been undergoing a steady but slow growth. Since the formative years of educational broadcasting in America took place during the nation's depression years, progress was retarded. When the man on the street spoke of "fads and frills," the time was hardly a propitious one for experimentation. Highly significant, however, is the fact that the support of a successful and continuous effort—Standard School Broadcasts—has been provided by commercial interests.

Obstacles to Overcome

From its very inception, formal school broadcasting ran into a series of difficulties. That radio eventually would supplant the classroom instructor was but the ranting of the "lunatic fringe." Yet some teachers in charge of classes receiving programs failed to realize the implications of the fact that the radio at best was merely a supplement to effective teaching. Teaching with radio, an auditory aid, requires careful preparation, as does any visual aid, and in most cases a thorough follow-up. Broadcasting operations, work sheets, visual materials, and an evaluation program not only require much additional time and effort, but a considerable financial outlay as well.

The factors mentioned earlier as limitations in the use of radio also apply as complications in the acceptance of this tool. These factors, it will be recalled, are (a) synchronization, (b) timeliness, (c) utilization, and (d) program form. There is a definite relationship between these difficulties and the establishment of radio stations owned and operated by schools.

With the modern departmentalized school, the problem of adjustment to schedule periods is aggravated. Particularly is this problem difficult when it is accepted that the radio program, in most instances, should be so spaced in the class period that there can be some time for preparation as well as for follow-up. Recognition of this problem

---

[10] W. B. Levenson, "The Use of Radio to Interpret the Schools to the Public," a study noted in *Educational Research Service*, N.E.A., September, 1939, p. 7.

meant, in a sense, that the radio programs could be better utilized in the elementary schools. In the lower grades it was an easier task to receive a particular program, since the division of time for the study of a given topic could be easily reallocated. Geography could be studied as easily at two-thirty as at ten-thirty.

The factor of timeliness is one which cannot be overlooked. From the classroom teacher's point of view, the radio material being presented has to fit in somehow with the school curriculum. The teacher is quick to point out that a program on the Civil War, though interesting, is of limited value if given while the students are studying the problems of the Revolutionary War.

From the very outset of school broadcasting this difficulty pointed to the fact that a formal school radio program presumed to fit in with a specific school curriculum would have to be confined to smaller and more compact geographical areas. In other words, since a similarity of curricular sequence was desired, the chances were greater that it would be found within selected localities. And for that reason the development of formal school broadcasting was confined largely to city school systems.

Many educators insist that whether or not the radio program is related definitely to the course of study is immaterial. The decisive factor, it is claimed, is whether the radio program provides, directly or indirectly, a desirable educational experience. There is general theoretical agreement with this point of view, but from the perspective of many classroom teachers it is a naïve assumption—what with tests, supervisors, and the pressure of time. The fact remains that if the classroom teacher who is voluntarily accepting the program actually believes that the time spent listening to the radio should definitely reinforce her classroom efforts, then any approach which presumes to be realistic must be cognizant of her wishes.

Lack of proper classrom utilization was another factor which handicapped the growth of school radio. When it was recognized finally that merely *hearing* the radio program was no more valuable than merely *showing* the movie, then a definite and worthwhile step in reaching educational objectives had been taken. Obviously the specific limitations mentioned earlier, such as synchronization and timeliness, definitely affect the quality of utilization.

The question of program form presented additional problems. The simplest thing was tried first, the lecture method. But it was soon evident that the pedant had much to learn from the "showman," for procedures that succeeded in the classroom required some modification when put on the air. When the novelty of listening wore off and the determining factor became program quality, the educational broadcaster had to learn the tricks of a new trade. During the process of apprenticeship the audience too often was lost.

Sustained experimentation in school broadcasting was handicapped by various factors: the indifference or undue conservatism of some administrators, the lack of satisfactory equipment, the pressure of time upon the broadcasting teachers, the absence of effective organization and experience as well as insufficient funds. In certain localities, nevertheless, where the vision and courage of the administration surmounted apparent handicaps, the broadcasting of school programs continued with varying degrees of success.

An Opportunity Appears.   On January 26, 1938, governmental action provided the opportunity for which some progressive schoolmen had been waiting. It was announced by the FCC that five channels in the ultra-high frequency band between 41,000 and 42,000 kilocycles had been allocated for assignment to noncommercial broadcast stations. Technical advance had made it evident that the ultrashort waves could also be used for broadcasting.

Speaking of the use of such school stations, former United States Commissioner of Education J. W. Studebaker, who played a leading role in securing FCC action, stated:

An educational agency with an ultra-high frequency local radio station at its command could, for instance:
1. Reach all teachers and classrooms any day instantly.
2. Project the message of the eminent visitor through his own voice to every school room and to the community no matter how unexpected the opportunity.
3. Take to every teacher in his classroom the model lessons prepared by master teachers.
4. Make the outstanding production of any school in music or drama the common property of all schools.
5. Eliminate the disadvantages which outlying schools suffer because of their location in contacts with the central office and other schools.

6. Act instantly in countless emergencies.
7. Cultivate new fields in educational radio experimentation under local initiative and control.[11]

The Commission's rules pertaining to such station operation are as follows:

Rule 1057. The term noncommercial educational broadcast station means a high-frequency broadcast station licensed to an organized nonprofit educational agency for the advancement of its educational work and for the transmission of educational and entertainment programs to the general public.

Rule 1058. The operation of, and the service furnished by, noncommercial educational broadcast stations shall be governed by the following regulations in addition to the rules and regulations governing high-frequency broadcast stations.

1. A noncommercial educational broadcast station will be licensed only to an organized nonprofit educational agency and upon a showing that the station will be used for the advancement of the agency's educational program.

2. Each station may transmit programs directed to specific schools in the system for use in connection with the regular courses as well as routine and administrative material pertaining to the school system and may transmit educational and entertainment programs to the general public.

3. Each station shall furnish a nonprofit and noncommercial broadcast service. No sponsored or commercial program shall be transmitted nor shall commercial announcements of any character be made. A station shall not transmit the programs of other classes of broadcast stations unless all commercial announcements and commercial references in the continuity are eliminated.

4. The transmitting equipment, installation and operation as well as the location of the transmitter shall be in conformity with the requirements of good engineering practice as released from time to time by the Commission.

5. Any rule or regulation governing high-frequency broadcast stations which permits or requires operation different from or in conflict with the provisions of this rule shall not apply to noneducational broadcast stations.

Rule 1059 which deals with channel assignments has been changed twice. In May, 1940, the FCC, while conducting a hearing relative to

---

[11] J. W. Studebaker, "Private Airways for Public Education," *School Life*, March, 1938, p. 7.

the use of frequency modulation broadcasting, affirmed the right of educational agencies to the exclusive use of radio bands. Because of the development and acceptance of FM, or, as it is sometimes designated, "staticless" broadcasting, the educational reservation was moved and five new channels were allocated for noncommercial educational use; stations were to transmit by FM. It was estimated that this decision would permit the erection of as many as three thousand local stations.

On January 15, 1945, the FCC announced that twenty channels, each 200 kilocycles wide, from 84 to 88 megacycles, would be allocated for educational stations.

At present such operation licenses have been granted as follows:

Noncommercial Educational FM Broadcast Stations

By September 1, 1951, licenses had been granted to nearly 100 Noncommercial Educational FM broadcast stations in 35 states—the largest number in any one state being 7, an honor shared by California, Indiana, and New York.

STATE AND CITY	CALL LETTERS		LICENSEE
Alabama			
Tuscaloosa	WUOA	(FM)	Board of Trustees, Univ. of Alabama
Arizona			
Phoenix	KFCA	(FM)	Phoenix College
Thatcher	KGIA	(FM)	Gila Jr. College of Graham County
Arkansas			
Siloam Springs	KUOA	(FM)	KUOA, Inc. John Brown Univ.
California			
Long Beach	KLON	(FM)	Long Beach Board of Education
Los Angeles	KUSC	(FM)	Univ. of Southern California
Oceanside	KOEN	(FM)	Oceanside-Carlsbad Union High School District
San Diego	KSDS	(FM)	San Diego Unified School District
San Francisco	KALW	(FM)	Board of Education of San Francisco
Santa Monica	KCRW	(FM)	Santa Monica School Board

STATE AND CITY	CALL LETTERS		LICENSEE
California			
Stockton	KCVN	(FM)	College of the Pacific
Colorado			
Colorado Springs	KRCC	(FM)	Colorado College
Florida			
Miami	WTHS	(FM)	Lindsey Hopkins Vocational School
Georgia			
Atlanta	WABE	(FM)	Board of Education, City of Atlanta
Atlanta	WGST	(FM)	Regents, Georgia Inst. of Technology
Illinois			
Chicago	WBEZ	(FM)	Board of Education, City of Chicago
Elgin	WEPS	(FM)	Bd. of Educ., Union School Dist. #46
Evanston	WNUR	(FM)	Northwestern Univ.
Urbana	WIUC	(FM)	University of Illinois
Indiana			
Bloomington	WFIU	(FM)	Trustees of Indiana University
Evansville	WEVC	(FM)	Evansville College
Greencastle	WGRE	(FM)	DePauw University
Huntington	WVSH	(FM)	School City of Huntington
Indianapolis	WAJC	(FM)	Jordan College of Music
Muncie	WWHI	(FM)	Wilson Junior High School
New Albany	WNAS	(FM)	School City of New Albany
New Castle	WYSN	(FM)	New Castle–Henry Township Schools
Iowa			
Ames	WOI	(FM)	Iowa State College
Iowa City	KSUI	(FM)	State Univ. of Iowa
Waverly	KWAR	(FM)	Wartburg Normal College of the ALC
Kansas			
Lawrence	KANU	(FM)	Univ. of Kansas
Manhattan	KSDB	(FM)	Kansas State College
Ottawa	KTJO	(FM)	Ottawa University
Wichita	KMUW	(FM)	Municipal University of Wichita

STATE AND CITY	CALL LETTERS	LICENSEE
Kentucky		
Lexington	WBKY (FM)	Univ. of Kentucky
Louisville	WFPL (FM)	Board of Trustees, Free Public Library
Louisville	WSDX (FM)	Southern Baptist Theological Seminary
Louisiana		
Baton Rouge	WLSU (FM)	Louisiana State Univ.
New Orleans	WBEH (FM)	P. G. Beauregard School
Maryland		
Baltimore	WBJC (FM)	Baltimore Jr. College
Massachusetts		
Boston	WBUR (FM)	Boston University
Boston	WERS (FM)	Emerson College
Boston	WGBH (FM)	Lowell Institute
Springfield	WEDK (FM)	School Community of Springfield
Michigan		
Ann Arbor	WUOM (FM)	Regents of the Univ. of Michigan
Detroit	WDTR (FM)	Board of Education, City of Detroit
East Lansing	WKAR (FM)	Michigan State College
Kalamazoo	WMCR (FM)	West Michigan College of Education
Minnesota		
St. Paul	WNOV (FM)	Northwestern Vocational Institute
Mississippi		
Meridian	WMMI (FM)	Meridian Municipal Junior College
Missouri		
St. Louis	KSLH (FM)	Board of Education, City of St. Louis
New Jersey		
Newark	WBGO (FM)	Board of Education, City of Newark
So. Orange	WSOU (FM)	Seton Hall College

STATE AND CITY	CALL LETTERS		LICENSEE
New Mexico			
Albuquerque	KANW	(FM)	Board of Education, City of Albuquerque
New York			
Floral Park	WSHS	(FM)	Board of Education, Sewanhaka High School
Ithaca	WHCU	(FM)	Cornell University
New York City	WNYE	(FM)	Board of Education, City of New York
New York City	WFUV	(FM)	Fordham University
Springville	WSPE	(FM)	Board of Education, Central School District #1
Syracuse	WAER	(FM)	Syracuse University
Troy	WEVR	(FM)	Veterans Vocational School
North Carolina			
Chapel Hill	WUNC	(FM)	Univ. of No. Carolina
Greensboro	WGPS	(FM)	Board of Trustees, Greensboro City Administrative Unit
High Point	WHPS	(FM)	Bd. of School Commissioners, City of High Point
Ohio			
Athens	WOUI	(FM)	Ohio University
Bowling Green	WBGU	(FM)	Bowling Green State University
Cleveland	WBOE	(FM)	Board of Education, City of Cleveland
Columbus	WOSU	(FM)	Ohio State University
Kent	WKSU	(FM)	Kent State University
Oxford	WMUB	(FM)	President & Trustees, Miami University
Toledo	WTDS	(FM)	Board of Education, Toledo School Dist.
Oklahoma			
Norman	WNAD	(FM)	Univ. of Oklahoma
Oklahoma City	KPSS	(FM)	Board of Education, City of Okla. City
Tulsa	KWGS	(FM)	University of Tulsa
Oregon			
Eugene	KRVM	(FM)	School District #4, Lane County

STATE AND CITY	CALL LETTERS	LICENSEE
Oregon		
Eugene	KWAX (FM)	State Board of Higher Education
Oretech	KTEC (FM)	Oregon Technical Institute
Pennsylvania		
Havertown	WHHS (FM)	Haverford Twp. Senior High School
Philadelphia	WPWT (FM)	Philadelphia Wireless Technical Institute
Pittsburgh	WDUQ (FM)	Duquesne University
Scranton	WUSV (FM)	Univ. of Scranton
Rhode Island		
Providence	WPTL (FM)	Providence Bible Institute
Tennessee		
Knoxville	WUOT (FM)	Univ. of Tennessee
Texas		
Dallas	KVTT (FM)	Texas Trade School
Dallas	KSMU (FM)	Southern Methodist Univ.
El Paso	KVOF (FM)	Texas Western College of the Univ. of Texas
Fort Worth	KFTW (FM)	Southwestern Baptist Theological Seminary
Houston	KUHF (FM)	Univ. of Houston
Plainview	KHBL (FM)	Wayland Baptist College
Utah		
Ephraim	KEPH (FM)	Snow College, Jr. College of Utah
Washington		
Seattle	KUOW (FM)	Regents of the Univ. of Washington
Tacoma	KTOY (FM)	Tacoma School Dist. #10
Wisconsin		
Chilton	WHKW (FM)	State of Wisconsin Radio Council
Colfax	WHWC (FM)	"
Delafield	WHAD (FM)	"
Holmen	WHLA (FM)	"
Madison	WHA (FM)	"
Wausau	WHRM (FM)	"

Effect of FM on Programs. To the schools which had been using commercial radio time for the presentation of classroom programs, the independently controlled station meant the following:

1. Sufficient radio time was now available to permit the presentation of a variety of educational programs.
2. Schools no longer found it necessary to adjust to a rigid radio schedule. It was now possible, to a greater degree, to adapt program time to class time. Moreover, by means of recordings and repeated programs additional synchronization could result.
3. Instead of rigid time limits for the educational broadcast (such as 14 minutes 30 seconds), it was now possible to adjust the length of the radio visit to the needs of the auditors or the type of script.
4. It was now possible to prepare programs with the school audience exclusively in mind. When the commercial station was used that practice obviously had to be limited. The educational broadcaster inevitably shared the station's natural concern for "holding" the adult audience. When that was done, some compromises invariably resulted.
5. With more radio time available schools could make much greater use of transcribed educational features. The supply of such material is increasing rapidly.
6. The opportunity to broadcast during evening hours meant that schools could plan systematized radio programs for home listeners. A rich cultural program structure could be designed to serve local community needs. The night school could be brought to the living room.

From the special services resulting from the school station it should not be inferred that the commercial radio interests in the past were noncooperative. On the contrary, many station executives have cooperated far more than even a liberal definition of the "public interest" clause could justify. However, no one will argue that the basic objectives of both commercial and noncommerical stations are synonymous. When the school program was shifted because of commercial commitments and the time desired was not always available, when the length of the radio visit was regulated artificially, then in spite of the magnanimity and sincerity of many commercial broadcasters it became obvious that for classroom programs the school-owned station had distinct advantages.

Franklin Dunham, long a network executive, stated the matter simply: "It is quite true that in the hands of good teachers, any radio program may be made a valuable adjunct to the learning experience, but it is likewise true that programs which may be 'tailor made' for teaching purposes should fit the school situation far better than the 'store suit.'"

Television in Schools and Colleges. Television, by nature of its high installation and operation costs, was not at first sought as eagerly by colleges and universities as was FM. Only Iowa State College at Ames, Iowa, has at this time secured its own television frequency. Other universities, notably Syracuse and American University in Washington, D.C., have planned for university-owned studios on the campus with a coaxial cable linking them to near-by commercial stations. This gives the college facilities for instruction, experimentation, and a moderate amount of air time to be filled each week. It also gives the institution far less expense and responsibility.

Yet another pattern, which becomes increasingly popular, involves a cooperative arrangement between a college and a local station in which the college offers television training, frequently with the help of local station personnel, and has occasional use of the station's studio facilities. This type of arrangement has proved popular across the land from the University of Texas to Boston.

The University of Michigan, in cooperation with WWJ-TV–*The Detroit News,* made an even bolder step in November, 1950, by offering a series of regularly scheduled courses of instruction by television, through its Extension Service. An hour each Sunday was divided into three 20-minute segments, and such "telecourses" as *Man in His World—Human Biology; Living in the Later Years,* hobbies for the aging; and *Practical Photography* were offered at nominal fees. Students received, through the regular correspondence-course machinery of University Extension, course outlines, supplementary reading material and lists, assignments and (for those who wished Certificates of Participation) a final examination. In addition, the University's Radio and Television department planned a third element, a series of "teletours" into the unique libraries and laboratories of the University. The unusual combination of correspondence courses combined with broadcasts, successfully presented by radio since 1945, thus went a step further by showing what was being taught.

However, as the structure of television programming took clearer shape, colleges and schools realized that they would have to assume greater responsibility and expense in order to guarantee the place of education in the television spectrum. Accordingly, the Joint Committee on Educational Television was set up on October 16, 1950, to represent seven large groups of American educators. Their activities, as described in the last chapter of this book, were directed toward securing the reservation of 209 television channels in the United States and its territories for educational use. As this book goes to press, the decision of the FCC in regard to this petition is not yet known. More than three hundred educational groups and institutions have filed statements signifying their intention to use these channels if they are reserved for education, and several states have blue-printed state-wide networks of five to eleven television stations.

Television stations have also cooperated with religious groups. The Protestant Radio Commission, under the direction of Dr. Everett Parker, inaugurated in 1948 a week's work-study seminar at Syracuse, for clergymen. In the 1949 seminar the "students" used the studios of WHEN-TV, operated cameras and other equipment, and climaxed their week's work by writing and producing a half-hour religious program which the station was proud to broadcast.

In this connection, it may be interesting to note that the Army Chaplain's School at Fort Slocum, New York, has added to its fine sound recording equipment a television camera and control units, so that the chaplains-in-training may be prepared not only for radio but for video service and services.

With this brief survey of the development of radio and television education in the American schools, several subjects more specific in nature will be considered. The first of these deals with the preparation of educational programs, first for radio, and then for television.

3

Preparing the Educational Radio Program

◇◇

What are the more common program forms used in educational broadcasting?

What are the merits and limitations of each procedure?

What are several suggestions for preparing scripts for classroom reception?

◇◇◇◇◇◇◇◇THE MERE IMITATION of commercial radio procedures would not necessarily result in the attainment of worth-while educational objectives. Even if the educator had the required finances and theatrical talent, that would still be true. Whereas the commercial broadcast is concerned with the question: Is this good (radio) theater?, the school broadcast is faced with the test: Is this teaching something worth while? Education and entertainment, though not exclusive, are not synonymous.

Does this imply, however, that, since the children are corralled in a classroom, the school broadcaster can proceed to be as dull as he pleases? Obviously not. If the pedagogue puts classroom procedures on the air without adaptation, he evidently is not taking advantage of the possibilities of a new medium. It is incumbent upon him to become acquainted with the various program forms commonly used and to know their merits and limitations. In this chapter the writer does not presume "to tell all" about script forms. Topics such as character delineations, plot development, transition techniques, methods of adaptation and condensation, sound effects and trick devices have been discussed fully by qualified radio writers.[1] The approach here is distinctly from the point of view of one who is writing for the school-room audience. The aim is to analyze school radio-script forms more in terms of general emphasis than in specific techniques.

Educational Script Forms

Purpose Is Determined First. A school radio script begins with a purpose and not with a form. What effect upon the learner do I want to create? the writer asks. In this program, am I primarily concerned with the acquisition of facts, concepts, and principles or have I another aim in mind? The goals of the radio visit may be multiple but some primary target must be established. Do I want especially to create appreciations and emphasize attitudes? Is my basic purpose at this time

---

[1] Special attention is called to Eric Barnouw, *Handbook of Radio Writing*, D. C. Heath and Company, 1947; Rome Cowgill, *Fundamentals of Writing for Radio*, Rinehart & Company, 1949; and Max Wylie, *Radio and Television Writing* (rev. ed.), Rinehart & Company, 1950. Other books in this field are noted in the bibliography.

the building of broader interests? Shall I try to stimulate pupil investigation? Is my chief objective the development of critical thinking and discrimination? Once the desired end of the broadcast has been determined, the writer can turn to the means, that is, the content and form of the script.

General Observations. Before turning to specific suggestions a few general comments are in order. An ever-present danger in the development of classroom scripts is the crystallization of procedures which at first seem to be successful but which become routine after repeated use. Particularly is this a danger in school broadcasting, since the listening there is generally more systematic. The children frequently hear an entire series prepared by the same writer, rather than isolated programs by numerous writers employing a variety of techniques.

This failure to present new materials may be especially true of the school program which makes use of comprehensive teacher guides and selected visual materials. In a desire to capitalize upon the investment in these materials there is a great temptation to present the same materials again and again. The difficulty is, of course, that in such cases, instead of thinking primarily of the listener's need, undue consideration may be given to the use of existing materials. School funds are seldom ample, and it is quite likely that such conditions will exist in spite of theoretical considerations. Nevertheless, whether or not the same visual or recorded materials are utilized, there is no reason why the scripts cannot be revised after each presentation. Points of emphasis can be shifted; new personalities can participate; dramatic excerpts, recorded or otherwise, can be incorporated; current data can be introduced; and various other changes can and should be made.

Another consideration is perhaps more pertinent, and that is the painfully pedantic style used in many educational scripts. Some of the difficulty that educators have in writing scripts for classroom reception is due to the concern they have for judgment by their fellow teachers. Too often they forget that the point of attack is the child and not the adult. In a desire to display scholastic attainment, the script writer sometimes employs unfamiliar terminology, an abundance of data, and an occasional Latin phrase. In so doing he perhaps identifies himself as a student but it is at the expense of his classroom audience.

Unfortunately the time is not yet past when he who would "popularize" a subject is invariably said to have but superficial knowledge of it. If to be profound implies that real learning cannot be transmitted, then radio education, among many other things, is doomed. However, when the educator is thought of primarily as an agent for the communication of learning, his ability to popularize a subject in a dignified manner is a necessary attribute. Without it effective educational scripts cannot be written.

Some Common Script Types. The more common script types may be classified as follows: (a) the straight talk, (b) interview, (c) panel or round table, (d) actuality, (e) quiz bee, (f) classroom "pickup," (g) forum or debate, (h) dramatization, (i) music, (j) demonstration lesson. There are variations and combinations of each but in general these types are most frequently used.

There are merits and weaknesses in each type of script form. The quality of a script, nevertheless, does not depend inevitably upon the category into which it falls. The good writer can produce a good script regardless of its theoretical limitations. He is not concerned with "rules" for radio writing. Generally he doesn't even know them. One thing he does know—the type of script that holds listeners. The rules and principles which evolve in any art exist largely as a help to benefit the average technician. In analyzing the creations of the gifted, rules are conspicuous largely because they are broken. And so though the novice may list, in comprehensive outline form, the principles of radio writing, in the final analysis the proof of the script is what it does to the listener. The following pages will be devoted to a detailed discussion of each type of script.

Script Types: Merits, Limitations, Preparation

The Straight Talk—MERITS. The script form most often used in educational broadcasting is the straight talk. Its advantages are apparent. Since only one person takes part and a minimum of rehearsal and studio equipment is needed, it is generally a simple program to produce. Certainly with a well-developed talk, a great deal of information can be given in a minimum of time. The form is direct and the responsibility is fixed. If the personality of the speaker is such that he commands attention and holds interest, the value of a talk can be great. For very small children who are just learning to listen, it has additional merit, since they can more readily grasp the message delivered to them by a single voice.

LIMITATIONS. The disadvantages of the talk may arise from the very elements which can make it successful. If the voice is poor, the manner artificial, then obviously the effectiveness of the talk will be limited. It is apparent, too, that the talk demands continual concentration from the listener and often it is too much like the usual classroom lecture. Unless the speaker knows how to use his voice well or has a naturally pleasant one, the talk may become monotonous and interest will lag. If one of the purposes of the talk is a supervisory one suggesting classroom procedures, then of course the constant use of the talk assumes that good teaching is not lighting a lamp but merely filling a bucket.

The straight talk has other limitations, which come from psychological handicaps. It is often more difficult for the inexperienced speaker to be as natural when speaking alone as when two or three are taking part. It is generally easier to secure the layman to answer questions than it is to have him present a talk. If the talk deals with a controversial subject and only one aspect of the given problem is presented, then from the point of view of evoking classroom discussion this may be unfortunate.

SCRIPT PREPARATION.   Writing for the ear differs in several respects from writing for the eye. The way a script *sounds* is far more important than the way it *looks* and reads. Whereas in the opening scenes of a long stage play it is commonplace to hear some preliminary comments, meet a few of the characters, and then slowly move into the plot—in radio such a procedure would be fatal. Attention must be secured at once and only when that is done can the broadcaster proceed to build upon the child's experience, adding new concepts to old until the objective of the radio visit is attained. Attention must be not only sought but caught. If the teacher-broadcaster would judge the quality of her proposed radio talk, perhaps the best test is to read it to her pupils and note their reactions, keeping in mind that "the disciplined attention of the classroom is an academic luxury" —one that is not enjoyed by broadcasters.

Long and complex sentences may be acceptable in some textbooks but they do not belong in a talk script, especially if it is planned for children. The use of familiar words which are concrete, specific and which aid the child to form mental images are essential. The script writer does not just speak of "the court jester wearing a hat." Rather, "he wears a long, green hat shaped like an inverted ice-cream cone with small brass bells attached. As he walks they tinkle like those of a tiny sleigh."

Analogies and illustrations taken from the child's experience can help to make the presentation a more vital one. "Inflation, as an economic term, means little to people; as pork chops at a dollar a pound it means a lot."

Humorous incidents incorporated into the talk can stimulate attention and illustrate meanings. The narration of selected anecdotes is enjoyed greatly by children, especially when the stories are related with direct quotation, dialogue, and occasionally dialect.

People like to hear about people. The child as a listener is no different. Situations involving an element of human interest appeal to children and the capable school broadcaster will capitalize upon that knowledge. The situations used need not be involved or lengthy in description. A simple reference to a recent experience, a comment by a friend, an observation on the way to school—just a brief mention of this nature enhances the script. In the same way the use of pronouns in the first person can be helpful. Any device which will "humanize" the broadcaster should be considered. When the school program is tuned in, the children should anticipate meeting an old friend, not an avalanche of information. In radio as in the classroom, if the teacher will "sell" herself first, the acceptance of her product will be facilitated. The superior radio talk is direct and personal. It resembles a tête-à-tête more than it does an oration. The skilled broadcaster will take the children into her confidence and talk with them as though she and the children are sharing an exclusive experience desired by many but reserved only for them.

An informal approach necessitates the use of an informal style. Expressions such as "of course," "to be sure," "you know," and others of a similar nature aid greatly in providing a conversational tone. Short sentences, rhetorical questions, and the use of contractions likewise serve this purpose.

In preparing a talk script for children it is important that only a few new concepts be presented in any one program. If the script attempts to cover too much, and that is the usual tendency, the chances are that the program will produce nothing but confusion in the child's mind, and at best a few isolated and generally unimportant facts will be retained. A reasonable amount of new material, vividly introduced in a variety of ways, should be the aim of the usual school radio talk.

The danger of "talking down" to children is well understood by experienced teachers. The same caution must be applied to radio. Perhaps the best measure of a school broadcaster—and, for that matter, the commercial broadcaster as well—is the degree of sincerity projected. If the children sense that they are being "sold a bill of goods" (and they have an uncanny ability to recognize this), then the radio talk is merely heard but not absorbed. True, the speaker's ability has much to do with this impression but the script form also is a factor. The language used must be the child's. At least it must be familiar to him. However abstract the desired concept may be, the words used can still be simple.

If statistics must be used, they should be used sparingly. Simple ratios and comparisons selected from within the child's experience will have more meaning than large figures and confusing data. To illustrate, consider the enormity of the figure one billion. Does that number mean much to children, or is it better understood by them if it is thought of as a sum about equal to the number of minutes which have passed since the birth of Christ? For clarity, also, there is little reason why round numbers should not be used without sacrificing accuracy. Incidentally, it is foolish to refer to "the data given above." There is no such thing as the "above" in a radio talk. Generally speaking, the radio script should not assume much recall on the part of the listener. Whereas in reading it is easy to look back and recall who so-and-so was, in listening that is not true.

In the radio program designed for schools, and perhaps elsewhere as well, a brief summary at the close of the talk is an effective aid.

The summary serves to recapitulate the material presented, it ties up the odds and ends that may otherwise confuse the child, and it calls attention to the major points of emphasis. If the summarizing statements occasionally are made in outline form—one, two, three, and so on—vague abstractions are avoided and the listener is rewarded with the feeling that he has learned something definite and probably worth while.

The following talk script is one of a series broadcast to the upper elementary grades. It illustrates some of the aforementioned principles, and indicates further how interest in current developments can be capitalized upon in the presentation of educational materials. The language is simple and direct, the concepts few and carefully developed, the manner informal.

BEHIND THE HEADLINES

Division of Social Studies—Television

Script: Dave Baylor

ANNCR: BEHIND THE HEADLINES!

THEME: Newspaper office sounds—*up, under, and out*

ANNCR: Headline . . . *FCC Proposes New Television Channels to Provide More Stations* . . . and to tell you the story behind this headline, we present Dave Baylor, manager of Station WJMO. . . . Mr. Baylor.

BAYLOR: Suppose you and your family are in Spokane, Washington, in, say the year 1960. Your father runs out of money, he knows no one in Spokane, and wants to cash a check. That's a tough spot to be in. But maybe by 1960, it won't be any problem. Here is just what he might do. He might go into a bank, write a check on his own account, on his own bank in Cleveland. The bank clerk in Spokane takes the check back to the television room. He switches on the set and signals the Cleveland bank that he is about to transmit to them. The bank teller in Cleveland turns on his television receiver. The Spokane bank clerk puts your father's check in front of a television camera, and in Cleveland the bank clerk looks at it, compares your father's signature on the television screen and with one he has on a card in his file. Then he presses a button on a microphone, and says: "That check is perfectly all right, Spokane. Go ahead and pay it."

Now that sounds a little unusual, and when you see a television receiver in a downtown store, or in your home, you don't think about its commercial possibilities. But there are hundreds of uses for television such as we have just described. And that is the story behind our headline.

The FCC, or Federal Communications Commission, is the body in Washington which regulates the frequencies, or channels, on which radio stations in the United States broadcast. That's the reason why you find different Cleveland radio stations at different places on the dial. The spot on the dial at which you find the stations is determined by the FCC.

Now, television is new. Few of you as yet have television sets in your homes. Let's just see. Raise your hands, all of you who have television receivers in your homes.

(*a pause*)

You see what I mean. Now all you who have seen television broadcasts, not from the WEWS studios, but on a television receiver, raise your hands.

(*a pause*)

Not very many are there? Now how many of you have heard a regular radio broadcast? Let's see your hands.

(*a pause*)

That's right, everybody. In fact you're listening to one right now. Now if we had asked that last question in 1923, practically none of you, if you had lived at that time, would have had your hands up. Because radio was as new then as television is now. So the FCC had to re-examine the situation with regard to the number of television stations they were going to allow, and where they were going to allow them, and see if they couldn't improve the service to television-set owners by changing some of the locations. Basically they decided that some of the smaller towns needed television stations too; towns which, under the old rules, wouldn't have had them. Therefore, more people will be reached by television, more people will have a chance to see television programs under the new setup than under the old.

Here's what will happen in Cleveland, for example. There were originally to be five television stations in Cleveland. Under the proposed reallocation of television channels there will be only four. One of the channels which was to have gone to Cleveland will go to Canton. Two of the television channels are already granted to stations. One to Scripps Howard's WEWS which is now operating, and the other to a company called the Empire Coil Company, out in Parma; but that station is not even under construction. You see, you have to ask the FCC to assign you a place on the dial before you can even begin to construct a station.

Nobody knows for sure the number of television receivers there are in Cleveland. . . . There aren't very many. But remember that in 1923 there weren't very many radios either. That may seem strange to you because you can't remember when you didn't have at least one radio in your home. Someday, television receivers will be just as common as radios are now. Television receivers are very much more expensive than radios are today. But back in 1923, radios, good ones, were almost as expensive as television receivers are today. So, as soon as the manufacturers of television receivers get them produced on a large enough volume, the price will come down, and almost everybody will have one.

The cost of operating a television station is also greater. For example it takes almost twenty times as many people to run a television station as it does a regular radio station like WJMO.

Things move very fast in the radio business, and it may be no more than five or six years, until television will cease to be a new thing. But let me give you a little hint. You won't be able to turn on the television set while you do your homework, the way you can your radio. You just can't look at an arithmetic book and a television screen at the same time. Not unless you have four eyes, which isn't very likely. So when you read from time to time about what the Federal Communications Commission is doing to change television channels, read it carefully, because it will certainly affect you. And remember the story about the check. That may someday be as common as regular listening to regular radio programs is today.

ANNCR: Thank you, Mr. Baylor, for today's BEHIND THE HEAD-LINES story.

THEME: *Up, under, and out.*

ANNCR: BEHIND THE HEADLINES comes to you each week at this time from Your School Station, WBOE in Cleveland.

Most of the principles mentioned in preparing the talk script are applicable to other types of conversational programs. However, a few additional suggestions may be helpful. The classroom and music program types will not be discussed here, since they constitute specialized approaches to be noted later.

THE INTERVIEW—MERITS.   Another common type of educational broadcast is the interview. If properly developed, this can be an exceedingly valuable treatment. As with the talk, outstanding personalities and well-known experts can be brought into the classroom. By raising questions, the "problematic situation" is developed and interest is aroused. Prominent people are "humanized." By carefully considering the interests of the listeners, the teacher can guide the discussion by the layman so that pupil benefits are greater. Since more than one person participates in the conversation, it has the merits of greater participation. Monotony is reduced by furnishing an opportunity to hear more than one voice.

LIMITATIONS.   However, the interview has certain disadvantages which must be avoided. Not only must the person chosen to be interviewed have a message of importance and value to the class, but his style of delivery must be adapted to the medium. Unless the questions are carefully developed, the whole program may sound stilted and artificial. Care must be taken so that vocabulary used by the "expert" is neither so mature nor so technical that it is not adapted to the capacity of the school child.

SCRIPT PREPARATION.   In selecting the person for an interview it is well to remember that what is considered a "great personality" by adults may not be considered so by children. In the matter of health, for example, the learned observations of a noted physician may not be so effective as the remarks (written for him) of a baseball star. The person or persons presenting the questions should be careful that the entire discussion does not go off on a tangent which may or may not be of value. Of prime importance in the presentation of a well-rounded interview is the facility and ease with which ensuing questions are related to the previous answers. Thus the comments can be presented coherently rather than as isolated bits of information. As in the talk script, a concluding or summarizing comment is of value so that the various statements are related into a definite whole.

Several methods of script preparation have been used for the interview program. A common procedure is to have the interviewer and the person interviewed engage in a preliminary conversation. At that time the interviewer notes which of his prepared questions seem to be most productive. Interesting comments may thus be evoked which the expert, because he is so familiar with his subject, may consider quite prosaic, but which the interviewer realizes his audience may find most enlightening. The questions which stimulated these comments can then be used in the program.

In some instances a transcript is made of the informal conversation and the script is prepared from a condensed version. The chief merit of this plan is that it presents pertinent data in the natural style of the person interviewed. Nevertheless, this process is a time-consuming one.

Another interview-script plan is to send the questions to the expert and when his answers are returned the material is edited for broadcasting. Here also, as much as possible, the language used is that of the speaker. The danger is that much interesting data may be overlooked in this manner. Occasionally the expert is asked to forward several pages of pertinent material such as former speeches and other prepared literature. This is analyzed into a question-and-answer script, bits of humor are added, analogies are drawn, and so on.

The ease with which tape recordings can be edited has led to their wide use in interview programs. Reality is added as the speaker's own comments are used. For timing purposes, specific questions can be inserted later. If there is a distinctive sound pattern at the site of the interview (harbor noises, machinery in background, and the like), that too can be incorporated for additional effect. Here is part of a simple tape treatment by Charles Gilbert.

ANNCR: WORK MADE EASIER—planned and written for classes in senior-high physics. Each week at this time we will show the way in which some principle of physical science has been put to work to aid men in their daily lives. Today, "Pascal's Law."

NARR: By means of a tape recorder you are going to hear from several city officials directly concerned with the problem of supplying water to our city. There were times during the summer when this task became a difficult one. Consider the report of a local newspaper on Friday morning, August 26th, for example.

SOUND: *Teletype*

REPTR: Washing of babies and other household cleaning duties were temporarily suspended last night in several areas of the city as water pressure went down to nothing. For the third consecutive day taps have been turned on, and the result varies from a "dry run" to a "teasing trickle."

NARR: People in outlying suburbs, who were most affected, jammed the telephones with complaints to City Hall, local water departments, and newspapers. Some turned to the Weather Bureau, but received little consolation:

FORECASTER: (*Telephone effect*) "There is no rain expected for this area in the immediate future. It looks like the start of a warm, dry week-end."

NARR: What caused the water shortage? Was it some weakness in the system of mains and pumps and reservoirs? Or was it just that too many people wanted water at the same time? For answers to these questions, I went over to City Hall and talked with Mr. George W. Hamlin, Commissioner of Water and Heat. His first answer to my question "Why the water shortage?" was:

HAMLIN: (*Tape*) . . . The water crisis has been brought about due to increased consumption. It is felt very particularly during the evening hours when, in addition to the normal daily load, we have the much greater load due to universal sprinkling.

NARR: "Universal sprinkling." There was the basic difficulty. During weekdays everyone spent the early hours of the evening putting water on dry lawns. It was at that time that the pressure dropped—in some areas—to nothing. The water shortage then was caused by what the engineers called "overloading the system." Now let us consider some causes of pressure drop that are present wherever water runs through long distances of pipe. I asked Mr. Hamlin:

QUEST: (*Tape*) . . . I wonder if we could follow out just exactly what happens along the mains when everyone starts turning on their lawn sprinklers at the same time.

HAMLIN: (*Tape*) . . . It causes trouble due to loss of pressure in this way: as you well realize, water consumers are supplied through water mains of various diameters laid beneath the public streets. If we can assume that the mains were in a quiescent condition— that no water was being used—water would be at the same pressure throughout the system for points of equal elevation. According to Pascal's Law. . . .

The Panel or Round Table—MERITS.   Another common form of educational script is the panel or round-table procedure. By presenting conflicting points of view the essence of drama is available. By giving the listeners a chance to hear authorities who themselves may disagree, it is easy to draw the inference that dogma must be avoided. If the language is informal, if the number of participants is small enough to enable the listener to follow the point of view presented by each one, and if in the entire program there is a sense of spontaneity, even if it be planned; then the panel may be productive.

LIMITATIONS.   However, if script is used, unless the participants are expert readers the program may be stilted and formal. Only the unusually gifted can extemporize successfully. The extemporaneous aspect of the *Chicago Round Table* is probably one of its great attributes. The round-table discussion presumes, of course, that the auditors have at least a minimum of facts concerning the issues, and to that extent, when broadcasting to the immature listener, this method has certain limitations. To broadcast the fact that there is disagreement among experts is of doubtful value when the listeners themselves know little about the subject. If a number of speakers are used, particularly if they are busy laymen, it is sometimes difficult to arrange for joint rehearsals, and as in the interview method, unless they be cautioned, their language is likely to be too advanced or too technical for some pupils.

SCRIPT PREPARATION. The effectiveness of the panel or round table is dependent to a large degree upon the selection of participants as well as upon the timeliness and significance of the topic. The choice of speakers should be based upon variance in point of view; that is, the speakers should each represent a distinctive approach or solution to the problem. Otherwise, if the participants all agree, the program misses its opportunity to challenge and stimulate listeners.

Occasionally experienced speakers may prefer to broadcast without manuscript. There is much to be said for that procedure, since it encourages informality and naturalness, but for classroom listening it should be used with caution. When experts discuss extemporaneously a subject in which they are deeply interested, they are likely to respond to each other on a common plane as expert to expert, neglecting the younger listeners.

Even if no script is used a good deal of preliminary work is required. All the participants must first agree upon the specific issues involved as well as upon the definition of terms. A difficult task is to get the specialists to limit the area of discussion. During the initial conference a tentative outline may be developed and a conclusion drawn. For younger listeners particularly, it is helpful to have the panel indicate common grounds of agreement even more than reasons for divergency.

A chairman is not always necessary, but if the subject is a rather specialized one some precautions may be needed to keep the participants from becoming too technical. *The Chicago Round Table* device of using an Inquiring Reporter to pose the layman's questions or to express typical man-on-the-street reactions serves to keep the experts in line. An experienced chairman also helps to put the speakers at ease, keeps the basic issue in the foreground, balances the discussion, and facilitates timing.

Whether or not a script is used, a recorded rehearsal is helpful. As the record is played the speakers may wish to note changes in their presentation, the outline may be improved, and time adjustments made. If the panel is composed of comparative strangers, the recording serves to break the ice and to create the spirit of informality so essential in this type of program.

If a script is to be used for the round table, every effort should be made to keep the discussion lifelike and conversational. One plan used with some success is to have the panel proceed with an informal discussion while shorthand notes are taken. Later these notes are edited into script form, submitted to the speakers for possible corrections, and then polished into a final script.

For younger listeners particularly, it is often desirable to "dress up" the introduction to the panel so that the listener's attention is caught and the significance of the topic underlined. Here is a panel introduction illustrated by Earl Heist.

SOUND: *(On cue) Train whistle*
NARR: *(Cue)* 3 thousand coming by train.
SOUND: *(Cue) Bus shifting gears*
NARR: *(Cue)* 20 thousand coming by bus.
SOUND: *(Cue) Streetcar*
NARR: *(Cue)* 135 thousand by streetcar.
SOUND: *(Cue) Auto horn*
NARR: *(Cue)* 272 thousand by auto.
SOUND: *Sneak in traffic roar after horn . . . pull up . . . fade under and out*
NARR: Yes, thousands are coming . . . by train, bus, streetcar, and auto . . . coming into downtown Cleveland every day: to work, to school, and to the stores. As they come, they emphasize one of our area's greatest needs: rapid, convenient transportation. As they come, they create one of Cleveland's most serious problems . . . traffic congestion.
ANNCR: CURRENT TOPICS has as its guests today three Cleveland officials who are concerned with trying to solve our transportation and traffic difficulties. But first, why have such difficulties become so acute? The Cleveland Press suggested an answer last week.
NARR: "The traffic sickness from which the City of Cleveland suffers

is the sickness that comes of pouring 1952 traffic down a street that was built to carry horse-and-buggy traffic."

ANNCR: There is the clew. Cleveland has outgrown its transportation facilities. What shall we do about it? Mr. Vernon Johnson, Mr. Donald Hyde, and Mr. John Howard have agreed to suggest answers to this question. Each is directly concerned with different aspects of the problem of local transportation. Mr. Vernon Johnson is in charge of traffic engineering in the Department of Public Safety. . . .

The Actuality Broadcast—MERITS. A fourth type of educational script is the "on-the-spot," or actuality, broadcasts of important events as they occur. This approach has a vivid emotional appeal; reality is present, and the unexpected may happen. Under such circumstances the maintenance of pupil interest is no problem.

LIMITATIONS. The limitations in the use of this method can be seen readily. There is liable to be much waste of time unless it is known definitely just when, and what aspect of, the event being described will be of educational value. More than once classrooms have been tuned in on the opening of Congress, for example, and for more than half an hour have heard nothing but the roll call. Often, too, much time may elapse between speakers or events. The specialized talents required of the announcer who handles the extemporaneous description may not be present. Moreover, from the technical point of view, the pickup may be exceedingly difficult, and thus adequate classroom reception may not result. However, these are the risks run when entirely spontaneous programs are used; for, although spontaneity can be a virtue, it is likewise a potential vice in program utilization.

SCRIPT PREPARATION. The nature of this type of program is such that it is not based upon script but upon an event itself. The selection of the occasion and the skill of the narrator determine the probable value of the presentation, but even here some script resources are helpful. Research data compiled into script form enables the announcer to present the significance and possibly the historical development of the event. Biographical notes assembled for ready reference serve to provide background and add interest to the program. Introductory comments of description, interesting side lights, color, and general fill-in, as well as questions for brief interviews with leading personalities, can be planned to some extent in advance.

The Quiz Bee—MERITS. A fifth type of conversational program that has enjoyed great popularity recently is the quiz bee. This type of program often is stimulating and as a type of game it can be very interesting, especially if the listener knows the answers which the performers may not. For school use, if the questions are related and built around the development of worth-while information, then its adoption as a supplementary device can easily be justified.

LIMITATIONS. The limitations of the quiz bee, aside from the fact that it may have been overdone commercially, are apparent. If the information called for is unrelated and unimportant from the point of view of the school, the time spent may not have been used to best advantage. Then, too, the competitive aspect is often overemphasized and learning, at best, is incidental. It is difficult to produce a successful quiz program that will run less than a half-hour.

SCRIPT PREPARATION. The quiz and other forms of audience-participation programs are misleading, since one may infer that the script job is a simple one. The contrary is true; these programs require a carefully evolved framework of written material.

The few precautions to be noted here will suggest the type of planning needed for a successful program. The rules for the contest or quiz must be stated as briefly as possible so that participation can begin quickly. Contestants must be identified but not at the expense of pace. If eliminations are to take place, the first questions should be such that the dropping out is not too great too soon. In general, early questions should be easier than those which come later. Pauses at the very beginning of the program are fatal. Here, too, simpler questions at the outset are helpful. Difficulty of questions should be gauged so that contestants are dealt with fairly.

Questions in the same field should not be used successively. Otherwise there may be a lack of variety in types of information and one contestant may keep the "spotlight." Questions that are to be answered in several parts require careful phrasing, otherwise they prove confusing to both contestants and listeners.

In an educational quiz program some relationship between questions is desirable. In any quiz, questions should be so stated that most of the talk will come from contestants and not from the quizmaster.

Too many school programs of this type become a teacher's monologue interrupted by an occasional "yes" or "no" from pupils.

A well-constructed quiz makes use of properly spaced "performance questions." These are questions which recognize the possibilities of the medium and are based on sound effects, music, dramatic interludes, humorous interpolations, etc. Such questions or responses help greatly to stimulate listener interest and provide relief from constant talk.

If the quiz is based upon the completion of a certain number of rounds rather than individual questions, it should be recognized that problems of timing are increased. For example, the time may be nearly up with the last round just beginning. A flexible structure is essential in that case.

In school broadcasts, particularly, the quizmaster should avoid embarrassing the child who misses an apparently easy question. The emphasis should be on successes rather than misses. In many instances, it may be better to select a team as the winner rather than an individual. A competition between boys and girls appeals especially to adolescents.

In the selection of questions to be used for programs it may be desirable to develop a simple questionnaire to be returned by possible contestants. Hobbies and special interests suggest areas of questioning which add interest to the program. Of course, this cannot be done when contestants are selected immediately before "air time."

The prayer of the quizmaster is that his answers be accurate. Variations in possible answers should be considered also, and these noted so that his information is complete. References to local and timely matters add color to the program. Thus it can be seen that preparation and research are necessary with this program-type as well.

Classroom. A sixth form of educational broadcast that has been tried is the teacher and classroom type in which an entire class is brought into the studio. The teacher conducts her class in the usual manner, as though there were no microphones present and the studio were simply the classroom. Its chief merit is that it suggests what is being done in the ordinary schoolroom, and as such may have a public relations value.

LIMITATIONS. Its disadvantages far outnumber whatever advantages this type of script may have. It is apparent that, since the classroom is brought into the radio studio, if the program is to go on the air at all the natural classroom situation can no longer exist. Arrangements must be made for a proper pickup and, since it cannot be heard, physical activity such as use of the blackboard must be minimized. Then, if rehearsals are to take place, the procedure becomes more and more formal until, by the time it is a smooth radio performance, it little resembles the ordinary schoolroom response.

The Forum or Debate—MERITS. The forum or debate type of script has been used frequently in certain types of adult education. As a technique for stimulating thinking and for the presentation of various points of view concerning the issue, the device is a splendid one, particularly if the speakers are carefully selected not only as to their knowledge of subject matter, but as to their speaking abilities.

LIMITATIONS. However, as in formal school debating, there is danger of confusing mere glibness with correct thinking. The debate presumes, too, that the listeners have some knowledge of the subject being discussed. Unfortunately, there is often a tendency to resort to an emotional presentation rather than a rational one. The selection of controversial subjects to be broadcast necessitates caution.

SCRIPT PREPARATION. Because of the growing interest in the *Junior Town Meeting* idea and the spread of programs of this type, the discussion here will deal with the pupil-presented forum rather than the conventional radio procedure using adults who are often experts. The suggestions to be made are perhaps applicable to assembly and classroom presentations as well as to radio. They are not limited to script but refer to production problems as well.

First, the general framework of the program. Like the quiz, a successful forum can seldom be presented in less than one half-hour. Three pupil speakers, and certainly no more than four, discuss a timely issue of national or international significance. On some occasions a vital issue of local concern may be the topic. A moderator, usually an adult, serves to link the speakers, the questioners, and the listening audience. At the conclusion of the formal talks, about three minutes each, the studio audience, composed also of pupils, proceeds to question the speakers. Variations of this plan have been tried by some schools. For example, one procedure is to permit speakers to question each other before the audience is invited to participate. The WAKR Akron school series used a panel of questioners, usually composed of pupils who would appear as speakers the following week.

The selection and wording of the subject for discussion is an important element of the forum. Special consideration should be given to topics in which young people, because of their personal experience, are particularly interested and on which they are qualified to speak with authority. Subjects such as "Shall the voting age be reduced to eighteen?", "Shall we have compulsory military service in peacetime?", "Delinquency—juvenile or adult?" will more often produce excellent discussion than will other subjects which are not close to youth. Usually the topic should be stated as a question. It should be so framed that the issue is clear.

The speakers, each of whom represents a distinct point of view on the topic, should be chosen on the basis of several criteria: knowledge of the subject, an effective delivery, good diction, a satisfactory voice, and the ability to stand up before a barrage of questions.

The talks to be prepared by the pupils should represent their own convictions and the students should be left to form their own judgments. Within that general pattern, however, some compromises may have to be made so that the speakers represent different shades of opinion. A forum program based on a controversial question in which there is no indication of controversy falls flat indeed. Acrimonius debate should be avoided, but representative points of view should be defined and supported by evidence. All this should contribute to an earnest search for a solution.

The moderator has a key role in the forum program. Upon him depend the smooth flow of the program, an atmosphere of geniality, the encouragement of audience questions, the ease of the speakers, a respectful but lively give-and-take, and in general a demonstration of the democratic process in action. It may be desirable that he be a student of world affairs; but it is imperative that he be at ease before the microphone, articulate, possessing a sense of humor, a minimum of political bias, and an abundance of good sportsmanship.

Some moderators prefer to open the program with a short statement concerning the significance of the issue to be discussed. Others prefer to have the station announcer do that, after which they begin by introducing the first speaker.

The use of biographical questionnaires which are given to the speakers asking their hobbies, ambitions, accomplishments, and so on, provides information which enables the moderator to add human interest values to his introductory remarks.

In the *New England Junior Town Meeting* series, this biographical information serves as the basis for two or three preliminary questions, put by the moderator before the pupil is formally introduced.

At the conclusion of each talk, a summarizing sentence or two by the chairman may serve to define more clearly the basic differences in point of view. When the talks have been given, the moderator turns to the question period, perhaps the most important part of the program.

A responsive audience is a necessary element of the forum, but the questions must be well put. They should be to the point and carefully worded. Duplications and speeches rather than questions constitute a problem frequently faced. To be sure, an experienced moderator can help greatly to guide effective questioning but experience has shown that with a youthful audience some advance preparation may be necessary. This preparation for the question period is highly desirable as an educational experience as well.

One helpful procedure is to send summaries of the talks to be given to the schools which have been invited as audience members. There the pupils have an opportunity beforehand to study the issue and to evolve questions which, to them, seem pertinent.

When the audience arrives at the studio, cards are distributed on which they can write their questions. Some pupils, on the basis of their previous study, may even compose their questions before the broadcast begins, but most questions will probably be written as the speakers present their arguments. Written questions are not necessary but they are highly desirable, especially if some monitor or guide is to approve questions first.

A typical question card may include the following:

<u>JONESVILLE</u> <u>HIGH</u> <u>SCHOOL</u> <u>FORUM</u>

Question Card

1. Write your question on this card.
2. Only pupils may ask questions.
3. Make questions brief and to the point.
4. Submit your question to a guide.
5. If you are given a colored card, your question has been approved.
6. Raise your hand with the colored card in it.

* * * * * * * * *

I have a question for _____
                        (insert first name of speaker)

My name is _____ of

_____High School

_____

_____

In the Cleveland student forum each speaker was identified by a colored tag pinned to his lapel. The members of the audience wishing to ask questions of particular speakers submitted their cards to the monitors for approval. If their questions were chosen they were then handed a slip of paper corresponding in color to the one worn by the speaker to whom the question was addressed. Perhaps the greatest aid provided by the colored slip is that it shows the moderator quickly for which speaker a proposed question is intended. Thus he can keep the questions rotating among the members of the panel.

In a discussion of a specialized nature where audience response may be limited, it may be necessary to "plant" several prepared questions among the audience. However, these questions should be used only as a last resort.

Aside from such special considerations, there have been other developments in the radio-forum technique which should be considered by school broadcasters. It may be found desirable to have the speakers state briefly at the outset how they define certain terms and also what they regard as the current status of the issue. To ensure that light, as well as heat, has been generated by the discussion, after the question period and just before the program ends, some moderators ask the speakers to state briefly their areas of mutual agreement.

The Dramatization—MERITS.   An eighth form of educational script is the dramatization. Its merits are many, for if the script is well developed and adequately produced, ideas can be presented effectively. The dramatization can result in a powerful emotional appeal. A great variety of subjects can be handled in this manner. Opportunity for expression is available to many and the impressions created are often memorable. With good script writing, the educational pill can be sweetened and yet a great amount of value retained. The dramatic element in the radio program serves as the "white space" in an effective advertisement. The adage that it is much better to be read (heard) by hundreds than overlooked by thousands is significant to the educator also.

LIMITATIONS.   But just as the dramatic script can have great merit, it can also be a waste of much valuable time. Generally speaking, a good dramatic script is more difficult to write than the straight talk. Even if the script is prepared, good production by school groups is still uncommon. Then, too, there is danger of so diluting the few facts or concepts to be presented that, aside from entertainment, little results. The fact that a program is dramatized by no means ensures greater interest. For, as Lazarsfeld points out in speaking of adult programs:

> Strangely enough, it is always assumed that people who do not listen to a good talk or a well-organized round-table discussion will listen to a dramatization of a serious topic, or some jazzed-up form under which information might be conveyed. There is no evidence, however, that dramatized education gets a much larger listenership than well-delivered straight talks. . . . The listener ratings of the dramatized informational programs are not much higher than those of the well-established talk and discussion programs.[2]

One additional comment should be made concerning the values and limitations of the dramatization. Granted that a dramatic situation can stimulate the child's emotions, it should not be assumed that all

---

[2] Paul F. Lazarsfeld, "Audience Building in Educational Broadcasting," *The Journal of Educational Sociology*, May, 1941, p. 535.

emotions are equally desirable. To be helpful educationally, emotional reactions must be directed.

SCRIPT PREPARATION.   There has been a good deal of controversy concerning this type of script for school use. Some hold that dramatic programs, though designed primarily for school consumption, should in no way suffer by comparison with commercial broadcasting standards. They point out that the children are well aware, from their out-of-school listening, of what radio can do to stimulate their interest and hold their attention. If the school program falls short of these standards, it is claimed the children will be apathetic and the radio as a distinctive medium will not be used to its fullest extent.

Others indicate, for example, that the modern textbook does not resemble an "Amazing Story" magazine. The fact that the latter may have a great circulation, that it may be read avidly by children, and be hidden under their pillows at home is still no proof that it must be imitated by educators. The school environment, they argue, is not just *any* environment—it is *selective* in its very nature. The school experiences which the child undergoes must themselves be selective and to the extent that they are selective they cannot be universally popular.

Whether the radio program has as its prime purpose the stimulation of learning or of purchasing, in either case it is necessary that the habits and interests of the potential listeners be known. Schoolteachers know a good deal about children, but as broadcasters they have been slow in modifying their radio program forms to capitalize upon pupil interests.

On the other hand, commercial broadcasters who have made extensive investigations into the psychology of juvenile appeal have been quite successful in developing programs which at least interest young listeners.[3] Speaking of the commercial program for children, Wylie says:

It is just as important for the writer of children's programs to know his own customers as it is for the commercial sponsor to know his. Both are selling something. Neither can command an audience until his show

---

[3] E. Evelyn Grumbine, *Reaching Juvenile Markets*, McGraw-Hill Book Company, p. 430.

is right for them, and the child will tune out just as quickly as the adult and he will do so the instant the program leaves his own sphere of reality.[4]

The fact that the typical American child, of his own volition and occasionally against the advice of his parents, spends more than two hours a day with his ears next to the loudspeaker, demonstrates that the interest of children can be captured by radio. The educational value of some of the means used to do so will not be debated at this point. Suffice it to say that when the mental traits of the desired listeners are studied, radio programs can be "custom built" to suit the purpose of the broadcaster.

The comments of the radio advertiser who has had extensive experience in fashioning programs for children are of significance to the school broadcaster. The following statement by E. Evalyn Grumbine is worthy of analysis:

The technique employed in the preparation and presentation of all kinds of programs created to appeal to a juvenile audience is of vital importance. A radio program for children that includes all the elements that hold the interest and enthusiasms of boys and girls may be a dismal failure if certain fundamental techniques in presenting the program are overlooked. Absolute clarity is the first essential. This may be achieved through simplicity of language and ideas. Children are not interested in what they do not understand. This does not mean, however, that it is necessary to employ baby-talk technique, for there is nothing quite so insulting to a child's intelligence as to have an adult talk down to him. By using simple sentence construction and language understood by the children of the age for which the program is designed, clarity will be insured. It is best to use short sentences, omitting words not necessary to the meaning. . . .

The new and very strange or the old and very familiar have the greatest appeal to children. "Read it again, Daddy," or "Tell me about it again, Mommy," is the plea of every small child. Over and over again, the familiar stories must be told. Stories about boys and girls exactly like themselves are particular favorites. They also like to hear about fantastic heroes and heroines who accomplish the impossible; the giant killers and beautiful fairy princesses are also an important part of their world of imagination at certain stages of their development. Hero worship is one of the instincts that may be used advantageously in building radio programs for children. It starts to develop from four to six years of age and increases materially from seven through nine years. It continues in girls from ten through

4 Max Wylie, *op. cit.*, pp. 251–252.

twelve and in boys from ten through thirteen years, though at this time heroes of their own age have the most appeal.

Interest and clarity in the material written does not solve the whole problem of achieving a successful juvenile program. The actual presentation plays a vitally important part also. Adult dignity must be thrown to the winds, and the performer must actually enjoy the thrilling stories he tells his young listeners. A lively imagination is absolutely essential as well as infinite patience. In addition to possessing these qualities, the successful performer on juvenile programs must also be able to project his personality and interest in his young audience through his voice when broadcasting. Children's confidence can be destroyed if a harsh note which suggests impatience is detected in the voice. Ireene Wicker, famous Singing Lady of the Kellogg Company, is the best example of a successful radio personality with children. Her voice projects a personality that inspires confidence in boys and girls and a feeling of security. This is accomplished because of her ability to project interest and patience through her voice over the microphone. . . .[5]

Juvenile radio programs which have met with success in the commercial field have not only recognized juvenile interests but have catered to them. For the child's love of adventure they have had them ride with the Lone Ranger and fly with Buck Rogers; for the mystery-loving youngsters they have invented secret codes and passwords; for the youthful "joiner" they have organized clubs and "exclusive" memberships; for the budding "collector" they have distributed good-luck charms and picture booklets.

Numerous surveys, some of which will be discussed later, have shown that adventure and humor are among the chief preferences of children in their out-of-school listening. To the radio educator this poses a question: To what extent should the school broadcast capitalize upon these preferences? Obviously schools should not operate upon the approved Hollywood principles of "giving the public [child] what it wants." Mature judgment, intelligent planning, and high standards must prevail. Surely, to be successful as a teaching aid, the school radio program need not be full of "blood and thunder" or of "gags"; and yet anyone who presumes to write "listenable" school programs for children must incorporate at least a modicum of the elements that make for attractive listening. Nor need there be great reluctance to do this, for even a cursory examination of the recognized

[5] E. Evalyn Grumbine, op. cit., pp. 232–234.

classic literature of children will provide plenty of supporting evidence. The recommended writings of Mark Twain, Robert Louis Stevenson, Washington Irving—just to name a few—abound with adventure and humor. The newer textbooks which make use of anecdotes and an abundance of photographs are indicative of this development in the schools. And in radio, also, the dramatic program is no less a valid educational experience because it is made interesting and attractive.

The script which follows, "The Mystery of the Mad Maltese," is one of an excellent series, *Dr. Tim, Detective,* presented under the auspices of the Colorado State Medical Society.[6] The writer, Jack Weir Lewis, skillfully introduces considerable information within a framework of suspense and mystery that serves to hold listeners.

DR. TIM: This is Dr. Tim, Detective, to bring you by transcription *The Mystery of the Mad Maltese.*

SOUND: *Yowling cat. Cover with:*

MUSIC: *Theme up and fade under and out*

DR. TIM: (*Cue*) The mystery of the mad Maltese is one of the most exciting cases I've ever had anything to do with. You see, a man's life actually hung on the slender thread of *time,* and that man had disappeared—as completely and utterly as if the earth had opened up and swallowed him. But let me start at the beginning. You see, I'm a sort of combination of detective and medical doctor. This particular morning I was in the midst of a complicated experiment in my laboratory . . .

SOUND: *Hissing of air, bubbling of liquid, background to cue.*

DR. TIM: . . . having to do with testing some material for blood stains. Just as I set the bubbling liquid aside to cool . . .

SOUND: *Fade out, and into cat yowling and kids' voices in excitement, background to cue*

DR. TIM: . . . I heard a commotion outside my window. I recognized the voices of my good friends Sandy and Jill. Jill's my landlady's daughter, and Sandy is one of the kids down the street. Both of them have helped me on a lot of cases.

SOUND: *Cat and kids up slightly*

DR. TIM: I couldn't imagine what was going on, so I raised the window. . . .

SOUND: *Raise window. Sound up full*

DR. TIM: . . . and called out. "Hey, you kids . . . what's up?"

SOUND: *Voices out. Fade out cat*

JILL: (*Off*) Gosh, Dr. Tim—something *awful's* happened!

---

[6] Presented with permission of Monarch Program Library, Inc.

SANDY: (*Off*) We're trying to catch a big old cat. He's gone crazy or somethin', I guess.

JILL: (*Off*) Uh huh—he just clawed a man somethin' terrible, and he bit him on the hand, and . . .

DR. TIM: (*Narrating*) My heart jumped up in my throat, as I called through the window: "Get out of that yard *and stay out!* Don't go near that animal!"

SANDY: (*Off*) But gee, Dr. Tim, he might be dangerous. He might hurt some *little* kid if we don't . . .

DR. TIM: Without stopping to argue, I grabbed up the nearest thing I could lay my hands on—it happened to be my topcoat—and dashed out into the yard.

JILL: Gee, Dr. Tim, what's the matter?

DR. TIM: (*Breathing heavily*) Get back, both of you, and let *me* handle this!

SOUND: *Cat yowls*

DR. TIM: (*Narrating*) In a moment I had the cat—a huge Maltese—backed up into a corner of the fence, and holding my topcoat before me the way a bullfighter handles his cape, I threw it over the furious animal . . .

SOUND: *Awful caterwaulings from cat*

DR. TIM: . . . and in a few seconds had it bundled up in such a way that the cat could neither bite nor scratch. Followed by Sandy and Jill, I rushed the cat into the laboratory and dumped it into a wire cage. Exhausted, the cat stretched out, white saliva dripping from its rigid jaws. I tossed the coat into a corner away from all of us, and then looked at my hands. There was no sign of a cut or scratch on them. I heaved a big sigh of relief. Jill, big-eyed with fright, spoke first:

JILL: Gee whizz, Dr. Tim . . . what's wrong?

DR. TIM: I'm not sure, Jill, but I'm afraid it's . . . rabies. I'm almost certain that cat is . . . *mad!*

MUSIC: *Tension curtain. Up full and out*

DR. TIM: (*Cue*) A few minutes later I was getting the whole story from Sandy and Jill.

SANDY: . . . and . . . well, we were playing out in the yard, and this man came walking up the street. Gosh, I don't know *where* the cat came from, but . . .

JILL: When the man came along, the cat dashed out under his feet, and he stooped down to push it away. . . .

SANDY: . . . and—and—the cat had a sort of—of a fit, or something. It bit him on the hand. . . .

JILL: . . . so we ran up and chased the cat into the backyard, and when we got back the man was gone.

DR. TIM: (*Solemnly*) Sandy . . . Jill . . . You know what rabies is, don't you?

SANDY: You mean like a mad dog? But this is a *cat*.

DR. TIM: Cats can have it too. So can squirrels, and rats, and . . . well, a lot of animals. Wolves, coyotes . . .

JILL: Gee whizz . . . you mean hydro . . . hydro*phobia*, that makes you go *mad*?

DR. TIM: I'm afraid I do, Jill.

SANDY: But what about that man he bit? What'll happen?

DR. TIM: Unless we can find him, and find him *in time*, he'll die one of the most horrible deaths known to a human being. Now you kids—are you *sure* you didn't touch that cat?

BOTH: No, honest we didn't.

DR. TIM: Good enough. And you're sure the cat bit the—the mysterious stranger?

JILL: Yes.

DR. TIM: Then first of all, I have to make sure the cat really is rabid.

SANDY: How?

DR. TIM: You see, rabies is a virus . . . a deadly agent so small that it can't be seen even with a microscope. So some very complicated tests are necessary. However, in my mind there's no doubt that the cat has rabies.

SANDY: How do you know?

DR. TIM: From the way it acts. Any animal that bites can always be suspected of having the disease, and that means that if you're bitten, the biting animal should immediately be put under observation.

JILL: What'll you do when you find the man he bit?

DR. TIM: Give him a series of inoculations . . . injections, with a material known as a vaccine.

JILL: But Dr. Tim . . . how are we going to *find* the man?

DR. TIM: Jill, we're going to have to turn detectives again. I'm afraid we'll have to stage a manhunt, and *time* is the most important thing. Those treatments have to begin as soon as possible—or nothing, nothing in the world, can save that man from dying. Now let's start tracking him down!

MUSIC: *Transition and under*

DR. TIM: (*Cue*) There wasn't very much to go on. Jill and Sandy both agreed that the man was a stranger in the neighborhood. He wore a blue suit, a felt hat, was about fifty years old, and he carried a bag. As Jill explained.

JILL: Well, it was sort of . . . sort of like the bag *you* carry, Dr. Tim, with all your medicine and things in it . . . only bigger.

DR. TIM: A suitcase?

JILL: No, it wasn't a *suitcase*. Gee whizz, I wish I could remember more. (*Fading*) I remember he set it down, and . . .

DR. TIM: (*Narrating a sigh*) An average looking man of fifty, carrying a bag. Not much to go on, but we all got busy. Sandy and Jill and I went all over the neighborhood. We rang doorbells. . . .

SOUND: *Doorbells and buzzers*

DR. TIM: . . . we talked to housewives, always asking if they had seen anyone who looked like the man bitten by the rabid cat. No one had. There was only one thing left to do—and that was to send out a general alarm!

MUSIC: *Up for transition, and fade under for background to cue*

POLICE: (*Radio filter*) Calling all cars! Calling all cars! Be on lookout for man bitten by cat with rabies. Will have claw marks on left wrist and hand. Was last seen carrying small handbag (*fading*) in neighborhood of Grant and Eleventh streets. . . .

ANNCR: (*News style. Fading in*) . . . and here's an urgent bulletin. Somewhere there is a man who has been bitten by a rabid cat and probably doesn't realize his danger. If that man is listening—or if any of our listeners know him—he should be taken at once to the nearest hospital. Only prompt treatment can save his life. (*Fading*) Now here's the story. This morning . . .

MUSIC: *Up and fade out under*

DR. TIM: Every doctor in town—every doctor in the state—was asked to report at once, anyone who appeared for treatment of scratches and bites. But no one answering his description had been heard of. By that evening, we were at a dead end. Time was running short . . . time, that important factor in treating rabies. With every hour, our chances of saving the unknown man's life lessened. As we sat around and tried to think of some new way to find our man, we were certainly a dejected crew.

SANDY: Gosh, Dr. Tim, you'd think *somebody* would be able to locate him.

DR. TIM: (*Sighing*) Especially with that state-wide alarm out. And I suppose by now the story has gone over the whole country.

JILL: What did you do with the cat, Dr. Tim?

DR. TIM: The health department came out and got him this afternoon.

JILL: Are they . . . are they *sure* . . . you know . . . ?

DR. TIM: I'm afraid so. It's rabies, all right.

SANDY: Gosh, *why* do animals have to go and get things like that?

DR. TIM: That's life, Sandy. We doctors have been working for thousands of years to conquer disease, but we've barely made a beginning. Of course, human carelessness has a lot to do with it, too.

JILL: How?

DR. TIM: Well, rabies could be completely wiped out, if . . .

JILL: If what?

DR. TIM: If people would just use their heads. You see, rabies can be prevented.

SANDY: You mean something could have been done to keep that cat from going mad?

DR. TIM: Of course. Just in exactly the same way that you and Jill will never get smallpox, because you were vaccinated against it—and because you'll continue getting vaccinated every few years just as a safety measure.

JILL: Do they vaccinate dogs and cats too?

DR. TIM: Sure they do. In some places it's the law that all pets which might develop rabies *must* be immunized.

SANDY: That's a swell idea!

DR. TIM: There'll always be strays, but the first thing to do is to stay away from animals you don't know. You don't even have to be bitten to get rabies.

SANDY: How do you mean?

DR. TIM: If you have a cut or scratch, just *handling* the animal might infect you. Did you notice what I did to that coat of mine that I used to capture the cat?

JILL: I did. You wouldn't let me touch it. Then you wrapped it up in heavy paper, and . . . why did you do that?

DR. TIM: Because the cat infected it. It was hissing and spitting and slobbering all over the coat . . . and anyone touching those places with a cut or scratch might get the infection.

SANDY: Gosh, we sure had a close shave chasing after that cat.

DR. TIM: You'll never know how close. . . . Well, you kids, it's getting late. Not much more we can do tonight.

JILL: (*Sighing*) Gee, Dr. Tim, I feel like we sure let you down . . . not remembering more about what that man looked like.

SANDY: Yeah. . . .

DR. TIM: It can't be helped. I probably couldn't have remembered much more myself—and I've been trained as a detective.

SANDY: I've been thinking. There was something *different* about him, but I don't know what it was.

JILL: It was something about his clothes, I think. Oh, darn!

DR. TIM: (*Narrating*) A vague idea was beginning to form in my head. But it was crowded out by visions of what that unknown man was going to be in for if we didn't find him in a hurry. It might be a a week, a month, maybe longer, when he'd begin to feel restless— there'd be an unaccountable sense of terror . . . (*Fading*) . . . irritation . . . I could almost see it happen.

VOICE: (*Extreme filter, changing to dream echo on cue. Heavy breathing.*) Something's the matter with me . . . all that light in my eyes . . . doesn't seem to help even when I pull the shade down . . . no! No!

. . . I . . . can't . . . open . . . my . . . jaws . . . ah, better.
. . . Acting like a hysterical old woman . . . wish I knew what to
do . . . there it comes again! . . . the light . . . the . . . the
noise . . . (*Echo*) I'm going mad . . . mad! What are those
sounds? . . . My face . . . my face is paralyzed! (*A scream building to multiple echo*)

DR. TIM: (*Cue*) I was so lost in my horror-struck thoughts that I hardly
noticed what Sandy and Jill were saying, until. . . .

JILL: No, it wasn't, Sandy. It was sort of an *old-fashioned* coat. Not like
the one my dad wears . . . or Dr. Tim.

SANDY: Well, that's what I meant . . . sort of. But there was something
shiny. I remember, because when we ran out on the walk, something flashed in my eyes. And it was on his coat.

JILL: Wait a minute, Sandy . . . I think I'm beginning to remember.
Buttons . . . that was it!

SANDY: (*Excited*) *Brass* buttons! Dr. Tim—he had *brass buttons!*

DR. TIM: Eh? . . . Sorry, I didn't . . .

JILL: Dr. Tim! The man who was bitten, what he wore was like a uniform—only it wasn't exactly.

DR. TIM: (*Mounting intensity*) Policeman. . . . ? ? ? ?

SANDY: I'm sure it wasn't a policeman.

DR. TIM: Bus driver . . . nope . . . no brass buttons there. That handbag. Let me think. . . . Dark blue suit . . . brass buttons . . .
no uniform cap, though . . . handbag . . . going out of town obviously . . . buttons . . . buttons . . . buttons. . . .

SOUND: *Train whistle in far-off distance*

DR. TIM: (*Suddenly*) I've got it! Sandy . . . Jill . . . we've got our man
. . . Let me get at that telephone, quick! His life is saved!

MUSIC: *Transition*

DR. TIM: (*Cue*) About an hour later, the phone rang.

SOUND: *Receiver off*

VOICE: (*Telephone filter*) Well, doc . . . we've found him . . . yes . . .
yes . . . that's right. He's a conductor on the Chicago run . . .
yeah, train's just pulling into Ivyville now. An ambulance is meet-
it . . . he'll be given his first injection inside thirty minutes . . .
nice work, doc . . . and congratulate those kids for me, too. They're
smart youngsters. . . . Thanks, and so long.

SOUND: *Receiver click*

DR. TIM: (*A huge sigh*) Well! That's that!

JILL: Was he really a railroad conductor?

SANDY: Did they find him? On the train?

DR. TIM: He was and they did. And a nicer piece of detective work I've
never known. It was all *your* doing, kids.

JILL: But how did you *know?*

SANDY: Yeah. . . . I didn't even get hep till you telephoned the railroad station.

DR. TIM: Well, when you have all the pieces, you can put them together and get a picture. A man in a sort of uniform, as you called it . . . with brass buttons . . . a small grip. . . . And then, just as I was beginning to get somewhere, one of those fool accidents happened . . . one of those crazy things that make all the difference in the world. I heard a train whistle in the distance. All of a sudden, I knew . . . and that's the story.

SANDY: And you can put it down in your records as the mystery . . . the mystery of . . . .

JILL: The Mystery of the Mad Maltese!

MUSIC: *Theme*

DR. TIM: Well, this is Dr. Tim, Detective, saying so long until next week at this same time, when Sandy, Jill and I will bring you *The Mystery of the Guest in Number Two.*

MUSIC: *Theme fill*

A writer who undertakes an elementary-grade series aimed to develop the health habits of younger children has a sizable job on his hands. The same is true of safety education, for the tendency in both instances is to become preachy and when that happens the young listeners in the classroom tune out—even though they may not touch the radio. The following script, dealing with safety at the elementary-grade level, deliberately makes use of tongue-in-cheek humor and adventure cast in a format familiar to many children. At the same time the writer presents a sufficient number of important safety concepts which are within the experience of the young listener.

MURDER ON WHEELS
Division of Safety Education

SAFETY-SAM, DETECTIVE   Script: Shirley Guralnik

CAST	MUSIC	SOUND
Announcer	Theme	Organ-grinder
Cardigan	Lively bridges	Window open
Safety-Sam		Window closed
Louie		Telephone ring and receiver click
Pin-Face Finney		Car approaching and skid
Curly Miller—a child		Car heard from inside
		Whistle—3 blasts
		Squad car and siren

ANNCR: The Division of Safety Education presents SAFETY-SAM, DE-TECTIVE in—*The Case of Murder on Wheels.* It's Safety-Sam who says:

SAM: Carelessness is a crime, so play it safe.

MUSIC: *Theme . . . in, under and out*

CARDIGAN: (*On. Absent-mindedly*) What did you say, Sam?

SAM: (*Off*) I said . . . Cardigan! What *are* you watching through that window?

CARDIGAN: (*On*) A monkey, Sam. A little monkey and an organ-grinder. Listen!

SOUND: *Window opened*

MUSIC: (*In abruptly*) *Grind-organ tune* (*hold under*)

CARDIGAN: I've never seen a monkey that could throw a ball into the air and catch it. Ha! He just caught it again. I hope the people toss a lot of pennies. . . .

MUSIC: *Stop abruptly*

CARDIGAN: Yipe! The organ-grinder was almost hit by that car.

SAM: (*Off*) Why?

CARDIGAN: (*On*) The monkey's ball rolled into the street and the organ-grinder darted out after it.

SAM: (*Off*) Did the monkey run after the ball, too?

CARDIGAN: (*On*) No, he's still on the hand organ.

SAM: Then the monkey has more sense than the organ-grinder. I'm sure the monkey would look both ways before he stepped off that curb.

CARDIGAN: Think so, Safety-Sam?

SAM: Yes, Cardigan, I think so. Anyone with any sense at all looks both ways before he steps off the curb. And running after a ball is a poor excuse for surprising a driver and getting hit by the car. Now, how about getting back to work?

CARDIGAN: O.K., Sam. They're leaving anyway.

SOUND: *Window closing*

CARDIGAN: That was a close call. The organ-grinder could have been hit . . . the way Mrs. T. Cunningham-Smythe was hit!

SAM: Oh no! The driver who hit her *meant* to do it.

CARDIGAN: But honestly, Safety-Sam, I don't see how anyone could *purposely* knock a woman down as she crossed the street.

SAM: Cardigan, my good man, that crime was part of a jewel robbery. The car knocked Mrs. T. Cunningham-Smythe down and came to a sudden stop so that the driver could get out and grab her diamonds. And make a swift get-away . . . which he did. So far, all my clues point to Pin-Face Finney and Louie the Lug.

CARDIGAN: Has that gang been operating around here, Safety-Sam?

SAM: Well, yesterday Curly Miller was delivering his newspapers. In the yard of the old Hamlin house, he saw a man who answers to Pin-Face's description.

CARDIGAN: Then what are we waiting for?

SAM: Cardigan, you've been in the business of private detection long enough to know that we have to have proof first. I told Curly it would be better for him to stay away from the place until . . .

SOUND: *Telephone ringing*

CARDIGAN: I'll take it, Sam.

SOUND: *Receiver being picked up*

CARDIGAN: Safety-Sam, Detective Agency. Cardigan speaking. Oh, hello Curly! What? Where are you? (*Pause. To Sam*) Sam, Curly's calling from a drugstore. He's just been at the old Hamlin house.

SAM: What? I told him not to go there. Was Pin-Face there?

CARDIGAN: Curly, Sam wants to know if you saw Pin-Face Finney. He was? Pin-Face and Louie both? (*Pause*) Sam, when Curly was delivering the newspapers today, Pin-Face and Louie were fixing a flat tire in the yard.

SAM: Ask him if the thieves saw him?

CARDIGAN: Did they see you, Curly? (*Pause*) You think so? What? When you were copying the license number? What? Oh no!!!!

SAM: Cardigan, what is it?

CARDIGAN: Curly was in the bushes behind the car getting Pin-Face's license number and he heard Louis say to Pin-Face "We've got to get this flat fixed and get out of this place with these hot jewels."

SAM: Jewels? Maybe it's the T. Cunningham-Smythe jewels. Here, give me the phone. Hello, Curly. Listen, Curly, you'll have to be very careful. Pin-Face and Louie are the toughest jewel thieves in the country. And this is our chance to trap them! Give me the license number. Right! I've got it. Our squad car will be watching for CY 657. Now, did they get a look at you? They did? Cardigan, Louie saw him and chased him until he ducked into a drugstore. Curly, listen. They'll be on the lookout for you. After they get that flat fixed, they might try to run you over. Are you listening? Good! You start out from the drugstore and walk down Bridge Street. I'll meet you at Maple and Vine Avenue, just beyond where they're fixing the street. Do you understand? Talk to no one and *walk carefully*. Now, if they follow you, lead them to us at Maple and Vine. We'll be around the corner with the squad car. We'll wait for the car with the license number you gave me. Right! 'Bye.

SOUND: *Click of receiver*

CARDIGAN: Sam, don't you think we should follow Curly with the car? Pin-Face and Louie are plenty tough. They might hurt him.

SAM: No, Cardigan. We'll let Curly bring the thieves right to us. Call the squad car, give them the license number CY 657 and have the car stationed on Maple and Vine Street, just beyond where you see the street-repair outfit. But remember, stay away from the street repairing. There may be loose wires and danger areas.

CARDIGAN: Right! Safety-Sam, right!

MUSIC: *Lively Bridge*

CURLY: I don't see why Safety-Sam had to tell me to walk down the street carefully. I always do. Now down Bridge Street. I'll walk to the cross-walk and not cross in the middle of the block.

SOUND: *Car approach , . . skid around corner and fade*

CURLY: Wow! If I hadn't turned to look for cars turning corners, that one could have knocked me down. Safety-Sam told me to walk carefully. Not that he needed to remind me. Say, here comes that same car again. Seems as though I'm being followed. Golly!

MUSIC: *Bridge . . Segue into—*

SOUND: *Continuous running on highway . . . car heard from inside*

LOUIE: There he is, Pin-Face! That's the kid I saw taking down our license number. Quick, stop the car, Pin-Face. Let me nab him.

PIN-FACE: You crazy? It's broad daylight. We'll let it seem like an accident. Just keep your eye on him!

LOUIE: Why?

PIN-FACE: Sooner or later, he's sure to run out from between parked cars.

LOUIE: Oh, I get it. Wait until he does that and then run him down.

PIN-FACE: Louie, you're a genius. Hey, he's walking to the corner.

LOUIE: And he's crossing with the light.

PIN-FACE: We'll get him yet. When he crosses, we'll make a right turn. Kids don't watch for turning cars.

LOUIE: Then we'll get him.

PIN-FACE: We're almost up to him. . . .

SOUND: *Car skids around the corner*

PIN-FACE: Missed him.

LOUIE: What do we do now, Pin-Face?

PIN-FACE: He'll be crossing again at the next crosswalk, Louie. Jump out and get him to stop and talk to you in the middle of the street. Leave the rest to me. Quick!

SOUND: *Car slows to stop*

LOUIE: (*Calls*) Hello there, kid. Wait a minute. I want to ask if you can tell me where the post office is.

CURLY: Sorry mister. I never stand in the middle of the street to talk.

LOUIE: (*Off. Calls*) Wait! I want to talk with you.

CURLY: (*Calls*) Nothing doing. (*To himself*) Now I *know* that's Pin-Face Finney's car. He was trying to hit me. I'll hop on this bus to Vine Street.

MUSIC: *Bridge*

SAM: Cardigan, it looks as though our young friend isn't going to get here.

CARDIGAN: Maybe he stopped to get an ice-cream cone.

SAM: A very improbable deduction, my good man. You don't know Curly if you believe that. As a Junior Detective, he's much more dependable than that.

CARDIGAN: Then maybe he was in an accident.

SAM: Then it wouldn't be because he doesn't know how to take care of himself in the street.

CARDIGAN: What do you mean, chief?

SAM: Well, he's careful. He knows enough to cross at crosswalks.

CARDIGAN: Oh?

SAM: And he knows enough not to step from between parked cars.

CARDIGAN: Oh, that!

SAM: And he knows that a good detective learns to watch for cars at corners. He observes what's happening in the streets.

CARDIGAN: I wonder where he is. If he's been picked up by Pin-Face, there's no telling what might happen!

SAM: (Softly) Cardigan.

CARDIGAN: What?

SAM: There he is!

CARDIGAN: Who, Curly? Where?

SAM: He's getting off that bus. Hope he stays in the Safety Zone.

CARDIGAN: Don't worry. Curly isn't running from the Safety Zone. See. He's waiting until the cars pass before he walks to the curb.

SAM: Look! That big black car is stopping and the license is CY 657!

CARDIGAN: Hey! Those men are going to force Curly into their car.

SAM: Quick Cardigan! Three blasts on the whistle. The squad car's around the corner.

SOUND: *Three sharp whistle blasts . . . squad car starts. Siren begins*

SAM: Look, they see the squad car.

CARDIGAN: But Pin-Face didn't get Curly. He's still in the Safety Zone. Look, Pin-Face is getting away.

SAM: No, Cardigan, the squad car's behind them. Don't worry. Pin-Face Finney will get caught this time.

CURLY: (Fade in) Safety-Sam, we've trapped them. We got them!

CARDIGAN: Good work, Curly!

SAM: Yes sir! You've led the criminals right into the trap.

CURLY: Those thieves will soon learn that crime doesn't pay.

SAM: And we can return the jewels, thanks to you.

CARDIGAN: Curly's going to be a detective, all right. He knows what to look out for in the street.

SAM: Remarkable deduction, Cardigan. And I liked the way Curly stayed in the Safety Zone until it was safe to cross to the curb. That showed good common sense.

CURLY: I almost stopped to talk in the middle of the street. But I didn't.

SAM: Very good work, Curly! Cardigan, don't you think Curly deserves to be one of our Junior Detectives?

CARDIGAN: I sure do, Safety-Sam. He knew enough to get the license number when he was sus—sus—

SAM: Suspicious?

CARDIGAN: Yes. And his power of obser—obser—

SAM: Observation?

CARDIGAN: Yes, observation—of seeing things—is mighty fine.

SAM: Curly, you are now one of my favorite Junior Detectives.

CURLY: Boy! Oh, boy!

SAM: You know, Curly, this was a rare case. Jewel thieves don't usually wait around corners to knock boys and girls down. But it isn't too unusual to have boys and girls knocked down by automobiles in traffic. No, it happens very often.

CARDIGAN: Oh, too often, Safety-Sam!

SAM: You know, Curly, I'm not worried about your safety habits. But I'd like to know whether our listeners are alert enough to answer these questions. Here's the first question, boys and girls. Why will you cross at crosswalks and not in between parked cars? (15 seconds) You have a sharp detective's eye if you said that stepping out from between parked cars is dangerous because the motorist isn't expecting you and may strike you.

So take the time to walk over to the crosswalk and cross with the light. Let's see if you can figure this one out. Why will you keep away from areas that are blocked off for street repairs? (20 seconds) Good deduction if you said that children can get hurt where men are working.

Often there's loose, shifting sand or live wires. So keep away from places where men are at work. Now, you're old enough to travel alone by streetcar or bus. Where should you stand and wait when you get off the streetcar? (15 seconds)

I hope you said that when you get off the streetcar you should remain in the Safety Zone until it's safe to walk to the curb.

CURLY: Safety-Sam, I've got a lu-lu of a question I'd like to ask them.

SAM: Go ahead, Curly. Ask them.

CURLY: Why is it foolish to dash into the street for a ball? (15 seconds) You're O.K. if you said that a motorist must never be startled or surprised by having someone run in front of his car. If you look both ways and then walk, the driver has time to judge how long it will take you to get out of the path of his car.

CARDIGAN: (Laughs)

CURLY: What's funny?

CARDIGAN: (*Laughing*) Safety-Sam, don't tell me you want to make all the boys and girls into detectives?

SAM: Why not? If they can learn to be sharp in the streets and observe the cars and traffic they can come with me on my next case.

CURLY: What's it going to be, Safety-Sam?

SAM: All the sharp, careful ones can start out with me on (*Pause*) *The Case of the Cold Bulldog.*

MUSIC: *Theme*

Another type of modified dramatization will now be shown. This also deals with a subject difficult to handle without becoming offensively preachy—personal regimen. The writer made clever use of an approach familiar to the high-school listener. He was wisely aware that the judgment of peers, male and female, means more to the adolescent girl than the possible displeasure of "old-fashioned" elders. It will be seen that the script is developed to make use of school radio-workshop pupils and that names are to be filled in when the cast is selected.

The sound of the gong followed by a ten-second pause, which is noted at the beginning of the script, is a device used by WBOE to enable the sound system operators in the various schools to throw the necessary switches. Without such advance notification, it was found that classrooms frequently missed the opening line or two of a program or sometimes they were tuned in much too early.

NO-HIT PARADE—NO. 2

Division of Home Economics

BOY DATES GIRL—Series V   Script: E. F. Helman

CAST

Gay Head—Helen Barr	NO-HIT 10: Man-Eater	3: Goldie
Girl	8: Gloria	9: Superman
Boy	6: Paula	7: Red Bellows
		4: Windy Bill

MUSIC: *E.T. Electrical transcriptions*

SOUND: *Phone receiver down*

BARR: Stay tuned to this Station for the BOY DATES GIRL program which follows in ten seconds.

SOUND: *Chimes*

BARR: (*Cue*) Hello there! This is Helen Barr speaking for the Division of Home Economics and for Gay Head who writes the column in

Scholastic magazine called "Boy Dates Girl." My broadcast today is a new edition of our popular "No-Hit Parade." I have several assistants on this parade of unpopular personalities. Four high-school radio-workshop actors hope you will think they are good character actors . . . and not being their natural selves! They are—

_____   _____   _____   _____
_____   _____   _____   _____

In addition to these actors there are two other high-school acquaintances who will help me identify the types in today's lineup of dates whom everyone would like to avoid.

BOY: I'm _____ of _____ High School. May I also introduce _____ of _____ High School.

GIRL. Thank you, _____. I'm very glad to be here to watch the No-Hit Parade. But I do think it would have been more polite had you let Gay Head introduce *me* first. At the head of *my* No-Hit Parade of Dates is the boy who doesn't have good manners.

BARR: But, _____, I *asked* _____ to introduce himself and you. Since some of our listeners have already met me, perhaps it would have been better etiquette had I introduced you first, myself; but in radio we like to have men's voices contrast with women's.

BOY: Personally, Gay Head, at the head of *my* No-Hit Parade comes the girl who finds fault with her date's manners in front of other people

GIRL: You and I aren't dating!

BARR: On every blacklist is the couple who squabbles in public.

BOY: Are you reprimanding both _____ and me in public, Gay Head?

BARR: Good heavens, I suppose I am! Now how did this happen?

GIRL: I think it's the adult in you.

BARR: I suppose it is. You and _____ would probably put at the head of your No-Hit Parade the adult who assumes an air of superiority and authority whenever she talks with young people.

BOY: I certainly would, except that this parade today is a no-hit parade of *dates* . . *high-school dates.*

BARR: Um-m. It's high time we begin this parade before I *feel* as old as you think I am, _____.

GIRL: Just a sec, Gay Head. You want _____ and me to try to identify each number on this parade, is that it?

BARR: Correct. And if either of you feels moved to make additional comments, let experience be your guide. . . . And now the studio lights are dimmed, the spotlight is turned on, the curtain parts before the chromium-plated microphone!

MUSIC: *RCA Magic Key introduction . . . Music up, under*

BARR: (*Cue*) BOY DATES GIRL presents the No-Hit Parade!

MUSIC: *Up and fade on Cue*

NO-HIT 10: (*Subdeb man-eater. On cue*) Hello there, _____. My, it's *super* seeing you again! You're looking *wonderful!* That *tie* you're wearing . . . it's positively *atomic! . . .* How come you never call me up any more you hour of charm, you! . . . Not that I'm *waiting* for you. Freddie has sewed up positively every minute of my time in the last ten days. Freddie's *cute.* He's so strong and *handsome* and *sweet!* But I don't think it's good for a girl to let a boy take up *all* her time, do you, _____? Not at our age! (*Breaks off: then calls*) Hi, there, Danny! (*Calling and going off*) Danny, just a minute, big boy! I haven't seen you in ages!

BARR: (*Cue*) Do you know her type? It's Number 10 on our No-Hit Parade.

GIRL: She should have stood higher! She's a man-eater. And apparently she once ate you, _____!

BOY: Just a light lunch.

GIRL: An hour of charm!

BOY: Could be. Still an' all, there's no real harm in Two-Timing Tess.

GIRL: Harmless as a boa constrictor.

BARR: Don't you mean *boy* constrictor? Why so venomous, _____?

GIRL: She gives all the rest of us girls a bad reputation.

BOY: How do you figure?

GIRL: Tess gives you boys the idea that all girls are as male-crazy and disloyal as she is.

BOY: Not on your life! A wooden Indian could see through her. She can't hold even a dope like Freddie more than two weeks.

BARR: She's her own worst enemy, is that it?

BOY: Bro—ther, I'll say! Once you hear her sweet-wording all the guys, you take off. And when she's with you, she's always talking *about* other fellows and *to* them. A date with her is like a night out with your gang!

BARR: Alias *Mrs.* Bluebeard. . . . Well, Two-Timing Tess was tenth on our No-Hit Parade. Here's Number 9.

MUSIC: *Boy theme . . . fade in, up, out under*

NO-HIT 9: (*Man rules the world . . . he's that dumb*) Hi-ya sugar. Took you long enough to get to the phone. It isn't on television yet. Guess who this is! . . . Whatcha doin' tonight? . . . No kidding! Haven't you finished *that* yet! I cleaned that job up in study hall. What problem you working on now? . . . Why, that's easy! A cinch. Of course, I suppose it is hard for you women. You gotta have a man's brain to get anywhere in science, honey. . . . Gee, there's no point in getting sore. After all, everyone knows that you women—it isn't that women aren't O.K. so far as they go, you understand—but this is a man's world, honey, and science is a man's subject! You girls shouldn't try stuff like that. . . . Well, for Pete's sake! Why, you can't even take a little bit of constructive criticism. Ah—you women are all alike! (*Receiver down hard*)

BARR: (*Cue*) Ever met up with a type like that, _____?

GIRL: *That is Superman!*

BARR: Superman?

GIRL: Or Supermanny! He thinks woman was made for man's ribbing! She's just around to pick up after him and to soothe his fevered brow!

BOY: Well, isn't that a good idea?

GIRL: You see what I mean, Gay Head.

BARR: Back in 1914, the old German Kaiser used to say that women should have only three interests: kitchen, children, and church. . . . Can you imagine three things harder to manage?

GIRL: You know, Gay Head, I think these Supermen lack confidence in themselves. If they were really so superior, they wouldn't have to go around telling us how good they are.

BOY: Say, how's this for an idea? Next time I date a girl, I'll treat her like a man!

GIRL: Why should you? She isn't one.

BOY: But you just said—ah, what's the use of arguing with you women. You're all alike!

BARR: No we're not, _____, not any more than men are all alike. Some of us are smart, some of us are . . . well, normal. But we *are* individuals. Of course, we're a different sex—but so are you. We aren't inferior in any respect, and the sooner you get that idea out of your head the better you'll get along.

BOY: But this is a *man's* world!

GIRL: Says *who?*

BARR: While you're thinking out the answer to that one, _____, we'll move along to Number 8 on our No-Hit Parade.

MUSIC: *Girl theme . . . up, down, under*

NO-HIT 8: (*Movie-queenishly*) Cheerio, all you nice people!

MUSIC: *Up and out*

BOY: (*Cue. Whistles in admiration*) Glamorous Gloria. Quite a babe, not?

GIRL: (*Sniffishly*) If you like them that way.

BOY: Jealous?

GIRL: Don't make me laugh. She's on the *No-Hit Parade*, isn't she?

BARR: And I wonder why. Your whistle seemed to indicate—well, admiration, at least. Yet the majority of boys turn thumbs down on Glamorous Gloria.

BOY: Sure. Gloria is nothing but scenic effect. She's so self-conscious about her looks that she's—well, sort of unconscious, if you know what I mean. She isn't herself . . . just an attractive high-school girl. She's her own homemade edition of her latest Hollywood craze. A boy who wasn't an imitation movie star himself would be scared away from dating her. I'll whistle at her, but I won't take her out. She's just a clotheshorse.

BARR: Her glamour defeats itself, is that it? I suspect you'd recommend that Gloria spend as much time on her brain and character as on her hair and costume.

MUSIC: *Boy theme . . . up, down, under and out*

NO-HIT 7: (*Loud-mouthed show-off*) Boy, I'm telling you, sister, I gave Tom a hotfoot to end all hotfeet. Yow-ee! You should've seen him after that. He'd've slugged me if I hadn't ducked out too fast for him. (*Laughs loudly*) Huh? Sure, everybody's looking at us, but who cares? You look all right to me, sister. . . . Hey, *girlie! Wait- ress!* . . . Where's that sandwich my girl friend ordered last week? Ya bakin' the bread or something? . . . Ow-w! Hey, sister, what's the idea of kicking my ankle. (*Fade*) You want I should walk you home with a limp?

GIRL: (*Cue*) Number 7 is an old enemy—let's call him Red Bellows! He's the humorous half-wit with the oversized mouth. Any girl who goes out with him once has the smallpox next time he calls up for a date.

BARR: The male with the arrested social development. He was cute at two; a holy terror at four. And he's stayed that age ever since.

BOY: I dated a *girl* like that . . . once! She was the life of the party. Al- ways yelling at someone on the other side of the room. Laughed like a hyena. If I had it to do again, I'd act like a radio comedian when I took her out.

GIRL: Like a radio comedian?

BOY: Sure. I'd carry around an old *gag* for emergency use! . . . On with the show!

MUSIC: *Girl theme . . . up, under and out*

NO-HIT 6: (*Between petulance and a whine*) Oh, so there you are, _____. Don't you dare speak to me. I've been waiting for days for you to call me up—and now what do I see? You're sitting there enjoying yourself with two other women! You're a two-timer, that's what you are. (*Fade*) Well, let me tell you I won't put up with that kind of business. . . .

GIRL: (*Cue*) Why, _____, you're a male Two-Timing Tessie!

BOY: (*In disgust*) Naw. That's Possessive Paula. I took her to a homeroom dance once and now she thinks she's staked out a claim on me. Hon- estly, Gay Head, I've never given her the least reason to think I wanted to go steady with her.

BARR: I know. That's why she's on our parade. Men just don't like women who try to rope and brand them—either with or without encouragement. Possessive Paula never does keep her man—but she *tries!*

BOY: And how!

SOUND: *Fade in and out female Indian war-whoop*

GIRL: *What* in the world was that?

BOY: What a question! If we were on television, everyone else would recognize that little number.

BARR: Number five on our No-Hit Parade!

BOY: Cosmetic Kate! Cosmetic Kate, the painted squaw . . .

GIRL: Her long hair streaming in the breeze!

BARR: On or off the reservation, she's a sight, isn't she? No wonder you boys keep away from her.

BOY: She ought to wear a sign: Caution! Wet Paint!

GIRL: Cosmetic Kate thinks all her pan needs to make it attractive is a layer of pancake make-up.

BOY: Plus red, white, and blue!

BARR: Kleenex for Cosmetic Kate . . . and on to Number four!

MUSIC: *Boy theme up and under and out*

NO-HIT 4: (*He loves himself*) Say, _____, did I ever tell you about the time I won the basketball championship for my homeroom? Well, believe you me, I made the rest of the team look like a bunch of statues. You know me, kid—fast as lightning once I get started. Why, those hicks playing against me couldn't even *see* the ball. Any angle—any distance—I sank one basket after the other till the score looked like the high cost of living. Afterward, the varsity captain came up to me and said, "How come you've never gone out for the school team, Bill?" I says, "You just aren't in my class yet." Boy, did that slay him! . . . Yeh, I expect to make the Honor Society (*Fade*) if there isn't any dirty work at the crossroads.

BARR: (*Cue*) Know him?

GIRL: He came in with the Big Blow. That's Windy Bill. He knows only one interesting subject and he sticks to it.

BOY: If he didn't talk about himself, who would?

GIRL: That's a fact.

BOY: I know *girls* who are just like him . . . talk only about themselves . . . and improve on the facts as they go. . . .

BARR: Why don't you try ear plugs?

BOY: No date at all is better!

MUSIC: *Girl theme . . . up, under and out*

NO-HIT 3: Greetings, _____. You *are* ____ _____, aren't you? Let's get away from all these humdrum people tonight, _____. Let's hit the high spots. I feel like orchids, and filet mignon, and the Gold Room. Can't you borrow your cousin's Cadillac? . . . You can't? Well, I'll try to be ready when you come in a cab. . . .

What! You're broke? Well, call me up sometime when you're in the money again. Toodle-oo.

BOY: (*Cue*) She's tops in *my* No-Hit Parade . . . Goldie Digger, the female bandit. She leaves you cold and your pocketbook flat.

BARR: Why do you fellows ever fall for Goldie?

BOY: The same reason suckers buy gold bricks. But we don't have to get socked more than once . . . usually.

BARR: As Lincoln said, "You can't fool *all* of the men *all* of the time."

GIRL: Gay Head, I'm all agog. We're ready for the Number Two No-Hit. Is it masculine or feminine?

BARR: I have no idea.

BOY: Why not?

BARR: Our broadcast parade stops right here. Our listeners will choose the two *top* no-favorites for themselves.

GIRL: Who do you guess they will be? . . . We've paraded Two-Timing Tess, Superman, Glamorous Gloria, Red Bellows . . .

BOY: . . . Possessive Paula, Cosmetic Kate, Windy Bill, and Goldie Digger.

GIRL: All the unpleasant female dates have their male facsimiles.

BOY: Except Cosmetic Kate!

BARR: But who are Numbers Two and One in *your* all-time no-hitters, friends in the classroom audience? Once you've decided, let the Division of Home Economics know—if you have the time. Just write your nominations to BOY DATES GIRL in care of Your School Station, WBOE, in Cleveland.

Several of the more elaborate dramatizations, prepared by commercial broadcasters and planned for classroom use, have been criticized by some teachers. It might be well to analyze the nature of these reactions and to see what implications there are for the educational broadcaster.

Occasionally teachers have indicated that the usual educational program prepared by the commercial producer begins with the assumption that learning is an unpleasant process. Thus, say the teachers, the program is highly dramatized, and adventures are concocted which are probable and otherwise, after which, assuming that interest has been aroused, a bit of information is presented cautiously. Some teachers point out that such a procedure, though it may be desirable for after-school listening, has little place during school hours. They emphasize that learning itself is not an unpleasant process, particularly if a sense of satisfaction accompanies the use of recently acquired information or skills. In a sense they echo Clifton Fadiman's observation: "The twelve-year-old level theory is advanced by those with a thirteen-year-old mentality."

The "overproduced" program designed primarily for school use is a common target of criticism. To teachers it is evident that the educational quality of a program is in no way related to its budget, to the size of the cast or the complexity of the script. The only test is the measure of desired influences upon probable listeners.

Teachers have observed that background music, subtle sound effects, filter mikes, echo chambers, and other tricks of the radio trade, unless used very intelligently, merely confuse the children rather than heighten the emotion. For example, the technique of fading characters and scenes may be obvious to adults, but to children it may seem to indicate reception has become poor. Dialect may be colorful, but to children it may be confusing or even prompt questions such as, "Anyhow, Teacher, why should Columbus always speak broken English?" Transitional devices may be clever and musical bridges quite brilliant, but a school program is hardly the vehicle for displaying techniques. In the first place, it may be wasted effort since the younger children generally are not mature enough to recognize and appreciate subtleties; and second, it may sacrifice comprehension to technique.

The following statements quoted in part from an excellent manual by Reid and Woelfel are further indications of the need for clarity, especially in a dramatized school program:

. . . The best technique in a particular instance depends upon three factors: the nature of the material to be broadcast, the purposes of the program, and the maturity level of the listeners. . . . The use of experimental techniques can be justified only in terms of the degree to which they succeed in making the content of a school broadcast more interesting and meaningful to the listeners. . . . In school broadcasts simple patterns are to be preferred to more complex structures. . . . No school broadcast should contain so many scenes and episodes that the listeners will have difficulty in following the continuity. . . . The prestige value of a quotation does not compensate for loss of intelligibility.[7]

---

[7] Seerley Reid and Norman Woelfel, *How to Judge a School Broadcast*, Ohio State University, 1940, pp. 4–8.

In producing the school program it is well to remember that the children are not listening to the program at home, where listener conditions are almost ideal. At home the listener's ear is close to the receiver and the room is almost acoustically perfect with draperies and rugs, but, in the classroom, reception conditions are altogether different. Generally, the acoustics are bad, with half the walls devoted to windows and blackboards. The hard plaster ceilings, the occasional noise in the halls and in the schoolyard, all tend to aggravate this condition. Even under the best conditions, some of the children are seated as far as thirty feet or more from the radio, often at a great angle. The radio receivers themselves are frequently not so good as they are in the home, since in the average school the portability of equipment is desired. If reception is to be had through a central-sound system, conditions are often worse.

Some teachers observe also that, when broadcasting to little children, it is not necessary to be concerned greatly about realism. "To tiny tots one feather makes an Indian." When the broadcaster, in a desire to add realism to a program, reduces its clarity he is sacrificing a major value for a doubtful improvement. For older children the above may not hold true (and they surely are quick to recognize inconsistencies) but for children in the primary grades the broadcaster need only "give them a dotted line and they will fill it in."

Does the above discussion imply that the producer is to sacrifice artistic standards? "No," say the teachers, "if you want to serve us and if you are sincerely interested in classroom use, then we trust that you will recognize these limitations. A simple production which results in greater utilization is far more valuable educationally than an elaborate cacophony with little reception."

Other observations by classroom teachers are perhaps not confined to the dramatic type of program. The question of program length is mentioned frequently. Some teachers indicate that, as a rule, they favor the program which is no more than fifteen minutes in length. They point out that, if it is agreed that before the program is heard there should be some classroom preparation for it and some utilization after it, then the program should be of such brevity that sufficient time is available during the average school period. If the program is a half-hour in length or more, by the time the class is seated, the roll taken, the assignment for the following day mentioned, and other routine matters handled, there is little time left for an adequate and intelligent use of the radio program.

Music. A popular organization of educational material is that built around music. Because of its nature such a program lends itself easily to presentation by radio. Since, aside from continuity development, the music program generally is not considered a script program, there will be no statement here of its merits and limitations.

Demonstration Radio Lesson. Another type of school program mentioned earlier will be discussed here more fully since it has not been described in the radio-writing literature as much as have the other plans. This procedure has been designated by a variety of terms such as demonstration radio lesson, cooperative broadcast, directed activity, or master lesson. Whatever the name used, this approach generally calls for activity on the part of the classroom teacher and pupils as they listen to the radio broadcast. The talk method with timed pauses is used often, but occasionally a dramatic sequence or some type of conversational script is included. Frequently the script content is planned to synchronize with visual materials such as lantern slides and charts, which are shown in the listening classroom.

MERITS. Among the advantages of this procedure are the following: it simulates more nearly a classroom situation; it makes possible a demonstration lesson and the display of teaching techniques; and it emphasizes the supervisory approach.

By providing the child with the satisfaction of participation and by avoiding what may be a merely passive attitude, the cooperative procedure requests the attention of the audience. It provides the classroom teacher with an opportunity to judge her pupils while they react to an expert teacher's suggestions. By synchronizing the voice with the lantern slide or other visual aids, this approach provides a multiplicity of sensory impressions. In fact, the radio lesson is not just a script and perhaps should not be regarded as such. The demonstration radio lesson makes a specific and definite application to a local course of study. Because it is planned by selected teachers for pupils at a certain level of accomplishment, it makes evident to the classroom teachers the manner in which radio is helping them to attain their own classroom objectives. The demonstration approach, while admitting that real listening is definitely an activity of the highest order, nevertheless holds that for the presentation of certain materials, especially among younger children, a tested form of occasional motor activity is helpful. It is believed by some also that the radio, if it is to serve as a demonstration lesson, must do more than merely "tell." During this type of radio program the activities of at least three individuals supplement each other: the broadcaster, the classroom teacher, and the pupil.

LIMITATIONS. The so-called "directed activity" method has been criticized as follows: Unless it is used cautiously there is but routine automatic reaction on the part of teachers and pupils. It is cautioned that it is unwise to assume that listening is not an activity itself, or that selected material well presented cannot hold interest without physical activity. This procedure, it is stated, requires a great deal of time and expense in the preparation of lesson guides and visual materials. Much of the activity called for may be meaningless and unproductive. It may interfere with the continuity of thought. The directions must be timed for the median group and others are neglected. The classroom discussion is liable to be artificial because of the rigid timing. The whole procedure after a while may become humdrum and crystallized. The broadcasters do not grasp the opportunity of utilizing to its fullest extent a medium that is basically dramatic, emotional, and imaginative. Instead of serving as a tool the radio may become a control.

Another limitation of this method is that, although such procedures may be of value for the formal classroom, the radio "lessons" cannot be used effectively for public relations since they have little nonschool interest. As most school broadcasting is still done under commercial auspices, this factor cannot be overlooked. There is slight doubt that most effective use of the cooperative broadcast requires independent radio-station control.

SCRIPT PREPARATION. As stated previously, this type of program is not widely used. Unfortunately its use has been described largely by those who have had but slight acquaintance with its objectives and accomplishments. Almost inevitably it has been compared with the radio "show" and because it is far less spectacular, the demonstration approach has been judged accordingly. With such unrelated criteria one might as well compare the typical educational film with the Hollywood success. Obviously any such comparison is meaningless. Each has its place and, if well done, each serves a purpose. If some descriptions of the demonstration radio lesson were accepted *in toto* it would seem that the auditors merely simulate automatons and that all mental processes are eliminated. Fortunately that need not be the case.

It is quite probable that the use of radio for supervisory purposes has limitations, but if the profit and loss involved in the use of this procedure are evaluated it is clear that educational dividends are being paid. Twenty years of continuous experimentation with this method have shown that the demonstration radio lesson has a significant role in radio education.

As noted earlier, the probable spread of frequency modulation broadcasting and the establishment of more school-owned stations will permit greater flexibility in school-program forms, and it is quite likely that various demonstration procedures will be evolved. It might be desirable, therefore, to discuss some aspects of this type of script preparation. Such discussion in no way assumes that the demonstration methods should constitute the bulk of school broadcasting. The well-planned radio service for schools will consist of many program forms. As yet no one can presume to prescribe the "best" form of a school script. What is best for one situation may be poor for another. A variety of factors must be considered—available talent and supplies, course of study requirements, and the attitude of teachers and supervisors, to name a few.

The skillful radio writer working at his desk can complete a successful dramatic script, yet in preparing the demonstration lesson a satisfactory presentation can seldom be written without preliminary experimentation in a classroom. Only by working directly with the children and teachers is it possible to determine what subject matter should be broadcast; what techniques and methods are best adapted to radio teaching; what age, grade, or type of children are most benefited by radio instruction; what type of listener participation is helpful; what the time elements are, what visual materials should be used; how much detail the radio lesson guide should contain, and what co-

With Radio, the underprivileged school becomes the privileged one.

Students listen to WDTR in a Detroit elementary school.

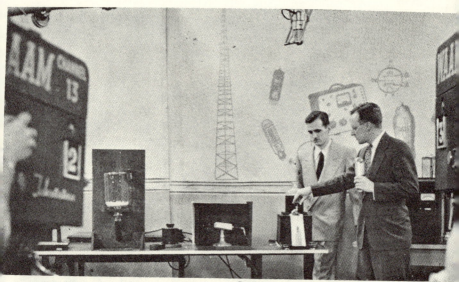

Above, The Peabody Award winning televisi
program, "The Johns Hopkins Science Review

Left, Dr. Roy K. Marshall explaining the
universe.

Below, Television in the junior high scho
classroom.

operation may be expected from the classroom teachers who are to receive the broadcast. The demonstration lesson seldom attains its objectives without a preliminary trial of the lesson in a typical classroom. For the same reason one who has not had actual classroom experience, though he be a gifted radio writer, cannot demonstrate expert teaching without help.

Where the demonstration radio lesson form has been used the preliminary procedures in script preparation are generally as follows:

In preparing the lesson, the material is selected to meet the needs of the pupils and teachers as well as the requirements of the course of study. It is then organized and a first draft written. The writer, supervisor, and often the principal then work together revising the manuscript until, in their judgment, it is ready to be presented to a class by means of the public-address system.

This experimental broadcast is received in a regular classroom, and in most cases the teacher who has written the lesson is in the classroom with the principal to observe the reaction and response of the children. Another teacher acts as broadcaster.

If there is a special supervisor for a given subject, he or she is invited to listen to the experimental broadcast. A conference follows each such trial lesson. Suggestions are made to clear away any difficulty that appears, and if important revision is made the lesson is tried again in another classroom. In certain fields, and if a school-owned station is available, a trial program is broadcast to three or four cooperating schools that act as judges of the proposed lesson. Suggestions for revision are received from these schools and are incorporated into a revised form.

This experimentation continues with each manuscript until all adults participating, and the children as well, are satisfied that the material is ready to serve the needs of the teachers and pupils throughout the city. The lesson is then given the final timing—generally fifteen minutes; however, with the school-owned radio station one important by-product is that no arbitrary time limit is required for a lesson. The entire series of broadcasts for each semester is ready weeks, and often months, in advance of the time for broadcasting, except those broadcasts dealing with current topics.

The choice of treatment for such proposed lessons is made in recognition of the need for variety. The general aim is to use the very best of classroom techniques with such adaptations as are deemed necessary for the radio. So far as possible, each radio lesson is presented in the form of a natural and vital learning situation. The essentials to be acquired, factual and otherwise, are developed inductively through experiment and observation. When this type of school script is used it is hoped that the dramatic element is neither overworked nor neglected.

There are several problems which the beginner may face in this type of writing. Generally there is a tendency to present too much information in one lesson. As noted in the discussion of the talk script, it is far more valuable to develop one important concept in a variety of ways than to attempt to present several less important aspects of a subject. The same need applies to the demonstration radio lesson.

The development of techniques for eliciting desirable pupil reactions during the radio lesson presents another difficulty. Just as in the use of sound effects the script writer seems to undergo three stages. First, he writes without a concern for any activities. Then he discovers that these pupil activities can be called for, and so, in unrestrained enthusiasm, he calls for them indiscriminately and often with poor results. However, with more experience, he finds that a limited amount of pupil participation, if carefully planned, can aid in effective lesson development. He becomes aware of the mistake, so often made, in which the teacher confuses physical activity with mental gain. Just as a thick notebook with pretty pictures and copious clippings is no assurance of learning having taken place, so there is but little correlation between the amount of pupil activity, the length and number of pauses which a radio lesson contains, and the degree of basic attainment. The experienced writer in this field plans for activities which are meaningful and which definitely aid in the achievement of the lesson's objectives.

Pupil participation should not be called forth as an apology for an uninteresting script or a humdrum presentation. If the script lacks general interest, it calls for more activity on the part of the writer and not of the child. Routine response by the pupils is no indication that they are sincerely interested. The well-organized demonstration lesson calls for as much imaginative writing as does the dramatization.

Presenting directions by radio is not easily done. It requires the ability to discern probable responses and that, in turn, assumes a knowledge of the child and his reactions when in a group.

Confusion may result unless the broadcaster's directions are stated clearly. For example, if several steps are involved in a listener's re-action, it is best to develop these one at a time and to await reactions sequentially. If several directions are given at once, not only is it difficult to judge the length of the broadcaster's pause but it necessitates recall on the part of the listener. Thus, if any one of the several directions has been missed, the child may not know how to proceed.

A pause which has existed for listener reaction should not be concluded abruptly by another direction which may not be heard by some children still at work. Rather, the previous act can better be concluded by some remark and then the next direction presented. If oral responses have been called for, then the use of rhetorical questions should be avoided, since they become confusing to the listeners who do not know whether to respond or not. In this script form particularly, the pace of presentation must be adjusted to the child. When the writer is in doubt, a slower pace is advisable. The alert classroom teacher can take up the lag with supplementary comments and explanations. In planning an activity, if the probable duration is an extremely difficult one to gauge—there may be too many variables present—it is best to eliminate the proposed activity and if it lends itself, perhaps suggest it as one of the follow-up procedures.

The demonstration type of script which follows suggests a review procedure helpful to teachers. The friendly uncle-like character featured in the series is familiar to the primary grade listeners since he also appears in their basic readers. The pauses noted in the script are for classroom activity which takes place during the broadcast. Only an experienced, skillful classroom teacher can plan for such responses. The use of two child characters, Michael and Judy, helps the youthful listeners to identify themselves with the story.

Station WBOE

NOW WE KNOW

Division of Health Education

GOOD HEALTH TO YOU

Program 8 . . . January 17, 1950

Script: Helen Margolis

CAST	MUSIC	SOUND
Narrator	Theme: I'm Healthy 'Cause	Footsteps
Mr. Carl	I'm Happy	

NARR: Good health to you and you and you!

MUSIC: *Theme*

NARR: Hello boys and girls. This is your health story teller, Charles Gilbert. The name of our program today is, *Now We Know.* It's true, isn't it, boys and girls, that *now we know?* We know we should keep our bodies clean, and eat the proper foods. We know that long hours of sleep help us to grow and that exercise makes us strong.

(*Slow*) Before we begin our program, I'd like to know if you have a letter on your desk. (*3 seconds*) Do you know who wrote that letter to you? (*5 seconds*) Yes, our good friend, Mr. Carl. Mr. Carl went away on a trip last week, and while he was gone he wrote you each a letter. But Mr. Carl didn't have the time to write your names. That's something you can do yourself. While we're waiting for Mr. Carl to get here, I think it would be a good idea if you'd write your first name on the line next to the word "dear." Your teacher will help you find the right place. (*10 seconds*) Just write your name and then put your pencil down. (*25 seconds*)

SOUND: *Fast footsteps off at first then bring in heavier behind*

NARR: I hear someone coming now. That sounds just like Mr. Carl.

SOUND: *Footsteps out*

NARR: It is Mr. Carl! Hello there, Mr. Carl! How did you enjoy your trip?

MR. CARL: Oh, fine and dandy. But my train was late coming in. That's why I couldn't get here sooner.

NARR: Well, you're just on time. The boys and girls are waiting for you.

MR. CARL: Hello boys and girls. (*3 seconds*) I've just returned from a wonderful trip down south. Would you believe it? I saw green grass, and green leaves on the trees, and I saw flowers too. Early every morning I could hear the birds singing in the trees outside my window. One sunny afternoon I even went fishing and was I ever lucky? Guess how many fish I caught? (*10 seconds*) I caught twelve fish! Yessir! I really did. And all the while I was enjoying myself, I thought of you. I wrote each of you a letter. I believe you have my letter on your desk right now. (*Pause*) I hope you have a pencil too, because this letter is not quite finished and you are all going to help me finish it. (*Pause*) Look at the first paragraph at the top of the page. (*5 seconds*) It says, (*Slow*) "I am just writing to tell you that I think about you every day, and hope you will grow to be strong and healthy. I want to wish you a happy year, and to remind you once more about all your good health rules. Eat all the good health foods that your mother gives you. Begin the day with a good breakfast." What do you think would be a good breakfast? Name some different kinds of breakfast foods? (*25 seconds*) It's always good to begin your breakfast with fruit juice, or a piece of fruit. (*Slow*) Here in the picture you see a half orange. Here, also in the same row, are pictures of two other kinds of food that are good for breakfast. These pictures are just made of dots, but you can take your pencil and draw a line from one dot to the next. Do that now. Draw a circle line all the way around right through the dots. (*45 seconds*) All right. Put your pencil down. (*10 seconds*) Who can tell what these two breakfast foods are? (*25 seconds*) One is a bowl of cereal, and the other is an egg! I hope you'll try to have these foods for breakfast every day.

(*Slow*) Now look at the next sentence. It says, "Drink about. . . ." What does that sentence tell you to drink? (*10 seconds*) Yes of course, it tells you to drink milk. In the blank space you are to write the number of glasses of milk that you think you should drink. Think first! Then put the number of glasses of milk you drink *right on the line*. All right. Do that now. (*10 seconds*) Who would like to read the sentence from your paper? (*15 seconds*) Very well, boys and girls. You may put your pencils down. (*10 seconds*) You will *not* need your pencils again until after the broadcast. As we read the letter together you can *think* about all the parts that are missing and when the program is over, you will have plenty of time to fill in the missing numbers. Ready! (*5 seconds*)

In the next picture, you see a brush. What kind of a brush is that? (*5 seconds*) Yes, it is a tooth brush and on the blank line you are to write the number of times you think you should brush your teeth each day. Don't do it now. You'll have a chance to do it later. Let's go on. What is the girl doing in the next picture? (*10 seconds*) The girl is taking a bath, isn't she? (*Pause*) The sentence reads, "Keep neat and clean. Take a bath about. . . ." And then you are to fill in the number of times a week, you think you should take a bath. In the next part of our letter, we see two children playing a game. Look at the verse next to the picture. There are four sentences. Point to each sentence. (*10 seconds*) Notice one word is missing in the second sentence, and one word is missing in the last sentence. The verse goes like this, "You'll grow stronger, every _____ (the missing word begins with *d*). If you go outdoors to _____" (the missing word begins with *p*). Does anyone know what the missing words are? (*25 seconds*) I hope you can write in the missing words so that your verse reads like this. "You'll grow stronger, every *day*. If you go outdoors to *play*."

Now let's look at the last part of our letter. If you will read that sentence to yourself, you will see that this sentence is about sleep. On the blank line you are to write the number of hours of sleep you need each night. Now look at the picture of the clock. (*5 seconds*) What's missing from the clock? (*5 seconds*) This clock has no hands. After the broadcast, you are to put hands on the clock to show what time you go to bed. Think carefully first, before you put anything down on the paper. Your teacher will help you with the words. When your letter is all finished, read it over to yourself. Ask your teacher if you can read your letter to the class. Perhaps the other boys and girls will tell you if your answers are just right. Then I'm sure you will want to take your letter home. You will want to read it to your brothers and sisters. You will want to teach them all about good health. And I'm sure you'll be anxious to read this letter to your mother. She will be happy to know that you are learning good health rules. I'm sure she will tell you that you are doing a fine job of taking care of yourself.

Well, I know you're anxious to get busy and finish the letter so I'll say, goodbye, and good health to you.

MUSIC: *Theme*

NARR: This program, GOOD HEALTH TO YOU, was the last one of the series for the current semester. This is Your School Station, WBOE in Cleveland.

The script writer, Miss Helen Margolis, points out:

Children are naturally attracted to game-like activities or exercises. The following worksheet was used with the last program of the series, *Good Health To You*, directed to pupils seven and eight years of age. These were dramatic presentations featuring Mr. Carl and the boys and girls living in his neighborhood, and also included active participation on the part of the listening audience. In his friendly way, Mr. Carl encouraged the pupils to follow the good-health practices presented in the broadcasts.

The worksheet served to give added emphasis to these ideas, and to sharpen up the basic concepts developed in the series. It also provided an important link between the radio teaching of health and home training, since with primary children it is more than likely that these worksheets were taken home and shown to members of the family.

In the last program Mr. Carl had just returned from a vacation during which he had written each child a letter. Following Mr. Carl's instructions the children helped Mr. Carl to finish the letter. The worksheet was clear-cut and simple enough so that it could have been used as an after-broadcast activity under the guidance of the classroom teacher.

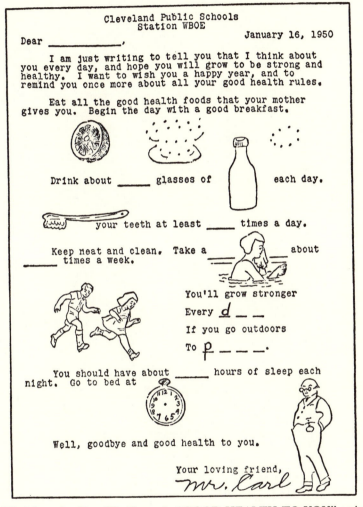

Worksheet for *Now We Know*, in "GOOD HEALTH TO YOU" series

4

Preparing the Educational Television Program

◇◇

How can schools secure the cooperation of a commercial television station?

What are some of the television formats which have proved acceptable?

What are the merits and limitations of each procedure?

What are useful suggestions for preparing educational scripts for televizing into homes or classrooms or both?

◇◇

◆◆◆◆◆◆◆◆AS NOTED IN THE previous chapter, one of the schools' worst mistakes would be to put classroom procedures on the air without adaptation. This would be true in radio, but television offers a double pitfall. The well-meaning teacher would be wrong to assume that he has only to create a classroom in the studio and plant cameras behind the last row of seats, to have a good program. The possible exception might be a public relations series, designed to show the public what is going on in the schools. He would be equally wrong to take a good radio script and turn cameras on the participants, or to show a series of still pictures as "illustrations" of the images called to the mind by a sound broadcast. It is once more necessary that the educator take advantage of the possibilities of the new medium, that he become acquainted with the various program forms already developed in the few years of the new industry's existence, that he know the merits and limitations of each form, and that he then proceed to build on this sound foundation new educational forms or variations thereof.

If that seems like a tall order, let it be noted that the challenge of television is a tall challenge, and cannot be met in short order. Teachers in a dozen cities have already met the challenge and, with each additional broadcast they prepare, they are learning new ways in which to use video for educational purposes.

The purpose comes first in educational broadcasting, both in television and in radio. If certain types of "lessons" or programs can be done better by sound alone, it would be a great waste to spend valuable time and money in doing the job less effectively in sight-and-sound. Already many broadcasters have begun to feel that news, for example, can be presented more immediately and possibly more satisfactorily by sound alone. Just hearing music (except for opera) is fully satisfactory to most people. Those with special interests, for example, in orchestration, conducting, or antique instruments, may get more value from seeing as well as hearing the performers. (One discounts for the moment the novelty value of the new medium or the impact of the sheer personality of favorite artists.)

When the purpose may best be achieved by sound and sight, however, no amount of effort is too great to achieve that purpose more

122

fully, granted that the necessary staff and the cooperation of the TV station can be secured.

Securing the Cooperation of the Local Station

According to Franklin Dunham, Chief of Radio, United States Office of Education, "Classroom lessons by television to help the teachers teach and the pupils to learn were being televised in New York, Chicago, Detroit, Buffalo, Philadelphia, Baltimore and Washington. . . ." This statement was made in 1950, when such activities were going on more or less regularly in the various cities mentioned. In most cases, local educators had gone to the managers or program directors of the station, or stations, in the city involved. In a few instances the station approached the schools first. That the programs reached the air, at considerable expense to the already strained resources of most stations, is an indication of the sincerity and willingness of the commercial broadcasters. But it is also a tribute to the resourcefulness and skill of the educators who had to persuade the broadcasters to use their precious time and facilities for educational purposes.

First the Written Presentation. Obviously, it is not very effective for an educator simply to say, "Let's do an educational series." The school man should have an outline of the proposed series in mind and *on paper!* In fact, if his city has had no previous school programs, he will do well to have several different formats and groups of potential programs outlined, neatly typed, and available in his briefcase before he writes or telephones for that first appointment. If possible, one typical broadcast in each series should be outlined in some detail.

Where is the teacher to get the know-how to prepare such a folder? True, there are few available courses in TV script writing and almost no books on script writing *per se,* although several books on production include program preparation and writing.[1] But the United States

---

[1] Max Wylie, *Radio and Television Writing* (rev. ed.), Rinehart & Company, 1950; Edward Stasheff and Rudy Bretz, *The Television Program: Its Writing, Direction and Production,* A. A. Wyn, 1951; Hoyland Bettinger, *Television Techniques;* Richard Hubbel, *Television Programming and Production* (2d ed.); others listed in the bibliography.

Office of Education reported, in 1950, that fifty-six great universities and city school systems were "interested in getting into television." Moreover, the AER Television Script Exchange has been distributing sample scripts since 1947. Perhaps the best way to begin is to study a series or two successfully presented by school systems active in video.

For example, the annual report of *Television Activities*, October, 1949–June, 1950, of the Philadelphia Public Schools listed the following:

Try It Yourself over WCAU-TV, 28 weeks
Science Is Fun over WFIL-TV, 32 weeks
Billy Penn, MC over WFIL-TV, 32 weeks
Career Forum over WCAU-TV, 28 weeks
The World at Your Door over WPTZ, 27 weeks
How's Your Social I.Q.? over WPTZ, 27 weeks
Formula for Champions over WCAU-TV, 12 weeks
Young Philadelphia Presents over WPTZ, 34 weeks

In addition, individual special broadcasts were listed and described. For each of the eight series, a descriptive paragraph gave the reader a quick summary of the content of the series. Since in education we are prone to share generously, and imitation is still considered sincere flattery, similarities in program ideas need cause no embarrassment.

A typical presentation of a series which the educator is trying to "sell" the station manager might look something like the following one, which was prepared by the Television Unit of the City of New York for submission to Station WPIX.

Presenting a Public Service Series

THIS IS YOUR CITY

To be produced jointly by
Station WPIX
and the
Television Unit of the City of New York

It is suggested that this series originate as a remote whenever possible and from the studios of WPIX when remote pickup is not feasible. Scripts, contact work, municipal personnel and props will be provided by the City; Director, Studio Personnel, Narrator and Studio Facilities will be provided by the station.

PROPOSED PROGRAMS

1   *New York City Housing Authority*—Mayor to open series; models and architect's drawings of new housing units; film showing demolition of old housing and construction work on new. Dramatization featuring young veteran couple to show need and solution. To originate from WPIX studios.

2   *Department of Hospitals*—to originate from Queens General Hospital. Work of doctors and nurses in City Hospitals; film sequences of ambulance calls, emergency room, wards. Live demonstrations of blood-typing in relation to RH factor; electro-cardiogram; portable X-ray; polio treatment.

3   *Police Department*—to originate from Police Headquarters. Film sequences of field activities—police planes and boats; training of mounted police and mounts. Live demonstration of captured weapons; ballistics bureau; physical training of rookies, including policewomen; Police Laboratory; Fingerprint Bureau.

4   *Department of Health*—to originate from Health Center near studios. Work of Baby Clinics; immunization; inspection of food-handlers and food implements; training in public health; disease prevention.

5   *Armistice Day Program*—to originate from Television Unit's Studio, using remote pickup crew from station. How the City received the news of the ending of two wars. Police executives on duty in Times Square on Armistice Day and V-J Day; military heroes from various municipal departments; chaplain who was overseas when the news came.

6   *Fire Department*—to originate from Television Unit as above. Live demonstration of historic equipment from 1857 to the present; uniforms and badges of the past century. Causes of fires in homes (live); film sequence, "Crimes of Carelessness." Fire Boxes (live) and the Fire Alarm Telegraph Bureau; danger of false alarms. Film sequence, "Smoke-Eaters." Demonstration of first aid by Rescue Company No. 1 (live) including inhalator. Work of the Uniformed Firemen's Association. Interview with outstanding and often-decorated hero.

7   *Department of Welfare*—to originate from WPIX studios. Purpose of department. Home visit to indigent family, aid and placement. Job placement service—work in office with worker and in field with prospective employers. Aptitude test. Work with the aged.

8   *Board of Education*—to originate from WPIX studios. To cover all levels of school system. Elementary: song-play as part of health education. Older Elementary: costumed dramatization of Henry Hudson and the Indians. Junior High School: Puppet play, "United We Stand," featuring brotherhood and interracial relations. Senior Academic High School: Round table discussion on atomic energy, using student-made models and equipment, including Geiger counter and

Wilson cloud chamber. Vocational High School: dress design and dressmaking. Adult Education; work among the foreign-born.

9   *Department of Public Works*—to originate from WPIX studios and film studio. Most of program to be on film owned by the Department of Public Works. Bridges: design, construction and maintenance. Sewage disposal plant. Building management and maintenance of all public buildings. Design and construction of new buildings: hospitals, health centers, courts, etc.

10   *The Arts in the Board of Education*—to originate from WPIX studios. Ballet Group from High School of Performing Arts. Modern dance choreographed by student. Orchestra from Midwood High School. Radio Drama by All-City Radio Workshop from WNYE. Choral numbers by Special Chorus of Fort Hamilton High School.

11   *Department of Parks*—to originate from WPIX studios. Film sequence showing over-all recreational facilities. Marionette Show from Park Department Touring Company. Square Dance and Minstrel Show. Physical Education: Boxing instruction for sub-teen-agers. Film sequence of beaches and special care given them to avoid contamination, and demonstration of life-saving. Barbershop Quartet—winners of Park Department Contest.

12   *Special Board of Health Program for Social Hygiene Month*—"VD"! Live posters and strip-film history of VD. Work of the Social Hygiene Centers shown in silhouetted dramatizations. Seriousness of VD as compared to polio, pneumonia, scarlet fever and TB. Demonstration of new use of penicillin. Results of untreated VD: accidents, paralysis, blindness. Blood test in connection with marriage license. Danger of quack treatments. (All dramatic vignettes to be shown in silhouette.) Procedure of treatment at Social Hygiene Centers. End on montage of posters, appeal to public to eradicate VD.

Beyond the Presentation. There are a few questions which the station manager or program director is likely to ask the educator, and the school man will be wise to have the answers ready. The broadcaster may ask whether the school can present a "dry run," a rough production of the program without technical facilities but with school-made "props," slides, film, or other visualizations. This may take place in a school auditorium, in the empty studio of the local station, or in the radio studio of the local school-owned station, if there is one. In any case, it will demonstrate to the TV station representative the potentialities of the program which is being offered to him. The educator will keep in mind, of course, the need for the program to be attractive and entertaining as well as informative; no station willingly airs a guaranteed "audience chaser." And if the program is to be scheduled for late afternoon or early evening, the station manager may suggest that it be made palatable to the general audience, as well as to the school population.

The matter of school personnel to be involved in the series or in the various programs may arise. The broadcaster will grant, sight unseen, the fact that teachers who are chosen to participate are good instructors and experts in their various fields and subject matters. He may wonder, however, about their appearance and personality. He will be delighted to hear of some with experience in radio, in amateur theatricals, or in lecture-platform demonstrations. He will probably ask that pupil participants be chosen not solely on the basis of IQ or high grades in the subjects being presented, but also with an eye to attractive appearance (not necessarily *beauty*), ability to express themselves readily, poise and presence.

There may arise the problem of remote pickups as against studio presentation. A "remote" involves sending several engineers and a large truck of equipment (the "mobile unit," which is a control room on wheels) to a given school. While this is an expensive operation, several smaller stations have very limited studio facilities and, if the remote crew is available on a given day, they may prefer to pick up the program from a centrally located school. For example, Station WOI-TV, owned and operated by Iowa State College and the first educational television station in the nation, if not in the world, planned a unique policy of development. In its first phase, WOI-TV will transmit all its programs from film and slide projectors, producing its own 16-mm. film as well as available materials. In the second phase, a mobile unit and field cameras will be used for remote sports broadcasts, meetings, laboratory activities, and classroom demonstrations. The third and last phase, scheduled for some time in the future, will be the construction of television studios. Many small commercial stations are following a similar pattern, sometimes compromising on one studio camera for "live" programming.

In the case of a remote pickup, the station manager will want one of his engineers to survey the proposed point of origin. Is there ample power for the strong portable lights which will be needed? Can cables be run through a window to the mobile truck parked outdoors? Is there height enough for the antenna of the microwave relay transmitter, which will send the program back to the station for amplification and rebroadcast?

And whether it be a remote or a studio program, what can the schools provide besides an idea and people? Are suitable visual materials available—slides, maps, charts, slide film, motion-picture film? Will students and teachers work on title cards, scenery, and props? If the program is to originate at the station, can the schools provide for the transportation of all materials?

As an example of the splendid lengths to which such cooperation may extend (not as an awesome example which may deter the prospective school producer), there follows one of the most elaborate lists of personnel and prop requirements the writers could find. It was prepared for a special program on VD, presented during Social Hygiene Month, 1950, by the Department of Health of New York City in cooperation with Station WPIX. The station provided studio facilities, director, announcer and studio personnel. The Department of Health and the city's Television Unit provided the following:

THIS IS YOUR CITY

(V.D.—Social Hygiene Month)

February 27—8:15 P.M.

CAST

Announcer (From Station Staff)
Commissioner Mahoney   Speaking parts
Health Dept. Doctor (Speaker)

AND

1. Physician who gives blood pressure test
2. His patient (a man)
3. Blackboard lecturer (a man)
4. Man for silhouette of cripple
5. Man for silhouette of blind man
6. Woman for silhouette of paralysis victim
7. Jack (a young man)
8. Mary (a young woman)
9. Marriage license clerk (a man)
10. Lucy
11. Frank (Lucy's husband)
12. Lucy and Frank's doctor
13. Quack doctor (shady-looking character)
14. Quack's patient (a man)
15. A nurse
16. A male patient (to get tests, etc.)
17. Examining physician
18. Doctor to give blood test
19. Laboratory technician
20. Another male patient

PROPS

Props requiring art work and lettering:

1. Letters "VD" painted large on a card.
2. Poster: "Gonorrhea can be cured—quickly, cheaply, painlessly, with new drugs"; this poster is *changed* in this way: The word "gonorrhea" is replaced by a strip of white with the words "Venereal Disease" lettered on it. Poster will then read "Venereal Disease can be cured . . . etc."
3. Large bar graph. This indicates the prevalence of different diseases. The graph should be wide enough so that the camera can pan the graph and only show one bar at a time. Each bar is labeled with the name of the disease and the number of cases.
4. Smaller bar graph. This graph is a smaller copy of the above graph made so that the camera can show all diseases at once.
5. Drawing: An outline drawing of an arm with an arrow labeled "Germ" bouncing off it.
6. Card with following lettering:

$$\text{Stages—1. Primary}$$
$$\text{2. Secondary}$$
$$\text{3. Tertiary}$$

7. Drawing of the microscopic spiral-shaped germ that causes VD.
8. Label for bottle. Label should be lettered "606."
9. Professional-looking label for bottle. Label should be lettered "Penicillin." (If have actual penicillin label with large lettering, this would be satisfactory.)
10. Anatomy chart (cutaway).
11. Anatomy outline chart. This shows the same outline as No. 10, but is covered with spots to symbolize the rash.
12. Poster: "VD saps human energy and reduces payroll." This poster is *changed* in this way: Eliminate the words "and reduces payroll," and paint in a white background around the man shown on the poster. This white background will make the man stand out more.
13. Sign "Marriage License Bureau."
14. Sign "Men's Special Doctor."
15. Label for bottle of phoney medicine. Label should read "Dr. X's Cure-All."
16. Poster "A Blood Test For All—Protects You—Against Syphilis." *Change* this poster by cutting off the words "Against Syphilis."
17. Circle graph labeled "97%."
18. Closing Credit Cards.

Props (pictures) that require photostatic enlargement:

19. Picture from Bartholomew Steber's book (from article reprint).
20. Picture of Jean Fernel (from article reprint).

21. Picture of Phillipe Ricord (from article reprint).
22. Picture of Fritz Schaudinn (from article reprint).
23. Picture of August von Wassermann (from article).
24. Picture of Paul Ehrlich.
25. Picture of Sir Alexander Fleming (Station converted these into 35-mm. strip film for convenience in handling on the air).

Other props:

26. Poster: "Risking VD is bad, neglecting it is worse" (large size).
27. Poster "Stamp out VD."
28. Film shots: Exteriors of hospitals.
29. Still photograph: A Hospital Ward.
30. Photograph of Alexander Fleming.
31. Photograph of Dr. John Mahoney.
32. Still or film of factory buildings.
33. Film of car riding along the road.
34. Photographic still of a car wreck.
35. Blood Pressure testing apparatus.
36. Two stethoscopes.
37. Notebooks, papers, pencils, cards, application forms, record sheets, etc.
38. Blackboard and chalk.
39. VD literature.
40. Bottle with liquid in it for penicillin label.
41. Hypodermic syringe to take penicillin from bottle.
42. Pointer.
43. Crutches.
44. Cane for blind man.
45. Dark glasses.
46. Wheel chair for paralysis victim.
47. Tables, chairs, desks.
48. Labeled bottles of quack medicine.
49. Spoon.
50. Wallet and money.
51. Sterilizer.
52. All equipment for taking blood sample.
53. Test tubes and bottles of chemicals.
54. Microscope.
55. Microscope slides.
56. Calendar.
57. Paint brush and black paint.

Television Educational Script Forms

In general, the formats that have proved successful in educational television's short life follow rather closely the forms of radio. There have been, however, a few variations which justify separate classification. Despite some slight overlapping, the following list gives a good working division for practical purposes: (a) talk, (b) interview, (c) panel, round table or forum, (d) actuality, (e) quiz, (f) dramatization and musical drama, (g) demonstration, particularly effective in art, science and music, (h) the demonstration lesson, (i) the simulated classroom, (j) the public relations program (to which an entire chapter is devoted later), (k) the musical program. As in the case of radio formats, there are variations of each and combinations. Music, for example, appears in three different categories above. But as a working basis, these divisions are in widespread use today. New forms will undoubtedly develop as television matures.

Script Preparation: General Observations. The wisest investment that can be made by the school broadcaster who is ready to "get his feet wet in television" is the spending of many afternoons and evenings at the studios of his local station, observing rehearsals and broadcasts. He should then familiarize himself with the equipment used at the station in which he hopes to present his programs. What are the limitations of space? How many cameras are in use? What film facilities are available? (All stations have 16-mm. projectors, some have 35-mm. as well.) How are slides handled? On 3- by 4-inch glass slides? On an opaque projector? On 2- by 2-inch glass slides? What size is preferred for "live" cards, which are shown on an easel and "shot" by a studio camera?

Armed with this information, the educator can then go back to his own armory—the storehouse of visual aids which most school systems have been collecting for years. He can take stock of the films, slides, slide films, charts, dioramas, models and demonstration apparatus which can be used to "visualize" the lessons he wishes to present on television.

Of course, not all this material is suitable for television. Slides in color, for example, are always suspect and must be tried on "system," that is, actually televised on a master control or film-studio monitor, before a staff director will consent to use them. Films, especially those with musical backgrounds and dramatic incidents, must be "cleared," since they were originally produced for classroom use and the television rights may not be held by the producer. While this means much correspondence with the company that made the film, it is the only way to avoid unpleasant complications.

Then the educator must be sure that he is planning his program around the needs of the viewers, not around the available material.

The temptation to do a program on whatever is best represented in
the Audio-Visual Aids Library is a strong one and must be vigorously
resisted, unless one is quite sure that the easiest program to produce
is also the best one for the students.

Now the teacher is ready to build a program—not so much to write
a completed script as to outline a series and perhaps the opening program of that series. Having secured the cooperation of the local station, he will probably have a director assigned to his project, and with
that director he will be working closely. In outlining the program for
the staff director, all available visual materials should be indicated, as
well as those additional props, easel cards and models which the schoolman feels confident that he, his colleagues, and his pupils can provide.

A word or two about the typographical format of the television
script will not be amiss here, since most published television scripts
have already been produced and show the work of the director as well
as the writer.

Basically, most stations prefer the two-column script, as will be seen
in the samples from various sources provided later in this chapter.
Again, in most stations, the left-hand column is devoted to "video—"
to that which is seen. Here the novice is tempted to put down every
wink of an eyelash, every movement of an actor's body. Since that
column on the left is also used by the director for marking his camera
shots, his cues, his warnings to his engineers, it is wise to indicate only
major changes of visual subject, and to list those as briefly as possible.

The professional writer sometimes makes so bold as to indicate
camera work, at least to suggest key shots, close-ups and the termina-
tions of scenes in "fade to black" or in "dissolve." The inexperienced
writer will be wise to leave all camera directions to the director and
to content himself with providing in his script, only essential information as to *what* is being shown. *How* to show it is the director's
job.

The right-hand column, which usually takes from half to two-thirds
of the page, is reserved for "audio"—the elements of the program
which are heard. This includes all dialogue, music and sound effects,
and, in many scripts, even includes the "stage business" of the actors.
"Business," of course, is visual, but its inclusion in the audio column
makes it easier for the performers to see their work as a whole, and

leaves that much more space in the video column for the director. Typographically speaking, the format is similar to that in radio scripts: characters' names, music and sound cues are all in capitals. In short, anything in the audio column which is not actually spoken should be in capitals.

Many programs, as may be noted on the following pages, are not completely scripted. Opening and closing material is provided in full, but the body of the broadcast is in outline form, with the actual words "ad libbed" by the teachers or other performers.

Visual appeal is important, and should always be kept in mind. Some beginners, however, may go to unusual lengths and drag extraneous illustration into what is best expressed by keeping the camera on the person who is speaking. The basic problem is to find visual material which enhances and reinforces what the program is designed to convey. For example, if still pictures and charts distract the viewer's attention and add nothing to clarity of understanding, they are not "good television."

Action and movement, again, are desirable. Static pictures of immobile participants are dull, as a rule, but a vigorous controversy from opponents at a table or in facing chairs is better than a weak discussion contributed by people who are moved artificially from chair to fireplace to sofa, just for the sake of movement. Again, there can be no set rule. When in doubt, consult the station director—he will have learned the hard way!

The Straight Talk. Strictly speaking, perhaps, there should be no such thing as a "straight talk" on television. If the speaker's voice conveys the entire message why use television when radio will serve? Good speakers do not need the added effectiveness of gesture and facial expression, while poor speakers seldom command them. Straight talks are effective on television only if the speaker has a tremendously vivid personality, if there is something to be gained by seeing as well as hearing a noted world figure, or if the talk is to be illustrated. In the latter case, we then wonder why it is called a *talk* and not a *demonstration*. It is indeed difficult to distinguish between Roy K. Marshall (who draws diagrams and displays models incidentally while he speaks of *The Nature of Things*) or Alexander Efron (who talks about his working models as his hands move quickly from one demonstration to another in *Science Today*), and the semi-interview, semidramatization used by "Mr. Science" in *Science Is Fun*, on WFIL-TV. It is, perhaps, a matter of degree, and once again the important thing is not whether we call it a talk accompanied by demonstration or a demonstration accompanied by necessary talk. What matters is whether students profit by exposure to the television screen.

Let it be noted also that the limitations and problems of the straight talk on radio also apply to television, with the additional problem of the speaker's appearance, which can be either an asset or a liability.

As we have just remarked, the talk, as such, has little place in television since it can be given equally effectively in radio. However, when the talk is illustrated at a blackboard or with models (preferably working models) and the speaker is an interesting person to watch, the talk becomes telegenic. One of the most successful practitioners of this form is Dr. Roy K. Marshall, whose science series, *The Nature of Things*, over the NBC television network, was one of the earliest "talk" programs to capture public interest.

The Interview. The television interview, while subject to the same pitfalls which confront the radio interview, has its particular advantage in the visual appeal of certain "interviewees"—the appeal of noted personages, or the novelty of foreign visitors who may wear native costume or who display handicrafts, games and other regalia.

SCRIPT PREPARATION. The interview format is particularly applicable to programs designed for social-studies classes. It is important to determine the age level of the anticipated audience and to keep the material and vocabulary within the range of that group. Preliminary discussion with interviewer and interviewee and a trial run-through before coming into the studio for camera rehearsal is most helpful in this regard.

As will be noted in the following excerpt from a program on Korea in the series *The World at Your Door*, the script is partly in full dialogue form, partly in outline form. The program was produced by Station WPTZ, Philadelphia, in cooperation with the Philadelphia schools.

THE WORLD AT YOUR DOOR—KOREA
November 17, 1949

VIDEO

AUDIO

ELSA: Our guest today is Mr. Han-Tardong, a native of Korea. At present he is studying in this country. Mr. Han, won't you

Students rise

come in? Mr. Han, may I present Robert Magetti, of South Philadelphia High School for Boys.

ROBERT: How do you do, Mr. Han?

MR. HAN: Hello, Robert. I'm very glad to be here. It was nice of you to invite me.

ROBERT: The pleasure is ours, Mr. Han. We should like to get some first-hand information about Korea.

MR. HAN: Well, tell me exactly what you want to know, Robert.

ROBERT: Elsa said that Korea was at the crossroads of the Orient. What is meant by that?

Mr. Han stands and points to map

MR. HAN: Perhaps I can explain that by pointing to the map. (*Explains*)

ELSA: It's easy to see why Korea has become such an important place.

ROBERT: Didn't Korea once have a different name, Mr. Han?

MR. HAN: Yes, it did. It was once called Chosen. This means "morning freshness." (*Explain further if you wish*)

ELSA: Do most of the Korean names have other meanings also?

MR. HAN: Yes, they usually do.

ROBERT: Then Korea itself probably can be translated to English.

MR. HAN: Yes, Korea means "high and beautiful." (*Explain further if you wish*)

ELSA: Well, speaking of names, Mr. Han, how about your name? Does it also have another meaning?

MR. HAN: Yes. Han means "authority" or "king." (*Explain further if you wish*)

ROBERT: That's very interesting, Mr. Han. We see a great deal about Korea in the paper today. Why has it become so important lately?

MR. HAN: That is a good question, Robert. But before answering that, you must understand more about the country itself. (*Explain Russia's dream of Korea and an ice-free port. Explain the following points in your own words—use map*)

Mr. Han points to map

1. Mountains in the north—industrial center.
2. Water power in the north, largest in the Orient. Supplies nation.
3. Country divided in two by the 38th parallel.
4. South—agriculture.
5. North and South depend upon each other

ELSA: How does the population of Korea compare with that of Pennsylvania, Mr. Han?

MR. HAN: Well, I don't know the population of Pennsylvania, but I can tell you that there are approximately 26 million people in Korea.

ROBERT: That is about 2½ times larger than the population of Pennsylvania.

MR. HAN: Thank you, Robert. Now I am learning something.

ELSA: What are your cities like, Mr. Han?

MR. HAN: (*Explain two or three cities in your own words*)

.   .   .   .   .

And so the script continues, with questions prepared, answers "ad libbed."

Panels, Round Tables, Forums. Television has tended to group all "discussion" programs in one basket, whether they be panels, forums or debates. In each case, the element of controversy, of difference of opinion, is the essential factor. Add to this the intelligence, charm and earnestness of young students and we may readily see why this type of program has been perhaps the most readily accepted by station managers and general public.

In television, such programs are rarely scripted. The moderator usually has an outline, and a preliminary rehearsal (often held in an empty room without lights or cameras) gives the participants adequate preparation. Student "discussants" should be amply provided with factual ammunition well in advance of the broadcast date, and several "dry runs" in a classroom or on the auditorium platform will accustom them to the give-and-take of the discussion.

Panels of experts pose one additional problem on television. An expert, once he warms to his subject, may embark on a lecture. Bad as this is in radio, it is worse in television where the viewer is aware that two or three other people are waiting to get a word in edgewise. The skillful moderator keeps the talk flowing and sees to it that no one person is on camera for too long a period at any one time.

SCRIPT PREPARATION. The ready success of high-school discussion programs on television (*There Ought to Be a Law* and *It's High Time* in New York; *Young Ideas* in Detroit) indicates that this format is a good one with which to begin a school system's television experimentation. Several items will contribute to the success of such a series.

Suitability of topic is the first consideration. The subject chosen must be potentially controversial, must have some immediate bearing on the lives of the young participants, and yet should have meat enough to warrant public airing. The literature of the Junior Town Meeting League is most helpful in providing a frame of reference.

Participants should be carefully chosen, not only for intelligence and academic standing, but for attractive appearance, fluency of extemporaneous speech, the ability to think on their feet. Television offers an opportunity for an automatic and subtle demonstration of good group relations, when children of various races, faiths and national origins are shown working together.

Advance preparation is perhaps the most important step. The students should, of course, have a thorough grounding in the facts about the chosen subject. They should be rehearsed in the mechanics of the opening and closing routine of the program, which frequently is standard on all broadcasts in the series. Such mechanical considerations as waiting for a microphone boom to swing over before launching into the body of one's contribution; sensitivity to the camera that is on the air; constant attention to the speaker (lack of which can be revealed in a group-reaction shot) can all be taught to a group without interfering with the spontaneity of the actual air show. If several rehearsals are possible, it is wise to use "dummy topics," (subjects used previously or not quite suitable for airing during the "dry runs") in order to avoid overdrilling. Many a team has left its fight in the locker room; many a discussion goes dry because the juice has been squeezed out of it by too many rehearsals, so that the responses become memorized and stale.

Most programs of this type use a standard opener and closer, and leave some 80 per cent of the air time to the ad libs of moderator and the students. One of the earliest samples of this type, produced by CBS and WNYE, the New York City school station, from 1945 to 1947, is given here. The "script," a few pages of mimeographed forms containing many blank spaces which were filled in for each program, is given as an example of the minimum "scripting" required for this type of broadcast.

CUE ANNCR: *There Ought to Be a Law!* And the young people of our city have plenty of new ones they'd like to introduce. WCBW [2] presents a new program comprised of outstanding students representing fifteen New York City high schools. Let them tell you why they think . . . *There Ought to Be a Law!*

CUE SPEAKER: (*Three gavel raps*) Will the members please take their places. This session will come to order. Mr. Clerk. . . .

CLERK: The _____ session of this house, Mr. Edward Stasheff presiding speaker.
(*To Stasheff*) First item on the order of business is Resolution _____ having been introduced by Representative _____ of _____ high school and favorably reported out of committee, will now be brought to this floor for final action.

SPEAKER: The chair will recognize Representative _____ of _____ high school for a period of two minutes to address the assembly and introduce the aforementioned resolution.

REPRESEN _____: (*Speaks for two minutes*)

SPEAKER: You have heard the Resolution. Is there a second? (*Biz*) The Chair will recognize Representative _____ of _____ high school for a period of one minute to second the resolution.

---

[2] WCBW is now WCBS-TV. This script is reproduced by permission of CBS TELEVISION, a division of Columbia Broadcasting System, Inc.

REPRESEN

_____: (*Seconds resolution*)

SPEAKER: The resolution has been proposed and seconded. It is now open for discussion.

(*Resolution is introduced and seconded from the floor. Floor discussion for 25 minutes*)

SPEAKER: The time remaining available for this session being limited, the chair will now entertain a motion on the question.

(*Motion is made, seconded, and voted upon from the floor*)

SPEAKER: The motion on the previous question having been carried, the clerk will please call the roll. Mr. Clerk.

CLERK: (*Reads*) Resolution No. _____ There Ought to Be a Law that

_____.

Members will vote aye or no in response to their names. (*Clerk calls roll very slowly and records votes. At conclusion of roll call, the clerk hands written tabulation to the speaker*)

SPEAKER: By a vote of _____ in favor to _____ opposed, this house votes that There Ought (Not) to Be a Law that

_____

The Clerk of the house will please read the resolution reported out of committee for action at the next session of this house. Mr. Clerk.

CLERK: Resolution No. _____, _____
introduced by Representative _____ of _____
high school having been favorably reported out of committee will be brought to this floor for action at the next session _____.

SPEAKER: This concludes all present business and the chair will entertain a motion to adjourn.

(*Motion made, seconded, and voted upon from the floor.*)

Motion carried. Mr. Clerk.

CLERK: The _____ session of this house, Mr. Edward Stasheff presiding, hereby declared adjourned until _____. (*Three gavel raps*)

CUE ANNCR: You have just heard *There Ought to Be a Law*, a spontaneous and informal program featuring outstanding students representing fifteen New York City high schools—the students are all members of the Board of Education's All-City Radio and Television Workshop. The opinions expressed by them are their own and in no way represent the official positions of their home schools or of the Board of Education. WCBW invites you to join them on _____ when once again they air their views as to whether or not—*There Ought to Be a Law!*

Another variation of the forum type, with just a dash of the interview, is the vocational series, *Career Forum*, presented by the Philadelphia Schools and Station WCAU-TV. Once again, the open and close are standard from week to week; the body of the program is extemporaneous.

Instructions to Master Control

VIDEO	AUDIO
OPENING:	*Et * Music*
Seal (*camera #1*)	ANNCR: Good afternoon . . . and welcome to
Title #1 (WCAU-TV CAREER FORUM) (*superimp. camera #2*)	the WCAU CAREER FORUM where high school students explore the highways to success in modern industries
Title #2 (*presented in cooperation* . . .)	and the professions. Today's seminar on "Hotel and Restaurant Practice" was transcribed in the studios of WCAU on Wednesday afternoon. . . . Six ambitious high school students are
Title #3 (H. & R. Practice)	seated around the guest speaker eager to ask questions about the varied (*Fade music*) Career opportunities open to young people in this field. . . .
Seal (*camera #1*)	(*Music out. Pause.*) . . . Here is Norris West, Assistant Director of Programs for WCAU and moderator of the CAREER FORUM who will introduce
(*Dis. camera #2 to West*)	our guest. . . . Mr. West.
(*West introduces Mr. Kenneth Baker, and then Mr. Baker speaks briefly . . . Question-and-answer period follows, length depending on time at this moment.*)	
CLOSING:	
Seal (*camera #1*)	ANNCR: In just a moment we'll tell you about next week's CAREER FORUM. . . .
	ET Music
Title #1 (WCAU-TV CAREER FORUM) (*superimp. camera #2*)	Today's program originated in the studios of WCAU on Wednesday afternoon at which time it was transcribed Cooperating with WCAU in presenting the CAREER FORUM are 14 presidents of universities and colleges in this area; 8 superintendents o

* Electrical transcription.

Title #3 (*produced & directed*)

Title #4 (*Military Service*)

Seal

public, parochial and private schools; The Chamber of Commerce and Board of Trade of Philadelphia (*Fade music*) and the Philadelphia Committee for Economic Development. (*Music out. Pause.*) Our guest today was Mr. Kenneth Baker, Manager of the Traymore Hotel in Atlantic City. . . . Next week the CAREER FORUM seminar will be devoted to "Military Service." Our guest speaker will be Brigadier General Hugh B. Hester, Commanding General of the Philadelphia Quartermasters Depot. So join us again next week at this same time. . . . This is _____ speaking.

The Actuality Broadcast. The impressiveness of the actuality on television is obvious; students see not "the photographed recent past," as in newsreels, but "the remote present," as one manufacturer has put it. Startling as television newsreels may be, thrown on the air within two or three hours of the actual event they picture, an "on-the-spot" broadcast has even more impact. But, as in radio, the subject is more important than the medium, for all the wonder of its immediacy. If students were given their choice, they would probably prefer the opening of the World Series to the opening of the United Nations or Congress, and some schools have been realistic enough to bring them both, using large-screen receivers in auditorium or gymnasium.

The important handicap of television actualities is their rarity; they wait upon events momentous enough to justify their expense. Similarly, the teacher must determine whether the importance of the event and the experience of seeing it as it occurs are such as to justify the disruption of the workday schedule, which must result, since great national and world events are rarely timed to coincide with the social-studies curriculum.

The tremendous expense involved in "picking up a remote event" necessarily limits its use to important occasions. The schools rarely have much to do with the preparation of such a program; their function is largely concerned with its reception. Again, it is difficult to provide a sample script, since much of the commentary must of necessity be impromptu, following events as they occur. One may assume, however, that director and commentator spent time in investigating the physical layout; that they secured an advance copy of the order of proceedings; that someone familiar with the participants was on hand to point them out and identify them; that some research went into securing background notes on the principal speakers.

Quizzes and Bees.   There is little point to repeating here the limitations of the radio quiz bee. If information is not education when heard, it is rarely more educational when seen. One point that may be made, however, is that questions which are presented visually, whether through actors, cards on easels, or objects and apparatus, are more likely to be remembered. The same is true of the answers.

Scripting the Television Quiz.   The television quiz, of course, should lean heavily upon visual questions. These may be drawings on an easel; charts or maps with blank sections to be filled in or identified, and other graphic illustrations. However, real objects are even more effective. Dioramas of historical scenes, to be identified; antique objects, hand tools, models of inventions, and the like, to be named and associated with industries or historic events; ancient costumes, to be associated with persons or periods, are all ways of "asking" a television question. In the field of science, a working model or experimental apparatus can be used to demonstrate a scientific principle, which participants must identify and explain. In short, a considerable amount of thought and effort must go into the preparation of a television quiz if the cameras are to avoid the constant repetition of shots of the MC, reading a question from a card. An example of a highly intelligent commercial quiz which uses all the elements mentioned above and a few more is the CBS program, *Winner Take All.*

Dramatizations and Musical Dramas.   The popularity of this form in educational radio has led to many efforts to use it in educational television. Yet the difference is obvious; drama of any kind is much more difficult in video, when lines must be memorized, sets built, props secured, costumes fitted, and the thousand-and-one details (given in Chapter 6) attended to. Accordingly, dramatization usually is limited to a simple introduction into the body of a program with pupils and teachers playing themselves, for the most part.

Radio workshop-ers can be quite effective when playing a wide range of ages and characters. Students on *television* are rarely convincing when playing older people. Professional actors, of course, are usually beyond the range of the school budget.

On the other hand, simple dramatizations, in which children play the parts of children and into which music is woven as an integral part, have both charm and impact. The fiesta of a foreign land, long a staple of the school assembly platform, has its place on the video screen when done with skill and taste. It should be noted, however, that both musical and dramatic material, unless composed by faculty members, must be "cleared" . . . that is, the school must get permission from the publishers or copyright owners to broadcast any material which is protected by copyright.

DRAMATIC—OR MUSICAL SCRIPTS. The attractiveness of this type of program, when it comes off successfully, tempts most educators beyond their powers of detachment. Yet it is the most difficult form to do well, since it involves so many factors, as we have shown earlier. It can be done well, however, if the writer will keep his script simple, within the range of talents of the performers and the limitations of the studio in which the program will be presented. One or two obvious bits of advice are:

1. Avoid mob scenes, except in dances, choral ensembles, etc. Keep dramatic dialogue in scenes involving two, three, or at most four characters.
2. Avoid using too many sets. Both space and setup time are limited in most studios.
3. Never end one scene with a certain character and begin the next with the same one; it takes time to get across a studio floor to the next set!

An inkling of the preparation involved in doing a thorough job may be gained from the following script on Italy produced in the *Operation Classroom* series over WCAU-TV, Philadelphia, under the supervision of Ruth Weir Miller.

OPERATION CLASSROOM
Social Studies Program
TOPIC: *ITALY*

STATION: WCAU-TV   DATE: March 30, 1949
SCHOOL: Lawton—6th Grade Class   TIME: 3:00–3:15 P.M.

TEACHER: Miss Whitaker
SOCIAL STUDIES COLLABORATOR: Mrs. Cassel
ART SUPERVISOR: Miss Roberts
MUSIC SUPERVISOR: Miss Lafferty
ACCOMPANIST: Mrs. English

SETTING

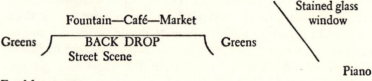

Houses

Fountain—Café—Market

Greens ⟋ BACK DROP ⟍ Greens
Street Scene

Stained glass window

Piano

Easel for narrator

SEQUENCE

Mrs. Miller's opening
1. Narrator—(Not seen) Camera on small relief map of Italy during introduction.
2. Scene I— Camera take in backdrop—rests on fountain (end of drop).
3. Scene II— Song (front at pilings—sea out front).
4. Scene III— Camera follows two children back to center back drop. Scene at table.
5. Scene IV— Camera moves to take in children at market.
6. Scene V— Camera center stage for song and dance.
7. Narrator— (a) Camera on children laughing and talking.
(b) Camera on close-ups of stained glass window, drawings on easel.
8. Music up to introduce scene.
9. Camera on large window and choir.
10. Scene VI— Children move into picture and kneel (FINALE).
Mrs. Miller's closing

PROPERTIES

From WCAU	*From School*
1. Framework for backdrop	1. School will send backdrop and window on Tuesday, March 29th.
2. Framework for stained-glass window brace to hold it erect	2. Hand properties, costumes, fruit etc.
3. Tubs (green with shrubs if possible at end of backdrop)	3. Accompanist.

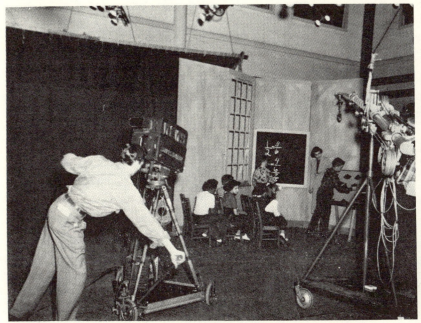

Cleveland students present their schools to the public over WEWS-TV.

Radio production as seen from inside of control room.

Above, Classroom
rehearsal.

Right, Television
rehearsal; control
room view.

Below, Student sound
effects men.

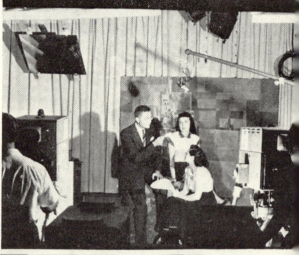

4. Wide steps—to put in front of
   window
5. Pilings and rope coils to represent street along wharf

ITALY

VIDEO	AUDIO
OPENING: *Title cards &* *music* OPENING: Mrs. Miller	
	MUSIC: *Italian music sneaks in—held under* *narration* MRS. MILLER: Hello, boys and girls. I'm Ruth Miller, here to welcome you to *Operation Classroom*. Don't you feel like going places on a lovely spring day like this? Well, *Operation Classroom* is taking you to Italy.
Dissolve to small relief *map of Italy*	NARR: (*Off camera*) This is Italy. The land of sunshine, lapped by the waters of the blue sea. This is the country we have studied. . . . Italy interested us because she has given to the world delicacies for our table; lovely ornaments for our homes; beautiful paintings and sculpture; and glorious music for the opera and church. It is of Naples we speak today, where blue and yellow houses cover the slopes of the bay, where little donkeys trudge along the streets to market. For Naples is a trading center for the fertile farms of her countryside.
Camera on fountain	And here, too, at the street fountain gather the women on bright sunny mornings.
	MARIA: Buon giorno, Nicolette, you too come for the water?
	NICOLETTE: Water and a little talk.
	MARIA: It's so sunny here, I like to watch the donkeys and oxen coming to market.
	NICOLETTE: I like better to taste the luscious fruits they bring.

Luigi and Nina come into scene from left	MARIA: Oh, here come Luigi and Nina.

Luigi and Nina come into scene from left

MARIA: Oh, here come Luigi and Nina.

NICOLETTE: Buon giorno, good friends.

LUIGI: And good morning to you this fine market day.

NINA: We've come into town to see the fish catch.

MARIA: The fishing boats are busy coming into the harbor, loaded with fish.

LUIGI: (*Walking toward camera*) Come, Nina, let's watch their sails in the sunlight.

Space does not permit our reproducing the rest of this script, but evidence of its richness and movement may be gathered from the photograph facing page 239. Song and dance were woven into the script, and the scene ended with a choir on the steps before the stained-glass window of the cathedral, as shown in the photograph.

On college level, a very unusual experimental script was prepared at the University of Nebraska by Paul L. Bogen and Gaylord Marr in 1948 and presented over the facilities of Station WOW. It was entitled *Man's Best Food . . . Milk!*

MILK!

TITLES

CAMERA 2

1. The University of Nebraska Presents—
   (*White letters on black screen*)
2. Through the facilities of Radio Station WOW—
   (*White letters on black screen*)
3. Man's Best Food—
   (*White letters on black screen—Camera zooms in to*)

CAMERA 1

4. MILK
   (*Lettered on milk can—Camera zooms in so the word "MILK" fills the screen*)
5. Cast Credits
   (*Lettered on milk can. Cans rolled by Milk Maids*)
6. Production Staff Credits:
   (*Lettered on milk can*)
7. Based on the research of Professor Arnold Barager
   (*Lettered on milk can*)
   (*Fade out . . . Fade in Scene One*)

SCENE I

| VIDEO | AUDIO |

We see the interior of a farm house bedroom. A slanted roof suggests that the interior room is on the upper floor of a story-and-a-half structure. Painted walls or wall-paper of an unobtrusive design. Old-fashioned iron bedstead with crazy quilt or patchwork quilt. Dresser against the back wall with an electric lamp. A plain shade keeps the lamplight from the eyes of the boy in bed. Medicine bottle and water tumbler with spoon are on the dresser, planted props to suggest the illness of the boy. A picture on the wall over the bed—Plockhorst's conception of "The Good Shepherd." Two straight-backed chairs.

Camera takes a doctor's old-fashioned satchel, open, on the floor. Pans up to the Doctor, his left fingertips are on the wrist of the boy in bed, taking his pulse. Doctor holds an old-fashioned watch in a pol-ished hunting case. Fa-ther's voice is heard— outside.

FATHER: He's pretty sick, isn't he, Doc?

Doctor looks up in the

*direction of the father's
voice and nods. He
closes the case on his
watch.*

DOCTOR: (*Nodding*) Yes, Jim, you've got a pretty sick boy here.

MOTHER: Can you tell us what it is, Doctor?

DOCTOR: Well—I've a pretty good idea. When is the first time he complained of not feeling well?

MOTHER: I noticed he didn't eat much for supper last night. I thought he had a fever when I put him to bed.

DOCTOR: Um-hum. I see.

*Doctor removes his
glasses, and polishes
them with his handker-
chief.*

FATHER: He ain't seemed up to snuff for the last couple days though. He's really a go-getter, that kid. Then all of a sudden, he just kinda seemed to lose interest in things. He forgot to feed his calf the night-before-last and I guess I kinda jumped on him for it. I asked him if he wasn't feelin' good, but he said he was all right.

DOCTOR: That follows the general pattern, ir-ritability . . . loss of appetite and in-terest. Tell me, Mrs. Walker, did he complain of anything . . . a stomach ache or anything like that?

MOTHER: He did say he had a headache, come to think of it.

*Doctor looks toward pa-
tient.*

DOCTOR: Headache, eh? Flushed face . . . fever . . . increased pulse rate and a rise in respiration.

FATHER: What's wrong with him, Doc?

DOCTOR: I can't say for sure, but judging by the symptoms, I'd say he has undulant fever.

MOTHER: Undulant fever?

DOCTOR: Yes, Mrs. Walker. Old-timers used

to call it "milksick" or the "trembles."

FATHER: Why, my grandmother died of the milksick. They tried everything . . . barks and jalap and boneset tea . . . but she died just the same. Doc, you don't think. . . .

DOCTOR: No, no . . . there's very little danger, Jim. Don't you go to worrying now.

MOTHER: You can't help but worry when you've got a sick boy.

. . . . .

Our interest and sympathy aroused, we are ready to learn what science has done to protect us from unwholesome milk.

Demonstration. Television's great contribution to educational broadcasting is, of course, its ability to teach skills. Commercial broadcasters were quick to see the possibility in demonstrations of cooking, sewing and interior decorating. In the more narrowly interpreted sense, educational programs in art and science have been highly successful in video because of their fundamentally visual nature. Music demonstrations, not so much in the skillful playing of individual instruments as in the visual reinforcement of the structure of a symphonic work, for example, have been popular to a lesser degree. In each case the problem is to build upon the foundation of the viewer's existing knowledge, which is often a difficult thing to determine. Most demonstration programs "begin at scratch" and review, briefly but interestingly, the basic principles involved in the body of the program.

SCRIPTING THE DEMONSTRATION PROGRAM. The values of the demonstration are self-evident. Almost anything can be shown to advantage on television if it is larger than a square inch, small enough to get into the studio, and if it does not depend for its effectiveness entirely on color. Highly polished metallic surfaces give trouble by reflecting studio lights, but even these can be toned down with a coat of clear lacquer or an application of pancake make-up.

In preparing a demonstration, one simply recalls that the camera gives every viewer a front-row seat right in the center of the demonstration table. A skillful demonstrator whose flow of talk is not too rapid and yet smoothly fluent, whose hands operate almost independently of his speech, and whose material is interesting, is the one sure-fire element. Young people, to whom he is presumably showing his wares and who may assist him in his operations, add an extra element of audience satisfaction.

Several short excerpts from scripts in various fields are provided herewith. First, a program on "Clocks," from the series *Science Is Fun!,* presented by the Philadelphia schools and Station WFIL-TV.

SCIENCE IS FUN!

TOPIC: *TELLING TIME (CLOCKS)*

STATION: WFIL-TV   DATE: January 27, 1950
TITLE: SCIENCE IS FUN!   TIME: 2:15–2:30 P.M.
SUBJECT: Telling Time (Clocks)

PARTICIPANTS

Dr. Joseph Zimmerman as Mr. Science
Dr. Armand Spitz, Scientist, of Franklin Institute
Curtis Arnold—Science Clubber, Patterson School

SEQUENCE

1. Title Cards.
2. Mr. Science greets audience.
3. Mr. Science and Curtis Arnold meet.
4. Mr. Science introduces Curtis to Mr. Spitz.
5. Mr. Spitz demonstrates the telling of time by the sun with upright stick and candle.
6. Mr. Spitz shows how time was noted with knotted rope and piece of punk.
7. A candle clock is shown by showing big buntz candle painted in alternate black and white bands.
8. Water clock is reconstructed with large washtub of water and various-sized cans that have been punctured.
9. Another type of water clock is made with a small, deep pie plate and a brace and bit.
10. Hourglass clock is demonstrated.
11. Pendulum clock demonstrated with aid of long piece of string and a small weight.
12. Wire-spring principle is shown by demonstrating with a thin piece of spring steel imbedded in a piece of wood.
13. Mr. Spitz shows picture of pig and clock.
14. Mr. Spitz shows piece of coiled wire (oscillating principle).
15. Mr. Spitz shows several clock models from Franklin Institute.

16. Curtis thanks Mr. Spitz and makes him an honorary member of club.
17. Mr. Science thanks Mr. Spitz and Curtis and signs off the show.
18. Title cards

VIDEO	AUDIO
1. *Camera on title cards —WFIL-TV*	MUSIC: *Theme (recorded)*
2. *Camera on—In co-operation with Phila-delphia Public Schools and Franklin Institute card*	
3. *Camera on "SCI-ENCE IS FUN!"*	MUSIC: *Theme out to*
4. *Dissolve to Mr. Sci-ence*	MR. SCIENCE: Welcome to the SCIENCE IS FUN CLUB of the air. . . . Today, January 27th, is our last Friday session for this term. It doesn't seem possible that four months have flown by since SCIENCE IS FUN called its first session together on October 14th. Yes, time certainly does fly, and speaking of time reminds me of today's topic— which is Telling Time . . .
Enter Curtis Arnold	CURTIS: That's why I'm here, Mr. Science, to find out about telling time.
	MR. SCIENCE: You must be our Science Clubber for today.
	CURTIS: Yes, Mr. Science, I'm Curtis Arnold from the Patterson School and I represent a group of boys and girls who are interested in finding out about the different clocks men have used to tell time.
	MR. SCIENCE: Well . . . you've come to the right place, Curtis . . . because over in Laboratory "B" you'll find Mr. Armand Spitz, from the Franklin Institute, and some interesting clock models.
	CURTIS: Are we going over there to experiment?
Curtis and Mr. Science step over to Mr. Spitz	MR. SCIENCE: We certainly are, Curtis . . . right this minute. . . . Mr. Spitz, meet

today's Science Clubber from the Patterson School—Curtis Arnold. . . .

Curtis and Mr. Spitz MR. SPITZ: Hello, Curtis . . . I'm glad to
shake hands meet a fellow scientist. . . .

CURTIS: And I'm especially glad to meet you,
Mr. Spitz, so I can find out about the
different kinds of clocks that men have
used for telling time . . .

*Mr. Spitz and Curtis go into body of show as listed in Sequence at be-
ginning of script.*

5. Mr. Spitz demonstrates the telling of time by the sun with upright stick
and candle.
6. Mr. Spitz shows how time was noted with knotted rope and piece of
punk. And so on.

Here is the *program outline,* since no *script* was used, of a demonstration of decorative flower painting, part of the *Try It Yourself*
series, again from the Philadelphia Schools and Station WCAU-TV.

DECORATIVE FLOWER PAINTING

OPENING:

INTRODUCTION TO PROGRAM: Teacher standing at easel; children painting
at table.
Show Matisse reproductions on easel. (Aim: to develop appreciation;
to show we all interpret differently; we too can paint.)

IDENTIFY CHILDREN

TEACHER AND CHILDREN SHOW MATERIALS NEEDED

TEACHER AND CHILDREN SIT AT TABLE TO TALK OVER WORK
Discuss nature of flowers.
Bowl of flowers on table prominent.

TEACHER AND CHILDREN GO TO EASEL
Discuss chart showing arrangements.
Plan arrangements on paper.

TEACHER AND CHILDREN RETURN TO TABLE TO PAINT FOR AS LONG AS TIME
ALLOWS

TEACHER AND CHILDREN GO TO EASEL TO DISCUSS FINE POINTS IN FINISHED
PAINTINGS

ENCOURAGE LISTENERS TO SEND IN COMMENTS, QUESTIONS, THEIR EFFORTS
ALONG THESE LINES

ANNOUNCE NEXT WEEK'S SUBJECT, AND TELL WHAT MATERIALS WILL BE
NEEDED

CLOSE

NEED

1 easel to hold Matisse reproductions, chart, and children's finished work.

1 easel to hold large paper on which flowers are pinned. (An identical arrangement of flowers on paper will be on table for children to study.

So many home economics programs are presented, particularly in the afternoon hours, that we should definitely expect a raising of the standard of the American-home cuisine. An interesting combination of interests brought to Chicago's Station WGN-TV and its *Women's Magazine of the Air*, a program segment, which had the support of the Radio Council of the Chicago Public Schools and National Fisheries. The subject, of course, was an unusual recipe for preparing fish, and the demonstrator was Esther Riff, a home economics student from Flower Technical High School. A portion of the script follows.

DEMONSTRATION PROCEDURE
FOR MAKING FISH TURBANS

INTRODUCTION: Fish turbans get their names from the way they look. They're fish fillets, each coiled around the inside of a well in a muffin pan, with the center of each turban filled with a sauce. The word "fillet" refers to the cut of fish. It is the sides of the fish which have been cut away from the backbone. You can broil, bake, sauté, or poach fish fillets. You don't have to fry them. But now to the turbans. Here's how to make them.

VIDEO	AUDIO
1. WORKING WITH TRAY NO. 1	
Sprinkle juice of 1 lemon over 6 fish fillets	I sprinkle the juice of 1 lemon over six fish fillets. Lemon juice adds to the flavor of fish, keeps it a good color and helps keep it from falling apart.
Coil each fillet around inside of a greased muffin well	Now I coil each fillet around the inside of a greased muffin well. You can use any kind of firm fish fillets such as sole, haddock, or ocean perch. They can be fresh or frozen. If they're frozen, you first have to let them thaw.

2. WORKING WITH TRAY
   NO. 2 AT RANGE

Melt 2 tablespoons butter or margarine in sauce pan

Now for the sauce that goes in the center of each fish turban. First I melt 2 tablespoons of butter in a saucepan over low heat. You can use margarine just as well, of course.

Add ½ cup soft bread crumbs. Stir until blended

When the butter or margarine is melted, I add ½ cup soft bread crumbs, and stir until the butter and crumbs are well blended. Takes but a minute.

Add ¾ cup milk, stirring constantly. Cook until thickened

Now I add ¾ cup milk, stirring all the time until the sauce is thickened.

Add a little of the thickened sauce to 1 beaten egg yolk

Now that the sauce is thickened, I take a little of it in a spoon and add it to one egg yolk which I have already beaten.

Add yolk mixture to cream sauce. Cook a minute longer

Then I add the yolk mixture to the cream sauce and cook a minute longer. The reason I added a little of the hot sauce to the egg yolk first was to keep the yolk from cooking into lumps when added to the hot sauce.

Remove from heat. Add ½ teaspoon salt, ¼ teaspoon pepper, ½ cup pimiento, and 2 tablespoons minced parsley

Now I take the saucepan from the heat and add the flavoring for the turban filling . . . 1 teaspoon salt, ¼ teaspoon pepper, and ½ cup pimiento.

Fold in beaten egg white

Next I fold in 1 egg white which is stiffly beaten. The way to fold in egg white is like this: down, under and over, with a spoon. When the recipe says fold in, never, never beat.

Fill coiled Fillets with sauce mixture. Bake 20 minutes in a moderate oven (375°F.)

Now the filling goes in the center of each fillet, and then I put the pan into an oven which is preheated to 375° F. It takes only 20 minutes for fish and stuffing to bake.

3. SHOWING FINISHED
   FISH

Show platter of stuffed turbans baked ahead, using pot holders as though hot

Because we don't have enough time to let them bake, I baked some ahead so you could see what they look like when they're finished. Pretty, aren't they, and so good for you. Fish, you know, is rich in protein, minerals and vitamins . . . and makes a very good low-cost main dish for dinner. Try baking these fish turbans at home and make your family proud of you!

PROPS NEEDED FOR FISH-TURBAN DEMONSTRATION

2 trays (1 for fish preparation, 1 for sauce preparation)
1 lemon-squeezer with pouring lip
2 muffin pans, each with 6 wells (1 pan for process, 1 for finished)
1 saucepan for making sauce
1 wooden spoon for stirring sauces
2 measuring cups (1 for bread crumbs, 1 for milk)
1 small bowl for pimiento and parsley, mixed together
1 set salt-and-pepper shakers, with tops off
1 small bowl for egg white

The Demonstration Television Lesson. The demonstration lesson has not as yet been used in television to a degree corresponding to its use in radio. The scarcity of opportunity to broadcast and the scarcity of receivers have combined to hold back its development. However, the Navy's experimental broadcasts, one of which is provided later in this chapter, have demonstrated the value of this technique. Baltimore schools did a successful series over stations WAAM, called *Baltimore Classroom, 1950.*

If the demonstration lesson on radio has among its values the spreading of expertness by the use of highly skilled teachers before the microphone, how much more true will this be when these teachers face the cameras! That this opinion is not confined to educational enthusiasts may be seen from a statement before the House Ways and Means Committee, in March, 1950, that "television will make it possible for the poorest and most isolated public schools to enjoy the benefits of the most modern teaching methods." The statement was made by P. T. Hines, General Manager of the Greensboro News Company, Greensboro, North Carolina, in connection with Station WFMY-TV. Mr. Hines described cooperation with the public schools of Greensboro and the University of North Carolina in testing methods of audio-visual education.

Most teacher-training institutions have model classes, taught by outstanding teachers, with student-teachers observing in the back rows. Television can give every student, or practicing teacher, access to the best in methods. But let us not make the mistake of planning demonstration lessons for the teachers who may be watching! They are meant for the classes which receive the program, and the effective demonstration lesson will have in mind a classful of students grouped about a TV receiver. Accordingly, anything that must be seen by the class must be large and taken in close-up. Material on the blackboard, charts or diagrams, should all be scanned slowly and clearly, and enough time provided for every viewer to assimilate what is being shown. In the case of text, reading it three times aloud to oneself, before rehearsal, usually provides the rate of the slowest viewer.

In general, all the suggestions and warnings relevant to the radio demonstration lesson on pages 110–115 apply equally well to the television counterpart. One factor to keep in mind is that the classroom will be partially or completely darkened, and that this will limit note-taking, writing and other activities of that nature. Such units may well be left for follow-up. A pause for response to a question is permissible, though even that may be difficult, since the teacher in the classroom may not be able to single out students who volunteer. The Navy Special Devices Section had a microphone in each classroom which permitted the students to ask questions of the television teacher in the studio miles away, but that is something most classrooms will not have for a long time, if ever. An excerpt from one of the experimental lessons in the Navy's project follows.

CROSS-COUNTRY FLIGHT
UNDER MARGINAL CONDITIONS

VIDEO	AUDIO
1. *Camera on instructor*	Today's lesson is to touch upon highlights of the programs presented during the past seven weeks, reviewing certain sections of CAR 60, Aerology, Plan 62, etc., which have a direct bearing on our flight today, at the conclusion of which a GCA demonstration will be presented.
2. *Map #1*	Today's flight is from SDC to Wright-Patterson AFB, Dayton, Ohio. Show how flight would be made if adhering to civil airways.

3. *Map #2*	High-priority cargo is to be picked up at Lancaster, Pennsylvania, Municipal Airport and flown to Wright-Patterson AFB. Therefore, pilots will fly direct to Lancaster and continue via civil airways to destination.
4. *Pilot and co-pilot at sectional map*	Show measuring mileage and determining true course from SDC to Lancaster. Also determining best check points en route and altitude as dictated by CAR 60304(b).
5. *Map #2A*	Show true course.
6. *Map #2B*	Show how true course would be corrected for magnetic variations giving correct magnetic course. Mention that magnetic heading is computed by figuring in wind drift.
7. *Map #2*	Show civil airways to be flown from Lancaster to Wright-Patterson.
8. *Form 423, clearance form*	Explain form while pilots plan flight.
9. *Weight and balance Form F (no cargo) SDC to Lancaster Form F (with cargo) Lancaster to Wright-Patterson*	Instructor explains filing of Form F for both legs of flight, duration of validity of Form F (90 days).
10. *Cross-country packet*	Explain use of BuSandA Form 459. Mention Air Force and Navy forms.
11. *Aerologist (5 min.)*	Aerologist briefs pilots on general weather situation using weather map, etc.
12. *BuSandA Form 459 (blown up)*	
13. *Mark 8 computer*	Instructor computes true air speed correcting calibrated air speed for temperature and altitude.
14. *E6B computer*	Instructor computes ETE and magnetic heading.
15. *Map #2C Map Hadley Field, N.J.* *Delaware River Pottstown, Pa.* *CU Hadley Field CU Pottstown*	Show check points to be used on first leg of flight.

16. *Aircraft flight report NAVAER 2429*	Explain use of forms. Mention that thorough visual check of aircraft should be made prior to starting.
17. *Instr.*	Review briefly steps pilots have taken to prepare for flight.
18. *Film*	Show aircraft taking off.
19. *Control-tower operator*	Calls Operations on intercom, gives "time-off."

The Simulated Classroom.   With remote broadcasts running into hundreds of dollars for technical expenses alone, it is often simpler as well as more economical to set up a classroom in the studio. Students and teacher then go about their business in as natural a way as possible with strong lights, cameras and microphone booms intruding in their "classroom." While blackboard work, flashcards, and other visual elements can be picked up readily, the necessary rehearsals make the situation artificial, and it is chiefly as a public relations element, in acquainting parents and taxpayers with what goes on in our schools, that this format can be justified.

The simulated class on television (usually simulated because it is easier and cheaper to set up a schoolroom in the studio than to bring mobile equipment to an actual school) differs in one basic important respect from the demonstration lesson—that is, of course, the presence of a class before the cameras.

There are two ways of preparing such a broadcast. One is to script the opening and closing announcements and to make the center and major portion of the class as impromptu as a real class would be. While this system has definite public relations value, as proved by such a series, *Baltimore Classroom—1950*, on Station WAAM, Baltimore, it is less effective sometimes in getting across an educational point than the completely scripted, or rehearsed, program in which the teacher can anticipate student response because it has been made in rehearsal. The danger here, again, is that the audience will be aware of previous preparation if students are too glib, too fluent, and never provide incorrect or partially correct answers. Moreover, it takes a very good student actor to ask that same question for the fifth time and really convince the audience that it just occurred to him that minute.

Nevertheless, classroom scenes have been made convincing on television, frequently by using a workshop group or a special class in television or drama to play the roles of students in physics or home economics classes, for example. Again, the general advice as to choice of subject and illustrations (awareness of the viewing audience, opportunity to see apparatus or models in close-up, opportunity to read blackboard material, charts and graphs) given in the previous section on the demonstration lesson, will be pertinent in the simulated classroom. An actual class might get the point a little more quickly than a simulated class; perhaps too quickly for the classes which are watching the receivers.

A sample of the completely scripted variety, produced by Station WABD of the DuMont Television Network and the television class of New York University in 1947 will show some of the advantages and problems of the latter type.

ATOMIC POWER [2]

VIDEO	AUDIO
*L.S.: Classroom set (Biz: Students seated . . . chatting idly . . . books, etc.	STUDENTS: (Ad lib conversation)
Dr. Clark enters . . . to upstage center, facing class . . .)	STUDENTS: (Quiet down). . . .
Ready C.U. Camera for work on blackboard and experiments with camera for M.L.S. kept there	CLARK: Our topic tonight relates to a general consideration of Atomic Energy. I presume all of you saw the newsreel pictures of the Bikini underwater atom bomb.
	ALL: (Answer affirmatively)
	CLARK: What did you think of the explosion?
	MARY: (Raising hand) It was a terrific explosion, and I'm confused as to how all that power was obtained from a rela-

---

* L.S. = Long Shot. C.U. = Close-up. M.S. = Medium Shot.
[2] New York University's production was the first student-written, student-acted, student-produced educational TV script. Professor Robert Gessner produced the program; Professor C. C. Clark of the Science Department appeared as the instructor.

tively small bomb. Just what is Atomic Energy?

CLARK: That's a large order, Mary; but let us note, first, a few basic ideas about Atomic Structure and then look into some of the processes whereby Atomic Energy is released and the Atom Bomb made possible. May I borrow a silver coin from one of you? A half dollar.

Biz: Students searching; Steve holds up one; rises and takes it to Dr. Clark. Resumes his seat

STEVE: Here you are, sir. By the way, Dr. Clark, what is that bone there on the table?

CLARK: That bone, Steve, has a very significant history and meaning. But we will come to it later. This is an ordinary half dollar, a piece of silver, made up of small invisible particles called atoms, too small to be seen even with the most powerful microscope. However, if we use our imagination as a microscope, we can enlarge this half dollar and magnify it as much as we desire. If we should enlarge this *until* its diameter is equal to the earth's orbit around the sun, how large would that be?

As Dr. Clark speaks, Dolly slowly in to show table and equipment . . . not students

C.U.: of half dollar in Clark's hand

JANET: 186,000 miles.

Dolly back to M.S.† of table

CLARK: On this scale of magnification the atoms would be a mile or so in diameter . . . and we would be able to see what the atoms really are. We would find that the silver atom is not a solid particle, but rather is composed of still smaller units, arranged in definite geometric patterns. Likewise, *all the materials on earth are composed of atoms and each different atom has a different number of these particles*. This cylinder contains some Hydrogen Gas. Hydrogen atoms are the simplest in structure of any substance on earth. John, step up to the chart and draw a picture of the

Biz: Clark picks up bottle labeled HYDROGEN

---

† M.S. = Medium Shot.

Biz: John rises, goes to board (chart) and draws pattern

Biz: Points to nucleus pattern he has drawn

structure of the hydrogen atom, and name the component parts.

JOHN: The hydrogen atom is made up of a nucleus . . . consisting of one particle with a *positive* electric charge called a PROTON, represented by a PLUS sign, and one extra nuclear particle with a negative electric charge called an ELECTRON, represented by a MINUS sign.

Biz: Dr. Clark picks up a bottle labeled HELIUM

CLARK: In this cylinder is some Helium Gas, the material now used in dirigibles. John, will you now diagram the Helium atom and explain its structure?

Biz: Students take notes

Biz: John again draws

JOHN: The Helium atom consists of a nucleus containing two protons, and also two other particles with NO electric charge on them, called NEUTRONS, represented by a PLUS and MINUS sign. Also outside the Nucleus there are two electrons, revolving around the nucleus at high speeds.

Biz: He draws

CLARK: What about the weight or mass of these atomic particles?

Biz: He writes figures

On board:
Mass proton + 1.0078
*   neutron ± 1.0090*
*   electron − 1/1800*

JOHN: The masses of the protons and the neutrons are about the same, each weighing about one atomic weight unit, while the electron weighs only about 1/1800th part of an atomic weight unit. Practically all of the mass of the atom is concentrated in the nucleus.

And on we go, with professor and students developing the nature of atomic energy.

Public Relations. In most cities, as television stations open, the public relations aspect of school broadcasting is usually the first to get on the air. It is significant that the outstanding Philadelphia setup originated as an aspect of the School-Community Relations Department and is still administered by that Bureau. The great advantage of this type of program is its ready acceptance; the disadvantage may arise from the desire to concentrate on this type of format, with its wide audience, to the detriment of more genuinely "teaching" programs. Both have their place, of course.

SCRIPTING THE PUBLIC RELATIONS PROGRAM. A chapter is devoted to Public Relations programming in the latter portion of this book, and a sizable part of that discussion deals with television. Nevertheless, it may not be amiss here to point out that, while there is no one format which is most effective, a program showing the work of the school or division we wish to publicize is perhaps the most popular. This may be done with film, either sound on film or silent footage to which a "live" narration is "dubbed" as it goes on the air, with sound effects and background music added as well.

Less effective than film, of course, is the use of slides or strip film, again with appropriate commentary. Where it is possible, a dramatic framework, in which film, still pictures, and studio demonstrations of special activities are interwoven, may prove the most satisfactory format of all.

Let us take as an example a public relations program produced by a specialized school, the School for the Deaf, supported by the Lutheran Friends of the Deaf. Produced at WPIX, New York, in November, 1949, it used all the elements mentioned above. One of its unique features was the giving of an audiometer test to a group of children with impaired hearing. As the child held the audiometer's earphone to her ear, a duplicate audiometer was patched into the audio console in the studio control room. Thus, by following a chart prepared by an expert for each child, the audio engineer was able to broadcast a close approximation of what that child was or was not hearing. The "heroine" of the program, a child with normal hearing who played the part of one isolated by increasing deafness, was one of those whose hearing difficulty was "discovered" in the course of the audiometer test. A portion of the script, "The Story of a Dream," follows.

SCENE: *Artist sketches at blackboard*

VIDEO	AUDIO
Artist outlines America	NARR: (*Off camera*) This is America, a mighty land inhabited by a great people, about

150,000,000 in the forty-eight States of the Union.

Among these many millions, there are many who are afflicted and many who are handicapped. Yet the plight of few troubled people in America is as serious as is that of the deaf. They are, to be sure, a relatively small proportion of our population, approximately 70,000 in all. Out of every million Americans, only 465 are handicapped by the total inability to hear.

Artist shades in one small area

Many others, though, have serious hearing defects. The number of those with impaired hearing is estimated to be between 10 to 15 per cent of our population.

Artist extends shaded portion to entire map, filling in ten per cent of area

SCENE: *Audiometer test*

NARR: To determine a child's ability, or lack of ability, to hear, he may receive an audiometer test like this one being conducted here.

Dissolve to classroom set. Teacher gives audiometer test to three children. First has normal hearing. Second has slight impairment. Third child is Mary who can hardly hear past second stage. Fade to black as Mary's impairment is definitely established. Fade up on living-room scene.

NARR: Sometimes it may happen that, if a child is given an audiometer test in school, she may bring home to her parents a note from her teacher, informing her of that which has been ascertained by means of the test.

MOTHER: John, I'm afraid that I have bad news for you this evening. Mary brought this note home from her teacher.

JOHN: (*Taking note*) What's this? Is Mary having trouble again in keeping up with her class? Just a few weeks ago Miss Bentley wrote that Mary was inattentive and that her work was below average. (*Reads note aloud*) Dear Mr. and Mrs. Jordan: In giving the annual audiometer test today, it was discovered that your child showed no response to the tests. She gives every indication of deafness. We suggest that you see your physician for advice as to treatment and procedure. . . . Jean. This can't be true, Mary can hear. You can hear me, can't you, Mary?

MARY: Yes, Daddy.

Hold pantomime scene over narrator's speech

NARR: It is true that children may show a greater response to those with whom they are closely associated, especially to members of their own family. For instance, if the impairment of the hearing has been gradual, they can be familiar with the expected responses by noting the expressions on faces.

JOHN: (*Holding watch closer and closer to Mary's ear*) Tell me when you hear it tick, Mary.

Pantomime scene
Fade out

MARY: (*No response—she bursts into tears and runs to mother*)

Music. Programs of pure music, as opposed to musical dramas, pose a serious problem on television. An orchestra is basically static, a chorus even more so. Many musical groups "don't look as good as they sound," and are better off on radio. However, with skillful camera work which focuses attention on each soloist in turn, or on that instrument or section of the orchestra which is important at any given moment in the score, a telecast of a concert can be made valid and valuable. In general, it must be admitted, radio can do so good a job that the trouble of getting a music-wise director who can mark his camera shots from a score instead of a script is rarely justified.

SCRIPTING THE MUSICAL PROGRAM. In no type of program is it

more necessary for the teacher-producer to be sure of the purpose of the broadcast than in the musical show. If the purpose is simply to broadcast fine music, radio can do it as effectively with far less trouble. If the purpose is to give young performers an opportunity to be seen and heard, we must be sure not to trespass on the patience of the viewing audience.

Perhaps our goal is music appreciation or a lesson in conducting given by a fine conductor. Here simply pointing cameras at an orchestra will not serve. The camera pattern must be worked out with the station director so that it will show the audience what it must *see* at any given moment to understand more clearly what it is *hearing*. Achieving this isn't as easy as it sounds.

Perhaps we are televising music not for its own sake but for what the music can tell us about our own or other cultures. Here we may combine music with social studies; illustrate it with dance; integrate it with painting or sculpture of the same period. It is this last use of music that many educators feel is the proper province of music on television. Here, as one example, is a script outline for a program in the *Operation Classroom* series, produced by WCAU-TV, Philadelphia, in cooperation with the Philadelphia schools. The program featured Mary Van Doren, concert pianist, and was entitled "Early American Scenes through Music."

VIDEO	AUDIO
OPENING: *Identification music and Flash cards*	
Camera on Mrs. Miller	MRS. MILLER: (*Opening—ad lib*)
Camera on Mary Van Doren at piano. Theme identification— Camera on Mary Van Doren and five pupils seated in school desks or chairs	MARY VAN DOREN: Opening remarks about music identified with Colonial Times and a musical visit to a Colonial Mansion. Dialogue between Mary Van Doren and pupils.
	MARY VAN DOREN: Introduction to first piece. Minuet—Haydn.
Camera on Colonial Room *4 Dancers—pantomime* *Camera on Mary Van Doren*	MARY VAN DOREN: Plays short part of selection. Speaks of minuet as a dance.
	Plays part that dancers will use. Introduces Dance.

Camera on dancers— *Minuet illustrated*	As Mary plays— MARY VAN DOREN: And now here is Joseph Haydn's "Minuet."
Camera on Mary Van *Doren and pupils*	MARY VAN DOREN: Introduction to—"To My Clock." Dialogue with children.
Camera on grandfather's *clock— One pupil in* *costume standing before* *it*	
Mary Van Doren's *hands on keyboard—* *Superimpose clock*	MARY VAN DOREN: Playing of selected parts— pupils participating in beating of rhythm.
Camera on Mary Van *Doren's hands on key-* *board*	Playing of selection—"To My Clock" by Charles Repper.
Superimpose picture of *grandfather's clock in* *close-up*	
Camera on Mary Van *Doren and pupils*	MARY VAN DOREN: Introduces "Spinning Song." Talk about spinning wheel found in colonial mansion.
Camera on spinning *wheel tableau*	Playing of selected parts to show whirr.
Camera on Mary Van *Doren*	Playing of entire selection—"Spinning Song" by Felix Mendelssohn.
	CLOSING: Saying goodbye to Colonial Mansion— Plays signature.
Camera on Mrs. Miller	MRS. MILLER: Closes program.
Camera on flash cards	
	MUSIC: *WCAU signature*

5

Presenting the Radio Program

◇◇◇

What are the more common direction and production procedures?

How must some of these be modified in the school radio program?

What mistakes have been noted in school broadcasting?

How can the talk be presented effectively?

◇◇◇◇◇◇◇◇THE BEST, AND PERHAPS the only, way to learn to produce radio programs is to produce them. Although some suggestions can be made which may minimize the trial and error process, merely reading about program production is only an incidental aid.[1]

Moreover, the techniques of radio production have been discussed in detail by qualified radio directors.[2] However, from the teacher's point of view, detailed analysis need not be necessary or even pertinent; the purpose of this chapter is simply to present some aspects of radio direction which are essential to all who attempt to produce school programs. Consideration will be given to the production problems met in (a) the dramatization and (b) the talk. These are the two most frequently used educational program types and the principles noted can be applied to other forms.

Production Procedures: the Tools Available

Knowing something about the equipment is not only desirable; it is imperative. The teacher may not be interested in things mechanical, yet as a producer of programs she should have a general idea as to the nature of the available tools.

Microphone and Studio. The basic tool is the microphone. It is an extension of the listener's ear. Although it is true that

---

[1] Recognizing this need, some courses in radio education include laboratory exercises in which use is made of studio equipment, radio programs are produced, recordings analyzed, and utilization practices demonstrated and evaluated. In some instances the course is divided into two phases. The first term's work is largely the collection of information such as is included in this text. During the second term opportunity is provided for expression. Each member of the class has as a project the development and production of an original script. In some cases the class members, who may be teaching, use their own pupils in the cast. Each of these programs is recorded and then presented to the class for analysis, evaluation, and a discussion of utilization procedures.

[2] John S. Carlile, *Production and Direction of Radio Programs*, Prentice-Hall, Inc., 1940.

Earle McGill, *Radio Directing*, McGraw-Hill Book Company, Inc., 1940.

Eric Barnouw, *Handbook of Radio Production.* D. C. Heath & Company, 1940.

Walter K. Kingson and Rome Cowgill, *Radio Drama Acting and Production,* Rinehart & Company, 1950.

Edwin Duerr, *Radio and Television Acting,* Rinehart & Company, 1950, and others noted in the bibliography.

168

fine school programs have been presented by teachers who did not know one microphone from another, even a limited knowledge of the "mike" can save a great deal of time and many last-minute changes.

Frequently one hears questions such as these from teachers who are to broadcast: "Does this mike pick up sounds from only one side, two sides, or from every position? How far back shall we stand from this one? How many members of my cast can I use here? Where shall I place the mike for the chorus?" and so on. To answer such questions it may not be necessary to know the mechanical details of the various instruments but it is a definite help to know a bit about the tonal and directional qualities of the common microphone types. These characteristics also have been discussed and illustrated by Abbot, McGill, and others.[3] It is evident, of course, that the only practical way to learn the nature of the equipment is to use it or, at least, to watch a demonstration of it.

A knowledge of studio acoustics also is of importance to the program producer, and the broadcasting teacher should know the basic principles involved;[4] but the "bottleneck" in school radio reception is not the acoustical quality of the broadcasting studio but the poor acoustical conditions which usually exist in the average schoolroom. The teacher-producer may make a fine distinction between the "live" and "dead" ends of his studios, he may talk learnedly about reverberation curves, his studios may be "floated," etc., but if what comes out of the classroom speaker invariably is distorted because of conditions in the classroom itself, then the experienced school-program producer soon learns that he need not spend too much time worrying about acoustical perfection in the studio from which the program emanates. It is not a question of complete neglect but rather one of understanding the probable returns.

However, for in-school public-address work, where programs often originate from more than one source, the acoustical differences which exist among the usual points of program origin require careful atten-

Waldo Abbot, *Handbook of Broadcasting*, McGraw-Hill Book Company, Inc., 2d ed., 1950, pp. 1–21.

Earle McGill, *op. cit.*, pp. 6–15.

Albert Crews, *Radio Production Directing*, Houghton Mifflin Company, 1944, p. 550.

John S. Carlile, *op. cit.*, pp. 344–350.

tion. The acoustics of the school auditorium will generally differ from those of the band room, the cafeteria, and the ordinary classroom. They should be tested and studied. A different microphone placement may be necessary for a program originating in each of these locations.

Sound Effects.   Another tool used by the radio director is the sound effect. Just as the stage director should know something about "props," so the radio producer must be acquainted with the "scenery" of a radio play—the sound effects.

There are several types of effects: those made by hand, such as the opening and closing of a door; those produced vocally, such as birdcalls and animal imitations; music effects which generally consist of original themes; acoustical effects; and the most common type—the recorded sound effect.

It is not necessary for the teacher to know how to create the various effects, for if she were to do so it would deny some child an enjoyable and perhaps valuable experience. Detailed suggestions for producing the more common effects are readily available elsewhere.[5] Aside from a few effects such as a door, which must be operated manually for exact timing and proper interpretation, it is quite likely that most school programs will find their sound-effect needs met by recorded materials. The equipment phase of this subject is discussed in the chapter, "Broadcasting Activities within the School."

Though the creation of the sound effect should naturally be of secondary interest to the teacher-producer, an understanding of its use in reinforcing the script is fundamental.

School program producers need to be cautioned to use sound effects with restraint. In the first place, a slight suggestion is enough especially if there is some verbal identification of the sound in the script. An overly enthusiastic use of a sound effect may divert the attention of the listeners from the script to consideration of the sound alone. Second, if there is a question as to the meaning of a sound then it should not be used, especially when broadcasting to children Certainly, a sound that is not entirely clear should be identified. T

---

[5] R. B. Turnbull, *Sound Effects*, Rinehart & Company, Inc., 1951. *Handbook of Sound Effects*, United States Office of Education, Washington, D.C., 1940.
Waldo Abbot, *op. cit.*, pp. 247–267.

illustrate: if the sound of the opening of a desk drawer is not perfectly clear, it is a simple matter to label it by a comment such as, 'Yes, it is here in the desk."

Clarity is of prime importance when broadcasting for classroom reception. Because two characters, for example, meet on the street and engage in conversation it is not necessary or even desirable to have the sound of traffic behind them constantly. If the scene is a long one, it tires the listeners and distracts attention from the dialogue which itself may be drowned out. It is far better, generally, to establish the sound effects so that there is no doubt as to the locale or the situation and then imperceptibly fade out the confusing background. It is not usually necessary to resort to circuitous methods to make this fading plausible. For example, in using the same traffic scene some teacher may deem it advisable to have the two enter a hallway so that the background can be eliminated. The dialogue necessary to accomplish this may be entirely irrelevant. When that is done the play is being written around the scenery.

The inexperienced director must avoid trying for too much detailed realism. If the teacher is in doubt as to the use of a sound, it is well to ask, "Does it contribute to the meaning of the script?" If the answer is in the negative, then the sound should be eliminated. Other comments concerning the use of sound effects will be made later in the discussion of rehearsals.

Music. The use of music as a tool in a dramatic program deserves some attention. A skillful selection and use of music can enhance the script greatly; on the other hand, a poor choice and awkward use of it can spoil even a superior script.

If the device of a musical transition, or "bridge," between scenes, for example, is regarded by the director merely as a relief from talk—a negative concept—then the results are inevitably poor. However, if atmospheric moods are to be established, then well-chosen musical interludes have no equal and the skillful director will build upon that fact.

The choice of musical selections is obviously subject to limitations in some school situations. The radio producer may have to make use of whatever selections the musical groups have rehearsed. If the effects desired in the radio play are considered paramount, however, then the use of the recorded music may be advisable. In almost every high-school group there will be at least one pupil who will be delighted to search for appropriate musical selections. After a few of these have been submitted the teacher can select those she deems particularly suitable.

Not only does the use of records make for greater variety, but it simplifies production. If many fades are to be used, if there is to be a delicate control of volume, then the use of the average school musical unit provides a difficulty even for the most experienced director. The arrangement and tonal balance of the instrumental group may take up much rehearsal time.[6] The use of "live" music may mean getting more pupils out of class. The transportation of instruments may present difficulties. In some communities union problems may arise. All these are considerations that must be understood if and when live music is employed. However, there is this to be said: if the radio program is regarded as a valuable educational experience, then participation in it should not be restricted unless very necessary. But that is always the problem of the schoolteacher in any field—whether to restrict an activity to a select few and elevate standards or to spread participation and accept what may amount to mediocrity.

If recorded music is used, the records must be analyzed carefully so that the desired passage is forthcoming—something like it is not good enough. This "spotting" of the records is sometimes poorly done. Too many teachers follow the practice of ending the recorded music by a fade that often is musically awkward and undesirable. Even if the music is to be brief, there is no reason why the record cannot be used at an appropriate passage which will bring the music to a natural conclusion.

Another mistake often made in using music to create a mood is to cut it too short. When broadcasting to children, especially, ample time should be taken in order that the atmosphere may be definitely established.

If the narrator is speaking with a background of music the musical volume should be kept low so that there is no need for shouting by the speaker. Competition for the listener's ear should be eliminated

---

[6] John S. Carlile, op. cit., pp. 60–110.

and the center of the stage—that is, the greater volume—should be given to the factor the director has in mind, whether it be speech, music, or a sound effect.

Recorded fanfares are generally poor and must be chosen with great care. However, a live fanfare requires considerable "finger-crossing" on the part of the director because there is nothing so devastating as a trumpet gone sour.

With the usual school group, orchestral fades require expert direction and careful microphone placement. An effective fade as a background to continued talk is difficult in a small studio, since each unit —the orchestra and the dramatic cast—must work on separate mikes, and the shorter the distance between the mikes the more difficult the fade. If one mike is turned down, there is the danger that the sound will be picked up on the other. For this reason a separate studio for each unit is often desirable, although this may complicate cueing or signaling procedures.

Much of what has been said applies also to the use of vocal music either as an interlude or as a program element. Whether it be a vocal or an instrumental unit, the use of live talent adds to rehearsal problems. However, the schools are doing much fine choral work that should not be neglected in planning the radio program.

There may be noted, perhaps, some advantages in using a vocal ensemble. No instruments need be transported, voice fades are easier to handle than instrumental; proper microphone placement is not difficult to get, and if labor union regulations are involved an *a cappella* group can be used.

Production Procedures: Preparatory Steps

Now let us discuss briefly the steps generally taken in presenting a typical school script. When a school production group is involved, commercial practices as such must be modified. For example, rehearsals can be longer, since no talent costs are involved. Modes of interpretation can and perhaps should be arrived at through discussion rather than imposing them upon the pupils. In order to spread pupil participation, the school cast can be larger and "doubling" minimized.

Conference with Station Personnel. If the program is to be presented over a local commercial station, several preliminary arrangements can save much effort later. Once the school group has been given time for a radio performance it should not be assumed that the need for close cooperation with the station staff no longer exists. The school director's obligation is to anticipate her activities so that by a conference or two with the station personnel she can develop a working relationship that will be of great value not only to the school but also to the station.

During the conference the teacher can discuss arrangements for such matters as the following:

1. A period for auditions. If the school has a public-address system this may not be necessary, since such preliminaries can be handled satisfactorily in the school.
2. A rehearsal period prior to the actual broadcast. The length of this final rehearsal depends upon the nature of the program. For the average school dramatization a period equal to three times the "air show" time is ample.
3. The services of an announcer, possibly a director, and whatever dramatic and musical talent the school cannot provide. Reasonable requests will generally be honored but it should be understood that it is the *school's* program.
4. The services of a control-room operator. It is desirable to have available for the rehearsal the same man who will be in charge during the air show.
5. The equipment that will be needed: microphones, sound effects, music stands, chairs, visitor accommodations, and so on. The chances are that this cannot be decided until production gets under way, in which case the final arrangements can be made later.
6. Program promotion. By working closely with the station's publicity staff the alert director can do much to build a local audience. The school's newspaper staff can be set to work on this as a project. Newspaper stories, photographs, posters, and other approaches can be used.

The United States Office of Education suggests that the teacher also discuss the matter of using school orchestras in connection with programs. "In some communities restrictions imposed by the musicians' union prohibit school orchestras or bands playing for broadcasting except upon the payment of 'stand by' fees to an equivalent number of union musicians." [7]

Music Conference at School.   Beginning with the script itself, the director may proceed in any one of several directions. If live music is to be used, the next step might be preparation for a conference with the music teacher. This step is suggested now so that there can be ample time for music rehearsals while the dramatic cast is getting under way. The music teacher, participating as he does, in concerts, football games, contests of various sorts, and special music lessons, is usually busy, and consequently he should be notified long in advance of the radio date.

In preparation for this conference the individual in charge of the radio program should know exactly how much and what music is needed. Copies of the script should be available and carefully marked with cues, fades, and interpretive suggestions. Obviously it will be a great help to the music director if the selections chosen for the program are those which the pupils have been rehearsing during the school year. In any case, the choice of selections must be dependent upon the ability of the school unit to play them adequately.

After the selections have been determined, not only from the musical point of view but also from the manner in which they reinforce the script, then the radio director can proceed with the next step.

Copyright Clearance.   Whether one follows the exact sequence of steps as noted here is immaterial, but one of the first steps should be to make sure that all program material, literary and musical, can be used without violating a copyright. Though this may not apply to in-school public-address work, nevertheless, if a commercial station is to be used, such caution is necessary. For purposes of this discussion it will be assumed that the school group is planning to present its material through a local commercial station.

Teachers occasionally are unaware that a stage play, a story, or a novel, either whole or in part, cannot be adapted or used in its original form without special permission from the copyright owner. To know

[7] *Radio Manual*, United States Office of Education, Washington, D.C., 1945, pp. 6–7.

whether material is in the "public domain" or whether the station subscribes to various musical societies is often not easily determined. If the teacher is in doubt, a phone call to the station may prevent some last-minute changes. While doing so it is wise to "clear" even the material that may not be used, so that necessary program changes later can be made without difficulty.

Planning Effects.   The next step in production can be the planning of sound effects. If one of the students is to be in charge, the script might now be discussed with him. As in the case of music, by doing this early, enough time is provided so that the sound effects can be collected and tested. And just as the music teacher must have his script carefully marked with all cues, so the pupil handling sound effects must know just what the director wants. If possible, script changes should be made before the music and sound effects men get their copies, and all subsequent changes on the director's script should be marked on *every* copy.

Casting.   When the script has been checked carefully and while the music and sound effects are being developed, the teacher can study the material for cast requirements.

In casting for a radio performance the teacher must be sure that the final judgment is made by her ear and not by her eyes. A child's physical resemblance to the character desired is no assurance that the voice will convey that impression to the listener. For example, it is quite possible that a girl can play a small boy's role and do it well. Even though a child may seem to have definite talent, no major role should be assigned without some preliminary audition.

Because young voices are often very similar, the director must be careful to cast the parts so that the listeners will not be confused. This is especially true if similar voices appear in the same scenes. The only safeguard is to listen; if two different characters sound alike, then casting should be changed. For the same reason "doubling" in roles must be used with caution.

If radio program production is to be a continuous school activity, then the teacher should not rely on hurried casting. Rather she should develop a simplified card file of school talent. These cards might note the following: the pupil's name, his homeroom number, the time he has available for rehearsals, a comment as to his voice quality, his ability rating in school roles previously played, and possibly the dialects he can use.

In casting the program, the director must avoid placing too much emphasis upon a distinctive voice *quality*. The ability to *use* the voice effectively is more important. A gifted child can use his voice with an amazing amount of flexibility. Without "pressing" too hard he can express his emotions with sincerity. His reading sounds conversational and his inflections denote understanding. A child thus talented may not possess a splendid voice but he may play the role superbly.

A question that has been debated by school directors is whether children should read adult roles. Those who favor the practice believe that it is perfectly proper to do so provided the program is planned primarily for a children's audience. As an indication that such casting can be used successfully they point to programs such as *Let's Pretend* in which the roles are taken by young people. Those who feel that such casting is undesirable argue that greater pupil participation can be secured in other ways, such as the use of choral groups.

This question is one which the director will have to settle. If the program is being presented as a distinct school enterprise, there may not be much choice in the matter.

Initial Reading. After the teacher has cast the program, it is well to mark each child's script with whatever notes or suggestions and points of emphasis the director has in mind. When the director is working with children the importance of the carefully marked script cannot be overemphasized. By analyzing each role and by anticipating difficulties the teacher can save much time and effort during rehearsals. For instance, if a cue is particularly important, if the child is to fade from the mike, if he is to double on a certain role or emphasize a certain line, the script should be marked accordingly. In mob scenes where so-called ad lib comments are needed, it may be necessary to write in such comments, especially with younger children. Unless the director is careful, their spontaneous comments may be not at all pertinent to the situation. The marked script, of course, should not be regarded as a clamp on individual interpretation.

When the pupils meet with the director for the first reading, no studio equipment is needed. A few general observations by the teacher as to the script itself and possible interpretations are helpful. As the children read the lines it may be found that certain word formations are difficult to handle, that excessive sibilants occur, that lines are ambiguous, and occasionally that the style may be unnatural. Such corrections should be made.

Script Discussion. When the first reading has been completed, the teacher may use the script as a vehicle for discussion. She may ask, "Are there various ways of interpreting the script? How shall *we* do it? What type of character is so-and-so? How can we emphasize that in our reading? Where can a change of reading pace improve the script? Are the transitions clear?"

While such a time-consuming procedure as that noted above may be unnecessary with a professional group, in school the radio program is a medium for providing an educational experience. The pupils should be encouraged in self-development. Obviously, characterization can be imposed on the young actor. As a mimic he has no equal, but if the teacher demands only *her* interpretation, then she is overlooking perhaps the greatest value of the school performance. Nothing is more fatal to a children's program than to have it presented by stiff, prim little imitators, rather than by "just kids," who are honestly enjoying the effort and in that enjoyment receive real benefits.

The comments of Nila Mack concerning the direction of children are enlightening. For more than fifteen years, the late Miss Mack directed children in the Columbia series *Let's Pretend*. She says:

First and foremost, children have taught me that talking down to them is fatal! It gets me nowhere fast. But an eye-to-eye conversation, using words and explanations they can understand, brings the same response that adults give. The same? I mean better.

Encouragement is far better than criticism. Confidence draws out better performances, rather than criticizing their first approach.

When a rehearsal begins on CBS "Let's Pretend," the youngsters sit around a table. The cast is assigned. Then we read the whole script straight through without stopping, so that each child gets a clear idea of the story first, along with a picture of his relationship to the other members of the cast. After that is over, and before we "put it on the mike," I discuss in an impersonal but business-like way, the characterizations they have given me. I listen to their ideas and try to learn just why they read as they did. If they are wrong, my answer will be something like "I see what you mean. But I believe in this instance, you can get more out of the part if you tackle it like this." I may read one line. But rather than have a group of parrots, I much prefer to recall a certain movie, or a story, or even another script wherein there was a character something like the one being discussed. The response is instantaneous and we start to build it along the lines I want. In the meantime, the child has not been humiliated and, while he plays it differently than he originally did, he doesn't feel that the first reading was unintelligent or that his ability was questioned.

Scolding is no good when there is a broadcast in the offing. It brings two definite reactions. To single out one child and scold or punish him creates a "gang" feeling. The child knows he mustn't come back with an argument and the others are embarrassed with and for him, with the result that they hang together in self-defense. The second reaction is an unsteady air performance wherein the child will very likely "fluff" his lines or miss his cues because he's thinking of the hurt he had.

Children, I have learned, have a clarity of vision that is amazing, an intuition that is comparable only to animals. They can sense the approach of friends or enemies, dangers or privileges. Children are unhampered by knowledge of sociology, economics, or involved human behavior so they are able to cut right through to the core and dissect the feeling and attitude of the person with whom they're dealing.

Let their teacher or director become nervous and jittery and the children immediately reflect the same condition. But bring to them a genuine interest, friendliness, good humor and a square deal and those same qualities come back to you 100 per cent.[8]

Timing the Program. Rehearsals without the microphone having been started, some consideration can now be given to timing the program. Getting the dramatic program off the air at exactly fourteen minutes and thirty seconds, particularly when working with young children who have had no previous experience, is not a simple task. Such exact timing is not necessary for an in-school presentation via the public-address system or even for broadcasts over many educational noncommercial stations, but, in presenting a program over a commercial station, exact timing is essential. In some instances the school program may be followed by a sustaining feature, the nature of which permits running over, but ordinarily the radio schedule allows no such liberties. Time is to the radio station what space is to the

---

[8] Nila Mack, "Talking Down to Children Really Fatal," *Cleveland Plain Dealer*, September 8, 1940, p. 27.

newspaper. And even that analogy must be qualified because the newspaper can add a page whereas the radio station can add no time.

The approximate length of the program can be determined during one of the early readings, additions or deletions can be made at that time. It is probably better to plan too little than too much. Many directors find that extending the length of time consumed by program units, that is, "stretching the program," is much easier than rushing it through.

When working with experienced adult actors, changing the pace during the broadcast itself is not particularly difficult, but with inexperienced children such effort on the part of the director may be confusing and often upsets their reading. As far as possible the broadcast pace should resemble the rehearsal pace. Theoretically, at least, the job of timing should be completed before the program begins. With young children, the use of "tentative cuts" (deletions to be made just before or after the program goes on the air) should be avoided.

For the school producer the simplest thing to do, perhaps, is to use some kind of "cushion"—an elastic part of a program. By means of a "cushion," such as the school song at the beginning and at the close of the program, it is a fairly simple matter to extend or reduce the time. If the program is of a continuous nature, such as a discussion, the easiest thing to do is to fade the discussion and continue it in the background while the announcer comes in with a concluding statement. A children's dramatic program composed entirely of talk calls for expert timing. With experience the task becomes much easier.

When programs are presented over commercial stations it must be understood by the teacher that the timing of the program is her responsibility and not that of the station staff. Every element of the program, music, announcements, and dramatic skits, must be carefully timed with a stop watch. By knowing the time of each element, it is a simple matter, during the dress rehearsal, to eliminate quickly a portion of the program and to know exactly how much time has been saved. If cuts are made, everyone concerned with the production should know exactly what they are. If possible, it is much easier to cut a block of the script than to make many small cuts, which must then be totaled and marked accordingly. Of course, essential plot action should not be eliminated. In the exceptional cases where that must be done planned narration has to be available as a "cover-up."

In marking his script the director may indicate the length of each program element and also, at the bottom of each page, the running time of the program. Some teachers mark the script at thirty-second intervals. Regardless of the procedure, the test of its merit is whether it enables the director to know at all times during the broadcast just how the actual pace varies from the rehearsed pace.

Microphone Rehearsals. The next step is the rehearsal with microphones. For the school producer this step involves certain difficulties, since the technical personnel and the school equipment used for rehearsals are not the same as the engineering staff and the broadcast equipment to be had at the radio station. The teacher may rehearse carefully with the pupil operators but later the professional technicians will take over for the air show. Voice levels can be adjusted to the school's public-address microphones but at the studio the instruments are generally more sensitive and the children frequently "hug the mike" and "blast" into it. Sound effects may sound fine in the school but at the studio they may have to be discarded. Obviously the best procedure is to do more rehearsing at the station, if possible.

This difficulty sometimes causes the school director to keep the production as simple as possible. Sound effects are minimized, as is the extensive use of "board fades." [9]

Dress Rehearsal. When school rehearsals have continued to the point where there is general satisfaction, then the cast can report to the station for the dress rehearsal. Frequently this will take place the same day the program is scheduled so that only one trip is needed and, if the program is during school time, fewer classes are missed.

School groups occasionally report to a station ready to go on the

[9] The "board fade" is to the radio play what the fall of the curtain is to the stage production. It terminates a scene by a reduction of volume and introduces another scene by a corresponding increase. This maneuver is handled by the control-room operator at the director's cue and therefore requires some rehearsal. The device is invaluable when a mass sound (a musical unit, a mob scene, or the like) is to be reduced or increased uniformly. Contrasted with this type of fade is the performer's fade in which he moves away from the microphone.

air and then some difficulty presents itself. There may not be enough scripts for all who need copies, not all the sound-effect materials may have been collected, there may be no certainty as to the number of microphones needed, cues may not be marked, the engineer's script may be confusing, the length of the program may have been greatly misjudged, certain musical numbers may not have been cleared, and so on. As indicated previously, many of these difficulties can be avoided by a careful preliminary analysis of the script and its require-ments, and much of this work can be done even before the casting begins.

When the group goes to the commercial radio station for a broad-cast the teacher must understand that her program is but one of many, and that the station is a place of business, and not a school. Unfortunately there will not be time, in most cases, for more than the "dress." All other rehearsing should have been completed earlier. If special equipment or station personnel is needed, then previous notice to the station would have been helpful.

The best way to get station cooperation is for one to admit that this is a new field. Nothing is more disturbing to the station staff than to be told where and how successfully the individual has broad-cast and then to learn, too late perhaps, that this person cannot even use the live side of the microphone.

Ordinarily the teacher can expect, and most likely will receive, courteous treatment. She can assume, having indicated her needs, that there will be ample time, a suitable studio and equipment, and station personnel available for a final rehearsal. She will find most radio men are tolerant of early efforts. After all, they know that teachers have been trained primarily to do something else, that their knowledge of production can come but gradually, and that profes-sional standards cannot be imposed upon the school group. They will have to evolve slowly.

Generally, the director plans to have the "dress" early enough before program time so that final checks can be made and noted. Punctuality in reporting to the studio is therefore essential and noth-ing can ruin the rehearsal like stragglers who delay proceedings.

If the production is a rather elaborate one entailing the use of live music, a dramatic cast, and so on, the distribution of the rehearsal time for each unit may cause some difficulties unless there is an understanding among the teachers beforehand just when each group is to be monitored (heard in the control room).

The teacher, probably unacquainted with the studio acoustics and technical equipment, will welcome any aid she can receive from the station personnel. Particularly on instrumental setups and proper balance will she seek counsel. The level of every element in the program must be heard and adjusted. A proper level in a radio program is as vital as the proper focus in a photograph.

During the "dress," all the elements of the program are blended: speech, music, and sound effects. That is the director's job. The proper timing of the program may depend upon someone else but the responsibility must be fixed.

Weaknesses will present themselves during the final rehearsal and the alert teacher will not rely upon memory to recall them during the conference later. Some directors note the errors on their scripts, others on blank sheets of paper. A few prefer to call them off to an assistant who has more time to write them out while the rehearsal continues.

Aside from the need to cut, stretch, or even add program bits for time adjustment, the director may notice a wide variety of imperfections. Some of these, she will recognize, cannot be eliminated at this late stage, but many can be handled by consultation with the performers, the engineers, or the station's production man. She may notice, for instance, that the perspectives which seemed proper when developed with equipment at school now require some readjustment. Improper mike placement may cause a performer, while fading from one mike, to walk on to another. The balance of the orchestra may require additional attention. If several mikes are being used, there may be poor visibility from the control room. If the director is shifting scenes by means of a few board fades, there may be need for more work with the control-room operator. The sound effects may present problems: cueing may be poor, some effects may require further definition, fixed perspectives in recorded effects may necessitate some adjustment. Background chatter may require attention, rustling of scripts may be heard, etc.

The real test of the director's ability is the extent to which all those involved in the production function at their peak. The methods used by various directors of course vary with their own personalities. Here, too, there is no one best way to get the most from actors. Techniques successful with one director may fail dismally if simply borrowed, without adaptation, by another. However, there are numerous procedures that have been productive. The following techniques have been found useful. In directing children they may need some modification but the basic principles apply whether the performers are young or old. Here are "Seventeen Ways to Make an Actor Act" as developed by Charles C. Urquhart of NBC.

These angles of approach are used after the actor has been cast and rehearsals have begun. They are not listed in order of importance. Individual directors use various methods, any or all or none, at any given moment, depending on the problem at hand.

1. "Primary" tactics. The simplest way of all—brief and succinct and basic, instructions such as "faster, slower, louder, older, younger, try again on a new tack, etc."
2. Physical description of character—he often talks and reacts the way he looks.
3. Inside the character's brain:
   (a) A cerebral analysis of his place in the scheme of the play;
   (b) His emotional chemistry;
   (c) His spiritual status.
4. The life history or biography of the character.
5. The use of the director's, or actor's, recollection, recalling other actors, people, parts, or literary figures as an aid to seeing the role.
6. Story line, past and future as a motivation for a character.
7. Conflict, if any, physical, mental, or psychic.
8. Relationship to other characters in the play—what do they "think" about each other.
9. The use of parables. "Have you yourself ever been in a situation where . . ."
10. Analyze down to one, single, elementary idea or purpose, then rebuild.
11. Break down various moods, separate them. Have actor do first one mood, then the other, then both together.
12. Russian system of fantastic exaggeration, after which actor can be toned down to reality.
13. Tempi—employing actual musical rhythms to establish your point:
    (a) Directorial use of unarticulated inflection.
14. Grammar—parse sentences.
15. Drive the actors to exhaustion or to anger. (Not recommended.)

16. Teach by rote, but only as a last resort.
17. Get another actor.

Final Preparations. At the conclusion of the dress rehearsal, the director, utilizing her notes, calls her performers together and presents her suggestions for improvement. As a teacher she is aware, of course, that embarrassment of any one child should be avoided. All cuts, due to time requirements, must be noted on all scripts. If there is any question about the sequence of musical numbers or any units of the program, having them listed on a large blackboard, visible to all in the studio, can be quite reassuring.

A few minutes before program time the children should be given an opportunity to relax and to leave the studio if necessary. Again, if the director's attitude is one of concern and anxiety, the children will react accordingly. A smiling, confident countenance is the best send-off for the program.

When the performers have reassembled, sound effects and music are ready, scripts arranged, the director takes her place in the control room. Upon a cue from the engineer she starts the program on its way.

On the Air. The director is fully aware that the children are dependent upon her, not only for cues, but for an alertness to meet any emergency. If mistakes are made, then the teacher realizes that they are not committed deliberately. Resentment that is made evident probably will upset the child and cause more slips. A finished performance is certainly desirable, but the capable school director tempers her zeal and occasionally her disappointment with an understanding of the fact that the radio play is but the means and not the end of an educational experience.

Direction and Production Procedures in the School Radio Program

Whether it be in the school or at the station, the principles of good production are the same. Even with public-address equipment the teacher who is aware of these principles can do much to provide the fundamentals that will be needed in the studio.

Some of the elementary concepts which need emphasis are:

1. There is perspective in sound as there is in sight.

2. During the performance the director plays the leading role. She is not a spectator.

3. The presentation can be judged adequately, in most cases, only from the listener's position.

A brief discussion of these items will illustrate the importance of each in radio production.

Perspective in Sound. The teacher who is inexperienced in this field invariably has the children read directly on, and equidistantly from, the microphone, regardless of script requirements. With such direction, if a character is supposed to enter a room or if a traveler disappears in the distance in an outdoor scene, the position at the mike unfortunately remains constant. The result is apparent. There is no depth. Everything is flat. The director is drawing a picture without perspective. But once she has drawn the parallel between visual and auditory perspective she is able to add another dimension to the radio play by adjustment to microphone distances. However, caution is needed, for an "off mike" position may reduce clarity.

It has been said that "radio's spotlight is volume." If every performer plays every scene in the same position, then the spot light disappears and attention is fixed on no one in particular. Every character has the center of the stage. The presentation itself becomes drab and monotonous.

When the producer learns that the microphone is really the listener's ear and that it must be utilized accordingly, then improvement in production can be expected, for, as McGill notes, "A dramatic broadcast is no better than the illusion of depth that is achieved for it by the director by building sound perspectively." [10]

To give certain characters the center of the stage in the radio play, in other words, to have them get the listener's primary interest, the director can decide just who is to be "on mike." For instance, as some of the audience at Gettysburg discuss Lincoln's appearance before he arises to speak, is the mike to be with them or is it to be with the introductory speaker? Obviously they should not all "play the mike" at the same distance. It is the director's function to determine where she wants the spotlight placed.

---

[10] Earle McGill, *op. cit.*, p. 131.

The Director Plays the Leading Role. During the performance the director plays the leading role. The need for emphasizing this second principle is due largely to the teacher's past experience in other fields. Since many of those who undertake to present school radio programs have had some experience with the coaching of plays for the school stage, it is reasonable to expect that they would transfer some of their stage practices to the radio studio. In many ways this stage experience is invaluable, for acting is acting whether it be behind the footlights or in front of the microphone. The need for interpretation, for example, is present in either case, and the elements of "good theater" remain the same.

However, in transferring practices from one medium to another some adaptation must be made. One of the most harmful of these transfers which must be avoided is the supposition that in radio as on the stage the director, having rehearsed the performance, can then sit back and become a spectator.

Occasionally inexperienced teachers come into a studio assuming the performers can "cue" themselves, that sound effects will be heard automatically at the right instant, that the "level" always will be perfect, that the engineer can guess just when "fades" are to take place, and that timing the program is somebody else's problem.

Obviously such detachment from the production itself is to be deplored, particularly when the performers are immature. Actually, the radio presentation moves entirely about the director and, as stated above, she always plays the lead. The dramatic and musical performers, engineers and sound effects personnel, depend upon her in final production as well as in rehearsal.

The director's manner in cueing the performers often sets the tone of the presentation. If cues are given in a hesitant and confusing way, the actors themselves, even if not confused, are sure to "let down." But if the director, having carefully planned his action, proceeds in a confident and decisive manner, an improved production will result. It is therefore essential that all cues be marked on every script and that when the time comes for the cue to be given it is the director's responsibility to see that it *is* given, clearly and without hesitation. At the exact moment she must point directly at the performer involved.

If the radio director is to hold the reins of the play in her hands, if sound effects and music, for example, are to be heard as they have been planned, it is apparent that a carefully marked script is a necessity. It is probably fair to say that a good indication of a school radio director's ability is the amount of preliminary paper work undertaken by her. A script that has been studied and plotted serves as a road map to a successful performance. All cues are clearly noted so that every move is anticipated.

Radio Program Must Be Judged from Listener's Position. Only from the listener's position can a radio program be judged adequately. That statement seems almost too obvious to require discussion, and yet too many individuals try to direct a program while remaining in the studio with the performers. Thus they depend largely upon a visual judgment of perspective, pitch, volume, blending of sound effects, and fades.

Even professional directors, who are well acquainted with studio acoustics and blessed with experienced dramatic and technical help, usually resort to earphones when they direct from the studio. The inexperienced director should be in a position where she can judge what the listeners will hear. That place is not the studio, but the control room, beside the engineer.

Sometimes one hears, "Yes, I know I should be in the control room but I have an acting role in this radio play." The answer is, of course, that unless this would-be actor-director has had a good deal of experience she had better forego such multiple responsibility and concentrate her efforts on one job. If she must remain in the studio, then someone else should be responsible for the direction.

The statement made occasionally that young children cannot be directed effectively from the isolated control room is, in the writer's opinion, of no validity. If the children are trained to work at the director's cue, the distance from her is of little importance as long as she is clearly visible.

As the rehearsals continue, the director works in close cooperation with the technical and sound-effects operators. At every stage of the play the director keeps them informed as to the effects she desires. Although, as indicated previously, the perspective developed at the school may require some change at the radio station, nevertheless, much preliminary work can be accomplished. The orchestra can meet with the dramatic cast, and necessary cues and fades can be checked. It can be determined how many and perhaps what types of microphones will be needed, the director realizing that as she adds microphones she generally adds problems. The fewer microphones the better. This necessitates less rehearsal with the station technicians and cueing is easier.

Mistakes Noted in School Broadcasting

Whether in school or at the station, many of the mistakes made by the children during rehearsals can be noted by the director and called to the attention of the cast. Some of the children may not be in a correct position with reference to the microphone. Some may be too close, others too far away, and still others off on a side. There may be crowding at the microphone so that it is difficult for the next actor to step up. Some child may not be ready when his cue is given. Occasionally a child may not wait for his cue from the director but read ahead, perhaps anticipating a sound effect which, when it comes, is out of place. A procedure which some teachers have found helpful is to caution the children never to read after any sound effect until they have the director's cue. When the exceptions to this rule occur they can be noted. Of course, proper cueing and adjustment of microphone position cannot take place unless the children are trained to keep one eye on the director while they perform just as though they were instrumentalists in an orchestra.

The simple "do's" and "don'ts" listed in a handbook issued by the Inglewood (Calif.) Radio Guild are clear and to the point:

"Do's"

Underline character's name each time it appears.

Speak directly into the microphone. Move away or turn head when calling.

Make "ad lib" speeches fit the scene. Say definite lines.

Follow the entire script even though you are only a part of it. When you are not at the mike, take your seat and watch for your cue. Be ready several speeches in advance of your entrance.

Stay at the mike as long as another actor directs his line to you. Helps him to keep character.

Pick up cues quickly.

Separate pages of script before final production.

Always bring a pencil to rehearsals and broadcasts. Mark all changes in script whether or not they affect your lines.

Check the order of your pages just before the broadcast.

Hold script at eye level (just to one side of mike) so that your voice will be directed into the mike.

Use a full voice at a little distance from microphone rather than a low voice a few inches away. Work for relaxation, informality, and sincerity. Contractions add naturalness (don't, I'd, and so forth). Get variety into your speech by inflections, changes of pitch and of tempo.

See the situation and break up your lines according to the natural meaning. "Talk" them.

Keep the same distance from the microphone during a speech unless you are fading in or out.

Be careful of diction, especially the ends of the words. Avoid mispronouncing the vowels sounds in short words (*wuz* for *was*, *fer* for *for*).

PAY ATTENTION TO THE DIRECTOR AT ALL TIMES DURING REHEARSALS AND BROADCASTS.

"Don'ts"

Don't touch any part of the microphone.

Don't rattle scripts or let them touch the mike.

Don't hold script in front of your face.

Don't clear your throat, cough, shuffle your feet, or carry on a conversation in another part of the room.

Don't wait for the actor ahead of you to finish his line before you take your breath to pick up your cue.

Don't "hog" the mike when others are using it with you.

Don't run into another actor when leaving the microphone.

Don't "blast" by calling, laughing, or speaking too loudly while close to the instrument.

Don't correct yourself if you mispronounce a word. Go on.

Don't drop your character.

Don't overact. Be sincere in your part.

Don't talk in a monotone.[11]

Other Production Types: the Talk

With some adaptations the procedure described above is generally followed in producing the dramatized program. In presenting other school program types, such as conversational scripts, some of the steps described can be eliminated but the basic principles re-

[11] *Handbook of Radio Play Production*, Los Angeles County Schools, 1939, pp. 7–8.

main. There is always need of a proper level, exact timing, effective pacing, and intelligent interpretation. Incidentally, the teacher interested in radio direction can probably make arrangements with local stations to witness rehearsals and productions.

The Speaker.   The problems frequently met in presenting the radio talk suggest productional procedures which are applicable to other school script types.

Assuming that the script has been prepared, the first question that usually arises is, "Shall the writer also do the broadcasting?" There are those who feel that, if it is at all possible, the writer should be the one to "speak" her material to the children. They state that, since a thorough understanding of the child and the material to be broadcast is essential, the teacher who has prepared the script, and who presumably knows her audience, should be the one to broadcast. A more effective pace and a natural use of the written style are suggested as additional reasons for such a procedure.

A reply to this position was made by C. L. Menser, who said:

Too many times, the speaker has been selected only because he is an authority on his subject. This is a little bit like asking Clem McCarthy to run in the Kentucky Derby because he happens to know a great deal about horse racing. This is undoubtedly a carry-over from a classroom method which has gone too long unquestioned. An honest survey of the effectiveness of many a classroom lecture would bring some appalling revelations. Many a time the man who is the best qualified, so far as material for the talk is concerned, has a woebegone delivery which completely nullifies his expert knowledge.

In a medium which is dependent upon sound alone, and in a technique in which that sound comes from the human voice, it is highly important that we put considerable emphasis upon performance. Textbooks badly printed with blurred and illegible pages would not be tolerated for a moment. No more should the speaker whose performance is rated far below the authority of the material presented. The personality of the speaker, as it is reflected in his voice, is as surely an important element in the talk as is the material itself. The fact that the word "personality" has been misused greatly does not in any sense alter the conviction that it must be considered when discussing the effectiveness of a talk on the air. Much discussion on methods of arranging material for maximum effectiveness is to be found. We have had too little discussion on the personality of the speaker as reflected through his voice.

The implications for educational broadcasts are far-reaching. There is no more reason to believe that a man who is qualified to write a speech on geography, for instance, should deliver this speech in an educational broadcast, than there is to believe that a playwright should deliver his own play. Maxwell Anderson may feel that he knows all there is to know about *Winterset*, but it took a good cast and an effective presentation to make it win a critics' prize. Even so common a technique as the talk may need casting in order that content not be hampered by ineffective presentation. Such casting demands a keen sense of discrimination and absolute intellectual honesty. By "discrimination" I mean sound judgment as to what constitutes effectiveness in the human voice; by "intellectual honesty" I mean the ability to make that judgment paramount to all other considerations, in order to rule out those who have every reason to be on the air except their ability to broadcast.[12]

An acceptance of this argument does not imply that a commercial announcer should be used to present a third-grade lesson in English. It does mean that, if the script-writer's voice and delivery are poor, it would be better to use another teacher in the presentation of the script.

Timing the Talk.   As in the dramatic program, when the script for the talk has been completed one of the first problems is that of timing. The speaker is asked to fill the assigned broadcasting period, less 30 seconds for station operation and whatever time will be needed for announcements. Assuming that the opening and close will total a minute, the actual speaking time on a 15-minute program is 13½ minutes, and 28½ minutes on a half-hour program.

By using the stop watch and clocking his normal rate of delivery the speaker can learn quite definitely just how long the script runs. If the total running time is placed at the bottom of each page and later checked during delivery at the microphone, even the nonprofessional can determine whether his normal reading rate is being maintained.

What constitutes a normal rate cannot be stated arbitrarily, for much depends upon the type of material, the speaker's personality, and the type of audience. Floyd Gibbons's rate was 180 words a minute but most broadcasters are slower than that.[13] An early study conducted by Lumley on rates of speech used in radio indicated that "The average syllable rate was roughly 240 per minute and the word rate 160

---

[12] C. L. Menser, "A Demonstration of Contrasts in Techniques for Education," *Education on the Air*, Ohio State University, 1936, pp. 159–160.
[13] *Broadcasting Advertising*, IV (November, 1931), p. 12.

per minute. Slight differences were shown to exist between the rates of delivery for speakers addressing adults and those addressing school children. Figures for news talks showed that they were delivered at a faster rate than other talks." [14] The school broadcaster especially must be careful that her pace is not too fast. Some of the vocabulary she uses, though familiar to the children, may not always result in instantaneous recognition. New concepts, however simply they may be stated, are not quickly grasped by all the listeners. A rapid reader generally overlooks the value of a well-timed pause. Breathing is liable to be poor. The degree of sincerity and the effectiveness of emphasis also are limited by rapid reading.

Projecting Enthusiasm. The teacher accustomed to facing her classroom audience may feel handicapped when broadcasting to an unseen group. The stimulation that comes to her from seeing reactions on the faces of children is absent when she is alone in the studio facing nothing but an instrument. When broadcasting she is likely to regard her gestures and facial expressions as valueless. She may feel unduly concerned about the preciseness of her speech, for some of her colleagues are listening, too. The result is, in some cases, that her radio talk becomes a formal, mechanical, and impersonal presentation. The words are there, but the spirit, the enthusiasm which she evidences in the classroom are sadly lacking.

With more experience the radio teacher learns that her gestures and facial expressions are as important in the radio studio as they are in the classroom. Perhaps more so. Any animation which helps to make her message more vital and more personal should be maintained. She becomes aware that her muscular reactions are manifested in her speech. When, as she speaks, the "lines" on her face are up, her voice reflects it. When she smiles as she talks, her speech is more pleasant. When she uses gestures (without striking the microphone) her presentation is more vital. When she reads and looks bored, her listeners react the same way.

The broadcaster soon learns that the test of good radio reading is whether it sounds like talking. When it resembles talk, the presentation sounds spontaneous, not rehearsed. It is natural, not perfect. It

[14] F. H. Lumley, "Rates of Speech in Radio Speaking," *The Quarterly Journal of Speech*, XIX (June, 1933), p. 403.

deals with ideas rather than words, with feeling rather than sentences. The result is a conversation and not an oration.

She learns, also, that in her "mind's eye" she must see her audience in the classroom. Not as thousands of children collectively, but as a single classroom. She must talk to them as though she were a guest visiting them. To this extent her manner may differ somewhat from that of the commercial broadcaster who is advised to think of his audience as constituting two or three people at home listening to the radio. Yet she does not take the child's attention for granted. There is a certain friendly persuasiveness about her manner.

Suggestions for Improvement.   All this is more easily said than done. The beginner may be nervous, her breath control may be poor, sibilants may trouble her, her phrasing may be inadequate, and her reading colorless. It is well to ask, therefore, what the prospective broadcaster can do to improve herself. There is only one answer—practice in reading aloud. "A person who is going on the air should sit down with a friend and tell that friend what he intends to say and then read a part of his talk. The listener can tell him just how his conversation differs from his reading style and tone. It would be a better test if the friend would close his eyes or turn from the speaker while listening." [15]

In some schools, teachers have used a similar procedure by reading their materials from the rear of a classroom. The comments of the children are frequently helpful.

Suggestions by others are helpful, but self-analysis is even better. For this the recording has no superior. If the teacher records her talk and then analyzes it as it is reproduced, she will note many things which can be improved. Her voice quality may displease her, and though the chances are that she may be able to do but little with it, nevertheless, her style of delivery can be vastly improved. She may not realize to what extent her inflections monotonously rise and fall, or how the final word in each sentence is lost, or even how strangely artificial her manner is. But an awareness of these defects is the first step toward improvement.

The ability to relax is a great asset to one who would broadcast. If the muscles of the throat and chest are strained, a normally good voice sounds hard and unnatural.

---

[15] Waldo Abbot, *op. cit.*, p. 25.

A proper position before the microphone can help to put the speaker at ease. If, because of poor placement, she must reach for the mike or lower her head to talk into it, the effect will be undesirable. She will be unable to relax the throat and the muscles of the jaw as she should. Some teachers can do better while sitting, others prefer to stand. Both positions should be tried. If standing, the speaker must be careful not to sway to or from the microphone. Tight-fitting clothes seem to trouble some speakers, particularly men. Some find that when they loosen their ties and unbutton their vests and shirt collars they become much more at ease.

Excessive sibilance is not easily overcome. If it is due to the position of the teeth, as is frequently the case, then perhaps the easiest thing to do is to look for synonyms to replace words with "s" sounds— "boat," "liner," "whaler," "freighter" instead of "ship," etc. In some instances it may help to stand farther back from the microphone than one ordinarily would. Talking past the instrument rather than directly into it is also helpful in some cases.

In the early days of radio much mention was made of "mike fright" as though it were something unique to radio. However, platform speakers knew the symptoms long before the days of Marconi. The truth is that nearly everyone experiences some tenseness before going on the air. In general those who are so impassive that the experience stirs no emotion in them invariably are lifeless in their delivery. Excitement before speaking, when kept under control, can be a desirable thing if it results in a dynamic presentation.

Various suggestions have been made by which this nervousness may be controlled. For some individuals a minor hint seems to be of real help; for others extensive rehearsals and even continued appearances are of little value. Some broadcasters state that if they establish a rhythm of breathing before they begin to speak they can perform in a more relaxed manner. Some teachers prefer to read their material facing someone in the studio. The presence of an individual before them seems to help make their radio presentation more lifelike.

The best thing for the broadcaster to do is to fix her attention on the script. If she permits her mind to wander, "fluffs" may occur, with the usual result that she will become self-conscious, pick up speed, upset her breathing rhythm, and then read in an even worse manner. For this reason there is some danger in knowing the script content too well. A script marked with pauses and points of emphasis helps to fix attention on the material being delivered.

Proper phrasing is essentially good reading. With a narrow eye span, intelligent interpretation is difficult. If the reader has such difficulties, a marked script is again a great help, though, of course, the use of short sentences is the best plan.

The teacher who has had occasion to broadcast for some time must be on guard to see that she does not "let down." Experience is of no value if it interferes with enthusiasm and vitality. Ben Darrow calls attention to another possible danger. "There are many cases in which a broadcasting teacher becomes less rather than more efficient with experience. This is true of those who begin their broadcasting with a salutary meekness but turn prima-donna after a bit of praise. They begin to think of themselves when they should be thinking of the listeners. They speak to themselves and think how beautifully rounded their phrasing has become. They often attempt characterizations beyond their power. To continue to improve, the broadcaster must center his attention upon his message and forget himself completely." [16]

There are other minor suggestions that may be made to the potential broadcaster, some of them rather obvious. If she finds it necessary to clear her throat, cough or sneeze, the head should be turned away from the microphone. The smacking of lips is unpleasant. The rustle of paper not only destroys the illusion of "telling" but it distracts the listener's attention. Onionskin paper should not be used. If the manuscript is clipped together, the clip should be removed so that there is no shuffling of pages. The microphone should not be handled. All mechanical adjustments should be made by the station personnel and then left alone. The speaker must avoid too much movement or else the voice may be off the "beam." When the talk is finished nothing should be said until she is certain she is off the air. The line, "Thank goodness that's over!" is hardly a suitable close for the school program.

In concluding this discussion concerning the radio speaker, one other qualification should be noted, one that is perhaps basic—the need for being able "to take it," a willingness to accept criticism. Temperament, it has been said, is a luxury that not even the most talented school broadcaster can afford.

---

[16] Ben Darrow, *Radio Trailblazing*, College Book Co., 1940, p. 122.

6

Presenting the
Television Program

◇◇◇

What are the more common direction and production procedures in television?

What tools are available?

What preparatory steps must be taken in presenting a television demonstration?

How must some of the preparations be modified in using faculty and student personnel?

What steps can be taken so that the school series will be "invited back for a return engagement"?

What mistakes have been noted in early school telecasts?

How much time will the preparation and presentation of a television program require?

◇◇◇◇◇◇◇◇FOR SOME TIME to come, educators will plan, prepare, and even rehearse television programs, but they will not direct them on the air. That will have to be left to a staff director at the station which broadcasts the show. The technique of directing a television broadcast is so complicated and involves so many feats of coordination and split-second timing that considerable experience behind the cameras, at least as an assistant or associate director, is required before one can assume the responsibility for putting a production on the air. Moreover, while the problems and techniques of radio direction can be solved to a considerable extent in a simulated radio control room, using fairly inexpensive equipment, the handling of television cameras (to name only one, but the chief factor) can be practiced only with professional and highly expensive facilities. With the exception of a few universities, such as Iowa State College at Ames, American University and Syracuse University, opportunities for such practice are not readily available to the teacher.

Accordingly, the educator's function is likely to fall somewhere between the roles of producer, script writer and assistant to the director, frequently involving a combination of all three, and invariably demanding a large fund of flexibility and tact. The emphasis in this chapter, then, is placed necessarily on the teacher's role in preparing the program out of the studio, anticipating the needs and demands of the studio situation, and delivering a "half-baked" product, which is ready to be done to a turn under the studio lights. In no sense does this mean that the educator abdicates all rights and controls over educational content, nor the use to which pupils may be put; it merely confirms the realities of the situation which requires that the station man shall take over once the program comes into the studio and shall have the authority and responsibility necessary for a smooth and successful production.

The most common, most obvious, and most successful system is the team of a director from the station staff and a teacher from the school or school system that is cooperating in the broadcast or series. The latter is frequently a member of the radio staff who has augmented his radio training by reading, observation, and (where feasible) participation in the field of video broadcasting. It is self-evident that experience in amateur theatricals and the making of teaching films will be valuable supplements. And it is even more obvious that the earlier in the life of the program that the team of educator and station director can be formed the better. Throughout, it will be the duty of one to tell the other what is good broadcast education; the duty of the other to say what is good (and physically practical) television. It will help, of course, if each has some knowledge of the other's problems, and to that end this chapter will concern itself first with the tools available and problems involved in the most difficult type of television program, the dramatization.

The Tools Available

Television directors are fond of pointing out that whereas the radio director has only three tools to use (and to worry about) the television director has over a dozen, each of which can lend an added value to his program, but each of which can go wrong at the crucial moment. The three basic tools of radio, of course, are sound effects, music, and the human voice. We may put an actor's voice through a filter, we can pass it through an echo chamber, but fundamentally it remains a voice. The simple or elaborate mechanism of the radio studio, its wall surfaces, acoustical treatment, and microphones are all there to serve the proper pickup of voices or of live musical instruments, meaning those actually played in the studio.

In the television studio there is a much more elaborate and much more confusing display of equipment: cameras, lights, microphones (on movable, flexible booms), easels, projectors, screens, drapes, flats, and so on, far into the night and even farther into the budget. Yet these machines and gadgets are there for one and the same purpose —to pick up the program, the voices, faces, bodies of the participants and the items of demonstration, illustration or visual explanation which the participants will handle or describe.

Television begins with radio's three fundamental tools—voice, sound effects, and music—and adds any or all of the following elements.

Actors. Using the term actor to include anyone who participates in a television program brings us more closely back to the word's original meaning—the doer. The successful television participant or performer is one who *does* something in the course of his few moments before the cameras. Television actors must *look* the part as well as *sound* it, which imposes definite limitations on the use of student casts, despite the magic of make-up. The camera is not as kind as the eye of the sympathetic auditor in a school auditorium.

Group Movement. While the small size of the average television screen (under 20 inches in most homes and classrooms) makes the scene involving two or three characters the preferred one, ballet, square dancing, group drills, and many other types of presentation involving the rehearsed movement of many participants have been very effective. In the educational program, these would seem to be most applicable to programs concerned with music, the dance, and health education; but other uses will undoubtedly be developed.

Scenery. While whole settings are usually provided by the station as beyond the power of the schools to provide, individual units or elements such as a stained-glass window or a puppet stage are frequently supplied by a school where making sets for the annual play, for example, is a popular activity. The slightly amateurish quality of the work lends atmosphere and charm, particularly if the audience is informed that such an item was designed and executed by the children. Dimensions and color values, of course, must be checked with the art director of the station.

Costumes and Make-up. Costumes, where called for, are often supplied by the school, particularly when they have already been made for use in a school play or assembly program. Renting professional costumes, in most cities, is an expensive and involved process, something that both school and station try to avoid, since budgets for educational programs can rarely stand this additional burden.

Projected Elements. Under this heading may be lumped all those types of visualization which are not picked up by a television camera in the studio, but which come from the projection room of the station. A typical example would be a 16-mm. motion picture of students pouring into a school building in the morning, used as the opening sequence of a Board of Education series. The elements which normally come from the projection room include motion-picture film, both silent and sound; drawings or photographs for an opaque projector; transparent slides of various sizes; and strip film or slide film (if is known educationally under both names), usually produced on 35-mm. film.

Many of these media are already familiar to the teacher who makes active use of audio-visual aids. Two important considerations must be borne in mind:

1. It is wise to find out just what projection equipment your particular local station has available, that is, can it handle 35-mm. film or only 16-mm.; does it use 3- by 4-inch slides or 2- by 2-inch slides; has it a "balop," or opaque projector?

2. It is wise to test even professionally made materials on system, that is, to preview them on a video monitor well in advance of the air date, to be sure that they are technically acceptable. Such matters as size, aspect ratio (relation of height to width), and color value (if the materials are in color) are all-important and should be checked by station engineers well in advance of the broadcast, so that they may be remade or replaced by other items if technically unsatisfactory.

Models or Miniatures. Television borrows from motion pictures in extensive use of scale models and miniature settings to save space and money. Still and working models, dioramas, and miniature replicas of many objects, other than planes and sailing ships, are to be found in the audio-visual aids library or in the supply closets of schools. So long as the miniature has been reproduced to scale—any scale—the television camera can come in close enough to make it look life-size.

Still Pictures. Still pictures (or *pix* in studio slang) are not so convenient as slides or strip film, since they must be "shot" by a studio camera. However, when the time or the money to make slides is lacking, stills can be mounted on cardboard and placed on an easel, ready for a "live" camera. Stills may be photographs, drawings, graphs, charts, or almost any form of graphic representation. Black and white is always safer than color, and larger stills (11 by 14 inches and up) are always more convenient than small ones. Once again, in preparing the stills the school director should seek the advice of the station's art director, although three standard rules will be helpful:

1. Always observe the 3 by 4 unit aspect ratio; 3 units high by 4 units wide.

2. Always leave a margin of 25 per cent of blank area around the subject itself.
3. Always use matte finish rather than glossy prints if at all possible.

"Pull-outs." "Pull-outs" are stills to which a rough semblance of movement is given. The classic (and outworn) example is the bar graph in which the various items are represented by windows in a skyscraper. As each bar is to be shown, a black shield is pulled out from behind that particular vertical row of windows. Light from behind the graph shines through translucent rectangles cut in the basic cardboard of the "pull-out," and the light seems to streak up that bar to the desired height. Many hundreds of variations, involving three and four sheets of transparent acetate, or "cellies," have been devised, with sheets of black paper interleaved between the "cellies," with additional material revealed as each sheet of black paper is pulled out in its turn.

Floor Animations. True animation, of the type associated with Walt Disney's film cartoons, is an expensive and lengthy process. Floor animation is television's attempt, often a bit rough, to add controlled movement to a drawing. One method calls for rear illumination, with the elements to be shown (on a ground-glass screen) cut out of cardboard so that a desired silhouette is outlined as the light shines through the space in the cardboard. Another variety is the Bretzicon, a front-illuminated ground-glass screen. For example, a map is drawn on the glass, or on architect's tracing cloth, and cut-outs made of white cardboard are pressed against the screen. The cut-out shows only when pressed against the screen; it may appear magically, and may be moved about on the screen by the black-gloved hand of an operator who becomes invisible to the camera. The value of such devices in the teaching of the social studies, for example, is obvious. Yet the enthusiastic educator must be warned that not all studios are equipped with such devices.

Special Effects. Whole books have been written on the subject of special effects. In no branch of television are the imagination and ingenuity of the artisan so challenged as by this catch-all division. Any particular effect which is not achieved by the other standard means described above is a special effect. It may range from some thing as simple as a small ring of fire which is superimposed about the 6-foot form of Mephistopheles or a bit of dry ice at the bottom of Faust's magic potion to cause it to "steam," to something as elaborate as an earthquake or a scene under the sea. In general, special effects are rarely at the disposal of the average educational program, since they are costly in time and effort, if not in materials. Unless given adequate rehearsal time before the cameras, they may backfire with disastrous and hilarious results.

Materials the School Can Supply.   In the previous chapter, we have described the wealth of televisable material to be found in any well-equipped audio-visual aids library. In the last few pages mention has been made of school-provided scenery and costumes. Still pictures can be furnished by school photographers; drawings, charts and graphs, signs and title cards can be drawn and lettered by students in art classes. Such cooperation, while imposing on the teacher in charge of the whole program the added burden of enlisting the aid of colleagues in other departments, has a double value. It earns the gratitude of the station, which realizes full well that it is getting the free use of material that would be prohibitively expensive to rent or make; and it gives more teachers and students the opportunity to be part of the program, to make a valuable contribution, to see their work on the air.

Again, at the risk of being boringly repetitious, the teacher is reminded to consult the staff director assigned to the program and the station's art director to ensure the technical acceptability of such items, be they props, film, or art work; and to be sure that anything purchased by the school from an outside agency for use in the classroom has been cleared for use on the air. This is not important in the case of standard maps and charts, but is of the utmost importance in connection with the video use of commercially produced film. One last item the school can frequently provide is transportation. Where a school truck from the bureau of supplies is available, in most cities, it must be reserved weeks in advance. When a station wagon owned by a cooperative parent or fellow teacher will be used, that too must be known. In any event, the station will appreciate receiving all material at least one or two days in advance of the broadcast.

Preparatory Steps

For purposes of covering the most elaborate production
routine possible, this section will discuss the steps involved in presenting a dramatization, the most complicated format on television as on
radio. Many of these steps, of course, are contracted, combined or
omitted in the production of simpler and easier formats.

Preliminary Conference. Once a station has agreed to
present a program or a series, it usually assigns a producer, a director,
or sometimes both, to this particular project. The teacher or teachers
who are to represent the school or school system, it is presumed, will
already have been selected by the appropriate school authorities. The
"team" convenes at the earliest possible opportunity, and its members
decide what they are going to do. The purpose of the program, of
course, comes first. Then the format which will best accomplish that
purpose, within the limitations of the facilities and studio rehearsal
time available for this broadcast, is determined. If the program is to be
scripted, rather than "ad libbed" about a central outline (see examples
in Chapter 4), the script writer must be selected. Is he, or she, to be
provided by the station or by the school? Perhaps the teacher assigned
to produce the program for the school will also script it.

Preparing the Script. Attention has been given to this
problem in Chapter 4. Let us assume that this program is to be scripted
by a writer from the school system who has had some television training. The rough draft of the script is gone over by the teacher-producer
for educational effectiveness, and by the station director for television
practicality. Then the three (producer, director, and writer) meet
again to pool their comments and work out solutions to problems. The
writer then completes a revised draft. Let us be optimistic and assume
that this second revision is approved by all concerned. It is now mimeographed (usually by the school) and a half dozen copies are provided
for the station's use. One copy will go to continuity acceptance to
make sure that the script is not contrary to any point of station policy.
Another will go to the production manager for the assignment of
technical facilities; a third to the art director. The director of the
program may want two or three for his own use and that of his assistants.

Who Is to Supply What?   It is most helpful to have a complete list of the personnel required ("cast" will do for lack of a better word) and a list of props, furniture, stills, and so on. The writer who takes the time to prepare an accurate inventory of the items needed for his script earns the gratitude of all hands. The team meets again and determines definitely which items can be supplied by the station and which will be provided by the school. It is good practice to make up a list, indicating clearly the source of each item to be used. This prevents misunderstandings and last-minute crises.

Floor Plan.   It may be possible for the director to have ready at this production conference the floor plan of his set or sets. This is a scale drawing, showing a bird's-eye view of the set with scenery and major furniture marked. From this plan the teacher can create a rough duplicate of the set in the classroom or auditorium in which the cast will rehearse. Chalk lines will do for walls, and school furniture has represented everything from the furnishings of a palace to the few sticks of a slum. If the floor plan is not available at the first production conference, after the acceptance of the script, it should be provided by the director at the earliest possible moment and before rehearsals have gone very far.

Casting.   When his crowded schedule permits, the station director will want to be present at the final casting. Usually he will be too busy and will have to trust to the teacher's judgment. By the time they have done two or three programs together, the teacher will know the needs of television, whether for a drama, a discussion program, or a simple demonstration. In general, suitability of appearance and voice, a convincing and natural quality, and flexibility are all more important than beauty or photogenic quality. Of course, a little talent and personality never hurt.

Music.   Once again, all hands must know whether music is to be provided by the station or by the school. If it is to be recorded music, the station may prefer to supply it from its own library. If the school is to provide the records, they should be fairly new copies which have not been played too often. When finances permit, one set of disks is used for rehearsals, with fresh copies reserved for dress rehearsal and use on the air.

Sometimes the station has a staff pianist or organist; sometimes the school provides a teacher-accompanist. Student musicians under the age of sixteen are usually given clearance by the local branch of the American Federation of Musicians, with whom almost all stations have contracts. For adults who are not members of the union, special permission must be secured. The selections themselves must be cleared by the station's music department, to be sure that these compositions are available for broadcast.

Sound Effects. While sound is rarely required for any but dramatic programs, it may, for example, be a part of a science demonstration. Directors of school radio workshops may be shocked to discover that their own sound effects departments excel those of many small television stations, particularly when it comes to manual effects. In any event, when sound effects are needed, it is wise to check with the station well ahead of time.

Rehearsals. If the station director can be present at the first "dry run" rehearsal, usually at the school, to block out the main lines of action and movement in terms of his cameras, that will be invaluable. If not, director and teacher may sit down together, prior to rehearsals, and "block the show" on a copy of the floor plan. The teacher then will continue to direct rehearsals in consonance with the working areas determined at this preliminary meeting. Possibly the director can be present to watch one rehearsal, plan his shots, and make some suggestions before the cast finally comes down to the studio. If not, he will count on making any necessary changes and marking his shooting script on the day of the broadcast. This sounds rough, and it frequently is, but television people work at high speeds. They have to.

A-Day—Air Date. Let us assume that all physical items— props, stills, and film—have been checked well before the broadcast date. While the set is being put up and the props placed where needed, the station director will probably want to go through one or more rehearsals in a "dry run" rehearsal room somewhere in the studio building. Here he will take over completely, and the wise teacher will have prepared the cast for such a situation. Any line changes in the script will already have been conveyed to the station director and marked by him in the scripts of all his staff. The director will have marked his basic "shots" in his script and will be changing them as he finally sees the cast go through its paces. He may change

positions, alter groupings, and rehearse special cues which the participants must give him accurately when film or slides are integrated with
the live material.

Sometimes it will be possible for the cast to go through the program
once without cameras but in the actual set and with the real props
and stills. Sometimes they will "go on camera" immediately after the
"dry run."

Where is the teacher to be during camera rehearsal? There can be
no question that future programs will benefit most by having the
teacher in the control room, standing quietly behind the director and
making notes, both mentally and in writing. Only by seeing the
director's problems from the control room can the educator anticipate
them and master them in subsequent productions. However, it is
often necessary to have someone known to the cast near them on the
studio floor, preferably someone with authority and control. A solution that is frequently used is to have two teachers work with the
cast all along, so that one can be with the students in the studio while
the other assists the director in the control room.

If the station's rehearsal schedule permits, the director will go
through the program at least twice: once to rough out his camera
movements, to acquaint his cameramen with their shots and moves,
and to familiarize the cast with the strange studio equipment. The
second run-through (or the third, under ideal conditions) is a dress
rehearsal, in which all concerned try to give the same performance
they will give on the air. In any event, after the last camera rehearsal,
director and educator go down to the cast, give them final corrections
and instructions, and polish any rough spots that still need smoothing
out. Sometimes this is done in 10 or 15 minutes just before air time;
sometimes the rehearsal has to be scheduled for the morning or early
afternoon, anywhere from a half-hour to a half-day removed from air
time. In the latter case, the cast will have ample time to take a light
once-over, to have a light bite to eat, to relax a bit (but not too much)
before going on.

As the program goes on the air, the teacher who has prepared it
will certainly want to see how it looks on the television screen. If she
is in the control room, an air monitor or line monitor will give her a
somewhat better picture than the one in the average classroom or

home. If she is standing by her charges on the floor, she may be able to watch a "jeep," or floor monitor, a portable television receiver with its sound turned off. On the screen of the average jeep she can see a somewhat inferior picture, as far as clarity goes, but she will know what the program is like. And therein lies the proof of the pudding —not how it looked in rehearsal, not how it seemed to go in the studio, but how it came over the air.

As the program ends, the well-trained cast will hold its places until released by the floor manager, and then leave quietly by designated routes through designated exits to an area outside the studio doors. Only then should mutual congratulations and self-reproaches be permitted, since other programs may be following immediately in the same studio. The cast cleans up, picks up *all* personal belongings, leaves the building with a minimum of disturbance to the rest of the station's personnel, and dashes for home to receive the congratulations of admiring family and friends. The teacher-producer hastens to telephone supervisors and colleagues from whom she may expect a more valid judgment, having first checked to determine when she may return to reclaim the school-owned materials which were used on the program. Many hours of work may still await her, but for the moment let us leave the postbroadcast activities until after we have discussed modifications of the schedule we have just described.

Modifications and Simplifications

It is reassuring to note that not all of the steps and procedures listed above are necessary for all programs. Any series, for example, which continues regularly will soon establish a routine of consultation and preparation. If the same general setting is used each week, which is true of most programs, there will be few technical problems to settle each time. Title cards and most of the art work will be repeated and can be stored at the station. The floor plan will not change, and the teacher-producer will soon know its dimensions by heart. Most educational programs, as we have observed, are not fully scripted but merely outlined, so that continuity acceptance is a simple matter. Music once cleared may be used again and again, and so on.

Above, Rochester's
Junior Town
Meeting.

Left, Student round-
table discussion.

Hawkins Street School kindergarten class at Radio Station WBGO.

Elementary school pupils do art work for the TV camera; parents watch.

The basic steps which can rarely be omitted are these:

1. A preliminary conference to go over the content of the program.
2. A list of the items to be supplied by each party.
3. A dry rehearsal (or several) away from the studio.
4. A dry run at the station, in the set if possible, if not in a dry rehearsal room.
5. One or more camera rehearsals (if there is time for only one, that *is* the dress rehearsal).
6. Revision and polishing; cuts or additions for the sake of timing; necessary changes.
7. Air show (and all that it entails).
8. Cleanup.

It must be obvious that a discussion program, an interview, or a science demonstration, while posing unique problems of their own, will not require the weeks of rehearsal and preparation involved in a dramatization. But even the simplest program involves a number of postbroadcast steps, and it is to this area that we now turn.

Ensuring a Return Engagement

If the hypothetical program we have been discussing was a "one-shot," a broadcast meant for one time only, or an experimental show done to determine whether a whole series would be worth doing, it is very much to the educator's interest to have the station want more. If the program was one of a series, the continuation of that series may depend on the program's cost, its success in terms of audience response, its ability to be produced without disrupting the entire operation of the whole station. The end of the series will bring the same thought to the minds of the station manager and the educational administrators: Has the whole thing been worth the cost? For it has cost both the school system and the station much, not in money, perhaps, but in man-hours and the disruption of normal schedules. What are some of the steps we may take to make everybody feel that the program was worth its price?

Cleanup. Nothing will keep the teacher-producer on better terms with his friends at the station and his friends at school than the prompt and thorough removal from the station of all borrowed materials and their prompt return to the libraries, audio-visual storerooms, and filing cases from whence they came. Television is a horizontal activity; it needs room in which to spread out, in which to store its myriad lares and penates. And most fire departments take a dim view of storing stuff in hallways and corridors! So prompt removal of material no longer needed is imperative.

Follow-up. Once the novelty of television has passed, all concerned must seek objective evidence of the program's value. If it was received in several classrooms, the evaluation techniques we have described earlier come into play. If the program was aired during evening hours, some evidence of its having been seen and enjoyed may be gained from letters or postcards from students and parents. These may quite ethically be suggested, but avoid the mechanical message which some well-intentioned teachers produce by assigning a letter of thanks or praise. Honest comment, especially when accompanied by constructive criticism, is of far more value.

The teacher who worked on the show, however, is thoroughly in order in writing to the station manager to thank him for the cooperation extended by the members of his staff. If she can enclose evidence of the program's value and acceptability, of the fact that the station's time and trouble were well invested, she has done much to ensure that return engagement. If supervisors are moved to write similarly, the station manager will cherish their correspondence for submission to the Federal Communications Commission as evidence of his serving "the public interest, convenience and necessity."

Evaluating Personnel. When the smoke and heat of the battle have abated, the educator and the director may want to meet again to discuss the participants of a program or a series, with an eye toward inviting some of them back for the next series. Television is an exacting medium, and gifted teachers may fail to project their personalities through that cold glass eye in the camera. Student participants, too, may have been exceptionally poor or exceptionally good, and while it is good education to give as many as possible an opportunity to face the cameras, it is not good policy to inflict poor talent on the long-suffering audience. There are numerous factors to consider, but they all boil down to the fact that some participants were easy to work with, took direction and "came across" on the screen; others did not. While not all the participants in the next series will be drawn from those who did well in the past one, since there are both tactful and technical reasons for discovering new talent, it will help immeasurably to have a nucleus of seasoned and capable veterans on whom to draw. It is wise to make up a simple card index of such people while the completed program or series is still fresh in the memories of teacher and director.

Some Early Mistakes

Histories of radio broadcasting tell us of the errors that were made by early educational broadcasters; errors that led the great majority of the early college-owned stations to abandon their frequencies. Similar errors have developed in television, but since everything in video seems to move at fantastic speeds, the recognition of such mistakes seems to be proceeding quite rapidly. There are a goodly number, but the four most frequent are discussed briefly here.

The Straight Talk. Despite the frequent asking of television's basic question, "What are they looking at now?" many program planners fell into the error of seating a capable lecturer before the cameras and having him talk to the audience. A few have succeeded, but it takes a tremendously attractive and persuasive personality to hold an audience simply by looking at them and talking to them. As for reading a prepared script or glancing down frequently to check an outline, that type of video behavior has been aptly described as an "audience chaser."

The most successful talks, of course, are ad libbed. They are frequently disguised as interviews, with a skillful professional drawing out the educator. And visual aids, such as working models, miniatures, slides and film, are needed here as much as, or more than, in any other program type.

Symposium vs. Discussion. Strangely enough, the discussion program, which would seem to be purely aural in nature, has proved tremendously successful in television. Its appeal seems to derive from the audience's ability to observe the reactions of the participants as they lock horns. Such programs as *Court of Current Issues, Meet the Press, On Trial,* and *Author Meets the Critics* point up one important factor, however—the necessary element is controversy, as conflict is the essential of drama. The well-meaning citizens who gather to make prepared speeches on the various angles of a given issue, even though they may differ slightly in the means they propose for solution, will not provide conflict. It is in the exchange of thrust and counterthrust between prominent personalities, in the rapier play of keen minds in sincere opposition, in the occasional heated exchanges of facts and opinions that the television discussion audience seems to find its chief enjoyment. All this, of course, applies to telecasts of adult discussion. Viewers of student discussion naturally are more likely to find keen interest in a vigorous exchange of conflicting points of view than in a harmonious series of forensic contributions, which differ only in minor ways and means, to the solution of a problem on whose major issues all participants are in agreement. The student minds, of course, may not be as keen as those of their elders, but their expression is frequently more forthright and engaging.

The Student Talent Show. The commercial success of amateur hours and children's song-and-dance competitions has impelled many local stations to seek a school program of similar nature. Insofar as it demonstrates the work being done by teachers of music and health education, such a broadcast may be justified. But station operators rarely want glee clubs and dance groups; they prefer soloists and dance teams, which usually reflect *training* rather than *education.* If we add the competitive emphasis, the stress on the number of votes received by each contestant, the value of the prize awarded the winner, we may or may not have entertainment, but we rarely have education. Many educational leaders seriously question whether a school system should lend its support to a program of this type, whether it be sponsored or sustaining. One may seriously wonder what such a show accomplishes, beyond attracting an undeniable audience.

The Student Quiz. Quiz programs have their value in radio, although again many leaders in the field remind us that "information is not education." The quiz program can bring out information in an attractive manner, and it may be genuinely educational both for its participants and its audience. When, however, directors yield to the temptation to increase the program's appeal by stressing the competitive angle unduly, so that the losing team feels it has disgraced its school, and when contestants are required to give brief, completely factual answers in order to "keep the show moving," the educational values are nullified. Giving a contestant ample time in which to perform an experiment and explain its basic principles or to find an area on the map and explain how its location has determined its economy and its culture may not keep the entire viewing public on the edge of its chairs, but will provide contestants and viewers with a more profitable experience.

Estimating the Cost in Time and Effort

It is difficult to guess at the number of man-hours required to prepare a program, to see it through from initial concept to completion and cleanup, even after the telecast is over. It is even more difficult to estimate what the average program of a given type will require in time and effort, since both the station facilities and school resources differ widely from city to city. In general, the more complicated formats, such as dramatizations, musical and dance programs, can be calculated as requiring the same amount of time needed to prepare a similar program for an assembly, *plus* 15 to 20 hours of application to television. Since the average assembly program usually receives a minimum of four afternoons a week for two or three weeks, we can see that producing such a show for television would be a fairly time-consuming undertaking.

An interview, on the other hand, might require little more time than it would need on radio: 2 to 3 hours of preparation, rehearsal, and air time, all told, once the guest for the interview had been secured. A discussion program involving a group of high-school students may consume 6 to 10 hours of student and teacher time, but much of that time is itself an educational experience. A skillful demonstrator, using scientific apparatus already developed for the classroom, could adapt his coverage of a specific subject in an hour, rehearse for half an hour and tack on a 15-minute broadcast for a total which would be under 2 hours, exclusive of time spent in waiting—something never to be eliminated, apparently, in the theater, motion pictures, or television. That is one of radio's great advantages—you rarely have to stand about waiting for the studio to be readied.

There are exceptions to all rules. In small stations, a staff director may be responsible for as much as 20 hours of air time a week, which will leave him but few moments to help an educator. The latter's consumption of time will go up accordingly. In the few cities which are doing extensive television programming for schools, however, members of the radio-television staff average two or three programs a week, with varying numbers of radio programs as well. While the formats are less ambitious and each series tends to follow a pattern, the results are good, and the average educator's time load per program would seem to be 3 to 5 hours per week.

In the average school system, where the teacher assigned to working on television programs would very likely be devoting a good share of her time to radio as well, the following generalization might provide a rough rule of thumb: for each television series undertaken, the producing teacher should be relieved of one-third of her previous weekly responsibilities, at least for the first year of operation. As she gains in experience, as each series shakes down into a more thoroughly mastered routine, she may undertake more than three programs a week; but for that first year of telecasting, three video shows a week will be all she can manage without flirting with a nervous breakdown.

7

Selecting and Using the Program

◇◇

What sources of program information are available?

How does the teacher select and use programs?

How does the teacher's purpose determine utilization?

Before the program begins, what preparatory steps are helpful?

What should be done during the program?

What are the most common objectives of the follow-up period?

Does all this apply to television programs?

How and to what degree should the teacher assign and utilize the out-of-school program?

◇◇◇◇◇◇◇◇IT IS A SIMPLE MATTER to suggest to the teacher that the value her pupils will receive from the radio program will depend largely upon the use she makes of it in the classroom. But the effective use of radio in the classroom is closely allied to several factors, some beyond the teacher's control.

What if she tunes in to find a program wholly unrelated to the abilities, needs, and interests of her pupils? Then effective utilization is largely wishful thinking. Or, if the desirable program conflicts with the school schedule, the same situation results.

Whether, and to what extent, these and similar problems can be solved by the use of recordings, school-owned and -operated stations, and other methods will not be discussed in this chapter. Such difficulties must be recognized, however, before there can be an honest discussion of classroom procedures. The solution to these problems will bring about general acceptance and widespread use of radio in education, but there can be no solution without a thorough understanding by the teacher of the problems involved.

To the capable teacher there is nothing new involved in the utilization of a radio program. Fundamentally, the procedures used are the same as those adopted by good teachers in the classroom use of many other materials: textbooks, films, maps, and so on. It is axiomatic that the best teachers make the best use of most teaching aids, and that the teachers who need these aids most use them least.

Use Begins with Selection

Unfortunately, the very nature of radio does not permit the teacher to pre-audit the program, unless recordings or repeat programs are available. There is, generally, complete dependence on whatever advance notices may be had. These notices are seldom thorough enough to be of very much value to the teacher. They are of some help, though, and may prevent *missing* a program of value; for once missed, a program can seldom be heard again.

Teachers should be familiar with the numerous sources of program information available to them. They will then make the most of all existing programs of educational value. There are two main classifications of advance program information: those that relate to a variety of programs and those that are concerned primarily with one program or one series.

Program Information: General

Newspapers. The daily schedule carried in the local newspapers is the most common source and generally the most accurate. It indicates what network programs are carried locally and mentions special broadcasts, yet from the teacher's point of view it is far from satisfactory, since the program notes, if any, are generally too brief for classroom use. Unfortunately most radio columns are merely a collection of press agent "blurbs." Some newspapers are obviously reluctant to promote a competitive advertising medium.

Local Radio Station Weekly Schedules. These schedules, though subject to change, are helpful, since they may provide the teacher with some time to plan for the reception of the program. They seldom include any description of programs. A few local commercial stations, such as Kansas City's KMBC, Philadelphia's WFIL and WIP, and Chicago's WLS, issue more detailed publications.

Magazines. One publication that teachers interested in radio should know is the *Journal of the AER* (Association for Education by Radio). It is published monthly during the school year and goes to all members of the association. It contains articles by leaders in radio education, a survey of local developments, a section on broadcasts for schools, an exchange department, and reviews of radio literature. (It is a sad commentary on American radio that there is no publication in this country comparable to the British *Listener,* which is prepared primarily to help the discriminating lay listener.) The trade weekly *Variety* carries reviews of radio programs though generally they are written from the point of view of the producer rather than of the consumer. However, some of these reviews are helpful in developing a list of standards for the evaluation of out-of-school programs.

School Systems and Universities. Several of the large school systems, state departments of education, and university-owned radio stations issue radio program logs, station schedules, and utilization handbooks which are of value to those schools within the areas of "coverage." An outstanding publication which includes information about motion pictures and the press, as well as radio, is *The News Letter*, published monthly, except June, July, August, and September, by the Bureau of Educational Research, Ohio State University.

The materials issued by the Wisconsin, Ohio, and Minnesota Schools of the Air, the Radio Council of Chicago Public Schools, the Texas State Department of Education, and the Cleveland, Newark, New York City, and Detroit Public Schools are noteworthy.

Networks. The major networks issue educational programs lists upon request. However, from the classroom teacher's point of view it is regrettable that the detailed bulletins and manuals formerly issued by NBC and CBS are no longer available. Of course, that is to be expected, now that *there is not a single classroom radio series in this country presented on a national network.* When an American, living in the wealthiest nation of the world, compares this state of affairs with the relative abundance of educational radio offerings available to Canadian children, the contrast is—and should be— disturbing.

Government Bulletins. The United States Office of Education issues materials which are extremely helpful in the school radio field. The Service Bulletin of the Federal Radio Education Committee is a splendid contribution. In addition, this office issues a radio manual, a bibliography, a radio glossary, a newsletter, extensive catalogues of scripts and transcriptions which are on loan, and numerous pamphlets on specific radio subjects.

Organizations. Various educational and broadcasting groups collect program information that is generally of interest to the classroom teacher. Some of the better-known agencies are:

Association for Education by Radio-Television, 228 North LaSalle Street, Chicago 1, Illinois.

Institute for Education by Radio, Ohio State University, Columbus 10, Ohio.

National Association of Broadcasters, 1771 N St., N.W., Washington, D.C.

National Association of Educational Broadcasters, Station WNYC, New York, N.Y.

Federal Radio Education Committee, United States Office of Education, Federal Security Agency, Washington, D.C.

Program Information: Specific

The second type of radio program information which teachers can use deals with a certain series or with a single program. These advance notices assume a great variety of forms, and for purposes of simplification they will be grouped here under the following heads: (a) those program notes issued by commercial radio organizations; (b) those developed by university-owned radio stations; (c) and those program guides developed by city school systems utilizing the radio as a teaching aid.

No attempt is made here to present what the writers consider to be the best radio program aids. The purpose is to discuss briefly features which were helpful to classroom teachers.

Publications Issued by Commercial Radio Organizations. Perhaps the most widely used publication of this type was the teacher's manual issued annually by the CBS American School of the Air. These programs have unfortunately been discontinued, and it is pointless to analyze in detail the items contained therein. A unique feature, however, will be mentioned, since the technique can be adapted to local broadcasts. The CBS series *This Living World* was of particular value to the alert classroom teacher. The program was constructed so that her own pupils could actively participate in the series, which was devoted to a discussion of current events and postwar problems.

An excerpt from the teacher's manual stated:

The typical *This Living World* program is composed of a presentation of the subject to be considered, followed by an eight-minute high school student discussion. This pattern will be followed during the coming year, except in the case of a few programs falling on school holidays.

Boys and girls will thus have regular opportunities to go on the air and talk about problems vitally affecting their future—problems which in a few years they will deal with as voters. One student group will be heard each Friday from New York. Other groups will be presented by local CBS stations, which will cut away from the network at the conclusion of the first part of the program, and give youth in their own communities a chance to participate. CBS encourages the activities of these local groups, which have numbered as many as forty during the past year.

Even if the teacher does not find it possible for her pupils to broadcast their follow-up discussion, a simulated broadcast in the classroom also has great value. The panel can be rotated each week so that by the end of the series every pupil has had at least one opportunity to participate.

Only one other teacher's manual of this type will be mentioned, the beautifully illustrated booklet which accompanies the Standard School Broadcast. The manual includes:

1. A summary of each broadcast.
2. Musical themes for the blackboard.
3. Lists of music to be played.
4. Vocabularies.
5. Biographical chart of composers.
6. Musical charts.
7. Reproductions of art correlations.
8. Photos of symphony musicians.
9. Pictorialized teaching instructions.

Teachers who reside on the West Coast, where this series is heard, find especially helpful the correlation which this series emphasizes between music, art, and social studies.

Postbroadcast publication of radio scripts has been used by a number of agencies in cooperation with the various networks. For advance information such procedures are of little value to the classroom teacher, although the possession of the transcript itself does contribute to improved utilization. A transcript enables one to study the material presented, serves as a source for future reference, and can be used to distribute information to those who may not have heard the program. Some scripts suggest a pattern for in-school programs.

Among the better-known postbroadcast publications are those issued in conjunction with the *University of Chicago Round Table* and *America's Town Meeting of the Air.*

The Round Table notes include not only the comments of the various participants, but also supplementary information, questions for analysis and discussion, objective questions for examination, excerpts from various speeches, letters from listeners, and suggested readings for future programs.

The Town Meeting bulletin presents the formal radio addresses and verbatim reports of the question-answer phase of the program. A selected bibliography of both current articles and books pertaining to the subject being discussed is also included. This postbroadcast publication is but one phase of the *Town Meeting* program publicity. The advance program information issued by this organization is quite complete.

To aid classes in utilizing this series the Town Hall Advisory Service issues a statement of the background of the topic to be discussed and the issues involved, an annotated reading list, and biographical sketches concerning the speakers.

Instead of script transcripts, a summary of the radio address has been used occasionally. For instance, CBS issued the magazine *Talks*, "a quarterly digest of addresses of diversified interest broadcast over the Columbia Network."

Program Guides Issued by University-Owned Radio Stations. Teachers who are within the range of university stations will find excellent classroom programs available. As would be expected, the material in the manuals issued by such stations is more specific in character and occasionally less formal. A good example of a guide prepared for teachers is the following excerpt from the popular series on elementary science, *Science Club of the Air*, presented by Station WOSU, Ohio State University.

LET'S FIND OUT IF IT'S TRUE:
FACT VERSUS SUPERSTITION

Our Problem: Are the weather myths, sayings, and folklore stories always true?

Do You Know:

1. If the ground hog can predict weather?
2. If the saying "Rain before seven, clear before eleven" can be proved scientifically?
3. Some of the myths and stories of olden times with which people tried to explain thunder, lightning, and other happenings?
4. The difference between a superstition and a fact?
5. What to do when someone makes a statement to explain something which doesn't sound right?

For the Broadcast:

People have always wanted an explanation of happenings, events, and other phenomena of their natural environment. This has resulted in many beliefs based on unscientific ideas and practices, long discarded as incorrect, but which are still being used to predict consequences.

Today's program will explore dramatically some of the more common superstitions to show how they are unfounded in fact and to point out the importance of seeking correct interpretations as a means of dispelling superstitions and ungrounded fears.

Related Activities and Experiments:

1. Start keeping a daily record of the weather including temperature, clouds, and wind, to see if the ground hog foretold the weather.
2. Make a list of superstitions and have the children check them.
3. The moon is often used to determine when the plant crops. Ask farmers who planted by the moon and those who did not what the crop yield was in each case.
4. Try to find some of the superstitions used by sailors or by people in fields such as medicine.
5. Check the weather forecast in the World Almanac with the actual weather reports as printed in a newspaper for a given period of time.

Publications Prepared by City School Systems.   The manuals issued by school systems which present classroom radio programs are among the most complete. The fact that in most cases the series is prepared with a specific course of study in mind makes it easier to incorporate detailed information. Teachers using these guides receive a complete lesson plan. However, adaptation to specific class needs is always essential.

In addition to the usual script synopsis and suggestions to be considered before, during, and after the broadcast, as well as suggested readings, some of the manuals include visual aids such as maps, photographs and charts. These can be used by the teacher to give "eyes" to the program.

In some communities the classroom teachers using the programs receive other types of assistance. For example, one of the series presented by Station WBEZ of the Chicago Public Schools is supplemented by special tours and lectures planned for classroom listeners. Tickets of admission are printed in the manual which permit student representatives to attend lectures at museums and Art Institutes that correlate with program topics.

The radio bulletins issued by the Rochester, New York, Schools aid teachers to secure a broad picture of radio education by including information concerning such activities in other communities. Brief reviews of current literature in radio, suggested reading for teachers, and comments concerning commercial juvenile programs also are discussed.

Some of the guides prepared for teachers suggest methods of classroom organization which are helpful in making effective use of the radio programs. For example, the series *Your Health Parade,* presented by the Los Angeles City Schools, lists the following projects:

Health dictionary: After each broadcast the children could select words from the program to be included in a health dictionary for the class.

Health dramatization: From the information that is presented on the broadcasts the children could write and produce a play or a radio script to show good health habits.

Health poster committee: Children in the class who enjoy art could make a poster, after each broadcast, which would serve as a health reminder for the class.

Health notebook: Each classroom listener may keep a health notebook with an illustration and a list of "check yourself" questions for each broadcast. Suggested items on which to "check yourself" will be on each study guide.

Health bulletin board committee: Members of the class may bring pictures and paragraphs about healthful living that they find in magazines and newspapers. Several children could be responsible for planning and arranging them on the bulletin board.

This above series, which was presented through Station KFAC in cooperation with the Los Angeles County Tuberculosis and Health Association, provided a separate list of suggestions for each of the programs. The following illustrates one of these:

HOLD THAT TEMPER

STORY THEME

This program will attempt to explain what goes on within us when we experience the emotions of anger, hatred, and fear, at home as well as at school.

Through experiences familiar to children, the program will portray the social and family life of two children who suffer emotional tensions because they do not understand the reasons for their instability in unpleasant situations.

BEFORE THE BROADCAST

Write the title of the program on the board and tell the children it is about a boy and a girl who had to learn how to make other children like them.

Suggest things to listen for in the broadcast:

Why do we sometimes feel afraid?

Why do people sometimes feel angry?

What do anger and fear do to us?

What did Jimmy and Laura learn that helped them to be liked by their playmates?

AFTER THE BROADCAST

Discuss the suggested listening topics before the broadcast.

Have you ever been afraid and then found there was nothing to be afraid of? Let the children tell of their experiences.

Are you a good friend to others? Think about these "check yourself" questions:

Do you do your part when there is work to be done?

Do you tell the truth?

Do you help others?

Do you go on playing even when your team is losing?

Do you show you are a good loser?

Do you admit when you are wrong?

Do you control your temper?

Do you remember never to tell tales on others?

ACTIVITIES STIMULATED BY THE BROADCAST

Develop a list of standards for a chart on good sportsmanship in games. The list might include:

A good sport does what the captain tells him.

A good sport knows and obeys the rules of the game.

A good sport helps his team win in every way that is fair.

A good sport does not blame others when his team loses.

Teachers using this California series were also provided with a correlated reading list and audio-visual materials.

In other parts of the country individual worksheets have been used. These are provided to each listener in preparation for a broadcast, and as the program is presented, the child uses the material thus furnished in the manner suggested by the radio voice. It may be writing, cutting, pasting, or any number of other activities.

Such worksheets must be used with caution, for certainly the teacher does not wish a standardized response in almost routine fashion. However, if this procedure is carefully developed, it can serve to make the listener an active participant, and it may reduce the gap between the all-too-often impersonal radio voice and the child. Wherever desirable such worksheets can suggest specific follow-up activities. Since these materials are usually furnished in local school systems, they can be planned to relate more closely to established courses of study. An example of the individual listener worksheet was shown with the demonstration lesson in Chapter 3.

Selection and Use of Program

When the teacher has become acquainted with some of the general and specific information concerning programs available in her district, the next consideration is to determine which of these programs shall be used. Some criteria for making selections are needed.

Selection. A committee of teachers under the supervision of Norman Woelfel listed the following elements which have been helpful in selecting programs for school use.

A. *Time:* The broadcast should be on the air at a time during the school day when major administrative adjustments will not be necessary in order that the program may be heard. The program should fit into the scheduled periods easily, unless it is possible to make satisfactory arrangements with other teachers for exchange of classes.

B. *Length of Program:* Since the realization of the educational possibilities of radio depends upon concentrated listening, broadcasts of 15-minute duration are probably preferable to those of a half-hour duration. This is particularly true with younger children. The teacher herself can best judge what length program is most satisfactory for her group in terms of the children's interests, attention spans, and physical needs. Because an integral part of the process of radio listening is the discussion or activity before and after the broadcast, the broadcast should not take up too much of the class period. A great deal of the benefit of the broadcast is lost if the class has to disband immediately after the program. While it is impossible for the teacher to govern the actual length of the program, she can choose programs which are of appropriate length, or, if possible, rearrange the class schedule to provide for discussion and activity time.

C. *Teacher Objectives:* The teacher should have clearly defined in her own mind the objectives which she wishes the broadcast to achieve. She should have checked with observations of previous broadcasts, public announcements, and any supplementary lesson manuals in order to judge the ways in which the objectives she has chosen are to be served. She should know whether or not the broadcast is designed for classroom use, what subject-matter content it aims to cover, and what social attitudes it seeks to influence. Those broadcasts should be selected which are, or can be made, relevant to the work going on in the classroom. Occasional exceptions to this are newscasts, actuality or spot broadcasts, foreign broadcasts, and special events broadcasts. There may be cases in which the teacher knows that her objectives and those of the broadcast differ. Under these circumstances she should plan such a utilization of the program as will best serve her objectives.

D. *Quality of Performance:* The teacher should select programs which are presented as effectively as possible in terms of the purposes she has determined upon. She must guard against the danger of selecting programs so poorly executed and presented that they may hinder the use of radio as a teaching device. No matter how worthy the content and objectives, a radio program is ineffective if poorly presented. The broadcast should be conceived and produced primarily in terms of the best modern radio techniques. That is to say, the broadcast material should be so chosen and assembled that it is more effective over the radio than if produced through some other educational medium such as the theatre, lecture hall, or classroom. When the broadcast attempts direct teaching, simplicity and vividness of terminology are prime requisites.

E. *Interest:* The material of the broadcast should be based on the interest of the students, and should serve to stimulate new interests as well as to deepen those already present. The arousal and maintenance of a high degree of spontaneous interests on the part of most listeners to the broadcast should be evident before any broadcast series is used regularly for school listening.

F. *Authenticity:* The teacher should use every means available to her for checking the authenticity of the broadcast content. She should know the source of the broadcast: if educational, what institutions are sponsoring it, if commercial, what organizations are using it and for what purposes. She should check the material of previous broadcasts from the same or similar sources. She should know how to help the students find references to corroborate, develop, or disagree with the material as presented.[1]

Use. After the choice of a program has been made the teacher can proceed with plans for its use. Beyond the application of common sense, there are no hard and fast rules for the use of a radio program.

David J. Heffernan emphasizes this fact:

I suppose there is no supplementary aid in education which has been so clouded with an air of mysticism as that surrounding radio in educa

---

[1] *How to Use Radio in the Classroom,* National Association of Broadcasters, 1939, pp. 5–6.

tion. There seems to be a feeling that the radio is a magic box, out of which comes material requiring a superintellect to interpret it to a class. As far as I can see there is not a great deal of difference between using radio as a supplementary aid and using textbooks, movies, slides, and other appurtenances so much a part of every good school. Radio is simply a very vitalizing stimulant. It is something to which we listen for fifteen minutes, and then spend hours in follow-up work. If we read a book, we can go back over pages for their sheer beauty, or because they stimulated us to thinking, or threw out some challenging questions. With a radio presentation we listen to as much as we can and then it is gone. Radio education, as far as the teacher is concerned, is part of education itself. We utilize radio as we utilize our educational knowledge. After we become familiar with the best of thought in the field, we then interpret it to our classes in the light of our own personality and our own experiences.[2]

The use of a radio program is in some ways related to its form. In discussing utilization techniques one may classify the various educational broadcasts as follows: (a) enrichment programs planned for school use; (b) special events broadcasts or other programs of general interest, planned primarily for the adult audience, which may be heard during school hours; (c) demonstration lessons based upon the local course of study; and (d) programs of educational value which may be heard out of school.

The use of these programs requires a somewhat different emphasis in each case. To illustrate briefly, an effective use of the enrichment program implies stressing the interrelationship of all subject matter. Drill procedures and questions calling for recall would be out of place and perhaps nonproductive, since the chief aim is the development of attitudes rather than the acquisition of information.

Use of the special events broadcast suggests an emphasis on the currency of the event, its causes, possible implications and effects. In utilizing the demonstration lesson the teacher is concerned not only with its contribution to the pupils but also with its values for her as a teacher. The emphasis in this latter instance is part of a specific course of study, whereas the out-of-school listening program is related only incidentally to a course of study, and its success depends largely upon the teacher's ability to stimulate interest in listening after school hours.

David J. Heffernan, "Proper Utilization of Radio," *Educational Press Bulletin*, November, 1940.

The Teacher's Purpose

The form of a program may suggest its manner of use but the determining factor is the teacher's purpose. What a teacher does with the program depends upon the objectives she has in mind. If the broadcast is being heard because of its timeliness, then it is that aspect which the teacher will want to emphasize. If the radio is being used because the teacher wants the children to participate in the occasion being broadcast, then classroom procedures will be modified accordingly. When the chief aim of the listening is to create desirable attitudes, then it is upon the emotional aspect of the radio visit that she will capitalize.

The teacher may decide to use the radio because it adds authority. In that case information is sought primarily, and even note-taking may be justified. If the broadcast is listened to because it can integrate experiences, then maximum opportunity for reference to other areas of study should be provided.

When the radio is used to challenge preconceived notions, the teacher may first survey the points of view generally shared in the class. After the program the class may investigate to what extent their beliefs have been challenged. A similar approach can be used with a program planned to develop standards of taste.

The teacher's purpose is not an afterthought in using radio programs; rather, it should orient and guide the classroom activities before, during, and after the program.

Before the Broadcast: Preliminary Considerations

School Clocks Need to Be Accurate.   The need for checking the clock seems obvious and yet occasionally a class will miss the opening minutes of a program because that has not been done. It is better to tune in early and to keep the volume down while the teacher prepares the group for the radio visit.

Reception in Auditorium Not Advised.   If possible the program should be heard in the classroom where materials are on hand rather than in an auditorium. Ben Darrow's early observation in this regard is still valid.

One of the greatest dangers to the success of radio for schools has been the receiving of the program in auditoriums. No blanket indictment is placed against them, because some of them are small and reception is sometimes claimed to be satisfactory. Nevertheless there are several reasons for cautious use of auditoriums.

(1) The acoustics are often bad.
(2) If only one speaker is used the volume is likely to be too loud for those close to the speaker or too low for those farthest away.
(3) Even though the loudspeakers are so placed as to give good audibility there are still the problems of:
    a. Lack of classroom helps, such as desks, maps, blackboards, etc.
    b. Too many pupils causing the loss of classroom leadership of the teacher.
    c. The tendency toward confusion whenever and wherever the discipline is not of a high order.
    d. Loss of time in marching to and from the auditorium.

Of course, some of the above objections are inoperative where a single class or comparatively small groups are taken to the auditorium. Nevertheless the classroom offers a more satisfactory place for listening. The interaction between pupil and teacher in their own classroom during the radio lesson is more natural and complete. No time is lost. The taking of notes, observing of maps and drawings, etc., is much easier in the classroom atmosphere.[3]

The problem of television viewing is even more critical. As receivers with screens over 4 feet in width come into wider use, it may be possible to use the auditorium for watching the program, although the postbroadcast discussion will still be more effective if conducted in the classroom. Any attempt, however, to use even a 16-inch or 19-inch television receiver in the auditorium would probably lead to improper viewing, with the children at the sides and the rear of the room getting a very poor view of the program. It will be difficult, while schools are limited to one or two receivers to a building, to resist the impulse to crowd 80 to 100 pupils in front of one screen, but that impulse should be resisted.

    Avoid Overcrowding. The practice of combining classes or radio reception also interferes with efficiency, but this is done generally because not enough radio sets are available. (The entire problem of equipment will be discussed later.) For classroom use of radio pro-

---

Ben Darrow, *Radio, the Assistant Teacher*, pp. 148–149.

grams, the ideal situation would be to have a radio set in every classroom. The relative merits of the individual receiver as contrasted with the use of a central sound system will be mentioned later. Of course, for reception of programs produced within the school some distribution system is necessary.

Correct Tuning Is Vital.   Although it would seem that teachers have ample practice at home tuning in their radios, yet frequently a visitor notes that reception in the classroom could be greatly improved if the receiver were properly tuned.

The knob should be turned until the pointer indicates the frequency of the desired station. The rotation should be continued until the program becomes indistinct and then the same operation continued in the opposite direction. The best position is generally halfway between these two points.

For speech, the tone control should be in the treble position. The use of the tone control in the bass position, although it may reduce some static, also reduces the clarity of both speech and music.

Some educational stations assist teachers in tuning receivers accurately by issuing detailed directions. These, of course, must be adapted to station frequencies and to the type of receiver used. An example follows:

1. Completely unwind the power cord from the back of the set and plug it into an *ALTERNATING CURRENT* (AC) plug.
2. Set BAND SWITCH (extreme right) to the FM position.
3. Turn SWITCH (extreme left) to ON position, and allow set to warm up for 30 seconds.
4. Adjust VOLUME control (left of center) until a sound is heard from the set.
5. Adjust TUNING control (right of center) so that the dial crossbar is very slightly to the *left* of 90 on the upper scale marked FREQUENCY MODULATION IN MEGACYCLES. (Our signal is 90.3 megacycles.) Vary TUNING control back and forth until WBOE is heard; then, for accurate reception, tune the set UNTIL THE GREEN TUNING EYE HAS AS SMALL A SHADOW AS POSSIBLE.
6. Adjust VOLUME control until there is comfortable hearing in all parts of the room. (The set should be at the listener's eye-and-ear level.)
7. Reception of FM stations, including WBOE, *may* be improved if

the position of the power cord is moved in height or in various directions after the station is tuned in. (The cord is an antenna.) Observe the tuning eye as you move the cord position to help gauge improvement.

8. To receive standard broadcasting (AM) stations, set BAND SWITCH on AM position and tune in station on the lower scale. (STANDARD BROADCAST BAND) with the aid of the tuning eye.

Placement of the Receiver. The placement of the radio set in the classroom perhaps deserves mention. Generally it should be in front of the room facing the class. If it is a small unit, it should rest on a table. Frequently teachers make the mistake of adjusting the volume to suit their own ears and their own position in the room. They overlook the fact that pupils at the rear and sides may require some other adjustments. The children should feel free to raise their hands when hearing is difficult. At such time the volume either can be adjusted or the child can quietly change seats. If it is known that certain children have hearing difficulties, they should be given preferred positions.

Occasionally in a kindergarten class, for instance, the children may be observed gathered at one end of the room listening to a radio placed at the other end. This is unfortunate, since the distance between the source of the sound and the listeners should be kept at a practical minimum. The radio program is uniquely intimate in its nature. One who has observed children at home listening to radio will have noted how close to the instrument they prefer to sit. Such intimacy, though not possible in the ordinary classroom, should nevertheless be kept in mind in placing the receiver. If necessary, and if safety precautions are heeded, an extension cord should be used.

With FM particularly, the difference between good and poor reception in a classroom may be a slight change in the placement of the receiver. Adjacent steel beams, the relationship to station transmitter site, outdoor traffic—these and other factors can determine optimum receiver placement in the room. The teacher should try the set in various parts of the room until she is satisfied that she has chosen the best. Obviously, this need not be done for every program.

Minimize Disturbances. Occasionally unnecessary disturbances interfere with effective listening, such as notices to the teacher, requests for certain pupils, etc. A small sign on the door indicating that a radio program is being received will help to minimize such visits, which can generally be delayed without harm. The Rochester schools call attention to the following:

> Pupils and teachers ought to feel a real responsibility for providing a most courteous reception for radio voice visitors. It would be ideal if attitudes toward radio guests were the same as toward visitors who come to the classroom in person. Guests should be admitted to the room when they arrive. Radios should be tuned in on time. Unnecessary movement of teachers and pupils about the room should be minimized during the broadcast. It may be necessary to go to the radio to increase its volume, or to point to a map as the broadcast requests. But it is unnecessary and discourteous to sharpen pencils, open or close windows, or aimlessly wander about while the radio is talking.[4]

When adjustments of a physical nature have been made, the teacher can turn her attention to the specific task at hand, that is, preparing the children for the program so that they will receive maximum benefit from it.

Before the Broadcast: Preparatory Activities

Prebroadcast activities can be of numerous types. As noted earlier, they will vary with the teacher's objectives and also with the program form and content. The demonstration lesson procedure, for example, involves definite preparatory steps, and the completion of each one is essential to the success of the lesson. On the other hand, a dramatized or musical enrichment program may be most effective with but a minimum of prebroadcast activity, merely a few comments to set the stage.

Although preparatory procedures are often necessary and helpful, it is apparent that only so much can be asked of the classroom teacher if she is to be sympathetic to the use of this tool. When there is danger of the preparatory activities becoming prescribed and burdensome to the teachers, it is best for the broadcasters and script writers to omit them, or at least to be realistic about the situation. Granted that the

---

[4] "Tuning In on the Rochester School of the Air," Rochester, N.Y., October 23, 1939.

broadcast is for the children, yet the attitude of the teacher on the receiving end should not be overlooked.

If the teacher comes to regard the radio as an added burden, it is inevitable that her children will react accordingly. If, on the contrary, she thinks of the radio as an assistant that is striving to serve her, then the probability is that both she and her charges will enjoy added service.

Sometimes the teacher's attitude may be such that it definitely limits whatever values the program may have. The truth is that she may regard the program largely as an opportunity to catch up on her clerical work or as a relief from her teaching duties. Obviously, the radio program cannot "do tricks" any more than a textbook can, and to have value, it too must be prepared for and used intelligently. Modern educational philosophy places full emphasis on what happens after an educational experience. Little of importance will result unless adequate preparation has been made.

If the group is to listen to a dramatized program, several suggestions might be made to the children, such as these: Is the language used in keeping with the locale and period? Are the sound effects, including the music, appropriate? Is the characterization sincere and correctly drawn?

The teacher, who is aware that the immature listener often misses the chief objective of a program when he concerns himself with unimportant details, may suggest these guides: See whether you can determine the chief purpose of this program. If the writer of the script had used an outline, what would it look like?

Preparation Activities. It is difficult to list prebroadcast techniques without knowing the specific situation in which they are to be applied. The following activities have been selected from a list compiled at Ohio State University and they are suggestive of the more common procedures which may be used before a program is heard:

1. Putting questions about the broadcast topic on the blackboard.
2. Discussing questions about the topic with the class.
3. Telling the class what the teacher knows about the topic.
4. Having students summarize what they know about the topic.
5. Discussing motion pictures related to the topic.
6. Using maps of various kinds.

7. Listing the things the class wants to know about the topic.
8. Looking at pictures or lantern slides illustrative of the topic.
9. Special exercises such as oral drills or dictation to make pupils more ear-minded.
10. Reading magazines, newspapers, or books about the topic.
11. Looking at specimens, models, or articles related to the topic.
12. Having illustrative or explanatory materials in pupils' hands before the broadcast.
13. Using the reference books for specific information.
14. Asking someone outside the class to tell about the topic.
15. A few moments of expectant silence just previous to the broadcast.
16. Taking an imaginary journey related to the topic.
17. Having students write out what they know about the topic.
18. Writing and defining key words related to the topic.
19. Imagining with the class what will be covered in the broadcast.
20. Studying the broadcast manual and attempting to carry out some of its suggestions.
21. Making books and magazines related to the topic readily available.
22. Visiting a radio station and seeing a broadcast.
23. Making illustrative and supplementary materials.
24. Making all necessary seating arrangements or room adjustments in advance of a broadcast.
25. Making plans to connect the broadcast with regular classwork.
26. Posting advance announcements of the broadcast.
27. Having students keep advance notes about the topic of the broadcast.

Activities During the Broadcast

The Teacher Is a Participant.   The commencement of the program does not mean that there can be a "letdown" on the part of the classroom teacher. In listening to a radio program, as well as in preparing for it, the pupils can be expected to evidence no more interest than the teacher herself exhibits. If the teacher manifests a vital interest in the material, even though she may have heard the program more than once, the children will react in a similar manner.

On the other hand, if, instead of listening *with* the children, she turns to do some clerical work or becomes otherwise occupied, she is being decidedly unfair to the children. She is not teaching *with* radio; rather, she is letting radio carry the load. In fact, she is interfering with its potential accomplishment. If the teacher does not give the program her complete attention, she has no right to expect, and will not receive, more from the pupils.

A capable teacher knows that the broadcast period provides her with a unique opportunity to observe the reactions of her pupils. If some difficulty in understanding appears during the program (and a good teacher can readily discern that condition), she notes the items that will require clarification. As she listens, new approaches to the subject or other aspects for discussion may occur to her. She notes these also. In other words, what she sees and hears during the program helps her to determine how she can most effectively follow up the broadcast.

Usually the teacher should be at the front of the room where the pupils may see her and share her interest, and where she can use whatever materials may be helpful.

Even if no program booklet is available, the alert teacher will perform whatever activities enhance the effect of the broadcast. In a news program she may point to the map as a certain region is discussed. During an English program a new word or two may be written on the blackboard. In an elementary music series she may demonstrate the suggested rhythmic activity. During an art broadcast she can show the pictures mentioned. As she performs these functions she is fully aware that too much activity and too much talk on her part may distract rather than help the listeners.

Required Materials Must Be Available. If, in the usual radio program, the role of the classroom teacher is important, it is doubly so when using programs closely correlated to a teacher's guide. Only to the extent that the teacher realizes that the broadcaster is dependent upon her can there be any reasonable success in the use of this procedure. When the program guide has suggested that certain laboratory and visual materials be assembled for the broadcast, then it is essential that such materials be in readiness; otherwise the presentation may result in a waste of time.

The need for assembling materials is but one phase of the teacher's responsibility. If lantern slides are to be used, a child must be instructed in the use of the projector. It may facilitate matters to have one pupil in charge of lights, another to adjust screens, shades, etc. In other words, the teacher must so prepare the class that there is absolute readiness for the radio visit, that a businesslike rather than a "show" attitude results, and that the teacher is free to reinforce, as she sees fit, the comments of the radio teacher.

The following is an excerpt from a guide prepared for teachers receiving radio programs in elementary science. It illustrates the preparations made for the use of visual materials to accompany the radio program.

USE OF SLIDES DURING THE RADIO LESSON

1. Lessons in which slides are used require the participation of the entire class. Any seating arrangement which permits all the children to see the picture projected on the screen will be satisfactory. In most cases, they will remain in their regular seats.
2. For lessons in which slides are shown, the following directions should be followed before the broadcast:
    (a) Try out the lantern in the room where you are going to receive the radio lessons to find the best location for it. The lantern must be focused:
        (1) So that the picture will be clear and large.
        (2) Where the children can see the picture.
        (3) Low enough that a child, using a pointer, can easily point to all parts of the picture.
    (b) Have the first and second slide to be used during the lesson placed in the slide holder of the lantern. Take the other slides listed for use out of the slide box and place them, *in the order in which they will be used,* near the lantern.
    (c) Draw all window shades down, and turn on the lights.
    (d) Arrange with some child to turn off the lights when the broadcaster asks that a slide be shown. The only direction that will be given over the radio in regard to turning the lights off and on will be—"Please show slide No. ___." Have this same child turn the lights on each time the lantern is turned off. There should be a substitute for this child if he is absent.
    (e) Slides that are used for a minute or longer get very hot and hard to handle. Therefore, it will be necessary to have, on the table or desk with the lantern, a cloth which can be used to take out the hot slides.
    (f) Place a pointer in the chalk tray near the screen.
    (g) If you have not used a lantern, try it several times until you become familiar with it.
3. The following directions must be followed during the broadcast:
    (a) When referring to the number of a slide, the number on the

red-edged oval label, pasted on the slide, will be used. For example, Slide No. 1 is "Autumn Children in a Garden."

(b) When you are asked to show a slide, do not turn off the lantern until you are asked to do so. There will be no danger of cracking the slide if it is put in properly.

(c) *Important:* When you put a slide in the lantern, be sure that the red-edge oval label is at the upper right-hand corner of the slide. This is essential to insure the right placing of the picture on the screen.

(d) If a child is asked to point to something on the screen, see that he uses the pointer, and stands at the side of the picture so that all the children may see.

Not All Programs Equally Suitable. What if the classroom teacher finds that the radio programs in a particular series are too difficult or are paced too fast for her class? There is but one possible answer. Her class should no longer receive that series. Just as the teacher would not suggest reading materials which are too difficult, so radio materials must be adapted to the child. There can be no radio program that is suitable for *all* children, even of the same age. The nature of the radio program implies that generally it will be aimed at the average in abilities. When it is evident to the teacher that her class differs appreciably from the norm, then the use of both tools and procedures must be modified.

When Is a Child Listening? The expectations of the teacher during the "listening period" may necessitate a word of caution. For instance, it would be a mistake for the teacher to think that the child is listening only when he or she is looking straight ahead at the loudspeaker. Some children do their most effective listening while they are seemingly gazing or merely drawing figures. A much better measure of effective listening is the reaction manifested in the follow-up period. By forcing children to accept stereotyped practices in listening, the teacher confuses a physical form with a mental state.

Note-Taking and Other Pupil Activity. Whether or not it is valuable to take notes during a radio program has not yet been determined conclusively. School broadcasters in Great Britain indicated that from their experimentation it was clear that "for these senior school pupils note-taking of any kind was an unprofitable activity. In several directions, particularly in tests of delayed recall, non notetakers have the advantage." [5] It seems clear that, if the basic purpose of the program is to create desirable attitudes, a mechanical procedure which interferes with continued listening would probably not contribute much. However, if the purpose is to accumulate facts, perhaps note-taking can be justified.

But the ability to take notes effectively is not easily acquired. The difficulties that even college students have can testify to that. Thus it seems reasonable that at the elementary school level the practice should be discouraged. The younger children not only have difficulty in writing and spelling but they generally lack the experience which enables them to note only that which is significant as contrasted with that which is irrelevant.

Just as points of emphasis are in some ways related to program form, so likewise are types of teacher and pupil activity. In a dramatized enrichment program it is quite likely that no motor activity will be called for aside from listening. In fact, physical activities may reduce the value of this type of program.

In some types of programs, where the presentation attempts to stimulate classroom procedures, a great variety of student and teacher activity may be used. As shown earlier, for any reasonable degree of success this program necessitates comprehensive radio lesson guides and planned pauses for auditor reaction.

After the Broadcast

The activities which follow a broadcast can be as varied and as valuable as those which precede it. Just which follow-up technique to use depends upon the teacher's objectives as well as upon the program and its results.

Some broadcasts may provide a real challenge for a worth-while discussion, others may present a fine summary for which even a brief test may be appropriate, while other programs may produce an emotional reaction for which any follow-up is unnecessary, if not actually harmful.

In any case, the postbroadcast treatment should be varied and care-

---

[5] "School Broadcasting in Great Britain," National Advisory Council on Radio in Education, No. 17, November, 1937, p. 51.

fully planned. Routine procedures will result in routine pupil reaction and the atmosphere of the class will be laden inevitably with a deadly indifference. A poor follow-up has spoiled more than one good program.

A good measure of effective utilization is the degree to which the teacher stimulates and provides an opportunity for the voluntary expression of her pupils. Inherent in any productive class discussion is the need for developing a critical attitude toward the materials which were presented, whether it was by sound or by sight. Parenthetically it might be noted that a critical attitude does not imply a general and uniform skepticism. The intelligent teacher recognizes that perhaps this aspect has been overdone in some instances, to the extent that skepticism becomes a defense for ignorance, and the superficial skeptic is mistaken occasionally for a sage. An honest critical attitude presumes a positive point of view as well.

Variation in Procedures Is Essential.   Perhaps the most common error made in the use of a radio program is to regard the follow-up only as an opportunity for testing the pupils to determine what facts they have acquired. In such cases the postbroadcast period becomes a dull "rehash" of the program itself, and nothing new is contributed. The method of pure recall, if overworked, enhances the value of the radio visit no more than does a question and answer drill implement of textbook. In each case the book becomes an end in itself rather than a means. If the radio program is to be a "springboard" for class activity, some leap forward is involved; otherwise the child merely sits down and the platform springs but to no avail. Education is more than training of memory.

Learning Must Be Integrated.   Another weakness in utilization, perhaps less frequent, is the failure to relate the radio material to the past experiences of the child. The psychology of learning, as it is applied to text materials, must also be applied to radio materials, and the learning derived from listening must be used to reinforce other classroom experiences. Whatever objectives may have been attained by the radio visit should not be isolated, but rather must be integrated to all other worth-while goals.

Lowdermilk's narration, though perhaps a bit overdrawn, nevertheless illustrates this point:

"You have just heard the seventh in this series of broadcasts. Listen in again at this same time next Tuesday for the eighth program of this series, 'The Internal Combustion Motor.' Remember—same time—same station," invites the announcer. " 'Everyday Science,' to which you have been listening, is a presentation of the _____."

Miss Hull quickly snaps off the radio in the 7B home room, and rolls up the large wall map of Eurasia on the front wall, exposing a list of twenty problems in percentage, neatly written on the blackboard.

"If you will get out your pencils and workbooks quickly," explains Miss Hull, "you will just have time to finish this list of examples before recess. Read each problem carefully, given in each example. If you have forgotten our three rules, you may refer to yesterday's page in your workbooks. Any question before we start?"

John, in the back seat of the second row, suddenly sits erect and waves his hand vigorously.

"Yes, John?" inquires Miss Hull.

"If we took some ether," begins John excitedly, "and then poured it over—"

"But what has ether to do with arithmetic?" asks Miss Hull.

"The man in the broadcast! Just now—what he was telling us about refrigeration—you know!"

"But, John," Miss Hull interrupts reprovingly, "this is your arithmetic practice period. Why, you haven't even got out your arithmetic workbook yet! Quickly, please, John! You know how you hate to take your unfinished work home for homework!" [6]

The principles of effective utilization as suggested earlier apply to practically all programs regardless of form, although the use of the demonstration lesson requires some additional comment concerning the follow-up period.

Though this procedure necessitates a comprehensive lesson guide, care should be taken not to prescribe postbroadcast practices. The manual can do no more than guide the teacher. The final choice must be made by her with the hope that she will adopt such procedures as serve best the specific needs of her class. To detail in routine fashion just what should be done by all teachers after each program would stifle initiative and destroy the aim of the radio series. A far more effective plan is to suggest several procedures any of which may be adopted by the teacher.

---

[6] R. R. Lowdermilk, "Teaching with Radio," Bulletin No. 16, Bureau of Educational Research, Ohio State University, pp. 18, 19.

Unit in Radio Communication: Control booth planned and built by sixth grade students.

Children prepare for a health broadcast from WBOE.

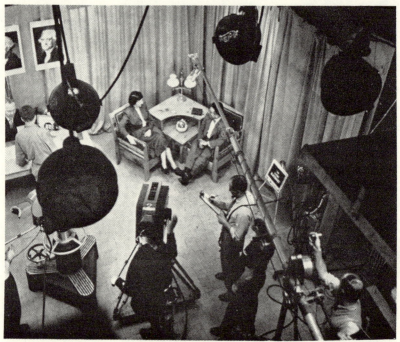

"The Living Blackboard" goes out to New York City's homebound high school students from WPIX.

Elementary school children taking part in Italian street scene for TV: background planned and executed by children.

For illustration, an extract from a guide used with radio lessons in safety education is shown. Notice that the suggestions are flexible so that individual differences are not overlooked.

FOLLOW-UP SUGGESTIONS

A. Permit other children to demonstrate how to extinguish a fire in one's clothing.
    1. A demonstration could be given to other classes.
B. Discuss and find other fire hazards in the home.
C. Prepare and check home inspection sheets.
D..Collect and check newspaper items to find the chief causes of fires.
E. Study data given in Course of Study, Safety Education, pages 15 and 16. (While these figures are not the current ones, they will serve as representative facts.)
F. Make fire prevention posters.
G. Read stories in "Road to Safety" Series:
    1. D–pages 54–65 (This is suitable for children having difficulty in reading.)
    2. E–pages 37–74
    3. F–pages 57–76
    4. H–pages 112–116, 241, 242

Radio Is a Guide, Not a Control. Occasionally class activities are suggested for completion between broadcasts rather than immediately following them. When this procedure is tried, there is the possible danger of putting too much pressure on the teacher if not enough time is available between programs. It cannot be repeated too often that both from the broadcaster's and from the classroom teacher's point of view it is far better to use effectively a few superior programs than to utilize indifferently an abundance of mediocre ones. Care must be taken not to make the radio programs the backbone of teaching activity, for even under ideal conditions they can provide no more than a periodic "lift."

The activities which may be used following a program vary greatly, and the selection of a specific technique can be determined only by a knowledge of the basic aims, the program, the teacher, the pupils, and the materials available. A teaching technique which is effective in one situation may prove to be of little value under other conditions.

The following is a summary of postbroadcast activities which have been observed in various classrooms using programs planned for the elementary grades.

SUMMARY OF CLASS ACTIVITIES

(Teacher and Pupils)

Activities Common to All Subjects

1. Brought in pictures of subject under discussion.
2. Checked-upon, or tested, material covered in radio program.
3. Compiled a vocabulary list of words introduced in radio programs.
4. Continued discussion of points stressed in radio programs throughout the week.
5. Encouraged pupil to do outside work in searching for materials relative to subject or in doing creative problems.
6. Filled in question sheets.
7. Finished work begun in radio program.
8. Helped children with individual problems.
9. Kept notebooks.
10. Read books suggested in teacher's guide in preparation for next radio program.
11. Summarized main points of broadcast.
12. Used suggested slides in supplementary reading material.

Other activities noted were:

Arithmetic

1. Continued discussion of activities introduced in radio program, i.e., calendar, dates, clock, telling time, counting coins, planning a garden, etc.
2. Directed class in making of and working with calendars.
3. Played number games suggested in teacher's guide.

Art

1. Compared slides, and then made sketches of them from memory.
2. Compiled a vocabulary list of words used to describe drawings.
3. Followed creative problem suggested by radio, i.e., work in wood, soap, clay, sketch, cut paper designs, silhouette portraits, studies made in pencil, crayon, paint.
4. Listened to a symphonic composition on victrola while studying a picture and described relation of two works.
5. Made dolls and costumes for them.
6. Wrote description of pictures studied.

Geography

1. Built typical Congo homes.
2. Demonstrated and practiced in winding a turban in connection with series of broadcasts on Sahara Desert.
3. Listened to African music and made Congo musical instruments.
4. Made a geography dictionary.
5. Performed experiments.
6. Planned an exhibit of mats, clay bowls, etc., that class had made.
7. Planned dramatization.
8. Played various word games suggested in workbook, used vocabulary learned in radio programs, i.e., anagrams, crossword puzzles, etc.
9. Traced routes on map.
10. Visited Natural History Museum.
11. Visited the Zoo to study the camel in connection with lessons on the Sahara Desert.

Handcraft

1. Collected pictures.
2. Constructed cork sailors.
3. Cut out cardboard tracings.
4. Decorated toys with crayon, colored pencil, or show card paints.
5. Designated and collected other toy patterns for future use in woodwork.
6. Designed ruler animals for measuring experiences.
7. Designed simple monograms on squared paper that were used on book-ends, towels, posters, etc.
8. Experimented with various animal patterns.
9. Made model miniature sailboats.
10. Made tops.
11. Made color designs.
12. Observed crafts of other people.
13. Practiced using rulers in measuring.
14. Read about and discussed making of kites before making them.
15. Sawed animal patterns out of wood, filed, and sanded them.
16. Started a hobby and joined a hobby club.
17. Worked at home and at school making patterns and drawing freehand.

Health

1. Checked individual weight charts.
2. Continued and repeated experiments begun in radio broadcast.
3. Gathered materials and illustrations for notebooks.
4. Weighed entire class and kept weighing records.

History

1. Conducted a debate in class.
2. Constructed a trading post and forts.
3. Drew cartoons of stories in history being studied.
4. Filled in outline maps.
5. Gave informal dramatizations.
6. Made (as a class project) a frieze showing sequence of historical events.
7. Rewrote important events in history in correct chronological order.
8. Told story from an outline.

Music

1. Completed teaching of songs introduced in radio program.
2. Continued work with rhythmic activities as introduced in radio broadcast.
3. Sang tonal patterns found in workbook.
4. Taught new songs and played recorded selections as suggested in the teacher's guide.
5. Completed work sheets.
6. Graded test papers and sent results to broadcaster.
7. Played games with rhythm patterns, i.e., sang, clapped, tapped rhythm patterns.
8. Used victrola records that tie up with particular song, composer, or period of music history being studied.

Primary Safety

1. Arranged class meetings and elected class members to take charge.
2. Became acquainted with the duties of a policeman.
3. Composed safety slogans, poems, and rhymes.
4. Conducted dramatizations and pantomimes suggested by slides.
5. Demonstrated proper clothing for rainy day, snowy day, etc.
6. Encouraged reports of practiced safety rules.
7. Entire class dressed suitably for a field trip.
8. Filled in work sheets under teacher's guidance.
9. Made individual booklets in which safety rules were written and illustrated.
10. Made class book or chart of safety rules stressed in radio program.
11. Planned a trip to a fire station.
12. Prepared dramatizations to demonstrate safety rules stressed during radio broadcasts.
13. Read stories on safety.
14. Told stories of travel.
15. Visited a safety patrol meeting.

Science

1. Added to science notebooks, i.e., drew pictures, wrote stories.
2. Carved animals, built a model farm, and made pin wheels.
3. Made collections of specimens, pictures, etc.
4. Performed experiments based on previous radio programs.

The following list issued by the Ohio State Evaluation study "was culled from many reports by teachers indicating how they have been utilizing radio in the classroom." It is not implied here that any or all these activities are considered uniformly effective.

Follow-up Activities Growing Out of This Broadcast

1. Drawing of illustrations on the blackboard by students.
2. Giving the class an information test on the broadcast.
3. Having students write what they got out of the broadcast.
4. Having students discuss the good and bad features of the broadcast.
5. Having students retell the most interesting parts of the broadcast.
6. Making assignments in texts or reference books.
7. Comparing prebroadcast expectations with the actual broadcast.
8. Discussing the new and unusual features of the broadcast.
9. Providing a relaxation or rest period immediately after the broadcast.
10. Holding an informal oral quiz on the broadcast.
11. Discussing the manner of speech and pronunciation of the broadcasters.
12. Drawing maps or pictures related to the broadcast.
13. Having students bring in things from home illustrating aspects of the broadcast.
14. Inviting some person who is an expert on the topic of the broadcast to speak to the class.
15. Putting on a similar make-believe broadcast in class.
16. Broadcasting a program over the school public address system.
17. Posting pictures and news clippings related to the broadcast.
18. Making critical comments in writing to the broadcaster.
19. Having a class dramatization of pantomime related to the broadcast.
20. Making comparisons of this broadcast with others heard.
21. Having students report on similar out-of-school broadcasts.
22. Discussing aspects of the broadcast with other teachers.
23. Answering student's questions about the broadcast.
24. Painting a picture of, or modeling with clay, something suggested by the broadcast.

25. Relating personal experiences along the line of the broadcast to the class.
26. Making a list of all the problems raised by the broadcast as a basis for the individual or committee reports by the students.
27. Planning a class excursion to some point of interest mentioned in the broadcast.
28. Appointing a committee to plan things to do as a result of hearing the broadcast.
29. Connecting the broadcast with the regular classroom activities.
30. Summarizing for the class the main points made in the broadcast.
31. Having the class write a radio script on a similar topic.
32. Planning an assembly program.
33. Making observations on the broadcast topic outside of school.
34. Planning interviews with people who know a great deal about the topic.
35. Demonstrating to another class or to parents the learnings resulting from the broadcast.
36. Carrying on an experiment to settle certain questions raised in the broadcast.
37. Keeping class or individual scrapbooks related to radio programs.
38. Forming class committees to take action on matters suggested by the broadcast.
39. Making available a number of interesting books about the topic of the broadcast.
40. Allowing the students to quiz the teacher about the broadcast or matters growing out of the broadcast.
41. Writing poems suggested by the topic of the broadcast.

It has been suggested by some that a carefully planned class organization for effective radio reception may enhance the efforts of the teacher in this direction.

The National Broadcasting Company called attention to the plan of pupil participation as introduced by Dr. Rollo G. Reynolds of Columbia University. Briefly, the organization consists of a Radio Program and Bulletinboard Committee, Radio Program Secretaries, a Radio Librarian, a Master of the Machine, and a Performance Committee.

The committee in charge of programs collects and scans advance program data and then lists them on the bulletinboard some time in advance.

The program secretaries take notes during a program when that is not required of the entire class. The Librarian finds information bearing upon the subject of the broadcast. The Master of the Machine is in charge of the radio and its operation, while the Performance Committee develops and presents to the class rules and regulations for "its own self-imposed conduct during a listening period."

Does all this apply to television programs?

While it is readily seen that all or most of the selection problems and utilization techniques of radio are applicable to video, with the possible exception of note-taking during the broadcast, one great difference presents itself immediately. In the opinion of the authors, it will be at least 1955 before the teacher will have much choice of programs within the school day in most cities of America. True, in Philadelphia, in February, 1950, the teacher had her choice of at least one program a day, two on Thursdays and three on Fridays, as the splendid monthly *Television Schedule* issued by the School-Community Relations Office of the Philadelphia Schools, shown on the following pages, will demonstrate. But Philadelphia was the exception that proved the rule, the example which educators in other cities were pointing out to local broadcasters.

In most cities, daytime programs included few that were specifically educational, with choice limited largely to the "housewife audience," from which the domestic-science departments might find cooking or homemaking lessons of unquestionable value.

By 1955, it is hoped, the example of Philadelphia will have been followed by other cities and the teacher who wishes to use television will have the same problems of selection, although with still a narrower field of choice, that now obtains in radio. The teacher will probably have the added problem of moving her class to the audio-visual aids room or the auditorium, since few schools will boast more than one or two television receivers.

The teacher will bear in mind that 6 to 10 feet is the most comfortable and practical viewing distance for receivers with 15- to 19-inch picture tubes, although television screens of that size will provide satisfactory viewing to children with normal vision as far as 20 feet from the screen. Audio-visual aids rooms will undoubtedly have provision for darkening the room, although it is well to bear in mind that current thinking seems to prefer a little light in the room, rather than absolute darkness, thus to reduce glare.

Teachers will also discover that newspapers carry program listings for the full week ahead, but that television stations have listings prepared two weeks in advance. The public relations department of a station will usually be willing to place the name of one teacher in each school on its mailing list, and from these advance listings a viewing schedule may be drawn up by a committee of teachers, or a list of appropriate programs may be posted on a faculty bulletinboard.

Reference was made earlier to the monthly *Television Schedule* which is issued to the Philadelphia schools by the School-Community Relations Office. It is so fine an example of preplanning and programming service that a typical schedule is reproduced herewith.

TELEVISION SCHEDULE [7]
February, 1950

NOTE
On February 28—4 to 4:30 p.m.—*Billy Penn M.C.* and *Science Is Fun* (from WFIL-TV) will be beamed to a meeting "Television and Education" in Atlantic City, in connection with the convention of the American Association of School Administrators.

Therefore, *Billy Penn M.C.* and *Science Is Fun* will *not* be scheduled on Friday, March 3.

. . .

Telecasts on Station WCAU will be omitted the week of February 27. There will be school telecasts on February 13 and 22.

. . .

TRY IT YOURSELF   WCAU-TV
Josephine D'Onofrio
(Note change in time)

This series explores the many creative approaches to art for all ages. It is designed primarily for elementary school pupils, but is directed also to homemakers. Simple materials are used in this adventure in art for fun, for expression, for utility, for appreciation. Many responses have been received from in- and out-of-school viewers.

---

[7] School-Community Relations Office, School District of Philadelphia, Department of Superintendence.

MONDAY, FEBRUARY 6, 1:45 P.M.   Valentines. Old-fashioned and new-fashioned—sentimental, nostalgic, heart-warming.

MONDAY, FEBRUARY 13, 1:45 P.M.   Hooked Rugs. We moderns take a page out of grandmother's book of handwork.

MONDAY, FEBRUARY 20, 1:45 P.M.   Tied—Dyed. An ancient art brought up-to-date and applied in many practical and beautiful ways.

MONDAY, FEBRUARY 27, 1:45 P.M.   No telecast.

CAREER FORUM   WCAU-TV
Ruth Weir Miller
(Note change in time)

High school boys and girls hear from experts in industry, business and the professions the opportunities and requirements in careers. Exceptional personalities appear this month.

WEDNESDAY, FEBRUARY 1, 1:35 P.M.   Military Service. Brigadier General Hugh B. Hester, Commanding General of Philadelphia Quartermaster's Depot.

WEDNESDAY, FEBRUARY 8, 1:35 P.M.   Automobile Industry. A representative of the Ford Motor Company will be present to answer any and all questions regarding the automobile industry.

WEDNESDAY, FEBRUARY 15, 1:35 P.M.   Science. Dr. Carl T. Chase, Assistant Associate Director of The Franklin Institute Laboratory for Research and Development.

WEDNESDAY, FEBRUARY 22, 1:35 P.M.   A civil leader will discuss many types of careers in public service.

OPERATION BLACKBOARD   WPTZ
William Helm, Gertrude Novokovsky, Martha Gable

Two fifteen-minute presentations for secondary schools will be included. Part I, "The World at Your Door," includes films, important guests, and visual material to highlight the problems of the various countries relating to world peace. The World Affairs Council and International House are co-operating in these programs. Part II, "How's Your Social I.Q.?" demonstrates proper social conduct in many situations in answer to teen-age questions.

THURSDAY, FEBRUARY 2

Part I. "The World at Your Door" 1:30 P.M.   Poland. Miss Adele Przybylowski of the International Institute will tell about the customs of Poland and illustrate with dolls and dancing.

Part II. "How's Your Social I.Q?" 1:45 P.M.   Number please! Good manners in using the telephone will be shown by Bell Telephone Company operators, under the direction of Mr. John Mott, General Commercial Supervisor.

THURSDAY, FEBRUARY 9

Part I. "The World at Your Door" 1:30 P.M.   Esperanto. Mr. R. Paul Montgomery of the Esperanto Club of Philadelphia will explain the mysteries of Esperanto, the World Interlanguage. It's really easy!

Part II. "How's Your Social I.Q?" 1:45 P.M.   All Aboard. Traveling manners, good and bad, will be seen from the point of view of an airlines pilot and hostess.

THURSDAY, FEBRUARY 16

Part I. "The World at Your Door" 1:30 P.M.   Ireland. Mr. William J. Gillen will charm you with tales from Ireland.

Part II. "How's Your Social I.Q?" 1:45 P.M.   It's a Party. The grapevine and proper ways of being a host and a guest will be demonstrated by the attractive Glover twins.

THURSDAY, FEBRUARY 23

Part I. "The World at Your Door" 1:30 P.M.   Persia. Mr. Karim Farman, a student at the University of Pennsylvania, will tell about his native land and show some interesting objects from that country.

Part II. "How's Your Social I.Q?" 1:45 P.M.   Date Manners. Everyone will be on his toes when Fred Niedland, manager of the Arthur Murray Studio, takes over.

YOUNG PHILADELPHIA PRESENTS   WPTZ
Martha Gable
(Note change in time)

Talented pupils in the music and dance arts are featured in the current series with Mrs. Emmeline Weakley who develops the story of the day in words and music. Each program is planned to enlarge the listeners' knowledge and enjoyment of music.

THURSDAY, FEBRUARY 2, 5:00 P.M.   Unfamiliar instruments will be played by experts.

THURSDAY, FEBRUARY 9, 5:00 P.M.   Familiar musical comedy numbers will be sung, played and danced.

THURSDAY, FEBRUARY 16, 5:00 P.M.   Miniatures in Music. Marionettes will dance, and young performers will demonstrate their talents instrumentally and vocally.

THURSDAY, FEBRUARY 23, 5:00 P.M.   Familiar Music of Presidents. The songs of our Presidents will be traced through history. This is an interesting sidelight on their interests and personalities.

FORMULA FOR CHAMPIONS   WCAU-TV
Martha Gable
(Note change in time)

The building of health and fitness in the schools—for youngsters up through high school and college—is demonstrated by a wide variety of activities. This program is designed particularly to stimulate interest in keeping fit, and participation in sports.

The boys and girls will be invited to join the "Club of Champions." A certificate and a button will be issued—on the receipt of a letter stating what sport he or she engages in—each day of the week. This will be further explained in the telecasts.

FRIDAY, FEBRUARY 3, 1:45 P.M.   Champion fencers from Northeast High School will show the difference between foil, épée and saber. Exciting dueling will be shown.

FRIDAY, FEBRUARY 10, 1:45 P.M.   Swinging a baton by drum majors and majorettes is an American addition to the sport scene. Skilled twirlers from Bartram High School will show how it is done.

FRIDAY, FEBRUARY 17, 1:45 P.M.   Vaults and swing exercises on the side horse by champions of South Philadelphia High School will show what can be done with good coaching and practice.

FRIDAY, FEBRUARY 24, 1:45 P.M.   Championship swimming techniques will be discussed by the world's breast stroke champion, Joe Verdeur.

BILLY PENN M.C.   WFIL-TV
Kathryn Fields Bovaird

During February the telecast will feature outstanding industrial activities in and near Philadelphia.

FRIDAY, FEBRUARY 3, 2:00 P.M.   Since 1865 the Stetson Company has been a leader in the making of all kinds of hats, soft hats, derby hats and the wonderful ten-gallon hats the cowboys wear. Program will show the fur pelts, hats in various stages of production, and finished hats.

FRIDAY, FEBRUARY 10, 2:00 P.M.   Just outside of Philadelphia at Ambler, the firm of Keasbey and Mattison processes asbestos fibers—fibers mined from rock that are cleaned, carded and spun into fabrics. This program will show the rock, the fiber, finished products—such as asbestos coverings, gloves, fire-fighter suits.

FRIDAY, FEBRUARY 17, 2:00 P.M.   Known the world over for its manufacture of automobile bodies, railroad cars, and mechanical parts for industry, the Budd Company is one of Philadelphia's foremost industries. Program will show models, samples and pictures of parts of this great plant.

FRIDAY, FEBRUARY 24, 2:00 P.M.   Philadelphia has long been a textile center. Early Colonial weavers came from England. Their skill built up the great rug-and-carpet industry. But their knowledge came as civilization moved from the Far East, westward. Program begins with native weaving in Persia—to the rag-rug loom typical of early America—to hand-hooked rugs and finally to the American carpets of today, woven in enormous power-driven machines.

TUESDAY, FEBRUARY 28 (4 TO 4:15 P.M.)   Activities of the Philadelphia

Navy Yard will be demonstrated. This telecast will be beamed to a meeting in Atlantic City of the American Association of School Administrators.

SCIENCE IS FUN   WFIL-TV
Lyda Ickler

The radio program which was so popular with elementary school pupils takes shape on television. Interesting personalities and materials will make scientific principles easy to understand.

FRIDAY, FEBRUARY 3, 2:15 P.M.   *A Bouncing Good Show!* The mysteries and properties of rubber and rubber-making will be demonstrated with the help of Mr. Armand N. Spitz of The Franklin Institute.

FRIDAY, FEBRUARY 10, 2:15 P.M.   Shakes and Shivers. What causes earthquakes? A miniature earthquake will be featured to show how, why and when, within the limitations of present information.

FRIDAY, FEBRUARY 17, 2:15 P.M.   Radio Sound Effects. Here you will see the manner in which sounds are imitated over the radio—doors opening, fires, waterfalls, gunshots, etc. Temple University Workshop students will show you how.

FRIDAY, FEBRUARY 24, 2:15 P.M.   Man Makes a Fire. Mr. Spitz will demonstrate the many ways of causing combustion.

TUESDAY, FEBRUARY 28 (4:15 TO 4:30 P.M.)   Energy—momentum. What causes it—how is it controlled—how does it work for us. Mr. Spitz will give a special demonstration for the convention of American Association of School Administrators.

Out-of-School Listening and Viewing

So far this discussion on utilization has dealt with programs heard within the school. Whether the broadcast be prepared specifically for a school or lay audience, and whether it be presented by recordings, public address, radio or television, the same broad principles of classroom use apply in each case. However, there is another type of radio listening which should be noted, the out-of-school, or "assigned-listening," program, as it is sometimes termed.

Much of what has been said concerning the use of the in-school program applies to the out-of-school broadcast. Here also, before the teacher can recommend such listening it is necessary that she know what programs are scheduled. The sources noted earlier will be helpful in this regard also.

When the teacher has determined what out-of-school programs are available, she is ready to make her recommendations for home listening. Her choice of specific programs should be based upon several criteria. She might ask herself these questions:

1. Is the program based on children's interests?
2. Does it come at a suitable time?
3. Is it technically well presented?
4. Is it emotionally satisfying?
5. Does it meet the particular needs of the child, or children, for whom I am recommending it?
6. Is it valid?
7. Is it of general interest?
8. Is it closely correlated to our work in school?
9. Do the programs which I recommend present a variety of experience? [8]

Following the establishment of a list of selective programs for out-of-school listening, the teacher can then decide how she plans to use the contributions from these programs.

This listening after school hours may either be suggested as a leisure-time activity or it may be used as an investigation for supplementary material. The two approaches are not mutually exclusive, and both can be used to further school ends.

Recreational Listening and Viewing. Selective leisure-time listening has been encouraged by teachers in several ways.

1. Surveys of pupil radio tastes have been conducted. Following the survey, studies have been made to determine why certain programs are popular and what the factors are that can contribute to better programs. Teachers have issued weekly lists of such superior programs.
2. The place of the listener as a consumer of radio advertised products has been analyzed. Advertising appeals have been evaluated.
3. Methods for the improvement of home listening have been studied with a committee of the Parent-Teachers Association or the local Radio Council. The results of the investigation have been reported to the faculty and the parents. (A more detailed discu: :on of such activity is found in Chapter 12.)
4. Some schools have incorporated in their school newspapers a radio log which calls attention to preferred programs.
5. In many classrooms a committee is chosen to place a daily radio schedule on the bulletinboard. Preferences and program notes are displayed.

6. In a few schools, announcements concerning select programs for the evening are broadcast over the public address system.

Thus, it is seen that the improvement of leisure-time listening should be encouraged in a positive manner. Good programs should be recommended rather than poor programs condemned.

Out-of-school *viewing*, as television people prefer to call it, will probably be more fruitful than in-school viewing in most communities for some time to come. The field of drama, especially valuable for the secondary-school pupils, will be a staple of network programming, and will by virtue of its expense continue to be an evening item, although the American Broadcasting Company began four series of half-hour dramas on Saturday mornings early in 1951. Half-hour dramatizations of short stories, whether "live" or on film, seem to continue in popularity. The "family programs"—*Mama, The Goldbergs*, and others—are wholesome fare. And while video's commercial programming for children, as discussed in a later chapter, has already created some alarm, the principle of recommending good programs rather than condemning poor ones holds equally good in television, so that guiding the younger children to *Mr. Wizard* or *Magic Cottage* is well worth the teacher's time.

Assigned Listening and Viewing. The second approach to out-of-school listening is to use it as a supplement to classroom activity. Numerous methods have been employed by teachers to guide such listening. Some of the procedures noted above can be used here also.

1. The most common procedure consists of individual reports which are made to the class, after which a discussion takes place.
2. The teacher may organize a radio committee, each member of which engages in selective listening, and then a joint report is presented.
3. A third plan, which has been used with some success in small communities, is the formation of a student listening group whereby several pupils meet at a home and listen collectively.

Whether the children have been asked to listen alone or as members of a group, worth-while results are more likely if the *purposes* for listening are clearly understood. If the teacher has aroused curiosity if a critical evaluation is to be made, and perhaps a class report is to be given, then out-of-school listening becomes a more meaningful experience.

The assignment of home listening requires a word of caution. In some homes the radio may be commandeered by other members of the family so that the pupil may not have an opportunity to hear the program assigned. With the spread of multiple-set ownership, however, that difficulty is disappearing. Care should be taken, too, that the choice of a program does not require the pupil to stay up too late. This is especially true in the lower grades. In some poorer districts the family may not possess a radio, and although that is becoming increasingly rare, the teacher should first be sure before any child is embarrassed. Particularly is this true of television, for television-set ownership, although increasing at a remarkable rate, is still not yet widespread enough to warrant general classroom assignments. Indeed, most teachers can truthfully align themselves with those who do *not* own video receivers. Accordingly, group listening in the homes of those who do have sets becomes even more logical, although the question of interference with the interests of other members of the family may become even more acute. However, the practice of having the neighbors' children in to watch television is so widespread that most set-owning parents are now conditioned to such invasions and will probably be surprised and pleased to discover that certain programs have teacher's approval.

Whether the child's listening and viewing be done in school or out, with elaborate organization or otherwise, the values of radio and television are in direct ratio to the classroom teacher's interest and activity. Would that all who plan to use a broadcast might follow the "ten commandments" as stated by the Wisconsin School of the Air:

1. Provide good receiving equipment! Poor reception can ruin the finest program.
2. Select program carefully to correlate with your regular work or to stimulate new activity.
3. Prepare the class for the broadcast. Build an eager listening attitude, and have maps, paper, or other materials ready.
4. Tune your radio and adjust the volume level well in advance of the scheduled time of the broadcast.
5. Give leadership in attentive listening and response throughout the program. Wait for the concluding announcement.

6. Follow up the broadcast with whatever discussion or activity seems needed to make the experience worth while and lasting.

7. Don't kill the pleasure of radio listening by compulsory notetaking, excessive testing, or tiring routine.

8. Don't expect the radio to do everything. Your skill in using a program is just as important as that of the broadcaster in presenting it. The program must be used, not only heard.

9. Encourage listening by parents. Discussions between parents and children form an excellent tie-up between school and home.

10. Relay your criticisms and suggestions to the broadcasters. They are striving to serve your needs.

The above suggestions relate specifically to radio, but the principles of good use are the same for radio and television, recordings, films, and even textbooks. In the following statement by John H. Griffith substitute any other teaching aid for the words *pictures* and *films*, and the cautions are still valid. The Director of Visual Education in the Galesburg (Illinois) Public Schools asks:

1. *Are you guilty* of going on a picture drunk? Have you been guilty of showing several complete film strips, sets of 2- by 2-inch slides, or several moving pictures all at one time?

2. *Are you guilty* of failing to prepare the student for that which you want him to see or understand?

3. *Are you guilty* of expecting a student to understand a picture, film, or diagram just because he looks at it? (A picture is not necessarily worth ten thousand words.)

4. *Are you guilty* of failing to follow up the use of each aid with an explanation of points not understood and a check on what has been learned?

5. *Are you guilty* of failing to place the new vocabulary to be encountered in the film on the board?

6. *Are you guilty* of failing to ask unanswered questions about what is to be seen in order that the student will be alert in finding the answers to those questions?

7. *Are you guilty* of thinking, that because a certain film is good, the whole school ought to see it whether it fits into their unit of work or not?

8. *Are you guilty* of thinking that a film which lasts only 10 minutes is a waste of time? (Attention span of many children is not longer than this.)

9. *Are you guilty* of thinking, "I won't have to teach today because we are going to have a film"?

10. *Are you guilty* of thinking that a child gets all there is in a film strip or moving picture by seeing it once?

11. *Are you guilty* of failing to realize that many of the words you use are empty, meaningless words to your students and that they will continue to be so unless you are able to put meat on these word-skeletons in the form of real and vicarious experiences?

12. *Are you guilty* of not realizing that materials in this field, which you may have considered worthless in the past, are now being replaced by excellent up-to-date materials?

13. *Are you guilty* of failing to think of visual aids as just one of the fine tools for learning and not a substitute for the teacher.

14. *Are you guilty* of believing that, because you have had bad experiences with poor films or strip films, poor projection, improper lighting, poor acoustics, failure to get materials at the time needed or failure to get them at all, no place to show them, etc., that this field can be of no future help to you? [9]

---

[9] John H. Griffiths, "Are You Guilty?" *Educational Screen*, January, 1948, p. 6.

8

Measuring the Results

◇◇◇

What are the more common objectives of the radio and television programs?

What types of measurement have been used commercially?

What are some of the values and limitations of each procedure?

In evaluating educational programs what procedures and forms are being utilized? What are the relative merits of each plan?

What forms are used in television evaluation?

◆◆◆◆◆◆◆◆THREE BASIC STEPS in the program enterprise have been discussed thus far: preparation, presentation, and utilization. A fourth and equally important step is evaluation, for only with some form of measurement can one tell what the program has accomplished. The aim of this chapter is to discuss briefly some of the more common procedures used to answer that need. With minor exceptions the methods used are the same for both radio and television broadcasts. Since the methods of evaluation and the degree of accomplishment are determined by the goals or objectives of the broadcaster, it is necessary, first, to ascertain what the objectives are.

Program Objectives

To the commercial advertiser the prime purpose of the program is to stimulate sales. The entertainment itself may relate only indirectly to a specific product and may be primarily concerned with the promotion of institutional good will; yet in the final analysis, its success can be measured only in terms of increased sales of the product. It goes without saying, however, that the sales promotion can form a genuinely educational program, for often the distinction between what is advertising and what is education is slight.

To the educator the recognition and general acceptance of objectives are not so easily attained. Not only are these objectives in a state of flux, but the degree of emphasis may vary with changing conditions. In fact, the development of objectives has been a major activity thus far in broadcast research.

Wrightstone has classified the chief goals of school programs into these categories:

1. Functional information; objectives dealing with the acquisition of facts, information, concepts, and principles in various fields.
2. Powers of critical thinking and discrimination; objectives dealing with ability to infer, to analyze, to apply generalizations, principles or standards.
3. Attitudes and appreciations; objectives dealing with the quality direction and consistency of beliefs, convictions, opinions and choices
4. Interests; objectives dealing with the building of broader, deeper and growing interests and preferences in each area of the curriculum

5. Creative expression; objectives dealing with self-expression in any media, including self-purposed experiments or investigations.
6. Personal-social adaptability; objectives dealing with emotional, personal, and social values and patterns of behavior.
7. Skills and techniques; objectives dealing with conventionally accepted "tools" or skills peculiar to a subject or discipline.[1]

If general acceptance of these goals can be presumed, it may be well at this point to discuss the methods of measurement generally in use. The first phase of the discussion will deal briefly with commercial research, since some of the methods used may be suggestive to the educational broadcaster and of general interest to teachers. Emphasis will be given to that phase of the subject which deals with the application of some of these procedures to education.

Methods of Listener * Surveys

Various surveys have been conducted by advertisers to determine whether or not the objectives of a broadcast have been obtained. From these surveys the broadcaster endeavors to learn whether he is reaching the audience he wants and whether the type of program planned is producing the desired effect.

Knowledge of the individual listener, his habits and interests, is of vital importance to the advertiser. A survey of listeners can be very productive, if it shows their number, geographical distribution, age, sex, intelligence, social and economic status. To determine the listeners' habits the survey may attempt to note their activities; whether they are regular or occasional listeners, whether and to what degree they have purchased the product, attended the concert or meeting, etc. In partial indication of interests the survey may attempt measurement of the listeners' preference for the program or the station. It may seek, also, to determine to what extent the audience associates the program with the product.

Although the accumulation of facts concerning the audience is perhaps the most common purpose of the survey, nevertheless, investiga-

[1] J. Wayne Wrightstone, "Evaluating the Production and Use of School Broadcasts," *The Phi Delta Kappan*, March, 1939, p. 333.
* In this discussion the term "listener" refers to viewers of television programs as well.

tions are undertaken for various reasons. The advertiser may want to know the effect of changes in program forms and personnel, broadcasting periods, networks, and even station power. He may want to compare the sales before and after a broadcast advertising campaign, or he may want to measure the sales response to different types of advertising media such as newspapers, billboards, circulars, magazines, as well as radio and television. It may be helpful for him to know the effects of signal strength and interference in a certain locality. In short, the advertiser seeks any and all data which enable him to provide maximum service for his client's dollar.

In conducting such surveys a variety of methods have been used. Perhaps the four most commonly used are: *analysis of mail, telephone surveys, automatic-recording devices,* and *personal investigations.* Regardless of the technique adopted, the basic principles of measurement must be understood and applied. In the collection of data a proper sampling and tested reliability are essential. In the selection of the survey form, the probable degree of validity of the conclusions must be understood, and in the formation of these conclusions an objective treatment is demanded. In broadcasting, too, no method of measurement has inherent qualities which cannot be destroyed by poor execution, or enhanced by scientific application.

Analysis of Mail. One of the methods often used commercially is the analysis of mail which may be either solicited or unsolicited.

As any listener knows, many ingenious plans have been used to stimulate audiences to write, such as free offers of samples and novelties, copies of talks, playing of request numbers, enrollment in clubs, contests and possible awards, reading of names, and even threats to discontinue programs.

Several procedures have been followed to analyze the resulting mail. By inspecting postmarks, the quality of stationery, the grammar, spelling, and punctuation of the written response, the broadcaster can judge, in some degree, the listener's occupation as well as his economic and educational standards.

It is conceded generally that mail response comes largely from classes on the lower economic level. An early analysis of mail by Durant led him to conclude that "most of the letters were sent in by

invalids, lonely people, the very aged, the very youthful, hero wor-
shipers, and mischievous children." [2] In England, mail received following a series of talks on psychology was said by Burt to have come
from "an excessive proportion of people who were obviously neurotic,
writing about their own mental troubles, or those of their children
or their friends." [3] Obviously this type of response may have been
elicited by the content of the talks presented.

However, the consensus of many performers is that the mail response indicates an increasing sense of discrimination and a slow but
gradual development of tastes. In spite of this gradual improvement,
the so-called "class" audience which is most apt to be critical is least
apt to write. The poor mail response to the Toscanini series was indicative of this.

There needs to be a greater emphasis placed upon positive rather than
upon negative comments. The broadcaster, though he wants to know
what is not liked, is also anxious to know what is desired. In either
case, if a definite listener judgment is apparent the public can expect
some program reaction, for, as Julius F. Seebach, Jr. indicates:

Do not underestimate the constructive value of intelligent comments.
We do not ask our audience nor could it help us very much, to solve the
details of schedule making, such as the hour or the day at which these
various programs should be presented. All of these things depend upon very
complicated circumstances such as availability of artists, previous commitments, and many other elements from which we alone can draw practical
conclusions. But if large numbers of people spontaneously like a certain
program and let us know of it, the result can only be favorable to its continuance. If they do not like a certain program, if it bores or annoys them,
and enough listeners let us know it, and an equal or greater number do
not actively approve of it, we are certain to change that program.[4]

Although the mail analysis technique is inexpensive and covers rather
quickly a wide geographic area, as a scientific tool of measurement
it has evident limitations. Karol points out that, at best, audience mail
is valuable only as a rough index. Large quantities of mail may reveal

Louis Reid, "Psychology of Fan Mail," Broadcasting, September 15, 1932, p. 10.
British Broadcasting Corporation, The B.B.C. Yearbook, 1932, p. 216.
Julius F. Seebach, Jr., "Did You Like the Program?" Education, June, 1940,
    629.

good or bad qualities of particular programs but its better function is to indicate listener location rather than numbers.[5]

Although the response solicited by questionnaires may be large, it does not necessarily result in good sampling. The validity of the mail response depends upon the degree to which it represents those who do not write. For objective evaluation, this representational degree must be determined; and, furthermore, as Lumley notes, if the evaluation of mail response is to be helpful, inducements for writing must be either eliminated or standardized, and the analysis that follows must be conducted by an impartial agency.[6]

Analysis of Telephone Calls. A second method frequently used in a broadcast survey is analysis of telephone calls. The calls may be either an unsolicited response from listeners, or solicited by representatives of the broadcasters.

Many station switchboard operators can provide ample testimony to the fact that listeners do not hesitate to phone when, for example, programs are changed without announcement, or the station accidentally goes off the air, or if the earth is "invaded."

Although these calls have real significance for the broadcaster, a better measurement of typical listener reaction is probably the planned telephone survey as conducted by the investigator. Various techniques have been used in conducting the telephone survey, but these can generally be classified into two methods, the coincidental and the unaided recall.

In the coincidental procedure, the telephone survey is made during the time in which the program is broadcast. This procedure has several merits. It secures information that is not distorted by the need for recalling it. It is especially helpful in providing quickly the listener reactions to a specific program. This coincidental use of the telephone, however, does interrupt listening or viewing, only a limited amount of information can be collected, and there is the danger of antagonizing the public by calling them too early or too late in the day or night.

The telephone survey using the method of unaided recall is less concerned with the element of time. The respondent is not aided in

---

[5] John J. Karol, "Measuring Radio Audiences," *Printer's Ink Weekly*, November 19, 1936, p. 16.
[6] F. H. Lumley, *Measurement in Radio*, Ohio State University, 1934, p. 87.

his recall by the mention of any specific program, performer, or product. Questions phrased carefully can be used to good advantage when widespread interviews must be made within a limited period. It probably permits greater analysis of listener reaction than does the coincidental call, although the factor of memory does become involved. Moreover, interviewers are prone to hurry the interview and there is a tendency for listeners to favor the programs which immediately precede the phone call.

Whether the telephone survey be made during or after a program, this method in general is a fairly inexpensive one. Such measurement is effective when the interviews sought are of a brief, unclassified nature. However, telephone interviews have several limitations. They are at a disadvantage when extensive information is sought, when analysis of the listener's attitude is wanted, and when further classification of the audience is desirable. There is also considerable listening by audiences that are not reached by telephones, such as in automobiles, out-of-doors, and in rural areas.

The weaknesses of proper sampling with the telephone have been recognized, for otherwise the assumption is that comments from telephone subscribers are typical of audience response in general. Thus, data based on interviews with this group cannot be regarded as typical, although comparative studies, in urban areas at least, have shown a close correlation between the results of surveys conducted both by telephone and by personal interviews.

The most widely used telephone service has long been provided by C. E. Hooper, Incorporated, through a coincidental telephone check of listeners in major cities. From these calls the following basic information is obtained: available homes, percentage of homes using sets, program choice at time of phone call, sponsor identification, and audience composition. Periodic reports include the familiar "Hooperating" which represents the percentage of set owners called in a given area who are listening to a certain program. Thus, for example, the report for New York City the first week in August, 1950, showed that *Toast of the Town* on television had a rating of 49.2.

Broadcast advertisers find these results helpful in several ways. They can pick the preferable day and hour whenever a choice of broadcast time is available; detect trends in the popularity of programs and types of programs; appraise talent by scrutinizing performance in ratings; determine whether a given season should be included or not; balance the value of daytime and night time programs; analyze program audiences by sections of the country, population groups, income levels, and the like; and evaluate the possible elements that contribute to high- and low-rating programs.

The rise of television and its cut into radio listening has complicated measurement techniques. Thus, for instance, accurate national ratings cannot be determined by simply averaging local data, since television does not yet exist as a competing service in all cities surveyed. This was one of the reasons that led the Hooper organization to emphasize its local rather than national service.

Automatic-Recording Devices. Automatic-recording devices have been in use for fifteen years. The device in one form or another is attached to the home radio or television receiver and records when the listener tunes in. The choice of station is also noted automatically. Thus data can be obtained as to frequency of listening and viewing, minute-by-minute reports during all hours, popularity trends, and so on.

The most widely used device of this kind is the one developed by the Nielsen Company, the Audimeter. These have been placed in a selected, supposedly representative cross section of all United States radio homes (with the exception of mountain states, which comprise only 3 per cent of radio homes). The national Nielsen sample at the time of this writing consisted of 1,500 homes.

The method has several advantages, since the recording is automatic and provides data for every minute of the year. The sample can be carefully chosen and controlled to a maximum degree. Subjective elements, such as faulty recall and poor question-phrasing, are reduced to a minimum.

It is apparent, however, that a premium is placed on exact, scientific sampling for the number of expensive recording devices placed in homes must necessarily remain very small as compared to the size of the total audience. There is some question also as to effective measurement in multiple-set homes, outdoor listening which is unrecorded, and other unusual conditions.

Personal Investigation. Another method of research used is that of personal statement, and here, again, the listener response may be either unsolicited or solicited.

Unsolicited comments of a casual nature frequently bear great weight with sponsors, but obviously it is imperative that a proper interpretation be given to them, for the comments heard may be far from typical. (Perhaps the poorest way to evaluate one's success as a broadcaster is to ask a friend for his opinion!)

Greater reliance can be placed upon the response which has been solicited through personal interviews, made either by unaided recall or by aided recall.

In the former method the listener is asked to recall, for example, what programs he heard during the day. The value of this procedure is lowered because the response depends upon the listener's ability to remember. By checking results against an automatic record of actual set operation, it was found that the average person was able to recall correctly only 31 per cent of the programs he heard the day before.

In the aided-recall method the listener often is provided with a list of programs and broadcast periods which he checks. Although this approach reduces the loss due to memory, it facilitates errors of commission due to checking full programs that are only partially heard.

However, in either case, with trained interviewers, questions carefully phrased, and a correct sampling, this measurement by personal interviews, although it is expensive, can provide a good deal of fairly reliable data from a relatively small number of persons. Several variations of this method have been used, including a panel of judges, a paid jury, and direct personal observation by the surveyor. These methods, since they have been used to a greater extent in educational research, will be discussed later.

Other Methods. In addition to the four methods of measurement noted above, other techniques have been employed by advertisers. It is evident that the proof of the advertising pudding is the volume of sales, and consequently the analysis of the market response is another measuring rod. This response can be gauged in several ways: by comparing the sales of similar items, one with broadcast advertising and others without it; by varying the types of advertising media and charting the sales; by relating the volume of sales to varying

expenditures on broadcast advertising; by analyzing sales in comparable areas using different advertising media; and by tracing the causes
of sales.

Other forms of research have attempted to demonstrate the relationship between audience response and purely technical factors, such
as signal strength. Some investigators have examined the effect on
the purchase of radios. Evidences of some modification of other types
of listener behavior, such as reading habits, election returns, and attendance figures, have been sifted and analyzed.

One of the problems confronting the broadcast research student
is the difficulty of adding "why" to "how many." The popularity of
a program can be determined, but the specific reasons for its success
are not so easily established. As C. A. Siepmann puts it, "We count
heads, but reckon little what registers *in* the head." [7]

Automatic-recording devices such as those referred to earlier have
been adapted for use in other forms of evaluation. Early experimentation by Lazersfeld and Stanton and more recently expanded by
Schwerin made use of the recorded likes and dislikes of laboratory
audiences as trial programs are pretested. Through such evaluation
before the program is actually broadcast the judgment of sample
audiences can be used to reduce possible program weaknesses. As
further experimentation with this "Program Analyzer" takes place, it
may be found extremely helpful in answering the question, "Who
likes what and why?" The results of such investigations are significant
to the advertiser, and to the educator as well.

As the use of television expands, specialized forms of measurement
specifically applicable to that medium will no doubt develop but at
present, as indicated earlier, comparable methods are generally used.
For purposes of illustration only one specialized television-measure-
ment service will be noted. Charles C. Flarida, Jr., Incorporated of
New York, for example, records commercials off the screen of 16-mm.
sound film, deleting the product's name. An assembly of "neighborhood people" observe the film and indicate their awareness or non-
awareness of the product's existence. Similar techniques are used by
other research groups.

---

[7] Paul F. Lazersfeld and Frank Stanton, *Radio Research* 1942–1943, Duell, Sloan,
& Pearce, 1944, p. 148.

School Broadcast Evaluation

Continuous evaluation is essential if the educator is to know which of the many school activities undertaken are actually productive. Without the knowledge of results, the time and effort spent in the radio or TV enterprise may well be questioned. An activity which takes up the time of great numbers must show conclusively its actual accomplishments if it is to merit support.

By collecting pertinent data concerning the programs, listeners, and the effects of listening, the evaluation can contribute much to the broadcasters and to the classroom teachers.

In the field of education the techniques of measurement and evaluation used by commercial radio require some adaptation. Not only are the goals of school broadcasting different and probably more intangible than those related to sales; but its audience, if not known definitely, is frequently a selective one with respect to ages, grades, interests, etc. Some of the measurement techniques used with the non-school program may be applied also to the school broadcast; but, whereas the advertiser's measurement has as its chief aim the determination of the size and type of his listening audience, with the educator that consideration may be incidental. In some instances, the school broadcaster may know in advance how many auditors she is to have and how much teacher material to prepare.

Measurement in this field is not so new as one might suppose. If psychological experimentation on auditory suggestion is included, and it may well be, contributions to the basic measurement of the educational value of radio were made long before commercial broadcasting began. As early as 1902 Pearce noted the comparative adjustments in his subjects to visual and auditory suggestions.[8] At least four other important studies in this same area are described in psychological journals before 1920, the birth date of modern radio.[9]

[8] Haywood J. Pearce, "Experimental Observations upon Normal Motor Suggestibility," *Psychological Review*, July, 1902, pp. 329–356.

[9] M. Schuyten, "Sur la validité de l'enseignement intuitif primaire," *Archives de Psychologie*, V (1906), 245–253.

F. Kuhlmann, "The Present Status of Memory Investigation," *Psychological Bulletin*, September 15, 1908, pp. 285–293.

J. Carleton Bell, "The Effects of Suggestion upon the Reproduction of Triangles

If the measurement of auditory memory is considered a field related to radio, then it is interesting to note that investigations such as those conducted by Whitehead and Kirkpatrick took place during the latter part of the nineteenth century.

However, the discussion here will be confined to procedures of measurement and evaluation which have taken place recently and which are definitely an outgrowth of radio broadcasting. Even here the scope of such efforts is so wide that only a cursory survey of the subject can be attempted. Much of the early research in radio in education was conducted by the National Advisory Council on Radio in Education, the National Committee on Education by Radio, the Radio Division of the United States Office of Education, the Bureau of Radio Research at Teachers College, the Bureau of Educational Research at Ohio State University, and the Harvard Psychological Laboratory.

In order to coordinate the research activities, Ohio State University in 1931 began to collect and report the various studies undertaken. This collection appeared in mimeographed form under the name *Research Studies in Education by Radio—Cooperative Group*. To suggest the nature of the projects included, a few typical ones selected at random are listed:

(1931) A study of the influence on certain of children's musical preferences of one year Series A of the NBC Music Appreciation Concerts conducted by Walter Damrosch.

A trial study of the effect of a radio program on children's reading interests.

An attempt to discover what mode of oral style in radio broadcasting is best suited to the recall of facts, on the part of college students.

(1932) A comparison of the mental processes of a group listening to material from a loud speaker with the mental processes of the same group face to face with the broadcaster.

To see whether a congregate group of listeners before a loudspeaker can correctly match the voices of three speakers with information concerning the personalities of the speakers.

---

and of Point Distances," *American Journal of Psychology*, October, 1908, pp. 504–518.

V. A. C. Henmon, "The Relation between Mode of Presentation and Retention," *Psychological Review*, March, 1912, pp. 88–94.

To study the effect of rate on comprehension.

(1933) A further study of the relative recall efficiency of visual and auditory presentation of advertising material.

Comparisons of actual operation times of receiving sets with listener estimations.

A survey of listening interests and tastes of one thousand high-school pupils.

(1934) Children's interests and reactions in radio programs: A study of the intermediate grade in the New York Metropolitan Area.

The psychology of listening as applied to an informational radio address.

Some effective conditions for broadcasting:

1. Is it better to present material in a very general way, in a specific way, or is some combination of general with specific presentation best?
2. What is the relative effectiveness of short and long sentences?
3. What is the most effective speed for broadcasting various types of material?
4. What is the value of repetition in the presentation of different types of material over the radio?
5. What is the optimum length for different types of broadcasts?

(1935) To develop listening guide charts of varying degrees of difficulty for use in junior and senor high school and colleges.

To determine the educational effects of a short summary included in a geography lesson presented as a drama concerning Manchuria by the *American School of the Air.*

(1936) The training of radio personnel.

(1937) To determine children's reactions to radio programs by means of student observers trained to detect evidences of interest in children's physical movements and changes in facial expression.

(1938) To determine the value of radio as an educational factor in the Detroit Schools.

To gather information as to the extent of radio guidance in the senior high schools of Minnesota.

This joint listing of research studies was discontinued when the following three major research projects in the field of radio education were launched by the General Education Board in 1937.

At Ohio State University, the Evaluation of School Broadcasts undertook a study, the expected outcome of which is described as follows:

1. The study will indicate what school broadcasts are accomplishing and where they are falling short.
2. The study will make possible a number of generalizations regarding the results to be expected from certain types of school broadcast programs.
3. The study will result in the establishment of a number of criteria helpful in building new programs.
4. Techniques will be developed which may be utilized by broadcasters and by other investigators in evaluating radio programs.
5. New instruments of evaluation will be developed which will be helpful not only in educational broadcasting but in general education as well.
6. It may well be expected as a result of the close cooperation of teachers and broadcasters in this work that the quality of school broadcasts will be improved.[10]

At the University of Wisconsin a project was undertaken which "attempted to measure the educational effectiveness of a series of radio programs heard in the classroom and intended to supplement the work of the teacher. Broadcasts in music, nature study, geography, community living, English and speech, planned by teachers of these subjects, were written and produced by trained staff members." [11]

The Bureau of Applied Social Research at Columbia University has published a series of excellent studies which deal with the role of mass media in the United States. The Institute of Public Opinion at Princeton is also publishing materials which are of value in this field. The *Journal of Applied Psychology* and the *Public Opinion Quarterly* report studies in the general area of mass communication.

In addition to the studies undertaken by various universities much of the research pertaining to specific school programs rather than general education broadcasts has been carried on by several school systems, which are presenting their own radio materials. Among these are New York, Detroit, Cleveland, and Chicago.

Whether the research in education by radio or TV be under the auspices of a university or a local board of education, the results of such investigations can be grouped into related areas: those studies that analyze program forms, those that consider listener preferences,

---

[10] *Conference Summary*, Evaluation of School Broadcasts, November 2–4, 1939.
[11] Lester Ward Parker, "The Wisconsin Study of School Broadcasts," *Education on the Air*, Ohio State University, 1938, p. 92.

those that are concerned with program effects and results, and those that consider methods of classroom utilization.

All these phases of investigation undoubtedly have value, and may be of some interest to the classroom teacher. However, unless she is actively concerned with the preparation and presentation of broadcasts, the chances are that her primary interest will be in judging the results of certain programs of which she and her pupils are consumers, and in determining the most effective methods for using these programs in the school.

Common Forms of School Program Measurement

Several procedures have been used to evaluate school broadcasts and, as Wrightstone indicates, each method suggests a different purpose for the evaluation. He has listed the following ways by which a local school system can conduct such measurement:

1. Using a panel of teachers who fill out a rating scale or check list for each of a series of broadcasts.
2. Using teacher-made tests for measuring such objectives as the acquisition of information, attitudes, and interests.
3. Using commercially available tests, such as those available for American history, literature, and for aspects of critical thinking.
4. Using tests, scales, and measures constructed by such research groups as the Evaluation of School Broadcasts Staff at Ohio State University or the WHA Radio Project Staff at the University of Wisconsin.[12]

Several variations of the panel technique noted above have been used in school program evaluation. These panels have been composed most often of teachers, though occasionally judgment by pupils, supervisors and principals has been solicited.

Use of Rating Scales or Check Lists. To collect the group reaction a variety of written forms has been used, the most common of which is the rating scale or check list. A major difficulty in the development of these forms has been to construct them so that they take but a minimum of the teacher's time and yet provide a maximum of value for the broadcaster.

The rating scales in use can generally be classified as follows: (a) those which can be applied to all school programs regardless of

---

[12] J. Wayne Wrightstone, *op. cit.*, p. 335.

content and form and (b) those which are planned to evaluate a specific series or an individual program.

GENERAL TYPE. To illustrate the first type, the general rating scale, the following form is shown. It is a report outline included in the *Evaluation Manual* distributed to a panel of teachers by the Radio Council of the Chicago Public Schools. This report, which was to be sent in each week, was prepared "in order that staff members of the Radio Council of the Board of Education may have an impartial and complete criticism of their work." The items listed in this report will be of interest to classroom teachers as well as to educational broadcasters, since they suggest specific standards for judging the effectiveness of a school program.

WEEKLY REPORT
RADIO COUNCIL BROADCAST

Date_____Series Title_____Broadcast Title_____
Teacher's Name_____School_____Grade_____
Size of Listening Group_____

                    High_____Average_____Low_____
Economic Rating of Class: _____
Intelligence Rating of Class: _____
Please check in the blanks the words that express your opinion. Base it as much as possible on student reaction.
(ALL)
   1. Student reaction indicated that this program was:
      ___ Excellent
      ___ Good
      ___ Fair
      ___ Poor
(PLANNER)
   2. This broadcast was related to the course of study:
      ___ in the current unit?
      ___ as a past unit?
      ___ as a future unit?
      ___ no unit?
   3. This broadcast served the following purposes:
      ___ Supplemented textbooks with timely material
      ___ Vitalized the subject matter of the course of study
      ___ Broadened student's background
      ___ Stimulated student activity or investigation
(SCRIPT WRITER)

4. This broadcast was:
   ___ Above the maturity level of my students?
   ___ Below the maturity level of my students?
   Explain!
5. The purpose or objectives of this broadcast were stated in the handbook; these purposes were:
   ___ Insufficiently emphasized
   ___ Overemphasized
6. The ideas or facts presented were:
   ___ Too numerous
   ___ Too few
7. The vocabulary used was:
   ___ Too elementary   (list objectionable words)
   ___ Too difficult
8. The program aroused and held student interest:
   ___ From the beginning of the program
   ___ Later in the program
   ___ At no time during the program
9. During the broadcast students manifested:
   ___ Intense interest
   ___ Some interest   (check by questioning students on content, etc.)
   ___ Little interest
10. The narrator's or actor's speeches were:
    ___ Too long
    ___ Too short
    ___ Too frequent
11. Changes of scene occurred:
    ___ Too often   (check by questioning students)
    ___ Too seldom
12. The entire program moved:
    ___ Too quickly
    ___ Too slowly
    Why?
(PRODUCER)
13. The music:
    ___ Contributed to the program
    ___ Most of the time
    ___ Part of the time
    ___ Never
    If it detracted, tell how:
14. Indicate characters who could not be distinguished because of lack of voice contrast.
15. List actors or speakers who talked too rapidly.

16. List actors or speakers who were not understandable.
17. List any sound effects which were intrusive or not realistic.
18. List any sound effects whose absence was noticeable.
19. List transitions which were not clear.

Excellent Good Fair Poor
20. The educational value of the content _____
The quality of the production techniques _____
The degree of interest and appeal _____

In addition to the weekly report, the panel was asked to fill in the following form at the conclusion of the semester:

END OF SEMESTER RADIO BROADCAST REPORT

This is the final report of the semester. Use the same methods of checking as in the weekly reports, giving *special attention* to questions requiring explanation. Include list made by student of class activities motivated by the radio broadcasts.

Answer the following as completely as possible:

A. How could the structure and format of the handbook be improved?

B. Suggest parts of the handbook which are inadequate or should be deleted.

C. Explain how you approached the broadcasts.

D. Mention additional procedures you used which aren't given in the handbook.

E. What was it that made the series effective?

F. What part of the series was lacking in sincerity?

G. List other in-school broadcasts you used.

H. What city excursions or visits to service institutions did any of your students make as a result of broadcasts?

I. List other grades and series for which this broadcast would be suitable.

Check the blanks which describe your opinion. Leave vacant if the statement does not express your opinion:

1. The Series as a Whole:

___ Fulfilled objectives in the handbook.

___ Aided in subject field instruction.

___ Contributed nothing good teacher covers.

___ Was above maturity level of students.

___ Below maturity level of students.

___ Was of transient value to students.

___ Was of permanent value to students, as:

The Series as a Whole—*cont.*:
___ Specific education.
___ Background enrichment
 ___ Improvement of attitudes.
 ___ Stimulated individual research.

Utilization and Handbooks:
2. The structure and format of the handbook were:
___ Practical and comprehensive.
___ Impractical.
3. The handbook contained:
___ Too much material.
___ Too little material.
4. To aid in preparation, the broadcast:
___ Should be summarized in handbook.
___ Should not be summarized
5. The suggestions for preliminary preparation were used:
___ Consistently.
___ Occasionally.
___ Seldom.
6. The post-broadcast suggestions were used:
___ Consistently.
___ Occasionally.
___ Seldom.

Participation:
7. Listener participation in the broadcast:
___ Contributed to student interest.
___ Increased student interest and attention.
___ Confused students.

8. Pupil activity during the broadcast (drawing, taking notes, etc.):
___ Aided student after the show.
___ Provided valuable motivation.
___ Made him lose part of the broadcast.

Program Content:
9. The broadcasts:
___ Were worth while.
___ Were timely.
___ Included subjects related to the child's experience.
___ Were unrelated and unsatisfactory.
___ Followed course of study closely.
___ Did not follow course of study.
___ Stories were suitable, interesting.
___ Uninteresting, of little value.
___ Children prefer familiar stories and subjects.
___ Prefer new stories and subjects.
___ Held students' attention.
___ Stimulated follow-up.
___ Covered too much ground.
___ Were at grade level in most cases.
___ Were above grade level generally.
___ Were below grade level generally.

Program Content—*cont.*:

10. The children and you:
    ___ Liked the series device.
    ___ Disliked the series device.

Program Pattern:

11. The device was:
    ___ Convincing and exciting.
    ___ Loosely connected.
    ___ Weak, obvious.

12. Children prefer the:
    ___ Interview type of show.
    ___ Dramatization.
    ___ Quiz program.

13. The introduction was:
    ___ Attention getting.
    ___ Uninteresting.

14. An occasional variation from the regular pattern of the broadcast would:
    ___ Make series more interesting.
    ___ Make confusion for the students.
    ___ Make no difference.

15. The radio reception was:
    ___ Consistently good.
    ___ Occasionally good.
    ___ Never good.

Forms Used in Television Evaluation.   While the results of program-evaluation research in television are less readily available, several interesting evaluation forms have already made their appearance. Mention has already been made of the United States Navy's research project at the Special Devices Center, Port Washington, Long Island. Evaluation research conducted by Dr. Robert D. Rock, Jr., of the Department of Education of Fordham University included the giving of pre- and postinstruction tests to classes involved in the experiment in order to compare teaching by (a) television; (b) television instructors face to face in the classroom; (c) normal classroom instruction; (d) kinescope recordings. (Kinescope recordings are 16-mm. sound films, photographed from the face of the kinescope, or picture tube, of a high-powered television receiver while the program is being broadcast. They are television's much more expensive equivalent of the disc or tape off-the-air recording of a radio program.)

In addition, Lieutenant Dana D. Reynolds, Head of Operations, Radio and Television Service of the United States Department of Agriculture, drew up the following "Scorecard for Telecasts," to be used by the students in a "post-mortem" analysis of each program.

An analysis of this detailed check list will be helpful also in guiding inexperienced television-program producers.

GENERAL SCOREBOARD FOR INFORMATION TV SHOWS

Subject of Telecast: ....

Station: ....

Date: ....

Length of Program: ....

I. SUBJECT OF TELECAST

	Excellent	Good	Fair	Poor
A. Is it of direct interest to TV audience?				
B. Is importance to audience clearly brought out?				
C. Is it timely in terms of: 1. Currrent news developments, problems?				
2. Seasonal problems?				
D. Is it suitable for this series of telecasts?				
E. Is it appropriate to time of day of telecast?				
F. Does the telecast further a definite, important function of originating agency?.				
G. Is it suitable for television?				

II. TO WHOM IS TELECAST DIRECTED

Is telecast primarily directed at:

Rural groups? ....
Urban groups? ....
Both? ....

Is appeal mainly to:

Men? ....
Women? ....
Both?   ....
Children? ....

III. OBJECTIVE AND APPEAL

A. What does telecast seek to accomplish? ....

....

....

	Excellent	Good	Fair	Poor
1. Does telecast accomplish objective?				

B. What is telecast's main interest appeal to viewer:

1. Make him feel well informed?   ....

    2. Offer background on matter currently in news? . . . .

    3. Save or make money?   . . . .

    4. Protect or improve health of self or family?   . . . .

    5. Personal improvement?   . . . .

    6. Solution to household or homegrounds problem? . . . .

IV. FORMAT

Indicate which of following formats was *used* . . . and which you think should have been used:

	USED	SHOULD USE
A. Interview	_____	_____
B. Group Discussion	_____	_____
C. Demonstration	_____	_____
D. Stills or movies with narration	_____	_____
E. Other	_____	_____

V. ORGANIZATION AND DEVELOPMENT

	Excellent	Good	Fair	Poor
A. Did telecast develop strong, central theme?				

    1. What was theme? . . . .
. . . .
. . . .

	Excellent	Good	Fair	Poor
B. Was subject logically developed?				
C. Was material fresh and informative?				
D. Was suspense employed to hold viewer to end of telecast for answer to question posed?				
E. Was conclusion strong? . . .				

F. Was there a call for the viewer to do something? . . Yes? . . . .; No? . . . .

    1. Should there have been such a call? . . . . Yes? . . . .; No? . . . .

G. Was telecast (or particular segment being considered):

    Too long? . . . .

    Too short? . . . .

    About right? . . . .

H. Was there too much detail? . . . .

    Too little? . . . .

    About right? . . . .

VI. TALENT
   A. Rate talent on following points:

	Excellent	Good	Fair	Poor
1. Personality				
2. Articulateness				
3. Authoritativeness				
4. General stage presence ..				

VII. AUDIO-VIDEO BALANCE

	Excellent	Good	Fair	Poor
A. Were the oral & visual parts "in balance"?				

   B. Would some of material presented visually have been better left to imagination?   Yes? ....; No? ....

VIII. PRODUCTION QUALITY

	Excellent	Good	Fair	Poor
A. Is there an intimacy (inherent in set, manner or talent, treatment of subject, that is in keeping with family-home situation)?				
B. Is there adequate motion in telecast? Movement of talent?				
Movement in visual presentations (e.g., drawing map or chart, rather than showing one previously prepared)?				

   C. Was there too much narration? ....
      Too little? ....
      About right? ....

   D. Rate language and delivery of audio part:

	Excellent	Good	Fair	Poor
1. Conversational quality ..				
2. Warmth and enthusiasm				
3. Change in volume, pace, pitch				

	Excellent	Good	Fair	Poor
E. Change of pace in show in general: Is there enough variety in show?				
Do action and "business" help "pace"?				
What about rhythm?				

Was show slow and draggy? . . . .

Too fast? . . . .

About right? . . . .

F. Was music used? Yes? . . . . . . No . . . . . . If so, did it add to program? . . . . . . detract? . . . . . . neither? . . . . . .

IX. VISUALS

	Excellent	Good	Fair	Poor
A. Titles				
B. Maps, graphs, charts: 1. Was lettering large enough and distinct?				
2. Could material presented be readily grasped?				
3. Were color tones pleasing?				
4. Were pictorial symbols used effectively?				

C. Diagrams, animations, cartoons—were they well used? . . . .

poorly used? . . . .

more needed? . . . .

D. Still photographs:
    1. Did photographs help tell story? . . . .
    2. Rate photographs according to:
        a. Amount of detail: Right? . . . . . too much? . . . . .
        b. Contrasting shade: Right? . . . . . too little? . . . . .
    3. Were too many stills used? . . . . too few? . . . . right number? . . . .
    4. Were stills held on screen long enough? . . . . too long? . . . .

E. Movies

	Excellent	Good	Fair	Poor
1. Did movies contribute to show?				

2. Rate movies according to:
   a. Amount of detail: Right? . . . . . too much? . . . . . .
   b. Definition: Good? . . . . . poor? . . . .
   c. Contrast   (black &
      white):   Good? . . . . . poor? . . . .

X. STUDIO SET

	Excellent	Good	Fair	Poor
A. Does set harmonize with the subject matter presented?				

B. Are there irrelevant materials on set?   Yes? . . . . No? . . . .

C. Is set well balanced (both props and talent)?   Yes? . . . . No? . . . .

D. Does set afford good contrast between actors and props . . . and background?   Yes? . . . . No? . . . .

XI. LIGHTING

	Excellent	Good	Fair	Poor
A. Do lights illuminate subjects adequately?				
B. Are lights localized to bring out areas of interest?				
C. Do lights model subjects to make stand out from background?				

XII. CAMERA ACTION

	Excellent	Good	Fair	Poor
A. Did cameras follow main subjects of interest?				
B. Did cameras show subjects big enough to insure instant recognition?				
C. Were there good transitions between close-ups and long shots, etc?				

	Excellent	Good	Fair	Poor
D. Was there good composition in shots?				
E. Did cameras give good orientation of set through distance shots?				

XIII. INTEREST

	Excellent	Good	Fair	Poor
A. Did telecast grab your attention right at outset?				

    1. If so, because of:
       a. Subject? ....
       b. Visual effects? ....
       c. Personality of talent? ....
       d. Other attention-getting factors? ....
  B. Would you tune in this program regularly?   Yes? ....
                                      No? ....
                                      Don't know? ...

XIV. OVER-ALL RATING OF SHOW

  A. What over-all rating would you give this show (the scale represents a range of 50 to 100):
    5_____6_____7_____8_____9_____10_____

One of the earliest forms of evaluation, drawn up in 1947, when there were fewer than a dozen television stations on the air and educational broadcasts were even fewer and farther between than now, was the "Yardstick" of the Education Committee of the American Television Society. Most of the members of the committee were professional workers in the commercial field, with a keen though extracurricular interest in educational programming. Their evaluation sheet reflects the point of view of the "inside worker."

AMERICAN TELEVISION SOCIETY YARDSTICK FOR EVALUATING TELEVISION EDUCATIONAL PROGRAMS

At whom was program directed?   3–6 yrs.?....; 6–10?....; 11–15?....; 15–18?......; college students? ....; Gen. public?....

Whom did it hit—in your opinion?
What did it try to teach?
Did it accomplish its purpose?
Was the subject important and worth learning?

Was the subject matter adapted and simplified for audience?

Did it make you want to do something more with the subject—or about the subject?

Did you learn anything? If so, what? New Information? . . . . . .
                                    New Attitudes? . . . . . .

Did it review known material? . . . . . . Dramatize known facts? . . . . . .

Did it maintain interest? . . . . . . In all or in part? . . . . . .

Would it have maintained interest of group aimed at?

Was the material presented visually?

Would this program have been as effective without the visual?

Did it try to give you too much information? . . . . . . Too much at once? . . . . . .

Was the script good? . . . . . . Format appropriate to subject? . . . . . .

    Lighting?_____ Cast?_____ Camera work?_____ Direction?_____

What per cent of the program was:

    Dramatization?_____ Lecture?_____ Demonstration?_____ Commentary?_____

What per cent would you prefer for this subject?

    Dramatization?_____ Lecture?_____ Demonstration?_____ Commentary?_____

Were the production techniques and devices effectively used to increase the understanding of the subject?

    (film, slides, etc.) If not, why not?

If there was background music, did you like it?

Any objectional features in content of production?

    Social?_____ Ethical?_____ Patriotic?_____ Moral?_____ Aesthetic?_____ Religious?_____ Technical?_____

Would you like to see another show in this series? . . . . . . On the same subject? . . . . . . Suggestions for another program?

Suggestion for improving this one?

    Another interesting evaluation sheet, on the school level, was drawn up by the Chicago Radio Council—WBEZ. Two forms are shown below, the first for the use of teachers and supervisors, the second for the use of students who have watched the telecast.

TELEVISION EVALUATION—RADIO COUNCIL
BROADCASTS

PROGRAM REPORT OF: .... PROGRAM TITLE: ....
        (School)   (District)

Reported by: .... PROGRAM SERIES: ....
    (Principal or Teacher or Supt.)

                      STATION: ....

GRADE: ...... SIZE OF GROUP: ... DATE OF PROGRAM: ....

INTELLIGENCE RATING OF VIEWING GROUP:
               High .... Average .... Low ....

ECONOMIC RATING OF VIEWING GROUP:
               High .... Average .... Low ....

PLEASE INCLUDE STUDENT OPINION IN YOUR ANSWERS
TO THE FOLLOWING WHEREVER POSSIBLE:

1. Is the maturity level of this program appropriate for your class?
   YES? .... NO? .... WHY? ....
2. In what ways was it a valuable educational experience?
3. What criticisms do you have of the educational value of this program?
4. In comparison with other television programs you have seen in this series, how would you rate its educational value?
5. Could the students hear the program easily?
6. Could the program be seen clearly by all present?
   Size of your television screen ....
7. Were any reception difficulties encountered? Explain, if any.
8. List parts of program (if any) which you consider:
   a. Too difficult ....
   b. Too simple ....
9. If students lost interest in the program and the attention lagged, indicate why and at what point.
10. Did any production techniques cause confusion?
    a. Visual Effects (Characters in costume, background effects, pictures, other properties):
    ....
    b. Sound Effects (Sounds, background noises, music, fading from one scene to another, and so forth):
    ....
11. Would this program have been as effective without the visual?
    YES? .... NO? .... WHY? ....
    ....
12. What parts of the program did the students enjoy most?
13. What parts of the program did they like least?
14. What preparation did you and the class make for today's telecast?

15. Did any activities grow out of last week's telecast? Describe briefly.
16. Have you any samples of television utilization that might be sent to the Radio Council?   YES? ... NO? ... Describe briefly: ....
....
17. What suggestions do you have as to further improvement of this type of program?
....
....
18. Your suggestions for further television programs suitable for class-room use:
....
....
....

STUDENT EVALUATION—RADIO COUNCIL TELEVISION PROGRAMS

TO THE TEACHER: Please ask your students these questions and send us a composite of their answers.

1. Is television as valuable to you in learning about new things as:
    RADIO? ....
    ....
    ....
    MOTION PICTURES? ....
    ....
    ....
    READING (Books, Magazines, Newspapers)? ....
    ....
    ....
2. Were the televiews (pictures) HELPFUL? YES? ...... NO? ......
    Give the reasons for your answer: ....
    ....
    ....
3. Did the Television Broadcast make you want to DO something more about the subject of the broadcast (further reading, research, projects, other activities)?
    ....
    ....
    Just what DID you do? ....
    ....

4. State briefly what the program meant to you: ....
....
....
....
This is the Report of: ....
(Student or Student-Group)
ROOM: .... GRADE: .... SCHOOL: .... DISTRICT: ....
PROGRAM TITLE: ....
PROGRAM SERIES: .... STATION: ....
DATE OF PROGRAM: ....

VALUES OF SCALES AND CHECK LISTS. There are several merits to the use of such teacher reports. They quickly provide the broadcaster with the collective judgment of teachers who are in classrooms utilizing the material presented. Thus the evaluation is made in a practical situation where success is measured in terms of actual effects rather than merely pleasant artistic forms.

The rating-scale method provides more people with an opportunity to express their reactions. It is certainly a more democratic technique than the application of a purely mechanical statistical measurement. For radio education particularly this is significant, since innovations can receive sympathetic consideration only if those who are to be influenced by the new development have an opportunity to present their views.

LIMITATIONS. The disadvantages of the radio check list are much like those of any questionnaire approach. If the lists are not prepared carefully they may take too much of the teacher's time, undue consideration may be given to unimportant details, and in any case the judgment may be a subjective one. There is always the temptation to tell someone what he likes to hear. Instances have been reported where teachers have even submitted evaluations of programs which had been canceled.

Evaluation to be effective should be continuous. Getting some judgment concerning every program may place an undue burden upon the teachers, and accordingly some school broadcasters have found it desirable to "stagger" the responses. A group of teachers is asked to evaluate different broadcasts. In this manner it is hoped that though the sample may be small, the reactions are more carefully studied. Surely it is more desirable to have several evaluations carefully made than many hasty judgments given indifferently.

OTHER PANEL USES.   Aside from check lists and rating scales, some investigators have used other devices in the form of a panel. In England, teachers kept weekly diaries. Wiebe made use of students' logs in evaluating a CBS music series.[13] In a Michigan study, individual "listening cards" were tried.[14] Gaudet utilized a panel of 600 high school students who responded to a series of questionnaires.[15]

An interesting variation of the panel method has been a change, not in the measurement form, but in the time at which the judgment is made. Proposed school programs are given a prebroadcast as well as a postbroadcast evaluation.

It is a mistake to assume that evaluation cannot take place until the radio lesson has been put "on the air." In fact, the assumption would simply be a waste of much time and effort for, if the radio material is to be of increasing value, the process of evaluation and revision must commence with the writing of the script and it must be a continuous process. Unless the proposed material is "prejudged," a waste of the listener's time is a probable result.

It is reasonable to assume that the most effective form of preliminary evaluation should take place in a situation similar to that in which the proposed material would be received later. Thus, it has been the practice to "preaudit" the rough draft in a typical classroom which corresponds in grade level, ability, size, equipment, and so forth to the usual listener situation for that particular subject. With the radio teacher and often the supervisor thus noting listener reactions to the new material, the conference which follows may result in important revisions. It is sometimes found, for example, that too much has been attempted in one lesson, or that the pauses for listener activity may not be properly timed, the vocabulary may be too difficult, the questions may not be clear, the directions confusing, and so forth. Certainly, it is less wasteful to experiment thus with one class than to broadcast doubtful material city-wide.

[13] J. Wayne Wrightstone, "The Status of Research in Education by Radio," *Education on the Air*, Ohio State University, 1940, p. 321.
[14] Roy Robinson, "Listening Habits of Michigan Children," *Michigan Education Association*, 1940, p. 20.
[15] Hazel Gaudet, "High School Students Judge Radio Programs," *Education*, June, 1940, p. 639.

The flexibility of the school-station schedule makes possible additional "preauditing." For example, in the science and music broadcasts so-called "tryout lessons" are presented by radio to three or four schools which thus evaluate the material before it is presented to all.[16]

Use of Tests. It will be recalled that the second and third methods of school-broadcast evaluation as listed by Wrightstone both have to do with the use of tests, either made by the teacher or available commercially.

The use of equated groups, some of which receive radio programs and others which do not, has been a common procedure in school-broadcast evaluation.

In Cleveland, for example, this method was tried as early as 1929 in conjunction with arithmetic lessons presented by radio. The first evaluation, which included Woody-McCall Mixed Fundamentals, Form I, and Cleveland Arithmetic Test—Problems, Test A, Form 2, was administered before the radio instruction was started, the second was given in conclusion of the radio lessons, using Form III of Woody-McCall, and Test A, Form I, of the Cleveland Arithmetic Test. Test Forms I and III, Woody-McCall, and 1 and 2 Test A, Cleveland Arithmetic Test—Problems, were equal in difficulty and the results comparable.

The results of that early study are presented statistically in bulletin form and a summarizing discussion is available in the Thirteenth Yearbook of the N.E.A.

Commencing in 1932 and continuing to the present time, each semester the Music Department has conducted a radio-testing program, the purposes of which are:

1. To measure to some extent, at least, the musicality and the achievement of individual pupils.
2. To give a basis for measuring progress in the advanced work.
3. To spur the children to further interest and achievement.

Copies of the tests used and the results obtained have been published and responses from teachers and principles who cooperated

---

[16] Station WBOE, *Report of Radio Activities*, pp. 76, 77.

during the first three years of the experiment were discussed at the Music Educators National Conferences.[17]

It is evident that not all types of programs lend themselves to judgment by tests. Those broadcasts which distinctly supplement courses of study and which emphasize the creation of social and scientific attitudes are more difficult to evaluate in this manner than are those broadcasts which relate more closely to particular school subjects and where the emphasis may be placed on the acquisition of facts. Nevertheless, tests have been developed and applied for both types of objectives. The literature published by the Evaluation of School Broadcasts included examples of such material.[18]

Occasionally the tests to be used in some type of evaluation are prepared by the broadcaster and included in the teacher's manual. This procedure has merits, since it not only saves the teacher's time but also aids the broadcaster to secure some evaluation of the particular objectives he has in mind. The manuals which accompanied the former Damrosch music series made use of this plan.

Another way for the local school system to evaluate broadcasts, it has been suggested, is by the use of tests, scales, and measures which have been constructed by various research groups.

Use of Research-Group Aid. Several such forms have been developed by research groups. As is the case with the check lists prepared by school systems, some apply to a specific program series and other forms are of a more general nature planned to be used with a variety of educational programs. Illustrative of the first type is the report form shown below. It was one of three used with a study planned "to determine (a) whether children acquire rhythmic skills better with radio lessons or without radio lessons and (b) whether teachers find the radio lessons in rhythmic activities a source of new music materials and of new teaching techniques."

Myrtle Head, "Three Years of Elementary Radio Music Instruction," *Music Educators National Conference Yearbook*, 1934, pp. 292, 294.

[18] "Publication List," *Evaluation of School Broadcasts*, Ohio State University, 1942.

RADIO TEACHER'S WEEKLY REPORT ON RHYTHM BROADCASTS

Date _____ Title of This Broadcast _____
Teacher's Name _____ Number of Pupils Listening _ _ _ _ _ _

Directions: Please check one item in each group, or answer the question in the space provided.

RADIO RECEPTION

___ Excellent
___ Average
___ Poor

Were the directions clear to the pupils?

___ Yes
___ No

PROGRAM TIMING

___ Too fast
___ Just right
___ Too slow

Was there any unfamiliar music on the broadcast which you liked especially? If so, give titles:

_____
_____

VOCABULARY

___ Too difficult
___ Just right
___ Too elementary

Did you get any new teaching techniques which you expect to use with your class? If so, indicate what they are:

PROGRAM AS A WHOLE

___ Better than usual
___ As good as usual
___ Poorer than usual

_____
_____

Did your children have difficulty with any of the muscular activities called for in the broadcast? If so, which ones?
_____
_____

What were the strong points of the broadcast?
_____
_____

What were the weak points of the broadcast?
_____
_____

An example of the general type of check list is now shown. It was prepared for application to a variety of programs.

TEACHER'S REPORT OF A BROADCAST

Teacher's Name _____ School _____
City _____ County _____ State _____
Subject(s) Served by This Broadcast _____
Grade _____ No. of Pupils Listening _____
General Title of This Program Series _____
Title of This Broadcast _____
Radio Station _____ Length of Program _____
Date of Broadcast _____ Time of Day _____

DIRECTIONS: Broadcasters are very much interested in getting your opinions of programs they offer for school listening. Hence, they would like your honest evaluation of this program. Please check ($\sqrt{}$) those items which most nearly express your judgment of the educational value of this program to your class.

Please note that this page should be filled in immediately after the broadcast. The rest should be filled in as soon as possible after you have completed your utilization of this radio program.

1. Could the broadcast be heard distinctly
   ___ a. all of the time?
   ___ b. part of the time?
   ___ c. most of the time?

2. For classroom use, would you rate this broadcast as being
   ___ a. very valuable?
   ___ b. suitable?
   ___ c. entirely unsuitable?

3. For your purpose, was this broadcast
   ___ a. too long?
   ___ b. too short?
   ___ c. about right?

4. For use at your grade level, was this broadcast
   ___ a. appropriate?
   ___ b. usable?
   ___ c. unsuitable?

5. Was this broadcast related to work which the class
   ___ a. has already done?
   ___ b. is doing now?
   ___ c. will do?

6. Was the main theme of the broadcast
   ___ a. well brought out?
   ___ b. poorly brought out?

7. Were the points that were emphasized in the broadcast
   ___ a. too many?
   ___ b. too few?
   ___ c. about right?

8. Was the vocabulary of the broadcast
   ___ a. too advanced?
   ___ b. too elementary?
   ___ c. about right?

9. Was the action in the broadcast
   ___ a. too rapid?
   ___ b. about right?
   ___ c. too slow?

10. Was the amount of dramatization
    ___ a. about right?
    ___ b. too much?
    ___ c. too little?

11. Did you always know which character or person in the program was speaking?
    ___ a. yes.
    ___ b. no.

12. Did the music in the broadcast
    ___ a. contribute to the enjoyment of the program?
    ___ b. detract from the program?

13. Were the transitions between scenes
    ___ a. confusing?
    ___ b. clear?

14. Did the sound effects used seem
    ___ a. effective?
    ___ b. ineffective?

15. From your observation of the pupils during the broadcast, would you say that the general appeal of the program to the class was
    ___ a. high?
    ___ b. average?
    ___ c. low?

An important function of evaluation is to stimulate more effective classroom use of programs. The following utilization report form also was prepared by the Evaluation of School Broadcasts group. Its questions are very significant to the classroom teacher who is receiving radio programs. She can use it as a check list to judge her own quality of utilization.

UTILIZATION REPORT

1. Did you have an opportunity to prepare your students for listening to this program before the time of the broadcast? ___Yes. ___No. If you did, when was this done?
   ___ a. Immediately before the broadcast began.
   ___ b. At an earlier time on the day of the broadcast.
   ___ c. At some time before the day of the broadcast.
   If you did, underline the number which most nearly approximates the number of minutes spent in advance-preparation activities:
   Less than 5   5 to 10   10 to 15   15 to 20   20 to 30   30 to 40   45 or more.

2. Check any of the following types of activity that were employed in preparing your class for listening to this broadcast:
   ___ a. The teacher consulted the printed manual about this broadcast
   ___ b. The teacher explained to the students what the broadcast was to be about.

___ c. Questions about which the broadcast was expected to provide information were listed.

___ d. Key words, names of people, places, or dates were listed on the blackboard.

___ e. Students discussed the subject of the broadcast.

___ f. Materials such as books, pictures, maps, clippings, etc., related to the topic of the broadcast were consulted.

___ g. Students maintained a few moments of silence.

3. Check any of the following things you did to facilitate listening:

___ a. Made sure window shades were properly adjusted before program began.

___ b. Carefully checked heat and ventilation of the room.

___ c. Allowed students to move to places where they could hear better (if radio set is located in the room).

___ d. Tuned in the station, beforehand, to check reception.

___ e. Turned on the program promptly at the beginning, and shut it off promptly at the end of the broadcast (if centralized radio is used).

___ f. Checked with the office to make sure the broadcast would be turned on as scheduled.

4. Check any of the following things which you did during the broadcast:

___ a. Checked reception in all parts of the room.

___ b. Permitted freedom of pupil activity so long as it did not interfere with group listening.

___ c. Kept a few notes on the broadcast for use in later discussions.

___ d. Wrote, on the blackboard, names, dates, new words, and the like, that were mentioned in the broadcast.

___ e. Pointed to locations on a map, or to words listed on the blackboard.

___ f. Listened attentively with the students.

. Were you able to allow time for a period of follow-up activities after the students had listened to the broadcast? ___Yes. ___No.

If so, when did these follow-up activities take place?

___ a. Immediately after the broadcast was concluded.

___ b. At a time during the day of the broadcast.

___ c. At some time after the day of the broadcast.

If so, underline the number which most nearly approximates the number of minutes spent in follow-up activities:

  Less than 5   5 to 10   10 to 15   15 to 20   20 to 30   30 to 40   45 or more.

Check any of the following types of follow-up activities that were employed in connection with this broadcast:

___ a. Students had a brief period of relaxation.

___ b. Students took part in a free discussion of the broadcast.

____ c. Students discussed points in the broadcast they considered important.

____ d. Students discussed the broadcast in terms of previously listed questions.

____ e. Students listed important points which the broadcast had failed to mention.

____ f. Parts of the broadcast were explained by the teacher.

____ g. Questions raised, but not answered, in the broadcast were pointed out for further consideration.

____ h. Sources where additional information about the topic of the broadcast might be found were suggested.

____ i. Students drew pictures or wrote about things suggested to them by the broadcast.

7. Write, in the space below, any observations which indicated that the broadcast (including preparation and follow-up) was a valuable educative experience for the students of your class.

Other Methods: Personal Observation

Judgment of the relative success or failure of a school broadcast is not confined to the use of written tests and questionnaires. As in commercial radio, a variety of techniques has been used to evaluate school programs. The method of personal observation, for example, has been used more in educational broadcasting than it has elsewhere.

The best way to judge the results of a school program is to visit the classroom and note pupil reactions. If there are questions about the mode of presentation, the suitability of content, utilization practices and materials, the most accurate answers can be determined at the point of reception. The success of a school broadcast cannot be judged in the control room. The administrator of a school-broadcasting enterprise can do no more than to insist that writers and producers visit classrooms regularly. Incidentally, with the increasing use of transcription facilities, such visitation even by performers should be encouraged. The programs can be recorded while their actual effects in the classroom are witnessed and analyzed. In England, recordings have been used to hear the audience reaction following a program, though it is apparent that such a plan tends to formalize the follow-up period.

Some evaluation by personal investigation can also be conducted in other ways. Some communities have arranged for the selection in each school of one teacher who seems especially interested in radio to act as the school-station representative. These radio representatives, as they are called, serve a definite function as a liaison between the program producers and the classroom consumers. They act as a sounding board. Comments concerning broadcasts that individual teachers for one reason or another would not volunteer ordinarily, are solicited openly and such suggestions have proved helpful in many ways. Periodic conferences of these representatives provide additional opportunity for the exchange of views. Not only in aiding evaluation but also in the development and maintenance of good will is this plan of teacher representation helpful.

Mail Analysis. The analysis of mail as a device for measurement has not been used as much in school broadcasting as it has in commercial radio. In the first place, there is not so much mail to analyze, and generally the school audience is better known. The usual school script does not attempt to stimulate such listener action, for there are not awards for "mail-pulling" contests. However, when mail has been forthcoming from pupils, teachers, and occasionally parents, it has been helpful to the broadcasters.

It should be noted, furthermore, that if letter writing is considered a genuine educational experience and if listener correspondence tends to create a more personal relationship between the broadcaster and the pupil, then there need be no hesitancy about encouraging it. If a school-mail delivery is available, it can be used to overcome the cost of postage which may prevent some children from writing.

Behavior Effects. The school broadcaster cannot measure his influence in terms of sales response; nevertheless, in addition to the result from tests and scales, personal observation, and mail, he has other means for discerning evidences of modified behavior.

If the broadcasts attempted to stimulate reading, as the series did in Fort Wayne, he can measure the effect of the series on library circulation. If a series in art or science were planned to encourage attendance at museums, as in Chicago, then such attendance can be determined. If the program has as a major aim the development of skills, the products made can be shown, as in Cleveland where an annual exhibit of such materials was held. If the radio visit is planned to stimulate the use of visual aids by teachers, the subsequent distribution of such material among teachers can be measured. If broadcasts of health information, for example, are planned to alter certain health habits, these changes can be analyzed, as was done in Sweden. Other evidences of the influence of school broadcasting can be noted: the effect on the purchase of radio sets and allied equipment, the formation of clubs, requests for auditions, activities of radio workshops, and the like.

Program Analysis. All these techniques for evaluation take time, and any measurement of educational growth is liable to be not only a slow but a complex process. Frequently there is a need for definite judgment concerning a program to be made rather quickly, in which case there must be some agreement as to standards and criteria.

To provide a basis for such judgment Reid and Woelfel have established definite criteria based upon their extensive experience. The following is but a brief summary of the bulletin *How to Judge a School Broadcast.*[19]

The merits of a school radio program, say the writers, can be considered under the following heads.

1. EDUCATIONAL VALUE

Maturity Level—A broadcast if recommended for a specific grade or grades should be appropriate for such use there.

Length of Broadcast—The proper length of the broadcast should be dependent upon its ability to hold interest as well as to allow time for the development of a unified presentation.

Leading Ideas—The broadcast should serve a definite purpose and its scope should be confined to the presentation of a few well-chosen concepts.

Educational Value—This can be judged by reference to the following criteria which are self-explanatory.

1. Social Significance
2. Historical Perspective
3. Integration of Learning
4. Cultural Understanding
5. Uniqueness of Presentation

---

[19] Seerley Reid and Norman Woelfel, "How to Judge a School Broadcast," *Bulletin No. 19,* Evaluation of School Broadcasts, 1940.

6. Democratic Values

7. Accuracy and Validity

II. CLARITY AND COMPREHENSIBILITY

Clear Reception—If, after careful tuning, the signal remains weak or indistinct then concentrated listening should not be attempted.

Radio Techniques—These should be experimental only as they add interest and meaning to the child, for with only few exceptions does the technique rather than the message have inherent value educationally.

Broadcast Structure—The pattern of the script should be discernible to the students and, if in doubt, any proposed variation should be subordinated to comprehensibility.

Number of Scenes—The use of too many scenes may destroy the unity of the program.

Vocabulary—Whether the vocabulary is appropriate can be thought of only in terms of the maturity of the potential listeners.

Generalizations and Quotations—These, too, must be used carefully if they are to be meaningful to the specific listeners in mind.

Large Numbers and Statistics—Confusion rather than comprehension may result from an unwarranted use of such material.

Universality of Appeal—If the program's coverage is regional or national its content should appeal to a variety of listeners.

Numbers of Characters and Casting—The need for comprehension may restrict the size of the cast; however, stereotyped speech should be avoided.

Fades—If fades are not used carefully they are apt to confuse the listener in the classroom.

Transitions—If the unity of the broadcast is to be maintained transitions must be definite and readily apparent to the child.

Sound Effects—If the effects do not enhance an episode but rather interfere with understanding they should either be changed or eliminated.

III. INTEREST AND APPEAL TO LISTENERS

Listener's Experience—The school program should present scenes and situations which are closely related to the experiences of the children for whom the program is planned.

Child Characters—The use of one or more young characters, since it usually stimulates interest among classroom listeners, should be encouraged.

Humor—Humor should be an integral part of the situation and so presented that it is related to the child's ability to appreciate it.

Dramatizations—The dramatized program is well received by classroom listeners, but it must meet well-established dramatic criteria.

Pace—The broadcast should move so that it catches and maintains listener interest.

The major difficulties in the field of program evaluation are much the same as those in other fields. The point at which the producer can end his investigations and the consumer can begin is a very indefinite one. The radio researcher also is liable to be disheartened at what seems to be indifference and a blind adherence to tradition. And in radio, too, the teacher in the classroom may question extensive research investigations which wind up either with obvious generalities or with conclusions so abstruse that a typically American response is evoked: "So what?"

However, in each case, research and application, developments are of necessity slow to come. In 1937, it was found that among the thirty largest universities, in the period from 1925 to 1935 inclusive, a total of 180 theses in the field of radio had been written. More than two thirds of these dealt with the radio as a machine rather than with its use. This field, too, is another instance where the social scientist has yet to catch up with his colleagues in the physical field. In the meantime the products of the technical laboratory continue to pour forth.

Each new development does not mean, however, that investigations need start anew. Frequently there is a carry-over. For example, in spite of the comparative newness of television, it would be a mistake to assume that research data with regards to its potential effectiveness is meagre. Aside from the positive factor of immediacy it is reasonable to assume that findings relative to motion-picture films are generally applicable to TV also.

The Forty-Eighth Yearbook of the National Society for the Study of Education, "Audio-visual Materials of Instruction," points out that "the following claims for properly used audio-visual materials in the teaching situation are supported by research evidence:

1. They supply a concrete basis for conceptual thinking and hence reduce meaningless word responses of students.
2. They have a high degree of interest for students.
3. They supply the necessary basis for developmental learning and hence make learning more permanent.
4. They offer a reality of experience which stimulates self-activity on the part of pupils.

5. They develop a continuity of thought; this is especially true of motion pictures.
6. They contribute to growth of meaning and hence to vocabulary development.
7. They provide experiences not easily secured by other materials and contribute to the efficiency, depth, and variety of learning.[20]

Whether the films are presented in the classroom through a projector or received via television the basic findings remain. As new products of technical genius become available to the teacher the mass of research data now being collected, though of course requiring modification, will again be applicable.

---

[20] N.S.S.E. *Yearbook*, 1949, p. 255.

9

Broadcasting Activities Within the School

◇◇

What are the purposes and activities of the school radio workshop?

What types of organization are used?

In what ways has sound equipment been used in the schools?

What plan of organization for one use of sound equipment is best?

What television experiences can be provided by the school workshop?

◇◇◇◇◇◇◇◇THE BROADCASTING ACTIVITIES within many schools have grown so rapidly that they now encompass a wide field. The discussion in this chapter will deal first with the school radio workshop, its purposes and forms. The second section will concern the use of sound equipment. Finally, the place of television will be considered.

The Radio Workshop: Its Purposes

The term "radio workshop" has been used frequently of late, though without general agreement as to its connotation. To Darrow the term means "the grouping of people interested in the better broadcasting of scripts now available or the production of better scripts." [1] To Lawton the workshop is "a place where a group gets a program ready," [2] while a much wider activity is assumed by the Committee on Radio Workshops of the National Advisory Council. This committee has defined a radio workshop as:

A laboratory for experimentation, training, and practice in broadcasting techniques and educational content. The experimental phase of a workshop deals with materials of learning suitable for radio use in terms of the interests of general radio listeners and of large special groups; with effective broadcasting techniques, including preparation of materials and their presentation; with methods of stimulating listener interest, of organizing listening groups, and of encouraging listener follow-up in learning; with ways of securing cooperation with existing social agencies, such as schools, civic organizations, governmental bodies, women's clubs, and commercial groups, and with improved use of studio equipment and radio facilities generally. [3]

It is thus apparent that there is likewise no general agreement as to the purposes of the radio workshop. Some have stated that if the workshop is to be truly useful it must train actors and professional radio workers, while others suggest that the workshop serves the same

[1] Ben Darrow, "Radio Workshops—The Next Step," *American School Board Journal*, December, 1938, p. 23.
[2] Thomas D. Rishworth, "Radio Workshops," *Education on the Air*, Ohio State University, 1940, p. 263.
[3] Ned H. Dearborn, "Report of the Workshop Committee of the National Advisory Council," *Education on the Air*, Ohio State University, 1937, p. 181.

function for a civic organization as does the advertising agency for a commercial firm.[4]

The Workshop Committee noted above submits these general objectives:

The selection of suitable material for educational broadcasting; the development of effective broadcasting techniques; the training of competent workers in the industry, the coordination of radio resources and facilities, the training of educational-radio leadership and competence among social agencies outside the industry; the production of improved programs of interest to the general public and to large special groups; and the advancement of radio standards generally.[5]

With such variance of purpose it is natural to assume that several kinds of radio workshops would evolve. And such has been the case. Workshops have been conducted by commercial broadcasting organizations as well as by governmental agencies, local radio councils, summer camps, universities, public as well as private schools, and even church groups.

The workshop activities of some of these groups, particularly those in several of the large universities, have been fully described elsewhere. The discussion here will be confined specifically to those activities undertaken in the public school which relate more or less directly to the field of radio or television, either in the production or in the consumption of programs.

The matter of equipment will not be considered until there has been a preliminary discussion of values and uses. This is done to emphasize the fact, although it may seem unnecessary, that desirable educational practices, in radio, television, or elsewhere, should not depend upon the equipment available, but rather that the nature of the equipment should depend upon the use to be made of it. Too frequently sound equipment has been installed in schools and then almost as an afterthought its use is considered. The result is that often the equipment is found to be inflexible and the teacher's activities are unnecessarily limited. The primary consideration is the educational goal, and the secondary one is equipment, not the reverse.

What, then, are the values of radio-workshop activity in a typical

[4] *Education on the Air*, Ohio State University, 1940, p. 265.
[5] Ned Dearborn, *op. cit.*, p. 182.

high school? First, let it be understood, though it may seem arbitrary, that the high-school workshop is not, and should not be, primarily vocational in its intent. The demands of the radio industry being what they are, both quantitatively and qualitatively, any attempt to do more than mention such employment is, in the writers' opinion, quite unfair both to the child and to the radio industry. Painful testimony is readily available at every graduation period when "hopefuls" besiege the studios. Radio-workshop activity even at the college level, many will agree, cannot afford as yet to be largely vocational in purpose. It may be that in the future, with the wider distribution of technical developments and perhaps certain types of legislation, such vocational opportunities will present themselves, but as yet it remains in a state of wishful thinking.

Granted that there is but a slight possibility that the child will be a radio producer, there is nevertheless no doubt that he is and will be a constant radio consumer.

The Workshop Aids the Pupil as a Radio Consumer.   Various studies of radio listening have been made by De Boer, Eisenberg, McKay, and others; and, although the figures vary with age and grade level, a conservative estimate of average listening of about two hours a day seems fairly accurate. It has been noted by some that the average high-school student in one year spends as much time listening to the radio as he does in school. Television has already reduced radio listening, but the total amount of time devoted to viewing and listening is greater than ever. If it is agreed that it is a function of the school to help the child to interpret his out-of-school experiences, the question then is obvious: Is there value in developing a greater awareness of such influence?

If the term "awareness" implies the need for critical thinking, intelligent discrimination, and appreciation, the values of the workshop become more apparent. There is but little doubt that in radio and television, too, a critical attitude is dependent upon knowledge and understanding. For unless the school furnishes a background upon which intelligent choices can be based, it merely turns out another dallying dilettante who waits for the "bandwagon" before deciding what is supposed to be good. But aside from artistic considerations, with radio the powerful agent for propaganda that it is, the need for the development of a critical attitude among listeners and consumers is of more than theoretical interest. It is a vital need in a working democracy.

Keith Tyler emphasizes this obligation upon the part of the school when he states:

An important part of this vital task of developing discrimination is in relation to radio. Our loudspeakers pour out upon us a withering barrage of propaganda—political, economic, and social—a flood of verbose sales talk, and great quantities of mediocre clap-trap. There are better programs on the air than there ever have been, but they are still greatly in the minority. Day in and day out our radio stations turn out a great deal of uninspired music, of cheap melodrama, of meaningless quizzes, and dull speakers. To distinguish the artistic, the lasting, the esthetic, and the genuine from among these miscellaneous offerings requires training. To detect propaganda, to look for hidden assumptions, to recognize glittering generalities requires guidance. To withstand clever psychological sales appeals based upon "keeping up with the Joneses," upon snobbery, upon feelings of inferiority requires consumer education.

Lumping these together, is it not clear that we must develop now on the part of boys and girls the ability to discriminate with regard to their radio listening? [6]

The need for the development of discriminating listening is discussed further in Chapter 12, "The Commercial Program for Children."

The Workshop Challenges Creative Abilities. The fact that the pupil probably will not become a professional broadcaster does not imply that he cannot benefit also from the creative aspect of workshop activity. For example, the school workshop offers excellent stimulation for many types of speech work, all aiming toward a greater degree of effectiveness. One radio workshop teacher says: "The pupils gain (a) knowledge of radio in general; (b) specific knowledge and understanding of radio production, speaking, and acting; (c) confidence in the use of the microphone; (d) ability to understand and reach the radio audience; (e) improvement in voice and diction; (f) improvement in intelligent oral interpretation of reading; (g) critical judgment in listening; (h) interest in and knowledge of effective writing; (i) technical training, with its accompanying value in vocational

---

[6] I. Keith Tyler, "Radio's Function in Education," *Educational Method*, January, 1939, pp. 152–153.

exploration; (j) ability to work with others in an exacting group project in which every detail has value."

Another teacher points out:

> There is the fascinating experience of carrying an idea through from its rough inception to its complex and finished production. This activity gives pupils a sense of useful and immediate accomplishment. . . . It makes the group voice-conscious. . . . A small class working for self-improvement is fun.

The workshop provides expression for a variety of literary forms, material which, with a certain amount of adaptation, can lend itself to presentation by radio. This "production for use," the chance that the pupil's story or poem may be broadcast, often provides the needed incentive. Even on the college level such stimulation is helpful, and there, too, as Darrow notes, is a need for channels of expression.

> Why should students write essays and papers only for the wastebaskets of professors? Why should not the students who are interested in geography and journalism, for example, be given an opportunity to write geography travelogues? Why should not the students interested in history and biography and also in dramatics, be given an opportunity to write some of the dramalogues so sorely needed in these fields? [7]

For the pupil, therefore, the radio workshop can serve as a practical project for the development of skills, in both writing and speaking. It is a "natural" for the teaching of English; it affords opportunities for the development of desirable attitudes, among them punctuality and reliability; it demonstrates the interrelationship in subject matter; and it provides experiences which in turn make for a more intelligent response to a major influence in modern life.

The Workshop Serves the School.   For the school, too, the workshop has definite values. As a school enterprise, which pleasurably yet effectively reinforces the teacher's efforts, it provides a "lift" for the classroom procedures.

As a vehicle for the promotion of more effective public relations broadcasting, the school workshop can perform a significant function. Carefully planned and produced school radio programs can be presented through local commercial radio stations. The radio group can

---

[7] Ben Darrow, *loc. cit.*

provide a real contribution if it aids the school in interpreting its activities to the community.

In discussing the values for the school, one workshop teacher writes: "From the school viewpoint, the radio workshop is a fine medium for molding school opinion and getting activities backed. We have inaugurated a 'Meet the Teacher' series which we feel has promoted excellent faculty-student relations."

Organizing the Group

Though the possible values of a school radio workshop are accepted, it by no means follows that the next step is the organization of a formal course of instruction. Perhaps several preliminary procedures are essential before this can be attempted, and it may well be that in some instances greater values will be derived if the workshop activity remains informal and extracurricular in nature. At any rate, an accredited course should not be attempted until the instructor has become sufficiently familiar with radio to warrant such a step. Furthermore, as the administrator knows, it is hardly wise to develop and offer a school course without some indication of pupil interest and demand. In the third place, the workshop course of study itself, if developed with only a limited background, will probably require an initial period of experimentation and revision.

An Informal Organization. All this suggests the desirability, in most cases, of launching the school radio workshop first as an extracurricular activity, and later, if conditions warrant, the workshop or club can be reorganized along more formal lines and finally offered as an accredited course. In the meantime the teaching personnel has had an opportunity to become acquainted with the field, the outlines of a workable course become more apparent, equipment needs are better understood, and student needs can be gauged.

In launching the radio group it probably will be desirable at first to extend membership to all pupils who wish to join. Those who are interested in speech and dramatics as well as in creative writing may find the activities of special interest, although there should be room also for pupils with more technical interest who may aid in the construction and maintenance of equipment, sound effects, etc. It is quite unlikely, however, that the same organization can serve satisfactorily those interested in the purely technical side of the radio, the would-be "hams," as well as those interested primarily in the program phase. In this instance, the "Radram Club" (radio dramatics) can no more serve the interests of the youthful radio technicians than can the school journalism staff serve the printer's apprentice. Where numbers make it possible, separate organizations are preferred.

There are in the radio field many types of informal club activities that can be followed. For example, an effective way of stimulating interest in the discussion of program tastes and in the need for discrimination has been to conduct a survey of program preferences either in the group or in the entire school. Following this, the analysis of the appeal of the more popular programs has been an interesting as well as a profitable undertaking. The organization of listening panels which report on various programs also has been helpful.

The discussion of radio's influence on various groups—voters, farmers, students, consumers, and others—can be used as the theme for research and several brief talks by members. Others may prefer to investigate and discuss such topics as the legal and economic basis of the radio industry, foreign broadcasting and the relative merits of the American scheme, simplified radio theory, radio personalities, and the use of transcriptions. Thus the group not only secures information concerning the Fifth Estate, but the members themselves secure additional opportunity for public speaking. And let it be noted that he who would learn to broadcast must first learn to speak. With this type of activity the radio group can be of real service whether or not the pupil will ever face a microphone in his later life.

Of particular interest to school children have been visits and guided excursions to local radio stations. Arrangements can be made either for the entire group to visit, or for individuals to interview key staff members and then report to the group. If properly planned, such a visit can be a real educational experience rather than a mere lark. The results of such trips, however, depend upon preparation.

Occasionally station personnel can be invited to visit the school to discuss topics such as the organization of a radio station, measuring the radio audience, preparing effective script and continuity, the role of the advertising agency, and related subjects. This type of presentation will help to dissipate whatever false notions the adolescent is inclined to have concerning the so-called glamour of radio.

In order to suggest an additional activity which may be undertaken, reference will be made to a personal experience with a high-school radio group. The following is an excerpt from a description of the enterprise which appeared elsewhere:

With the cooperation of one of Cleveland's leading radio stations, a rather unusual procedure was developed. One Saturday, late last spring, was set aside as West Tech Day. For the duration of that day all programs were to be planned and produced by students. Of course, commercially sponsored programs and announcements were not to be included. Every member of the station staff from general manager to page boy was to have for that day a West Tech student as an understudy. A chart of the station personnel was developed and by conference with teachers a staff of interested and capable students was finally selected.

Fortunately, West Tech makes rather extensive use of its own public address system, operates its own amateur radio station, and conducts classes in "Radio English," so that the selection of an interested student staff was not a difficult task.

To serve on the engineering staff of the station, students were selected from among those taking technical courses. The public address system operators were also utilized. Likewise for typists and switchboard operators, the choice was made among commercial students. Those posts dealing with music, such as the musical director, music librarian, and others, were filled by students recommended by the department of music. The journalism courses took care of the posts dealing with station publicity and news.

Most stations make use of hostesses who serve as guides for station visitors. To publicize West Tech Day throughout the school, a popularity contest was conducted by the school newspaper. The four winners were selected as hostesses.

Having organized the staff, the officials of the station were notified so that the entire station force knew of the plan. Each of the students arranged for private interviews with the individual whose post he was to "take over." The conduct of these individual visits was of great value to the young folks. For the first time, many of them learned that behind the glamour of the microphone there is a great deal of planning, organization, and rehearsal.

After these interviews and observations, radio literature was analyzed during after-school hours. Each student sought to learn more concerning his specific post. The by-product, an increased appreciation of radio as a medium for communication, was inevitable.

In the meantime preparations were being made for the actual programs to be produced. To the school band went a request for a half-hour musical program. Opened and closed by school songs, accurately timed, and of a varied nature, the project served to provide the band with an active but pleasant week of rehearsals. From the "Radio English" classes came a dramatization. Continuity was written, sound effects developed, and again the "bug-bear" of radio, careful timing, was essential.

The popular "amateur hour" was arranged using the school's outstanding talent. Auditions for the hoped-for appearance at the station were held previously at West Tech. There, a board of student judges did the selecting and also evolved the final draft of the continuity for this particular program.

After a week or two of rehearsals, special programs were published, newspaper pictures taken, and finally West Tech Day arrived. The school band gathered at the Public Square and paraded to the station led by a police escort. The student officials were at their posts; the general manager beaming—he had a private secretary! The popular hostesses showed curious parents just where "Johnny" was to broadcast. The engineers sat at their controls—of course, under the supervision of the station engineers. The musicians and performers collected, and the programs were presented according to schedule. Thus West Tech Day became a fond memory.

Well, let's take stock. What were the values of the experience? It may have been a gay adventure, but did it really provide anything substantial?

The writer sincerely believes that it *was* a most worthwhile experience. In fact, he believes that it might well be suggestive to other schools who may care to undertake a similar enterprise.

Surely it opened the eyes of the students to the vocational possibilities in this new field. Prior to this time the entertainment feature of the industry had been their chief and perhaps only interest.

By producing radio programs one receives a keener appreciation of what good programs really are. The need for improved appreciation of both radio and movie productions need not be reiterated here.

The project, if we may call it such, certainly provided the school with favorable publicity. It established cordial relationships with another powerful medium of influence, the radio. The results of such good will are evident.[8]

As a phase of the group's activity, the discussion of the question "How Shall I Listen to a Radio Program?" is of great value and the subsequent analysis may lead into an investigation of the whole field of propaganda, the place of legitimate advertising, the influence of the sponsor, the consumer's defense, the need for and danger of gov-

---

[8] Wm. B. Levenson, "Exploring Radio," *Ohio Schools*, October, 1937, p. 359.

ernment regulation. And thus, through these and many other activities, the radio group considers its privileges and obligations as a consumer of radio.

However, teachers who have engaged in this type of activity will agree with Tyler that "A unit on radio discrimination which narrows itself merely to a discussion of programs soon runs dry. Pupils are curious; they want some understanding of how programs are produced as well as insight into consumer values. And appreciation of a product is heightened by an understanding of the conditions under which it is produced. A boy with sandlot-baseball experience appreciates the big-league game the more because of his perception of the difficulties and thrills of the sport. Those who themselves took music lessons have a deeper appreciation of the rendition of a complicated symphony." [9] Thus, a phase of the club program can be devoted to creative aspects, the planning, development, and presentation of radio materials.

If possible, this preparation can be pointed toward actual production through a public-address system or over a local station, but if necessary the program can be produced visually—with "dummy" mikes. At least it is a beginning, and the project itself should encourage the study of some of the literature, the United States Office of Education radio materials, and perhaps some of the simpler texts in radio writing and production.

It is difficult, if not foolish, to indicate specifically what activities can be undertaken by an extracurricular group in this field. To have value and to "hold" the children, the plans made will have to evolve from within the membership and the needs and interests peculiar to it. The chief attribute of any such successful enterprise is that its program has a maximum of flexibility and yet be consistent with worthwhile goals definitely established.

As noted earlier, there is no reason why, in some instances, the radio workshop cannot continue as an extracurricular activity. However, it is interesting to note that several forms of curricular organization have been used.

A *Formal Organization.*   In some schools a unit of a conventional subject such as English, public speaking, or civics has been

[9] I. Keith Tyler, "Developing Discrimination with Regard to Radio," *The English Journal*, February, 1937, p. 125.

devoted to radio. In such units radio's relationship to the field is analyzed and in turn it is hoped that the work in the subject field itself will be stimulated.

The contents of such a radio unit in a high-school economics course, for example, have been described by Stenius as follows:

> The consumer viewpoint is stressed in the unit which attempts to bring certain aspects of radio to the attention of the student who is studying economics. Just how true is the statement that programs which the student hears in his home come to the family absolutely free? Can he judge as clearly the sales argument which he hears as that which he reads in a magazine? And what, to him, is the significance of the contest which demands that a boxtop be sent in with every entry? These are questions which a student may have asked himself many times, or it may be that they never have occurred to him. Whichever may be the case, a high school course in economics should recognize that radio is such a vital force that to explain to the students the law of diminishing utility without making him pause to reflect upon questions such as those just listed is not an action in line with modern educational philosophy.[10]

Some schools have confined the unit to a consideration of radio appreciation. In other instances the unit includes a section on the motion picture. The chief objectives of such units incorporated into a speech class, for instance, have been noted by Ross:

1. First of all, both units, but especially the radio, offer so many opportunities for speech activities, and a tremendous incentive to the pupils to increase the flexibility and power of their own speech mechanisms, their voices.
2. The second reason why both the radio and the movies are worthwhile to tackle, is that work with them interests all types of students and gives opportunity for so many varied talents to be exercised.
3. And thirdly, teaching the appreciation of radio and the motion pictures teaches for better living, right now and later, for both these arts are a part of all students' daily experience, and more intelligent use of them means surely a fuller enjoyment of life.[11]

The unit on radio and motion-picture appreciation has been expanded into an elective course in several schools. The aims of such a course have been listed by Child and Finch as follows:

---

[10] Arthur Stenius, "Radio Units and Courses in High Schools," *Educational Method*, January, 1939, p. 172.
[11] Jeanette Ross, "The Speech Teacher Keeps Abreast of the Radio and the Motion Picture," *The Quarterly Journal of Speech*, October, 1940, pp. 431–433.

1. To make students more aware of the sociological, economic, and international aspects of the motion picture and the radio.
2. To aid the pupils in shopping for worth-while movie and radio programs.
3. To help the pupils to enjoy these programs to the greatest possible degree by extending their appreciation of the arts involved.
4. To improve the writing and speaking abilities of students with the radio and motion pictures as centers of interest.
5. To teach some of the skills involved in amateur motion picture and radio production.
6. To discuss the literary aspects and social problems present in film and radio programs.[12]

Occasionally the radio material is related closely to an existing field and a synthesized course of study is followed. Often this is termed "Radio English" or "Radio Speech."

The radio classes taught by Miss Frances M. Beck at Cleveland's Collinwood High School utilize the following courses of study:

RADIO ENGLISH I

(One semester; 5 points credit; one period daily)

The purpose of this course is fivefold:
1. To furnish an introduction to radio and television
2. To improve voice and spoken English
3. To develop an appreciation of the best that is on the air by learning to criticize, judge, and enjoy
4. To prepare talented and ambitious pupils for Radio English II, which is a course in radio production
5. To discover talented pupils

The course stresses the improvement of voice quality and diction and emphasizes interpretative reading.

1. Voice: With the understanding that the radio speaker is dependent entirely upon his voice, our goal is a rich, full voice. Emphasis is laid upon correct breathing, resonance rather than volume, direction of tone, inflection, and the elimination of individual voice defects.

2. Diction: Clear, crisp enunciation is the goal. Use of lips, tongue, and teeth in formation of words is taught. Particular attention is given to enunciation of consonants. Correct grammar and pronunciation are emphasized.

3. Interpretation: Stress is placed on the conversational style; on the

---

[12] Eleanor D. Child and Hardy R. Finch, "Motion Picture and Radio: An English Elective." *Curriculum Journal,* October, 1939, p. 253.

projection of personality; on phrasing according to meaning; on the use of the intelligent and purposeful pause; on
proper pace; on the sustaining of thought; on emphasis
of key words and phrases; and on learning to mark a script
for use.

The following assignments are used in this course:

1. Read individual selections of one minute in length in order to
   establish familiarity with the microphone. (Record voices to permit
   the pupils to analyze their own voices.) Repeat this type of exercise a number of times.

2. Present radio talks giving information gathered from research in
   various phases of radio and television.

3. Give one- to three-minute discussions of current radio programs
   (Talks are timed exactly, and pupils are taught the importance of
   the time element in radio.)

4. Attempt imitations of radio performers.

5. Give news talks.

6. Give discussions of radio commentators, analysts, and reporters.

7. Learn to edit news. (The class is divided into several groups, and
   each group is given 15 minutes to edit the news they have brought
   into class. Each group chooses its own reporter to read the radio
   report over the microphone. The reports are always followed by
   class discussion and analysis.)

8. In a good class each pupil writes a weekly radio broadcast in which
   he strives to develop an individual style of writing and speaking.
   Suggested subjects are sports, fashions, theatre, news, humor. A pupil might represent a bookstore or library and give talks on books.
   Another might represent a record shop.

9. Develop a book review, incorporating short dramatized scenes.

10. Examine professional dramatic scripts in order to develop familiar-
    ity with the form.

11. Select and prepare for production suitable dramatic scripts, both orig-
    inal and professional. The teacher directs the first one. The pupils
    are then taught to handle all phases of production. The last month
    is used for production, and pupils are taught by actual practice the
    details of procedure in the production of a radio show. They are
    ready for Radio English II.

12. Keep notebooks containing
    a. mimeographed material
       exercises in voice work
       exercises in enunciation
    b. a record of listening and evaluation of programs
    c. reports on reading that pupils have done in radio and television
    d. all talks and other scripts which the pupil has presented at the

microphone, in order to provide a record of material used in his development

e. scrapbook section: clippings from current radio and television publications to be arranged according to subject matter—advertising, music, dramatic shows, news—as the pupil desires

Radio English II (Production)

(One semester; 5 points credit; one period daily)

The work of the course divides into five parts: (1) Evaluation of Pupils' Voices and Abilities, (2) Evaluation and Appreciation of Professional Radio and Television Programs, (3) Script Writing, (4) Production of Programs, (5) Additional Special Workshop Training.

1. Evaluation of Voices and Abilities: At the beginning of the term considerable individual work is done at the microphone, so that each pupil's radio ability may be judged. His classmates learn in what parts he can be best cast when they begin to produce their own shows, and his teacher is enabled to analyze his shortcomings in order to assist him to improve. Individual microphone practice is given in interpretative reading, news reports, panel discussions, round-table discussions, and talks on current radio programs.

2. Evaluation and Appreciation of Professional Radio and Television Programs: Current programs are discussed critically in microphone reports by individual pupils or by the class after all have heard or seen a particular program. Reports are given at the microphone on various radio and television topics from material gathered in newspapers, magazines, and books, or from visits to the stations. Each pupil keeps a notebook which contains clippings on radio and television, copies of the scripts of all broadcasts in which he has participated, and his own criticism of all class broadcasts and of certain professional broadcasts. Pupils gain a critical appreciation of the coordination of activity which goes into a radio production and are enabled to evaluate their own participation with greater understanding.

3. Script Writing: Considerable freedom is permitted in this phase of activity. After the pupils have discovered their own talent or interest, they are permitted to concentrate to a certain extent in that line. Script writing includes scripts for special occasions and campaigns, continuity for school bulletins, originals, adaptations for radio of short stories, episodes from novels or biographies, and one-act plays.

4. Production of Programs: Workshop pupils are trained to prepare and present
a. bulletin broadcasts to the entire school

b. scripts for special occasions, broadcast to the entire school
c. scripts written by members of the class and broadcast over local stations
d. professional scripts produced for class practice
e. studio demonstrations presented on the auditorium stage for assembly programs
f. demonstration programs before civic groups for the purpose of information and entertainment
g. commencement scripts written and produced by radio students

5. Additional Special Workshop Training: All pupils are given experience in creating sound effects. Ingenuity and imagination are emphasized. The studio has assembled a library of sound-effects records and music records. Pupils select and plan the use of music for their shows. At times the music department furnishes a choral group or instrumental music for the Workshop programs. The Radio Workshop provides unlimited opportunity for pupils to experiment in writing, acting, and directing. Many of their programs have been produced by local stations.

The rather complete outline of a proposed high-school course, "Radio Speech," prepared by a committee of Texas teachers is included in Bulletin No. 4 issued by the Federal Radio Education Committee, *Schools of the Air and Radio in the High School Curriculum.*

The half-year course contains these units and pupil experiences. Objectives and suggested teaching procedures also are listed:

UNIT I   HISTORY OF THE DEVELOPMENT OF RADIO

Experiences: Acquiring knowledge of the historical development of radio, listening to a discussion of radio by the teacher, discussing the various steps in the development.

UNIT II   THE SCOPE OF EDUCATIONAL RADIO

Experiences: Becoming acquainted with educational broadcasts and listening to network educational broadcasts, making reports on programs heard, thus drawing conclusions as to the value of educational broadcasts.

UNIT III   A KNOWLEDGE OF RADIO SPEECH

Experiences: Pupils listen to radio speech and practice before a microphone with newscasts.

UNIT IV   STANDARDS FOR JUDGING EFFECTIVENESS IN PRESENT-DAY PROGRAMS

Experiences: Pupils become acquainted with current radio programs, classify musical programs, classify radio advertisements study educational programs, set up standards of evaluation of radio programs, along with developing a chart for judging radio programs.

UNIT V   OBSERVATION OF A RADIO STATION

Experiences: Pupils observe the radio studio and the microphones, also the staff of a radio studio, by

    a. Studying work of announcers

    b. Learning work of program manager

    c. Visiting the control room

    d. Visiting with the continuity writers

    e. Learning what goes on in the manager's office, etc.

UNIT VI   THE RADIO CLASS AS A PRODUCTION UNIT

Experiences: Organizing the class into a production unit like that of a real broadcasting studio with pupils acting the various parts of a radio staff. Pupils study the "Radio Glossary" for peculiar terms used in connection with radio broadcasts. Pupils can produce a radio play by

    a. Having tryouts for the play

    b. Casting the play

    c. Preparing for the performance

    d. Giving the play

UNIT VII   CREATIVE RADIO DRAMATICS

Experiences: Writing and producing an original radio play.

UNIT VIII   THE RADIO SPEECH

Experiences: Developing criteria for judging radio speeches by writing and giving an original radio speech.

UNIT IX   AN ACTUAL BROADCAST

Experiences: Pupils participate in a radio broadcast after making arrangements with the studio. Pupils perform in the studio.

UNIT X   A SURVEY OF POSSIBLE AVENUES OF RADIO WORK

Experiences: Investigating possible avenues of work which have been opened up through these units of radio study. Communicating with studios.

A separate and distinct course in radio broadcasting has as yet been tried in but few high schools. In the colleges and universities, however, such courses are quite common. A list of these is presented annually in the *Broadcasting Yearbook*.

Using Sound Equipment

The broadcasting activities of the modern school as applied to the use of sound equipment can be classified into three categories: (a) administrative, (b) instructional, and (c) extracurricular.

Administrative Uses. In discussing administrative uses, the term "radio" is a misnomer, for the equipment serves as a public-address system, in fact, as a glorified telephone, rather than as a radio. A more accurate term is "the central program-distribution system." However, in this discussion the more common names will be used— public-address or central-sound system.

One of the most frequent uses of such equipment is the presentation of announcements. In the modern schools, large as many of them are, the difficulty of presenting simultaneous announcements to the entire student body is often a perplexing one. Too, the task of home-room teachers in many schools, sad to relate, is seldom more than the mere recital of routine announcements. With a proper use of the central-sound system, the responsibility for such routine shifts from the teacher to the pupil. Once an announcement is made, the directions are his to follow. No longer does he cry, "But Mrs. Adams didn't tell us that." Of course there are instances when some future references may be made in the announcements and in such cases the material still must be written.

In a good many schools the auditorium can accommodate only a part of the student body. Although a certain program may have interest and value for some of the others, because of limited space they may have to forego attendance. By means of a school hookup, however, the speaker's voice can be brought into every homeroom. Though not every type of assembly program can be broadcast effectively, there are talks and musical presentations that can be relayed in this manner. Some schools have gone further and have "piped" the program to a local radio station, which then broadcasts it city-wide.

Incidentally, in some auditoriums which are poor acoustically, amplification of the speaker's voice even for the visual audience is more than welcome. Furthermore, the loudspeaker unit can be used with a motion picture installation.

Some principals have noted that, since the central-sound system facilitates brief comments by them to the entire student body, these "appearances," if well handled, can serve to "humanize" the administration—something often neglected in the large school.

In some schools, building tests have been administered by means of the public-address system. Where this has been tried, it has been noted that not only is time saved, but control factors are more easily handled. The administrative uses of this tool should relate closely to the needs of the school, and consequently they are many and varied. For example, one school in a small community mounted a loudspeaker on top of the building, and with the appearance of the school's musical groups as well as with the use of recordings, the whole community was provided with Christmas music.

Instructional Uses. The instructional uses of sound equipment in the school are perhaps more common than administrative applications. The most frequent use is the classroom reception of radio programs distributed from a central receiver, reproduced from a recording, or presented "live" before school microphones.

A common activity is the presentation during the homeroom period of a news broadcast. In some schools the script for this daily five-minute broadcast is prepared by students, and in others a social studies teacher prepares the material. A well-prepared newscast for school reception minimizes the "gossip" aspect and emphasizes the relationship of current events to the pupil's knowledge of history. It presents an historical perspective, calling attention to cause and effect rather than to a presumptive knowledge of "things to come." If the script is dramatized, use is made of members of the radio workshop or pupils in the public-speaking classes.

Elizabeth Laine has noted the value of news programs for the pupil:

> For the school such broadcasts have inestimable value; they not only keep students informed of the significant happenings in the world, but they also create an infinitely closer contact between these students and the world than could be obtained in any other way. This use of the radio imparts to the listener an intimate knowledge of current history, and creates in him a genuine feeling of world membership.
>
> Newspapers, magazines, newsreels, and books interpret and record for public consumption the vast succession of developments in national and world affairs, in scientific discoveries, in social life, in literature, and in art.

The news broadcast, though in a sense but one reporter of current history among many others, is none the less one having certain unique advantages.

In the first place, the radio transmits news items more rapidly than the press or the cinema. That special feature of radio which enables listeners to participate in world events as they take place has already been noted. The rapidity of the radio in transmitting news of recent occurrences is almost as remarkable. The radio can inform the world of all that is taking place in a miraculously short space of time after the event has happened, and thus keep the public up to the minute in developments of general interest. This feature of the news broadcast is important for the school from the point of view of keeping a living contact with the outside world.

Another advantage in the news broadcast, especially from the standpoint of the school, is its selective power. The broadcaster can present news items of significance and omit items of lesser journalistic value. In this way students are helped to distinguish between the worth while and the trivial, and are stimulated to take an interest in national and worldly problems. And finally, the news broadcast, because it is an oral presentation, facilitates interpretation. By means of voice modulation, inflection, accent, and the use of pauses, the intelligibility of news articles is increased and the value of the current-history lesson is enhanced. An excellent news broadcast should furnish an incentive to students to follow up subsequent developments in world situations in magazines, books, and newspapers. It should serve to set students to thinking and reading about such vital subjects of contemporary interest as unemployment, disarmament, slum clearance, and the problem of preserving the democratic form of government.[13]

In some schools recorded music has been used with success in typing and in physical education classes. In the operation and maintenance of the equipment valuable experience is provided for pupils in electrical classes.

The glamour appeal of radio and dramatics has been used by skillful teachers to motivate ordinary classroom work. Contrast two types of assignments.

In one room a pupil is asked to report the next day on the life of, let us say, Thomas A. Edison. Some research is involved, but even more deterring with some pupils is their reluctance to get up in front of class. As the assignment is made there seems to be little enthusiasm to undertake the task.

---

[13] Elizabeth Laine, *Motion Pictures and Radio*, McGraw-Hill Book Company, Inc., 1939. pp. 94–95

In another room the teacher had borrowed the school microphone for use in her room. It will not be connected actually, but even as a stage "prop" it serves her purpose.

"Next week," she says, "we are going to have a series of interviews. With our microphone we are going to stage two or three broadcasts. Bill, suppose you find out what you can about Henry Hudson. Mary, here, will interview you. We will have that broadcast on Monday. On Friday, Current Events Day, we are going to discuss the subject 'Inflation.' Let us try a round table. Tom, will you play the role of a manufacturer? You give us the industrialist's point of view. Martha, surely you know the housewife's point of view. Suppose you ask your mother what she thinks and you take part in the round table, presenting the housewife's reaction to the cost of living. Bob, your dad works in the steel mill. Let us get labor's point of view. Sam, you have told us that your father worked for the government. You will be the fourth member of this panel. Suppose you, as a committee, meet and plan for this broadcast."

The use of "mock radio" has been found successful even at the elementary-grade level in conducting drills in the form of quiz programs, dramatizing storybooks, and the like.

The public-address system provides the radio workshop and other groups with an opportunity to present programs to the rest of the student body. Selected lessons have been distributed in this manner, which either launch or summarize a unit of study.

Illustrative of this application is the following script, one of a series prepared for 10B English classes. The material was written and presented over the public-address system at John Adams High School in Cleveland under the direction of Mr. Edwin F. Helman.

THE ADAMS FAMILY CONSIDERS VOICE
Lessons for the 10B Semester
Lesson One: Voice and Personality

CAST

Announcer	Peggy Adams ⎱ tenth-graders
Henry Adams, the father	Jack Adams ⎰
Martha Adams, the mother	Warren Adams, a college sophomore

TIME: 14 minutes

SOUND EFFECTS: subdued noises of china and silverware

ANNCER: Good day. The English Curriculum Center would like to introduce the Adams family.

PEGGY: How do you do? I'm Peggy. I'm a *twin*, worse luck!

JACK: "Worse luck" is right! I couldn't have described you better myself! . . . Oh, hello! I'm Jack, the *better* half of the luck!

WARREN: The twins are tenth-graders. I'm in the class of '42 at *college*. I'm Warren.

MR. A: And I'm Henry Adams, the father of this tribe. May I present my wife, Martha?

MRS. A: How do you do?

ANNCER: Now that etiquette has been observed, join us in a call at the Adams home. Or, better still—since the family is at dinner—let's just *listen*.

MRS. A: Jack! Jack Adams! Come to dinner at once!

MR. A: What in the world is a good dinner in comparison with *Lil' Abner*, Martha? . . . Son, you heard your mother. We're waiting for you!

JACK: (*Off mike*) O.K.! (*Coming on*) What's the rush, dad! You haven't even started to serve!

PEGGY: Mother, look! Jack hasn't washed his hands yet.

JACK: Shut up, Peggy! What're my hands to you, anyway?

MRS. A: Children! . . . Peggy, don't say another word. . . . Jack, go wash your hands this minute.

JACK: Ah-h, ma! Why don't you make Peg take that stuff off her fingernails! (*Fade*)

SOUND: *Slight noises of china and cutlery at intervals from here to end*

WARREN: I don't see why we have to start every meal with this sort of rumpus, mother. It's hard on the digestion.

MRS. A: It *is* unpleasant, Warren. I often wonder what the people upstairs think of us.

PEGGY: Lots they have to crab about! The way she stands out on the porch and yells, "HA-ROLD! HAR-RO-LD!"

MRS. A: Now, Peggy, I suspect that when we really get to know them, we'll find they're just as nice as we know *we* are.

MR. A: No doubt of it, Martha. In spite of all the years I've been a salesman, I'm still surprised at the difference between a customer's *voice* and his *personal appearance*.

WARREN: You've got something there, dad! Have I ever told you about the girl Jimmie got for me on a blind date at the Phi Gam dance last year? Boy, was she a honey! So long as she kept her mouth shut, she knocked us all cold!

JACK: Just like Peg! Huh, Warren? . . . Ouch! . . . Ma, Peg kicked me!

MRS. A: Children! . . . What do you mean, Warren?

WARREN: Oh, you know, mother. She was pretty, and a swell dancer; but her voice would have stopped a truck.

MRS. A: "Her voice was ever soft, gentle, and low—an excellent thing in woman." . . . Shakespeare to you, Jack.

JACK: Oh, that guy! Too bad Peg never heard of him.

PEGGY: Dad, make him stop teasing me. Anyone with a voice like his ought to be calling hogs, anyway.

MRS. A: Not another word from either of you! I declare if I didn't hope you both would grow out of this squabbling, I'd wish you were—orphans!

WARREN: "Her voice was ever soft, gentle, and low . . ."

MRS. A: What? . . . Oh, I'm sorry! I suppose it's catching.

MR. A: That's right, Martha. You're in rare form tonight!

MRS. A: Henry Adams, what *are* you talking about?

MR. A: A minute ago you said that people's voices are often less attractive than their persons, and just now you said that a bad voice is catching. Two excellent points.

WARREN: Sounds like a lecture coming on, dad. Make it snappy! . . . And I'd like another potato, please.

MR. A: All right, son. Pass your plate. . . . I have no lecture; I'll leave that to your professors. But a man who's been a pretty fair salesman for twenty years can't help having some ideas about the voice. I've had to depend on it to make a living! It's my firm conviction that most people pay too little attention to the importance of having a likable voice.

PEGGY: My English teacher says that *radio* is improving speech all over the country.

MR. A: She's right, of course, Peggy. That is, radio *could* improve speech if we paid any attention to what it can teach. Most of us don't. Jack, what are your favorite radio programs?

JACK: Um-m. Lone Ranger and Jack Benny.

PEGGY: Don't talk with your mouth full, stupid.

MR. A: Peggy, your mother will take care of Jack's manners! . . . I haven't heard the Lone Ranger except when he comes floating in from your room, Jack. But would you say he was a likable person?

JACK: Huh?

MR. A: I said, would you say that the Lone Ranger was a likable person?

JACK: Sure, he's a swell guy!

MR. A: How do you know?

JACK: Well, he's always saving people! And then he *sounds* as if he were a real guy.

MR. A: Exactly. And I'm sure we all think the same thing of Jack Benny. His jokes may fall flat every once in a while, but all America likes Jack Benny because he *sounds* like a fine fellow. The voice is mighty important.

WARREN: I suppose your idea is, dad, that since we can't *see* these people, they impress us with their voices; and that those voices do the job as well as though we could see them. I've noticed, in dialing different stations, that I never need more than a few seconds to decide whether I'm listening to someone I like. These radio voices sure have to carry the old appeal, or—click—on you go to somewhere else.

MRS. A: But what about Rochester on the Benny program, Henry? He certainly hasn't a nice voice—and, for that matter, neither has Mary Livingstone!

PEGGY: Oh, I like *her* very much, mother. I know her voice is sort of thin and in the nose—but she sounds as though she would be *fun* to know.

MR. A: I agree with you, Peggy. There are certainly more beautiful voices over the air than Mary Livingstone's, but her voice is alive and she does sound as though she had a sense of humor. As for Rochester, Martha—part of the reason we all laugh at what he says is the quality of voice he uses when he reads his lines. By the way, what do you imagine he looks like?

MRS. A: Big and clumsy, I suppose.

JACK: And sly!

MRS. A: But good-natured.

PEGGY: Andy Devine has a terrible voice, but he sounds full of pep and fun.

WARREN: Come to think of it, dad, everyone on that program, from the big jolly announcer to the adolescent tenor, sounds like a good egg!

MR. A: That's my point! If these people can sell themselves to millions of others by means of their voices, it's time you and I realized that our own voices are worth cultivating. Every time we speak, the sound of our voices gives someone an impression of our personalities. We ought to try to make that impression a good one.

JACK: But, gee whiz! Jack Benny and all those people are professional actors. Maybe they're not so nice in real life as we think they are. You don't want *us* to *act*—and be hypocrites, do you?

MR. A: Hypocrites? Suppose someone who couldn't see you had been listening to you and Peggy a while ago. What sort of person would they imagine you to be?

JACK: They'd think Peggy was a stuck-up, fussy old—

PEGGY: They'd think Jack was a loud-mouthed . . . loud mouth, that's what!

MR. A: I don't doubt it!

JACK: Ah, dad!

MR. A: But are you really like that, Jack? And are you actually a stuck-up fussy female, Peggy? In spite of all your squabbling, I don't believe you think that of each other; and I'm sure your mother and I don't Let's hope your friends at school don't either.

JACK: Gosh, no! That's just the way we talk here at home.

MRS. A: Your father said a bit ago that I was right when I said that bad voices are catching. If you talk that way to each other day after day, I should think it might get to be a habit without your knowing it. Suppose you should take on that tone of voice when you're walking home with Bill Johnson someday, Peggy?

JACK: Ya-ah, ah! Bill Johnson!

MR. A: What chance would you have to be elected president of your club, Jack, if you used that tone of voice to your friends?

WARREN: But, isn't this off the line of argument, dad? We talk nicely to people we like or want to please. The people we don't care about we talk to in any way.

MRS. A: Of course, Warren, you seem to be assuming that most of the time none of us care about our own family!

MR. A: All I meant, Warren, was this: Which voice is yours? Voice is fundamentally a product of our character, and of our way of living. More than that, you and your voice are a sort of ring-around-the-rose of cause and effect. Improve your character and you improve your voice. Improve your voice, and—by thunder—you help improve your own nature! People who make themselves talk calmly when they are angry are very like to calm themselves down. People who try to make their *voices* sound full and clear and pleasant are influencing their inner selves as well.

MRS. A: Bravo, Henry! . . . but it's time to clear the table. Jack, you take off the plates; and, Peggy, bring in the dessert, please. . . . Now no fuss. Let me sound like the loving mother I hope I am. . . .

SOUND: *Dishes stacked*

. . . No, Jack! Don't stack the plates. . . . Oh, dear! . . . (*Laughs*). I couldn't help remembering your aunt Genevieve while you were talking, Henry. That poor, thin, whining voice of hers. Of course, there was that big house and all those children; but even after they were grown and away, she had the same whine and nag as ever. I always thought your uncle John was a martyr.

MR. A: Aunt Genevieve was used to sounding that way, I imagine, and never thought of it as whining or nagging. That was the way it was with your cousin Albert, Martha. What rows he used to have with his wife because she claimed he was speaking sarcastically. Some little turn in his tone of voice which he never seemed to be aware of. Of course, he was a school teacher!

WARREN: Let's drop these family comparisons, dad! Safety first! . . . Still, these people whose voices don't fit them worry me! Afraid I might be the same way, I suppose. Now there's a fellow in my class who's one of these big tough guys. . . . He really is! . . . Yet he talks with a thin, piping voice—like a boy. I tell you it really embarrasses him. And that girl I was talking about—the one on the blind date. She wasn't at all a bad number. When you got to know her, you discovered that her voice didn't fit either her figure or her personality!

MRS. A: Yes, and, Henry, there's Mrs. Hal Wright in my club. She's one of the new members. She's quite plain, and doesn't put herself forward, but last week she got up to speak on a motion and made a tremendous impression. My nominations committee has already started to consider her for an office next year. She has one of those clear, quiet, intelligent voices that tell you right away, "Here is somebody!"

MR. A: Right, both of you. The world is full of people who are excellent citizens and fine friends but whose voices handicap them with every new acquaintance; just as there are plenty of men and women who make themselves felt by the personality of their voices when they wouldn't be given a second thought without that quality. That's why radio has changed the old campaigning methods in politics so much. We used to read candidates' speeches and look at their pictures. Now we gather round the loudspeaker to make up our minds through their effect on our ears. . . . Mmmm. This is the kind of pie I like, Martha . . . and so was the whole meal.

MRS. A: Thank you, Henry. I'm glad you have the kind of voice that makes customers buy enough goods to make this meal possible!

JACK: But, dad. Suppose you *want* to have the right kind of voice, and you *don't have it.* What can you do about it? How about that tough guy with the squeak, Warren was talking about?

PEGGY: And that girl who hadn't the kind of voice Shakespeare said a woman ought to have?

MR. A: Why don't you have a talk with your English teacher, Peggy? And, Warren, one of those professors in your speech department at college ought to have something to say which would help answer these questions. Suppose we talk over the how's of the voice after you've consulted them. Just now it's almost time for Lowell Thomas. There's a chap whose voice is his fortune. Other news reporters have as good or better stories of the day's events, but there's only one with Lowell's voice, isn't there? (*Fade*)

ANNCER: This concludes our first visit with the Adams family. However, they haven't yet settled this business of acquiring a voice that fits personality, so we'll be listening again sometime soon.

Extracurricular Uses. The extracurricular uses of sound equipment in the school have been many. By broadcasting advance information concerning forthcoming school events, effective publicity is provided. One principal has noted that within a short time he paid for the equipment by the increased attendance at such events. Not only is greater participation stimulated but many opportunities are provided for the recognition of outstanding accomplishment both in the classroom and out.

Music for school functions, dances, and parties has been furnished by the system. Loudspeaker and announcing units for athletic events either in the gymnasium or on the football field have been relayed to various rooms. Entertainment has been provided for parent-teacher organizations.

An interesting development has been the use of a "radio hall," or listening center. Students who are assigned to a study hall and who have completed their work are permitted to enter this radio hall where they can hear selected musical and educational programs brought to them by either radio or recordings. The hall is administered by members of the Student Council.

A frequent use of public-address and studio equipment in the school is the rehearsal of workshop programs which are to be broadcast later through local radio stations. To rehearse adequately for such a presentation without a minimum of equipment is a difficult task, and even with school materials, as was shown earlier, a good deal of adjustment must be made.

Certain types of equipment make possible a variety of specialized uses. The recording machine, for example, has been used in schools in several ways. Programs have been taken off the air and used later to overcome schedule difficulties, pupil efforts in speech and music have been recorded for analysis and comparison, sound effects have been developed, a library of "documentary sound" has been organized. This library may include talks by contemporary leaders, outstanding news events, and like materials. These and other uses of recordings will be discussed more fully in the next chapter.

Obviously not all uses of the public-address system and its allied equipment have equal value. Some applications have special merit while other methods of utilization are less valuable if not actually negative in effect. Of the latter type is the unwise use that is sometimes made of the "talk-back" unit.

When this feature is incorporated with the equipment it is possible, boast some salesmen, to hear what is going on in the classrooms. This use of the sound system by an administrator without the knowledge and express permission of the teacher is deplorable. To mistake this form of "snoopervision" as having any values in supervision is foolish. It is false to assume that qualities of teaching can be determined largely by what is or is not heard. It is common knowledge that in many instances the noisiest room is the one in which most learning is taking place. Fortunately the talk-back unit device is not generally used in this manner, but where it is, the debilitating effects on teacher morale are not hard to imagine.

Plan of Organization for Use of Sound Equipment

Plans for Administration. The best form of organization for using the central-sound system and allied equipment depends upon the specific needs of the individual school. In some smaller schools the equipment is controlled directly by the principal. In larger schools maintenance and operation may be assigned to one teacher, while the program activities are directed by a dramatics teacher or someone else similarly qualified. Several schools have vested authority in a Radio Committee, which frequently includes the principal, journalism adviser, music and drama teachers.

If the two-teacher plan is used, the duties may be allocated as follows:

A. Duties of the teacher in charge of equipment:
   1. The care of technical equipment.
   2. The analysis of technical equipment to suit school needs and the selection of new equipment and replacements.
   3. The supervision of public-address and radio reception, including the routine check of individual classroom reception.
   4. The selection, management, and supervision of pupil personnel assisting in technical operation.
   5. The management and handling of the public-address or radio equipment when it is used outside the school's studios.
B. Duties of the teacher in charge of program activities:
   1. Informing class teachers of prospective public-address or radio programs.

2. Setting up the daily broadcast schedule to be followed by control-room operators.
3. Editing and producing scripts used in homeroom bulletins or in other administrative announcements.
4. Editing, producing, and sometimes writing scripts used in special drives or in advertising other extracurricular activities.
5. Editing, producing, and frequently writing scripts used for holiday programs or similar occasions.
6. Editing and producing scripts used by various departments of instruction within the individual school.
7. Managing and producing all other in-school broadcasts, such as the broadcast of assembly programs and talent shows.
8. Directing occasional programs given by the individual school over local radio stations.
9. Selecting pupils to take part in outside-school radio programs not under the teacher's direction.
10. Arranging for and directing the recording of voices or other sound in connection with in-school classwork—actual recording being handled by the technical staff.
11. Maintaining and cataloguing a library of transcriptions for in-school use by all departments of instruction.

Precautions in Use of Equipment. The indifference of classroom teachers to the use of the public-address system is as yet quite common. A device that has potential merit has come to be regraded in some schools as a distraction and a plaything. It is not difficult to account for this attitude when, in some instances, the legitimate activities of the entire school are halted to hear some announcement which is either trivial or of interest to but few students. There is no excuse for interrupting the school to state, for example, that an article has been lost. An announcement that consumes the time of the entire student body should be of general interest.

If programs are broadcast during homeroom time the administrator must make certain that enough time remains for the teachers to complete their routine duties. If this "gadget" comes to be regarded as a competitor for class time, then, needless to say, no general acceptance can be expected.

Before an announcement is given, some slight warning is helpful; otherwise the sudden interruption provides quite a jolt and some of the announcement is missed. A melodious chime has been used frequently. When machines and other noisy equipment are being used in the class, either a preliminary pause or a repeated announcement is essential.

Perhaps the basic rule for the teacher in charge of the address system to follow is that the device be used sparingly and only as occasion demands. High standards of presentation must be maintained, for inevitably there is a comparison by the listeners between what they hear at home over the radio and what the school offers. Certainly the best way to develop an attitude of cooperation among the teachers is to enlist their aid in program planning.

Some time ago, the writers asked several teachers associated with public-address equipment to indicate what they considered the most important precautions to be observed in the use of the equipment. These were some of the comments verbatim:

1. One teacher should be in charge of the operation, adjustment, and care of the public-address system. This would be the technical side. This person should also be in charge of public-address schedules, for seeing that the programs are coming through properly, for announcements, etc.
   One teacher should be in charge of producing programs such as plays, etc. This teacher will have to work in very close cooperation with the one in charge of the technical side.
   Caution—do not scatter the above responsibilities and be sure to select two teachers who can work together. Do not let any one else "play" with the public-address system. Make everything pass through the hands of the appointed teachers.
2. Neither the principal nor any teacher should talk too much over the public-address. Too frequent use causes them to lose their effectiveness.
3. Use pupil announcers whenever possible but train them so they are good. Make them realize that they are always on the spot and must always give as near a perfect performance as possible.
4. Classes should not be interrupted for announcements during the day except in an emergency. It should require the approval of either the principal or the assistant principal for such interruption.
5. Do not rely too much on the boys running the public-address system. They should be used but should work under the close supervision of a teacher. Pupils will not see to it that the broadcast is done well enough.
6. All announcements, plays, etc., sent over the public-address should

be done well or not at all. A careless presentation should not be permitted.

7. Do not permit anything which will cause teachers and pupils to consider the public-address system an annoyance rather than a help.
8. Do not feel that the public-address system must be used in order to get your money's worth. If you do not have a legitimate use for the public-address system, let it remain silent.

Selecting and Guiding Pupil Operators. Most high schools and many junior high schools depend upon pupils for the operation of the school's sound equipment. In some instances the operators are chosen from science and electrical classes. Many schools prefer to use volunteers who serve a period of apprenticeship and are then placed on the regular staff. Several large schools organize the operators into a service club headed by a "chief operator." Occasionally secretaries are also chosen to handle the daily schedule form, check operator's attendance, and perform other clerical duties for the teacher in charge of equipment.

Written codes of rules for pupil operators have been developed, and they are helpful in establishing standards. A representative list of such duties given to pupils includes the following:

Code of Rules for Control-Room Operators

1. The chief operator is responsible to the faculty adviser for the general efficiency of the sound system and the cooperation of period-operators.
2. Each of you is responsible for the efficiency of the system and the technical excellence of a program presented during your period of duty; consequently, you must cooperate closely with the directors and assistants in charge of each studio program. You must follow the requests made by the chief operator.
3. The principal daily job is to "monitor" broadcasts so that they may be heard in the classrooms at the best volume and with greatest possible clarity. No one—or no other occupation—should keep you from listening to *every* program you send out.
4. Report promptly at the beginning of your period of duty. If you know in advance that you must be late or absent tell the chief operator so; explain later to the teacher in charge.
5. Do not leave the control room until the next operator reports. If it appears that he is absent, report the fact at once to the faculty adviser.

6. Help the operator who comes after you. If a broadcast is scheduled soon after he is due to report, anticipate his difficulties; set up his switchboard for him. If there is a "rookie" in the group, give him the advantage of your experience.

7. Pay attention to the broadcast schedule. Know on Monday what you may have to do on Tuesday, etc. Anticipate demands on your skill.

8. Get programs started on time. Check the school clock for accuracy.

9. Throw off the switch as soon as the program is completed.

10. Check classroom reception occasionally to see that teachers are satisfied.

11. Make careful notes of complaints or any requests for schedule or change of schedule, and—if necessary—see that such requests are communicated promptly to the chief operator.

12. See that no one is present during a broadcast except those directly concerned with its production.

13. Refuse admission—as politely as possible—to any pupils who may wish to "visit" the control room or the studios.

14. See that the broadcasting rooms are kept clean and in good order.

15. Follow instructions on handling equipment and records; keep performers or hangers-on from touching any property for which you are responsible. Microphones and other studio property are under your supervision during the time you are on duty. The chief operator will check on the condition of the studio equipment at the end of the day.

Recognizing that efficient operation of sound equipment is a vital factor in determining the success of the school's broadcasting activities, teachers have tried numerous procedures such as giving awards to pupil operators. Some schools provide special certificates. Several institutions grant school letters and pupil-designed insignia. A few schools grant credit towards membership in the National Honor Society. Scholastic credit is given in few instances.

Equipment Notes. As was noted earlier, the factors of need, value, and utilization determine the type of equipment. If the radio activities of the school are to be confined almost entirely to reception of outside radio programs, it is probable that individual sets are superior to inflexible public-address loudspeakers. If a major phase of the school activity is to be the development and presentation of programs, then some form of central-sound system is essential. If transcriptions are to be used frequently, turntables suitable as to size and speed must be available. If, in addition to program production, a radio workshop is planned, then some modification of the equipment may be needed.

Several years ago under the joint sponsorship of the United States Office of Education, the Cleveland Board of Education and the Radio and Television Manufacturers Association, a group of leading manufacturers met with representative educators familiar with the general problems of school audio-equipment design. One of the writers was privileged to serve as a member of this group. As an outgrowth of this meeting and others which followed, several helpful brochures were published which summarize basic standards.[14] The following is from the first-named publication:

SPECIFICATIONS FOR SCHOOL SOUND SYSTEMS

It is proposed that Sound Systems for Schools be broken down into the following general systems, it being recognized that the proper performance of the Systems is contingent upon favorable acoustic treatment for Sound Conditioning as well as design of equipment for temperature and humidity conditions normally encountered.

I—A two-channel centralized system.
II—A single-channel centralized system.
III—An auxiliary system for use in auditoriums and/or gymnasiums, and/or cafeterias.
IV—An auxiliary system for workshop.

I. DETAILS OF TWO-CHANNEL CENTRALIZED SYSTEMS

The two-channel centralized systems shall include the following:
1—Control Unit
   This unit shall be styled in a modern functional design suitable for installation in a centrally located school office or preferably in a "radio workshop." It should not be over forty-three inches high in order that the operator may have full vision to observe live talent. It shall contain all speaker line keys or switches, a clock, a volume control for each channel, all radio tuners, talk-back and other controls. It preferably shall be large enough to accommodate a dual speed sixteen-inch transcription player and all preamplifiers. Adequate ventilation for any power amplifiers which may be housed in

---

[14] "School Sound Systems," "Classroom Radio Receivers," and "School Recording and Playback Equipment." These brochures are available from either the Radio Section, United States Office of Education, Washington 25, D.C., or the Radio and Television Manufacturer's Association, 1317 F Street, N.W., Washington 4, D.C.

this unit shall be provided. For larger installations, power amplifiers and associated equipment, other than essential operation-control equipment, may be housed externally.

2—Channels

Two program channels shall be provided.

Input circuits from at least four (4) low impedance microphones, two (2) radio tuners, one (1) turntable and two (2) incoming lines shall be terminated in the control unit, with provisions for routing and simultaneous mixing of any four of these into either or both of the two program channels at the option of the operator. Microphone lines may be supplied to some or all of the following: the administrative offices, the auditorium, the music room, the speech room, the English room, the language room, the gymnasium, the bus-loading area, and other special-purpose centers.

Provisions for outgoing lines to other schools, radio stations, athletic fields or playground speakers should be made, if required.

3—Radio Tuners

The radio tuners shall combine FM tuning for the educational and FM broadcast channels and standard AM broadcast reception. Adequate international shortwave bands are desirable. Adequate frequency compensation shall be provided for, working in combination with the centralized-system amplifiers. Adequate antenna equipment shall be provided for these tuners.

4—Monitor Speaker

A monitor speaker shall be provided at or built into the control unit, with switching to permit monitoring either channel.

5—Keys or Switches

Keys or switches to control the speaker line to each classroom and to each other area served shall be provided in the control unit which shall also contain a master key or switch for emergency anouncements to all areas.

6—Talk-Back Provisions (Optional)

Where talk-back circuits are called for, to permit intercommunication between teacher and operator or teacher and principal, a separate amplifier and suitable controls shall be provided.

7—Flexibility

Consideration shall be given in the design of this equipment so as to provide flexibility of switching and to permit a reasonable amount of deviation from standard "package units." It should permit substitution without redesign.

8—Loudspeakers

Provide suitable speakers for adequate coverage of classrooms, music room and/or library, auditorium, gymnasium, cafeteria and bus-loading terminals. These speakers should be of modern design, capable of faithfully reproducing the source material. Provisions shall be made to assure substantially the same volume regardless of number of rooms that are being used.

II. DETAILS OF A SINGLE-CHANNEL CENTRALIZED SYSTEM

The single-channel centralized system shall include the following:

1—Control Unit

This unit shall be styled in a modern functional design suitable for installation in a centrally located school office or preferably in a "radio workshop." It should not be over 43 inches high in order that the operator may have full vision to observe live talent. It shall contain all speaker-line keys or switches, a clock, a volume indicating meter, all radio tuners, talk-back and other controls. It preferably shall be large enough to accommodate a transcription player and all preamplifiers. Adequate ventilation for any power amplifiers which may be housed in this unit shall be provided. For a large installation, power and amplifier and associated equipment other than essential operation-control equipment may be housed externally.

2—Channels

One channel shall be provided.

Input circuits from at least three (3) low impedance microphones, one (1) radio tuner, one (1) turntable and one (1) incoming line shall be terminated in the control unit with provisions for simultaneously mixing of any four (4) of these. Microphone lines may be supplied to some or all of the following: the administrative offices, the auditorium, the music room, the speech room, the English room, the language room, the gymnasium, the bus-loading area, and other special-purpose centers.

Provisions for outgoing lines to other schools, radio stations, athletic fields or playground speakers should be made, if required.

3—Radio Tuners

The radio tuners shall combine FM tuning for the educational and FM broadcast channels and standard AM broadcast reception. Adequate international-shortwave bands are desirable. Adequate frequency compensation shall be provided for working in combination with the centralized-system amplifiers. Adequate antenna equipment shall be provided for these tuners.

4—Monitor Speaker

A monitor speaker shall be provided at or built into the control unit.

5—Keys or Switches

Keys or switches to control the speaker line to each classroom and

and to each other area served shall be provided in the control unit which shall also contain a master key or switch for emergency announcements to all areas.

6—Talk-Back Provisions (Optional)

Where talk-back circuits are called for, to permit intercommunication between teacher and operator or teacher and principal, a separate amplifier and suitable controls shall be provided.

7—Flexibility

Consideration shall be given in the design of this equipment so as to provide flexibility of switching and to permit a reasonable amount of deviation from standard "package units." It should permit substitution without redesign.

8—Loud Speakers

Provide suitable speakers for adequate coverage of classrooms, music room and/or library, auditorium, gymnasium, cafeteria and bus-loading terminals. These speakers should be of modern design capable of faithfully reproducing the source material. Provisions shall be made to assure substantially the same volume regardless of number of rooms that are being used.

III. DETAILS OF AUXILIARY SYSTEM FOR THE AUDITORIUM, GYMNASIUM, AND CAFETERIA

It is recommended that the sound system provided for the auditorium and/or gymnasium and/or cafeteria be designed and installed to provide:

1—Tying the auditorium microphones and/or speakers into the centralized system.

2—Tying the gymnasium speakers and/or microphones into the centralized system.

3—Tying the cafeteria speakers and/or microphones into the centralized system.

4—Well-balanced sound diffusion throughout the entire auditorium, yet retaining the auditorium-stage direction as the effective source of all sounds.

5—Adequate mixing and volume control facilities at a point where the auditorium volume can be ascertained.

6—Amplification of ample power and fidelity for music and speech.

7—Consideration shall be given in the design of this equipment so as to provide flexibility of switching and to permit a reasonable amount of deviation from standard "package units." It should permit reasonable substitution of equipment without the necessity of complete redesign.

IV. DETAILS OF AN AUXILIARY SYSTEM FOR WORKSHOP

Suitable means shall be provided for:

1—Local pickup of plays or programs.

2—Broadcasting of the above over tie-line into the centralized and/or auditorium systems, or to local-broadcast station.

3—Recording of the above and feeding transcribed programs over tie-lines into the centralized and/or auditorium systems, or to local-broadcast station.

V. ACCESSORIES COMMONLY REQUIRED FOR COMPLETE SYSTEMS

1—Record and Transcription Players

(a) Transcription Players

This equipment shall be designed to feature noise-free reproduction transcriptions with the best fidelity practicable. A pickup suitable for lateral-cut transcriptions with optional provisions for vertical-cut transcriptions shall be provided. The transcription player should be capable of playing 12-inch and 16-inch transcriptions at either 78 or 33⅓ RPM.

(b) Record Players (Manual)

This equipment shall be designed to feature noise-free reproduction of good records with the best fidelity practicable. It should be provided with a suitable light-weight pickup with good wide-range response.

(c) Automatic Record Changers

A well-built disc automatic-record changer, preferably of the drop type shall be provided. It shall be as nearly foolproof in design as possible and shall be equipped with a permanent-point pick-up head, capable of reasonably good reproduction.

2—Recording Equipment (All Types)

Provide adequate recording and playback facilities, either permanent or portable, to record and play-back programs picked up in the auditorium, any classroom or by radio.

3—Microphones

Provide microphones of low-impedance types designed to give maximum-frequency response for voice and music reproduction. The microphones shall be of rugged design capable of withstanding normal hard usage.

VI. PROTECTION TO CONSUMER

The consumer should expect the supplier to furnish a strong warranty covering the equipment under normal usage for a period of time, usually ninety days. In addition, an instruction manual containing complete wiring diagrams and essential information for the care and operation of the equipment should be supplied with the equipment. The responsible supplier will probably be eager to offer an annual service or maintenance contract at a nominal charge. These indications of faith and good will serve to protect both the consumer and the supplier.

On systems standard with the manufacturer, the seal of approval of the

Underwriters' Laboratories, Inc., should be displayed on each piece of equipment involving fire or shock hazard. Major standard elements of custom-built systems should also display this seal. Similarly, all wiring and the installation should be examined and approved by the local- or state-approval agency.

Installation Considerations

The proper location of equipment will contribute to the integration of the use of audio devices in the instructional program as regular tools for learning—not as occasional, extra or supplementary devices.

Central Equipment

The permanently installed major pieces of equipment should be located in a quiet area inasmuch as ordinary school noises may be picked up by a live microphone at the control unit if the announcements are originated at that point. At the same time they should be installed as near as possible to the geographic center of the school even if this means they must be remote from the administrative office in order to effect a saving in wiring costs and in amplifier power.

Adequate conduits should be installed at the time of building construction. Separate conduits should be provided for loudspeaker and for input lines to each location presently considered and also for any anticipated expansion.

Studios and Control Room

Where space considerations permit, a school should have a studio large enough to accommodate a musical ensemble or dramatic cast. Often a smaller adjacent studio is planned for use by individuals, quartets or other small groups. These rooms can be effectively separated by a "control room," independently reached, equipped (if remote from the centralized-control unit) with mixers, preamplifiers, and line amplifiers. A "sound lock" type of hall for entry to the studio(s) and control room is desirable. For a large school it is recommended that a control room for the studio area be remote from the control unit of the sound system. This permits greater flexibility in distributing radio and recorded programs to some classrooms while studio programs are in progress.

This studio and control-room area will need special consideration and treatment to meet the purposes for which it is designed. The following is a list of criteria which should be met:

1. Location should be in the quietest part of the school plant—as far as possible from shops, cafeteria kitchens, and other sources of noise.

2. Air conditioning is needed in studios and control areas for comfort and so that heat generated by the equipment will be dissipated. Thus protected against extreme conditions of temperature and humidity, the equipment will serve for a longer period of time.

3. Sound conditioning of the entire area, to effect the best possible acoustic values, should be planned and supervised by an engineer experienced in acoustics. This is not a matter of either guesswork or sound-deadening. Ceilings, walls, and floors all will need careful treatment to achieve the desired end and to contribute to the elimination of audible interference from all sources. Conduits, both intake and exhaust, should be baffled, as well as insulated, and, where possible, floated to eliminate any danger of noise transmission.

4. A means of communication between studios and control room should be readily available at all times. This can be accomplished through separate communication facilities between the control room and the studios.

5. Doors leading from the studios to the sound lock and from the sound lock to the hall should be of a quiet-closing and sound-insulated type. Two doors, 36 inches wide, meeting at a removable center stanchion, allow for the easy passage of grand pianos.

6. Storage facilities for microphones, portable turntables, sound props, and other accessory equipment should be so located that such material is readily available to the student operators.

7. Plate-glass windows should be part of the wall separating studios and control room. These should be double, each of ¼ inch thick plate glass with a minimum of 1½ inch dead-air space between the panes. It is not necessary to provide a viewing area lower than about 36 inches above floor level or higher than 66 inches above floor level. However, the viewing area should be wide enough from side to side to afford as nearly full vision of the studio as possible.

8. Conduits, adequate to accommodate all required circuits between the Central-Control Room, Studio-Control Room and Studio(s) should be provided.
   1″ or larger, from the exterior of the building to the control room, will be needed to provide exclusively for telephone and other communication services.

9. Clocks with sweep second hands are of primary importance in each studio and in the control room. These must be quiet in operation and so installed that they are readily visible to the performer and to the operator.

10. Transformer starters, where used for fluorescent lights, should be located outside the studios to avoid interference with microphones.

11. "Studio-in-Use" warning signs, prominently displayed in the hall and sound lock, should be lighted when silence is required.
12. Outlets, both for microphones and service current in studios and and control rooms, should be high enough from the floor for protection against dust and water resulting from cleaning.
13. Control of all lighting in the studios should be centralized in the control room.
14. Service wiring having a minimum capacity of 20 amperes will be needed in studios and control room.
15. Control panels should be independently lighted.
16. Troughs or overhead supports for microphone cables should be used to prevent damage.
17. Studio windows in outside walls should be double-glassed (preferably plate) and sealed.
18. A signal light fitted to the microphone stand should be so installed that students have positive indication when individual microphones are alive.

Classrooms

The location of the loudspeaker in each classroom presents an individual problem for which no simple, easy, and foolproof answer can be indicated. Generally a location in or on the front wall is best, sufficiently above the blackboard so as not to interfere with visual aids commonly used in classrooms. In any event, the loudspeaker should be located and directed to provide maximum-listening ease. Two loudspeakers will give better coverage than one, especially for the front corner seats in large or oddly shaped classrooms.

The acoustic properties of the classroom may limit the effectiveness of the sound system and seriously injure the utilization potential. This is a matter of wall and ceiling treatment in all new construction or alteration. Large amounts of wall space with sound-absorbing surfaces will not always suffice. Scientific application of sound-absorbing materials will result in a classroom well balanced for easy listening—neither too "dead" nor too reverberative. The conditioning of classrooms—in fact of all parts of the school building—is a matter for the consideration of an experienced acoustical engineer.

Administrative Offices

The administrative offices of the school should be so equipped that by simple key or switch manipulation the administrator can monitor any channel or Studio at his discretion. Further, there should be a microphone line (reserved for emergency uses) direct from the administrator's desk to the control panel.

Auditorium

In new construction or alteration, attention should be given to the proper acoustical conditioning of the auditorium. Of equal importance is the proper installation of sound amplification and reproduction equipment so that is can be used to best advantage. Where possible the mixing and control of volume should be done at the rear of the auditorium. The greatest care should be given to the proper shielding of the audio equipment and wiring, to prevent interference. This shielding can be practically accomplished by isolating the audio equipment from the variety of other electrical stage equipment such as banks of switches, transformers, electric motors and other power-operated devices found in most auditoriums.

There should be a sufficient number of loudspeakers in the auditorium to offer complete coverage. Ideally, these should be installed over the proscenium arch so that the illusion of direction can be maintained. However, if this is impossible, they should be placed on each side of the proscenium. It may be necessary to install additional loudspeakers in certain auditoriums.

Gymnasium

Gymnasium activities make special demands on the sound equipment. Loudspeakers should be placed high and should be enclosed for protection. Extra volume and speaker coverage should be provided to take care of the higher-ambient noise level.

Cafeteria

A quiet and restful atmosphere is desired in the cafeteria. Consequently, the number and location of loudspeakers should be such that sound and music are heard throughout the room at a uniformly pleasant background level. Diners should not be disturbed by the sound or forced to raise their voices to override it.

Music Room

Because only highest-quality sound reproduction can be considered acceptable in music rooms, both selection and installation of loudspeakers need careful attention. The greatest degree of listening comfort combined with highest-fidelity reproduction is essential. Record and transcription reproducers may be wired to the central-control unit but, preferably, an independent system should be supplied in the music room so that the instructor will have complete control of volume at all times.

Library

Two specialized types of installation serve well in the library. Group-listening rooms, where small groups of students can listen to selected broadcast or transcribed material without disturbing others, are desirable. Listening booths, each supplied with either a headset or a loudspeaker, facilitate individual-study purposes. The development of the audio aspects of the library adds to the material available to the student for research and study.

Television Activities

As in every aspect of television, the factor of expense is the great limitation when it comes to providing opportunities for pupils to "do" television. Whereas sound-system equipment, suitable for intramural broadcasting and for practice use by the radio workshop can sometimes be assembled under three figures, a television camera chain (as the unit of camera, power supply, control unit, monitor, and other parts is called), is something that begins with five figures and climbs rapidly upward. So it will be a good many years before any individual school or even a school-system's radio station can afford real television equipment.

Educational Experiences the School Can Provide. Colleges, of course, can do better, as noted in Chapter 13, "The School Radio Station," though even here the exception still proves the rule when it comes to securing a frequency and operating a television transmitter. But for the average school the chance to "play television" with genuine equipment is far off in the distant future. What legitimate educational experiences can a school provide?

VISITING A TELEVISION STATION. For one thing, the central-radio workshop of a school system, or even each radio workshop in each school, can manage to visit a television station and watch rehearsals and broadcasts. To ensure continuance of the privilege, visiting groups should be limited to twenty to thirty pupils at a time and should be accompanied by adequate faculty escort. The visits, too, should be spaced at two-week intervals between one school's workshop and the next, except for the few stations which have large "studio theaters," capable of accommodating several hundred spectators at one broadcast.

STUDY OF TELEVISION SCRIPTS. Study of television scripts is profitable, particularly when most or all the students have seen the broadcast of the particular script, and can translate the cryptic symbols on the mimeographed page into meaningful memories of what was seen on the screen. Discussion and analysis of a program viewed the night before by all or most of the class are most valuable in developing discrimination and taste, as we have already noted. Since few stations can afford to distribute scripts widely, perhaps one representative of the school system can do the "securing" and arrange for duplication for school use, always with the permission of the station, and with the understanding that the scripts will be used for study purposes only. Members of the Association for Education by Radio can secure many good examples from its Television-Script Exchange.

In time, these scripts can be bound in manila folders and made part of the radio workshop's bookshelf, along with copies of suitable books on television, such as *The Television Program, Its Writing, Direction and Production,* by Edward Stasheff and Rudy Bretz, Rudy Bretz's *The Techniques of Television Production,* and others listed in the bibliography.

Books on television have a terrifying rate of obsolescence, but those mentioned here should prove valuable for some time.

STUDY OF KINESCOPE RECORDINGS OR FILM TRANSCRIPTIONS. One activity which would be most helpful, where it is practical, is the classroom viewing and subsequent discussion of kinescope recordings or film transcriptions of television programs, run off on ordinary classroom 16 mm. sound projectors. However, as noted in more detail in the next chapter, there may be some question as to the legality of showing such filmed programs in the classroom, and securing clearance from the organizations involved may prove too slow and difficult a process. Eventually, if the history of similar developments in radio serve as an example, arrangements will no doubt be made to make such film transcriptions available for school use.

TALKS BY WORKERS IN THE FIELD. Talks by workers in the field of television are usually good fun and always valuable. The toilers in the television vineyard are full of their subject and usually have a fund of interesting anecdotes to illustrate their points. However, they are busy people, frequently working 60-hour weeks and wondering how to get along on 24 hours a day. Speaking to a group of thirty "Radio Workshoppers" may seem a burden, but arranging a meeting of several workshops in a centrally located auditorium is a possible solution to this problem.

HANDLING AND TUNING SETS. In those schools fortunate enough to possess television receivers, handling and tuning the sets is a valuable experience for a squad of skilled and devoted students (always under competent faculty supervision, since television receivers are not only expensive and fragile—they are run by high voltage and the student's impulse to "open the back" and tinker with the set must be firmly discouraged). Yet as early as November, 1949, South High School in Columbus, Ohio, using a minimum of television equipment, had taken the first steps toward a television workshop. Philip Lewis, of South Shore High School, Chicago, built up a television workshop with dummy cameras and working microphone booms.

PREPARING AND REHEARSING FOR AN ACTUAL BROADCAST. Of course the most valuable in-school experience is preparing and rehearsing for an actual broadcast from the studios of a local station, with the experience of really being on the air the most impressive of all. In the dozen cities already mentioned as being active in television, hundreds of pupils in all grades have faced the cameras. While some series may use a scant score of central workshoppers again and again, other programs involve a group from a different school each week.

However, special classes devoted to television are likely to follow the hundreds of radio courses now given in high schools. In the South Shore High School of Chicago a class devoted to video writing, lighting, make-up, research and program criticism was organized in the spring of 1950. The workshop course was organized after a survey showed that 500 of the school's 1,600 pupils came from homes having television receivers.

Educational Experiences on College Level. On the college level, opportunities are even greater. Iowa State College is already on the air with Station WOI-TV; Cornell, University of Iowa, Concordia College of St. Louis, and Harding of Memphis had already applied to the FCC for construction permits before the assigning of frequencies was temporarily "frozen" in 1949. Other colleges and universities—Syracuse, Creighton, Nebraska, American University in Washington, D.C., Michigan, Western Reserve, Temple, to name only a few—either had campus studios from which they could "feed" programs to local commercial stations or had working agreements with local stations for a continuing series. The University of Miami, for example, did a 26-week series of sustaining programs over Station WTVJ, Miami, and followed that with another series under the sponsorship of a local construction company. In addition, the Radio and Television Department was at work on a film dealing with student life on the campus, stressing the unique educational and academic advantages of the University, from its specially designed, tropical architecture to its marine-laboratory work. The University of Michigan uses about twenty college students a week in its three 20-minute programs over WWJ-TV, Detroit.

In short, while television activities within the school building will probably not equal the opportunities offered to many students by sound broadcasting, there will be a number of valuable experiences open to the few students who are particularly gifted and interested in broadcasting.

10

Recordings

◇◇

What are the methods of recording and playback?

What advantages have recordings that make them of significance to classroom teachers?

Are there any limitations that should be noted in the use of recorded programs?

What suggestions have been made for using recordings effectively?

From what organizations can teachers secure information concerning educational recordings?

What of television recording? How may film recordings of television programs be used?

What seem to be the major trends in the educational recording field?

◇◇◇◇◇◇◇◇THE ANCESTOR OF the modern electrical-transcription cutting machine was invented by Thomas Edison in 1877. It is noteworthy that even then the "Wizard of Menlo Park" predicted the educational application of the "voice writer." By means of preserving the voices of famous statesmen, through records of books read by elocutionists, through the music box, and by various forms of dictation he saw that this could be achieved.

To imaginative teachers the early phonograph records had educational possibilities, and long before radio broadcasting as such began records were being used to some extent in schoolrooms. However, the production of recordings by the school itself was not common until the past decade when recording processes were reduced in cost so that the means of making satisfactory recordings was placed in the hands of educational institutions. It is evident that the rapid development of the radio industry in both programs and equipment did much to stimulate increased interest in recordings as a teaching tool.

The terms "records," "recordings," "transcriptions," and "transcribed programs" are often used interchangeably, though there is some distinction that should be mentioned. The Federal Communications Commission indicates that transcriptions are made for broadcast purposes only and for sale to radio stations, while records are for sale to the general public.

Methods of Recording and Playback

Without going into excessive detail the general principles presented here are from one of the helpful brochures, "School Sound Recording and Playback Equipment," developed jointly by the United States Office of Education and the Radio and Television Manufacturers Association Committee on Standards for School Audio Equipment.

Methods of recording and reproducing sound may be classified in three major groups:

1. Mechanical, which covers the engraving and embossing methods: the engraving, in which a varying groove is cut into a suitable medium by means of a sharp edge of an engraving tool; and the embossing

350

in which a varying groove is formed in a suitable medium by the rounded tip of an embossing tool.

2. Magnetic, in which the sound is recorded magnetically on a suitable moving medium.

3. Photographic, in which the sound is recorded photographically; this method finds its greatest usefulness in sound pictures, the sound record being usually on the same film as the picture, but at times on a separate film operating synchronously with a picture film.

Mechanical Recording and Reproducing

Mechanical recording is used almost exclusively in the present-day phonograph industry, in electrical transcriptions for broadcast purposes and general-utility recorders. Most mechanical recording is made on discs varying in diameter from 6 inches for general utility equipment to 16 inches in broadcast transcriptions. In general, there are two types of disc recorders; the lateral type of recorder where the stylus moves parallel to the radius of the disc, and the vertical type where the stylus moves at right angles to the face of the disc.

On some discs the recording is made "inside-out"; that is, the groove starts at the inside of the disc and the cutting head or playback needle travels toward the outer edge of the disc. This is the reverse of what is done on standard phonograph records and is usually found only on 16-inch transcriptions. The direction of play should be indicated on the recording label.

The recording material in general may be divided into two classes:

a. The wax disc, intended for subsequent processing and duplication, used by large record-manufacturing companies. This type of recording is not well adapted for school recording and therefore will not be described in detail here.

b. The instantaneous media, disc or otherwise, intended mainly for reproduction directly from the embossed or engraved masters. The latter are occasionally used for subsequent processing and duplication.

Instantaneous-Playback Discs

This term covers a multitude of plastics and metals which lend themselves to easy engraving or embossing. In the higher-quality field of instantaneous recording media, the 10, 12, and 16-inch lacquer-coated discs of glass or metal are most common.

In the general-utility field, recording discs are most commonly made of vinylite or vinylchloride, or lacquer-coated paper. Gelatin and soft metals such as aluminum are also used.

Mechanical-Recording Media Other than Disc

Although the recording medium on most general-utility recording machines takes the form of a disc, two exceptions worthy of note are made. The first of these is film on which the recorded grooves are embossed on an endless loop of safety-film base. The other exception is the well-known wax cylinder, now principally used for office dictation.

Magnetic Recording and Reproducing

Although the process of recording on a magnetic medium for later reproduction has been long known, other recording devices have been more thoroughly exploited and, as a result, have come into wide usage. The earliest record of magnetic recording is credited to Poulsen who in 1900 described his "Telegraphone." Since that time, though much has been learned and vastly improved results have been obtained, extensive use of the method as a recording process of great potentialities was not achieved until the war years of 1941–1945.

The magnetic-recording method offers certain unique advantages. The mechanism may be rugged and simple to operate. The record can be played practically any number of times with no perceptible loss of fidelity or volume. The recording may be erased and the medium reused as often as desired.

Magnetic recording involves three fundamental operations or processes: (a) erasing, (b) recording, (c) playback. Erasing is the process by which the magnetic-recording medium is either neutralized or saturated magnetically to obliterate any audible signal previously recorded. In the early phases of development saturation by a strong d-c field was used. More recently, neutralization by an inaudible high-frequency a-c field has been used.

The process of magnetic recording consists of impressing on the moving magnetic medium a varying magnetization which is directly proportional to the instantaneous value of the recording-head current. The recording head is usually associated with an amplifier so designed that the recording currents are independent of the impedance characteristic of the head. In most applications recording currents are small, and very little power is required. In certain applications electronic amplification is not used and the recording current is obtained directly from an energized-carbon microphone.

Playback is accomplished by passing the recorded medium over a magnetically sensitive head, at the same velocity and in the same direction as in recording. The voltages induced in the head are then amplified and equalized to obtain the desired-frequency characteristic. All these processes may be accomplished with the same head.

Magnetic-Recording Media————Physical Forms

Most of the early magnetic-recording equipment employed a solid homogeneous-steel wire or tape as the recording medium. Recent refinements in the art of electroplating magnetic alloys and developments in the use of magnetic power-coated paper and plastic materials have removed many of the restrictions on the form of the recording medium. Although there are some technical differences between the media, the choice of physical form in general is determined by the desired application.

Magnetic wire is generally used wherever a very long playing time is required or when compact equipment is necessary. The wire diameter commonly used is between 0.004 and 0.006 inch in diameter. Splicing in some machines can be accomplished by tying a square knot in the wire.

Metal tape is useful for applications requiring a continuous record-playback-erase cycle. In such applications the tape is prepared in the form of an endless belt. Whenever a more-extended playing time is required the tape is reeled in a manner similar to motion-picture film. Recording equipment has been commercially produced, using 0.002 by 0.050-inch tape and offset-recording and reproducing-pole pieces, in which an extended frequency response and dynamic range is realized at a comparatively low-operating speed.

Paper or plastic tapes coated with magnetic material, since they are necessarily more bulky than wire, are applicable to all uses where requirements of playing time are not excessive. The material is inexpensive to manufacture and, if cut, may be easily spliced by cementing. The material is usually 0.0013 to 0.0025 inch thick. In contrast to steel wire and tape, when a reel of the material is removed from a machine, there is little danger of free uncoiling. Eliminating this danger is very desirable in classroom applications.

The use of powdered-magnetic materials applied to paper or plastic bases has recently received considerable attention in this country. Such a recording medium is comparatively cheap to manufacture and may be produced with very uniform and stable properties. Various magnetic materials in powder form are being investigated for properties advantageous to magnetic recording. One such material, black magnetic iron oxide, is commercially available in the required finely divided form. The powdered material is normally dispersed in a plasticized lacquer and applied to the base to a thickness of approximately 0.0005 inch. When the powdered-magnetic material is very finely divided and uniformly dispersed in the binder excellent results have been obtained both in extension of frequency response and reduction of background noise.

Photographic Method

The photographic method of sound recording finds its greatest field in sound motion pictures. Aside from this use, the photographic method is not at present widely accepted in schools and therefore will not be treated in detail here.

Two Major Methods of Recording————Merits of Each

Engraved Disc Recording

Advantages

1. It is universally used and well established.
2. The medium lends itself to easy filing and storage, provided reasonable precautions are taken to prevent warpage caused by improper support, high temperature or high humidity.
3. Only one process is necessary, after which as many pressings as required can be made without having to re-record the copies individually. For large quantity duplication the disc method is the best as of today. Excellent reproduction may also be obtained from instantaneous recordings provided a relatively short life is satisfactory with respect to the number of possible playings.
4. Because of the established position of engraved-disc recording, huge libraries of recorded material are now available. Pressed-record discs are standardized for interchangeability and use on all school-playback equipment.
5. With the disc it is relatively easy to locate and replay desired parts of a program.
6. The disc has excellent characteristics in that it can be made to cover a wide range both in frequency and in volume.

Disadvantages

1. With prolonged use, the fidelity of disc-type recordings becomes progressively poorer, and the "scratch level" becomes more noticeable.
2. Disc-type recordings are susceptible to damage from handling.
3. In the case of the longer-playing disc recordings (i.e., the 16-inch program transcriptions), playback equipment becomes too heavy and bulky for easy portability.
4. Disc-type recordings cannot be readily edited—an error necessitates starting over again and means lost time and a wasted disc.

Magnetic Recording

Advantages

1. Permits recording and playback without any processing whatsoever. Signals are permanent, permitting thousands of playings—only restriction is wear of wire or tape.
2. It is readily portable because, for either playback or recording, there is no need for heavy, bulky equipment.
3. The initial recording may be transferred to some other medium, making the medium available for future recordings.
4. The machine can be operated in any position or while in motion and under a wide range of climatic conditions.

5. It is easy for an inexperienced person to make a recording with a magnetic system.
6. Magnetic recordings require relatively little storage and shipping space, are light in weight, and are not subject to damage due to heat, humidity or careless handling.
7. Development work very active now—offers great possibilities for expansion and improvements.

Disadvantages

1. A desired portion of the recordings cannot be easily and quickly located for playback.
2. On many machines it is necessary to take time to rewind the wire or tape before the recorded program can be played, and to rewind after each playing.
3. It is expensive to make duplicates of magnetic recordings at the present time.

Evaluation of Recordings

Special Values. In the discussion that follows, the term "recording" will be used as indicating all materials which are recorded, either on phonograph records or on transcriptions, as contrasted with programs which are being presented "live" from a radio studio. Since wire, tape, and film recorders are as yet comparatively rare in the schools, most of this discussion will relate to the disc type of recording.

The educational values ascribed to the use of selected radio programs apply as well to the judicious use of carefully chosen recordings. They make real and vivid what may seem abstract; they dramatize what may appear prosaic; they provide a pleasurable yet very worthwhile experience.

FLEXIBILITY AND PERMANENCE. Two features of the recordings make them of special significance to the schoolteacher: flexibility and, to some degree, permanence.

The flexibility of the recording makes it possible for the teacher to use it at a time when she believes it will serve the children most. In this manner it is possible to overcome somewhat the limitations of broadcasting: (a) the difficulty of adjusting to rigid radio schedules and (b) the problem of securing programs that relate closely to the curriculum. If the teacher has in her possession a program which has been recorded, it is of little concern to her that the same program is broadcast at a time when her pupils might be studying some other subject or that it is given in the evening. She merely plays the record when she pleases. The same is true of the latter difficulty. If the recorded program deals with a topic that will not be touched upon in the course of study until later in the school term, it is a simple matter to delay the use of that program until such date as it will serve best. However, if the program were broadcast rather than recorded, this opportunity would not exist.

This flexibility of use is of additional importance, since it thus becomes possible for the teacher to hear the program before she presents it to her class. If the proper use of a teaching aid requires a preliminary knowledge of the material to be presented, then this opportunity to preaudit the program is significant to the conscientious teacher. The lack of information relative to forthcoming radio programs, it was mentioned previously, presents a real obstacle to a more effective use of such radio programs. By means of recordings, the teacher can secure the advance data she requires. Thus, she can become acquainted with the scope of the program, the points to emphasize, the follow-up procedures to undertake, as well as the most propitious time to use the recordings.

The comparative permanence of the recording suggests other values. It is perhaps the major tragedy of radio that once a program is given, no matter how excellent, it is seldom heard again. With the recording that experience is captured and made to serve repeatedly. Jacobsen calls attention to this phase of radio weakness: "The radio broadcast, unless recorded, is gone forever with the announcer's signature. If textbooks vanished page by page as the student read them, if only one set of books could be used at a time, and then only at a certain hour of the day, taxpayers and schoolmen would be feverishly searching for a less expensive and more permanent vehicle." [1]

The permanence of the recorded program further enhances utilization by making it possible to repeat the program. Since, for some slower groups, such repetition may be essential, and since, too, with the recordings it is possible to interrupt the program for class discussion relative to a certain point, it becomes apparent that permanence is a definite factor in facilitating effective use.

The production and use of radio programs by school groups as com-

[1] Philip A. Jacobsen, "Transcriptions and Pictures," *The Phi Delta Kappan*, May 1940, p. 431.

pared with the production and use of recorded programs have been discussed in educational circles for some time. There are those who feel that because of the merits of recordings, some of which were noted above, the place of radio broadcasting in the schools is but a limited one. It is pointed out that, whereas with a single transmitter only one school program at a time can be broadcast, with recordings any number of programs can be used simultaneously in the various classrooms. The only limitation is the number of recordings and playback machines available.

But, like many other things in education, both the radio programs which are broadcast and those which are recorded have a place in the school picture. There are advantages and limitations to each. A radio broadcast can provide materials which are current and up-to-date, while with recordings there is a danger that the materials may become obsolete. As in the case of textbooks, teaching objectives and procedures may become dependent upon existing materials, rather than the materials dependent upon aims. The quality of permanence, although it is an asset in the use of recordings, can also prove to be a limitation. If the recorded materials continue to be used after they are out of date or after they are technically imperfect, such utilization is deplorable. "When such lectures become canned and stereotyped, they should be thrown out—not immortalized on wax." [2]

With recordings it is necessary to have satisfactory playback equipment, something yet scarce as compared with radio receivers, which are available in many schoolrooms. Then, too, if every program that is to be used must be purchased or recorded, there is a danger of restricting program plans because of the cost of recordings and processing records. The question of comparative cost of radio or recording is by no means a conclusive one. If recorded copies of every broadcast are to be made available, let us say, to one hundred schools, it is quite likely that the total cost of this enterprise might at the end of the year be larger than the operation of a small broadcasting station which could present those materials by radio. Certainly it is more convenient to tune in a program by radio than to use a recording disc which itself has but a limited life, is easily marred, and requires delicate handling. The adoption by schools of the newer type of wire and tape recorders may alter this picture considerably.

Edgar Dale, *The Phi Delta Kappan*, May, 1940, p. 411.

Aside from these and other factors, it is probably true that radio will be used to a larger extent in the lower grades, and the recordings may find increased utilization in the junior and senior high schools. Obviously, the operation of a school station does not preclude the extensive use of recorded materials, for the development of a station with its access to network lines and programs may be an essential step in the organization of a comprehensive recording library in the schools. The use of recorded materials in a school station will be described later.

Limitations. Judging by teacher and pupil comments, it would seem that in general the criticisms made with reference to commercial radio programs designed for classroom use apply to recordings as well. An inordinate number of production techniques may reduce comprehensibility. Excessive and inappropriate music and sound effects, confusing dialects, too many scenes, too large a cast, fades that are likely to confuse the child, and a strange vocabulary are among the deficiencies noted.

However, it is pointed out that even the recordings generally rated as excellent are not very productive when poorly utilized by an indifferent or unskilled teacher. Granted that there is a need for improvement in recordings planned for use in the schools, there is likewise a vital need for better use to be made by the teacher of the stimulating experiences furnished by many of the records. Through careful planning the skilled teacher can greatly enhance the value of even a mediocre program.

In this connection it is interesting to note the manufacturer's point of view concerning educational recordings:

Two major problems of the manufacturers of recordings are those of (a) acquainting classroom teachers with the wide variety of recordings available, and (b) training teachers to use recordings in the numerous situations for which they are suited.

Thousands of teachers who enter the profession each year have received little or no training in the proper use of recordings as teaching aids. These teachers should be trained, but it is a job which cannot be accomplished by any manufacturer. The constant change in teaching personnel makes it difficult to reach these people with the information they should have. Therefore, it is the function of those agencies which regularly train teachers.

Another major problem is the wide divergence of real or imaginary requirements of school users. Unfortunately, there seems to be nothing approaching unanimity among classroom teachers and supervisors as to what they would like to have on records. One desires a certain series of subjects, treated in a specific way; another might like the series, but not the treatment; and still another wouldn't like either. This somewhat general confusion among potential users of recordings is further indicated by the hundreds of different suggestions received from school people concerning recordings which should be made.

The general problem of providing desired educational recordings is not solved merely by finding out what school people want. Research to determine what is needed; additional research to determine how the subject should be treated; selection of cast or artist; high quality manufacture; announcing and advertising the records among hundreds of thousands of teachers; making the records readily accessible for hearing and purchase through convenient sources—all these require expenditures of time and money which will not be returned unless a great many schools actually purchase the recordings.

One solution might be to charge more for special educational recordings than for other phonograph records; another, to be less careful about quality of production. Neither would seem to be desirable, if the non-musical teaching records are to be used among schools as commonly as standard musical recordings are used today.

The future availability of additional recordings to meet the requirements of schools will be determined largely by the extent to which schools actually purchase and use the best records now available. No manufacturer can long continue to produce teaching aids which fail to find a ready market. Classroom experience with recordings is the best guide to manufacturers, so the closest possible cooperation between school users and manufacturers is highly desirable.[3]

The producers of recorded materials for the schools face other problems. The chief among these have been listed by Miles and Tyler as being:

a. The selection of content that is appropriate, educationally significant and adaptable to presentation by sound,
b. the choice of the method of treating the selected content,
c. the discriminating use of dramatic license in insuring the appeal of the program,
d. the selection of program technique and of the dramatic cast in terms of making the program understandable and interesting for listeners at the particular maturity level intended, and

Ellsworth C. Dent in *Education by Radio*, Third Quarter, 1941, p. 34.

e. the problem of publicizing, selling, and distributing the completed programs.[4]

To collect data which may aid these producers to meet schoolroom needs, the Ohio State project has evolved several report forms. One of these is shown on pages 363–364. The form is also suggestive to teachers who may wish to establish criteria for the purchase of educational recordings.

PURCHASING EQUIPMENT. In contemplating the purchase or loan of recorded programs such as noted earlier the teacher must first make certain that her school has the equipment needed to reproduce the material. The conventional phonograph cannot always be used.

The authoritative pamphlet referred to earlier, "School Sound Recording and Playback Equipment," lists the following considerations for the purchase of playback as well as recording equipment.

Portability

Among the many problems which must be considered is the question of portability. If portable equipment is required, factors of weight, dimensions and case structure are important. In order to be accepted as "portable," equipment should be so designed that it can readily be carried by teacher or student. The case should be ruggedly built to protect the equipment, and the handle designed and located so as to promote ease of carrying.

Versatility

In purchasing recording and playback equipment, one should bear in mind the fact that some equipment is designed for one purpose only, while other similar units are designed to perform two or more functions. For example, some types of recorders serve to record only, whereas other designs permit the same instrument to be used for recording and playback. Similarly, there are several features which certain recording and playback equipment may offer which are not included in other types of design. For example, some magnetic-recording and playback units are provided with an input jack to permit their use for re-recording programs originally made on discs, or to permit using them with a radio tuner for making "off the air" recordings of radio programs. Similarly some units are regularly provided with such features as a final-output jack to permit plugging in an external loudspeaker (for applications where maximum playback fidelity is desired), or a "zero level" output jack to permit feeding the playback output into an external amplifying system, such as the school's central-

---

[4] Miles and Tyler, *op. cit.*, pp. 9–10.

sound system. Where these features are desired, the purchaser obviously will need to make sure whether or not they are offered in the machine he selects. If he has any intention of using his recorder in conjunction with other communications equipment items (such as the central-sound system, the speech-input equipment of a school program-production workshop), he will need, also, to consider the electrical-matching characteristics of the input and output connections that are provided. All of these are important and all must be taken into account. Selection will not be made alone on this basis, but the factor of versatility of application should be given due consideration in making comparisons of value.

For practically all school applications involving disc-type playback, it is desirable to purchase dual-speed playback equipment rather than one machine for standard phonograph records (78 revolutions per minute) and a second machine for transcriptions (33⅓ revolutions per minute). The increasing availability of sixteen-inch transcriptions for use at all levels of learning will serve further to enhance the desirability of dual-speed equipment.

Performance

There are many factors which combine to determine performance of audio equipment. Not only power-output and frequency-response range but also such factors as distortion, dynamic range, "wow" and "flutter" content, etc., must be taken into consideration in order to evaluate overall performance. Wow and flutter (change in pitch usually caused by irregularity in the speed of the recording medium) are often present to an annoying degree in recording and reproducing mechanisms. These undesirable characteristics can be readily noted in playing back recordings containing sustained musical notes. Leading record companies offer recordings of sustained notes which serve to detect or demonstrate wow and flutter. It is also imperative that the playback machine operate at the same speed as that of the recorder.

Over-all recorder and playback performance depends on many factors, beginning with the proper selection of equipment to do specific school jobs. In a climate where high heat and high humidity prevail for even a few days in each year, one may well specify that equipment be designed specifically to meet these conditions so that, although the cost may be slightly higher, the useful life of the machine will probably be greater.

Even so seemingly simple a matter as the proper selection of needles for any particular machine is important because both the dynamic-range and the frequency response may be unnecessarily limited by an unwise selection. The manufacturer makes specific recommendations and these should be carried out. In the event that a change is contemplated, the manufacturer's advice should be solicited.

Needle pressure has a direct relation to the useful life of both the needle itself and the records played. In general, lighter pressures mean longer record life. A needle pressure, as rated by the manufacturer, of not more than one and one-half ounces may be considered satisfactory for general use.

Trying to prolong needle life beyond the manufacturer's recommendation is usually a false economy. A worn-out or damaged needle may do irreparable damage to a new or only partially used record and thereby create a situation necessitating the replacement of both the needle and the record.

Simplicity of Operation

Different types and designs of recording and playback equipment vary greatly with respect to the amount of time, effort, and skill required in operation. Other things being equal, the best machine is the one which is easiest to operate. Simplicity of putting on, playing, and taking off recordings is of primary importance. In the case of portable equipment, one should also note the nature, number, and sequence of operations required in setting up the equipment for use and in packing it for transport.

Foolproof Design

The equipment should be so designed as to eliminate insofar as possible injury to (a) the equipment, (b) the recording, and (c) the operator through improper handling. For example:

(a) In the case of disc-type machines, it should be impossible to swing the pickup across to the opposite side of the center pin so as to permit the sound groove to turn against the needle tip.

(b) In the case of magnetic-wire machines correct design will help prevent accidental erasure of the recorded program.

(c) All types of equipment should be so designed that the operator receives maximum protection from shock. Approval of the equipment by Underwriters' Laboratories offers good evidence that the manufacturer has taken steps to assure the minimum shock and fire hazard.

All equipment should be so designed and manufacturered as to provide the maximum number of hours of operation with the minimum amount of servicing. Proper designation of controls and components, as well as clearly written servicing instructions, is essential. Points requiring lubrication or adjustment should be clearly indicated and easy of access. The machine should be so designed that expendable items such as tubes, fuses, and drive belts are easy to replace.

Integrity of Manufacturer and Dealer

Purchasers should bear in mind that the integrity of any manufacturer is reflected in the over-all quality of his product and in the extent to which his distributor-dealer organization has been picked, organized and trained toward the goal of assuring continuing owner satisfaction. In other words, the prospective purchaser of a recorder or a recorded-program player should give careful consideration to the reputation of the manufacturer— his reputation for basing equipment design and construction on careful study of the conditions under which the equipment will normally be used; his reputation for putting out equipment known for endurance and trouble-free performance; his reputation for continuing to supply replacement parts throughout the useful life of the equipment; and the like —plus the reputation of the local factory-authorized dealer or distributor on whom he will necessarily depend to keep the equipment in proper working order.

Only by keeping these factors in mind will the purchaser be assured of getting a product properly designed for its intended applications, and of getting full dealer-distributor cooperation in the continued satisfactory performance of the equipment.

REPORT ON RADIO TRANSCRIPTION

Name _____ School _____
City _____ County _____ State _____
Subjects for Which Transcription Might Be Used _____ Suggested Grade ____
General Title of This Program Series _____
Title of This Broadcast _____ Length of Program _____

DIRECTIONS: Recordings or transcriptions of radio programs in special subject-matter fields are being increasingly made available for school use. In order that a solid body of reliable information about their usefulness can be built up, it is very important that you appraise or evaluate this particular transcription with utter frankness. Please check these items which most nearly express your judgment of the educational value of this program to your class.

1. Was the transcription clear and distinct
___(a) all of the time?
___(b) part of the time?
___(c) most of the time?

2. For classroom use, would you rate this transcription as being
___(a) very valuable?
___(b) suitable?
___(c) entirely unsuitable?

3. For your purpose, was this transcription
___(a) too long?
___(b) too short?
___(c) about right?

4. For use at your grade level, was this transcription
___(a) appropriate?
___(b) usable?
___(c) unsuitable?

5. Was the main theme of the transcription
___(a) well brought out?
___(b) poorly brought out?
___(c) no main theme apparent?

6. Were the points that were emphasized in the transcription
___(a) too many?
___(b) too few?
___(c) about right?

7. The vocabulary in the transcription would be satisfactory at
___(a) the elementary level
___(b) the intermediate level
___(c) the junior high level
___(d) the senior high level

8. Was the action in the transcription
___(a) too rapid?
___(b) about right?
___(c) too slow?
___(d) not enough action?

9. Was the amount of dramatization
___(a) about right?
___(b) too much?
___(c) too little?

10. Did you always know which character or person in the program was speaking?
___(a) Yes.
___(b) No.

11. Did the music in the transcription
___(a) contribute to the enjoyment of the program?
___(b) detract from the program?
___(c) the music neither added nor detracted.
___(d) no music in the program.

12. Were the transitions between scenes
___(a) confusing?
___(b) clear?

13. Did the sound effects used seem
___(a) effective?
___(b) ineffective?

14. Would you say that the general appeal of the program for the majority of students at the suggested grade levels was
___(a) high?
___(b) average?
___(c) low?

Use of Recordings

Several uses have been made in the classroom of both records and the recording procedure. The former, the use of recorded programs, is to a great degree dependent upon the material chosen. The supply is gradually increasing.

Nearly all the criteria suggested for the selection of a radio program apply also to the choice of recorded programs. Some of the most important of these standards were noted in the chapter, "Selecting and Using the Program." Before using a recording, it is essential for the teacher to understand the purposes of the program. The length of the program also is important to her, as is the quality of the performance, the appeal to pupil interest, and the authenticity of the information presented. It is frequently difficult to tell at what point fact ends and fiction begins. Before the teacher can presume to contribute authentic materials to the class, she should have a fairly good idea of the sources responsible for the recorded broadcast. Two or three of the criteria noted above which apply specifically to the recorded program will be discussed further.

As in selecting other teaching aids, an important criterion is the relationship of the recorded material to the educational objective the teacher has in mind. Unless the recording presented has a bearing upon classroom work, the time spent is hardly productive.

Selection of Recordings. A wise selection of recordings in turn implies a knowledge of the material that is available. Suitable material presents needed information. Through vivid dramatizations, reproductions of voices of leaders past and present and discussions of important issues, the recordings can serve to stimulate classroom activity of various sorts. However, this is possible only if the recorded material is related to classroom studies. Enrichment, yes, but not just a "show." Out-of-school listening provides plenty of the latter, and yet the anticipation that accompanies the pleasurable experience can be used to good purpose, for, as Donald L. Cherry notes, "Perhaps the most significant aspect of the assistance which recordings can bring to the social science (or any other) teacher is that which springs from the fact that the idea of recording carries with it a connotation of entertainment in the student's mind. If this preliminary favorable attitude on the part of the class can be capitalized upon, recordings may help to bring life and drama, with their stimulation to critical thought, to the social science classroom." [5]

The successful teacher is well aware that the material she selects for use in the classroom must not be based primarily upon *her* own needs and interests, but rather upon the needs, capacities, and interests of the pupils in her charge. The recordings selected should have a definite appeal for the students who are to hear them. That is not to say that the degree of pupil interest is synonymous with the

[5] Donald L. Cherry, "Recordings in the Social Science Classroom," Federal Radio Education Committee. Release, November 24, 1941, p. 4.

value of the program, but rather to indicate that in addition to content, the form of the program should be an interesting one.

QUALITY OF RECORDING A FACTOR IN SELECTION. Further, it is apparent that a recording can serve no worth-while purpose if it is technically imperfect. If the recording is of the instantaneous-transcription type and not a more durable pressing, these difficulties are likely to be quite common. If the surface noise is great, if there are awkward repetitions in the recording, then in most cases the record had better not be played at all. The technical quality of the recording is therefore another criterion in making a wise choice.

The wise choice of recordings is the first and perhaps the most important step in making effective use of them. Once the selection has been made, the broad principles of good pedagogy apply here as elsewhere. As with the utilization of radio programs, the best use of recordings is made by the best teachers. To a skilled teacher nothing unique is required in using either type of teaching aid. Paul Reed puts it this way: "In fact, as an instructional tool, the transcription has much in common with the motion picture and other materials of instruction. Practices that produce best teaching results are common to all. Speaking particularly of transcriptions and motion pictures, both should be stimulating experiences productive to clearer understandings and meanings leading to desirable attitudes, worth-while habits, or meaningful generalizations. Pupils should be ready for the experience when it comes. It should be related to previous experiences. There should be opportunity for discussion, inevitably stimulated, and for clarification of misconceptions, if any persist. Opportunity should be provided for the further learning activities that flow normally from the visual or auditory experience." [6]

With recordings, as with radio programs, it is well to remember that mere exposure does not constitute effective utilization. Merely playing the recording does not ensure learning. The skillful teacher will regard the listening experience as but a means to desired ends whether they be the acquisition of facts, the development and expression of skills, or perhaps the most important, the formation of attitudes.

---

[6] Paul Reed, "Experience Transcribed," *New York State Education*, April, 1941, pp. 517, 566.

HEARING THE RECORD IN ADVANCE.   In the use of recordings one caution in particular should be emphasized and that is the need for hearing the record before it is played to the class. There are two important reasons for this. First, unless this is done the teacher overlooks a great value of the recording as compared to a radio program. Second, if the teacher attempts to play the recording without a preliminary audition, it is quite possible that she may find the quality of the record so poor as to lack intelligibility. Rather than subject the children to this type of wasteful experience it is much better to make a check beforehand. The acetate recording is quite fragile and requires delicate handling of the type not always present in a school building.

The following is a notice used to seal the package in which recordings are sent to the various Cleveland schools:

IMPORTANT

This record has been inspected by our engineers. Please play it *immediately* upon receipt. If any defects are noticed in the record, communicate with Station WBOE. No class should be asked to listen to a record without a preliminary audition. In this way, it is hoped that not only will class disturbances be minimized, but that the teacher will be able to make better use of this recording.

Miles and Tyler, who have reported quite extensively on recordings, have noted the following suggestions which were recommended by teachers who have used recordings:

1. Teachers should know the content and maturity level of recordings in order to estimate what purposes they may serve; i.e., whether to use them as an interest-creating overview at the beginning of a unit, or as an enriching experience during the unit. Knowing what is contained in a record is essential to devising appropriate uses.
2. Recordings often lead to discussions or debates during which portions of the program are repeated.
3. Recordings should be considered as an integral part of a whole group of learning experiences and not in isolation; i.e., recordings are good or bad in terms of the uses made of them in a total unit.
4. Recordings stimulate student concern to a high degree when appropriately used. Teachers and administrators must be prepared to take advantage of such stimulation and to encourage, both in and out of school, the learning activities which the programs suggest.
5. The selection and servicing of equipment is a vital problem for

which some teacher or committee of teachers should be made responsible. Careful instruction in the use of equipment by teachers or students is necessary. Programs often fail when a playback is run too fast
or too slow, with improper needles, or with a quality lacking either
high or low frequencies.

6. Recordings and "live" radio programs may often be used to comple-
ment each other. Auditory aids used in school frequently suggest out-
of-school programs which can be as logically assigned as a book,
magazine, or movie.[7]

Uses of Recordings in School.   The recorded program has
been used successfully in the school in a number of ways. Some teachers have introduced the material in order to supplement their classroom activities, either as a stimulation for further activity or as a summary of a certain unit of work. Some have presented the program as
a vehicle with which to encourage critical thinking. The children
compare the recorded information with factual data. Even commercial
"plugs" are analyzed as to sales claims, the psychology of selling is
discussed, the implications for the consumer are noted.

DRAMATIZATION.   Dramatizations by famous artists have been used
in many schools to stimulate an interest in Shakespeare. Nickerson has
reported a study in this connection, the purpose of which was to
test the effectiveness of a set of such recordings accompanied by a
handbook. Four methods of utilization were employed. Judging from
pupils' comments, Nickerson suggests:

One of the best ways of using the recordings is for the instructor, without actually reading or discussing the text extensively, to clear up major
language difficulties, to furnish essential knowledge, to set the general
mood, and then to play the recordings while pupils follow in the texts;
finally to utilize this visual-auditory experience as a basis for complete
discussion and interpretation.[8]

ANALYSIS.   In some school-radio workshops recorded commercial
broadcasts have been presented for analysis. Instead of merely speaking about sound perspective, boardfades, pacing and timing, the stu-

[7] J. Robert Miles and I. Keith Tyler, "Recordings, a Significant Aid in Teaching,"
Scholastic, March 31, 1941, p. 13.
[8] Paul S. Nickerson, "A Study of the Value of Recordings in the Teaching of
Shakespeare," *Radio and English Teaching*. D. Appleton–Century Co., 1941,
p. 205.

Left, KBPS transmitter operator at the recorder.

Below, KBPS student staff member operates studio controls.

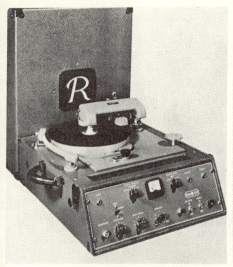

Challenger DeLuxe Disc-Recorder by
Rek-O-Kut.

Portable tape and disc recorder.

Tape recorder, studio console model.

Portable Ampex Tape Recorder.

dents audit the program. A discussion follows which is generally much more valuable than a theoretical discussion of textbook suggestions.

The installation of public-address systems in many schools has served to stimulate the use of recorded material since the repetition of programs throughout the day to various rooms is thus made feasible.

A common use of the recording process in the schools has been the analysis of speech, dramatics, and music. The recording and subsequent analysis of pupil performance before and after a period of training have been undertaken in numerous schools.

Many schools have used their recording equipment to take programs "off the air," that is, they record radio programs which unfortunately are presented at a time when they cannot be heard in the classrooms. Once the recording is made, it is added to the recording library and thus becomes available for use. This procedure is a practical one if the school plans to establish an extensive library of sound.

DOCUMENTATION. Some school workshops have used the recording equipment to "document" school life. They record scenes from the annual play, a football rally, and similar events. Other groups have "documented" activities of their local community. The sequences are later combined into an effective program.

VOICE STUDY. Many teachers of shorthand are making effective use of recordings to acquaint the students with a variety of voices, modes of delivery, and other characteristics.

In foreign-language classes the recording approach has proved of great value in making clearer to the learner, as he listens to himself and others, the possible differences between his pronunciation and inflection and that of a native.

RECORDING OF A UNIT ACTIVITY. At the elementary-school level some teachers have used recordings at the culmination of a unit activity. The preparation of pupil reports, simple dramatizations, and musical performances which grew out of the activity are thus recorded.

FOR EDUCATIONAL EXPERIENCES OUTSIDE SCHOOL. Several educational stations such as WBEZ and WILL have prepared effective programs by means of "tape tours" to local industries in which the comments of management and labor, the authentic sounds and processes of industry, are brought into the classroom. Stations WOI, WLS, and others have developed noteworthy programs using transcription exchanges with foreign countries, particularly in Western Europe. Questions related to themes of interest to youthful listeners are submitted in advance to the overseas broadcasters, and the recorded replies are then integrated at home into effective educational experiences which span the seas.

Specialized Uses—IN THERAPY WORK.   Many specialized uses of recordings have been undertaken. In the field of psychotherapy recordings enable the psychiatrist to study the patient after the interview. Columbia University has used this device in its psychiatric laboratory. Recordings have also helped the counselor analyze his guidance procedures.

In several Veterans' hospitals, the music therapist works hand in hand with the psychiatrist in dealing with patients undergoing insulin or electric shock. Some hospitals use music in the waiting room before, as well as during, surgery. At the Crile Hospital, WBOE provided educational transcriptions which were "piped" to individual beds by means of earphones. A choice of three channels was available.

The Central Institute for the Deaf in St. Louis uses sound-effect records with earphones that amplify sound to the level of the pupil's hearing. Children can now hear trains whistling, lions roaring, and bacon sizzling in the pan.

IN COMMERCIAL FIELDS.   Recordings are useful in many commercial fields. Several life insurance companies use recordings to train salesmen. The Yale Law School uses them in lectures, debates, and practice court work. It is said that no matter how carefully the new lawyer prepares his first case when the opposing counsel says, "I object!", the entire brief goes out the window, so to speak. The Air Corps and Submarine services found that fewer personnel cracked up in crises if they provided practice in speaking and listening during simulated airplane noise. A ruling in Cleveland divorce courts now makes recording mandatory when no court stenographer is present.

Recordings play an even more important part in the operations of a school radio station than they do in a commercial station, since for the school the "repeat program" is a common practice.

Sources of Educational Recordings

An effective use of recordings in the classroom does not necessitate the operation of either a school station or a transcription studio. There are many educational recordings available through purchase or loan from several organizations. Many fields are covered: science, social studies, foreign languages, speech, safety, and English.

The list noted here does not presume to be a complete one but it can serve to provide some preliminary selection. Information concerning educational recordings can be secured from the following:

Educational Radio Script and Transcription Exchange, Federal Radio Education Committee, United States Office of Education, Washington 25, D.C.
United States Treasury Department, Washington 25, D.C.
North American Service of the French Broadcasting System, 501 Madison Avenue, New York 23, New York.
United States War Department, Recruiting Publicity Bureau, Governors Island, New York.
United States Department of Agriculture, Farm Credit Administration, Washington 25, D.C.
United States Department of Agriculture, Forest Service, 623 N. Second Street, Milwaukee 3, Wisconsin.
Royal Norwegian Information Services, 630 Rockefeller Plaza, Room 1825, New York 20, New York.
National Mental Health Foundation, 1520 Race Street, Philadelphia 2, Pennsylvania.
Netherlands Information Bureau, Netherlands Museum, Holland, Michigan.
Training Aids, Inc., 7414 Beverly Blvd., Los Angeles 36, California.
Citizens Committee on Displaced Persons, 39 E. 36th Street, Los Angeles 15, California.
Institute for Democratic Education, 415 Lexington Avenue, New York 17, New York.
Masterpiece Reproduction Society, 667 Madison Avenue, New York 21, New York.
British Broadcasting Corporation, 630 Fifth Avenue, New York 20, New York.
Gloria Chandler Recordings, Inc., Box 1112, Grand Central Station, New York, New York.
RCA Manufacturing Company, Inc., Camden, New Jersey.

Radio Transcription Company of America, Ltd., Hollywood, California.

World Book Company, Yonkers, New York.

N.A.E.B. (National Association of Educational Broadcasters) Tape Network, University of Illinois, Urbana, Illinois.

Minnesota Tape Service, Audio-Visual Supervisor, State Department of Education, St. Paul 1, Minnesota.

A good way to begin the selection of recorded materials is to examine the bulletin published by the Recording Division of the New York University Film Library, entitled *A Catalogue of Selected Educational Recordings*. The address of this organization is: 71 Washington Square South, New York City. The bulletin includes a subject index of recorded materials, brief notes, and a price list.

Several teacher organizations have compiled sources of recordings for use in specific fields. Among these groups are the National Council of Teachers of English and the American Association of Teachers of French.

The Federal Radio Education Committee is outstanding as a clearing house for educational radio information. Its publication *Transcription Service for Schools* should be in the hands of all teachers who are interested in the classroom use of recordings. The booklet contains a list of transcriptions available for sale or for loan and in addition it presents sources of information on educational recordings and equipment.

At least two other nonprofit organizations have made significant contributions in this field: the former Committee on Scientific Aids to Learning, 41 East 42nd Street, New York City, and the Evaluation of School Broadcasts, at Ohio State University, Columbus, Ohio. The latter organization has conducted an intensive appraisal study of educational recordings. Several hundred recorded programs suitable for school use have been audited and appraised by the Ohio State staff. A list of these recordings and an indication of their contents are available in the publication *Recordings for School Use* by J. Robert Miles. *The News Letter* issued by Ohio State University also includes current recording information.

An excellent source of selected recordings, including the judgments of them by qualified teachers, is found in *The Journal of the AER*, 228 North La Salle Street, Chicago 1, Illinois. In 1948 twelve local rotating committees were established throughout the country to appraise recordings in terms of their suitability for educational use. The summaries of these panel judgments are detailed each month in the "AER Record Review," listed in the *Journal*.

The column conducted by Max U. Bildersee in *Educational Screen* entitled, "Records in Review," is a good source of record and transcription information.

In the *Scholastic Teacher*, helpful data in this field are found in the articles by William J. Temple of Brooklyn College.

Film Recordings of Television Programs

Television's equivalent of radio's "electrical transcription" is the television recording, also known as the "kinescope recording," the "video transcription," the "television recording" and by several other names. It is a sound motion picture photographed from the face of a kinescope or picture tube, with the picture portion of the program being filmed simultaneously with the recording of the audio portion on the sound track of the film. The result, frequently called "kinescope recording" or "kine" (kinney) from the tube on which the film camera is focused, is a relatively accurate reproduction of the original program.

It would be reasonable to suppose that duplicate prints of these sound films which reproduce television programs could be made available for classroom screening, and some day they undoubtedly will be. At the present time, however, there is very little classroom use of such films, and for a variety of reasons. For one thing, the quality of these films is barely adequate for reproduction by means of television on the comparatively small screen of the average television receiver. Another problem is the matter of "clearance," which is complicated by the contracts now governing the making of these transcriptions. Musicians and other performers are paid for the initial broadcast, and for single repetitions of the broadcast via transcription within thirty days of the original air show. They do not receive payment comparable to the fees paid in the making of motion pictures for theatrical or nontheatrical screening, and so broadcasters are understandably reluctant to lend film transcriptions for use in auditoriums or classrooms, since such showings might be considered violations of basic contracts.

Undoubtedly, educational programs in the not-too-distant future will be recorded on sound film and, when the original program is broadcast in the evening, the transcription will be used during school hours on the following day. Contracts with performers will probably contain provisions for such "repeats." However, even for noncommercial and purely educational purposes, the permission of the various organizations involved will have to be secured before these filmed telecasts can be loaned to schools and colleges for showing in classroom and auditorium.

The technical quality of the kinescope transcriptions is increasing steadily, and they will soon approach original telecasts in sharpness and clarity. In time the contractual difficulties will undoubtedly be ironed out so that the wealth of filmed material in the vaults of the broadcasters can be put to use in the schools of the nation, provided problems of distribution and careful use can be worked out.

Recordings in the Future

The place that the recording will come to have in the modern school is perhaps much like that which will be accorded other auditory and visual aids. In some schools, these aids will be wisely selected and intelligently utilized. In other schools, unfortunately, this equipment will be purchased indiscriminately, and then will be used poorly—after which the inevitable complaint will be heard that these "gadgets" have little value. Like the Liverpool weavers of the eighteenth century, some in education may entertain the ill-founded fear that they are to be replaced by the machine and will deplore man's inventive genius. Yet these same individuals will doubtless agree that the school in preparing for life in a changing society must be dynamic, not alone in its objectives but also in its methods.

To do their job well, tomorrow's teachers (and there will be more rather than fewer) will need all the help they can receive. Jacobsen's observations apropos of the above are stimulating:

If, after all, the teacher is so precious and there is no substitute for student-teacher contacts, then why not increase the ratio of time spent with students to time spent at subprofessional tasks, by outfitting the teacher with time and energy-saving aids comparable to those thought necessary for the engineer, the salesman, the doctor, and even the house-wife. The present practice of handling increased activity by hiring addi-tional cheap help and diluting salaries should certainly be re-examined. A business which employs a million people and instructs one in every four of the nation's inhabitants probably needs mass-production tools. But unlike the American industries, which have challenged the world with their production techniques and superlative products, education is ex-pected to carry on and save democracy to boot, without most of the out-standing productive tools created by its own scientists and engineers.[9]

The organization of additional education transcription services is a likely development in the near future. These groups will either rent or sell selected recordings to the schools, much as do the commercial-transcription firms to the broadcasters today.

Such an effective recording service to the schools will require the collection of materials from various sources: broadcasting organiza-tions, transcription firms, as well as schools and universities.

The collection of such material is but the first step. It has been noted that a program first broadcast to the general public and then distributed to the schools in recorded form is not the best way to furnish auditory aids. The recordings will have to be edited and graded, teacher materials developed, and corollary visual aids prepared. Even then the recordings will not be ready for best classroom use. A careful evaluation will have to be made of the recordings in actual classroom situations. When these preliminary steps have been completed, press-ings, wire and tape, or films can be made and distribution to the schools undertaken.

Unless educational recordings are developed in some such manner, the schools will be asked to consider their needs as being secondary and to make use of existing materials. The fact is that educational needs are paramount and any worth-while school recording service should adjust to them. Only then can recordings be of maximum service to the teachers.

---

[9] Philip A. Jacobsen, *op. cit.*, p. 435.

Several obstacles will have to be overcome before the development and widespread distribution of educational recordings become common. Some of these were noted earlier. Teachers will have to be trained in the utilization of such materials. The broadcasting organizations will have to solve several perplexing problems relative to copyrights and performer wage scales. The fragile nature of the present-day recording with its limited life presents further difficulties. However, it may be that eventually the magnetic recording or sound on film will be the accepted form. The cost of recordings will have to be reduced. Just as textbooks are now furnished free by most states, transcription services may be made available to all schools with the aid of state funds. The experiment in Minnesota by which the State Department of Education duplicates and distributes tape recordings to schools may be a forerunner of this type of development. The rapid growth of the N.A.E.B. tape network will be discussed in the final chapter.

It may not be foolhardy to predict that someday most schoolteachers will have at their disposal a library of carefully prepared materials for the ear just as they now use the library of printed materials for the eye. Thus the child will converse, in a sense, with the great minds past and present. He will be stimulated by leading dramatists and musicians. For him, history will not be "a story of dead people" but a living human adventure.

To continue this crystal gazing, if such it be, the school library of tomorrow will be so outfitted that the child will be enabled to hear his homework as well as to read it. This is not so novel as it may seem to some, for already several of the larger municipal libraries are equipped with "listening rooms" where patrons enjoy musical programs of various types. As noted earlier, in some schools "radio halls" have been organized. Pupils who have been assigned to study halls but who have completed their work are permitted to come to this acoustically treated and well-equipped room where they hear a prepared program of educational recordings, musical and otherwise. Frequently, radio programs are also presented. The enterprise is administered by members of the Student Council. How much better to do this than to subject the child who has completed his work to attendance at a study hall which is frequently wasteful, and where, because of a desire "to kill time," disciplinary problems are likely to arise.

The fact that an adequate supply of choice transcriptions is not yet available should not be a deterrent to action in this direction. As others have noted, the use of recordings in the schools must not be measured against perfection but against the alternative of having none at all.

In education, too, there has been an evolution in methods and tools. The forms may change. They may be recordings, radio, the sound film, television, or facsimile; but whatever these tools are, one thing is certain, auditory aids are here to stay.

The Well-Equipped School. Mention has been made of "tomorrow's" school. How should it be equipped for effective use of audio-visual materials? Or, if a wing is to be added to an existing building, what would be an admittedly idealistic plan? The sketch shown on the end papers contains several features of interest: [10]

TYPICAL CLASSROOM. This classroom, typical of classrooms in the entire school, has no special architectural devices to fit it for audio-visual purposes. Following modern classroom design, there are electrical outlets at both front and rear of the room. All lights operate from one switch. Seats are movable.

In the back is a three-tiered rubber-tired truck which carries equipment and films to and from the storeroom. It is also the projection table. On its top stands the 16-mm. sound projector; on the second shelf, film, film-strips, extra reel, and literature supplied with the films; on the bottom shelf, a filmstrip projector to be used following the movie. At the front of the room stands the portable screen with two small loudspeakers, one on each side and about even with the middle of the screen. Such loudspeaker arrangement provides better acoustical qualities.

On the teacher's desk is a special device for projecting teacher-drawn diagrams and other materials overhead onto a screen.

As the room is air-conditioned, room darkening presents no prob-

---

[10] Sketch and description furnished through courtesy of *Scholastic Teacher*. Illustration by Eva E. Mizerek. Text by William D. Boutwell, Edward G. Bernard, Vera Falconer and William J. Temple.

lem; opaque shades suffice. Were it not, ventilation would be provided simply. The opaque shades slide in metal runways to prevent light leakage. Opaque-painted glass deflectors on window sills permit opening the window without admitting light.[11]

Chairs are arranged so that the first row is at least two screen lengths from the screen itself. The front corners, which have undesirable visibility, are left vacant. The screen's bottom edge is at eye level of the seated class, permitting unobstructed projection. No neck-craning necessary.

Suppose the teacher wants an audio setup? Again the equipment truck rolls in—this time to the front of the room with playback, recorder, or radio on its top shelf; records and other materials on the bottom shelves. The chairs are rearranged around it in semicircles.

Bulletin boards run the length of one wall. Here are posted charts, posters, clippings, still pictures, and other materials, frequently changed and never cluttered with too many things at one time. There is a classroom library, also a table for models and mockups.

SPEECH-LANGUAGE ROOM.   First, acoustic treatment gives the room good speaking and listening conditions whether there are two or 102 people in it. This room has acoustic material above the blackboards as well as on the ceiling.

The speech room has recording and reproducing equipment. It has magnetic tape for economical day-to-day use and for uninterrupted half-hour or full-hour programs. It has disc-recording machines useful for making records to be filed for before-and-after comparisons and for the students to take home for study. This well-equipped room can re-record from tape to disc and from disc to tape. It has one or more microphones with a talk-back connection into the radio-control room.

It has an AM-FM radio receiver for listening to broadcast programs. Connections to recorders make it possible to capture a good program and use it over and over again. For language students a shortwave receiver picks up programs from foreign countries.

For maximum clarity and quality of reproduction the room has a permanently installed, separate, high-quality amplifier and high-quality loudspeaker.

---

[11] Francis Noel's new pamphlet, "Setting Up an Audio-visual Program," recommends a curtain hung from the ceiling, parallel to, and 18 inches from, the window.

There are turntables and earphones (singly and in gangs) for individual and group listening. For individual drill and practice in pronunciation, there is a magnetic recorder modified or rebuilt for short-span recordings. The room has space to store records and other supplies, with locks.

THE RADIO CONTROL ROOM.   The school's central-sound system operates from here. It connects with numerous pickup points in the principal's office, auditorium, gymnasium, etc. It serves loudspeakers mounted in the corners of each classroom. The same control equipment also serves for real broadcasts, mock broadcasts, recording concerts, and other purposes.

The control room is acoustically isolated from the radio-workshop studio but has windows into both the studio and speech rooms. It contains a control console for switching and monitoring the programs that originate before the studio microphones or on the transcription turntables in the control room, recording equipment (disc recorders for continuous recording, besides tape equipment), and the amplifiers which send the program out to the transmitter, or the sound-distribution system, and the monitor loudspeaker. There is also a talk-back circuit for communication with studio or speech room.

RADIO-WORKSHOP CLASSROOM.   Because this room serves as the school radio studio it has a double door "sound lock" entrance. It is soundproof. It is air-conditioned, or it has some kind of forced ventilation. Acoustical material covers the ceiling and some walls. Large, double, soundproof windows open on the radio control room and the listening alcove. From the control room a radio-program director can direct actors, using the talk-back system. This radio workshop has microphones and a rubber-tired sound-effects console with two, or preferably three, turntables for mixing recorded sound effects. Here also are some manual sound effects made by the industrial arts department, including the inevitable sound-effects door. Large storage cabinets contain manual sound-effects equipment and records. Also a piano. The music department uses this room too. The window to the listening alcove allows for audiences.

The class in radio meets in this room. Here also the school-radio guild presents in-school programs and prepares other recorded programs for local commercial or school stations.

LISTENING ALCOVE. This alcove permits the age-old library plan of individual use of books to be extended to music. Around the walls are shelves containing albums of music, poetry, and drama. One shelf holds reels of tape recordings of symphony concerts, outstanding radio programs recorded from the air—great events, foreign-language broadcasts (for training), and dramas. Other shelves contain books on music, radio, poetry, and drama. In the center of the room is a table with turntables almost flush with the table top. These turn at $33\frac{1}{3}$, 45, or 78 rpm, with suitable pick-up heads. A student selects a record, puts it on the turntable, and listens over earphones. Or he may use a tape playback. In one corner stands a high-fidelity speaker for small group listening.

VIEWING ALCOVE. A student also should have the right of personal access to visual materials. Here he may throw a filmstrip or 2 by 2 inch slides on a small screen. Or turn to the inexhaustible resources that a microfilm projector opens to him. This viewing alcove contains files of prints, photographs, and pictures protected with lamination. It has cases with wide, shallow drawers for large color prints and maps. The old stereograph has returned in a new, simple lightweight hand viewer, permitting the student to see national parks, cities, etc., in full, natural, three-dimensional color. A field-trip file contains guides on where to go and what to see.

INSTRUCTIONAL RESOURCE CENTER. Where will the school's central collection of visual and auditory materials be housed? Where will teachers preview films and prehear recordings and transcriptions? Where will the professional staff committees meet for curriculum planning work?

For these functions the well-equipped school has four rooms:

(a) Instructional-Aids Library and Conference Room
(b) Equipment-Storage Room
(c) Instructional Resource Workroom
(d) Audio-visual Director's Office

INSTRUCTIONAL-AIDS LIBRARY. This serves as a repository for visual aids and a preview room. Here will be found the school's permanent collection of films, filmstrips (other than those for individual student use), and slides. Also records, tape, disc, or wire recordings for teacher use. Cabinets contain collections of laminated pictures, photographs, models, dioramas, mock-ups, and foreign-language flash cards not readily storable in classrooms. The library annex also serves as a handy library anteroom for books, for teachers, and for receipt of new books for the library. The librarian keeps the aids in usable order; the audiovisual director has easy access to them for previewing.

EQUIPMENT-STORAGE ROOM.   In this "well-equipped school" very little audio-visual or radio equipment remains in the classroom. It rides on rubber-tired trucks to classrooms as needed. In between times it is stored in the equipment room on shelves. This room is adjacent to the Resource Room where repairs and tests can be made. On the shelves are film projectors, filmstrip and slide-film projectors, opaque and slide projectors; recorders, record players, and playbacks for tape, wire, and discs; amplifiers; loudspeakers which may be used either for sound films or records; portable screens; etc. Double doors to the hall make it easy to roll the instructional aids "pushcarts" in and out.

RESOURCE WORKROOM.   Teachers of the school are not content to rely solely on instructional aids supplied from the "outside." They like to "roll their own" to suit their special teaching problems. Students also like to work on projects for science, history, or other subjects that require model-making, pictorializing, or other devices. To serve teachers, students, and even their parents in the evening, the resource workshop is located strategically adjacent to the industrial-arts shop and the photography darkroom. That brings close at hand the bandsaws, lathes, clamps-for-glueing, enlargers, and similar equipment.

But the resource workroom itself has benches and tables for cutting, splicing, and editing films or filmstrips; for trimming and mounting photographs; for making slides; for a laminating press to encase flat pictures in transparent plastic for permanency, etc.

This workroom is also the headquarters of the school's Student-Operators' Club. Here they receive training as projectionists. Here they learn how to make repairs and keep equipment in good operating condition. Here these budding engineers learn about audio equipment by acting as custodians, repairmen, and operators.

This room is also headquarters for the Camera Club. On occasion there is organized instruction in photography. More often the club members work from study outlines carrying forward their step-by-step learning in darkroom laboratory work and bringing their products to the club advisor for check and questions.

11

Public Relations Broadcasting

◇◇◇

What advantages have the schools in public relations broadcasting?

What are several guiding principles to be noted in this type of enterprise?

What types of public relations broadcasts are there?

What mistakes have been observed in public relations school broadcasting and how may they be corrected?

How can the "spot announcement" be utilized?

How can television be used in the field of public relations?

◇◇◇◇◇◇◇◇THE USE OF RADIO as an effective means of creating institutional good will has long been recognized among commercial organizations. The manufacturer's product may not even be mentioned in the program, yet cautious advertisers see enough value in this indirect appeal to warrant the expenditure of large sums. For education this fact has real significance. Just as radio can distribute the message of the commercial house, so can it encourage desired attitudes concerning the schools. Every school activity is by its very nature a public relations enterprise, but the skillful use of radio can serve the objectives of school publicity with great effectiveness. Properly planned and carefully produced, the school program can be used:

1. To interpret school activities to the public.

2. To pave the way for the understanding of new policies and methods.

3. To prevent misunderstanding.

4. To explain the need of financial support.

Even if necessary school levies were never defeated and all teachers were adequately paid; even if classes were of the right size and supplies sufficient, there would still remain a need for interpreting school activities to the community. Schools cannot have a surplus of good will.

Some Advantages Schools Enjoy

In using the radio as a public relations agency the school system has certain advantages that the advertiser has not. Perhaps one advantage enjoyed by the school broadcaster is that the process which he discusses is more or less familiar. Nearly all the listeners at one time or another have shared in the school experience. Furthermore, nearly all the potential listeners agree that the American schoolhouse is the nursery of the democratic spirit. To many of the listeners —the parents—the welfare of their children is a vital concern. Equally important is the fact that the school is a public investment and as such the taxpayer should know just what dividends he is receiving. "Where a man's investment is, there is his heart."

Another advantage available to the school broadcaster is the fact that there occurs a certain prestige that can be capitalized upon: well-known public figures can be invited to participate in the school series, the schools can be used to publicize the programs, and the radio time itself can generally be secured without cost.

By virtue of the "public interest, convenience, and necessity," clause included in the government broadcasting license, many local radio stations will contribute to the Board of Education a reasonable amount of radio time, since the school program provides an inexpensive sustaining feature.

A *Typical Case.* Let us consider a hypothetical case. The Board of Education of Capitol City has been offered free a half-hour per week of radio time. The radio station authorities have indicated that the schools may use this period in any way they see fit. Naturally, it is expected that the programs will be somewhat educational in nature, and at the same time attractive enough to "hold" the listeners. Since the broadcasting period given to the school happens to be out of school hours, the programs will be intended primarily for an adult audience. The Board of Education of Capitol City welcomes this opportunity for increased publicity. In a short time the citizenry of that community will be asked to vote on a school-supporting tax levy, and friends of the school are aware that too frequently this publicity campaign has been a last minute pre-election effort. They know now that good "advertising" should be continuous the year around.

What are some important considerations to be noted in the development of Capitol City's "good-will" school program?

Several Principles to be Observed

Continuity and Effectiveness Are Closely Related. The first of these has already been mentioned—the need for continuity in the enterprise. Whether the medium used is written, visual, oral, or social, the public relations activity should be a continuous effort. Concerning this need the comments of F. J. Moffitt are quite pertinent:

Many a young school executive has discovered to his dismay that the newspapers are eager to exploit his theories and his more sensational experiments. The skyrocket of interpretation goes into space with a boom, there are pyrotechnical displays with personal photographs and egotistical headlines, there is shouting from a small group of onlookers. Then darkness, and the show is over. No school has been materially benefited by flamboyant publicity. No profession has ever been uplifted by half-baked discoveries enunciated through the columns of the press. Interpretation of the school must be interesting, yes, but not spectacular. And above all, it must be continuous, not flaring forth and dying away.[1]

As applied to radio not only should publicity efforts be continuous, but, if possible, arrangements should be made for a definite, fixed period so that listeners can expect to hear the school program in accordance with a fixed schedule. The development of a listening audience is a cumulative effort and irregular scheduling is a definite obstacle. Some limitations exist when the radio period is offered gratuitously, but unless the school system is willing to purchase time or, perhaps, operate its own radio station—a possibility to be discussed later—these limitations are inevitable. The "best" hours, seven to ten in the evening, are in greatest demand and it is quite likely that commercial commitments will exclude their use by the schools. If a good evening period is available for a while, it is probable that some shifts may have to be made later and thus continuous scheduling sacrificed.

Programs Must Have Broad Appeal. A second principle to observe in using the radio for this purpose is that the programs must be designed to have a broad appeal. He who would broadcast and be heard must realize that competition for the listener's ear is exceedingly keen. Commercial programs using professional entertainers appear simultaneously on the air. Hence, some element of attraction, some "showmanship," if you like, must be present in a competing program. That is not to say that the schools should be represented by professional entertainers, but rather that school officials must understand that it is perfectly possible to be dignified without being dull, and that the test of the program is not whether it is broadcast but whether it attracts attention.

All the comments made earlier concerning effective script writing for classroom listening apply to the public relations program with increasing emphasis. The schoolroom audience is in a situation in which the use of instructional materials is more easily justified than

[1] Frederick J. Moffitt, "Some Shalt Nots of School Interpretation," *Education,* June, 1938, p. 610.

when the listeners are adults who are at home and perhaps primarily interested in entertainment.

The need for appealing to personal interests, the effectiveness of simple language, the use of a minimum of statistics, the development in many ways of a single idea rather than the presentation of an abundance of concepts—all these are vital if the program is to be heard as well as broadcast.

Developing radio scripts which are informative yet entertaining requires skill. Not every school system may have the talent required. If, after some trial and error, it is discovered that such is the case, then perhaps the schools can utilize successful scripts which have been used elsewhere. Helpful script materials can be borrowed from various agencies, among them the Script Exchange of the United States Office of Education, the university stations, and the various school organizations which have had some experience along this line. With suitable adaptations to local needs and interests it is quite possible to produce a satisfactory series which can be used by even the very small school units. If production facilities are lacking it is quite possible that recorded programs can be borrowed and perhaps pertinent comments by local representatives "dubbed in." In any case, to an alert administration cognizant of radio's possibilities, numerous applications are evident.

Programs Must Be Publicized. A third principle in using the radio for interpreting the schools is derived from "the mousetrap fallacy" which assumes that if educators will just build a good program people will beat a path to it. On the contrary, the program itself must be publicized and promoted in a variety of ways. People must know about it and know about it in advance. Listening must not be left merely to the dialer's chance.

"If the program has the elements of audience appeal that warrant putting it on the air at all, it has the qualities that audience building can use to win listeners for it out of the large and valuable margin between its *normal* and its *potential* audience." [2]

The importance of program promotion has been greatly neglected among school broadcasters although, as has been noted earlier, the

[2] Douglas Duff Connah, *How to Build the Radio Audience*, Harper & Brothers, 1938, p. 11.

schools have unusual opportunities for announcing their radio offerings. The school series can be "tied up," for example, with displays in the libraries of the community and in the school buildings themselves. The school newspapers can be used to publicize the programs. Photographs and brief program notes can be furnished to the newspapers and particularly to the radio editors.

In publicizing their programs the schools can secure a good deal of help from the publicity department of the radio station itself for as these people publicize the school program, which is to be broadcast over their station, they are also publicizing their own institution.

A good title can greatly facilitate program promotion and should be chosen with several criteria in mind. It must corral attention, it must be easily remembered, and, incidentally, it must fit into the radio schedule space of a newspaper.

The programs noted below which were broadcast by the Spokane Public Schools illustrate the use of interesting titles:

Station KFPY,	Spokane, Washington	(7:45—8:15 P.M.)
Jan. 27	"The School of Miracles."	
Feb. 3	"Reading—Then and Now."	
Feb. 10	"A Trip to the Iron Works."	
Feb. 17	"I Stutter, Can You Help Me?"	
Feb. 24	"Who Pays the Bills?"	
March 3	"The School Plant."	
March 10	"Spokane's Smallest Hospital."	
March 17	"Just Fads and Frills."	
March 24	"An Adventure in Democracy."	
March 31	"Washington's Golden Jubilee."	
April 7	"How We Learn Music."	

Another incidental but valuable means of publicizing programs has been used successfully by several school systems. Arrangements are made for the Radio Players to appear before community groups where visual radio programs are then presented. To many people who have never seen a program "go on the air," such a presentation holds real interest and, at the same time, acquaints them with the programs being broadcast.

Members of various local groups can be furnished with printed invitations to witness the programs (tickets increase the desire to attend an event though it may be free to all), recordings can be made of some of the programs and played to certain community groups and thus the program can be "institutionalized." Every agency should be utilized in order that the values resulting from the radio program may be multiplied. Obviously this does not imply using high-pressure methods to overcome sales resistance—nothing of the sort. It simply means that our educational institutions, in spite of natural reluctance, must operate on realistic principles made necessary by the publicity medium they employ. Their motive is certainly no less sincere.

Timeliness Is Significant. There are many school activities that provide excellent radio material if the factor of *timeliness* is given consideration. The "nose for news" that is so essential in journalism is likewise important in broadcasting. A school program which presents the winning soloists of a vocal contest on the day the awards are announced is of greater interest than one which presents these boys and girls in a musical program one month later.

If scholarship awards have been granted to local students, as they are annually, this event can be capitalized upon with its evident implication: "the schools of our town are doing a good job." If conservation is of concern to the community, then the school's contribution to it can be discussed. If an exhibit is to be held, if some innovation has taken place in the schools, the time to incorporate the facts into a script is *now*—not when it is no longer news.

Timeliness is significant, not only in terms of program *content*, but also in terms of program *form*. A school broadcaster worthy of the name knows the recent developments in commercial-program practices. He seeks their implications for his enterprise. For example, some school broadcasters, noting the success of the serial story, have utilized this form to interpret school activities. This excerpt from the Radio Bulletin issued by the Toledo (Ohio) Public Schools illustrates one such application:

Station WSPD

THE EDUCATION OF THE ADAMS FAMILY

Tues. Jan. 31, 2:00 P.M. The Adams Family move to Toledo and begin to acquaint themselves with our schools. Kindergarten unit furnishes the educational background. This program should be heard as the necessary preface to the series of twenty, but it is quite entertaining by itself.

Thur. Feb. 2, 2:00 P.M. Episode two relates the experiences of Martha, a generous, sweet girl whose enthusiasm for a unit in home economics, "Bathing a Baby," infects her entire family—except her brother Fred.

Tues. Feb. 7, 2:00 P.M. Fred's school experiences have been not so wholly satisfying as were Martha's. In the fifth grade Fred "wows" the class with his knowledge of cotton and share croppers, frequently asserting "my father says," but comes a cropper in reading.

Thur. Feb. 9, 2:00 P.M. Fred is reconciled somewhat to remedial reading, because he finds it different from what he had expected. The racial backgrounds of his class are used to develop a unit in social science.

When community singing was in vogue the alert school broadcaster incorporated it into his series. When "vox-popping" and "quizzing" were the mode, he was not far behind. His program plans are based upon a firm belief that he is no longer a schoolteacher who can close the doors of his room and demand attention. Now he is in competition, and his rivals for the American listener's ear are perhaps the most skillful in the world.

The most effective form of a public relations broadcast can be prescribed no more than can a radio program for any other purpose. The dramatization, the interview, the audience participation, the musical, the documentary, the variety, the forum, and even the unduly criticized talk program—all these and others have a place in the school series—*provided* they are well done. The form of a program is but the means; the "pay off" is the end result.

A Theme Is Helpful. It is the writers' belief, though it may not be accepted generally, that a definite relationship between programs is essential. A haphazard mélange of unrelated facts will not result in any desired attitudes. That "repetition makes reputation" is a well-known maxim in the advertising world. It applies no less to school broadcasting. All through the series there should run a common thread; for example, the programs might include information concerning the difference between the traditional and the modern curricula, the heterogeneity of the present-day school population, the effect of compulsory universal education, and the implications of all these on school costs.

Since the school broadcaster enjoys the enviable position of being able to enlist the aid of the community for his series, he would be negligent if he failed to do so. It is unwise perhaps to confine the list of speakers to school officials, teachers, and students. It might be desirable to include several local leaders, parents, clergymen, and others. The values of this procedure are:

1. The propagandistic aspect of the program is minimized while efforts to promote good will are increased.
2. Unusual speaking talent is utilized.
3. Greater listener appeal is present because of "big names."
4. Indirectly, it allies the speaker with the aims and interests of education.

Radio is a medium for the communication of sound. When the term "pleasant" is added to "sound," then of course music is suggested. It is evident that music can play a leading role in almost any program plans. And although it is not essential that music be a part of the individual program, yet the use of music may contribute greatly to the success of the series.

1. It increases the number of participants.
2. It results in a keener interest on the part of parents whose youngsters are participating.
3. It provides an element of universal appeal.
4. It serves to break up the "talk" in the broadcast.
5. It provides an avenue of expression and stimulation for the many musical groups of the schools.

Listener Interests Must Be Known. The good broadcaster knows his audience, their interests and prejudices. An understanding of listener interest is a prerequisite to program planning.

As one who would win listeners and influence people he is keenly aware that there is no such thing as *a* public but rather that there exists *several* publics. And, as L. B. Johnson has noted:

. . . This becomes even more apparent when the subject to be presented is as large as education. For example, there is a public composed of wealthy and influential citizens, who either have no children or whose children are in private schools. There is an entirely different public of well-educated socially-minded citizens with moderate incomes, who may or may not have children in our public schools. There is another public of laborers and manual workers, who may not be well educated, but want good education for their children.

With each of these groups and with twenty or thirty other publics which could be listed, different methods of approach must be used. One group may be swayed by statistics which would be meaningless to another. One group may be reached by visual education, which could include movies, graphs, pictures, posters, charts, etc. Another group wishes to participate in activities and becomes interested in a larger program of education by such participation.

Publicity should be planned in terms of people's interests.[3]

As applied to radio, an acceptance of this principle implies that the school programs be not only "tailor-made" for public relations but that they be planned with a specific section of the listening audience in mind. A cosmopolitan center with a large foreign element might do well, for example, to present a Christmas program to which various nationality groups contribute and in which "good will to man" becomes more than a seasonal phrase. The purpose of such a program, and it can be expanded into a series, might be to call attention not so much to the differences that exist, but rather to indicate how all these national patterns when blended together by our schools create the amazing mosaic that is America.

One large school system even presents a series of foreign-language programs on Sundays during which time high-school students of foreign parentage discuss the schools, using their native tongue. As can be expected these programs are popular among the foreign-born population.

The following excerpt from the broadcasting schedule of the Philadelphia Schools presents another application of this principle:

Tuesday   9:15–9:30   WPEN   JEWISH PROGRAM
Feb. 7   P.M.   (920)   Talk—"Keeping Your Child Well"—Mr. Harry Hershman, teacher, McIntyre School

Wednesday 8:30–8:45   WPEN   POLISH PROGRAM
Feb. 8   A.M.   (920)   Talk—"Keeping Your Child Well"—Miss Jane Czarnecki, teacher, Emlen School

---

[3] Lawrence B. Johnson, "Interpreting the Schools," *N.J. Educational Review,* 1940, p. 48.

Thursday   10:15-10:30   WPEN   ITALIAN PROGRAM
Feb. 9   A.M.   (920)   Talk—"Keeping Your Child
                                   Well"—Miss Anne Marzucco.
                                   teacher, South Philadelphia Girls'
                                   High School

Certain cautions should be noted in broadcasting material of this type, for it is quite likely that some elements of the population prefer not to be thought of as isolated groups, and so it is wise to end every program of this type on a positive note with the promotion of American ideals as the theme.

Good Will Is Often a By-product.   It should not be assumed that a radio program is productive of good will only when it sets out to create it deliberately. Good will is often a by-product. A program presented over a commercial station and planned for school children, yet which is heard in the home, is also a public relations program.

Speaking of the results obtained from this "indirect" approach, Harold Kent, formerly director of the Radio Council, Chicago Public Schools, said:

. . . Now Mrs. Bailey, who is a Chicago mother, has just happened to have tuned in station WIND. She happens to hear the introduction to a radio broadcast designed for students from grades seven to twelve. And as the story of, let us say, Vincent Van Gogh unfolds, she finds herself becoming more and more interested in the tragedy and magnificent victory of the great artist. Then, at the close of the program she hears: "This has been a production of the Radio Council of the Chicago Public Schools." What is her reaction. In all probability, her first one is that of relief, then gratitude sets in, and finally, curiosity and healthy interest. When her children return from school that afternoon, she questions them as to what the Radio Council is and what their teachers have instructed them as to the purpose and the functions of the Council; then Mrs. Bailey takes her questions to the principal on her next visit to the school or, perhaps, brings it up before her local parent-teacher organization. And what does she learn? She learns that the Chicago public-school system of which she is a direct supporter through taxes is using a new tool to increase the efficacy of the educative process. She learns that the principle of radio in education, as far as the Chicago system is concerned, has for its main objectives the training of the child in good listening habits, the achieving of taste and discrimination in the selection of radio programs and the substitution of worth-while, entertaining material for the sensationalism that has been cluttering up the air lanes. So much has Mrs. Bailey learned, through inquiry and sincere interest. And what is her further reaction? If she is the normal, intelligent, American mother she says to herself: "Now there's something valuable! It's a great, forward step from the days when I went to school and our horizon was limited by the three 'R's.' Our school system is, indeed, using its funds and its time to advantage if this is any indication." And millions of words that have been written, vilifying the system and its administrators are neutralized, for Mrs. Bailey, at least, by a fifteen-minute radio program! [4]

Although it is quite apparent that every school program has public relations possibilities, it is equally obvious that, if a program is to achieve to a maximum degree a specific purpose, the program must be planned with that aim in mind. In this instance, too, the rifle is more effective than the shotgun.

Progressive school broadcasting organizations will make use of both types of program material: that which is aimed directly at creating desirable public relations and that which is productive of the same end in an indirect manner, the classroom program.

Types of Programs

The school radio programs planned specifically with public relations in mind generally fall into two categories: (1) those which are concerned with the activities of one school and are prepared and presented by the faculty and students of that school and (2) those which deal with the school system in general and are frequently produced by a central broadcasting unit.

There are certain values to each of these types that should be noted here. The first—the appearance on the radio of a school group —is likely to encourage a keen neighborhood interest in the program if it is well publicized. Furthermore, by rotating these appearances among the schools many children share in the values of such participation. Moreover, adults like to hear children perform, provided their efforts are skillfully handled.

It generally follows, however, that as participation is spread, artistic standards are somewhat lowered. Unless the program is well done and

---

[4] Harold Kent in address before School Public Relations Association, Milwaukee, Wisc., June 29, 1940.

unless the school recognizes the radio appearance as a privilege rather than as an added burden, this type of public relations effort should be minimized.

The second type of program organization—that which deals with the entire school system and its numerous activities—provides the listeners with an understanding of the relationship of all these school functions. Generally, because a select and perhaps a more mature cast can be used, the production is more finished than the first type. Of course, as a compromise, children also can appear in minor roles or as members of a school musical group—vocal or instrumental. System wide casting permits greater choice of talent.

Regardless of the program type, it should be understood that, since the production of a radio program requires somewhat specialized ability, all scripts to be used and perhaps even the final rehearsals should be supervised by individuals chosen for that work. This should not be regarded as a form of censorship but as an attempt to maintain a high standard of performance. If the programs are worth doing, they are worth doing as well as possible.

While television programs, in general, will fall under the same two categories mentioned above, the more limited opportunity for appearance on TV tends to throw emphasis on the second type, the program or series which deals with the entire school system. While individual school groups appear frequently, they are more likely to provide one small segment of a given program, although an extended series might well feature, in any one broadcast, the work of one school selected for its outstanding performance in a given field. In either case, it is most important to have some person with experience in television assigned to assist the teachers who are preparing the various elements of each program and to make their presentations "telegenic."

Some Common Mistakes and How to Correct Them

Some of the precautions to be noted seem to apply particularly to that type of school public relations program which is prepared by the individual school and which generally deals with the activities of that school.

All too frequently such a program overlooks the fact that it is not necessary to discuss the entire school and all its numerous activities in one radio appearance. Instead, the script attempts to touch upon every phase of the school's work, and the unfortunate result is that what might be both an informative and enjoyable experience for the listener becomes a rather dull catalogue of the school's clubs, subjects taught, number of classes, and the like.

If dramatics is attempted with the same purpose in mind, the script generally calls for many doors opening and closing while the supposedly curious radio visitor peeks his head into a classroom, quickly hears what is taking place, and then dashes out before the door is slammed. That such a treatment is not only trite but often ridiculous is quite apparent.

A basic principle of educational script writing noted earlier applies here as it does elsewhere—a single concept, one worth-while theme developed simply, will result in a better program than an overly ambitious effort that gets nowhere. Rather than provide a superficial glimpse at its many projects, it would be far better for the school producing the program to select one of its activities of which it is especially proud and to devote the entire program to it. It might be its orchestra, its newspaper, its student government, or even a national issue as it applies to a school function. Thus the script can be just to the school, to the activity, and above all, to the listener.

Another elementary consideration sometimes overlooked is that a radio program should be thought of as a *unit* not as a vehicle for displaying 8 minutes of work by the English Department, 15 minutes by the Music Division, and 6½ minutes by a history class. Such a resulting hodgepodge is liable to be a boomerang as far as effective public relations broadcasting is concerned.

A program so conceived and so dedicated to the listener becomes a production man's nightmare. Invariably the program is not accurately timed, and when it comes to cutting parts of the script there is obvious reluctance to do so since each department thinks of its own contribution as a well-rounded unit. There is no fixed responsibility for the program. No one is primarily concerned with the quality of the program in its entirety. But instead each confines his efforts to his own contribution. It is therefore not difficult to see why the station production man who sets out to be a kind counselor becomes a tyrant and is thereafter referred to as "that horrible man."

But what is perhaps more important, the elements of the program themselves are often not related. The program opens with a student representing the history classes who recites the Gettysburg Address. Then the English class presents a heart-rending romance. This is followed by the Music Department, which seals the marriage vows with 15 minutes of martial music by the band. A gross exaggeration? Certainly. But to a lesser degree this type of program organization is not so rare as one would like it to be.

Some time ago one of the writers outlined a series of fifteen programs which, with some adaptation, may be suggestive to a school system considering the use of radio as an agency for interpretation.

SUGGESTED SERIES
I. Your Schools
A. Program Aims
　1. To introduce the series.
　2. To secure newspaper publicity for the programs.
　3. To show (indirectly) that the time is not bought by the schools.
　4. To create interest in the future programs.
B. Procedure
Following a musical prelude, the management of the radio station formally donates the time to the schools. The superintendent of schools accepts, and is interviewed by a local newspaper man. The scope and the purpose of the series is set forth. To create an air of expectancy is the aim.

II. What Are the "Frills"?
A. Program Aims
　1. To justify the expansion of the curriculum.
　2. To distinguish between wise and unwise school economy.
B. Procedure
A dramatization in which a well-known alumnus visits his former school and notes the changes that have come about. The principal indicates that a dynamic society requires a changing education. The terms "fads" and "frills" have been used to mean different things at different times. The verbal comment is interspersed with musical selections by student performers.

III. The Three R's
A. Program Aims
　1. To show that the three R's are still being taught at least as effectively as ever.

2. To describe newer methods of instruction.

3. To show that the "core-curriculum" is in constant flux.

B. Procedure

A dramatization with a parent, teacher, and student. The work in the three R's is traced through the elementary grades, the junior high, and high schools.

IV. Do You Belong?

A. Program Aims

1. To interest more parents in the work of the PTA.
2. To develop mutual understanding between the home and school.
3. To provide the PTA with an opportunity to take part in an educational enterprise.
4. To introduce the PTA leaders to the public.

B. Procedure

An interview with the local PTA President. Musical selections, if possible by PTA members.

V. Our Schools, "A Melting Pot"

A. Program Aims

1. To create interest in the schools among the various nationality groups in the community.
2. To recognize the process of educating "the new Americans."
3. To show the importance of education in a democracy.

B. Procedure

Brief talks by several students, each representing a different nation. Folk songs and other characteristic music used. The chairman is a well-known immigrant in the community who "made good." This subject might be expanded into several programs, each devoted to a specific nationality.

VI. What Happened to the Truant Officer?

A. Program Aims

1. To describe the work of the Bureau of Attendance.
2. To indicate a modern point of view that is taken toward delinquents.
3. To indicate that the function of a modern school system is a constantly expanding one.
4. To suggest that if these worth-while functions are to be undertaken increased financial support is essential.

B. Procedure

A series of dramatized sketches depicting some of the cases handled by the Bureau of Attendance. At the conclusion of each scene a comment is given as to treatment.

VII. The Meaning of Report Cards

A. Program Aims

1. To inform the parents of the meaning of grades.
2. To suggest the methods by which grades are determined.

3. To indicate possible parental cooperation when failing work is evident.

4. To gain sympathetic understanding of a school function.

B. Procedure

A parent asks questions pertaining to the subject. These are discussed and analyzed by selected school representatives of the elementary, junior-high, and high-school grades.

VIII. What's Your I.Q.?

A. Program Aims

1. To point out the heterogeneity of modern school population.
2. To indicate the need for classification.
3. To describe briefly the methods of testing.
4. To show the uses made of these test results. The implications financially of individual differences.

B. Procedure

A dramatized discussion between several parents and the school psychologist. Interludes of music included.

IX. Education for All

A. Program Aims

1. To describe the manifold activities of the schools in providing education for special groups: (a) Adult evening classes; (b) Crippled children; (c) The blind and deaf; (d) Recreation groups; (e) Delinquents.
2. To show that such special education was rare some years ago.
3. To note the effect of this type of education on school costs.

B. Procedure

A series of brief messages by selected representatives of each of these "special" groups. The music to be provided by organizations developed within such groups. An entire series can be developed from this theme.

X. Health Is Happiness

A. Program Aims

1. To describe the work of the various health agencies within the school system, such as the doctor, nurse, dentist, and psychiatrist.
2. To indicate that the school is doing much that was formerly done at home.

B. Procedure

Several scenes in dramatic form. Johnny visits the school doctor; or perhaps the dentist comes to school. Musical interludes offered by a school orchestra. Summary made by the Director of Health.

XI. Learning "To Take It"

A. Program Aims

1. To provide a particular attraction to the school broadcasts.
2. To describe the athletic activities in the educational system.

3. To relate this activity to the programs on "Health" and "Citizenship."

B. Procedure

An informal discussion between several outstanding local athletes of recent years. A sports writer or coach might act as toastmaster. This is a period of reminiscence—the spirit of good will the keynote.

XII. Meet John Q. Public, Jr.

A. Program Aims

1. To describe the various agencies in the school which provide citizenship training.
2. To describe the extracurricular activities in the modern school.
3. To discuss the objectives of these activities.
4. To provide certain school groups with a worth-while project.

B. Procedure

This program is to be largely a student enterprise. A city-wide competition among high-school dramatic groups might be conducted and the winning groups in this contest present the program themselves, under expert guidance.

XIII. The Little Red Schoolhouse

A. Program Aims

1. To contrast the school of yesterday with the modern institution.
2. To imply the inevitable increase in school costs.
3. To interest certain civic leaders in the school series.
4. To provide an unusual attraction to the school programs.

B. Procedure

Selected civic leaders take part in an informal discussion. Each relates a series of humorous experiences of their school days. Humor and geniality are prevalent.

XIV. Who Teaches Our Children?

A. Program Aims

1. To create an appreciation of the preparation and the requirements for a teaching position today.
2. To develop a sympathetic understanding of the teacher's problems and her attitudes.
3. To inform the public of the existence and the goals of the various teacher organizations.

B. Procedure

The heads of the various teacher organizations are interviewed by several well-known parents. Musical selections by teachers are used after each interview.

XV. Educational Dividends

A. Program Aims

1. To summarize the previous broadcasts showing the need for public support if these services are to be adequate.

Left, Miami television
students rehearse at
Station WTVJ.

Below, UCLA students make
a film for television.

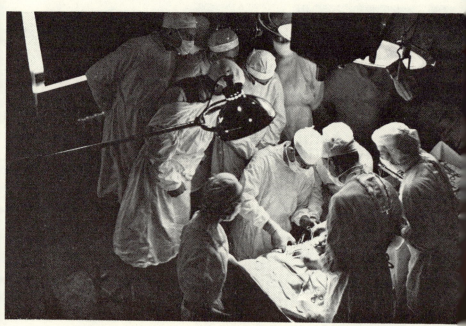

The TV camera watches surgeons performing an operation.

Naval lessons by television.

2. To describe the present methods of financing public education.
3. To enlist the cooperation of the public in the process of producing an educated citizenry.

B. Procedure

A conversation is presented in which the school treasurer, a high-school student, and a leader in PTA work take part. Selected choral groups serve to break up the "talk."

There are numerous school activities other than those already noted that might be developed into superior programs. To list just a few:

"Never Too Old to Learn"
The aim and function of the division of adult education. If such a program is scheduled at the time registration is taking place in evening schools some of the newer courses can be noted.

"Your Child's Safety"
What the schools are doing to aid children in the development of safety habits.

"Training for the Machine Age"
The place of the industrial arts in the school curriculum.

"Meet the Graduates"
Comments concerning the value of education by students who are about to leave the schools.

"New Teaching Aids"
The use of visual and auditory aids in serving the learner.

"Tomorrow's Job"
The activities of the guidance and placement department.

"Young Artists"
Featuring the talents of outstanding school instrumentalists and vocalists.

"Hobbies Are Fun"
What the school extracurricular groups are doing to encourage the worthy use of leisure time.

"We Are Proud of Them"
Presenting the winners of recent scholarship awards.

"Your Child Celebrates"
Illustrating how the schools celebrate various state and national holidays.

In the hands of a good script writer even the most abstract platitudes can become real and meaningful to all. The script now shown

which was prepared by the Department of Visual and Radio Education of the Detroit Public Schools illustrates how vital is the proper
training for the duties of citizenship. As a public relations program,
especially if scheduled early in November, it not only interests the
adult voter but it adds an "amen" to the efforts of the schools in
that direction.

Station WJBK

Series: THE AMERICAN SCENE
Program: ELECTIONS

VOICE: Order in the court! Order in the court! The case of the people of
 Detroit versus John Doe. Mr. John Doe take the stand. Mr. John
 Doe take the stand!
SOUND: *Rapping of gavel*
 Mr. Doe, do you swear to tell the truth . . . the whole truth . . .
 and nothing but the truth?
DOE: I do.
VOICE: Take the witness stand, please.
JUDGE: Clerk, what is the charge against the prisoner?
VOICE: He is charged with evading his civic responsibilities by failing to
 vote, Your Honor.
JUDGE: Failing to vote, eh? Very well . . . Mr. District Attorney, exam-
 ine the witness.
DIST. ATTY: One moment, Your Honor. If it please the court, may I say
 that it will be impossible for the jury to understand the testimony
 of this witness unless we first examine other important evidence.
 The accused is charged with failing to vote. Before he is examined I
 think it would be wise to give the jury a little information about
 our election system here in Detroit and about our Election Commission.
JUDGE: An excellent suggestion, Mr. District Attorney. Will you give the
 jury such information as you deem necessary?
DIST. ATTY: Thank you, Your Honor, I will, but, before I address the jury
 I'd better say just a word to our radio audience. . . . Boys and girls,
 ladies and gentlemen . . . as you might suspect from the name of
 the accused, Mr. John Doe, the trial you are about to hear is entirely
 fictitious. However, in a moment we will continue the trial and
 recall Mr. Doe to the stand. Later on, we'll also examine another
 individual whom we trust you'll find equally as interesting as Mr.
 Doe. Now, on with the trial. . . . Ladies and gentlemen of the
 jury. Mr. Doe has been accused of failure to vote. In order to more
 fully understand the gravity of his offense, let's take a brief look at

Detroit's voting system. We find the following paragraph concerning this system in the Social Studies test, *Citizenship in Detroit:*

VOICE: "The persons in control of the election system are the most important part of the system. An honest, civic-minded group can produce a sound, honest system . . . whereas gangsters and crooks can ruin a perfectly well-planned organization." Let's see who controls Detroit's Election System, ladies and gentlemen of the jury.

DIST. ATTY: In Detroit the city charter provides for an election commission consisting of three men . . . the city clerk, the recorder of Recorders Court, and the president of the Common Council. The general powers and duties of this commission are . . . Number one:

VOICE: To appoint registration boards.

DIST. ATTY: Two:

VOICE: To provide places for voting.

DIST. ATTY: Three:

VOICE: To prepare and print election ballots.

DIST. ATTY: Four:

VOICE: To have general supervision of all elections in the city, with full power to prevent any and all manner of fraud or dishonest conduct.

DIST. ATTY: Five:

VOICE: To act as a board of city canvassers for the examination of votes cast at all city elections.

DIST. ATTY: Six:

VOICE: To provide public examinations of all applicants for inspectors or other election officials appointed by the commission.

DIST. ATTY: Besides these and other duties, this three-man election commission also has power . . .

VOICE: To employ or discharge the full staff of district officials.

DIST. ATTY: Ladies and gentlemen of the jury . . . you have heard what an excellent commission our charter provides. In opening the case against Mr. Doe, I want to remind you that his offense . . . failure to vote . . . is one often committed by thousands of others. We are sorry to say that there have been elections in Detroit in which only 15 per cent of the registered voters cast a ballot.

Many Europeans who have visioned America as the very home of democracy would be amazed if they were aware of how lightly some of us hold this privilege of the ballot. In fact, one little democracy of Europe, that was newly born following the World War, passed laws making it a misdemeanor for any citizen not to vote. Citizens failing in this respect were fined.

Failure to vote is one of our definite civic problems, but the solution of the problem is the personal job of each individual. And, now, we'll call Mr. Doe to the stand. Let's hear this fellow, who won't take the trouble to cast his ballot. Let's find out just why he is that way.

JUDGE: Mr. District Attorney, the accused has already been sworn in. You may examine him.

DIST. ATTY: Thank you, Your Honor. Just be seated, Mr. Doe.

DOE: I want to say right now I'm here to witness in my own defense. What if I did fail to vote? That's no crime.

JUDGE: (*Pounds gavel*) The witness is out of order. The witness will please speak only when questioned.

DOE: Huh? Oh, . . . yes, Your Honor.

DIST. ATTY: Mr. Doe, since you failed to vote, can we assume that you weren't interested in the outcome of the election?

DOE: No, sir! You can't. I certainly was interested. But, after all, let's be practical. I haven't the time to go down to that crowded booth and stand in a long line waiting for a chance to write out my ballot. Yeah . . . and did you ever stop to think . . . just what possible difference can one vote make? Huh! . . . Tell me that . . . just what difference will *one vote* make?

DIST. ATTY: I'll answer that question! Listen, Mr. Doe, around about this season of the year, reputable witnesses have heard you say:

DOE: (*Filter*) Say! I wouldn't miss that football game Saturday for a million bucks! Look at the two tickets I have . . . right on the fifty-yard line. I had to stand in line for two hours to get them . . . but it was worth it.

DIST. ATTY: So you see, Mr. Doe . . . you, who are so worried by the crowd at the voting booths, think nothing of waiting two hours to get football tickets! Well, that's fair enough. *Most of us* enjoy a good football game . . . But the point is this:
You spend a great deal of effort in order to see a football game. But, it just doesn't occur to you that you have a civic responsibility to cast your ballot, which deserves, at least, an equal amount of effort. Why, apparently you're more interested in whether Harvard beats Yale than you are in the laws you live under or the public officials who represent you in office. You don't even vote!

DOE: What are you talking about? What difference does *one vote* make?

DIST. ATTY: The same old excuse . . . Admittedly, one vote wouldn't make any appreciable difference. But when eighty-five people out of one hundred fail to vote—as occurred in one Detroit election—it makes a great deal of difference. Do you realize that you are not just *one* citizen . . . but one of a group of thousands of citizens, saying the same thing? What difference will one vote make? And in the South we hear . . .

SOUTHERNER: (*With accent*) Ah can't see what diff'ence mah vote'll make.

DIST. ATTY: And in the East . . .

WOMAN: (*With accent*) I really can't see that one vote matters so much.

DIST. ATTY: And in the West . . .

MAN: (*With accent*) Ah reckon as how mah vote cain't mattah much.

DIST. ATTY: And so, from the Atlantic to the Pacific Ocean we hear the theme song of the poor citizen . . . "What's one vote?" Quite obviously, Mr. Doe, it's not a matter of one vote, but a matter of millions of votes. Now let's return to our original case. Ladies and gentlemen of the jury. The scene I am about to bring you will show you Mr. Doe's behavior following the election in which he failed to vote. We see him arguing with his friends. Listen!

DOE: (*Fade in*) Fine town this is . . . Look at the good man they defeated for state representative. Huh! A qualified man runs for office and what happens? People don't vote for him.

VOICE: Whom did you vote for?

DOE: (*Aggressive*) Whom did I vote for! Whom do you think? I voted for the best man . . . the man who . . . (*Suddenly remembers he didn't vote*) uh . . . er . . . well, what I mean is I didn't . . . er . . . vote . . . (*Recovers*) But get this . . . if I *had* voted . . . well, I would have voted *right*.

VOICE: (*Very rational and cool in contrast*) You mean to say you didn't vote?

DOE: No, I didn't.

VOICE: (*Slightly shocked*) You didn't? . . . Aren't you a citizen?

DOE: What do you mean? I'm 100 per cent American!

VOICE: I'm sorry . . . I didn't mean to offend you . . . but . . . uh . . . well, aliens, of course, haven't the privilege of voting, and I thought . . .

DOE: (*Insulted*) Aliens!

VOICE: Well, why didn't you vote? Were you ill?

DOE: No . . . not exactly . . . (*Muttering*) I was pretty busy, and . . . uh . . . the election booths were crowded, you see . . .

VOICE: You mean to say you didn't take the trouble to vote for this candidate you admire so greatly . . . just because the election booths were crowded? Why, you actually contributed toward his defeat . . . And then you have the nerve to complain about it.

DOE: Aw, the voters haven't any sense in this town.

VOICE: They have enough sense to vote, anyway. That's more than you can say. I might have guessed it. The man who complains the loudest about the results of an election is usually the man who didn't even bother to vote.

DOE: What's one vote?

VOICE: Look here . . . What if they passed a law that all persons who failed to vote at the last election could never vote again?

DOE: Heah? Let them try it! It's unconstitutional! They couldn't take my rights away from me. Our forefathers fought . . .

VOICE: Precisely! Our forefathers fought for a democratic system of government. And the Constitution does defend your privileges. No, they couldn't take your rights away from you. You'd fight back. But when those same rights and privileges are laid right in your lap, you don't even bother to use them. You're a fine one to complain about the results of the election. As far as I can see, you're just a zero when it comes to being of any civic worth to this community. (*Fade*)

DIST. ATTY: And that, ladies and gentlemen of the jury, is an example of Mr. Doe's behavior. Let me go over the important points in this case: First, Mr. Doe fails to vote . . . in itself, a fine example of poor citizenship! But is he ashamed? Oh, no! Not Mr. Doe! Instead of admitting his own failing, he has the colossal impudence to criticize the selections of citizens who *did* vote. He says the voting citizens have no sense. Well, ladies and gentlemen of the jury and friends of the radio audience . . . I'll leave it to you to decide just who is the senseless one in this case. And, finally, in an attempt to excuse his strange undemocratic behavior Mr. Doe asks: What difference does one vote make? Well, I can pity a man who gives such a weak excuse as that for failure to make his contribution to our American form of government. Mr. Doe, you may leave the stand . . .

JUDGE: Is your case finished, Mr. District Attorney?

DIST. ATTY: No, Your Honor, at this time I would like to put another culprit, Jane Roe, on the stand.

JUDGE: Clerk, call Jane Roe.

CLERK: Yes, Your Honor . . . (*Calling*) The case of the people versus Jane Roe! Miss Jane Roe take the stand!

SOUND: *Of gavel*

CLERK: Miss Roe, do you swear to tell the truth, the whole truth, and nothing but the truth?

JANE: I do.

JUDGE: Proceed, Mr. District Attorney.

DIST. ATTY: Thank you . . . Your Honor, ladies and gentlemen of the jury . . . John Doe was accused of evading his civic responsibilities by failing to vote. The case of Jane Roe is slightly different, but not less serious. The state will attempt to prove that she has not evaded . . . but abused . . . her civic responsibilities. I believe this will become clear as I question the witness.

JUDGE: Proceed, Mr. District Attorney.

DIST. ATTY: Yes, Your Honor . . . will the accused give her name please?

JANE: My name is Jane Roe . . . and I don't know *what* this is all about.

DIST. ATTY: Miss Roe, the other day I overheard you make a remark to a friend about the manner in which you voted. Would you mind repeating that statement?

JANE: Not at all. I said I didn't know whom to vote for; so I just looked over the ballot and picked out the candidates whose name sounded the best and marked an "X" after their names.

DIST. ATTY: Yes, that's what you said. Now, Miss Roe, tell us, do you use the same system when you buy your new fall hat? I mean, do you merely pick up an order blank and place an "X" after the name of the hat that sounds the best?

JANE: Why, how silly! Certainly not! I want to know what I'm getting when I buy a new hat.

DIST. ATTY: Ladies and gentlemen of the jury . . . please note. Miss Roe says that she wants to know what she's getting when she buys a hat. But by her own admission, she doesn't think the same common sense applies to picking out public officials . . . Miss Roe, don't you ever attempt to familiarize yourself with the records and qualifications of candidates for public office?

JANE: I don't guess I do . . . I merely place an "X"—(D.A. joins in)— the names that sound the best.

DIST. ATTY: After the names that sound the best . . . Yes, you explained all that. . . . Miss Roe, can you name the city, county, state, and national officials whom you voted for in recent elections?

JANE: Well let's see . . . I know the names of the president . . . and the governor . . . and the mayor . . . and . . . one of our senators . . . and . . . uh . . . I guess I can't think of any more right now.

DIST. ATTY: In other words, you know all the principal officers. Do you know who your representative is in the House of Representatives at Washington?

JANE: I can't remember.

DIST. ATTY: You voted for a representative, didn't you?

JANE: Oh! Yes, I voted for one, all right.

DIST. ATTY: Can't you remember the name of anyone else you voted for?

JANE: Oh! I remember another . . . a man running for a city office named . . .

DIST. ATTY: Never mind his name, Miss Roe, but tell us . . . what were his qualifications for the office?

JANE: Qualifications? . . . Search me.

DIST. ATTY: Well, then, was his past record a good one?

JANE: How would I know?

DIST. ATTY: Very easily, Miss Roe, if you took the trouble to study such matters. You read the newspapers, don't you? And candidates do speak on the radio . . . and there are magazines and pamphlets and many other such sources of information to which a good citizen can refer to enable him to vote intelligently. Let me tell you a story, Miss Roe. To teach the citizens of a certain community a lesson, a group of men nominated a mule for sheriff . . . and the mule was elected, too.

JANE: A mule?

DIST. ATTY: That's right. There were enough people around who merely marked an "X" after the name on the ballot . . . the name that sounded the best . . . and in this case it was the name of a mule. Does that make you realize how important your ballot is, Miss Roe?

JANE: I guess it does. I wouldn't want to elect a mule for sheriff.

DIST. ATTY: Your ballot and the manner in which you use it has more effect on your life than you realize. Consider how many things your ballot determines . . . whether taxes will be large or small . . . how they'll be distributed . . . what laws will be made to regulate traffic . . . or entertainment . . . or social problems . . . perhaps the number of hours you'll work a day . . . our foreign policy . . . the size of our navy . . . high tariffs or low tariffs . . . the efficiency of our government . . . of all branches of government . . . our Health Department . . . how much money will be spent for education . . . and a thousand other things. Perhaps your ballot does not determine all this *directly*, but your ballot does elect representatives who will determine such matters. And you, Miss Roe . . . you! Aren't you ashamed to confess that you merely pick out the names that sound the best and mark an "X" after them? . . . (*Fade*) You may leave the witness stand, Miss Roe.

JUDGE: Mr. District Attorney, will you now sum up this case for the jury?

DIST. ATTY: I will, Your Honor . . . Ladies and gentlemen of the jury. The secret ballot guarantees Miss Roe the right to make any selection she wishes when voting for a law or for a candidate. That's her privilege. However, we're not concerned with *what* selections Miss Roe makes . . . but, we are deeply concerned with *how* she makes those selections. The community demands that Miss Roe have enough civic responsibility to familiarize herself sufficiently with amendments and candidates and issues so that she might cast her ballot in the light of intelligent study.

So, in conclusion, let's not forget these two individuals . . . First, Mr. Doe, who says . . .

DOE: What difference does one vote make?

DIST. ATTY: And second, Miss Roe . . . who says . . .

JANE: I just put an "X" after the names that looked the best.

DIST. ATTY: It has been said that Detroit, because of its present election system, is almost a perfect democracy . . . Ladies and gentlemen of the jury . . . Let's take every advantage of utilizing this election system, so as to bring a continually increasing amount of civic responsibility to the American Scene . . . Your Honor, the people rest!

JUDGE: Thank you . . . (*Gavel*) Court is adjourned until next week at this same time.

MUSIC: A *March* . . . *up a moment* . . . *into closing*

The above script is illustrative of the type that can be adapted easily to meet local requirements. Most, if not all, school systems will cooperate in the exchange of script materials.

Using Spot Announcements

A discussion of school public relations broadcasting should emphasize that it is not essential for the school system which is planning to use radio to have a large production staff. Nor is it necessary to develop and produce complete script programs. Radio can serve in other ways.

Some of the most noteworthy "success stories" in the radio industry have resulted not from presenting entire programs but from the use of well-placed "spot announcements."

To the school broadcaster who generally is handicapped by limited production facilities this fact should be of real significance. Unfortunately, it is one which, with few exceptions, has been grossly neglected. Considering the ease of production, the ends gained in terms of listener influence are noteworthy.

These spot announcements are brief statements generally less than one minute in length presented between programs. They may be read by the announcer, or, if not read, a transcription is used. Occasionally the announcement may assume the form of a simple dramatization or even an entire program in miniature.

It is a comparatively easy matter to develop several such announcements and generally arrangements can be made with the local stations to have them presented as they do their commercial "spots." In some cases the voices of children making the brief announcements will have additional listener appeal. The child, for example, presents a personal invitation to his parents asking them to attend his school during American Education Week, two pupils discuss the fun they had with arithmetic as it is taught in the modern school, and so forth. These comments can be recorded and replayed by the station as the spots are scheduled. In this manner it eliminates the necessity for the participants' presence in the studio.

For these announcements, as with complete programs, selective scheduling is important since it will determine to a large degree the size of the potential listener audience.

The early evening periods are most desirable and if the spot can follow a very popular program, there is a definite inheritance of listeners. An announcement preceding a popular program is also desirable, but it is quite likely that these choice spots have been contracted for commercially. The cost, however, to the school in terms of time and effort is so small that this opportunity should not be overlooked.

Announcements of various kinds can be utilized, such as quotations by famous men concerning the value of education in general, as well as statements by pupils and laymen concerning the local schools in particular.

These examples may be suggestive:

Dear Mother and Dad. Our schools are celebrating American Education Week this coming Monday. I spend five hours each weekday away from home. Wouldn't you like to see how I am making use of my time? I know you're interested.

"What sculpture is to a block of marble, education is to the soul." This is American Education Week. Visit your neighborhood school.

Every school day morning [number] children attend our schools. You, the taxpayers, have made this possible. Visit your schools during this American Education Week.

Education is the first line of Democracy. Next week is American Education Week. Visit your neighborhood schools and see Democracy in action.

FATHER: I can't understand it. Johnny actually likes arithmetic. Why, when I . . .
MOTHER: Well, he ought to with the methods they use nowadays.
ANNOUNCER: Visit the schools next week and see these methods being applied.

The above are indicative of the various applications that can be made of the spot announcement. The manner in which the material is presented is also important. If the announcement is made in a sincere and conversational tone, the result will be desirable. If it is read with a bombastic, unduly aggressive delivery, the result, as almost any listener knows, can often be a negative one.

Television, too, has its noncommercial spot announcements, and while other local agencies and equally worthy causes—Boy Scouts, Girl Scouts, Community Chest, March of Dimes, etc.—will all be competing for the few available spots, schools have an important claim. But television spots must be *visual* as well as verbal. Good visualization costs comparatively little. It may take the form of four-to-six still pictures, showing various school activities. These may be shown directly on a "live" television camera, in which case the station will appreciate good 8- by 10-inch prints with a dull, not a glossy, finish. For television, pictures should be in the same aspect ratio as the television screen, that is, wider than they are high. Transparent slides are even more convenient for station use, since they do not "tie up a live camera." Most stations use 2- by 2-inch or 3- by 4-inch slide projectors, and it is wise to consult the local station before making up material. Another variation is slide film or strip film, a series of individual frames on 35-mm. film. Most school systems have facilities, in their audio-visual aid departments, for making up such slide films from glossy photographs, and these are even less expensive than slides. There are schools and school systems with 16-mm. motion-picture facilities and clubs, and the creation of a 16-mm. film running one minute, for example, might well be a project for such units. It is safest to "shoot them" in black and white, and silent film will do, if narration is carefully written to fit and supplied to the station. A staff announcer may read the commentary, or possibly the station will permit a talented high-school student to provide the voice behind the picture.

Obviously, an imaginative, attractive visual presentation, accompanied by narration which also contains good showmanship will be more welcome to the station and will have greater impact on the audience.

Using Television in the Field of Public Relations

It is an interesting fact that in several cities, noted for co-operation between the local school system and television stations, public relations programs were the first type attempted, with purely educational programs coming later. These public relations broadcasts fall into two classifications: individual, "one-shot," special broadcasts which are presented occasionally as circumstances warrant, and those which come in a regularly scheduled series.

In the first class of irregular, occasional programs are school-supplied elements of established programs, such as the appearance of the Superintendent of Schools to welcome parents to Open School Week, or to announce innovations at the beginning of a school year. Sometimes stations will go to the trouble and expense of sending a mobile unit to a school during Open School Week. Students who have won prizes in athletics, scholarship or the creative arts are interviewed on news programs or interview shows. Student leaders occasionally appear on the evening before a major athletic contest to invite the support of the general public.

While such irregularly scheduled broadcasts do not have the continuing impact of a series, they are one way of keeping the schools in the public eye, and a skillful public relations director working with the school system can easily "get the schools on the screen" at least once or twice each month.

Far more valuable, of course, are the regularly scheduled programs in a definite series. These are usually devoted to showing parents and citizens the workings of the school system as a whole, although specific elements and units may come from particular schools, and special departments or divisions may be features in any given single program.

The schools of Schenectady probably led the way in this field with programs from WRGB, Schenectady, as far back as 1944. In 1945, the Board of Education Station, WBEZ, and the Chicago Radio Council began several series over WBKB. One, A View of Education, covered a different grade level and subject area each week, and tied in definitely with the course of study of the grade level selected, while showing parents new methods in education. Another series, Young Chicago, featured high school units. In the words of Elizabeth

Marshall, of WBEZ, "It showed everything from art classes, debating teams, physical education groups and student councils to chemistry experiments. Each school selected an outstanding activity and featured it."

Student discussion programs have been most successful in the sense that any program which shows the citizens and taxpayers boys and girls who are the end-product of school training, may be considered as helping in public relations. *There Ought to Be a Law,* begun in 1945 by CBS and WNYE, the New York City Board of Education Station, ran for two years and won an award from the American Television Society. *Young Ideas,* another discussion program involving high-school students of the Detroit Schools under the supervision of staff members of WDTR, the Detroit school station, was presented as a radio program for two semesters, then went on television over station WWJ-TV in 1947.

St. Louis schools began a public relations series designed to acquaint citizens with the special services of their schools in 1947, and continued on into 1948 on Station KSO-TV. One of the most effective broadcasts was the demonstration of the first steps in teaching deaf children to speak, shown by Mrs. Florence Russell, a teacher at the Gallaudet School. Three totally deaf children were televised as they were taught to speak and taught the regular school curriculum at the same time.

Meet Your Schools is presented by the Cleveland Board of Education every Tuesday evening over station WEWS. This series, in which the Superintendent, Dr. Mark C. Schinnerer, serves as M.C., has earned high listener ratings.

In Philadelphia, the entire (and very extensive) television program is under the supervision of Martha A. Gable, of the Office of School-Community Relations. This division began its study of television in September, 1947; was on the air with experimental programs by February, 1948, and by the end of the following school year of 1948–1949, had arranged 210 telecasts in which there appeared 2,500 pupils from 145 schools, over stations WFIL-TV, WPTZ and WCAU-TV.

While Philadelphia's more recent schedule of twelve television programs a week is largely within school hours and designed for in-school viewing, the programs of 1948 were largely in the field of public relations and were "designed to tell the story of the schools to the public." Both *Here's How* (WFIL-TV) and *Young Philadelphia Presents* cut across all school and divisional lines, and featured the activities of boys and girls from kindergarten through the twelfth year.

"HERE'S HOW"   WFIL-TV   MONDAYS 5:45–6   36 WEEKS

Boys and girls of all ages demonstrated how to make a wide variety of articles and how to develop appropriate skills. Vocational activities such as the use of power sewing machines, airbrush, and cut-all, the art of hairdressing, baking, dressmaking, and upholstering were included. Dance, art, instrumental music, agriculture, and animal husbandry also were featured. A one-minute film with commentary, taken in various classrooms and shops, was used as an opening each week. A basement-workshop scene was built by the station for this series. All sorts of applications from children who wanted to participate on "Here's How" came to us during the year.

"YOUNG PHILADELPHIA PRESENTS" WPTZ TUESDAYS 4:45–5 32 WEEKS

This cut across the entire school system from kindergarten to college, and included nearly every subject. Reading, rhythms, art, music, dance, social studies, health, drama, safety, and history provided interesting topics. A series of Philadelphia "first" included dramatic episodes in the beginnings of the Curtis Publishing Company, the Pennsylvania Hospital, and the Baldwin Locomotive Works. The Chamber of Commerce became interested and assisted in the procurement of materials. When the new report card for elementary schools was issued, a skit which explained the card and its use was presented.

An interesting variation on the public-service angle is another Philadelphia school program, *Billy Penn, MC*. This series, over WFIL-TV, tells the story of local industrial activities, from the Philadelphia Mint to manufacture of hats or storage batteries. Such a series serves the double purpose of acquainting students with the industries of their own community, and of making industrial leaders aware of the activities of the schools.

A genuine "television tour of the schools" is provided the citizens of Baltimore by the schools and station WAAM. A series called *Baltimore Classroom—1950* used a replica of a typical classroom and brought actual classes, doing typical classroom work, into the studio. Pupil participants have been complimented by the trade paper, *Variety*, for their "surprising disregard for lights, cameras and so forth." The Board of Education and the staff of WAAM cooperated in covering all grade levels and all parts of the city. An interesting by-product was the discussion of each broadcast by teachers' and PTA groups, with emphasis on the methods observed.

Toward New Horizons
By Eleanora Bowling Kane *

The teacher was preparing her classroom for a lesson. She arranged the little tables and chairs in informal groupings. She placed a piece of paper with a mimeographed assignment on each desk. From a large cardboard carton she drew a collection of children's paintings, and prepared to pin them on a side wall. A man in dungarees and plaid shirt, bucket in one hand, and paint brush stained with gray in the other, wandered in and waved her off. With deft, sweeping strokes he began to paint the dark gray wall a lighter shade of gray. The teacher put aside the children's art efforts until later and turned to the task of writing on the board. A blonde beauty in a blue bathrobe, with her hair wound tightly on aluminum curlers, drifted in and stared at the assignment the teacher was writing.

In a room across from the teacher's, another blonde, in slacks, carefully clothed a dummy leg in a sheer stocking. She straightened the seams and arranged the model in a showcase. Behind her, a refrigerator door banged, and a grinning youth emerged with a bottle of milk.

The teacher finished writing on the board and turned to prop up an easel against the wall. Just as she set it in place, the wall suddenly folded up and walked off, apparently of its own volition. A man on the other side of the erstwhile wall could be heard intoning: "So ladies, tear off the top of your nearest grocer." . . . There was laughter, silenced by a request over the "talk-back." The teacher's former classroom wall reappeared on another set. Brilliant lights flared. The bathrobed beauty took her place on the set. She yawned, stretched, went through the motions of a person just awakening.

The teacher continued with the arranging of her classroom. In a little while the freshly painted gray flat that represented one wall of her classroom would be dry and she could put up the children's pictures. The other wall, a "two-fold" now doing duty for an audition show, would reappear in her classroom as quickly and miraculously as it had left; and in a short time the set would be ready for another telecast in the series *Baltimore Classroom—1950*.

It would be a fairly safe bet, too, to assume that this teacher and her children would, that evening, do a fine job of showing parents what goes on in their children's schools.

Baltimore Classroom—1950,† presented every Friday evening from Feb-

---

* Specialist in radio education. The article appeared originally in the *Baltimore Bulletin of Education.*

† And its successors, 1951, 1952, and so on.

ruary tenth through May nineteenth over WAAM-TV, is something new and different in the way of television programs. Designed to interpret schools to the public, it features classroom procedures at all levels, from kindergarten through Junior College, and brings to the TV screen actual classroom situations. The lessons are unrehearsed. The teacher and the children are in the studio, using their own classroom equipment, transported to WAAM especially for this purpose. Two microphones hang overhead. Two, and sometimes three cameras pick up at close range the interesting classroom activities. The resulting programs have been good entertainment and have served a valuable means of worthwhile public relations.

Before each class has come before the cameras at seven o'clock on Friday evening, a great deal has preceded their appearance. What goes on before each program is indicative of fine station and school cooperation. Months before the show reached the screen, Joel Chaseman of WAAM's staff, accompanied by the school's radio and TV specialist, visited regularly in the schools, often several times a week, observing lessons, teachers, and children. Careful notes were taken, lessons discussed, and certain activities selected for presentation over television. Then, after the schedule had been set up, there were meetings with the "television teachers."

"What color shall I wear?"

"What about make-up?"

"When shall we let you know what materials we need?"

"Should the children stand when they talk?"

These other questions settled, we moved closer to production. Before any lesson is put on the air, a second conference is held. Every Tuesday morning, Dennis Kane, director of *Baltimore Classroom—1950*, and Joel Chaseman and Eleanora Bowling Kane, producers, visit the teacher who is scheduled for the following Friday evening. They discuss the teacher's plan, and may make some changes to fit the limitations of the TV medium. They look at the furniture and materials that will be needed, and then Dennis Kane's experienced fingers fly over the paper creating a stage set. Every piece of furniture is placed on the drawing. The teacher's position at the beginning of the show is indicated. Her movements from group to group can sometimes be plotted in advance so the director can have his cameramen ready to follow her. All material must be placed so that the children can see it and still not present their backs to the cameras. The audience must also be able to see the material the children are handling. This creates problems in arranging furniture and each lesson offers its own peculiar difficulties. At the time of this conference, the director also talks to the children and urges them not to wear their party dresses and their best suits. He tells them that they are going to school Friday night and they should wear their school clothes. He points to a plaid shirt, or a sweater.

. . . "That's just the thing," he says, and a child glows. He does not need to admonish the children to ignore the microphone dangling over their heads, or to be too conscious of the cameras. They have already seen these things. They know all about them, for a pre-telecast trip to WAAM for each class is one of the planned activities of the project.

The teacher, though, has still another job to do. At twelve-thirty on the day of her telecast, she joins the director and the school radio specialist at WAAM to set up the stage for the evening's program, as was mentioned at the beginning ot this article. When the bus rolls up the hill to the station and disgorges its eager load of children at 6:30, everything is ready. The youngsters crowd to the glass window to watch Kitty Dierken go through her paces. They speculate on how their teacher will look when she comes in wearing her television make-up . . . and then . . . the magic hour has arrived and they are summoned to their TV classroom. There are a few minutes for final instructions. The cameras roll up. The boom shoots its mike over the head of the class. The stage manager throws a cue to the teacher, and the show is on.

Baltimore Classroom—1950 is an important part of our program in public relations. In addition it offers children and teachers interesting and new experiences, opening up to them wide and new horizons. The use of the word horizons is an appropriate one here. Television waves move straight out toward the horizon instead of curving with the earth, and television has certainly, in a short and exciting time, opened new horizons to educators. One of these is the use of TV as a teaching medium. Baltimore is one of several cities experimenting in this area, and is one of the pioneers in the field.

Students in the radio and television departments of the University of Miami undertook as a project for the 1950 school term the making of a documentary film, stressing the advantages of their institution. The film portrayed undergraduate recreational activities unique to southern Florida and featured such unusual subject areas as progressive teaching methods, specially designed tropical architecture, radio-television courses, tropical-food research, marine-laboratory work, and other unusual aspects. The film will be used for nontheatrical and television showing.

The Milwaukee Public Library instituted the use of television in 1950, over station WTMJ-TV. A quarter-hour weekly program, *Your Library Story* features stories for children from five to ten years old, visualized by illustrations from the books. A five-minute *Library Quiz* is built around the most interesting questions asked of the research and reference department, and calls attention "to the fact that the public library is always happy to be of service to them in answering any question for which they may need reference."

Clearly, television can be a powerful medium for public relations. It can show parents and taxpayers how their money is being spent and can effectively highlight such physically impressive things as new school furniture, equipment, and teaching aids. In more subtle fashion, it can show how teaching has changed "since father's time" and can win the support of the public not only for school funds but for new school policies.

12

The Commercial Program for Children

◇◇◇

Is it of any concern to the teacher to know what programs her pupils listen to after school?

What are some of the conclusions found by surveys made in this field?

What aspects of some juvenile programs have been criticized?

What have been some contributing causes of poor quality programs?

What can the schools do to encourage selective radio listening?

What improvements can parents, teachers, and broadcasters make?

What new problems has television introduced?

◇◇◇◇◇◇◇NO PROGRESSIVE TEACHER who is serving youth today will doubt that it is one of her functions to guide her pupils in the worthy use of leisure time. Nevertheless, all too often such phrases as "worthy use of leisure time" are tossed glibly about and in actual classroom practice too little is done to achieve these accepted goals. Instead, the more typical procedure is to wrestle with the minutiae of a course of study while harboring the hope that somewhere along the line the youngsters will acquire the attitudes that make for wholesome, successful living in a changing society. As Professor W. A. Orton of Smith College once stated:

But in regard to the culture, the intelligence and the morale of our democracy, we still believe for the most part in the genial destiny of good luck . . . so we expose our young to commercial stimuli of a mechanized culture—to the syndicated comic strip, the funnies, the commercial movies, commercialized sport, commercial radio . . . and we assume that out of all this they will "naturally" develop intelligence, morale and a sense of values equal to the demand that modern citizenship will make upon them.[1]

What influences a child's thinking? The sum total of *all* his experiences. Are these educative experiences confined to the classroom? Obviously not. Some, perhaps most, take place during his so-called leisure time. In general, to the degree that these informal learning processes are guided, they make for mental growth in desirable directions. Many psychologists hold that the formation of attitudes is essentially emotional rather than intellectual in character. When the child is permitted to undergo an emotional experience without regard for its influence upon his attitudes, it is quite likely that some of the attitudes thus developed will be definitely undesirable.

Is it of concern to the teacher that one of the child's every four waking hours is spent at the radio? Of course it is. And it is not so much the amount of listening as the quality of it that is important. If, as Edgar Dale notes, "The average high school student listens to the radio two hours a day, sees a movie a week, and reads the paper for about thirty-five minutes daily,"[2] then all these influences in terms

---

[1] W. A. Orton, "Education by Radio," *Education on the Air*, Ohio State University, 1935, p. 65.
[2] Edgar Dale, "Open Letters," *The News Letter*, December, 1940, p. 2.

of their qualitative conditioning of the child are significant to the teacher. This is especially true since these great educational influences are in the hands of noneducators.[3]

In the American scheme of broadcasting, the commercial program designed especially for children is planned directly or indirectly to stimulate the purchase of certain commodities.

E. Evalyn Grumbine, in *Reaching Juvenile Markets*, says:

Few people realize the broad scope of the juvenile market as it exists today. It is estimated that one-third of all merchandise sold in this country consists of products consumed and used by children. Manufacturers of a wide variety of goods are producing an ever-increasing number of articles for children. The list includes foods of all kinds, wearing apparel which stresses a complete ensemble for the child from undergarments to properly matched accessories, beverages from chocolate food drinks to fruit juices, household appliances that may be used easily and safely by children as well as adults, toilet accessories with an appeal through health and school activities built around the use of certain soaps, tooth paste, etc., home furnishings for the greater comfort and pleasure of children, books, and toys. Transportation companies, including those operating railroads and airplanes and steamships, as well as great gasoline and oil companies, also have developed appeals to the juvenile.[4]

The influence of broadcasting upon the child is recognized by advertisers perhaps even more so than it is by teachers. The same author notes:

The salesmanship of the juvenile is irresistible. His prospect is usually mother, father, or a doting relative anxious to grant any reasonable and many unreasonable requests. If a child is intrigued by the offer of a premium described in glowing terms over the radio or pictured in an appealing manner in comic-strip or juvenile magazine advertising, adults rarely refuse to purchase the product so that the child may have the coveted prize. We know that this not only gives pleasure to the child but also to the adult, who feels that by granting these requests he is contributing to the happiness of the child.[5]

However, in justice to the advertisers, Grumbine's following comment should be included:

---

[3] John De Boer, "Radio and Children's Emotions," *School and Society*, September 16, 1939, p. 369.
[4] E. Evalyn Grumbine, *op. cit.*, p. 6.
[5] *Ibid.*, p. 21.

When children are saving box tops or labels to secure a bigger prize, mother continues to buy the necessary cereal or the product as long as the youngsters will eat or use it. This is true, of course, only when the product is a good one that offers fair value for the money spent. Parents will not continue to purchase cheap merchandise even to satisfy the desires of the juvenile.[6]

Children's programs, like those planned for adults, are of various types but generally they may be classified as follows: (a) legends and fairy tales, (b) dramatized adventures, (c) musical programs, (d) sketches, (e) song-stories, (f) comic-strip serials, and (g) novelty programs.

Local stations have presented a large variety of programs for children. Among the more successful forms are the following as listed by Grumbine:

1. *Programs Featuring Local Amateur Talent.*—Boys and girls are invited to come to the radio station and take part in the broadcast. Some of the children sing, others tap dance or recite.

2. *Interviewing Local Children Over the Air.*—In order to test out reactions to this type of program, a station reaching about 150,000 homes interviewed a four-year-old child. She was taken into the studio, where the microphone was alive. By talking to her casually, the announcer drew many amusing comments about her home life—how her mother burned the pies, how she did not have to go to church because she was only four years old, that she was going to visit her grandmother that afternoon, that she had fallen down and hurt herself the day before, etc. From this two-minute interview scores of letters were received both from people who knew the child and from others who did not know her.

3. *Birthday Clubs for Boys and Girls.*—Children are asked to write in and tell their birthday date so that it may be announced over the radio on that day. In some cases requests are made to have certain songs played or sung. When time permits this is done in addition to the birthday announcements. Birthday cards or buttons are sent to the children by some stations.

4. *Safety Clubs.*—Children who belong pledge themselves to be careful at all times while crossing the streets, riding their bicycles, roller skating, or playing games at home and at school. Announcers urge boys and girls to take all possible precaution to avoid any kind of accident. Safety club pins are proudly worn by members of the club.

5. *Story Hours.*—A good storyteller over the radio is sure to hold the

---

[6] *Ibid.*, pp. 21–22.

interest of a juvenile audience. Stories of all kinds should be selected—those with thrilling adventure, light mystery, and interesting heroes of all ages being the most popular.

6. *Spelling Bee.*—In some states spelling bees are conducted by radio stations, sponsored by local merchants and the Chamber of Commerce. Winners are then sent to finals held in the state capital or other large cities in the state.

7. *Contests.*—Many different kinds of contests are promoted to interest boys and girls and include essays, drawings, best letters about given subjects, identifying musical selections of popular tunes played, etc.

8. *Health Club.*—Local dairies particularly have promoted many successful health clubs among boys and girls. Drinking a certain amount of milk daily is usually a prerequisite for members of these clubs. Needless to say they receive the hearty support of parents, who are glad for assistance in getting children to drink an adequate amount of milk. In addition to membership cards and buttons, prizes are given by entering contests to save bottle tops and labels from dairy products consumed by the family during various periods of time.[7]

Programs such as the above are generally scheduled in the early morning, late afternoon, or early evening. The late afternoon period is currently the most popular.

What the Surveys Have Shown

To what programs do children listen? What are their preferences and dislikes? Numerous surveys have been made to determine these and similar facts. A brief mention of the conclusions of only a few of these will be made here.

K. H. Baker (1937), on the basis of information gained from the distribution of 10,000 questionnaires to Minnesota children, concluded that they prefer emotionally charged or exciting programs whether they were written for children or adults.[8]

W. L. Gottenberg and R. L. Neal (1940), in a questionnaire survey of 963 children, submitted these conclusions:

1. Regardless of the economic status of their homes, 903 out of 963 pupils reported possession of a radio to which 819 of them listened

---

[7] *Ibid.*, pp. 220–221.
[8] K. H. Baker, "Radio Listening and Socio-Economic Status," *Psychological Record*, 1937, p. 138.

daily. 582 of these pupils did their listening between the hours of six and nine-fifteen o'clock in the evening.

2. The type of program that is preferred by youth is one that possesses considerable dramatization.
3. The findings of this investigation suggest that children are not especially interested in juvenile broadcasts. Two facts show that they prefer adult programs: first, they listen for the most part between the hours of six and nine-fifteen in the evening during which time the programs directed mainly toward adult audiences are on the air; and, second, most programs which they prefer are designed primarily for adult consumption.
4. The children in this investigation showed a definite preference for cowboy, old time, band, fast, and national folk music rather than for classical, vocal, slow, and romantic.
5. This study shows that children do gain information by listening to the radio, since the average number of items listed by them was 1.6. This conclusion is further substantiated by the fact that 90% of these children believed that they had acquired some information.[9]

Roy Robinson (1940) reported the results of a survey made in Michigan of the radio listening for one week of approximately 2,000 elementary school children:

1. This study shows that the average pupil in grades four, five, six, seven, and eight listens at least one and one-half hours per day to the radio.
2. He listens a less amount on Saturday and Sunday than on other days, even though he is home a greater time.
3. He listens, as would be expected, more to evening programs than to afternoon programs.
4. If he lives farther from a large metropolitan station he is likely to tune in a greater variety of stations, but not necessarily a greater variety of programs.
5. His listening is confined largely to network programs.
6. Eight stations in this region supply 85.5 per cent of the total radio programs listened to.
7. Forty-eight single programs and thirty-one continuing programs provide 47.5 per cent of the total week's listening.
8. This study does not show, among other things, why children like these programs, nor that they are of the children's own selection;

[9] W. L. Gottenberg and R. L. Neal, "Radio at Home." *The Phi Delta Kappan,* May, 1940, pp. 418, 421.

it merely shows that they are the ones children record that they listen to.[10]

A comprehensive study made in 1939 by the Wilmette, Illinois, PTA was productive of some interesting material. Questionnaires were filled out by 1,825 pupils in grades 1 through 8. A few of the findings were:

1. Children listen to the radio about sixteen hours a week.
2. Even in grades one to three, children follow 13.5 different programs.
3. There are few programs produced *for children* that appeal to children beyond the third-grade level.
4. Exciting first and then funny. These are the two chief requisites of a radio program if it is to satisfy the majority of our youngsters.
5. It is evident that girls demand excitement fully as much as boys at the lower ages, but less from the fourth grade on. The peak of this desire for excitement comes at the fourth grade level for both boys and girls and wanes from then on.
6. According to statements of the children themselves, more than one-third of them are subject to some parental restrictions on their radio listening. There is less restriction as the children grow older and more on the girls than on the boys.[11]

A. L. Eisenberg (1936) made a thorough study of more than 3,000 children in the New York metropolitan area. Among his conclusions were the following:

Radio listening is preferred by children to such competing activities as listening to a phonograph, reading, playing a musical instrument, and solving a puzzle. Going to the movies, listening to an orchestra on the stage, and reading the "funnies" hold greater attraction for them than does the radio. In this expression of preference the only disagreement evidenced between the boys and girls is with regard to ball playing. The boys would much rather engage in this activity, while the girls prefer listening to the radio. . . . Children are directed to programs by the following means, arranged in order of greatest frequency: (1) recommendations by friends, 42 per cent, (2) radio sheet, 29 per cent, (3) random dialing, 24 per cent, (4) advertisements, 4 per cent, (5) adult guidance, 1 per cent. . . . In tuning in, the children make no distinction whatever between the so-called

---

[10] Roy Robinson, "Listening Habits of Michigan Children," *Implications of the Radio in Education,* 12th Yearbook of the Department of Elementary School Principals, Michigan Education Association, p. 32.
[11] "The Home Radio Listening of Wilmette Grade-School Children," Bulletin issued by Wilmette, Illinois, PTA, pp. 8, 10, 24, 25, 30.

adult and juvenile programs. The time of broadcast determines whether
or not a program will have a child audience. Little is done by the teacher
in directing children to worth-while programs. Only one third of the children report that their teachers ever directed them in their radio listening.[12]

John De Boer (1939) studied the listening habits of 1,000 Chicago
school children. An excerpt from his report indicates:

While mystery and horror stories are conspicuously absent among the
programs consistently popular with children of all ages, child-adventure
series lead the list of radio programs preferred by all children. Some,
though not all, of these programs deal with the detection of crime and the
apprehension of criminals, but the qualities common to all these programs
are action and suspense. A notable element in the programs which are
preferred by young children is the presence of child characters in the story.
But probably the most important conclusion that may be drawn from the
evidence is the fact that children do respond intensely to radio drama and
that they respond to an extremely wide diversity of types of situations.[13]

Two major, and perhaps obvious, generalizations can be drawn from
such surveys: (a) children listen to many adult programs; (b) the
exciting story is especially attractive to children.

How significant are surveys of listener preference? Is it not true that
the quality of appreciation is determined largely by the type of exposure? Edgar Dale says,

Tastes are developed by the kind of things which we taste. "If children
are brought up on a diet of excellent music, they prefer it. If they have
been brought up on a diet of salt pork and beans, they prefer that. If they
are used to trash and sentimentality in reading, they prefer that. If we
honestly wish to develop good taste in reading, radio listening, and the
movies we shall have to pay the price, namely, to make excellent things
available to children.[14]

Some Common Criticisms

It is evident that there has not been general satisfaction
with the commercial radio program for children. A similar reaction
that has developed with television will be noted later in this chapter.

---

[12] A. L. Eisenberg, *Children and Radio Programs*, Columbia University Press,
1936, pp. 184–185.
[13] John De Boer, *op. cit.*, p. 370.
[14] Edgar Dale, in editorial comment to *The Phi Delta Kappan*, May, 1940, p. 411.

First, concerning radio—what have been the most common criticisms?

Since the radio through the human voice provides a more intimate approach than does cold print, the influence upon the emotions, especially those of children, is greater. Investigations have shown that a tense moment in a program may cause, among some children, an acceleration in pulse rate from 80 to 130 beats per minute, accompanied by sudden changes in blood pressure.[15] Others have complained that radio interferes with meals, the performance of household tasks, and normal bedtime. The children will postpone these while listening with rapt attention to another thrilling adventure. Some parents claim to have traced poor sleeping habits to such over-stimulation. After listening to an exciting mystery or ghost story, children have awakened screaming with terror from a horrible nightmare.

According to F. L. Redefer, some of these broadcasts have been criticized as "appealing to low motives, exhibiting poor taste, as inculcating poor English, as exploiting immature children through advertising statements, and using unethical means to sell the sponsor's product." [16] The situations portrayed are unreal and beyond providing cheap entertainment—they have no worth-while purpose. De Boer indicates that "many psychologists believe that the programs portraying crime and the pursuit of criminals actually contribute to delinquency because the emotional satisfactions inherent in struggle and vicarious escape are more influential than any reasonable disapproval of crime that may be introduced into the story." [17] Variety of September 18, 1940, reported that some of the leading police chiefs condemned such crime dramas. Efforts to boycott them were encouraged.

Dr. I. Keith Tyler has summarized some of the problems resulting from home radio listening as follows:

(1) There is the competition of radio with more physically active play, (2) competition of radio with other types of worth-while activities; music lessons, reading, etc., (3) effect upon the child of being emotionally stimulated without being provided with an outlet, (4) through the continued use

---

[15] John De Boer, op. cit., p. 371.
[16] Frederick L. Redefer, "Radio Programs for Children," Education on the Air, Ohio State University, 1935, p. 129.
[17] John De Boer, op. cit., p. 371.

of stereotyped plots and casting, the child receives false notions about people and situations. . . . Such programs are educating children for a kind of world that doesn't exist, and making it more difficult for them to be really effective as citizens in the kind of world in which they actually do live, (5) there is the interference of the child's listening with home routines, and (6) effects of such listening upon vocabulary and speech habits.[18]

The most common complaint made concerning these programs has not been so much that they are specifically harmful, but rather that they are generally useless. A tremendous influence for good upon the growing generation, it is stated, is not being fully utilized. Dorothy Gordon, a veteran radio artist, put it this way: "It is not so much what *is* on the air that is dangerous to the youth of America—it is rather what is *not* on the air." [19]

Several Contributing Causes

Lack of Experience. It was probably lack of experience in broadcasting for children that caused some of the earlier advertisers to err in this field. Certainly no national business institution would deliberately develop a program that might cause some resentment among parents. The measure of effective commercial broadcasting is the degree of good will created. If there is some doubt as to this achievement, let alone a negative development, then sponsors are well aware that the advertising dollar is wasted.

In addition to this lack of knowledge in a rapidly growing field, other causes for such difficulty with children's programs may be discovered. And perhaps these difficulties are not confined to juvenile programs but to all phases of the radio program structure.

Broadcasting Necessitates Quantity Rather than Quality. The microphone gobbles up words so quickly that a premium is placed upon quantity rather than quality. Whereas a good child's story is sold and resold and royalties may be forthcoming for years, a children's radio program is presented but once and is gone. Under such circumstances one could hardly expect the best writers to perspire while they grind out five high-quality programs a week or sixty-five for

[18] I. Keith Tyler, "Teaching of Discriminate Listening," in *Implications of the Radio in Education*, pp. 55–56.
[19] Dorothy Gordon, *All Children Listen*, George W. Stewart, 1942, p. 15.

THE COMMERCIAL PROGRAM FOR CHILDREN

the conventional thirteen-week contract. If quality is to be a major concern, radio writing will merit greater rewards.

Advertising Exercises Too Much Editorial Authority. Another cause of the low cultural level of some of the programs has been attributed to "radio's complete identification with the machinery of advertising, which limits it as an instrument for diffusing culture." [20]

Merrill Dennison, the noted radio writer, while praising the great contribution that radio has made toward an elevation of American cultural life, complains, nevertheless:

> Of all programs the commercials will continue to arouse the loudest protests as long as the advertising agency occupies the dominating position it now does in the selection and production of sponsored programs. Half by accident, they have come to exercise editorial authority without responsibility. Could the agency return to the same position it occupies in the magazine world, most of the broadcasting industry's unhappy relations would automatically disappear.[21]

Students of broadcasting have stated that the radio networks, being private enterprises, have been unusually aware of their responsibilities and obligations as vital social forces. But as they become increasingly subordinated in their program policies to the wishes of advertisers, their constructive efforts are limited.

General Indifference of Listeners. The general indifference of listeners is another cause of mediocre programs. As noted elsewhere, listeners may complain but they seldom suggest. Investigations such as the Wilmette Survey have shown that only a minority of the parents regard the radio as sufficiently important to warrant their attention and guidance. The children have few standards for judgment and there is a crying need for the development of discriminate listening among youth. The school's function as it relates to the latter will be discussed more fully at a later point.

Some teachers have pointed out that if children's programs were less often in serial form there might be less of that "must listen" feeling.

---

[20] Clarissa Lorenz, "Radio's Ugly Duckling," *The Horn Book*, September, 1939, p. 280.
[21] Merrill Dennison, "Soap-opera," *Harper's Magazine*, May, 1939, p. 498.

Schools Can and Should Help in Developing Better Broadcasting

See the Broadcaster's Viewpoint. However, the broadcaster's point of view should be considered before one attempts to pass judgment concerning juvenile programs. In the first place, any blanket statement as to their quality is foolish. There are excellent programs for children as well as poor ones. Thus to be an intelligent critic one should first be a listener. Ask most critics what programs they have heard recently and for what length of time, and their answer generally suggests that they do not know what is available.

Some broadcasters have indicated that even the critics cannot agree which programs are objectionable and which are not. It is difficult to state just how much excitement is too much. Children differ and their reactions vary accordingly; therefore, much depends upon parental guidance at home.

Generations of children have survived ghost stories, dime novels, and the exploits of Nick Carter and Jesse James. A dull intellectual diet is not enough. At the close of the school day, the child seeks relief and, like most of his elders, he wants entertainment. Children have always sought adventure. These days, especially, when many a child is reared within the confines of modern urban living, some outlet must be provided for a naturally healthy and adventurous spirit. So runs the argument.

Even the accepted children's classics, it is shown, were full of thrilling adventures. C. L. Menser observes:

I have been tremendously interested in children's programs. Indeed, one of the most successful programs with which I have been connected was a children's program, in which a number of boys caught another little boy and stuffed him into a furnace, and then hammered on the outside of it. Maybe there were a number of children who did not sleep that night. I do not know—I wonder sometimes, however, what would have kept them awake if the radio had not been there to do it for them. That episode was lifted almost intact from a well-known book. You will know it when I tell you the boy put in the furnace was named Georgie Bassett. Two of the children hammering were Penrod and Sam. It was written by a notable gentleman from Indiana named Tarkington. I think it would be just a little silly to rise up against Tarkington for writing interesting and entertaining episodes the like of which happen every day in backyards of America.[22]

Psychologists do not agree as to the effect of programs. Arthur T. Jersild of Columbia University, who has served as a consulting psychologist for one of the major networks, makes these comments concerning children's programs. They are excerpts from a talk on this subject broadcast several years ago:

Any scheme for good programs for children must necessarily build upon children's interests. This raises a problem right from the start, for the things children have liked best in dramatic sketches have also been criticized most. Now, who are wrong, the children or the critics? Actually, both may be largely right. Children have a right to their likes and interests. Broadcasters have a right to meet these interests. But critics (or anybody else) have a right to object if program-makers, instead of dealing constructively with children's interests, merely exploit them.

Perhaps someone will protest, why not let the kids be kids and give them what they want? Fair enough. This slogan is just the thing. But when we apply it to other things in daily life, we try to do so with a sense of proportion, and with the child's welfare in mind. If a child has a sweet tooth, we do not feed him only on candy. If he likes an exciting story, we do not proceed to scare the daylights out of him. If he is ignorant on a subject and comes to us in good faith, we do not take advantage of his ignorance, but attempt to give him a good answer.

The same sort of sincerity may rightfully be expected in a children's program.

Standards can, of course, be too rigid, just as they can be too lax. The typical child is not a highbrow, steeped in culture and art. He is just a healthy-minded, somewhat naive youngster with a live curiosity and a strong desire, among other things, for vicarious adventure. . . .

Actually, this problem of excitement seldom comes along. If a broadcast has to depend upon terrifying suspense, it usually will have other questionable features. The important thing is the underlying quality. The more ably a children's script is prepared and produced, the more genuine its appeal, and the less it will try to inflame the child in order to hold his interest.

Another thing that children like is a story that involves conflict.

We know that conflict and opposition are vital to all drama, whether for children or adults. An easy way to meet this interest is to give the child nothing but crime. Of course, a child can hear about crime without thereby acquiring a motive for committing crime but the usual "crime formula" has no place in a children's program.

---

[22] *Education on the Air*, Ohio State University, 1935, p. 141.

There is not much good to be learned from sham battles with criminals. On the contrary, it may be quite unwholesome constantly to emphasize vice, to advertise the techniques of crime and tacitly to convey the impression that the way to be a hero or to get a thrill is either to chase a crook or to be one.

Again, in solving this crime problem, the important thing is the basic content of the program and the general formula on which it is built.

In a well-written serial for children, conflict and opposition will enter into the story, just as will other issues and themes. It will not be built merely upon suspicion and vindictiveness, but will give play to a wide range of human feeling. Although there may be a crime in genuine drama, the most valid forms of opposition will not be found in the antics of criminals. . . .

When we look once more at our hypothetical child, we notice that he spends his time on many things that don't interest grownups. In like manner, he may enjoy a radio program which to his parents seems utterly inane. Here we may note one of the most frequent criticisms of children's programs is that they are trashy, cheap, artificial and absurd. When this criticism is made, it should be remembered that a thing may not suit adult needs and still be suitable for children. When a boy gets a pair of pants that are just right for him, do we object if they don't also happen to fit his father? This point is often overlooked when criticisms are made. But it can also be abused. If a child is not as wise as he might be, and is somewhat undiscriminating in his tastes, this does not mean that we should ply him with humbug. . . .

If a program is based on fantasy, legend, or fairy tale themes, let it be true to its pattern. If it purports to deal with real events, let it be substantially true to its setting, even though it is fictional timing and detail. If it dramatizes a literary classic, let it reproduce some of the qualities that made the story a classic, rather than select only the spiciest parts.

To be authentic, a story need not reproduce all the plodding details of everyday life, but it cannot be made authentic simply by patching a few items of truth on an unsound structure. If a program is artistic in its treatment of fantasy, or gives a genuine treatment of historical or contemporary events, it also has cultural values, even though it frankly is meant to entertain and not to teach. . . .

It must also be remembered that children's broadcasts seldom come singly. Let one be trashy and trade upon a child's ignorance and you thereby have lowered the standards for all. You also make it harder for a worthwhile program to succeed. . . .

The principle of good workmanship, both in the writing and in the production of a program, covers also the matter of grammar and diction. Bad grammar and poor diction obviously are open to criticism if simply dragged in for artificial effect. A well-rounded production will, however, present people pretty much as they are, and will not portray all manner of persons as purists in their speech.

A pressing problem in some homes is that children want to listen to the radio when parents feel that they should be doing something else. Behind this there sometimes is a conviction that what the child listens to is not worth his time. To the extent that this is true, it is only natural that parents should resent the extra problem which radio brings to the home. It is the broadcaster's responsibility to supply children's programs that are worthwhile. Broadcasters cannot, of course, go beyond this to decide how much time a child should spend at the radio. Sometimes the difficulty is caused by children's interest in adult broadcasts. Here, of course, there likewise is a limit to what the broadcasters can do, for the audience would object if everything broadcast during the day or night were planned solely from the point of view of children. . . .[23]

Even if such radio fare is admitted to be generally harmless and, as some have insisted, useless as well, then that fact is significant to the schools. The cultural measure of any influence, be it radio or otherwise, is "not whether it produces applause, but whether it is worth applauding." An experience which an average child undergoes more than two hours daily and which proves to be innocuous does not per se imply acceptance. An absence of harm is not the criterion for judging the worthy use of a leisure time. Rather, what merits has the experience? What contributions does it make? It is perhaps chiefly on this score that the commercial radio program for children requires improvement.

Educational Leaders Should Work with Radio Executives. It is commonplace in the radio industry that "everybody thinks he knows the business." But the point is that radio broadcasting is more than just a "business." It is a dynamic social force for good or evil dependent upon the ideals and the intelligence motivating it. To that extent, teachers have not only a right, but an obligation as well, to see that this major influence on the child's personality is used in a socially desirable manner.

Perhaps John De Boer points the way when he says:

I believe more progress would be made if the educational leaders would say to the radio officials: "We do not hold you responsible for the instruction of children in the facts of history, or geography, or mathematics, or English grammar. We will take care of these matters in the schools or in

---

[23] Arthur T. Jersild, "Children's Radio Programs," *Talks,* CBS, April, 1938, pp. 3–7.

special educational broadcasts. If your entertainment is artistically prepared and presented, we are confident that it will contribute to the enrichment of children's experience background and make them better informed. But your particular, though not exclusive, province is the emotional life of the child. We expect you to present programs which will assist children to meet the problems arising out of their social contacts and to develop those attitudes which are needed in the complex social environment of today." [24]

Others who have studied the influence of commercialized entertainment upon children have stated that it is only to be expected that the level of pupil taste in one medium, for instance, the radio, cannot be much more advanced than it is in other fields, the movies, magazines, comic strips, etc.

Speaking of both radio and motion pictures, Edgar Dale raises an interesting question.

Here is a problem which needs a concerted attack by school people. We need to use the approach that we have used with the public libraries. Through the public library we make available to the children not the good with the bad, but only the good that has been carefully selected. And we support that good by public taxation. Should we not in the same fashion make available to children the best in radio and motion pictures at public expense through children's theatres, and perhaps also through local radio programs? I don't know the answer to this problem, but I believe that the tastes of children are so important that we need to think as honestly about radio and movie tastes as we have about tastes in the field of books.[25]

That there has been some improvement in children's programs no fair-minded parent or teacher will deny. Much of this improvement is due no doubt to the reactions of adults at home and elsewhere. Nevertheless, a share of this credit should go to the broadcasters and advertisers, for if there is anything that distinguishes American industry it is its ability to feel the public's pulse. Progress has been made and will continue to be made provided that there continues an evident consumer desire for such improvement.

Planning for Improvement

Broadcasters Have Taken Steps for Improvement of Juvenile Programs.   Each of the leading networks, as well as the National

---

[24] John De Boer, *op. cit.*, p. 370.
[25] Edgar Dale, *op. cit.*, p. 411.

Association of Broadcasters, has developed a code of practices and program policies that recognizes and attempts to forestall some of the difficulties related to the broadcasting industry. Of course, the skeptic may observe that the presence of rules and regulations does not *ipso facto* guarantee high quality. That may be, but if pleasing the public is only good business sense, then it is quite probable that such rules do modify practices. True, there may be some differences as to the definition of terms but that is to be expected when generalizations must be employed.

The following is the section on children's programs as included in the code of program standards developed by the National Association of Broadcasters (in effect as of July 1, 1948).

Children's programs should be based upon sound social concepts and should reflect respect for parents, law and order, clean living, high morals, fair play and honorable behavior.

They should convey the commonly accepted moral, social and ethical ideals characteristic of American life.

They should contribute to the healthy development of personality and character.

There should be no appeals urging children to purchase the product in order to keep the program on the air, or which for any purpose encourage children to enter strange places or to converse with strangers.[26]

The following material is taken from the book entitled *NBC Program Policies and Working Manual,* copyrighted by The National Broadcasting Company in 1944, with whose permission this material is reprinted:

POLICIES APPLICABLE TO CHILDREN'S PROGRAMS

In addition to all policies and standards of the Company being applied to children's programs, especial care should be exercised where the values of right feeling and good taste are concerned.

A. RESPECT FOR LAW

All stories must reflect respect for law and order, adult authority, good morals and clean living.

The hero or heroine and other sympathetic characters must be portrayed as intelligent and morally courageous. The theme must stress the importance of mutual respect of one man for another, and should emphasize the desirability of fair play

---

[26] *Broadcasting Yearbook,* 1949, p. 37.

and honorable behavior. Cowardice, malice, deceit, selfishness and disrespect for law must be avoided in the delineation of any character presented in the light of a hero to the child listener.

B. ADVENTURE

Adventure stories may be accepted subject to the following prohibitions:

No torture or suggestion of torture.

No horror—present or impending.

No use of the supernatural or of superstition likely to arouse fear.

No profanity or vulgarity.

No kidnapping or threats of kidnapping.

In order that children will not be emotionally upset, no program or episode shall end with an incident which will create in their minds morbid suspense or hysteria.

C. COMMERCIAL COPY

It is consistent that fair play and considerate behavior be reflected through the commercial copy as in the script itself. Advice "to be sure to tell mother" or "ask mother to buy" must be limited to twice in the program. The greatest possible care must be used to see that no misleading or extravagant statements be made in commercial copy on children's programs. When promises are made as to the benefits to be derived from use of the product advertised, it will be necessary to submit proof that such promises are valid and truthful and will be kept.

D. CONTESTS AND OFFERS

Contests and offers which encourage children to enter strange places and to converse with strangers in an effort to collect box tops or wrappers may present a definite element of danger to the children. Therefore, such contests and offers are not acceptable.

E. DRAMATIZED APPEALS

No appeal may be made to the child to help characters in the story by sending in box tops or wrappers; nor may any actor remain in character and, in the commercial copy, address the child, urging him to purchase the product in order to keep the program on the air, or make similar appeals.

F. SECRET CLUBS

The forming of clubs is often introduced on children's programs. Sometimes initiation requirements and other rules of such clubs are disseminated in code form. Full details concerning the organization of children's secret society or code must be submitted to the

National Broadcasting Company at least ten business days before its introduction on the air.[27]

The Columbia Broadcasting System and others have adopted policies which are similar and so it will not be necessary to include them here.

Parents Must Help If There Is to Be Improvement. Constructive efforts which will contribute to the improvement of juvenile programs need not be confined to the activities of broadcasters and advertisers. Intelligent parents recognize their responsibilities in this endeavor.

Parental efforts in this direction perhaps can be considered as being twofold: those which relate to the consumer, that is the child, and those which relate to the producer, the broadcaster.

A knowledge of some of these forms of parental guidance in home listening is important for teachers since they are occasionally asked by parents just what can be done at home. An offhand reply such as "listen to the better programs" is not satisfactory. What, then, can parents do to help?

PARENTAL ACTION AS RELATED TO THE CHILD. First, the parent should be aware that, whereas the child at home can read only those materials which are available, with the radio the child has access to all programs including those not planned for him at all. Therefore, some guidance is needed, and the influence of parents can be very significant in determining the values that result from home listening.

If the child is to develop a growing sense of discrimination in all the arts—music, literature, drama, and others—both parents and teachers have an important job to do. It is simple enough to ask the schools to do this too (and the trend is always in this direction); yet an intelligent adult accepts this as one of the responsibilities of parenthood.

Putting the child before the radio and commanding him to listen to a certain program, because the parent has heard somewhere that this program has merit, will not result in discriminate listening. Nor will it come by abruptly shutting off the radio because an objectionable feature is being presented. Real guidance is a cooperative effort and

---

[27] "NBC Program Policies," National Broadcasting Company, 1944, pp. 20–21.

only by listening with the child and then calmly discussing the program with him, its merits and faults, can such efforts actually prove helpful. Intelligent guidance does not emphasize denial. A positive approach is needed. If the parent, after a reasonable amount of listening, has selected several programs she deems specially valuable she will call these to the child's attention at the time they are broadcast. More than that, she may even develop, as some have done, a simple program log which she posts beside the radio, thus further encouraging selective dialing.

The modern parent recognizes that the emotional stability of the child is related closely to his state of health. If the youngster is fatigued or ill, any listening to a very exciting broadcast should certainly be discouraged. Many parents make a preliminary examination of their child's reading material but they frequently neglect to give similar attention to an even more stimulating medium.

Even aside from overstimulation, the influence of home listening upon the child's physical condition should not be neglected by parents. If the child listens to the radio daily, there is danger that the youngster's playtime outdoors is being reduced and perhaps needed exercise is being neglected.

Here also the parents will want to organize the home environment so that listening to the radio is but one of the child's many activities. Perhaps tuning in during the afternoon hours should be discouraged. Opportunities for group play should be provided in the yard or in the house. Nothing will do more to encourage such play at home and the visiting of friends than the provision of play space for the youngster's own use. These, therefore, are some of the suggestions the teacher may have for the parent.

PARENTAL ACTION AS RELATED TO THE BROADCASTERS. A second type of parental action concerning juvenile programs is that which deals with the broadcasters.

In general, such activities can be classified as being either of a negative or positive nature.

Among the former have been various written and vocal complaints made to the broadcasters, some by organizations and others by individuals. As noted, even consumer boycotts have been threatened. Some critics have indicated that when the broadcaster informs parents to tune out the programs they deem offensive the problem remains.

for there is little that can be done at home if the listener's choice is limited.

The values of listener's protests have been emphasized by some and minimized by others. Dennison, for example, observes that "an articulate minority, even if microscopic, can wield more influence than a vast quiescent mass of the public. This is particularly true in broadcasting, where a single letter of disapproval carries more weight than 1,000 letters of affirmation." [28] On the other hand, some have stated that if the multitude remains indifferent there is little likelihood of a change. The vagueness of most complaints, the frequent disagreement as to faults, and the lack of understanding of radio advertising operations tend to reduce the effectiveness of such protests.

A positive approach to the problem has been tried in some communities with genuine effect. In the first place, some studies have shown that parents approve far more programs than they disapprove. Before condemning juvenile programs universally, an attempt is made to discover what their actual effects are. Surveys are conducted to determine what children and parents think of the programs, specific suggestions for improving them are noted, then forwarded where they may be most productive, guidance hints for parents are listed, etc.

A survey of this type undertaken jointly by the school and community can be of real educational significance. It can serve to acquaint indifferent parents with the concern that others feel for making home listening a meaningful as well as an entertaining experience. As applied to the children, the survey can help to make them aware that there exist varying standards in radio as in other art forms. For the organization an enterprise such as this provides an educational experience of benefit to all who participate.

It should be understood that a constructive approach of this nature does not require huge funds or even a large membership. The home listening survey, noted elsewhere, which was undertaken in Wilmette, Illinois, a community of 15,000 inhabitants, is an excellent example of the modest but meaningful type of investigation that can be undertaken by a progressive parent-teacher association. An excerpt from the questionnaire used in this survey for grades 4 through 8 is shown on the following pages.[29]

---

[28] Merrill Dennison, *op. cit.*
[29] Furnished through the courtesy of the Wilmette, Ill., P.T.A.

Name _____ Age _____ Boy ____ Girl ____
School _____ Grade _____ Teacher _____
How many people are there in your family? _____
How many radios? _____
Do you have a radio all your own? _____
Are there any programs to which you are not permitted to listen? _____
    What programs? _____
    _____
Do you usually study or read with a radio going? _____ If so, does it
    bother you? _____
Is the radio on while your family has dinner? _____ If so, what
    program is on? _____
Do you like to listen to stories that are exciting? _____
Do you like to listen to stories that scare you? _____
Which do you like best? (Check one) Each broadcast to be a complete
    story _____ A serial _____
Do you ever worry about what may happen to the hero after the story ends
    for the day? _____
Do you ever dream about a story you have heard over the radio? _____
    What program? _____
What are your three favorites and why do you like them?
    (Write answers below)

                                        Why do you like it?
1st choice _____   _____
2nd choice _____   _____
3rd choice _____   _____
Are there any programs to which your family listen together? _____
    Which programs? _____
    _____
Which radio program do you think is the funniest? _____
Which do you think is the most exciting? _____
Have you ever taken up any hobby because you heard about it over the
    radio? _____
    What? _____

Put a check after *each* kind of program you like.

Stories or Dramatizations	Music
adventure _____	popular "hit" songs _____
animals _____	ballads, folk, art songs _____
detectives _____	classical songs _____
hobbies _____	hill-billy songs _____
interesting people _____	grand opera _____
scientific things _____	swing, dance orchestra _____

history _____   piano _____
                                                      symphony orchestra _____
                                                      organ _____
                    fun, comedy, variety programs _____
                    quiz, question bee programs _____
                    plays _____

Check in the proper space to tell about how much time you listen to the
radio each day: (You should have one check in each column).

School Days (MON—FRI)	Saturday	Sunday
None		
15 min.		
½ hour		
¾ hour		
1 hour		
1½ hours		
2 hours		
2½ hours		
3 hours		
3½ hours		
4 hours		
4½ hours		

What product is advertised on each of these programs?
Jack Benny _____ Charlie McCarthy _____
Burns and Allen _____ Jack Armstrong _____
Jolly Joe _____ Amos and Andy _____
Have you ever sent in something (as a box top or label) for a prize? _____
        Were you satisfied with what you got? _____
Has your mother ever bought a product because you heard it advertised on a
        radio program and asked her to buy it? _____ What? _____
We want to know what programs you listen to. Put a check (√) in the
        proper column.

Do you listen to: Sometimes   Always   Never
        [List of current programs is given]
Write the names of any other   _____
programs to which you listen   _____
and check in the proper space.   _____

Radio stations want to put on the kind of programs their listeners like.
        What shall we tell them you would like to have?

This sample survey may be suggestive to others. Another form was used in the lower grades.

It has been the characteristic fate and perhaps the opportunity of the American school that parents, when confronted with a perplexing problem concerning their children, soon look to the teacher for aid. Whether it be character development, habits of safety, or skills of all types, numerous personal achievements are expected as a result of school attendance. The same has been true of home radio listening. Surveys such as that reported by Robinson indicate that a majority of the parents (62.7 per cent) feel that the school should attempt to guide their children's radio listening.[30]

Teachers Must Help If There Is to Be Improvement. The modern teacher does not require such comments from parents to recognize that the guidance of out-of-school influences also is a phase of her activity. Education is primarily training in discrimination. The encouragement of a more critical understanding of literature and music, among other things, has long been a province of the school.

Tyler makes a penetrating observation when he points out: "Practically every high school includes in its work with literature, a study of drama, ranging from Shakespeare to the moderns, yet most of our high-school students have never seen a professionally produced stage play. These same boys and girls, on the other hand, are listening to radio drama almost every day of their lives, yet we ignore it completely in our serious study. We spend years attempting to develop critical reading tastes as we unquestionably should, yet we fail to see the implications of the fact that students do much less reading than radio listening. Altogether we have been singularly blind to the possibilities and necessities of dealing in school with the vital elements of the pupil's everyday experience. Yet we could rather easily incorporate these experiences into the curriculum and thereby make our school work much more meaningful and effective in his daily living." [31]

Recognizing that the guidance of home listening is a problem for both home and school, what activities can the teacher undertake? Some of these activities were discussed in Chapters 7 and 9.

---

[30] Roy Robinson, *op. cit.*

[31] I. Keith Tyler, "Developing Critical Listening," *The Phi Delta Kappan*, March, 1939, p. 349.

First, she should find out to what programs children are listening. Second, she should develop an understanding on the part of the children, an understanding of how radio influences them. For if an individual recognizes that he is being influenced by someone or something, he is more likely to be concerned with the quality of the association than if he otherwise remains ignorant of it. Thus a second step for the teacher is to develop such an understanding on the part of the children. It is simple enough to demonstrate how the radio is influencing the children's speech, causing them to use pet expressions, setting a pattern for pronunciation, affecting their tastes in music, and so on. Perhaps this influence manifests itself in other ways. They might be asked where they get their new ideas about many social problems. Are their opinions about men, nations, and races also being influenced? Should they be aware of such influence? Or, the discussion might be developed from another approach:

> Do you go blindfolded into the open-shelf room of the public library, grab a book, then sulk at home because the book doesn't hold your interest? Do you look for a lighted façade of the movie house, then go in, and complain that the picture is without merit? Do you eat the first four dishes in line at a cafeteria, and then wail that the meal is unbalanced? . . .[32]

Discussions of this type can lead to an understanding of the need for selection in radio programs as well. Once the need for such discernment has been established, the teacher can proceed to a consideration of standards and the establishment of simple criteria for judgment. Some of these standards can apply to a judgment of performance, such as in a dramatic program: proper casting, effective portrayal, genuine dialect, appropriate sound effects, and dramatic pacing. Other criteria —and these are more important to the educator—can apply to an analysis of content such as: significance of the theme, intelligent dialogue, realistic situations, tasteful advertising, and objectivity of presentation.

As important as the criteria themselves is a knowledge of their relative significance. As noted above, not all criteria are of equal value. The sound effects may be poorly selected, the acting immature, but if a program is an honest treatment of an important theme, then it is

---

[32] Clara Nelson, "Preferred Listening," *Minnesota Journal of Education*, October, 1938, p. 65.

far more desirable as an educational experience than a tense professional drama loaded with sound and fury which signifies nothing.

From the teacher's point of view the important factor is not how complete the list of criteria is, but rather the manner in which it is developed. If these standards for judgment are genuinely the child's and actually determined by the entire class and not alone by the teacher, then there is a greater chance of manifesting some improvement in the child's listening.

The ability to recognize quality in radio programs is neither easily nor quickly developed. The process need not be confined to a mere discussion of merits. The imaginative teacher will use a variety of methods, some vivid and concrete. Nor is it necessary to wait until the children are older before steps are taken in this direction.

Even at the elementary grade level the teacher can stimulate the pupil's observation of important differences. The sooner the child becomes conscious that he must discriminate, the better. Ideally it should begin when he first listens to radio. If programs are being received in the classroom, such an analysis should be a phase of the follow-up activity. In considering home listening, the teacher can occasionally refer to some of the recent programs which the children may have heard. Suggestions for the use of such programs were given in the chapter, "Selecting and Using the Program."

In the higher grades, teachers have made use of many procedures to aid their pupils in selective listening. As noted in an earlier chapter, "Broadcasting Activities within the School," these procedures occasionally have been organized into a formal course, while in other schools a unit of the English curriculum is devoted to radio and perhaps motion-picture appreciation. Some institutions sponsor an extracurricular group which deals with radio dramatics.

Though forms of organization vary, it is frequently found that among the upper grades some consideration is given to the pupil as a producer of programs. The child, like an adult, develops a more intelligent appreciation of an activity if he knows more about the conditions under which the activity was expressed. It is not necessary to be an outstanding artist to appreciate a good painting, yet it is probable that if one has attempted some painting both his judgment and enjoyment of it have increased. Thus the production of simple radio programs by the pupils, whether it be over their school's public-address system, a local radio station, or even within the classroom, can serve to make their radio tastes more discerning.

Some instructors have organized pupil tours to radio stations where the group witnesses programs being broadcast. Broadcasting personnel and newspaper radio editors have been invited to address the children. Some teachers have used recorded programs as a medium for analysis, and many have planned their lessons in order to correlate home radio listening with classroom activities. School libraries have arranged a shelf devoted to the literature of radio program production as well as to the better fiction which is to be dramatized in forthcoming broadcasts.

As a result of activities such as the above, the pupils can establish their standards of judgment concerning radio programs. At this point the class will find it profitable to apply these standards to their listening habits as indicated by the survey taken previously. Therefore, as a third step, the teacher might stimulate a class discussion on questions such as: How are our choices altered as a result of our more recent experiences? What did the survey indicate concerning our former standards? What evidences are there of growth in discrimination?

The encouragement of discriminate listening requires continuous effort on the teacher's part. A momentary interest and thereafter general neglect of the problem will not be productive. If listening habits are to be fixed, they need to be practiced with regularity. Continuous guidance by the teacher, and an occasional reference to a superior program, can serve to remind the child of the need for selective dialing.

In order to provide this needed continuity, schools have undertaken various projects. Some maintain a radio log of suggested programs. These are noted on a large bulletin board in a corridor or in the various classrooms. Occasionally this log is printed in the school newspaper along with a column of radio reviews by a budding radio editor. Teachers have encouraged letter writing to the broadcasters commending the better programs and criticizing others. Unusual radio presentations have been called to the pupils' attention via the central sound system. Teachers have suggested group listening to certain out-of-school programs. When the material relates to classroom activity, the instructor has assigned individual or committee reports on such listening. The aim of all such procedures is to establish a continuity of effort.

It is thus evident that the school can do much to aid parents in guiding home listening. And yet a development of radio tastes may not be an entirely satisfactory answer. Like the parent, the teacher is concerned with the health of the child. As noted earlier, poor listening habits at home may deprive the child of needed physical exercise. This aspect of the problem should not be overlooked. Perhaps there is not much the individual teacher can do here. But certainly the school and the community will want to examine their accomplishments in the establishment of substitute activities for the children.

To be realistic one should recognize that few teachers will have the time or perhaps the ability to follow through on an elaborate plan of improving radio tastes. After all is said and done, multiplication tables must still be learned, reports kept, and examinations given. The teacher's time in school is already taken up with a multiplicity of activities, most of them worth while. How, then, one may ask, can new functions be expected of the teacher? The answer is that it is not a question of substitution but rather one of emphasis. The alert teacher recognizes that if she will corral the influences to which her charges are already being subjected, and use these influences to serve her ends, she will be aided in accomplishing more effectively the very things she is attempting to do. No one can assume that, even though the school day is a busy day, every minute is being used most effectively There is still time available to do many things that need to be done. It may well be that the teacher cannot devote as much time to these matters as she would like, but what is more deplorable is the fact that many teachers are as yet unaware of the need that exists for such efforts on their part.

If it can be assumed that commercialized entertainment will continue to play a leading role in fashioning the minds of American children, then our teacher training institutions have an important task awaiting them. Prospective teachers will have to be made aware of the influences of out-of-school listening and seeing. The recent development in some states of a required teacher training course in the utilization of radio and the motion picture is an encouraging sign in this direction.

However, the burden of effort does not remain with the teacher alone. If the radio program for children is to serve the individual and society, more concerted action on the part of the home, the school, the broadcaster, and the advertiser will be necessary.

The rapidly growing Radio Council movement will serve to focus attention upon more successful program ideas. The radio activities of the Association of Junior Leagues of America and similar groups throughout the country are already contributing to the improvement of leisure-time radio for youth by presenting experimental programs for young listeners in numerous communities.

Program Trends. Several trends are discernible in children's programs for leisure-time listening which may suggest the pattern of others to follow. One of these is the development of programs based upon national origins and folklore. For a time several local stations had experimented along this line and more recently at least one network has moved in this direction.

Another development in leisure-time programming for children is the specially designed newscast. Such programs have long been presented for classroom listening, but for home listening this development is a comparatively recent one. The Mutual Network tried the *Junior Newscaster* which, although it met with a good deal of approval, was discontinued after thirteen weeks. Station WSAI, Cincinnati, has presented such a program each school day in the late afternoon. Several other local stations are now presenting this type of program for home listening. Evidence is rapidly accumulating to indicate that the news period for children is here to stay, at least on a local-station basis.

A third trend in children's programs, and one which has long been getting under way, is the dramatization of children's classics. The success of the CBS series *Let's Pretend*, which is now sponsored, may encourage more programs of this type. The programs planned by the Junior League in Pittsburgh and Seattle are especially noteworthy in this development.

Other Proposals for Improvement. Aside from program planning, several proposals have been made which may contribute to the improvement of home listening by children:

1. The production and distribution of selected transcriptions for children would be welcomed by smaller stations particularly. The use of

transcriptions would also enable stations to adjust to local schedule needs.

2. The FCC could recommend that every local station devote at least a half-hour daily during the late afternoon to children's programs. These could be sponsored or sustaining. At least children would have a greater choice of programs which are planned for them.
3. The networks could set aside a definite period daily for continuous experimentation in juvenile programming.
4. Broadcasters could agree to present crime programs at late hours only.
5. The radio industry might consider lowering time-rates for children's programs. The assumption is that such programs are directed to a special audience and also represent an element of public service.

This problem, however, will not be solved by mere resolutions, codes, and parental indignation. What is needed is a mature attitude toward the responsibilities and obligations of broadcasting in a democracy. Recent events have again shown that young people, like their elders, need a faith to live by and ideals to strive for. It is becoming trite to say that liberty is not a gift but a triumph to be achieved by each generation. Yet it must be said, and said repeatedly.

In this continuing search for freedom, broadcasting has a breathtaking opportunity. The fictitious heroes of the superman stripe are no more exciting than the Tom Paines and Nathan Hales. Synthetic adventures are no more thrilling than the realities of life in terms which the child can understand. It is lamentable that the "know-how" of American broadcasting is being wasted on drivel, while a great service to the nation's children is being neglected.

Television Introduces New Problems

It was to be expected that television, which could show not only the product to be sold but the premium which the youngster might "win" by sending in box tops, would soon bid for its share of the youthful audience. Commercial programs for children were among the most successful, financially, of television's early days of 1947–1948. It was not surprising that although dramatic and variety programs drew most of the attention of press and public, children's programming and sports led the list in terms of program time occupied. In 1949, for example, NBC devoted 346 hours of a total of 1,922 hours on the air, or 18 per cent, to programs for the little ones. Sports followed with 16.5 per cent, drama with 15.2 per cent, and variety programs with 11.8 per cent. Let it be remembered that the 346 hours, or 18 per cent, mentioned above were programs *designed* for child viewers; the children also stayed on to see a program or two *not* designed for them, and thereby started all the trouble.

For the programs planned for children are on the whole praiseworthy. Television writers and directors made many claims for the quality of their "kiddie shows" when television first began to go really commercial, and by and large, with some justification. Television stations set out to make children's programs voluntarily subject to such codes of self-censorship as the NAB and NBC policies, with the visual restrictions of the motion-picture industry's Johnson-office thrown in for good measure. Both on the networks' coaxial cable and in local stations, puppet shows flourished. Characters such as Kukla, Howdy Doody, Foudini the Magician were nationally known stars in a year. The Singing Lady returned to the air, her charming stories acted out by marionettes. A new type of live program was introduced: *Mr. I. Magination*. And numerous "amalgams" of live and film followed the pattern set by Bob Emery with his *Small Fry Club*. True, much of the air time of this latter type was occupied by cartoon films and ancient comedies, but these were innocuous enough, if not particularly valuable. Wherein, then, lay the "menace of television," as irate parents, educators and editors were to call it? What caused the initial wave of enthusiasm for "children's entertainment in the home" to turn into a denunciation of the family receiver?

The answer is twofold. First, while many stations cooperated by scheduling most of their juvenile programs between the hours of five and eight, many, if not most, children took to staying up past eight o'clock to watch television. And the adult fare that begins at eight has had rather startling effects on the child viewer. In an editorial in *The Saturday Review of Literature*, Norman Cousins cited a nine-year-old who was interested in a box of poisoned chocolates for his teacher; a six-year-old who asked his policeman father for real bullets to use on his little sister, and a seven-year-old who was caught in the act of sprinkling ground glass into the family's lamb stew. All had been inspired by television. Commented Mr. Cousins,

In the one year since television has been on an assembly-line basis, there has been mass-produced a series of plodding stereotypes and low-quality programs. Behind it all, apparently, is a grinding lack of imagination and originality which has resulted in the standardized television formula for an evening's entertainment: a poisoning, a variety show, a wrestling match.

The broadcasters retaliated with the claim that such programming was not meant for the eyes of innocent little children; that the young had no business being out of bed at such hours; that it was the parents' responsibility to get them to bed and away from the receiver. In an article in *Variety*, television people pointed proudly to programs of classical music, ballet, and fine drama—notably Shakespeare. To all of which Mr. Cousins had already provided an answer in his editorial in *The Saturday Review of Literature*, December, 1949, when he wrote:

. . . for every half-hour worth seeing, there are literally days of wrath and writhing. For every *Kukla, Fran, and Ollie* program, which stimulates rather than stultifies the imagination of children, there are countless unskilled and ear-shattering kiddie shows and an even larger number of terror-and-torture specials.

Clearly, something was wrong somewhere. Television was not only not doing better things for children than radio had done, but it was accused of being far worse. Some bitter critics went so far as to say that television had managed in a year or two to acquire all the worst qualities which radio had taken twenty years to develop. Bernard Smith, outspoken writer and speaker on broadcasting, and an attorney specializing in radio and broadcasting, said, in an address to a large convention of educators in November, 1949:

While many observers are inclined to expect that the quality of television programs will improve as the number of sets increase, the fact is that television broadcasting today from a cultural point of view is better now than it ever will be again so long as advertising remains the sole source for its support . . . commercial television . . . must inevitably follow the pattern of radio broadcasting, which means that the advertisers will ultimately spend their dollars only on those programs that are calculated to reach the largest possible audience at the lowest possible cost.

To these disquieting statements a new element was added as metropolitan areas and their suburbs broke out in a rash of television aerials. Teachers began to observe a disturbing condition in their classrooms.

The cause? A new disease among children whose families had recently acquired television sets. The chief symptoms were drowsiness in the classroom; inattention; a marked increase in the number of pupils who came to school with homework poorly done or not even attempted.

Once again, the surveys were called upon to prove that havoc was being wrought. As educators sent questionnaires home, they discovered that mothers were adding to the two basic elements of loss of sleep and neglect of study a third accusation: television was interfering with the dinner hour! Children refused to stay in the dining room when the television screen was out of sight in the living room. Changing the evening meal hour to avoid conflict with a favorite program did nothing to help—a later or earlier hour meant loss of some other favorite!

True, reports did differ. A survey conducted in New Jersey found that 279 out of 562 students had sets in their homes, an increase of 100 per cent over the previous year. Earlier, 9 per cent had been doing unsatisfactory work. As the number of television sets doubled, the percentage of failure also doubled to 20 per cent. On the other hand, the United Parents Associations of New York found a more diverse series of effects. Children between the ages of five and seven showed little loss in study habits, but nearly a third of the group suffered loss of other recreation and were affected adversely in eating habits and emotional well-being. Seven-year-olds showed some loss in study, more in recreation, and about the same dietary and emotional difficulties. Very few eight-year-olds and nine-year-olds studied poorly, but this group showed an increase of mealtime trouble and the beginning of nightmares and difficulties in getting to bed. Ten-year-olds suffered in homework, but only moderately in recreation and diet; parents of eleven-year-olds and children on up to thirteen reported roughly about one-eighth of the group affected, with marks, recreation and eating habits suffering almost equally. The questions which the individual parents' associations affiliated with the United Parents Associations were asked are as follows:

1. Child's age.........Sex.........School attending?
2. School grade?
3. Listening time devoted to TV?

4. Type of program most interested in?
5. Have your child's study habits been affected?
6. Is this evident in the child's marks or in some other way to have drawn your attention?
7. Have your child's recreation habits been affected and how has this been manifested?
8. Teachers have complained that children come to school late, having been up the previous night viewing television. Also, that their eating habits have been affected, since so many of them are served in front of the television sets. Have you noticed any change in their eating habits and do certain tense situations in the shows react unfavorably?

At about the same time, the principal and vice-principal of the Burdick Junior High School in Stamford, Connecticut, conducted a survey which indicated that 79 per cent of the student body watched television on a regular basis, although only 50 per cent had sets in their own homes. The latter group spent an average of 27 hours a week or 3.86 hours a day at the receiver. As for effects, while definite conclusions were drawn, the following findings were significant:

1. A majority of the pupils and their parents believed that television *may* interfere with the completion of homework.
2. A majority of children from time to time had their supper while watching a show.
3. An overwhelming majority of children reported a sincere belief that television had increased their interest in events outside the home and school.

From the opposite side of the American continent came conflicting comment on the influence of television. FCC Chairman, Wayne Coy, in an address at the Annual Conference on Station Problems, University of Oklahoma, March 14, 1950, quoted a report sent to him in a letter of complaint from the Tenth District (Los Angeles) of the California Congress of Parents and Teachers. A questionnaire sent to some 300 pediatricians, sociologists, neuropsychiatrists and psychologists resulted in the following consensus of opinion:

90 per cent said that radio crime programs have a detrimental psychological effect on children;
93 per cent said radio thriller shows and programs ending in suspense have a bad effect;
81 per cent said that present-day radio programs contribute to children's delinquency or anti-social behavior;

63 per cent conceded that American children need an emotional escape, but 83 per cent said that such emotional escape *cannot* be safely provided by thrilling radio programs.

Now all this, of course, was in relation to radio. Turning to television, the Chairman of the FCC described a survey of television programs scheduled between 6 P.M. and 9 P.M. on Los Angeles stations for one week. The surveying group, the Southern California Association for Better Radio and Television, found no crime programs on KFI-TV, but found on the other stations:

91 murders, 7 stage hold-ups, 3 kidnappings, 10 thefts, 4 burglaries, 2 cases of arson, 2 jailbreaks, 1 murder by explosion of 15 to 20 people, 2 suicides, 1 case of blackmail. . . . Also cases of attempted murder . . . action in saloons . . . brawls . . . drunkenness, crooked judges, crooked sheriffs, crooked juries.

Much of the last named, of course, were shown on the ancient western films which have become so much a part of television fare. But such a report was a far cry from the proudly proclaimed purity of children's television which marked the late-afternoon programming of the live shows specifically designed for children at most stations. It revealed, too, the familiar "eight o'clock fallacy"—the concept that young children would not be watching television after eight o'clock, because wise parents would send them to bed at that hour.

On the other side of the picture, there came a reply to Commissioner Coy's statement, in which the radio-television chairman of the Tenth District California Conference of Parents and Teachers announced that the Commissioner's information must have come from sources other than official PTA groups.[33] Of twenty-nine children's programs surveyed by her group, not one had been found "outright objectionable," although some parents had "viewed certain elements in kid shows as questionable," said the rejoinder. Moreover, executives of six local (Los Angeles) stations had met with individual PTA groups and "had shown interest in keeping crime and other 'objectionable adult' programs off the air during early evening hours."

Completely reversing the "viewing with alarm" technique, Dr. Bruce Robinson, psychiatrist and Director of the Child Guidance Bureau of the Newark, New Jersey public schools, came to the defense

---

[33] *The Billboard*, April 8, 1950.

of television. In an address before the Metropolitan New York Chapter of the Association for Education by Radio, in 1950, Dr. Robinson described television as potentially no more dangerous for this generation of children than dime novels, motion pictures, radio, and comic books had been for their parents. He pointed out that vicarious violence and adventure had been a part of the child's experience from the days of Hans Christian Andersen and the Brothers Grimm, and suggested that such stimuli and vicarious outlets were healthy for the normal child. Indeed, television may call the child who needs special care to the attention of his parents, if programs leave him unusually disturbed, just as television has directed attention to numerous cases of eye deficiency which might otherwise have gone unnoticed. As for the problems of late retirement, eating at the receiver, or quarreling with siblings over which program was to be tuned in, Dr. Robinson found television providing a challenge to parents and an opportunity to develop a healthy working relationship within the family that would stand parent and child in good stead when the more serious problems of adolescence present themselves. While many parents at that meeting did not agree entirely with Dr. Robinson, the great majority were reassured by his calm suggestion that the parent was more likely to be upset by the effect of video on the child than the child himself.

Parents and Television. Most of the suggestions made earlier with reference to radio apply also to television. Additional health factors involved in overuse of the video receiver are the problem of eye strain and digestion. While oculists have, on the whole, found no grave danger even in two or three hours of sitting in a darkened room and staring at a glowing screen, they do recommend that the set be focused properly, with a proper degree of contrast and brightness. They urge that children sit at some distance from the set—six times the height of the screen is minimum viewing distance—and that some slight illumination which does *not* reflect from the surface of the screen be present.

The other health factor is digestion, although there is no evidence to confirm the belief that eating at the set is injurious, however harmful it be to manners and to family life. Some bewildered parents reported that their children ate better when watching programs!

But the basic factors of over-stimulation and lack of out-door exercise are likely to be even more present in a "television home" than one equipped only with radio. These problems disturb many parents.

In the final analysis the question is whether parents will permit television to rule in their homes or whether they will control it. As George E. Condon, Radio-Television Editor of the Cleveland Plain Dealer, has put it:

It seems to me that the critics are guilty of shallow thinking when they point the accusing finger at the radio or television set and lay the blame for the drop in scholastic achievement on either media or on the students.

This world is full of distracting things for youngsters. One may list sports participation, the candy store, motion-picture theater, the street-corner gang, the soda fountain or just the outdoors.

Youngsters may go to the theater too often, they may stay outside and play baseball too late or they may hang around the soda fountain too long.

Where, then, does the blame go if the students' grades drop?

It seems obvious that final responsibility for a student's lack of attention to his school work rests with the parents, no matter what specific distraction is luring him away from the books.

A bit of parental discipline will keep the child away from radio or television until the homework is completed. The whole problem would appear to center about the notable lack of discipline in the home rather than in the insidious nature of radio or television.

Teachers and Television. Again many of the comments made concerning radio are applicable here. In television, however, most parents seem to realize that teachers alone can do little to correct dangerous tendencies in video viewing. Judging by the surveys and resolutions reported by parents' associations, they seem to be turning directly to the broadcasters or to governmental agencies, or spurring magazines and newspapers to join them in possibly improving the situation.

It will be some time, of course, before the percentage of teachers who own sets will equal that of pupils who have access to television, and that factor alone has made many teachers hesitate to tackle the always delicate problem of student preferences. Many teachers are naturally hesitant to discuss programs which they have not seen themselves.

Every evidence available indicates that good television programming will be in need of at least equal assistance from the teacher, with the resources of the community marshaled behind her, if the television industry continues in the patterns it has already revealed. Television seems to have added two new problems: the conflict between dining with the family and having supper in front of the television set, and the temptation to stay up even later for television than the child would for radio. Teachers will, of course, concern themselves with the child who is listless and sleepy in class next day, who shows marked "television pallor," whose preparation for classwork has suffered. But the cautious teacher will make sure that other factors or home conditions are not responsible before she blames television. Once she is certain, consultations with the child's parents and the taking of concerted action on the part of the school and the home will at least present the pallid pupil with a united front in favor of keeping television viewing in reasonable bounds.

In general, the progressive teacher will show an interest in television, will capitalize on its merits, rather than condemn it wholesale and thus lose the opportunity to steer her class's viewing habits in the right direction. Outside of school, she is subject to the duty all conscientious "consumers of broadcasting" impose upon themselves: to praise the broadcasters for presenting the programs they favor and to criticize those they find objectionable. In addition, the conscientious teacher will unite herself with leaders of educational and parent groups who are working for better programming through surveys, correspondence with stations and sponsors, and the support, through public commendation and recommendation, of the programs they want the children to see. But let it never be forgotten that a program, first of all, must please the child, else no amount of suggestion and recommendation will bring him to watch it regularly. It is the contention of many, borne out by the success of many wholesome programs, that the child's captivation and the parents or teacher's approval are not necessarily incompatible.

Trends in Children's Television Programs. While television has not yet developed sufficiently to offer a clearly defined pattern of the future, several trends have made themselves evident. Those programs which are planned for children, with the exception for some parts of old Western films, are usually either praiseworthy or at worst innocuous. They lean heavily upon puppets or upon film cartoons, frequently, but usually stress wholesome fantasy and fun. Puppet characters such as Kukla, Foudini, Howdy Doody, and Beany have caused at least one writer (Jack Cluett of *Woman's Day* magazine) to "resent the fact that my kids pay more attention to TV characters than they do to their own father and mother. Maybe I'd have better luck if I dressed up like a cowboy and herded them off to bed with a six-shooter, or fitted my wife with strings, like a marionette, so the children would pay a little attention to her when she says, 'Eat your oatmeal.' " Yet it is not the program planned for children to which most parents and teachers take exception, but the one planned for adults which children all too often get to see—and continue to watch avidly thereafter.

The Singing Lady's puppet-animated fairy tales are not a new trend, of course, but comforting evidence that an old trend has survived the transition to a new medium. And NBC's *Watch the World,* a Sunday-afternoon newsreel for children, was certainly wholesome entertainment, if sometimes too widespread in its content to be truly educational. Our old friends, the magicians and the circus performers, are with us on television and provide thrills without bloodshed for hundreds of children who rarely get to see the real Big Top. And the growing number of child-talent shows, while they may or may not have unhealthy effects upon their steady participants, surely do no harm to their thousands of viewers, even though the latter be drawn to identification and emulation. Thus, children's programming in television has received at least the negative compliment due its avoidance of the harmful, at the worst, while at its best, it has revealed an imagination, originality and freshness which augurs well for the future. As Jack Gould, radio editor of the *New York Times,* remarked in an address before the Metropolitan New York chapter of the AER,

> . . . in the case of television, the cry for variety in programming is not an academic bit of intellectual thinking, as the broadcasters might imagine, but an absolute necessity. Television absorbs so much in such a short time, that I don't think it will have any real choice but to try and exploit what now may be minority preferences but could very easily be made into majority preferences.

Mr. Gould's remarks referred to general programming, of course; they are equally applicable to programs for children.

Secondary-School Principals' Report. The National Association of Secondary-School Principals speaking for 25,000 school communities has issued a statement recently on "The Role of the Motion Picture, Radio, and Television in Education." The motivation for this report was the belief that "alert citizens are becoming more sharply aware of a serious divergence in the matter of values, particularly between the school and the commercial fields of audio-visual entertainment." Comments relating to television in this report were as follows:

Too recently available to the general public, too limited as yet by unsolved technical and production problems to be evaluated in terms of its present influences, television is perhaps the most potentially significant communicative invention in the history of the world. Combining the powers of the motion picture and the radio, it brings directly into the home not only actual happenings as they occur, but provides a vehicle by which the entire gamut of musical and dramatic art may be brought within its compass. Indeed, the news magazine *Fortnight* (October 8, 1948) states candidly: "The Television Research Institute reported . . . that motion-picture exhibitors may be entirely out of business by 1955 as a result of television developments." Whether or not this prediction is accurate, it cannot be questioned that television will have revolutionary effects upon the motion-picture and radio industries. Certainly the social problems confronting it will be a combination of those now facing its two earlier forebears.

By way of prophecy, it may be observed that certain characteristics inherent in any entertainment medium will govern the use of television. One of these characteristics has to do with the degree of privacy available to the audience; another involves the source of sensory appeal. Among the communicative arts, literature has traditionally enjoyed the greatest latitude both in the choice of its subject matter and in its candor of expression. Reading is chiefly a private occupation. Its emotional reaction is an indirect product, dependent upon the imagination and sharply limited by the extent of the reader's personal experience. Motion-picture attendance is at least partially a public activity, as a result of which its scope of topic and manner of presentation is much more circumscribed than are those of literature. Radio, except when the listener happens to be alone, is subject to the criticism of an intimately related and mutually self-conscious social group. Of all the well-developed arts of the present day, it must be the most circumspect. But television, once out of its experimental infancy, will doubtless be even more highly restricted. In fact, the opinion can scarcely be avoided that, insofar as television enters the dramatic field, its every program will have to be of the "family" type. To the young and immature, this will be a valuable restriction; to the adult, it will not only be an annoyance but a definite artistic and educational handicap as well.

As educators, the authors of this statement suggest that those who have the destiny of television as their interest and responsibility consider not only what they feel will be an "acceptable" type of program, but that they seriously ponder the matter of what will best serve the broad interests and needs of society at all age levels. Too cautious a procedure might easily vitiate the far-reaching influence for greater human understanding and social cooperation which this new communicative agency should exert. To prevent this, it is further suggested that the industry invite laymen to join with it in formulating a code of principles, policies, and regulations for the governance of its entire entertainment program. Not only would this bring about better adjustment between the industry and society from the point of view of qualitative value; it would almost certainly benefit the industry from the standpoint of sheer profit. The producers and advertisers could scarcely do better than to consult their audience and their market.

13

The School Broadcasting Station

◇◇

What preliminary steps are suggested in establishing the school station?

What aspects of station relations are emphasized?

What are the three basic principles in planning a classroom program service?

What can the station do to encourage effective utilization practices?

How have recordings been used by the school station?

How can a complete record of station activities help?

Can the station add television to its services?

◇◇◇◇◇◇◇◇THE STEADILY GROWING number of applications to the FCC indicates a spreading interest in school stations. The aim of this chapter is to discuss several principles and suggestions for the establishment and operation of such educational stations. Primary consideration will be given to those stations operated by a public-school system. However, the general principles are applicable to the school functions of university-operated or state department radio organizations.

The suggestions to be made are based upon a twelve-year period of school-station operation. The activities of Station WBOE Cleveland, with which one of the writers is associated, will serve as the basis for analysis and the development of possible suggestions.

Initial Steps to Be Taken

A radio committee should be chosen to survey the needs of the schools and the community. The decision to apply for a station license should be based upon the answers to the following questions:

1. What educational needs have we that can be met to some extent by radio broadcasting?

2. Can our broadcasting efforts be more effective with our own station than with the use of commercial-station facilities made available to us?

3. How can our station be used most effectively? Shall it be planned primarily for classroom listening groups or for adult education and public information, or for both?

4. Shall the support of schools in the surrounding territory be enlisted?

5. What are the experiences of such stations elsewhere?

6. What are the probable installation costs for the type of radio service we have in mind? What can we expect the maintenance and operational costs to be?

7. Have we the financial resources to undertake this project?

8. Have we or can we secure the needed personnel?

After a preliminary study has led to a decision to apply for a station license, the next step is to secure the appropriate FCC rules. Those most applicable to school stations were listed in Chapter 2.

The following statement by George P. Adair, formerly chief engineer of the FCC, is helpful.

PROCEDURE FOR OBTAINING EDUCATIONAL BROADCAST FACILITIES [1]

With so much interest developing in the use of radio in education, particularly the establishment of new stations for this purpose, it is an opportune time to mention briefly some considerations in the filing of applications with the Federal Communications Commission for station authorizations. I would like to point out not only the main factors which suggest themselves but also to mention some of the other problems encountered by educators in proceeding to construct a station of their own.

A point which has been emphasized before but which merits repetition is adequate planning. Before the filing of an application and before making arrangements for the purchase and installation of equipment, it is essential that a determination be made of exactly (a) what radio service is desired; (b) how it is to be obtained technically; (c) how it is to be financed; and (d) how it is to be used. If necessary, go outside of the school staff for personnel skilled in the design, installation and use of a radio system that will be tailored to fit your needs. A properly engineered system that will do the job proposed may often effect economies that will more than offset added expenditures incurred in the beginning.

Along these lines you may want, perhaps, to first have a station that will serve a limited area or a single school system, but later to provide county-wide service or include possibly several school systems. The United States Office of Education undoubtedly can be of great assistance in your planning, and possibly coordinate your plans with those of other school systems in your vicinity or in your state. Consider the part your station will play in plans for state or regional networks of educational FM stations. Some applications have been received by the Commission where it appeared that rather nebulous if any plans had been made, even as to the area that the station was expected to serve.

Having determined the coverage you desire and the transmitter, power, transmitter location, and antenna system necessary to provide it, you are in a position to go ahead with the supplementary details, to estimate more accurately the cost of the system, and to have a proper basis for obtaining an appropriation for it. Other factors enter in, of course, such as the number and size of studios, the construction work and acoustical treatment involved, and the studio amplifiers and transcription equipment required.

Only after this groundwork has been laid should you file your application with the Commission. In addition to specifying the channel assignment you desire and a description of the facilities you propose to install, the application should include an adequate showing of the service you in-

---

[1] Presented at Fifteenth Institute for Education by Radio, May 6, 1944.

tend to provide. This should describe the extent of the school system or systems you intend to serve, as well as other areas you intend to include. List the plans and purposes of the station, including tentative programming, both as to the service which would be provided to schools and as to other projects such as adult education. Describe how your station would fit into a coordinated plan or network, if such is proposed for your region. Supply in your application the proper showing as to any local authorization needed for filing the application, such as the resolution of the school board, and of the money appropriated or made available for construction and operation of the station. Be sure the application includes duplicate copies of all exhibits, such as resolutions, maps of station location, etc.

In some cases applications for new noncommercial educational broadcast stations have been filed where construction is not proposed in the near future, due to wartime conditions, but where the school system or university desires to have the application pending for future actions. Such applications where there is sufficient evidence that the applicant fully intends to proceed to complete the application as soon as possible, have been accepted. However, such a procedure does not reserve a channel for use at some later time, and I wish to emphasize that the assignment of a channel is based upon the granting of an application and not merely for the reason that an application may be pending. It is not the policy to issue construction permits where construction may not be completed for an indefinite period of time, and applications in this category would probably be retained without present action by the Commission.

In some cases applications have been filed in incomplete form without, for example, specification of all the transmitting equipment proposed to be used. Although such applications are normally not acceptable for filing, they have been accepted on the basis that the missing material will be submitted when required by the Commission at a later date. It is expected that such applications be as complete as feasible at the time of filing and that a showing be included regarding incomplete portions. Some applications in this category have been received and returned for additional information, generally in cases where it was evident that it was available and overlooked or where certain portions of the form had not been answered. No action will be taken until the application is complete and the filing of incomplete applications in no way reserves a frequency or speeds the obtaining of a construction permit.

As to the actual mechanics of filing an application for construction permit, application forms should be requested from the Federal Communications Commission, Washington, 25, D.C., or from one of its field offices. Before attempting to complete the application, however, applicants should obtain copies of pertinent portions of the Commission's Rules which describe application procedure and the rules under which educational stations operate. It is therefore suggested that the following portions of the Rules be obtained from the Superintendent of Documents, Government Printing Office, Washington, D.C., which are available at the prices indicated:

Part 1, Rules of Practice and Procedure .... 10¢

Part 2, General Rules and Regulations .... 10¢

Part 4, Rules Governing Broadcast Services Other than Standard
Broadcast .... 10¢

Part 13, Rules Governing Commercial Radio Operators ..... 5¢

Upon filing of the application and the granting of the construction permit by the Commission, a permit is issued which specifies required dates of commencement and completion of construction, normally two and eight months, respectively, after the date of grant. Upon the completion of construction, certain tests are permitted before the station license is issued, as indicated by Sections 2.42 and 2.43 of the Commission's Rules. The license application must be filed with the Commission before the completion date specified by the construction permit.

Summarizing these comments, may I say that a little extra time and expense in planning today should reap rich dividends in the better performance and reduced cost of your radio system tomorrow. Radio in education depends upon the use we make of it, and so let us plan carefully now for the benefits it will bring in the time ahead.

Preliminary Planning. The technical phase of station planning constitutes an extensive discussion in itself, and will not be undertaken here.[2] The advisory services of a competent engineer, consultation with the staffs of other educational stations, analysis of the literature issued by the United States Office of Education, and guidance from reputable equipment manufacturers can all be utilized with benefit.

The technical facilities for an FM school station do not differ much from those used by commercial FM stations. A few distinctions, however, can be made.[3] The need for extended coverage is not so great if it has been determined to serve only the local schools and not the outlying area. The transmitter site of the school station may have to be located within the school district, although a more desirable site on a higher elevation may be available elsewhere in the neighboring area. The location of studios may have to be determined by available school-building space. The proposed use of the station as a technical

[2] *Report of Radio Activities, Station WBOE, 1938–1939*, p. 111–163.

[3] On Sept. 16, 1948, the FCC issued more lenient rules for educational stations which permit low power (ten-watt) installations.

laboratory as well as a broadcasting medium may suggest the establishment of the station within a technical or trade school. The restrictions imposed by a limited budget may necessitate housing the studios and transmitter in the same building. If this is done at the sacrifice of elevation, space, and convenience, some limitations will result, but at the same time operational costs will be reduced through savings in telephone-line rentals and the salary of personnel at the transmitter. Compromises with the highest technical standards usually have to be made. The nature of these modifications can best be determined by consultation with a technical expert.

Construction Costs.   The cost of transmission, studio, and control-room equipment is dependent to a large degree upon the type of service planned. A limited program schedule for a small compact community will obviously require a smaller outlay for equipment than an extensive service for a large sprawling cosmopolitan area. For the former, a small studio or two and a control room may suffice. Power requirements are small, rehearsals are few, and studio traffic is easily handled. In the larger city a more powerful transmitter may be needed. An elaborate program load calls for more studio space, audition facilities, etc. A floor plan such as is shown on page 467 may be found desirable for efficient operation.

Because of these variations in location and program service as well as in other factors, such as local wage scales, it is difficult to make close estimates of probable station costs. Current cost data can be secured by writing directly to the Radio Division, United States Office of Education in Washington.

Maintenance and Operating Costs.   Maintenance costs also vary with the type of installation and program service. A simple low-powered unit operated a few hours during the school day, and approximately 190 days a school year, will be maintained at a much lower cost than a high-powered installation used day and night throughout the calendar year.

Annual maintenance costs for a 250-watt station will probably range from $500 to $1,500, depending upon the factors noted above. Other elements should also be considered in estimating these costs. An account of the early experiences at WBOE may be informative in this regard, though current costs are higher.

Radio Station WBOE
Board of Education
Cleveland Ohio

The separation of studio and transmitter was necessitated by local topographical conditions. This increased not only construction and personnel costs but the expense of operation as well. The telephone-line charge between these points (six miles apart) for two circuits—one broadcast and one emergency talking circuit—is $61.80 a month. For an eight-hour operating day, computed on twenty-two days per month, this increased cost of operation is approximately 35 cents an hour.[4]

Power charges for operation of the transmitter are nominal. For a three-phase, 230-volt supply the average cost per hour is 15 cents, 6 kilowatts at 2½ cents per hour. Installation charges for a power supply similar to that mentioned were not included, as this supply was available already to the school building in which the transmitter is located. This will probably prove true in most stations of this type as the power-supply classification is one in common use and is usually required for the operation of fan and ventilating-system motors. Commercial power requirements for transmitters rated at 1-kilowatt radio-frequency output are usually low. This seldom exceeds 6 kilowatts.

Exclusive of salaries, a close estimate of technical operation costs for WBOE, including all items—tube replacement, line charges, tools, small parts—is slightly more than $1 per operating hour.

A variety of factors determines program-production costs apart from technical operation. The size of the station staff is, of course, the major item. If the plan is to use a good deal of pupil help or other volunteer aid, production costs can be held at a minimum. A suggested yard-stick for computing the annual over-all station-operation cost is to assume that it will approximate the initial cost of installation. This estimate is true only for a limited type of station activity. An elaborate program service which entails a subscription to a music library, a news service, line rentals for "remote" programs, a music staff, a large consumption of transcription blanks, and so on, would certainly run into a far greater expense. The one perhaps obvious generalization that can be made is that higher costs and greater program services are closely correlated.

Organizing the School Station

The organizational pattern of a school station is the result of the point of view which led to its establishment. A station considered primarily as a public relations instrument will differ in organiza-

---

[4] The installation of a beam-type relay to send the signal from studios to transmitter would be more economical in the long run, since it eliminates the use of telephone lines.

tion from one whose chief activity is classroom broadcasting. A station in one community which is expected to plan, present, and evaluate programs will differ in its administrative operation from another station which is regarded primarily as a medium of distribution to be used by instructional agencies already established. The best organizational form cannot be determined arbitrarily. Local needs are basic.

If the station is to be used primarily as an instructional force, one feature in particular should be emphasized. It should function as a service agency available to all departments of supervision and not as a separate entity. It is the writers' belief that the basis of an efficient school-station organization is its close relationship to the supervisory and teaching staffs. In the final analysis its program service is an extension of the efforts of the latter. Only by cooperating closely with the subject supervisors can the station staff better serve valid educational objectives. If the program producers mistakenly regard themselves as a separate instructional unit and proceed forthwith to draw up, produce, and even evaluate programs in various specialized fields, they foolishly assume an unusual degree of wisdom. The objectives to be reached and the desired content of classroom programs are usually better known by those who work closely with the teachers and children in the classroom. The form of the programs, the attractive elements, can be suggested by the radio department, but certainly it should not presume to determine what is needed in various fields and at different grade levels. If it is at all possible, the initial stages of program planning should be developed with the help and guidance of supervisors and teacher committees. The effect of this procedure on utilization and general acceptance in the schools of the district should be evident.

The plan of station organization shown on page 470 may serve to suggest several principles of use elsewhere.

The directing supervisor's general function is to direct the operations of the station staff and to utilize the facilities to attain the maximum educational returns. Specifically he aids in developing the broadcasting schedule, planning and preparing programs, consulting with individual schools as to their equipment and programs, suggesting evaluation procedures, preparing reports, and maintaining a cooperative relationship with local radio stations. The effective use of any

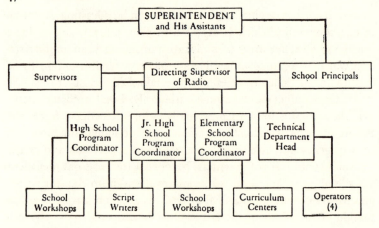

new tool involves a preliminary period of education as to its possibilities and limitations. Thus, a phase of the director's work has been, first, to inform himself of current experimentation in this field and, second, to interpret to both educators and the public the contributions of radio in education.

It will be seen on the chart that three program coordinators are used. Each one is responsible for the programs presented in his division. These coordinators discuss program plans with supervisors, confer with script writers and school radio-workshop teachers, and direct most program production.

Many of the productions for the elementary schools are handled by the radio teachers assigned to that function, and in these cases the station producer acts only as an adviser. Since her production duties are not so great, the elementary-school program coordinator has been assigned the responsibility of arranging the daily schedule and assigning studios for rehearsals.

The script writers are selected teachers who are assigned to WBOE as part of their teaching day. They develop scripts and teachers' program guides and also plan evaluation techniques with committees of teachers.

The technical-department head supervises the technical staff, develops specifications for the purchase of new equipment, and directs procedures for the operation and maintenance of station facilities. He is responsible for the servicing of school receivers, acts as consultant to schools contemplating the purchase of additional sound equipment, and conducts research activities of an engineering nature.

Four technical operators are employed at WBOE:

1. CONTROL-ROOM OPERATOR.   It is her major responsibility to send the program on its way to the transmitter properly monitored. She also tabulates the returns from weekly log sheets of school reception.

2. TRANSMITTER OPERATOR.   The operation of the transmitter and its maintenance are his responsibility. During the summer months he is used in reconstruction and expansion activities.

3. RECORDING OPERATOR.   Since the preparation of recordings, both for use over WBOE and through the central sound systems of the schools, has become an important function, it is found desirable to assign an operator to that specific job. Therefore, the recording operator is concerned primarily with the preparation of recordings. He is given a schedule of the records to be made and when these are completed he inspects them and has them sent to the schools which have requested them. Those which are to be rebroadcast at some future date are placed in the studio file and entered in the recording log.

4. RECEIVER REPAIRMAN.   Whereas the usual station engineering staff is concerned only with the studio and transmitting apparatus, in the Cleveland school station the staff has as an important function not only the aforementioned responsibility, but it is also concerned with the satisfactory operation of receivers in the schools. All receivers used in the Cleveland schools are serviced by the WBOE technical department. Weekly reception-report forms are sent to the various schools, asking them to indicate programs received and the quality of reception. These responses are tabulated and, wherever unsatisfactory reception is noted, the operator is scheduled for service calls. To facilitate more rapid service and to make it unnecessary for any schools to miss radio programs for an extended period, several additional receivers are stored in the studio workshop, ready for installation while the replaced receiver is being repaired.

The functions of the school workshop and curriculum centers also shown on the organizational chart will be discussed in a later section.

A program service of high quality requires an adequate staff. The school-station director should recognize the danger of trying to accomplish too much with too little. It is wiser to transmit two hours of good material than to attempt to produce a full day's schedule with mediocre programs hastily prepared.

It is natural to desire a complete, well-staffed organization but in launching this new enterprise the director should start on a modest scale. The staff should be kept at a workable minimum; otherwise the inevitable and natural questions of expense will arise and the burden of evidence will rest upon the station. Necessary staff additions can be made in better faith when the value of the service is demonstrable though it be on a limited scale.

Realistic station operators will recognize that a segment of the public has yet to learn the values of radio in education. A sizable increase of the school budget due to the introduction of radio certainly will not help the movement.

The part-time use of teachers and volunteers, as well as the sharing of station costs among the schools, should be considered, at least at the early stages of growth. The measure of good management in this instance, too, is maximum output with minimum costs.

The next subject, station relations, is a vital one in determining the success of the radio enterprise. Relations with several groups will be considered, each of which has an important contribution to make to the educational station: school principals, school workshops, local commercial stations, the library, and other community agencies.

Station Relations: School Principals

The importance of working closely with subject supervisors has already been indicated. The same can be said of the station's relationship to school principals. Without their interest and understanding, the school use of programs is limited. The principals should be informed of the station's purposes, programs, and allied services. The station staff should earnestly seek the counsel of principals. The attitude to be desired is not that the station is an authoritative blare from school headquarters, but rather that *our* station is the voice of all our schools. It is a mutual enterprise whose success depends upon the interest and guidance of the entire school community.

A procedure that has been found helpful in enlisting the cooperation of principals is the establishment of radio committees among the principals in each school division: elementary, junior high, and senior high.

These radio committees have been helpful in numerous ways: suggesting the best broadcast times, selecting occasions for special programs, exchanging information concerning school-radio equipment, recommending uniform bell schedules, promoting better utilization practices, encouraging the establishment of school-radio workshops, releasing teachers and pupils for program participation.

The alert station staff receives and likewise extends cooperation. It seeks every opportunity to help the individual schools not only with programs but also through other forms of assistance. It may repair school equipment, provide technical advice regrading proposed purchases and building alterations, help in local program production, advise in selection and training of radio-workshop teachers, present visual-radio programs during school assemblies, give talks to faculties on utilization and new technical developments, arrange courses of instruction for pupil-operators, and advise on administrative plans for program reception.

Station Relations: School Radio Workshops

The use of pupil talent in station program production is both an obligation and an opportunity. A pupil who appears in a program as technician or performer shares a vivid, meaningful experience. As an educational agency the station should seek to distribute such values.

The availability of pupil talent—dramatic, musical, technical, literary—affords the station an opportunity. It can undertake a type and extent of program production it could not otherwise afford.

Plans for utilizing pupils in station programs vary. In some stations a central radio workshop composed of carefully selected pupils meets at the station. Most program roles are taken by these pupils after audition.

A second plan is to use the local school-radio workshops as individual production units. Many program series are arranged so that specific broadcasts can be delegated to the schools. Usually broadcast dates and general program content are made available to the groups for an expression of individual preference. The entire program is cast and rehearsed in one school. Final rehearsals take place at the station under the direction or at least guidance of the station staff. Under this plan the school workshop may be compared to a station affiliate served by a network.

The central radio workshop has several merits:

1. It makes possible hurried casting and rapid production since a selected group is on hand.
2. In a serial type of program where continuity in a role is needed the rotating plan would not be feasible.
3. Greater selection made on a city-wide basis makes possible the maintenance of higher production standards.
4. A chosen few undergo an intensive radio experience which is not available in the usual school workshop.

The second plan, the use of local production units, should be considered for several reasons:

1. Program appearances provide stimulus to school-workshop activities.
2. The school group has a valuable opportunity to follow through on a project from script plan through final production. By listening to other programs in the series it can judge its comparative achievement.
3. Participation encourages interest. Greater listening results when the purposes and plans of a series are shared. The difficulty is the maintenance of standards.
4. The station, and radio education in general, benefit from direct contact with more teachers and pupils.
5. Workshop teachers gain experience and secure an opportunity for creative expression.
6. In the long run a better "screening" of pupil talent takes place since more performers appear.

The best plan is a combination of the two—a pool of available talent for special programs and those in which a continuity of roles is needed, and the use of school workshops for delegated programs. The script shown in Chapter 3, "No Hit Parade," illustrates how this combination plan can be used.

In addition to providing opportunities for program participation, there are other activities which the station can undertake that are very helpful to the radio-workshop teachers and pupils:

1. A library of appropriate scripts for school production can be developed and catalogues distributed to the schools. A loose-leaf form for later additions is desirable.
2. A transcription library is likewise helpful. The station will probably find that only pressings and tape can be circulated, since the instantaneous transcriptions are easily marred. However, copies of these may be made available to the schools upon receipt of a blank disk or tape.
3. Periodic demonstrations of the newest radio equipment are particularly helpful to those teachers who maintain school equipment.
4. The station staff can take the lead in forming a local chapter of the Association for Education by Radio. Thus, it can help keep teachers informed of latest developments in the field.
5. To stimulate pupil effort the station in cooperation with the English department can sponsor an original script-writing contest each year. The prize-winning play may then be produced on the air.
6. "Production Clinics" held periodically at the station, and often with the aid of commercial radiomen, serve to encourage workshop teachers to strive for high production standards.
7. Recognizing that careless operation of the school's central-sound system can be a bottleneck in classroom reception, the station staff can encourage efficiency by making awards to pupil operators.

Station WBOE issues an inscribed certificate to those pupil operators who have been recommended by the radio-workshop teachers.

Station Relations: Local Commercial Stations

In most communities the men who operate commercial radio stations are public-spirited citizens who take pride in their schools. They will usually regard the establishment of a school radio station as a progressive step in a modern educational system. Some commercial broadcasters welcome the school station because it relieves them of a burden. The classroom programs they may have carried hitherto invariably had a limited appeal to the general public.

However, whether the welcome be for positive or for negative reasons, harmonious relations can be beneficial to the radio educators, for the local commercial stations can be of assistance in several ways:

1. They can advise in filing FCC applications and in technical planning.
2. They can provide lines from the school station to their own control rooms, thus enabling the schools to relay selected local programs and possibly sustaining-network features.
3. They can occasionally record special programs for use later by the school station. This is particularly helpful when the educational station is closed as it may be during the summer, week ends, and possibly evening hours.
4. They can conduct demonstrations and lectures on various aspects of radio broadcasting. A summer workshop for teachers can be conducted jointly by school and commercial stations.
5. They can provide radio time for school public-relations programs planned for adult listeners.

Assistance of this type can be reciprocal. School broadcasters will do well to offer whatever cooperation they can. For example, they can do the following:

1. They can see to it that whenever school personnel is scheduled to appear on a commercial station, performances are smooth and constitute "good radio."
2. When such appearances are to take place, the school broadcasters can effectively publicize the programs, thus benefiting themselves and also contributing to more good will for the commercial station. Methods to be used were discussed in Chapter 11.
3. They can keep local stations informed of outstanding pupil ability, particularly in the technical field.
4. If school regulations permit, they can lend certain radio equipment for which there may be an emergency need.

The radio educator, like many of his colleagues, must be careful that he does not adopt a supercilious attitude whereby everything "commercial" is *ipso facto* inferior. This does not imply that all commercial practices have educational merit. The right to make constructive criticisms should be guarded and exercised. The criticisms, however, should be based on demonstrable facts and not on a general attitude.

Once the school man attempts to operate a radio station he becomes a hybrid, educator and showman combined. He must learn to speak the languages of both.

Station Relations: Community Agencies

A noncommercial educational station is a democratic agency which presents programs all of which are sponsored—by the people. The people, too, can be called upon to provide many of the program resources. In every locality there are numerous community enterprises which can be of immense help to a school station. Since these stations ordinarily operate on a limited budget, such assistance is doubly welcome. A preliminary survey of community resources is therefore highly desirable. Groups which can contribute to a rich program service include: museums, local newspaper staffs, government officials, little-theater groups, university faculties and students, musical organizations, racial groups, social-service agencies, medical and bar associations, women's clubs, radio councils, and libraries.

The help which the station can secure from such organizations is apparent. Dramatic talent can be found among the amateur-theatrical groups. Specialized information for use in a health series can come from medical associations. Many newspaper staffs can provide qualified commentators. They can aid in publicizing programs and in preparing such visual materials as maps.

The values of such cooperative relations can be illustrated by a description of the assistance the Cleveland Public Library has given to Station WBOE:

1. In the past few years five series of programs have been presented by members of the library staff: *This Week's Review, The Story Hour, Stories of the Friendly Nations, Keep Up to Date,* and *The Story Lady.*
2. The library staff suggests reference materials which are included in teachers' guides.
3. Special bookshelves are arranged correlating with programs to be broadcast.
4. Printed posters and bookmarks have been prepared and distributed jointly. The bookmarks distributed to listeners of a story series listed books and programs for leisure-time reading and listening.

Periodically the station conducts demonstrations, lectures, and auditions which are helpful to the library. Its staff recognizes the growing interdependence of two educational mediums—the library and the radio.

Program planning which does not use community resources effectively is likely to be barren and routine, as well as expensive.

The Classroom Programs of a School Station

Several of the principles pertaining to program planning have already been mentioned. However, three in particular should be emphasized: (a) a variety of programs, (b) meeting local needs, and (c) developing from school situations.

It is the writers' belief that a good program service resembles that of a good library. Programs should be of many types and presented in many ways. It is a mistake to assume that all programs should be purely supplementary. It is no less a mistake to present demonstration lessons only. Dramatizations and talks, forums and interviews, quizzes and musicals—every broadcast form has a definite place on the station schedule. Variety of content and form is the first principle in program planning.

A school station secures a license because it presumably will serve local needs. Unless these specific needs are known and programs planned in response to them, the primary purpose for station operation is not satisfied. If the programs presented are no more suitable to the classrooms of the district than those already available on other stations, then it is hard to justify school-station support, at least on the basis of classroom broadcasting. In planning for a maximum classroom reception it is utterly unrealistic, for example, to rule out the requirements of local courses of study. A second principle to consider, therefore, is the need for developing programs planned to serve specific needs.

The third principle is closely related to the foregoing. The successful manufacturer knows that acceptance of a product depends to a great degree upon its practical utility. He engages in consumer research. His blueprints are modified by his findings. The same is true of program planning for school consumption. Program ideas that originate in a swivel chair and look fine on paper had better be examined by teachers and supervisors before production begins. The question to consider is not what is the artistic effect in the studio, but rather what is the probable result in the classroom. The third principle in planning school programs is the need for securing the judgment of those on the reception end: pupils, teachers, principals, and supervisors.

Current WBOE Programs and Their Preparation. The following description of current WBOE programs is presented with the hope that it will illustrate some of the principles noted earlier.

As has been indicated, Station WBOE is a "service agency" for the divisions of instruction of the Cleveland Public Schools. A division of instruction is responsible for any decision to use radio as a classroom aid, for general planning of a resulting series, and for the specific content of individual programs. Practically speaking, this responsibility is usually carried out by the supervisor and a teacher-committee, assisted by the WBOE coordinator and a script writer assigned to the series. The basic responsibility of the school station is to produce programs that will best convey the content decided upon by the division.

Several of the elementary-school radio series are prepared by "curriculum centers" or laboratory schools. At each of these schools experimentation takes place in the development of improved methods for the various subject areas, such as safety, health, music, arithmetic, and science. To these schools there have been brought those teachers who appear to be especially interested and capable in the teaching of their subjects. As a reservoir of techniques and procedures is developed at the school, and as thought then is given to the distribution of these methods to the other elementary schools, various agencies of distribution are employed. The radio station is regarded as one of these.

When a curriculum center is responsible for a radio series, the script writer usually works at the center and tries out the radio lessons first with classes at that center. These series have become known as "participation lessons" since their radio techniques often involve participation by pupils in the classroom under the direction of a "radio teacher," with the classroom teacher acting as observer and guide.

Broadcast series offered by the divisions of instruction at the junior and senior high-school levels are usually planned directly by the supervisor, radio coordinator, and script writer; however, they follow the advice of a teacher-committee which has met first to plan and then, later, to evaluate. Like the elementary-school series, these programs are carefully coordinated with the development of a course of study, amplifying or enriching its content in the direction considered necessary by a division of instruction.

Script writers are selected by the division of instruction with the advice and consent of Station WBOE. They are usually teachers who have had successful classroom experience and are able to adapt their skills in writing to radio communication.

Volunteer adult groups and school radio-workshop talent are used to present the programs. The production and direction of the broadcasts is in the hands of WBOE coordinators and directors. Coordinators also act as script editors, although program content is determined entirely by divisional supervisors.

In 1949–1950, three series produced by outside radio agencies or networks were also selected and recommended by divisions of instruction because they were closely related to classroom work. For almost all of their series, divisions sent utilization guides to teachers for each program offered; this in addition to advance announcements about the series. Pupil worksheets were also available for some of the elementary-school series. As will also be noted, several of the series used selected lantern slides which were synchronized in the classroom with the broadcast.

During the spring term of 1949–1950 the following program series were offered by divisions of instruction:

DIVISION OF ART

Elementary-School Series

Art Appreciation is presented weekly to sixth-grade classes. Lantern slides assist the broadcaster to point out the artist's understanding and use of design. The series emphasizes the fact that design is the shaping of material into forms suitable to the material itself.

Junior High-School Series

A 7A series investigates various media used by the artist, such as wood, soap, plaster, linoleum, and textiles.

An 8A series aims at developing a discriminative observation of creative work and an interest in the creative problems of artists. Programs deal with water colors, drawings, cartoons, and the decorative use of figures.

DIVISION OF ENGLISH AND LANGUAGE ARTS

Elementary-School Series

The Storybook is planned for six-and-seven-year-olds and once a week tells old favorites and new stories in a simple dramatic form or by narrative enlivened by sound.

The Poetry Parade once a month presents a selection of poetry for upper-primary classes, in direct response to requests from primary teachers for poetry by radio.

Story Lady, directed to fourth-grade classes, is presented weekly in cooperation with the Cleveland Public Library. The stories include traditional favorites as well as those recently published; they are told by expert storytellers from the Children's Department of the Library. The series is planned in the belief that listening to a well-told "unadorned" narrative is of value at this age in the teaching of language arts.

The Treasure Chest of Poetry is broadcast to upper-elementary classes every two weeks. Poetry readers—a man and woman—weave the poetry into conversation around a central theme, such as "In Merry Mood," "Spring's Around the Corner," "Poet's Portrait Gallery," etc. Multiple voices, music, and sound effects are added to heighten dramatic interest or to create mood. Art spontaneously resulting from the series is exhibited at WBOE for the appreciation of visiting teachers and pupils.

Junior High-School Series

Passing in Review presents, in some programs, a dramatized book review as a means of stimulating the reading of books of a similar type; other programs present poetry of interest to this age group.

Weigh Your Words demonstrates how language can be made more effective in many of the customary activities of junior high-school boys and girls, such as making introductions, conducting a club meeting, writing a letter, applying for a job, etc.

Senior High-School Series

The American Story dramatizes short stories by American writers dealing with the American scene. The acting in this series is done by professional actors of the Cleveland Play House, a nonprofit community-repertory theater.

Fun from the Dictionary provides a systematic development of vocabulary through brief dramatic scenes which are analyzed for word meanings by a pupil panel. Each program uses production talent from high-school radio workshops. Teachers receive in advance an outline of program content and supplementary material.

DIVISION OF FOREIGN LANGUAGES

Elementary-School Series

Elementary French presents a native of France who, in weekly conversational meetings by air, introduces a basic vocabulary to children who are still in the "imitative stage" in which bilingual learning comes readily. French folk songs are also taught.

Elementary Spanish, like the French programs, presents to children a conversational vocabulary and simple folk songs.

Junior and Senior High-School Series

German and French series are intended for intermediate classes which are taught both in junior and senior high school. The programs are developed and produced by junior or senior high-school classes under the direction of their language teachers.

A Spanish series is intended for intermediate classes and is presented either by Spanish classes and their teachers or by Spanish or Latin-American visitors interviewed by pupils.

DIVISION OF HANDCRAFT

Elementary-School Series

The Village is a series of weekly lessons for upper-primary children which aims to stimulate interest in construction and to develop manual skills and the ability to follow directions. Stories about village life lead to the construction of miniature buildings such as the general store, post office, church, and school. Schools receive materials, instructions, designs, and patterns so that the children may participate actively in the broadcasts.

DIVISION OF HEALTH

Elementary-School Series

Good Health to You consists of eight programs which present to middle-primary children basic concepts in cleanliness, rest, exercise, and diet. The series is a "serial" story of the adventures of two seven-year-old children.

DIVISION OF HOME ECONOMICS

Senior High-School Series

Boy Dates Girl receives its title by permission of *Scholastic*. A radio representative of Gay Head, the *Scholastic* columnist, discusses with high-school young people those problems in family and personal relations which have been suggested by listening classes. Dramatized scenes are used to "take-off" into discussion.

DIVISION OF INDUSTRIAL ARTS

Senior High-School Series

The March of Production describes the steps in the development of a new automobile model from the "idea" through progressive stages of design, manufacture, and sales. The series is prepared to help high-school boys understand the tremendous organizational planning and cooperation which lie behind American mass production.

DIVISION OF KINDERGARTENS

Once Upon a Time introduces kindergartners to school radio listening. The weekly series includes both old folk tales and new stories and is planned by a group of kindergarten teachers. Several programs are illustrated by lantern slides during the story period.

DIVISION OF MATHEMATICS

Elementary-School Series

Primary Arithmetic consists of six participation lessons involving such arithmetic processes as carrying in addition, making change, and telling time.

4B Arithmetic aims to give meaning and understanding to number of experiences of children at the fourth-grade level by suggesting activities (i.e., reading time schedules, shopping from a price list, using a vertical bar) which motivate the arithmetic processes and skills and develop quantitative thinking.

Junior High-School Series

Get the Answer Right! consists of eight biweekly programs designed to stimulate interest in simple mental-arithmetic skills for seventh-grade pupils. Junior high-school pupils in the studio compete to get the answers to problems in mental arithmetic which are presented in dramatized situations. Opportunity is given for simultaneous participation by listening classes. The final program is a competition among listening classes for the mental math championship.

DIVISION OF MUSIC

Elementary School Series

Music for Young Listeners, in a weekly series of listening lessons for upper-primary classes, presents a carefully chosen repertory of little masterpieces. Professional musicians are used. The aim is to develop discriminate listening and a taste for good music.

Rhythmic Activities is planned for second-year classes and is presented weekly by a qualified music teacher who uses carefully chosen selections for rhythmic experiences. It is a participation-lesson series.

Rote Songs is planned to aid the first-year teacher by presenting a variety of methods of procedure and selected songs for first-year children. This participation series aims to help develop good vocal habits as well as careful habits of listening.

Song Study is planned to guide teachers of fifth-grade classes in the wise use of a new music book which emphasizes singing, listening, playing, rhythmic, and creative experiences.

Junior High School Series

Musical Highways and Byways—Master Composers gives an opportunity for junior high-school choral groups to present illustrative songs in programs which are based upon brief biographies of great composers.

DIVISION OF SAFETY

Elementary School Series

Safety-Sam, Detective emphasizes safety rules through the medium of a detective-mystery format. "The Case of the Cold Bulldog," for instance, recalled winter-sport safety regulations to its upper elementary-school listeners.

DIVISION OF SCHOOL GARDENS

Elementary-School Series

The Garden Club brings advice each month to elementary-school enthusiasts by experts of the Division.

DIVISION OF SCIENCE

Elementary-School Series

Fourth-Grade Science, a weekly series based on the course of study, presents participation lessons which suggest recommended teaching techniques. A detailed guidebook accompanies the series. Units included are "Why do living things need air and water?", "Why do we have days and nights?", "How do magnets work?", etc.

Junior High-School Series

Adventures in Research, as produced by the Westinghouse Research Laboratories, is correlated with the junior-high course of study. This series presents dramatically the stories of great scientific experiments and experimenters.

Science for Better Living uses talks, interviews, and dramatizations to explain some law or principle of science as it is put to use in home or in industry. This series is intended for 9A general-science classes.

Senior High-School Series

Biology for Living Today is broadcast to 10A biology classes. Each

THE SCHOOL BROADCASTING STATION

program explains some law or principle evidenced in the biological sciences or dramatizes rules governing physical and mental health.

Work Made Easier follows closely the course of study as outlined in the "Curriculum of Physics." Tape recordings of field trips and on-the-spot discussions with industrial and research experts help explain the practical use of some law of physics.

DIVISION OF SOCIAL STUDIES

Elementary-School Series

Behind the Headlines is in its fifth year of bringing to fifth- and sixth-grade children authoritative commentators who explain the background of some news story of current interest. This series is one of three which the Division offers as a radio springboard for the discussion of current problems; it is the first in respect to the age-level to which it is broadcast.

Leaders of Colonial America, for 5A classes, dramatizes the contributions made by men and women famous in the settlement and colonial life of America. The selection of leaders correlates with those emphasized in the course of study.

The Story of Early Cleveland is based on a book read by upper-primary classes. The series provides both participation lessons and dramatic programs which deal with events and social conditions in the early years of Cleveland's history.

Junior High-School Series

The News: Places and People chooses each week an important problem of local, national, or international significance and presents by narrative-dramatization an understanding of the persons and issues involved.

The Ohio Story is a selected rebroadcast of programs originally presented by the Ohio Bell Telephone Company. These entertaining dramatizations of incidents in Ohio's past enrich the work done in state history at this grade level. The sponsor and radio station permit the Division to select the programs of value to the course of study, record them for the Division's use over WBOE, and permit all advertising to be deleted.

Senior High-School Series

Current Topics has been for twelve years the stimulus which a large proportion of social-studies teachers has chosen to open the weekly discussion of current news. A visiting authority or local expert may be invited by the Division to explain and comment on the selected topic or issue or it may be presented by dramatization or round-table discussion. Carefully developed utilization guides supply additional factual information and a bibliography to assist further discussion by classroom listeners.

You Are There, the noteworthy CBS series, is rebroadcast over WBOE for school use with the permission of the American Federation of Musicians, the American Federation of Radio Artists, and the network-affiliate Station WGAR. It has been possible for the Division to schedule the programs in two series: (1) for classes in world history; (2) for classes in American history.

UN Story describes the work of its various agencies by a dramatic application of their work in some part of the world.

SPECIAL EVENTS

WBOE presents special programs in observance of various holidays, observances, and campaigns. The following are illustrative: Edison's Birthday, Brotherhood Week, UN Week, Pan-American Day, Constitution Day, the Community Chest and Red Cross campaigns, Thanksgiving Day, Christmas, etc.

PROGRAMS FOR TEACHERS

From time to time, supervisors present meetings-of-the-air in which they initiate discussion of general problems by departmental groups gathered in individual schools. Programs to elementary teachers are usually presented twice: late in the lunch hour and after school; those to junior and senior high-school teachers come at the end of the school day.

PROGRAM FOR ADULT LISTENERS OUTSIDE THE SCHOOL

Music for Masters broadcasts to its home- and office-listening audiences an hour's concert of symphonic or chamber music from 4:00 to 5:00 P.M. each school day.

Five Centuries of French Music, produced and transcribed by Radio Diffusion Francaise, presents weekly an unusual program of instrumental music by French composers.

"BBC Transcription Service" brings to WBOE's adult listeners serial dramatization of famous English novels, and two music programs: *London Studio Concerts* and *British Concert Hall.*

Festival Weeks—Station WBOE's broadcasting calendar cannot coincide exactly with that of the classroom year. The closing and opening weeks of a semester are usually not suitable for classroom broadcasts which are integrated with the courses of study. Consequently, during the last week of the first semester and the opening week of the second and during the final week of school in the spring, the School Station broadcasts to those adult listeners at home or in offices who have become regular listeners to the Station's after-school programs. These "Mid-Year Anniversary Festival" and "June Festival" weeks present recorded music of all types (opera, chamber music, orchestral concerts) and dramatic and informational programs, most of which are transcribed. These festival weeks are designed to present unusually high-quality programs for adult listening and are heard during the Station's entire broadcasting day from 8:00 A.M. to 5:00 P.M.

Schedule Preparation. Numerous methods are used in schedule development as in program preparation. In the elementary schools the following are the steps generally taken in planning the schedule for the coming term. First, the subject supervisors indicate in what areas radio programs are to be given. They are asked at that time to indicate their preferences as to the periods for scheduling. Frequently, a conference then is held at which time the radio schedule is developed.

In organizing the schedule for the lower grades several factors are considered. Generally no more than one major program a day is scheduled for any specific grade. A pupil's average listening time is thirty minutes a week. Obviously there can be too much radio. A limitation of three major programs per week for each grade level has been suggested. This is exclusive of purely supplementary material, such as dramatized stories.

If a program in sixth-grade art, for example, is scheduled at 9:30, then no other sixth-grade program is scheduled at that time during the remainder of the week. This enables the classes to have their art lessons at the same time each day. Of course, no programs are scheduled during the recess period. Ample class time is left before and after programs so that proper use can be made of the broadcasts. This would be more difficult with programs of greater length.

Classroom listening is entirely voluntary. Teachers should have the same freedom to select radio programs as they have to choose other teaching aids. It is much better to have a teacher use but one or two programs a week, and use them enthusiastically without feeling the undue pressure of time, than to have her tune in for several programs a week and utilize them indifferently. At the same time the choice of radio offerings should be great enough so that she can select whatever suits the specific needs of her class.

In the secondary grades, where synchronization with individual school schedules is more difficult, the above procedure is modified. The principals have helped greatly by moving toward a more uniform city-wide bell schedule. In scheduling a certain series, the program coordinator, working with the supervisor sponsoring the series, analyzes the school schedules and periods of optimum reception are chosen. By means of transcriptions the programs are repeated as often as ten times and, in addition, recorded copies are made available for school use.

When individual schools purchase newer types of recorders such as the magnetized tape unit, it will be possible to eliminate these repeat programs. The program will be presented once, recorded at each school, and repeated there as often as it is desired. Since the recorded material can be erased, the cost of discs will be eliminated. The inevitable noise increase resulting from repeated playings also will be overcome.

ILLUSTRATIVE DAILY SCHEDULE
WEDNESDAY, MAY 17, 1950

7:59		Sign On	
T * 8:00		Bulletin Board (Junior and Senior High)	
* 8:05	(ET)	The American Story—"THAT GREEK DOG"	(KM)
8:20		Music	
* 8:25	(ET)	Passing in Review—"A FACE, A FIGURE, A CHANGING"	(ESH)
8:40		Music	
* 8:50	(ET)	The American Story	
T * 9:05		Bulletin Board (Elementary)	
* 9:10	(ET)	Behind the Headlines—DR. GOOD: "RECENT DEVELOPMENTS IN MEDICAL RESEARCH"	(RF)
9:20		Music	
* 9:25	(ET)	Poetry Parade—"LET'S GO TO THE COUNTRY"	(RF)
* 9:40	(ET)	Passing in Review	
* 9:55	(ET)	The American Story	
T * 10:10	(ET)	5B Song Study—"A PLEASANT SURPRISE"	(RF)
* 10:30	(ET)	Passing in Review	
10:45		Music	
* 10:50	(ET)	The American Story	
* 11:05	(ET)	Story of Early Cleveland—"SCHOOLS OF LONG AGO"	(RF)
* 11:20	(ET)	Passing in Review	
* 11:35	(ET)	The American Story	
11:50		Music	

* 12:00	(ET)	Passing in Review
T 12:15		Music
* 12:20	(ET)	The American Story
* 12:35	(ET)	Passing in Review
12:50		Music
* 1:05	(ET)	The American Story
1:20		Music
* 1:25	(ET)	Passing in Review
* 1:40	(ET)	Behind the Headlines
* 1:50	(ET)	The American Story
* 2:05	(ET)	Passing in Review
* 2:20	(ET)	Once Upon a Time—"VERY STYLISH FARM" (RF)
		Music
* 2:35	(ET)	The American Story
* 2:50	(ET)	Passing in Review
3:05		Music
3:15	(ET)	Five Centuries of French Music—"MILHAUD AND POULENC" (KM)
* 3:45	(ET)	Ohio Story—"BOYHOOD OF A BIL-LIONAIRE" (ESH)
* 4:00		Music of the Masters
5:00		Sign Off

A brief analysis of such a day's broadcasting schedule will indicate several features of this type of school-station operation.

It will be seen that, whereas the usual radio schedule is divided into quarter-hour, half-hour, and hour periods, the WBOE schedule varies so that some programs, for example, end at 9:40 A.M., others begin at 1:25 P.M., and so on. This is done because the length of the school-radio program is not rigid. If the program runs short, then either recorded or live music is used to fill in. To give the school broadcaster a reasonable amount of flexibility, a "tight" schedule is avoided if possible. Regular programs (those marked with asterisk) must, of course, begin on time.

As indicated earlier, the repetition of programs is another feature of this type of schedule. It will be seen that the program *Passing in Review* is presented nine times, once for each class period.

The letter *T* shown at the left in the schedule indicates when the correct time is to be given by the studio announcer. This is done several times daily, since it is important that the school and station clocks be synchronized lest a part of a program be missed. The initials to the right indicate the staff member who is responsible for the specific program.

Related Activities. In addition to the presentation of classroom programs, a school station can undertake the challenging task of providing cultural materials for home listening. This type of program service will be discussed in detail in the closing chapter. There are, however, additional allied activities which relate to pupils and teachers, which the educational station can perform.

Consider a few emergency uses. When there was talk of impending air raids, the public, parochial, and suburban schools of Greater Cleveland established continuous-listening procedures whereby WBOE could alert the area in a few seconds. When the teachers were engaged in rationing, daily bulletins were broadcast to the rationing centers answering questions which had arisen. In February, 1944, Cleveland teachers were supplied with income-tax blanks, and after school they listened in their buildings as a tax expert, using a hypothetical case, went through the forms step by step. A visual audience in the studio, also composed of teachers, asked questions informally. The school station made friends that day.

The radio is used to administer city-wide tests; for example, high-school shorthand-dictation tests, the Seashore Test of Musical Aptitude, and the Kuhlman-Anderson Intelligence Test are broadcast each semester. Pupil forms and teacher guides are used. The Bureau of Educational Research indicates that the results are much more objective in centrally controlled, expertly administered radio tests than from the individual classroom procedure where many variables inevitably exist.

During the Second World War preinduction needs were met to some extent with the help of the school station. For example, lessons in code were broadcast, using Signal Corps transcriptions. A Saturday morning class in communications was established at WBOE and instructed by the technical staff. Pupils used the studio equipment as a technical laboratory. Certificates were granted upon completion of the course. Two series of interviews with local authorities in aviation and another with members of the Selective Service office and other government officials also contributed to such orientation.

The school station can do much to stimulate interest in speech—even on the elementary-school level. For instance, the station has built several portable public-address systems which circulate in the schools on a definite schedule. The teachers use the equipment in any way they wish. However, at the conclusion of each period, each school sends in audition rating cards to the station, where upon further screening takes place in an original playlet rebroadcast to the school. In this way a "talent pool" is being established in the elementary schools, and the file made available to program producers.

A Saturday morning elementary-school radio workshop was conducted for one year, using children from the major work classes—those of very high intelligence.

In a large school system radio can help to humanize the administration. Occasionally, not too often, the superintendent addresses all the teachers of the city.

At the conclusion of the term, graduation-day greetings were presented by the assistant superintendent in charge. The children were then welcomed by the administrator of the division which they were about to enter. These programs were made a part of the regular graduation-day exercises at the various schools.

The radio station also can serve as an "oral house organ." For example, WBOE carried a series for several semesters called *Know Your Schools.* These 10-minute talks were presented once a month after school hours as the opening phase of school faculty meetings throughout the city. A discussion led by the principal followed. These subjects are illustrative: "Your School Custodian," "Meet the School Secretary," "Some Ohio School Laws Every Teacher Should Know," "How Our Schools Are Financed," "The Kind of Teacher a Parent Admires." In 1950–1951 a series of city-wide faculty meetings on "Mental Health in the Classroom" was conducted by a psychiatrist.

Arrangements were made with the Washington branch of the Association for Education by Radio whereby Cleveland pupils can ask questions of leading government officials. Recordings of the interview were made with the cooperation of the Washington schools for use over WBOE.

The series *Home Safety* was designed for listening by parent-teacher groups meeting in the various schools. This series, developed in cooperation with the Safety Council, featured the appearance of physicians, firemen, policemen, and others. A certificate was awarded to each parent who listened to the entire series.

A city-wide oral spelling contest is broadcast in cooperation with a local newspaper. Election returns are edited for schoolroom listening. Drives and other civic enterprises are often launched by the school station. Thus it is seen that a school broadcasting organization can perform a great variety of helpful services.

The Preparation of Classroom-Teacher Manuals

One of the tasks frequently undertaken by a school station is the preparation of program guides for classroom teachers. The purpose of the discussion here is not to list in detail what should be included in these guides but rather to suggest several general principles.

A brief examination of the materials issued by the radio departments of the Chicago, Detroit, New York, Cleveland, and Rochester public schools, as well as the guides issued by several university-owned radio stations, will be helpful.

The classroom guides prepared for reception of network programs must be more general than the lesson guides planned for a local radio series to be used within a specific school system. The objective of the national series must be a supplementary one, since there cannot be a close relationship between the series planned for nation-wide reception and the specific needs of a local course of study. Therefore, the suggested activities in the manual accompanying the network radio series must also be of a supplementary nature. A flexible organization of teaching materials is necessary because certain local limitations may interfere. The national radio presentation generally cannot assume any fixed preparatory procedures and materials in the classrooms, since the wide variety of reception conditions precludes any probable uniformity. For greatest voluntary acceptance by the classroom teacher the supplementary network program cannot demand additional effort from the teacher, and consequently the aim must be to serve the teacher most in the simplest way.

In the local system, however, radio reception and effective program utilization can well be regarded as a part of classroom teaching duties and, therefore, there can be a more justifiable expectation that the teacher will attempt, at least, the suggested preparatory and follow-up activities. Since the local broadcast is more closely related to the local course of study, the manual can be more specific and it can refer to definite materials which are available locally. It can relate to other subject areas which are taught in the local schools and it can be planned for more specific classroom use.

One type of detailed guide might include the following:

1. Introductory Information
   Advance listing of all programs, dates, etc.
   The purpose and plan of the radio program
   Suggested seating arrangement
   Suggestions for distributing materials
   Reception in the classroom—the teacher's **function**
   Hints for teaching with radio
   General follow-up techniques
   Suggestions for using visual aids
2. The Individual Program
   Objectives of the program, possible outcomes

Before the Broadcast
   Materials needed—the teacher's responsibility
   If pupil worksheet is used, copy is attached

During the Broadcast
   Activity by the teacher
   Type of student participation

After the Broadcast
   The teacher's responsibility: immediately after the program; between radio programs
   Pupil's responsibility: individual progress chart
   Scope and summary of the program
   Suggested references: for teacher, for pupil
   Optional tasks for superior pupils
   Related vocabulary to be emphasized
   Test questions; key for grading

In the preparation of program guides, several principles merit attention. In the first place, it should be understood that the degree of detail in a manual is determined by the purpose and the nature of the program. A presentation distinctly supplementary in its scope usually requires less advance information than does a program planned to adhere closely to a local course of study.

In the preparation of the guide there is the problem of not providing the teacher with enough information; there is also the danger of including too much. The purpose of the guide is to assemble selective data which will help the teacher to utilize the program. If the material assembled is so unwieldy and so detailed that it requires undue effort in further selection, then the guide has not been of maximum value to the teacher. In fact, if the material accompanying a program is so comprehensive, even though it be scholarly, that it is actually formidable, a natural temptation on the part of the teacher is to throw the whole thing away and proceed with her other duties.

The teachers' guides used with the demonstration-radio-lesson technique are generally quite detailed. That fact in itself is not a weakness, in view of the purpose of the programs, but it is important that the teachers should not be asked to assemble more materials for any radio lesson than are absolutely necessary and that the materials required should be easily obtainable. Once the items have been collected, the classroom teacher can expect that the broadcaster will suggest a use for every item called for in the guide. The good will of the classroom teacher is indispensable in school broadcasting. Anything tending to alienate her interest and support is regrettable. A well-planned guide which makes clear to the teacher just how the broadcaster is attempting to help her contributes to this necessary interest and cooperation.

The program should not prescribe; it should suggest. Whenever possible, optional procedures should be noted. Not only does this stimulate planned and personal rather than automatic and perhaps indifferent utilization, but it facilitates adjustment to classroom differences in terms of varying pupil abilities and interests.

An opening statement of the philosophy underlying the radio series is desirable and it is essential that reference to this philosophy be made all through the guide. All too frequently opening comments are merely scanned, when in reality they may be the keystone of the entire enterprise.

The manual should usually contain a synopsis of the program to be presented. To some extent this can help to overcome one of the chief limitations in radio utilization—the inability to pre-audit the program. The synopsis, however, should be very brief.

Once the manual has been prepared and distributed to teachers, no major changes should be made in the program. Last-minute unannounced changes, though sometimes unavoidable, tend to destroy the teacher's interest in radio as a reliable teaching tool.

Finally, one other suggestion should be mentioned. Not many classroom teachers can write effectual radio scripts or direct satisfactory programs, but they probably do know effective classroom procedures. To the extent that they share in the planning of the manuals they become more vitally interested in the success of the programs. The guides thus prepared are more functional than those drawn up by someone at a radio station who has had little or no classroom experience. The alert broadcasting organization will make every effort to spread this participation and, even if in the final analysis the work still will be done by a few, the approach is a sound one.

It is easy to understand how a classroom teacher receiving a manual and seeing in it the names of some of her colleagues would be more sympathetic to the enterprise than if it were merely some more mimeographed paper to be filed and gather dust. At least the teacher would not be so likely to claim that the programs and guides are impractical and not related to her classroom needs. A well-prepared program guide is not only a collection of "advance tips" for improving classroom utilization, but it should also serve to stimulate interest in radio as an educational tool.

Advance Bulletins.   In addition to classroom manuals, the school station usually finds it desirable to issue advance program bulletins. The lack of time prohibits the preparation of guides for every program, especially for those scheduled on short notice. Repetition of program times serves as a reminder; also there may be last-minute changes.

Two types of bulletins have been used with some success. One is the "Bulletin Board"—a daily five-minute broadcast in which a forecast of the day's radio schedule is presented. These Bulletin Boards are scheduled early in the morning and each school arranges to have a pupil or teacher listen regularly so that announcements can be forwarded as needed.

A second type of bulletin, which appears weekly in mimeographed form, is illustrated on pages 497 to 502. Several copies are sent to each school: principal, head of each department, radio teacher, and office for posting. The distribution of these bulletins varies from school to school. In some places they are distributed by the department heads so that all teachers may see the forthcoming schedule. In several schools a pupil's service club circulates the bulletin. In a few cases a special radio bulletin board has been constructed on which the weekly announcement is posted. In the secondary grades the responsibility for informing teachers of future programs is usually assigned to the radio teacher. In the elementary schools the principal or her assistant undertakes this task.

Encouraging Effective Use of Programs

The measure of a school station's success is not how many programs it presents, but how many programs are received and to what extent they serve educational objectives.

The station's activity does not end at the microphone. Its primary objective is to provide educative experiences. If school broadcasters will remember that, they can effectively stimulate the use of their presentations.

The most effective way of encouraging teachers to utilize radio programs is to make the value of the programs evident to them. If a classroom broadcast is conceived as a radio "show" with educational value incidental to entertainment, then the station staff has no right to complain that teachers are indifferent to "educational" radio. Occasionally when such a comment as the preceding is made, vociferous objections are raised that artistic forms are sacrificed, that listener appeal is overlooked, that routine pedagogy is advocated and so on. No qualified school broadcaster would argue that the use of effectual radio forms should be neglected. The appeal made here is for a sense of proportion —educational content as well as effective radio. When that proportion is achieved an increase in the use of programs is likewise attained.

Studios
Administration Bld'g.
Sixth Floor

WBOE

Transmitter
Lafayette School

CLEVELAND PUBLIC SCHOOLS
90.3 M.C. (F.M.)

WEEKLY BULLETIN OF PROGRAMS

WEEK OF APRIL 24, 1950   *BULLETIN NO. 11*

* * * * * * * * * * * * * * *

*   GREATER CLEVELAND COUNCIL FOR
THE SOCIAL STUDIES   *

*   "The F.E.P.C. Ordinance: What It Means"   *

*   Tuesday, April 25—3:30 to 4:00 P.M.   *

* By transcription, Station WBOE carries a half-hour of the *
panel discussion by distinguished local authorities which
* took place on Thursday, April 20, at the Board of Education *
Auditorium, under the moderation of Clyde F. Varner, di-
* rector of community forums.   *

* * * * * * * * * * * * * * *

Monday, April 24

BULLETIN BOARD—8:00, 9:20

GET THE ANSWER—RIGHT!—8:05, 8:50, 9:40 (For Junior High
Mathematics Classes)
"Fractions"—Eight mental arithmetic problems involving the use of
fractions are presented in dramatic form. Pupils in the studio solve
the first four and then discuss their methods for working such problems quickly.

THE NEWS: PLACES AND PEOPLE—8:25, 9:05, 9:55, 10:30,
11:20, 12:00, 12:35, 1:25, 2:05, 2:50 (For Junior High Social-Studies
Classes)
"Traffic Control and Safety"—Discussion centers on a problem of
growing importance: provision of adequate parking facilities and better control of traffic flow to decrease street congestion and increase
pedestrian safety.

PRIMARY ARITHMETIC—9:25 (For Levels 11, 12)
"Making Change for a Quarter"

RHYTHMIC ACTIVITIES—10:10 (For Middle Primary Classes)
"New Music in Duple and Triple Meter"

BIOLOGY FOR LIVING TODAY—10:50, 12:20, 1:05, 2:35 (For Senior High Biology)
"Henry's Backyard"—Based on the publication, *The Races of Mankind,* this program helps to disprove the importance of so-called "racial characteristics."

6TH GRADE ART APPRECIATION—11:05
"Glass Can Be Shaped into Fine Designs"

STORY LADY—11:35 (For 4th Grade Language Arts Classes)
"Clever Elsie"—Cyrille Levenson of Harvey Rice Branch Library returns to tell a Grimm fairly tale.

LEADERS OF COLONIAL AMERICA—1:40 (For 5A History Classes)
"Paul Revere, Baron Stiegel, Duncan Phyfe"

GOOD HEALTH TO YOU—2:20 (For Middle Primary Classes)
"Learning to Cook"—The importance of milk in the daily diet is stressed in this program.

ELEMENTARY FRENCH—3:05—Lesson No. 24

ADVENTURES IN RESEARCH—3:45 (For Supplementary Listening)
"The Purple Vapor"—Napoleon's demand for better gunpowder for his armies led to the discovery of a new chemical element, iodine. This is a transcribed production by Westinghouse Research Laboratories.

MUSIC OF THE MASTERS—4:00–5:00 (For Home-Listening)
Boccherini: Suite, "Scuola di Ballo"—London Philharmonic Orchestra
Dohnanyi: Variations on a Nursery Theme—Cyril Smith, pianist, with Liverpool Philharmonic Orchestra

Tuesday, April 25

BULLETIN BOARD—8:00, 9:05

MARCH OF PRODUCTION—8:05, 8:50, 9:55, 10:50, 11:35, 12:20, 1:05, 2:00, 2:35 (For Senior High Industrial Arts Classes)
"Final Assembly"—With the completed installation of all assembly lines in the factory, test runs are made to assure safe and rapid operation. The program covers the final steps of preparation as the factory is made ready for the manufacturing of the new automobile.

BIOLOGY FOR LIVING TODAY—8:25—Rebroadcast of Monday's program

4TH-GRADE SCIENCE—9:10—"Air: What Is It? Where Is It?"

MUSICAL HIGHWAYS AND BYWAYS—MASTER COMPOSERS—9:40 (For Junior High Music Classes)
"Songs of Schubert"—Miss Naomi Holz directs the Girls' Ensemble and Triple Trio of Alexander Hamilton Junior High School in a program of four songs by Schubert: "To Music," "Who Is Sylvia," "Wandering," and "Ave Maria."

MUSIC FOR YOUNG LISTENERS—10:10 (For Upper Primary Classes)
"Instruments Sound Well Together—Woodwind Trio"

GET THE ANSWER—RIGHT!—10:30, 11:20, 11:50, 12:35, 1:25, 2:50
Rebroadcast of Monday's program

TREASURE CHEST OF POETRY—11:05 (For 5th- and 6th-Grade Language Arts Classes)
"Pictures at an Exhibition"—Helen Barr and Edwin Helman read poetry descriptive of places and people.

6TH-GRADE ART APPRECIATION—1:40—Rebroadcast of Monday's program

STORYBOOK—2:20 (For Lower and Middle Primary Classes)
"The Twelve Wild Ducks"—Lena Donald, supervisory assistant at Paul Revere School, tells an old Scandinavian folk tale.

ELEMENTARY SPANISH—3:05—Lesson No. 25

COUNCIL FOR THE SOCIAL STUDIES—3:30–4:00 (For Supplementary Listening)
"The F.E.P.C. Ordinance: What It Means" (See Box, page 1)

MUSIC OF THE MASTERS—4:00–5:00 (For Home Listening)
Mozart: "Eine Kleine Nachtmusik"—Berlin Philharmonic Orchestra
Brahms: Eight "Hungarian Dances"—Pittsburgh Symphony Orchestra
Tchaikowsky: Overture, "Romeo and Juliet"—N.B.C. Symphony Orchestra

Wednesday, April 26

BULLETIN BOARD—8:00, 9:05

FUN FROM THE DICTIONARY—8:05, 8:50, 9:55, 10:50, 11:35, 12:20, 1:05, 1:50, 2:35 (For Senior High English Classes)
A panel of students from Glenville High School assist "Mr. Webster,

Jr." in the presentation of useful words in this vocabulary building program.

WEIGH YOUR WORDS—8:25, 9:40, 10:30, 11:20, 12:00, 12:35, 1:25, 2:05, 2:50 (For Junior High English Classes)
"Out of Order—Come Results"—A new student chairman has difficulty in conducting a meeting. He redeems his mistakes by studying and applying parliamentary rules of order.

BEHIND THE HEADLINES—9:10, 1:40 (For 5th-and 6th-Grade Social Studies Classes)
Ray Gillespie, feature columnist, Cleveland Plain Dealer, is this week's guest commentator.

GOOD HEALTH TO YOU—9:25—Rebroadcast of Monday's program

5B SONG STUDY—10:10—"Very Different Composers"

LEADERS OF COLONIAL AMERICA—11:05—Rebroadcast of Monday's program

ONCE UPON A TIME—2:20 (For Kindergarten Classes)
"Blaze and the Forest Fire"—Dr. William B. Levenson, assistant superintendent, tells the story of how a little boy and his pony spread the alarm about a forest fire.

FIVE CENTURIES OF FRENCH MUSIC—3:15 (For Supplementary Listening)
"Quintet by Gabriel Pierne; Songs by Capedevielle, and Granjany"—This transcribed program is prepared and produced by the French Broadcasting System.

OHIO STORY—3:45 (For Supplementary Listening—Social Studies Classes)
"The Promise of Apple Creek"—Soil conservation turned rundown property near Wooster into one of the best-producing farms in Ohio. The Ohio Bell Telephone Company tells the story in this transcribed production.

MUSIC OF THE MASTERS—4:00–5:00 (For Home Listening)
Beethoven: Sonata No. 24 for Piano, op. 78——Rudolph Serkin
Scarlatti: Sonatas for Piano—Robert Casadesus

Thursday, April 27

BULLETIN BOARD—8:00, 9:05

WORK MADE EASIER—8:05, 8:50, 9:55, 10:50, 11:35, 12:20, 1:05, 2:00, 2:35 (For Senior High Physics Classes)
"A History of Home-Lighting"—This first of two programs dealing

with artificial lighting in the home traces development from the pine knot and oil lamp to the electric light. Colored slides are synchronized in the classroom with this program.

These broadcasts are presented in cooperation with the Division of Art.

OHIO STORY—8:25, 11:20, 12:00—Rebroadcast of Wednesday's program

4B ARITHMETIC—9:10—"Uneven Division"

MUSICAL HIGHWAYS AND BYWAYS—9:25, 10:30, 1:25 Rebroadcast of Monday's program

ONCE UPON A TIME—9:40—Rebroadcast of Wednesday's program

ROTE SONGS—10:10 (For Lower Primary Classes)
"Balloon Song"

BEHIND THE HEADLINES—11:05—Rebroadcast of Wednesday's program

YOU ARE THERE—12:35–1:05, 3:15–3:45 (For Supplementary Listening)
"Defense of the Alamo"—This transcribed program is made available through the courtesy of Station WGAR, the Columbia Broadcasting System, the American Federation of Radio Artists, and the American Federation of Musicians.

HANDCRAFT—1:40 (For Upper Primary Classes)
"The Village Houses"

TREASURE CHEST OF POETRY—2:20—Rebroadcast of Tuesday's program

STORYBOOK—2:50—Rebroadcast of Tuesday's program

U.N. STORY—3:45 (For Supplementary Listening)
"SS. Delta Queen"—Efforts of the U.N. to improve labor conditions on boats are explained in this transcribed program produced by the Radio Division of the United Nations, Lake Success, N.Y.

MUSIC OF THE MASTERS—4:00–5:00 (For Home-Listening)
Mozart: Quartet No. 2 in E Flat for Piano and Strings—George Szell and members of the Budapest String Quartet
Beethoven: Quartet No. 14, op. 131—Budapest String Quartet

Friday, April 28

BULLETIN BOARD—8:00, 9:20

CURRENT TOPICS—8:05, 8:50, 10:05, 10:50, 11:35, 12:20, 1:05, 1:50, 2:35 (For Senior High Social Studies Classes)

"Is the Primary the Best Way to Select Candidates?"—While many voters consider the regular November elections of considerable importance, they frequently fail to vote in the primary. This program indicates the civic problems created by present primary procedures.

SCIENCE FOR BETTER LIVING—8:25, 9:05, 9:40, 10:30, 11:20, 12:00, 12:35, 1:25, 2:05 (For Junior High Science Classes)
"The Long-Distance Telephone Call"—One of the progressive steps in the use of electricity for modern communication needs is illustrated by long-distance telephone developments.

TREASURE CHEST OF POETRY—9:25—Rebroadcast of Tuesday's program

BEHIND THE HEADLINES—10:20, 1:40—Rebroadcast of Wednesday's program

ONCE UPON A TIME—11:05—Rebroadcast of Wednesday's program

GOOD HEALTH TO YOU—2:20—Rebroadcast of Monday's program

STORY LADY—2:50—Rebroadcast of Monday's program

"GREAT EXPECTATIONS" by Charles Dickens—3:15–3:45 (For Supplementary Listening)
Installment No. 10—A serialized dramatization produced by the BBC

SONGS OF FRANCE—3:45 (For Supplementary Listening)
"Round-up in the Pyrenees"—Part 2—Transcribed in France, this program is made available through the courtesy of the French Broadcasting System.

MUSIC OF THE MASTERS—4:00–5:00 (For Home-Listening)
Haydn: Symphony No. 93—London Philharmonic Orchestra
Wagner: Love Duet, "Tristan und Isolde" (Act II, Sc. 2)—Helen Traubel, Torsten Ralf, Hertz Galz with the Metropolitan Opera Association Orchestra

It should be recalled that radio broadcasting did not arrive on the American scene until many, if not most, of the present generation of classroom teachers and administrators left college. It would be highly optimistic to assume that within so short a time these teachers generally would adopt the use of this new tool. The task of educating the educators remains. In this process the school station can play an important role.

What are some specific procedures that can be used?

1. The preparation of program guides developed with the help of teacher committees has already been discussed. The emphasis should be on the use of programs in practical classroom situations.

2. Before some of the radio series begin, an introductory broadcast planned for teachers and presented after school hours has been found helpful. In this "preview" program the script writer, supervisor, an outstanding teacher, and an assistant superintendent can discuss the purpose of the series, its form, and primarily the best ways of utilizing it in the classroom.

3. Periodic demonstrations to which teachers come and witness a classroom being handled by an expert teacher before, during, and after a program have been of great value. A special Demonstration Studio, for example, has been constructed at WBOE. In addition to teaching procedures, demonstrations are held of the latest radio equipment. The use of an instrument such as the ordinary playback machine, even the proper tuning of radio sets, particularly the more critical FM receivers, is facilitated by specific instruction.

4. An annual "Radio Exhibit" where some of the outcomes of the radio programs can be shown has also been helpful. The exhibit should be announced early in the school year so that materials can be saved and later assembled.

5. Station staff members should seek teaching opportunities in extension courses and teachers' workshops where better utilization methods can be encouraged. The cause of radio education needs missionaries who with enthusiasm and skill can combat pedagogic inertia.

6. Some school principals who visit classrooms during radio periods have need themselves of additional information concerning radio and its classroom uses. A small pamphlet prepared specially for administrators can be of value. It should include criteria for judging effective classroom use of radio, suggestions whereby the principal can help the teachers, equipment notes, methods of program-bulletin distribution, scheduling, and similar information.

7. This seventh suggestion, which may serve to increase and improve the classroom use of radio, is not a device but rather a philosophy. By establishing the school station as an instructional force, by evolving its plans with the help of teachers and administrators and thus integrating it to the school system at large, the station can offer radio pro-

grams which come to be considered not as isolated novelties but as educational experiences which should be incorporated into the school life of the child. This concept so fundamental to the effective operation of a school station determines to a large extent the use that will be made of its programs.

Participation Creates Interest. The establishment of a school radio station in the typical community will not be eagerly welcomed by everyone. A "show-me" attitude among some skeptics both in and out of the school system will probably exist.

The best way to do the "showing" is to provide a genuine educational service by radio. However, the station director also knows that one good way to win friends for the new station is to plan programs with participation in mind. As individuals and groups take part in broadcasts and become closely allied, even for a brief period, with the aims of the enterprise, they become more understanding of it.

A series such as *Our School Name,* in which various schools dramatize the origin and significance of their names, provides a good vehicle for participation. As a part of the program, the school principal can interview the PTA president of his school district. Other members of the PTA can be invited as a studio audience.

Talented members of various parent groups can be used on several types of programs. A Christmas broadcast to the schools, for example, featuring choral numbers by a community musical group has been used successfully.

The microphone appearance of business leaders, newspaper writers, and other influential community representatives provides excellent resource material for a high-school series as *Views of News.* There is also a by-product of good will from such appearances which has value for the schools in general as well as for the station.

A word of caution in this regard should be offered. Participation planned for participation's sake alone is hard to justify. Program standards must be maintained. Good will is not worth the price of integrity.

Use of Recordings

The preparation and use of recordings are important functions of the school station. If these activities are undertaken with imagination and a knowledge of school needs, they can greatly extend the station's services. Several suggested applications include:

Analyzing Musical and Dramatic Performances. The music department can make effective use of recordings for teaching purposes. After the soloist or ensemble has performed and the recordings are completed, the selection is heard and analyzed by the performers themselves. With selected groups these recordings can be edited and combined into a station program for later use.

A modification of this approach has also been helpful. The school group plays and records a selection. The pupils then hear the same selection as it was recorded commercially by a leading professional ensemble. When that is completed, their own record is played—with the usual reaction. This type of self-analysis, which makes evident the desired standards, is extremely valuable as a teaching procedure.

A specialized use of recordings in the field of music has been to illustrate the effect of a proper "pickup" as contrasted with one where microphones are poorly chosen or improperly placed.

Similar procedures have been used successfully by teachers of speech and dramatics. By recording individual accomplishment before and after a period of instruction the teacher as well as the pupil has an opportunity to judge progress.

Repeating Programs in Order to Meet School Schedules. As noted earlier, the difficulty of broadcasting a program city-wide that will synchronize with classroom time has been an obstacle, especially in the upper grades. One solution is the repetition of programs by means of recordings. These recordings and repeat programs may be handled by the station or, better, by the individual school. In the latter instance the station's broadcasting schedule is freed so that other programs may be presented. Incidentally, whereas the commercial station must announce the fact that a recording or transcription is being played, it is not necessary for a noncommerical educational station to do so.[5] This is rather important in the operation of an educational station, since psychologically, perhaps, the children might be less interested if they knew that the voice coming from the loudspeaker had been recorded. By avoiding such announcements it is

---

[5] FCC, regulations state that recorded programs intended primarily for use in classrooms need not be identified as transcriptions.

generally assumed that the speakers or the performers are actually in the studio.

Providing an Opportunity for the Radio Teacher to Judge Classroom Reactions to His Presentation.   Unless the radio teacher can visit the classroom occasionally, he has little opportunity to judge his own radio presentation and the reaction of the children to it. The occasional use of his recorded program makes it possible for him to be on the receiving end as well. Nothing is more conclusive of general program effectiveness. This opportunity to hear the voice as others hear it is made available by the recording. Script writers and program producers who may be inclined to judge educational effectiveness by control-room sounds rather than by classroom reactions are thus given additional opportunities to evaluate their efforts.

Recording Voices of Visiting Speakers Who May Be Unable to Appear at Program Time.   The inconvenience caused by asking community leaders and others to contribute their services at the microphone can be minimized by recording their comments at a time when they are available. The chance to hear himself is usually welcomed by the layman and to some extent it adds an inducement for his appearance.

Recording (with Permission) Selected Network Programs of an Educational Nature.   It is unfortunate that many excellent programs are given but once and then lost forever. Many programs of great interest to the schools are presented at a time in the evening when organized listening is difficult. The recording of these programs makes for more effective utilization.

"Dubbing in" to New Program Forms Existing Recorded Dramatic and Musical Sequences.   The production facilities generally required for effective dramatic presentation suggest the practice of utilizing selected dramatic sequences which are already available in recorded form. By editing recordings and adding script it is possible to condense the recorded materials into new forms.

Recording the Voices of World Figures and Special Events.   By hearing the scene as it actually happened and listening to the voices of world figures living and dead, the means are available for "making history breathe." Thus, a file of auditory aids to supplement visual aids may be built up.

Developing a File of Broadcasting Talent   The recorded

voice is more helpful in casting the program than is a brief card. The auditions of talented teachers and pupils are recorded and program producers file this material for future needs.

Preparing Copies of Recordings for Schools. Until more schools own their own recording equipment the school station may be called upon to furnish recording assistance. Even then the station may find it desirable to continue this service since the "master" records from which copies are desired may be limited in number.

Other applications of the recording procedure will no doubt occur to the staff. The above list is suggestive of possible variations.

Some Forms Found Helpful

Forms are most effective when evolved to serve local, specific needs. However, the following suggest the type of material which has been found serviceable:

Transmitter Log. The Federal Communications Commission requires all noncommercial educational radio stations to keep a complete log of transmitter operations and procedures. This log must include items such as readings of the amount of power supplied to the transmitter antenna, a record of the carrier-wave frequency, and deviations in frequency which occur with modulation. These items must be noted by the transmitter operator and written in the log at frequent and regular intervals throughout the broadcasting day. The transmitter log must include space for a complete record of all meter readings connected with operation of the transmitter. These must be recorded at least once during each broadcasting day. If transmitter difficulties make it necessary to discontinue operations at any time during the daily schedule, an exact record must be kept of such loss of time. Details of transmitter log forms must vary with the type of transmitter used. However, in general, the items indicated here are essential for all transmitter operations.

Studio Log. All noncommercial education radio stations are required by the Federal Communications Commission to maintain complete studio logs. This log should state the origin of each program: studio, network, transcription, and so on. If a mobile unit is available, an almost unlimited number of sources may be possible. The title and exact time at which each program begins and ends must be stated.

The exact time of all station identifications should be included. Space should be provided for any necessary special comments concerned with irregularities or technical difficulties which interrupt the daily schedule. There must be a record of the operator in charge during all periods of the broadcasting day.

Radio Receiver Repair Order. Since the technical department of a school station may be responsible for maintaining radio receivers in individual school buildings, a standardized radio receiver repair form will be found useful. The form shown below in-

RADIO RECEIVER REPAIR ORDER

School _____ Date _____
Make of set _____ Serial No. _____
Description of trouble (not technical) _____
_____
WBOE set requested _____ Call received by _____
Set loaned—serial no. _____
School will bring set in _____ To be picked up _____

SHOP REPORT

Set inspected by _____ Date _____
Technical report on trouble found _____
_____
_____

Materials Required	Order From	Cost

_____ Total cost of material _____
School notified by _____ Date _____
Work sanctioned by _____ Date _____

SHOP TIME

Work done by _____ Number of hours _____
_____
_____
Total number shop hours _____
Set inspected and OK'd by _____
Set delivered to _____ By _____ Date _____
Was WBOE set returned? _____

cludes typical items which it has been found desirable to record in connection with this type of service. Any such form should include at least the following items: (a) space for the manufacturer's name and the serial number of the radio receiver; (b) the type of difficulty reported by the school at which the receiver is used; (c) the materials required to effect repairs; and (d) the cost of replacement parts required.

Weekly Report of Quality of FM Reception. The use of this type of form is needed to determine reception conditions in the various schools. No less important, however, it provides a quantitative measurement of the classroom listening audience. This log sheet is sent weekly to each secondary school. It is filled out by pupil operators and occasionally by teachers, as individual programs are received.

Return to   WBOE LOG SHEET   School _____
STATION WBOE   Senior High-School Broadcasts
School Headquarters   Second Semester, 1949–1950   Week of _____

OPERATORS: PLEASE FOLLOW THESE INSTRUCTIONS
IN FILLING OUT THIS LOG SHEET

1. Indicate the number of classes listening to air broadcasts from WBOE each period.
2. Indicate radio reception quality. (See Note *)
3. Sign log in space provided for each listening period.
4. If *any* WBOE program is heard at any time in a classroom by *tape, wire,* or *disc,* please indicate on the log at the bottom of Column 1. If individual teachers use the transcriptions at any time after the WBOE air broadcast, ask those teachers to report complete title of program and number of classes listening to you, the operator. Write this information on the log sheet for that week.
5. Please return all logs, completely filled out, at the end of each week.
(*) QUALITY OF RADIO RECEPTION: Place an "X" in the RECEPTION Column to indicate *noisy, distorted,* or *fading* reception If reception is satisfactory, leave this space vacant.
(**) MISCELLANEOUS PROGRAMS are *any* WBOE programs not otherwise listed.

BROADCAST TIMES	NO. OF CLASSES LISTENING	(*) RECEPTION	OPERATOR'S SIGNATURE
MONDAY 10:50 Biology			
12:20 Biology			

BROADCAST TIMES	NO. OF CLASSES LISTENING	(*) RECEPTION	OPERATOR'S SIGNATURE
1:05 Biology			
2:35 Biology			
TUESDAY 8:05			
8:25 Biology			
8:50			
9:55			
10:50			
11:35			
12:20			
1:05			
2:00			
2:35			
WEDNESDAY 8:05 English			
8:50 English			
9:55 English			
10:50 English			
11:35 English			
12:20 English			
1:05 English			
1:50 English			
2:35 English			
THURSDAY 8:05 Physics			
8:50 Physics			
9:55 Physics			
10:50 Physics			
11:35 Physics			
12:20 Physics			
1:05 Physics			

BROADCAST TIMES	NO. OF CLASSES LISTENING	(*) RECEPTION	OPERATOR'S SIGNATURE
2:00 Physics			
2:35 Physics			
FRIDAY			
8:05 Social Studies			
8:50 Social Studies			
10:05 Social Studies			
10:50 Social Studies			
11:35 Social Studies			
12:20 Social Studies			
1:05 Social Studies			
1:50 Social Studies			
2:35 Social Studies			

(**) MISCELLANEOUS PROGRAMS

Program Title	No. of Classes Listening	Operator
Adventures in Research		
Five Centuries of French Music		
Ohio Story		
You Are There		
U.N. Story		
Great Expectations		

WBOE PROGRAMS REBROADCAST IN THE SCHOOL BY WIRE, TAPE, OR DISC (See #4 Above)

Program Title	No. of Classes Listening	Dept.	Operator

Teacher in charge of Operators _____

Technical-Trouble Report. For purposes of record it is highly desirable that both the person in charge of radio activities and the individual in charge of technical operations have written reports of the exact nature of all technical difficulties requiring interruption of the daily schedule. The form shown here is typical. Any such record should include space to record the exact time of the difficulty and the amount of air time lost. It is also important to record an explanation of the nature of the trouble and repairs required. Such a technical-trouble report form should provide space for recording all of the information relating to the difficulty that is entered in the transmitter log.

TECHNICAL TROUBLE REPORT

(This report to be made out in duplicate, one copy to be given to the Director, the other to the Technical Supervisor.)

Time trouble occurred _____ Date _____
Program during which trouble occurred _____
_____
Air time lost _____ From _____ To _____
Complete explanation as to nature of trouble and repairs required _____
_____
_____
_____
Operator on duty _____ (Signature)
Announcer on duty _____ (Signature)

(Essentials of above report should be entered in Day's Log)

Request for Use of Studio. This form is one of the most frequently used. Its use and function are self-evident. The block shown is for a rough sketch of desired studio arrangement. The technical department is responsible for meeting requests.

Adding Television to the School Station

The future of educational television will depend to a very great extent on the allocation for educational purposes of TV channels in 209 communities, as requested by the Joint Committee on Educational

REQUEST FOR USE OF STUDIO

Date of: Recording—Broadcast—Meeting   Producer

SERIES TITLE

PROGRAM TITLE

* * * * * * * * * * * * * * * * * *

STUDIO   A B C D
STUDIO SETUP READY BY _____ A.M. _____ P.M.
___ SOUND OPERATOR: manual ___: records ___ (In Studio by ___)
___ SUB-CONTROL OPERATOR   (At Controls by ___)
___ LIVE AT _____
___ RECORDING at _____ (Approximately)

* * * * * * * * * * * * * * * * * *

Tentative Studio Set-Up

REMARKS: _____
_____
_____
_____
_____
_____

Equipment Needed
Microphones: (Use Symbol)
___ boom (B)
___ table (T)
___ stand (S)
___ sound (SE)
___ filter (F)
___ unidirectional (U)
___ nondirectional (N)
   (new)
Sound Wagon _____
Playback   _____
Piano   _____
Chairs   _____
Earphones _____
Other equipment: _____

Television. There is an obvious decision to be made between commercial interests, who wish to operate TV channels for normal reasons of profit, and educational groups, who would use the same channels for reasons of public service.

The JCET (see next chapter) has actively concerned itself with securing frequencies for educational groups. It is important to remember at the moment that not all the interested groups are prepared to build and operate TV stations immediately. They ask the FCC to reserve the frequencies for a suitable number of years, at the end of which period educational institutions would be prepared to build and operate their own stations or to relinquish their reservations. These interested groups fall into three categories: colleges and universities, State Departments of Education which plan state-wide TV networks, and the school systems of metropolitan areas.

If the FCC should not reserve frequencies for education, the schools and colleges would be compelled to go on as they have during TV's first five years—pensioners on the bounty of the commercial broadcasters, whose only access to television is made possible by local stations who see the value of programs produced in cooperation with educational institutions. The following pages will discuss both types of operation. Station WOI-TV, owned and operated by Iowa State College at Ames, Iowa, is the only example of the university station on TV at this writing. Many other institutions are quoted as examples of the cooperative type of TV programming.

Television on the College Campus. While courses in television, both in programming and engineering, were springing up on the campuses of many universities as soon as the Second World War ended, the first college-owned station to be granted a frequency and to begin broadcasting was Station WOI-TV. WOI had been active in educational broadcasting for twenty-seven years prior to entering the video field. It had added FM first, and then embarked upon television in a carefully planned series of graduated steps. The first stage concentrated on film and slide programs, postponing live programs, both studio and remote, for a later period. The second phase involved a mobile unit and field cameras, to be used for remote sports broadcasts, meetings, laboratory activities and classroom demonstrations. The construction of television studios and the ambitious undertaking of a schedule of live studio programs was reserved for the third and final stage at some time in the future. Iowa State College is also unique in being located in a service area in which it was the only television station on the air, when it opened, because the "freeze" on new channels initiated by the FCC in 1949 prevented Des Moines and other nearby cities from securing television outlets. Accordingly, for the first few years of its existence, it was in a position to supplement its own programming with television programs from all four commercial networks.

Approximately 300 educational groups filed final statements with the FCC during September–October, 1951, signifying their interest in getting into television. Many of them had already taken preliminary steps which looked forward to the time when they might own their own stations and train students for TV as well as for AM and FM broadcasting.

A unique television situation exists in Washington, D.C., where the transmitter and tower of WMAL-TV are located on the campus of the American University. This university had already developed an extensive radio curriculum when WMAL began looking for a transmitter site, and its campus offered one of the highest hills in the District of Columbia.

A cooperative agreement was drawn up whereby American University obtains a regular amount of air time and the use of studios and equipment for instructional purposes in exchange for the use of the site. This contact is not a hindrance to the university in obtaining the cooperation of other Washington outlets; in fact, Willett Kempton, American's director of radio and television, feels that the relationship with WMAL-TV has prestige value in the university's relationship with the three other TV stations in the nation's capital.

American University has been originating television shows since 1947. One half-hour discussion program, *District Viewpoint*, has been televised weekly for a year and a half and a few students participate in each program.

Other series produced by the University during the past three years feature faculty members. Student dramatic shows are televised from time to time.

The University of Illinois began construction of a new 400-foot steel tower, of sufficient strength to support a future television antenna. For the immediate present, it will supplant one of the two present towers of the University's AM station, WILL, and will increase the coverage of its FM outlet, WIUC. Stephens College modified its old auditorium, when a new assembly hall was built, so that a stage area became a studio, with the area backstage converted into an announcer's booth, a control room, film-projection room and studio classroom. Plans included expansion, for the following year, by installation of two camera chains and a noncommercial closed circuit with receivers located only on the central campus of the college.

This would seem to be the arrangement most likely to fit the needs of most universities until they have their own outlets—a studio which provides students with experience under professional conditions, with programs "piped" to a limited number of receivers on the campus.

Syracuse University, though it does not hold a television license, seems to have developed an effective working relationship with commercial telecasters. In exchange for transmitter time through the facilities of the local NBC-TV affiliate, the university allows the commercial station to use its studios for the production of its own local programs. Because the floor crew—everyone except the director—are students (either seniors or graduate students) and because the local station uses the university floor crew for all its local programs, sustaining and commercial, Syracuse students are actually working in television while they learn. The local station has been protected against error as much as possible by careful training for a month before any student is put on an air show.

Until television equipment, under the stimulus of American ingenuity and the increasing influence of mass production, reaches a price within the reach of school system budgets, the educational studio is likely to be the intermediate step between present facilities and a full educational television station. In most communities, commercial broadcasters will be delighted to provide the time for several broadcasts a week, and the school system or college will find that two to four programs are all it can turn out, if quality is to be maintained. So long as programs are worth while, the commercial outlet will probably underwrite line costs for "piping" the program to its transmitter or for picking them up by microwave link (the small relay transmitter now used to send a remote program from the mobile unit in the field back to the parent station).

Still another development has been the production of educational programs on film, for broadcast on television stations at later times. Mention has been made of the 20-minute documentary film dealing with student life on the campus of the University of Miami, which was written and produced by students of the Radio and Television Department of that institution. The college's Television Workshop also presented a live 26-week series over the facilities of WTVJ, Miami, under the sponsorship of a local building firm. In New York City, the city's own Television and Film Unit added to its live series, *This Is Your City* over WPIX, films dealing with the work of various city departments for broadcast by the other stations. Where specifically made for noncommercial public-service use, such films can easily be cleared for showing in classrooms.

In short, for some years to come, television activities of school radio stations are likely to consist largely of part or all of the following:

1. Planning and producing programs for broadcast from the studios of local commercial stations.
2. Providing adequately equipped studios of their own for the training of teachers and students in which they can also produce a limited number of programs each week for relay to commercial stations.
3. Producing educational film which can be used both for television broadcast and classroom projection.

Ultimately, school systems may have their own stations, but only when the costs of television have come down to the point where maintaining a schedule of even one or two hours of air time per school day would not require more for one year than is now spent on setting up an FM station and running it for a decade.

14

The Changing Scene

◇◇

What is the current status of frequency modulation?

What is the NAEB Tape Network?

In what ways may facsimile broadcasting serve the home listener?

What are some of the problems facing television?

What are the implications of these developments for education?

◇◇◇◇◇◇◇◇SO RAPIDLY HAS modern broadcasting evolved that even to describe its current status, let alone to contemplate its future development, is an extremely difficult task. In the days before the Industrial Revolution an invention was a surprise, pleasant or, occasionally, unpleasant. In the twentieth century man has come to expect technical advances. In some instances he has a name for the invention before it actually appears. The impatience with which some awaited television is a case in point. There are three basic developments in the broadcasting field that appear to have significant implications for the educator: frequency modulation, facsimile broadcasting, and television.

Frequency Modulation

The first of these, frequency modulation, has already been mentioned in the discussion of school-owned radio stations. It may be well, however, to describe in a simple, nontechnical manner some of the characteristics of this type of broadcasting, since it is the nature of these characteristics that makes a large increase in number of radio stations technically possible.

The so-called "staticless" quality of FM, its reduction of program fading, and increased tonal range have been described fully in the public press and elsewhere. Of particular interest here is the selective nature of the FM receiver.

There are 105 radio channels available between 550 and 1,600 kilocycles on the conventional dial. At the present time there are approximately 2800 stations using these channels. Stations on the same frequency or channel, although miles apart, tend to interfere with each other. They produce a disturbing hum or cross-talk.

On the other hand, when two FM stations broadcast on the same frequency, the FM radio receiver selects the stronger of the two and "blacks out" the weaker one. Engineers estimate that there will be no interference between two FM stations on the same frequency provided the stronger signal is twice as strong as the weaker one. With conventional broadcasting (amplitude modulation), interference exists unless the stronger signal is at least twenty to fifty times as strong as the weaker one. In addition, interference occurs because there is

520

no clearance between channels and one station's program often overlaps its neighbors.

FM stations, on the other hand, broadcast in the upper region of the spectrum where there is more room. Each FM station has been assigned a "roadway" 200 kilocycles wide, or twenty times wider than a conventional one. Only 75 per cent of these channel widths need be used for the program, thus leaving a safety zone between adjacent channels to guard against overlapping. The net result is that technically hundreds of FM radio stations can be established throughout the country without necessarily causing interference.

In spite of the apparent technical superiority of frequency modulation over that of conventional radio, amplitude modulation, the blunt fact is that the commercial development of FM did not materialize. Enthusiasts had envisioned thousands of commercially licensed FM stations mushrooming in the post-war era. Actually, after a short spurt a reverse trend set in, many commercial FM stations suspending operations and relinquishing licenses. At the same time educational FM stations appear to be holding their own and slowly increasing in number, particularly in the low-power range. The present plight of commercial FM, however, has implications for education which will be noted shortly.

What were some of the factors which prevented the wide acceptance of FM? The dramatic growth of television is certainly a basic cause. However, other reasons have been advanced. The FCC ruling which permitted the duplication of programs over both AM and FM transmitters reduced consumer interest in the purchase of newer and more expensive receivers capable of receiving FM broadcasts. In most urban communities there seemed to be little reason for purchasing an FM set when it received only the same programs. Many AM stations' operators secured FM licenses largely as insurance, and there was a reluctance to promote and publicize the newcomer.

The superiority claimed for FM, freedom from static and higher fidelity, was argued by some broadcasters to be largely theoretical. They stated that disturbing static is infrequent in most areas; also that most of the listening public is insensitive to the need for increased frequencies at the extremes of the listening range. The difficulties of precise FM tuning, they insist, offset whatever qualities may be present.

Proponents of FM have pointed out that relatively few genuine FM receivers have been manufactured, wider tonal range was not incorporated in many, few had automatic frequency controls, most brands were not "drift compensated," built-in antennas were often not satisfactory.

Still others have decried the shifting of the FM band which made many existing receivers obsolete and, they claim, "served to kill FM at its birth." With bitterness, too, some have remarked that "competitive interests sabotaged FM in a variety of ways."

Whatever the real reasons, FM commercial broadcasting at the present writing, except for isolated instances in smaller communities which previously had little or no local radio service, seems to be on the decline.

What does this mean to education? When the earlier edition of this volume appeared at the time of FM's introduction to the public the two following paragraphs were included:

These new stations, educational and commercial, have a great opportunity. The present broadcast structure is based on the premise that to be successful the broadcaster must fashion his product, that is, his program, to suit the masses. American radio has performed notably in that regard. There is no question about it. But, as emphasized earlier, there is no one "public"—there are "publics." In the striving for mass circulation the tastes of the discriminating listener have generally been neglected. The measure of a program's success has been its popularity, not its value, culturally speaking. To be sure, a program cannot have value without listeners, but no one can deny that there is a segment of the American public that wants radio to be a cultural as well as an entertainment medium.

In many urban areas there are enough listeners to warrant a specialized radio service. The success of a New York commercial station which has devoted itself to quality programs, though not typical, is nevertheless significant in this connection. The spread of FM stations will result in a greater emphasis being placed upon a limited—yes, but a selective listening audience. The selection eventually may be at the top and bottom, in terms of tastes, as was the case in the magazine field.

A profound wish may have been father to the thought. Today the possibility of specialized FM radio programming, which could have meant more listening by selective groups, appears slight. Parenthetically, and perhaps wishfully, it might be pointed out that the impact of TV on AM radio may bring about this situation. More of this later.

THE CHANGING SCENE 523

Another effect of FM's halt has been reduced opportunity for many local groups to participate actively in program production and experimentation.

A third result may have far reaching influence on educational stations. With comparatively few FM sets purchased or even made, the potential adult audience for the educational FM station seems limited. In fact many institutions, particularly universities, are considering with care the proposed expenditure as they realize this limitation. School systems, however, since they are in a better position to secure receivers for their listeners—largely in classrooms—may wish to operate, as most have done, without much concern for home listening.

It has long been the dream of radio educators that some day networks of educational stations could be developed so that production costs could be shared and the best programs made available to distant listeners. If such cooperation was needed in commercial radio it is doubly so with the typical low-budget educational station.

Numerous efforts have been made, many with the stimulation of the United States Office of Education. The usual result has been a spark of interest, a meeting of a few interested school men, a map showing possible station locations, and then general apathy. In a few instances where effective progress was possible broadcasters fearful of a competitive radio system in their state successfully blocked the enterprise.

Two exceptions to the above should be noted, the Wisconsin State Radio Council and the Empire State FM School of the Air.

The former is a public body, created by the Wisconsin Legislature to "plan, construct, and develop a state system of radio broadcasting for the presentation of educational, informational, and public-service programs." The following excerpt from a Wisconsin publication relates to a basic question,

DO THE STATE STATIONS COMPETE
WITH PRIVATE STATIONS?

For Advertising Revenue? No. They sell no time.

For Air Channels? No. They use frequencies set aside specifically for non-commercial use.

For Programs? No. They offer programs of a type and length not attractive to advertisers or commercial stations.

For Listeners? Only occasionally. To overcome this any station may re-broadcast without charge programs from the state stations which it fears may endanger its own listening audience.

At the present time the Wisconsin educational network, so typical of the rich traditions of that state, seems to be well established. Pro-vided with outstanding leadership and the uniquely successful Station WHA its future seems encouraging. State-wide coverage of eight sta-tions is projected. Whether by full-network operation (day and night, supplementing its existing AM service with FM transmission) the pioneering Wisconsin broadcasters will be able to overcome FM's general decline and thus a limited potential home audience, as well as the later TV impact, remains to be seen. Friends of education will wish the project well.

Another type of state-wide educational radio network is the Empire State FM *School of the Air.* This project is essentially "grass-root" in origin and cooperative in nature. Eighteen commercial FM stations donate time for classroom programs which are prepared by schools, libraries, universities and radio stations. Fortunate in having the in-terest and motivation of capable radio and educational personnel, the project seems well underway. But here, too, aside from budgetary needs, the future of FM may jeopardize the network. If the commer-cial FM stations now carrying these programs find it necessary to sus-pend operations then, unfortunately, the existing school network may go with them.

THE NAEB TAPE NETWORK

The NAEB Tape Network is a cooperative organization devoted to the distribution of outstanding radio programs. It is operated by the National Association of Educational Broadcasters for its member stations, which are owned by educational institutions, municipalities, and other public service agencies. It provides for the mutual exchange of the best programs of its member stations and procures and dis-tributes programs from other agencies engaged in the production of radio programs of serious purpose and mature content.

An exchange network service has long been considered and dis-cussed by educational broadcasters. The NAEB Tape Network began in January, 1950, when the director of New York City's municipal station WNYC, Seymour N. Siegel, offered to a limited group of stations a tape recorded program series titled, *We Human Beings*. Within six months it had grown to an efficient exchange service supplying 35 stations. However, the manifold problems of finances, personnel, and time became increasingly acute. An offer to assume custodianship of the network was made by the Division of Communications of the University of Illinois. In January, 1951, headquarters for the operation was moved to the Illinois campus. In the months that followed, the network grew to 75 participating stations. The schedule expanded to seven program hours per week.

How Does the Network Operate?

To date, programs used have been produced by member stations, the British Broadcasting Corporation, Canadian Broadcasting Corporation, the Cooper Union, the Twentieth Century Fund, the Lowell Institute, the Rocky Mountain Radio Council, commercial stations and networks, university-sponsored conferences and symposia, and various public service institutions. The programs are selected by a program committee composed of representatives of member stations in various parts of the country.

The programs are assembled at network headquarters, where they are checked, edited, and made ready for duplication. Eight copies are then made of each program. As the name implies, the entire operation is carried on through the use of magnetic tape. The copies are "bicycled" around eight geographical "legs," each made up from seven to ten stations. The network will soon have a duplicating machine capable of reproducing ten copies of a program per run-through, and at fast speed. This mass duplication will permit the discontinuing of the time-consuming bicycling technique. A copy of each program will be made for every station, permitting operation.

Before the processing of the tapes begins, the stations are advised of what will be available and are supplied with complete information about the programs. A tentative schedule is suggested, and it is modified into the final broadcast schedule on the basis of acceptance by the stations. The individual stations are free to accept or reject programs on whatever basis they choose. There is no option time and no restriction or pressure on the stations in the use of available programs.

A Glimpse at the Future

The network is currently being organized on a permanent, business-like basis. When this organization is accomplished and the headquarters is completely equipped, it will be possible to expand the schedule to as much as 500 hours of programming per year. A constant search is carried on to find new sources of meaningful program material.

A stimulating prospect for the future is exemplified by the recent grant to the NAEB by the Adult Education Fund of the Ford Foundation, for the purpose of producing four series of programs. On a scale hitherto impossible, people with extensive experience in both education and broadcasting will have the opportunity to bring together outstanding subject-matter experts and the finest radio writers and producers. The programs will be authoritative in content and as suitable to the medium of radio as the best talent can make them. They will be heard on the NAEB Tape Network.

The network is now planning the distribution of programs specifically designed for in-school listening. The wide use of radio for classroom instruction indicates that this undertaking will be a major step forward in the network's service.

The National Association of Educational Broadcasters is hopeful that its network will continue to grow and enlarge its position as the chief source, in the United States, of mature, intelligent, and provocative radio programs.

One other type of educational station will be noted which probably will be influenced. Adult education agencies such as JUNTO, Inc., of Philadelphia and the Louisville Free Public Library have recognized the potential values of radio. Both are licensees with the latter already operating its 10-watt station, WFPL. Though optimism is tempting, the sober truth is that, unless the present state of FM changes radically, a *rapid* widespread use of specialized educational radio services is very doubtful. A *slow* growth is likely.

Facsimile Broadcasting

Less publicized than television or even FM, another technical advance which may prove of value to education is the use of facsimile broadcasting.

The term "facsimile" as used in this sense can be simply defined as the broadcasting of printed material. Like television, it has to do with sight; but, unlike television, it leaves a copy of the original material which can be referred to at any time.

The operation of facsimile broadcasting is analogous to that of regular sound broadcasting. At the sending end, instead of employing

Weather map recorded from a daily transmission by Radio Station KE2XER, New York. From an original recording on Timefax ND paper.

(Courtesy of Times Facsimile Corporation.)

a microphone to pick up sound waves, the facsimile system employs a photoelectric cell, or electric eye, to pick up the variations in light waves reflected from graphic copy (such as pictures, text, maps, or drawings) that is being scanned by the electric eye. These electrical impulses are amplified and transmitted through standard broadcast transmitters.

At the receiving end the facsimile signals are picked up by the radio receiver, but instead of being used to produce sound waves through a loudspeaker they are made to actuate the printer mechanism and produce black and white half-tone marks in accordance with the original material at the transmitting end.

Thus, the owner of a facsimile set while listening, for instance, to a cooking school program can also receive copies of the recipes by facsimile. A talk on new dresses can be illustrated by photographs and even patterns which can be used later. A news commentator while discussing world events can supply his listeners with maps for reference. Numerous other uses are apparent. The written material is reproduced on a roll of paper which has been placed in the facsimile unit.

In accomplishing this wireless printing, various reproduction systems have been used such as the photographic, the electrochemical, and the carbon-paper printer methods. It is likely, however, that the teacher's chief interest is not in the techniques used but in the possible applications to the furtherance of education.

Facsimile broadcasting has been tried experimentally in several communities. Before World War II the McClatchy radio stations on the West Coast, for example, conducted a comprehensive survey during eleven months of facsimile transmission.[1]

Sets were placed in 580 homes representing every income group, type and degree of intelligence and education. Approximately one-fourth of the reports indicated that the homes were enthusiastic over facsimile and wanted to buy sets at once. A little over one-third were interested in it "as a permanent addition to their daily lives." A similar number were mildly interested, and only 11 per cent were completely indifferent to it. It is interesting to note that 91.5 per cent of the persons receiving the facsimile material reported that even this prewar reproduction was considered good.

[1] *Broadcasting*, May 1, 1940, p. 28.

Technicians, however, felt existing systems were too slow, material limited in size and quality of reproduction in need of improvement.

During the war facsimile was used by the military services to send maps, orders, photographs and weather charts. Impetus was given to research which led to material improvements.

Recently standards of "fax" operation have been established as to speed, page widths and quality. Today the eight-inch page size permitting a four-column newspaper is standard. It was felt that speeds should correspond to the normal reading speed of the average person. Twenty-eight squares a minute is the adopted rate.

Other developments continue apace. The sending in full color of photographs, "colorfax," has been demonstrated. "Ultrafax," an RCA creation which combines film and TV, is capable of sending literally millions of words with breathtaking speed.

The most extensive use of "fax" has been made by the editors of the Miami *Herald*. Their three years of recent experimentation with "fax" has been described in detail.[2]

Facsimile receivers have been developed which are combined in one cabinet with a conventional radio set. The whole unit does not cost much more than a better grade radio receiver. It is automatic in its operation so that, whenever the transmitting station desires to send a bulletin or a photograph, the receiver in the home can be turned on electrically by a given signal.

Advertisers were among the first to recognize the possibilities of this new medium. Illustrated advertisements can be inserted among the news items or the cartoons and continued stories which are transmitted to the home. Coupons can be distributed. Facsimile space can be sold as is radio time. Some advertisers have considered printing their messages on the back of the paper which is then furnished free to the homes as refills for their facsimile receivers.

Facsimile can have numerous applications in the business field. With speed being the great factor that it is in various transactions, it will be possible for facsimile broadcasting to facilitate rapid correspondence at low rates. Blueprints, checks, specifications, and various other business papers can be transmitted in a few seconds. If copies of the material are required instantly, several recorders can be used.

---

[2] Lee Hills and Timothy J. Sullivan, *Facsimile*, McGraw-Hill, 1949, pp. 319.

In the police and military services, it is apparent that facsimile can aid in many ways through the transmission of photographs, fingerprints, maps, etc.

The educational services of facsimile broadcasting seem to be largely in the field of adult education. Some of the possible applications were mentioned earlier. Its use in presenting the news is quite evident. It should be remembered that with facsimile, unlike radio and television, it is not necessary to listen in continuously to avoid missing some important development. One need merely refer to the roll of paper coming from the receiver to see what the latest bulletin is. The reproduction of explanatory maps, charts, and photographs to accompany the text can quickly provide even the rural farmhouse with its own newspaper. The rural listener can receive written records of weather reports, news bulletins, and market prices which were printed in his home while he slept.

The effectiveness of educational radio in serving the listener at home can be increased greatly by the use of facsimile. Music appreciation programs can be preceded by the distribution of the annotated musical score to be performed. The geographer can provide the listeners with a map of the region to be discussed. The technician can discuss the blueprints which are in the hands of his listeners. After his presentation, they can continue with their follow-up activity. The English teacher can discuss effective writing and at the same time furnish the listeners with illustrative written text. The art instructor can discuss the facsimile photographs which have been distributed—incidentally, a good facsimile photograph has many of the qualities of an etching. Listeners will not have to send in for pamphlets and reprints. Some of the material can be sent to them quickly. Postage is no problem.

The use of facsimile in the schools has not been attempted to a great extent, although Station WBOE did conduct an experiment with this device in February, 1939. Administrative announcements, maps, lesson assignments, and student newspapers were distributed to the schools by using the school station transmitter and a temporary facsimile installation. The evidence is by no means conclusive, yet it appears that a large school system equipped with ample duplication and delivery facilities may find facsimile of limited value. The emergencies are not so frequent that the written materials cannot be provided in ample time by the ordinary methods. In rural areas, however, where distribution problems are more difficult, facsimile broadcasting may be of real service. If a school station undertakes a broadcasting service to the home, the correlated use of facsimile has great possibilities.

An institution operating an FM radio station needs only to install a facsimile scanner to print its own newspaper, for example, over the air. By using the "multiplex" system it can print materials for the eye and transmit sound for the ear simultaneously.

Television

An exercise enjoyed often by many Americans is jumping on the bandwagon. The extent to which television early captured the imagination of the public is a prime example.

There is no question as to television's industrial output and its mass movement into the living rooms of the fifty large American communities now being served. However, when one assays, prematurely to be sure, present television programs as an indication of future educational values then there is need to pause.

The same economic factors operate here as in radio except to a greater degree. With television's higher operating and production costs there is greater need for more advertising revenue. More revenue depends largely upon more circulation. Wider circulation requires mass appeal. Mass support, by and large, means an emphasis on entertainment, and whether school people prefer it or not, entertainment at a mediocre level.

This summary may be oversimplified but past events support the contention that modern communication media regard service to fringe listeners, readers, and viewers as a luxury. The hope is, and there is evidence for it, that in the long haul the mediocre tastes of the many can slowly be elevated to the interests of the relative few. But that as yet remains largely a hope. There is little doubt that television will continue to expand rapidly. However, radio should not be sold short. There are still over 40 million radio homes as compared with 5 million television equipped homes. In 1950 radio tuners were still outselling television, in terms of units.

Will television eventually replace radio? Not if history can be used to predict. The telegraph was not banished by the telephone, nor was the cable replaced by the wireless. Each has its own values.

When one attempts to evaluate the impact of television on AM radio then some form of crystal-gazing is required. Already in one American city, Baltimore, a recent Hooperating indicated the shape of things to come when an evening survey revealed that television viewers exceeded radio listeners. The shift of major radio programs to daytime hours and the raising of daytime radio rates has begun. Whether keener competition and a greater sharing of the advertising dollars may mean more service for the specialized audiences referred to earlier, remains to be seen.

One final word on the all-important factor of economics. If television costs continue to rise, if advertising revenue is limited or possibly reduced, other forms of support may be found necessary.[3] Some have suggested that a "box office" be added to television. One such system is Phonevision, in which a telecast is transmitted in the usual fashion. Ordinary television sets can receive the signal, but because a fraction of the total signal is withheld, the image vibrates and flickers so that the program is unintelligible. This key part is sent via the regular telephone lines. One who wishes to see the Phonevision program must call the operator and have his television connected. The cost is added to the regular telephone bill.

Even aside from the opposition of motion-picture interests, which is evident, acceptance of this plan seems doubtful when one recalls that a similar proposal was made with reference to "subscription radio."[4] In the television situation, however, the very weight of economic pressures may compel some such development.

---

[3] The Faught Company, Incorporated, of New York, in a comprehensive study entitled *Some Billion Dollar Questions about Television*, raises the question, "How much of what kind of television system can be built, and how will it be programmed, if the whole phenomenon is to rest on the economics of advertising"? They estimate one year's operation of a national Television system would be $1,740,352,500 —three times that of the national radio systems.

[4] Robert M. Hutchins, "The State of American Radio," written for the *BBC Quarterly* and reprinted in *Variety*, May 10, 1950, pp. 22, 34.

Television's Next Steps

The two developments in television broadcasting which will probably mean most to education are not as publicized nor as spectacular as color television or large-screen receivers. One is the development of the industry, both in economics and in labor relations, to the point where programs of educational value can be recorded (via kinescope transcription) and rebroadcast during school hours. Added to that is the hope that duplicates of such sound films can be reproduced inexpensively and the prints made available for classroom showings. These two steps, which would increase tremendously the availability of television to the classroom, would be linked with the development of low-cost television receivers, a field in which progress is already rapid.

However, it would be wrong to pass too lightly over the importance of large-screen receivers and of color. For the average classroom, a screen the size of a newspaper is considered the minimum by many authorities. Present large-screen sets depend on picture tubes which are 19 inches in diameter or larger and correspondingly expensive, on magnifying lenses placed before the screen and not satisfactory for viewers at the sides of the room, or for some type of enlargement or projection of the picture received on a small tube and thrown on an enlarging screen. One system of theater television makes a motion picture of the program as it is received, develops it, dries it and projects the film on to a normal theater screen with a modified theater projector, all in a matter of seconds—a process obviously too expensive for the classroom. Thus, while no one of the present enlarging systems meets the school's need for clarity, sharpness and economy, all indications point toward the development of a satisfactory classroom receiver before many years have passed.

Color Television. Color television was available in the laboratories even before Pearl Harbor. One of the writers of this volume was able to see the CBS color camera in action in 1945, when CBS began to move its color process out of the laboratories and onto the air. A controversy arose, however, whose merits it is not our place to discuss here. Opponents of the CBS color system claimed, in 1947 and again in 1949–1950, that color was not sufficiently perfected, that the public did not want to wait a few more years but wanted black-and-white television immediately. In 1950, however, the FCC ruled, after intensive and exhaustive tests and research, that CBS color had been perfected and was ready for the general public, and licensed CBS to broadcast commercially in color.

Opponents of the CBS system, notably RCA and Du Mont, claimed that their color systems were more practical and would be ready in a very few years. They pointed out that the CBS system required a whirling disc, between the viewer's eye and the picture tube, and that broadcasts in color could not be received on existing receivers without additional "converters" and "adapters." All-electronic color, however, could be received in black and white on existing receivers and would require only a single converter to change a black-and-white set into a color-receiving set.

Nevertheless, the FCC held to its decision and CBS began broadcasting in color in the late summer of 1951. Several manufacturers began to turn out CBS color sets at that time. In December of that same year the Office of Defense Mobilization requested that manufacture of color receivers be stopped in order to preserve critical materials. CBS not only stopped manufacture but discontinued broadcasting in color for the duration of the international crisis.

Shortly after this event, however, there came the announcement of still another color system, developed by Dr. Ernest O. Lawrence, a Nobel prize winner and inventor of the cyclotron. The Lawrence tri-color tube is said to produce either black-and-white or color pictures for any size screen, and to work with either the CBS, the RCA or any color system after relatively minor adaptations.*

The implications for education are self-evident.

Color will prove of tremendous value, of course, in educational programming. The field of art instruction, for example, will be intensified when color is in common use. An example of its value may be gained from the following script, written by Dr. Henry Cassirer and broadcast in color by the Columbia Broadcasting System from the National Gallery of Arts in Washington, D.C., early in 1950.

---

* Within a year, the FCC reversed itself and standardized American color broadcasting on the RCA "compatible system" which permits standard black-and-white receivers to get, in black-and-white, programs which are broadcast in color. This system is now used by all networks.

AN EVENING IN THE NATIONAL GALLERY [5]

OUTLINE OF PROGRAM:
1. Opening truck-in on gallery
2. Emerson: opening words and Mr. Finlay
3. Moroni: Gentlemen in Adoration, K 132, Room 24 (framed reproduction)
4. Botticelli: Portrait of Youth, M 20, Room 8 (reproduction)
5. Emerson: transition
6. Della Robbia: Christ Child, original bust. Room 27, K
7. Holbein: Edward VI, Room 39 (reproduction)
8. Lute player and singer—2 songs, in costume
9. Cantena: Portrait of a woman, K 101, Room 28 (original)
10. Emerson talks about Cantena painting, shows own fashions
11. Bust of Aretino, (original)
12. Fragonard: Game of hot cockles, K 168, Room 53 (original)
13. Emerson and models in Rococo type dresses
14. Fragonard
15. Romney: Mrs. Davenport, M, Room 56 (original)
16. Jan Steen: Dancing couple, W 53, Room 47 (original)
17. Folk dance
18. Emerson transition to modern France
19. Cézanne: Still life, CD 71 (original)
20. Van Gogh: La Mousms (reproduction) CD 76, Room 83
21. Renoir: Dancer, W 109, Room 76 (original)
22. Ballet dancer
23. Emerson
24. Van der Weyden: Portrait of a Lady, M 55, Room 39 (reproduction)

AN EVENING IN THE NATIONAL GALLERY
Written by Dr. Henry Cassirer
From broadcast January 19, 1950; 9:45 P.M.

VIDEO	AUDIO
LS of Room—pan around paintings	ANNCR: We welcome you tonight to spend with us an evening in the National Gallery of Arts. There is an air of expectancy here tonight—expectancy of the people who will fill these halls tomorrow to enjoy the world of art. And there is expectancy of a broadcast which for the

70536 TEACHING THROUGH RADIO AND TELEVISION

first time will bring these paintings to
you by color television.

These paintings belong to us, all of us, in
this *national* gallery, they are part of our
life, our enjoyment, not just dusty relics
of the past. They are the work of masters who sought to grasp the heartbeat
of the world through Art. They are with
us today as living art, and it is in this
spirit that we pay a visit to the Gallery.
To introduce the broadcast, here is the
director of the National Gallery of Arts,
Mr. David Finlay, and Miss Faye Emerson.

(Mr. Finlay makes a formal opening
statement, then turns the show over to
Miss Emerson.)

EMERSON: I feel a little overwhelmed in this
gallery, with Renoir and Botticelli surrounding me and introducing the first
color broadcast from an art collection.
But most of these paintings were not
created for awesome admiration, but
rather to give enjoyment and inspiration to us in living with them. We want
to see these paintings and sculptures as
living contemporaries who never cease
to have a fresh meaning to us. The artists
echo the color, the music, the dance and
the customs of their time, and all of
these live on today with us in our enjoyment of the arts.

Emerson steps to Maroni

The adoration of a painting is sometimes much like the adoration of the
Madonna by this young Italian noble-
man. There is a world that separates us,
yet there is an inner intimacy which
gives us inspiration and enjoyment.

*Come in to CU of man's
head*

ANNCR: This picture, painted by Giovanni Bat-
tista Moroni in 1560, shows in a way
the transition from the Middle Ages,
dominated by the church, to the modern
world of realism and individual personality.

Pan to Madonna

And yet this man is in intimate communication with the eternal Madonna and her Child. Her dress and her pose are timeless.

Truck out to show entire picture

The pale white shawl, the red sleeves and the blue costume stand out against the adorer who has his back turned to us and is dressed in a dark suit. The artist has created a mood of devotion in this painting.

Pan to Botticelli, Portrait of Youth

The intriguing mixture of romanticism and realism in the work of Botticelli, of sadness and of wistfulness speaks to us through his portrait of a youth. Here is a young man drawn in delicate lines and pure colors, of seemingly golden hair and almost painted red lips. He looks effeminate and soft, and yet the characters of this Machiavellian age could at the same time be ruthless in the intrigues of politics. It was a time when men were as careful of their dress as women are today, and many of their costumes are copied in current fashions.

A time as complex as our own, of intellectual revolution, of anarchy and war and of romantic beauty lives with us in the work of Botticelli.

Pan to Emerson

EMERSON: There is much that we have in common with the buoyant, romantic and hard-headed age of the Renaissance. It was an age in which lived some of the greatest and broadest minds of modern times, Michelangelo and Leonardo da Vinci, who laid the foundations of the modern concepts of man and of science. And there is something also that brings us close to the Florence of the Renaissance—their love of children.

Goes to della Robbia statue

The love of Italians for the bambino, the child, is always touching, and rarely has this love found as beautiful expression as in this Christ Child by Giovanni della Robbia. The National Gallery has the richest collection of Renaissance sculpture this side of the Atlantic, and this is one of its prize possessions, which came to it from the Kress collection.

CU *of bust*   EMERSON: (*Reads*) This bust was created in the thriving workshop of the Della Robbia family, which was always busy making plaques and reliefs for new buildings of the Renaissance. It is modeled in ordinary clay which was baked into a brick-hard statue of terra cotta, or cooked earth. It is painted with enamel glaze which blended its substance with the clay during the baking. The choice of colors is typical of Della Robbia statues and plaques: no red, for they had not yet found a bright red glaze. But rich green, blue and purple.

The statue is called Christ Child—quite a worldly Christ! It is of course the idealized child of the rich and successful rulers of Florence, dressed in noble garments and expressing the sensitivity and haughtiness of his age. Yet it is more, it is the finely chiseled face of a child— any child.

Pan to Holbein   ANNCR: And now to another child of the sixteenth century, a painting whose purpose is not to express eternal childhood but impressive royalty. This painting of young Edward the VIth, the son of Henry the VIIIth of England, by Hans Holbein the Younger, almost glows with the purple and gold of royalty.

Characteristic of Holbein is the flat design, with the colors set one against the other, and the light coming from the front. The relationship of light, shade and color in creating drama and realism had not yet been discovered by the art of painting.

Obviously, such a program would have lost much of its effectiveness in black-and-white transmission. So, too, in the field of medicine and medical education, color plays an important part. The medical profession first saw color demonstrated in the televising of surgical operations during the 1949 meeting of the American Medical Association. As reported by Warren Cheney, Film and Television Consultant of the National Institute of Health of the United States Public Health Service:

". . . the CBS color television equipment beamed a series of surgical operations and clinical reports (from the Atlantic City Hospital) to Convention Hall where twenty color receivers were set up. During the five days of the convention more than thirty thousand medical personnel witnessed the tests, and their reaction was immediate. For the first time many surgeons saw operations in more complete detail and thoroughness than they had when assisting at the same operations themselves. The television camera view was so excellent that more of the operating area was visible than anyone but the operating surgeon ever sees during an operation. And with the addition of color, identification of delicate membranes, nerves, muscle tissue and fascia was increased, picturewise, to within ninety percent of equality with direct observation of the original subject."

Mr. Cheney sees the future teaching application of the color camera, in the field of surgery for example. He describes it as follows:

Here then, is a full class of one hundred students every one of them seeing the operation on the screen at greatly enlarged scale at the same time they witness the full scale activity of the surgeon and his assistants. The color TV camera, like the current CBS equipment, is mounted on a boom and focused by remote control by the operator at the control board, seen in the foreground. The man behind the boom is used to propel the camera and compose the field, but he gets orders from the control-board operator via telephone line. The surgeon wears a throat microphone so he may comment as he works.

Many other fields, particularly in the sciences, may well profit by such a setup. Used within a university laboratory, for example, it can spread close-ups of the demonstrator's table to receivers at key points on the campus. Relayed to a nearby station (on subjects other than operations, of course) it can be broadcast to extension classes, other universities in near-by cities or to schoolrooms when the subject matter is appropriate.

Subscription Television. Several years after television's

full-scale commercialization a number of interests began to question whether the tremendous production costs of television could be met by revenue from advertising. One of the alternative methods of financing broadcasts was "subscription" broadcasting, whereby the viewer would pay for his entertainment directly.

A number of methods of collecting the revenue were proposed, all built around some method of making the broadcast capable of reception only by subscribers. The Skiatron Corporation proposed *Subscribervision* which works on a coded-card principle. Paramount Picture Corporation offered *Telemeter*, which works with a coin-operated box attached to the television set. Perhaps the most widely tested was Zenith Radio Corporation's *Phonevision*, which was tested by some three hundred families in Chicago from January to March of 1951. The *Phonevision* system sends out a picture over a regular television channel with one of the elements missing. This results in a scrambled picture at the ordinary receiver. But subscribers who have *Phonevision* attachments on their sets can call their local telephone operators and "order" the particular program desired. The telephone company then sends the missing element over the telephone line to the subscriber's set, and a clear picture results. Subscribers are charged for this service on their regular telephone bills.

The implications for educational broadcasting of such methods of financing television are not immediately apparent. Educational institutions would not charge for their broadcasts, nor could the average school afford to pay for such a service. Whether the growth of subscription television will alter the existing advertising-supported structure of television, and whether such an eventuality would provide more or less educational broadcasting from the conventional stations is still a matter of speculation.

Television Channels for Education

Perhaps the most significant development in educational broadcasting is the growing demand for the reservation of channels for education. In March, 1951, the Federal Communications Commission proposed that some two hundred channels (10 per cent of those available) be reserved for noncommercial educational television stations. Educators had failed to act in concert in the early days of radio, and frequencies were lost by default. Schoolmen and educational broadcasters, determined that this must not happen in TV, formed the Joint Committee on Educational Television.

The JCET, consisting of representatives of seven national organizations,* lost no time in providing the nation's educators with a background of information about the complicated procedures of the plan whereby these 209 frequencies might be allocated to the needs of education. As a result, colleges, universities, and local communities filed with the FCC more than 300 petitions in support of noncommercial TV facilities, affecting more than 230 individual communities and thousands of educational institutions. At least five states projected state-wide video networks: 5 stations for Connecticut, 6 for New Jersey, 11 for New York, 6 for Pennsylvania, and 12 for Wisconsin. In many cities, those who supported the projected stations envisaged cooperation in both financing and programming by local colleges, school systems, libraries, museums, and other public service organizations.

Cost and time in which to meet the cost were (and still are) the crucial factors. Educators hope that the educational frequencies will be reserved for a "reasonable period," a number of years in which states and schools may marshal their resources. Estimates for station construction costs vary from $106,000 to $400,000; annual operating budget estimates run from $18,000 to $300,000. The most ambitious construction plan, that of the Board of Regents of New York State, runs to some 3½ million dollars—the cost of an average high school in a large city.

Those opposed to the reservation of the channels hope that the FCC will insist that educators take up their claims and file their plans within ninety days. Those supporting the allocation plan maintain that such channels should be declared national resources—similar to national parks, forests, oil, and mineral reserves.

As this book goes to press, the decision of the FCC is not yet avail-

---

* American Council on Education; Association for Education by Radio and Television; Association of Land-Grant Colleges and Universities; National Association of Educational Broadcasters; National Association of State Universities; National Council of Chief State School Officers; National Education Association.

able.* If the channels are reserved, education will be faced with its greatest challenge of recent years. It must justify its right to TV stations of its own, or forfeit forever its opportunity to possess them. If the channels are not reserved, then educational televison will remain a pensioner on the bounty of commercial broadcasters and will have to continue its present uphill fight to prove that educational telecasts are not only in the public interest, but can and do interest the public.

In Conclusion

Thus far three major developments have been discussed which have significance for the educator. It is safe to say that many more scientific, auditory, and visual aids will be produced which can be used to assist in the function of education. Even at present, the use of wired radio and micro-wave broadcasting may suggest important applications to the schoolman of vision.

Though the nature of the tools may change, certain fundamental considerations will remain constant. The machine itself, however brilliant an achievement it may be, will have little value unless it is used judiciously. Even the best teacher can be helped by an intelligent use of the modern tools at her disposal. But the most ardent enthusiasts in the use of scientific aids to teaching must recognize that an undue use of these devices may "dehumanize" what is basically a personal relationship. No mechanical device can eliminate the factor of effort from successful teaching and effective learning. The well-known proportion of inspiration to perspiration will not be altered considerably by turning a switch or pushing a button.

Sometimes those in educational broadcasting are inclined to forget that the enterprise is a small, though admittedly important, part of the whole educational scheme. Many in specialized fields develop an enthusiasm which, if they are not careful, can readily overlook the nature of the conservative institution called education. Sometimes their emotional pendulum swings rapidly from gratifying achievement to discouraging frustration. One may forget that even the invention of printing took hundreds of years to make its way into general educational use. This enthusiasm is, of course, an indispensable quality for men

* Since this time, 257 channels have been reserved for noncommercial educational service, and about 10 per cent of these have already been put to use.

and women pioneering as they are. On the other hand, one must be careful that, to borrow Santayana's definition of a fanatic, "we do not redouble our efforts long after we have forgotten the original cause." Kept uppermost in mind should be the aim of improved education. Radio and TV have a veneer of glamor, and some may be enticed by the mere surface. The danger is that one may confuse means with ends.

Within one generation there has developed a powerful influence in American life. When it is recognized that the American home is tuned in several hours a day—when the school child during the year hears and views radio and TV more than he does his teacher; and no qualitative distinctions will be made here—then it is understood why broadcasting today is one of the three great mass communication media.

More and more teachers are using broadcasting in conjunction with other classroom aids. Equally important, they are learning to use these means more effectively. A steady flow of literature in the field is noticed on library shelves. Teacher training institutions are slowly but surely adding courses in radio education. Several states have already required that potential teachers complete a course in audio-visual aids prior to receiving a teaching certificate.

Yet, a skeptic who looks at educational practices and procedures can easily draw the conclusion that educators lag at least one generation behind society at large. Examine the superior printing and photographic work in many magazines. Compare them with school texts, and note that only in recent years has there been a reasonable improvement in the technical quality of printed materials for classroom use. Hollywood is fully aware of the tremendous power of a film in conditioning the minds of millions. Educators, too, recognize the influential role of film during war, as used by our armed services. Now, contrast those contributions with the applications made of visual education in the classrooms. In visual education, also, one can easily become discouraged. Some two thousand commercial radio stations have been established in this country. Compare them and their operating budgets with the number of educational outlets now on the air. A sense of discouragement is almost an inevitable result. But, are we being realistic? Can we actually expect publicly supported education to move much faster than it does?

Social institutions require many years to make effective use of technical developments. This so-called lag may be deplored, but on the other hand it is naïve enthusiasm to assume that within one generation a still-evolving instrument, such as broadcasting, could be fully exploited in terms of socially desired aims.

Education, rightly or wrongly, moves slowly. Sometimes the reasons are not apparent to the layman. A school system wishing to establish a television station, for example, cannot—like a corporation for profit—issue stock and quickly capitalize. Before budgeting a special service it is imperative that its stockholders, the general public, understand the reasons for such action. All too often the tag of fads and frills is given to forward-looking steps. It would be pleasant to move quickly and to spend tax dollars as educators believe best. However, we know only too well the lag that exists between a social vision and general acceptance of it. Yet that lag may be inevitable and, in fact, a safeguard in a social order that depends upon popular support.

A necessary phase of this seemingly slow process is the development among many people of the disposition to use a new and unfamiliar instrument. The imposition of television on classroom teachers not ready to use it well would largely negate its value. But change is inevitable.

The more than 25 million boys and girls in our American schools may not realize that they are living in greatly changing times brought on partly by the impact of electronic energy. To those charged with the responsibility of fashioning their mental, social, and emotional growth the very presence of radio and television is both a challenge and an opportunity.

Most school administrators are fully aware that schools are only one type of educational institution. However, parents are turning to the school daily to provide much that perhaps should be given in the home.

The schools find themselves in a dilemma. Shall they limit themselves to that which they know they can do, or shall they assume additional tasks thus spreading their energies as well as their funds?

Actually, they have no choice in the face of mounting social pressures. The ivory tower of yesterday is a luxury they cannot afford. The whole social arena has become their province.

In that province they find the powerful mass communication media affecting the minds and emotions of their patrons. It would be easy to stand back and permit the values of American life to be fashioned by those whose primary interest is not to foster growth but to sell merchandise. Were educators so inclined and so content, there would not have been the remarkable display of interest and action on behalf of American education in the allocation of television channels for noncommercial use. The utilization of closed circuit television, which permits the teaching of large numbers of students in widely spread rooms equipped with television receivers "fed" from a central studio, is another new note. It makes possible the use of an institution's most expert and effective teachers by a "class" larger than any which could be accommodated in a huge amphitheatre, yet gives every student "a seat in the front row." While the effectiveness of such instruction is still being evaluated at a dozen institutions, early results have been most encouraging. As has been stated earlier, this may well prove to be the most valuable solution to the problem of the rapidly approaching teacher and classroom shortage.

Now that closed circuit television is receiving financial support for experimentation, now that the FCC has reserved 257 noncommercial channels for community and educational use, the American public will observe with interest and perhaps concern the actual performance that follows in the wake of the many promises made.

General Bibliography

◇◇◇

Abbot, Waldo. *Handbook of Broadcasting.* 3rd ed. New York: McGraw-Hill Book Company, Inc., 1950. Pp. 494.

Audio-Visual Materials of Instruction. 48th Yearbook, Part 1. National Society for the Study of Education. Chicago: University of Chicago Press, 1949. Pp. 320.

Barnouw, Eric (ed.). *Radio Drama in Action.* New York: Rinehart & Company, Inc., 1945. Pp. 397.

———. *Handbook of Radio Writing.* New York: D. C. Heath & Co., 1947. Pp. 336.

———. *Handbook of Radio Production.* Boston: D. C. Heath & Co., 1949. Pp. 324.

Bettinger, Hoyland. *Television Techniques.* New York: Harper & Brothers, 1947. Pp. 237.

British Broadcasting Corporation. *The B.B.C. Yearbook.* London: British Broadcasting Corporation (annually).

Broderick, Gertrude G. *Radio & TV Bibliography.* Washington: United States Office of Education, 1948, Pp. 33.

Brooks, William F. *Radio News Writing.* New York: McGraw-Hill Book Company, Inc., 1948. Pp. 195.

Bryson, Lyman. *Time for Reason about Radio.* New York: George W. Stewart, Publisher, Inc., 1948. Pp. 127.

Callahan, Jennie Waugh. *Radio Workshop for Children.* New York: McGraw-Hill Book Company, Inc., 1948. Pp. 398.

Cantril, Hadley, and Allport, Gordon W. *Psychology of Radio.* New York: Harper & Brothers, 1935. Pp. 266.

CARLILE, JOHN S. *Production and Direction of Radio Programs.* New York: Prentice-Hall, Inc. 1939. Pp. 297.

CARLISLE, NORMAN V., and RICE, CONRAD C. *Your Career in Radio.* New York: E. P. Dutton & Co., Inc., 1941. Pp. 189.

CHAPPELL, M. N., and HOOPER, G. E. *Radio Audience Measurement.* New York: Stephen Daye, 1944. Pp. 246.

CHARNLEY, MITCHELL V. *News by Radio.* New York: The Macmillan Company, 1949. Pp. 198.

CHASE, FRANCIS, JR. *Sound and Fury.* New York: Harper & Brothers, 1942. Pp. 303.

CHASE, GILBERT (ed.). *Music in Radio Broadcasting.* New York: McGraw-Hill Book Company, Inc., 1946. Pp. 152.

CHESTER, GIRAUD, and GARRISON, GARNET R. *Radio and Television: An Introduction.* New York: Appleton-Century-Crofts, Inc., 1950. Pp. 556.

CHILDS, H. C., and WHITTON, J. B. *Propaganda by Short Wave.* Princeton: Princeton University Press, 1942. Pp. 355.

CONNAH, DOUGLAS DUFF. *How to Build the Radio Audience.* New York: Harper & Brothers, 1938. Pp. 271.

COTT, TED. *How to Audition for Radio.* New York: Greenberg, Publisher, 1946. Pp. 142.

COULTER, DOUGLAS (ed.). *Columbia Workshop Plays.* New York: Whittlesey House, 1939. Pp. 378.

COWGILL, ROME. *Fundamentals of Writing for Radio.* New York: Rinehart & Company, Inc., 1949. Pp. 301.

CREWS, ALBERT. *Radio Production Directing.* New York: Houghton Mifflin Company, 1944. Pp. 550.

———. *Professional Radio Writing.* New York: Houghton Mifflin Company, 1946. Pp. 473.

DARROW, BEN H. *Radio, the Assistant Teacher.* Columbus: R. G. Adams and Co., 1936. Pp. 274.

———. *Radio Trailblazing.* Columbus: College Book Co., 1940. Pp. 137.

DEHAVEN, ROBERT, and KAHM, H. S. *How to Break into Radio.* New York: Harper & Brothers, 1941. Pp. 160.

DRYER, SHERMAN H. *Radio in Wartime.* New York: Greenberg, 1942. Pp. 384.

DUERR, EDWIN. *Radio and Television Acting.* New York: Rinehart & Company, Inc., 1950. Pp. 417.

DUNLAP, ORRIN E., JR. *The Future of Television.* New York: Harper & Brothers, 1947 (rev.). Pp. 194.

EDDY, W. C. *Television—the Eyes of Tomorrow.* New York: Prentice-Hall, Inc., 1945. Pp. 330.

EISENBERG, A. L. *Children and Radio Programs.* New York: Columbia University Press, 1936. Pp. 234.

EWBANK, H. L., and LAWSON, S. P. *Projects for Radio Speech.* New York: Harper & Brothers, 1940. Pp. 158.

FRENCH, F. F., LEVENSON, W. B., ROCKWELL, V. C. *Radio English.* New York: McGraw-Hill Book Co., 1952. Pp. 350.

FROST, S. E. *Education's Own Stations.* Chicago: University of Chicago Press, 1937. Pp. 481.

————. *Is American Radio Democratic?* Chicago: University of Chicago Press, 1937. Pp. 234.

GILMORE, ART. *Radio Announcing.* Hollywood: Hollywood Radio Publications, 1948. Pp. 248.

GORDON, DOROTHY. *All Children Listen.* New York: George W. Stewart, 1942. Pp. 128.

HARRINGTON, RUTH LEE. *Your Opportunities in Television.* New York: Medill McBride Co., 1949. Pp. 199.

HARRISON, MARGARET. *Radio in the Classroom.* New York: Prentice-Hall, Inc., 1937. Pp. 260.

HARTLEY, WM. H. (ed.). *Audio-Visual Materials and Methods in the Social Studies.* 18th Yearbook, National Council for Social Studies, N.E.A., 1947. Pp. 214.

HAYES, J. S., and GARDNER, H. J. *Both Sides of the Microphone.* New York: J. P. Lippincott Company, 1938. Pp. 180.

HEATH, ERIC. *Writing for Television.* Los Angeles: Research Publishing Co., 1950. Pp. 325.

HENNEKE, BEN G. *The Radio Announcer's Handbook.* New York: Rinehart & Company, Inc., 1948. Pp. 264.

HERZBERG, MAX J. *Radio and English Teaching.* New York: Appleton-Century-Crofts, Inc., 1941. Pp. 246.

HILL, F. E. *Listen and Learn.* New York: George Grady Press, 1937. Pp. 248.

————, and WILLIAMS, W. E. *Radio's Listening Groups.* New York: Columbia University Press, 1941. Pp. 270.

HILLS, LEE, and SULLIVAN, TIMOTHY J. *Facsimile.* New York: McGraw-Hill Book Company, Inc., 1949. Pp. 319.

HOFFMAN, W. G., and ROGERS, R. L. *Effective Radio Speaking.* New York: McGraw-Hill Book Company, Inc., 1944. Pp. 241.

HORNING, J. L. *Radio as a Career.* New York: Funk & Wagnalls, 1940. Pp. 212.

HUBBELL, RICHARD W. *4000 Years of Television.* New York: G. P. Putnam's Sons, 1942. Pp. 256.

————. *Television Programming and Production.* 2d ed. New York: Rinehart & Company, Inc., 1950. Pp. 240.

HUTCHINSON, THOMAS H. *Here is Television: Your Window to the World.* New York: Hastings House, 1948. Pp. 366.

JONES, C. R. *Facsimile.* New York: Rinehart Books, Inc., 1949. Pp. 422.

JONES, V. C. *Short Plays for Stage and Radio.* Albuquerque: University of New Mexico Press, 1939. Pp. 191.

KAUFMAN, WILLIAM I. *The Best Television Plays of the Year.* New York: Merlin Press, Inc., 1950. Pp. 317.

KEMPNER, STANLEY. *Television Encyclopedia.* New York: Fairchild Publishing Co., 1948. Pp. 415.

KINGSON, WALTER KRULEVITCH, and COWGILL, ROME. *Radio Drama Acting and Production,* Rev. ed. New York: Rinehart & Company, Inc., 1950. Pp. 373.

KERBY, PHILIP. *The Victory of Television.* New York: Harper & Brothers, 1939. Pp. 115.

KOZLENKO, WILLIAM. *One Hundred Non-Royalty Radio Plays.* New York: Greenberg, 1941. Pp. 682.

LAINE, ELIZABETH. *Motion Pictures and Radio.* New York: The Regents' Inquiry, McGraw-Hill Book Company, Inc., 1939. Pp. 165.

LANDRY, ROBERT L. *Who, What, Why Is Radio?* New York: George W. Stewart, 1942. Pp. 128.

————. *This Fascinating Radio Business.* Indianapolis: The Bobbs-Merrill Company, 1946. Pp. 343.

LA PRADE, ERNEST. *Broadcasting Music.* New York: Rinehart & Company, Inc., 1948. Pp. 256.

LASS, A. H., McGILL, EARLE, and AXELROD, DONALD. *Plays from Radio.* Boston: Houghton Mifflin Company, 1948. Pp. 342.

LAWRENCE, JEROME. *Off Mike.* New York: Duell, Sloan & Pearce, 1944. Pp. 195.

LAWTON, SHERMAN PAXTON. *Radio Continuity Types.* Boston: Expression Company, 1938. Pp. 529.

————. *Radio Drama.* Boston: Expression Company, 1938. Pp. 404.

LAZERFELD, PAUL F. *Radio and the Printed Page.* New York: Duell, Sloan & Pearce, 1940. Pp. 354.

————, and STANTON, FRANK. *Radio Research,* 1941. New York: Duell, Sloan & Pearce, 1942. Pp. 333.

————, ————. *Radio Research,* 1942–1943. New York: Duell, Sloan & Pearce, 1944. Pp. 599.

————, and KENDALL, PATRICIA R. *Radio Listening in America.* New York: Prentice-Hall, Inc., 1949. Pp. 178.

————, and FIELD, HARRY. *The People Look At Radio.* Chapel Hill: University of North Carolina Press, 1947. Pp. 217.

LEATHERWOOD, DOWLING. *Journalism on the Air.* Minneapolis: Burgess Publishing Co., 1939. Pp. 101.

LEE, ROBERT E. *Television: The Revolutionary Industry.* New York: Essential Books, 1944. Pp. 229.

LEVERTON, GARRETT H. *On the Air.* New York: Samuel French, 1944. Pp. 259.

LOHR, LENOX. *Television Broadcasting.* New York: McGraw-Hill Book Company, Inc., 1940. Pp. 274.

LOIZEAUX, MARIE D. *Library on the Air.* New York: H. W. Wilson Co., 1940. Pp. 364.

LOWELL, MAURICE. *Listen In.* New York: Dodge Publishing Co., 1937. Pp. 114.

MCGILL, EARLE. *Radio Directing.* New York: McGraw-Hill Book Company, Inc., 1940. Pp. 370.

MACLATCHY, JOSEPHINE H. (ed.). *Education on the Air.* Yearbook of the Institute for Education by Radio. Columbus, Ohio: Ohio State University, 1930–1946.

MARSH, S. C. *Educational Broadcasting,* Proceedings of the First and Second National Conferences on Educational Broadcasting held in Washington, D.C. (1936–1937). Chicago: University of Chicago Press.

MORGAN, ALFRED. *Getting Acquainted with Radio.* New York: Appleton-Century-Crofts, Inc., 1940. Pp. 285.

MORRIS, JAMES. *Radio Workshop Plays.* New York: H. W. Wilson Co., 1940. Pp. 322.

NAGLER, FRANK. *Writing for Radio.* New York: Ronald Press Co., 1938. Pp. 160.

New Horizon in Radio. Philadelphia: Annals of the American Academy of Political and Social Science, Vol. 213, January, 1941. Pp. 253.

NUNMAKER, FRANCES G. *The Library Broadcasts.* New York: H. W. Wilson Co., 1948. Pp. 166.

OBOLER, ARCH. *Plays for Americans.* New York: Rinehart & Company, Inc., 1942. Pp. 271.

———, and LONGSTREET, STEPHEN. *Free World Theatre.* New York: Random House, 1944. Pp. 270.

OLSEN, O. JOE (ed.). *Education on the Air.* Yearbook of the Institute for Education by Radio. Columbus, Ohio: Ohio State University, 1947, 1948, 1949 . . . to date.

PARKER, LESTER WARD. *School Broadcasting in Great Britain.* Chicago: University of Chicago Press, 1937. Pp. 160.

PORTERFIELD, J., and REYNOLDS, KAY. *We Present Television.* New York: W. W. Norton & Company, 1940. Pp. 298.

ROBERTS, HOLLAND, RACHFORD, HELEN FOX, and GOUDY, ELIZABETH. *Airlanes to English.* New York: McGraw-Hill Book Company, Inc., 1942. Pp. 501.

ROGERS, RALPH. *Do's and Don'ts of Radio Writing.* Boston: Associated Radio Writers, Inc. 1937. Pp. 104.

ROLO, CHARLES J. *Radio Goes to War.* New York: G. P. Putnam's Sons, 1942. Pp. 293.

ROSE, C. B. *National Policy for Radio Broadcasting.* New York: Harper & Brothers, 1940. Pp. 283.

SAUER, J. L. *Radio Roads to Reading*. New York: H. W. Wilson Co., 1939. Pp. 236.

SELDES, GILBERT. *The Great Audience*. New York: Viking Press, 1950. Pp. 299.

SELIGMAN, MARJORIE, and FOGLE, SONYA. *Solo Reading for Radio and Class Work*. New York: Dramatists Play Service, 1941. Pp. 56.

SEYMOUR, KATHERINE. *Practical Radio Writing*. New York: Longmans, Green & Co., 1938. Pp. 308.

SIEPMANN, CHARLES A. *Radio's Second Chance*. Boston: Little, Brown & Company, 1946. Pp. 282.

———. *Radio, Television and Society*. New York: Oxford Press, 1950. Pp. 410.

SKORNIA, HARRY J., LEE, ROBERT H., and BREWER, FRED. *Creative Broadcasting*. New York: Prentice-Hall, Inc., 1950. Pp. 407.

SOUTHWELL, JOHN. *Getting a Job in Television*. New York: McGraw-Hill Book Company, 1947. Pp. 120.

SPOSA, LOUIS A. *TV Primer of Production and Direction*. New York: McGraw-Hill Book Company, Inc., 1947. Pp. 237.

STASHEFF, EDWARD, and BRETZ, RUDY. *The Television Program: Its Writing, Direction and Production*. New York: A. A. Wyn, Inc., 1951. Pp. 355.

STEWART, IRVIN (ed.). *Local Broadcasts to Schools*. Chicago: University of Chicago Press, 1939. Pp. 239.

STRAUSS, HARRY, and KIDD, J. R. *Look, Listen and Learn*. New York: Association Press, 1948. Pp. 235.

THORNE, SYLVIA, and GLEASON, MARION NORRIS. *The Pied Piper Broadcasts: Radio Plays for Children*. New York: H. W. Wilson Co., 1943. Pp. 380.

TOWNSEND, M. E. *Audio-Visual Aids for Teachers*. New York: H. W. Wilson Co., 1937. Pp. 131.

TYLER, KINGDON S. *Telecasting and Color*. New York: Harcourt, Brace and Company, 1946. Pp. 213.

WALDROP, FRANK C., and BORKIN, JOSEPH. *Television—A Struggle for Power*. New York: Williams Norrow and Co., 1938. Pp. 299.

WALLER, JUDITH C. *Radio, the Fifth Estate*. Boston: Houghton Mifflin Company, 1950. Pp. 483.

WARNER, HARRY P. *Radio and Television Law*. New York: Matthew Bender & Co., 1949. Pp. 1100.

WARREN, CARL. *Radio News Writing and Editing*. New York: Harper & Brothers, 1947. Pp. 439.

WEAVER, LUTHER. *The Techniques of Radio Writing*. New York: Prentice-Hall, Inc., 1948. Pp. 593.

WEISER, NORMAN S. *The Writer's Radio Theatre*. New York: Harper & Brothers, 1942. Pp. 210.

WHEELING, K. E., and HILSON, J. A. *Audio-Visual Materials for Junior and Senior High School Reading.* New York: H. W. Wilson Co., 1941. Pp. 98.

WHIPPLE, JAMES. *How to Write for the Radio.* New York: McGraw-Hill Book Company, Inc. Pp. 425.

WHITE, J. R. *Let's Broadcast.* New York: Harper & Bros., 1939. Pp. 266.

WHITE, LLEWELLYN. *The American Radio.* Chicago: University of Chicago Press, 1947. Pp. 111.

WHITE, PAUL W. *News on the Air.* New York: Harcourt, Brace and Company, 1947. Pp. 398.

WILLEY, ROY D., and YOUNG, HELEN A. *Radio in Elementary Education.* New York: D. C. Heath and Company, 1948. Pp. 450.

WISCONSIN RESEARCH PROJECT. *Radio in the Classroom.* Madison: University of Wisconsin Press, 1942. Pp. 203.

WOELFEL, NORMAN, and TYLER, I. KEITH. *Radio and the School.* New York: World Book Co., 1945. Pp. 358.

WYLIE, MAX. *Best Broadcasts of 1938–1939, 1940–1941.* New York: Whittlesey House, 1940–1941.

———. *Radio and Television Writing*, Rev. ed. New York: Rinehart and Company, Inc., 1950. Pp. 640.

Index

555